CW00863729

Police Station Referencer 2011

Andrew Keogh, LL.M

Solicitor

Published in 2011 by CrimeLine Training Limited

Registered office: 1st and 2nd Floor, 7-9 Mesnes St, Wigan WN1 1QP

Tel: 01942 40 52 61   Email: admin@crimeline.info

For further information on our products please visit:

www.crimeline.info

Crown copyright material is reproduced with the permission of the Controller of HMSO
and the Queen's Printer for Scotland

All rights reserved.

ISBN 978-1-4466-2297-1

Introduction

The aim of this book is to provide police station lawyers with a portable and comprehensive reference guide to the key PACE issues that can, and often do, arise at the police station.

The emphasis is on the practical as opposed to theoretical, with the most common issues anticipated in the texts key points. Unlike many previous books on this subject area the full PACE Codes of Practice are included along with the main provisions of PACE 1984 (as amended). This ensures that in the event that a more detailed analysis is required, the adviser has the primary resources at his or her fingertips. I have seen little point in simply rewording the primary material in the main text and have therefore resisted the tempataion.

Whether the aims of this project have been met must be for the reader to judge; to that end I would appreciate any constructive feedback that you feel able to offer, and in particular comments on anything that you feel ought to be included in the next edition.

The text states the law as of 31st January 2011, however the changes to PACE which take effect on 7th March 2011, along with new Codes A, B and D have been included in the text. Excluded from the text is consideration of provisions that relate to the detention of armed services personnel.

This book is dedicated to my wonderful family.

Andrew Keogh

Manchester, January 2011.

Email: Andrew@crimeline.info

Contents

Arrest, power of

Arrest without warrant

Section 24 *PACE 1984* provides:

A constable may arrest without a warrant--

(a) anyone who is about to commit an offence;

(b) anyone who is in the act of committing an offence;

(c) anyone whom he has reasonable grounds for suspecting to be about to commit an offence;

(d) anyone whom he has reasonable grounds for suspecting to be committing an offence.

If a constable has reasonable grounds (for which see *Armstrong v CC West Yorkshire Police* [2008] EWCA Civ 1582) for suspecting that an offence has been committed, he may arrest without a warrant anyone whom he has reasonable grounds to suspect of being guilty of it.

If an offence has been committed, a constable may arrest without a warrant--

(a) anyone who is guilty of the offence;

(b) anyone whom he has reasonable grounds for suspecting to be guilty of it.

Necessity

An arrest for any of the 3 reasons above must be necessary s. 24(4) *PACE 1984*):

(a) to enable the name of the person in question to be ascertained (in the case where the constable does not know, and cannot readily ascertain, the person's name, or has reasonable grounds for doubting whether a name given by the person as his name is his real name);

(b) correspondingly as regards the person's address;

(c) to prevent the person in question--

(i) causing physical injury to himself or any other person;

(ii) suffering physical injury;

(iii) causing loss of or damage to property;

(iv) committing an offence against public decency (subject to subsection (6)); or

(v) causing an unlawful obstruction of the highway;

(d) to protect a child or other vulnerable person from the person in question;

(e) to allow the prompt and effective investigation of the offence or of the conduct of the person in question;

(f) to prevent any prosecution for the offence from being hindered by the disappearance of the person in question.

It is questionable in most cases where a suspect attends or offers to attend at a police station voluntarily, whether there is in fact a necessity to arrest. English case law on the subject pre-dates the amendments to section 24 and the new *PACE Code G*. For an authority from the High Court in Northern Ireland (the lead judgment given by a judge who is now a member of the UK Supreme Court), see:

R v Alexander and others [2009] NIQB 20 - www.bailii.org/nie/cases/NIHC/QB/2009/20.html.

It is not however proper to seek injunctive or declaratory relief in advance of an arrest (*R (OAO Kaler-Haw) v Commissioner of Police for the Metropolis*, CO/3546/2007 – reported by Stephen Field, Barrister).

Arrest, not at a police station

A suspect must be taken to a designated police station as soon as is reasonably practicable following arrest (s.30 PACE 1984). Exceptions to this rule are to be found in s. 30(3), (4) and (5) *PACE 1984*.

Other statutory arrest powers

S. 26 PACE 1984 repealed almost all other statutory arrest powers. The following powers remain:

- Arrest of armed forces absentees and deserters;
- Arrest under emergency powers;
- Arrest of absconders and those who have broken bail;
- Arrest of certain persons under Immigration Act powers;
- Arrest of persons under the Mental Health Act 1983;
- Arrest of certain persons in connection with election offences.

Common law powers of arrest

The common law power to arrest for breach of the peace is retained by PACE. A breach of the peace is committed when harm was actually done or was likely to be done to a person or in his presence to his property, or whenever a person was in fear of being so harmed through an assault, affray, riot, unlawful assembly or other disturbance (*Howell* [1982] QB 416). Whilst breach of the peace is not a criminal offence and aspects of PACE are not engaged, it should be noted that the main provisions of *Code C* apply. If a person is arrested in order to prevent a future breach of the peace, he must be released as soon as detention for that purpose is no longer necessary (*Chief Constable of Cleveland Police v McGrogan* [2002] EWCA Civ 86).

Cross-border arrests

Where a power to arrest exists in the home country a constable can arrest that person in another part of the United Kingdom. There are some restrictions on the powers available to a British Transport Police officer. In the absence of malice damages will not lie in relation to wrongful arrest and false imprisonment (*McGrath v Chief Constable of the Royal Ulster Constabulary* [2001] 2 AC 731).

Section 137 *CJPOA 1984* provides:

(1) If the condition applicable to this subsection is satisfied, any constable of a police force in England and Wales who has reasonable grounds for suspecting that an offence has been committed or attempted in England or Wales and that the suspected person is in Scotland or in Northern Ireland may arrest without a warrant the suspected person wherever he is in Scotland or in Northern Ireland.

(2) If the condition applicable to this subsection is satisfied, any constable of a police force in Scotland who has reasonable grounds for suspecting that an offence has been committed or attempted in Scotland and that the suspected person is in England or Wales or in Northern Ireland may, as respects the suspected person, wherever he is in England or Wales or in Northern Ireland, exercise the same powers of arrest or detention as it would be competent for him to exercise were the person in Scotland.

(2A) The powers conferred by subsections (1) and (2) may be exercised in England and Wales and Scotland by a constable appointed under section 53 of the British Transport Commission Act 1949.

(3) If the conditions applicable to this subsection are satisfied, any constable of a police force in Northern Ireland who has reasonable grounds for suspecting that an offence has been committed or attempted in Northern Ireland and that the suspected person is in England or Wales or in Scotland may arrest without a warrant the suspected person wherever he is in England or Wales or in Scotland.

(4) The condition applicable to subsection (1) above is that it appears to the constable that it would have been lawful for him to have exercised the powers had the suspected person been in England and Wales.

(5) The condition applicable to subsection (2) above is that it appears to the constable that it would have been lawful for him to have exercised the powers had the suspected person been in Scotland.

(6) The conditions applicable to subsection (3) above are--

(a) that the suspected offence is an arrestable offence; or

(b) that, in the case of any other offence, it appears to the constable that service of a summons is impracticable or inappropriate for any of the reasons specified in subsection (3) of section 138.

(7) It shall be the duty of a constable who has arrested or, as the case may be detained, a person under this section--

(a) if he arrested him in Scotland, to take the person arrested either to the nearest convenient designated police station in England or in Northern Ireland or to a designated police station in a police area in England and Wales or in Northern Ireland in which the offence is being investigated;

(b) if he arrested him in England or Wales, to take the person arrested to the nearest convenient police station in Scotland or to a police station within a sheriffdom in which the offence is being investigated or to the nearest convenient designated police station in Northern Ireland or to a designated police station in Northern Ireland in which the offence is being investigated;

(c) if he detained him in England or Wales, to take the person detained to either such police station in Scotland as is mentioned in paragraph (b) above, or to the nearest convenient designated police station in England or Wales;

(d) if he arrested him in Northern Ireland, to take the person arrested either to the nearest convenient designated police station in England or Wales or to a designated police station in a police area in England and Wales in which the offence is being investigated or to the nearest convenient police station in Scotland or to a police station within a sheriffdom in which the offence is being investigated;

(e) if he detained him in Northern Ireland, to take the person detained to either such police station in Scotland as is mentioned in paragraph (b) above, or to the nearest convenient designated police station in Northern Ireland;

and to do so as soon as reasonably practicable.

(8) A constable--

(a) arresting a person under subsection (1) or (3) above, may use reasonable force and shall have the powers of search conferred by section 139;

(b) arresting a person under subsection (2) above shall have the same powers and duties, and the person arrested the same rights, as they would have had if the arrest had been in Scotland; and

(c) detaining a person under subsection (2) above shall act in accordance with the provisions applied by subsection (2) (as modified by subsection (6)) of section 138.

(9) In this section--

"arrestable offence" has the same meaning as in the Police and Criminal Evidence (Northern Ireland) Order 1989 ("the 1989 Order");

"designated police station" has the same meaning as in the Police and Criminal Evidence Act 1984 or, in relation to Northern Ireland, as in the 1989 Order; and

"constable of a police force", in relation to Northern Ireland, means a member of the Royal Ulster Constabulary or the Royal Ulster Constabulary Reserve.

(10) This section shall not prejudice any power of arrest conferred apart from this section.

Arrest of armed service personnel

Arrest of armed service personnel who are absent without leave or have deserted may be authorised by a magistrate or under s. 314 Armed Forces Act 2006:

(1) An officer of a UK police force or British overseas territory police force may arrest without a warrant a person ("a relevant suspect") who is reasonably suspected of being a person subject to service law who has deserted or is absent without leave.

(2) If an authorised person is satisfied by evidence given under oath or affirmation that a relevant suspect is or is reasonably suspected of being within his jurisdiction, he may issue a warrant for the arrest of the relevant suspect.

(3) In subsection (2) "authorised person" means a person who has authority in a relevant territory to issue a warrant for the arrest of a person suspected of an offence.

(4) A person arrested under this section must as soon as practicable be brought before a court of summary jurisdiction in the relevant territory in which he was arrested.

(5) In this section "relevant territory" means-

(a) England and Wales;

(b) Scotland;

(c) Northern Ireland;

(d) the Isle of Man; or

(e) a British overseas territory.

Arrest other than by a constable

A citizen retains the power to arrest without warrant, see s. 24A *PACE 1984*.

Information to be given on arrest

S. 28 *PACE 1984* details the information to be given on arrest.

Bad character

Questioning as to

It is perfectly proper for an officer during interview to seek to question a suspect in relation to his antecedent history. There is no valid argument that such questioning is not to do with whether an offence has been committed and if so by whom, since the whole purpose of the 2003 statutory scheme is to introduce bad character for the very purpose of proving the latter. Similarly, arguments that bad character is not relevant unless and until admitted by the court is simply not credible.

That said, there is no inference to be drawn from a refusal to discuss or admit prior misconduct, and it is questionable as to whether there is any advantage to be gained by doing so at the interview stage.

It should also be borne in mind that a defendant at trial is entitled to take steps to establish his innocence in relation to a previous conviction (for recent case law on this see *R v C*, Court of Appeal, 17 December 2010).

Care will be needed to ensure that the suspect does not unwittingly create a false impression (s. 105 *CJA 2003*), or attack the character of another (s. 106 *CJA 2003*). Advisers should be alert to s. 105(3) which provides for a person to disassociate themselves from or withdraw a false impression).

It would appear that the 2003 Act is being more strictly interpreted than previous law in relation to attacks on character. For example, in *Lamalatie* (2008) 172 JP 249 an allegation that the complainant started the violence was considered to be an allegation of reprehensible conduct. There is no provision allowing for a defendant to disassociate themselves from an attack on another's character, therefore it cannot be assumed that comments in interview can simply be edited out (see for example *Renda* [2006] 1 WLR 2948; and also *Nelson* [2006] EWCA Crim 3412 where the court did not support the practice of adducing parts of an interview merely to engage a bad character gateway).

Bail

Pre-charge

There is obviously no power to refuse bail pre-charge (although detention can and most often is authorised, and should not be confused with a refusal to grant bail).

The main powers in relation to pre-charge bail are:

(a) Street Bail, with or without conditions – s. 30A, 30C(3) *PACE 1984*. If new evidence comes to light then the suspect can be re-arrested (s. 30C(4) *PACE 1984*).

(b) A suspect can be bailed to return to a police station in order that the police complete further enquiries. Conditions can be imposed (s. 37(2) *PACE 1984*).

(c) A suspect can be bailed in order for the CPS to determine whether there is sufficient evidence to charge. Conditions can be imposed.

(d) A suspect can be bailed on expiry of any limit on his detention.

Appeal against pre-charge bail conditions

An appeal can be made direct to the police, or to a magistrates' court. Funding for magistrates' court appeals is under advocacy assistance provisions (CDS3).

Post-charge

As a starting point a suspect who has been charged ought to be released on bail, with or without conditions, unless some exception applies.

Murder

Police have no power to grant bail in respect to a person charged with murder (s. 115 *Coroners and Justice Act 2009*). Where a person is likely to be granted bail in such cases it is important that they are prepared for the time in custody that will inevitably follow once they are charged. Wherever possible advance arrangements should be made with the court in order to expedite arrangements.

Serious Offences

Persons facing retrial for serious offences (see s. 88(1)(b) *CJA 2003*) are subject to modified bail procedures including a requirement that if they are bailed that they must appear before the Crown Court within 24 hours.

Section 25 Criminal Justice and Public Order Act 1994 provides that where a person is charged with one of the offences below and has previously been convicted of an offence in that list (which need not be the same as the one now charged) or culpable homicide (but see s. 25(3A)), he shall not be granted bail other than in exceptional circumstances. Foreign convictions count. There is no definition of exceptional circumstances. Home Office Circular 34/1998 states:

In any such case where a decision to grant bail is made by the police, the custody officer will wish to consult a more senior officer before authorising the release of the suspect on bail. It is also advisable to consult the Crown Prosecution Service before reaching a final decision to grant bail in exceptional circumstances and to make a record of the reasons for granting bail on the custody record.

s. 25 No bail for defendants charged with or convicted of homicide or rape after previous conviction of such offences.

(1) A person who in any proceedings has been charged with or convicted of an offence to which this section applies in circumstances to which it applies shall be granted bail in those proceedings only if the court or, as the case may be, the constable considering the grant of bail is satisfied that there are exceptional circumstances which justify it.

(2) This section applies, subject to subsection (3) below, to the following offences, that is to say--

(a) murder;

(b) attempted murder;

(c) manslaughter;

(d) rape under the law of Scotland or Northern Ireland;

(e) an offence under section 1 of the Sexual Offences Act 1956 (rape);

(f) an offence under section 1 of the Sexual Offences Act 2003 (rape);

(g) an offence under section 2 of that Act (assault by penetration);

(h) an offence under section 4 of that Act (causing a person to engage in sexual activity without consent), where the activity caused involved penetration within subsection (4)(a) to (d) of that section;

(i) an offence under section 5 of that Act (rape of a child under 13);

(j) an offence under section 6 of that Act (assault of a child under 13 by penetration);

(k) an offence under section 8 of that Act (causing or inciting a child under 13 to engage in sexual activity), where an activity involving penetration within subsection (3)(a) to (d) of that section was caused;

(l) an offence under section 30 of that Act (sexual activity with a person with a mental disorder impeding choice), where the touching involved penetration within subsection (3)(a) to (d) of that section;

(m) an offence under section 31 of that Act (causing or inciting a person, with a mental disorder impeding choice, to engage in sexual activity), where an activity involving penetration within subsection (3)(a) to (d) of that section was caused;

(n) an attempt to commit an offence within any of paragraphs (d) to (m).

(3) This section applies in the circumstances described in subsection (3A) or (3B) only.

(3A) This section applies where--

(a) the person has been previously convicted by or before a court in any part of the United Kingdom of any offence within subsection (2) or of culpable homicide, and

(b) if that previous conviction is one of manslaughter or culpable homicide--

(i) the person was then a child or young person, and was sentenced to long-term detention under any of the relevant enactments, or

(ii) the person was not then a child or young person, and was sentenced to imprisonment or detention.

(3B) This section applies where--

(a) the person has been previously convicted by or before a court in another member State of any relevant foreign offence corresponding to an offence within subsection (2) or to culpable homicide, and

(b) if the previous conviction is of a relevant foreign offence corresponding to the offence of manslaughter or culpable homicide--

(i) the person was then a child or young person, and was sentenced to detention for a period in excess of 2 years, or

(ii) the person was not then a child or young person, and was sentenced to detention.

(4) This section applies whether or not an appeal is pending against conviction or sentence.

(5) In this section--

"conviction" includes--

(a) a finding that a person is not guilty by reason of insanity;

(b) a finding under section 4A(3) of the Criminal Procedure (Insanity) Act 1964 (cases of unfitness to plead) that a person did the act or made the omission charged against him; and

(c) a conviction of an offence for which an order is made discharging the offender absolutely or conditionally;

"convicted" shall be construed accordingly;

"the relevant enactments" means--

(a) as respects England and Wales, section 91 of the Powers of Criminal Courts (Sentencing) Act 2000;

(b) as respects Scotland, sections 205(1) to (3) and 208 of the Criminal Procedure (Scotland) Act 1995;

(c) as respects Northern Ireland, section 73(2) of the Children and Young Persons Act (Northern Ireland) 1968; and

"relevant foreign offence", in relation to a member State other than the United Kingdom, means an offence under the law in force in that member State.

(5A) For the purposes of subsection (3B), a relevant foreign offence corresponds to another offence if the relevant foreign offence would have constituted that other offence if it had been done in any part of the United Kingdom at the time when the relevant foreign offence was committed.

General exception to the grant of bail

In deciding whether or not to grant bail a custody officer must have regard to the same considerations that a court would have (s. 38(2A) *PACE 1984*).

S. 38(1) and (2) provide for bail to be refused in the following circumstances:

1 (a) if the person arrested is not an arrested juvenile--

(i) his name or address cannot be ascertained or the custody officer has reasonable grounds for doubting whether a name or address furnished by him as his name or address is his real name or address;

(ii) the custody officer has reasonable grounds for believing that the person arrested will fail to appear in court to answer to bail;

(iii) in the case of a person arrested for an imprisonable offence, the custody officer has reasonable grounds for believing that the detention of the person arrested is necessary to prevent him from committing an offence;

(iiia) in a case where a sample may be taken from the person under section 63B below, the custody officer has reasonable grounds for believing that the detention of the person is necessary to enable the sample to be taken from him;

(iv) in the case of a person arrested for an offence which is not an imprisonable offence, the custody officer has reasonable grounds for believing that the detention of the person arrested is necessary to prevent him from causing physical injury to any other person or from causing loss of or damage to property;

(v) the custody officer has reasonable grounds for believing that the detention of the person arrested is necessary to prevent him from interfering with the administration of justice or with the investigation of offences or of a particular offence; or

(vi) the custody officer has reasonable grounds for believing that the detention of the person arrested is necessary for his own protection;

(b) if he is an arrested juvenile--

(i) any of the requirements of paragraph (a) above is satisfied (but, in the case of paragraph (a)(iiia) above, only if the arrested juvenile has attained the minimum age); or

(ii) the custody officer has reasonable grounds for believing that he ought to be detained in his own interests;

(c) the offence with which the person is charged is murder.

2. If the release of a person arrested is not required by subsection (1) above, the custody officer may authorise him to be kept in police detention but may not authorise a person to be kept in police detention by virtue of subsection (1)(a)(iiia) after the end of the period of six hours beginning when he was charged with the offence.

Conditional bail

A surety or security can be required pre-release (s. 47(1) *PACE 1984*).

Conditions can be imposed post-release:

(a) to secure that he surrenders to custody,

(b) to secure that he does not commit an offence while on bail,

(c) to secure that he does not interfere with witnesses or otherwise obstruct the course of justice whether in relation to himself or any other person,

(ca) for his own protection or, if he is a child or young person, for his own welfare or in his own interests,

(d) to secure that he makes himself available for the purpose of enabling inquiries or a report to be made to assist the court in dealing with him for the offence.

(e) to secure that before the time appointed for him to surrender to custody, he attends an interview with a person who, for the purposes of the Legal Services Act 2007, is an authorised person in relation to an activity which constitutes the exercise of a right of audience or the conduct of litigation (within the meaning of that Act)

The following conditions cannot be imposed:

(a) Condition to reside in a bail hostel (s. 3A(2) *Bail Act 1976*),

(b) Condition to attend a medical appointment or upon a person compiling a report.

Variation of bail conditions

An application to vary conditions can be made to the police (s. 3A(4) *Bail Act 1976*) or to a magistrates' court (s. 43B *MCA 1980*), but note that on a variation more onerous conditions may be imposed.

Charge and other disposals

No further action

This brings the investigation to an end and the suspect is released with no future requirement to attend the police station. If further evidence comes to light the investigation can be restarted and there is no legitimate expectation that the suspect will not be proceeded against.

Cautions

There are 2 types of caution:

(a) Simple cautions

(b) Conditional cautions under the *CJA 2003*

Simple cautions

A caution can be offered if the following conditions are met:

1. The suspect is at least 18 years of age at the time the caution is administered;
2. There is a realistic prospect of conviction and a prosecution would be in the public interest;
3. The offender has admitted the offence;
4. The offender has given informed consent to the caution;
5. The circumstances of the offence and the offender are such that a caution is an appropriate disposal (see: *ACPO Gravity Matrix* at Appendix 3).

A simple caution will not be appropriate:

•   Where a person has not made a clear and reliable admission of the offence or has otherwise raised a defence. This includes occasions where intent is denied, there are doubts about their mental health or intellectual capacity, or where a statutory defence is offered. An admission which may be qualified - where, for example, an offender commits an offence while under the influence of alcohol and cannot remember the full circumstances, but evidence of involvement is agreed either through supporting witness evidence or other evidence (such as CCTV) - may be considered a full and frank admission if all evidence is accepted by the offender.

•   If someone refuses to accept it.

In addition, a simple caution cannot be viewed as an appropriate method of disposing of offences committed by serving prisoners or those subject to prison recall. It is also not appropriate to use a simple caution when the offender was on court bail or subject to a court order at the time of the commission of the offence. In general, it would be more appropriate to prosecute in these cases (or for such offences to be taken into consideration in relation to any other ongoing prosecution of that offender).

Further recommended reading:

The ACPO gravity matrix reproduced at Appendix 3.

ACPO guidelines in relation to charging of knife crime offences:

www.acpo.police.uk/documents/crime/2009/200907CRIKCO01.pdf

Conditional cautions

The Director of Public Prosecutions has issued a code of practice in relation to conditional cautions which is reproduced at Appendix 5.

Basic criteria for a conditional caution:

- that the offender is 18 or over at the time of disposal;

- that the offender admits the offence to the authorised person; and

- that there is, in the opinion of the relevant prosecutor, evidence sufficient to charge the offender with the offence.

It is important that your client is advised fully as to the consequences of breach, for which see paragraph 10 of the code of practice.

Youth conditional cautions

The CJIA 2008 provides for conditional cautions in relation to those aged 10-17 years. At the present time the scheme is only in operation for those aged 16 and 17. There is a separate code of practice for youth conditional cautions that contain additional safeguards (such as the presence of an appropriate adult in some cases and the input of local YOT's teams).

A copy of the code of practice in relation to youths can be viewed at:

http://tinyurl.com/5sxrj2j

Reprimands and final warnings

Section 65 Crime and Disorder Act 1998 provides:

(1) Subsections (2) to (5) below apply where--

(a) a constable has evidence that a child or young person ("the offender") has committed an offence;

(b) the constable considers that the evidence is such that, if the offender were prosecuted for the offence, there would be a realistic prospect of his being convicted;

(c) the offender admits to the constable that he committed the offence;

(d) the offender has not previously been convicted of an offence; and

(e) the constable is satisfied that it would not be in the public interest for the offender to be prosecuted.

(2) Subject to subsection (4) below, the constable may reprimand the offender if the offender has not previously been reprimanded or warned.

(3) The constable may warn the offender if--

(a) the offender has not previously been warned; or

(b) where the offender has previously been warned, the offence was committed more than two years after the date of the previous warning and the constable considers the offence to be not so serious as to require a charge to be brought;

but no person may be warned under paragraph (b) above more than once.

(4) Where the offender has not been previously reprimanded, the constable shall warn rather than reprimand the offender if he considers the offence to be so serious as to require a warning.

In deciding whether or not it is in the public interest to warn or reprimand, as opposed to charging the suspect, regard will be had to the *ACPO Gravity Matrix* reproduced at Appendix 3.

Penalty notices for disorder

Upper Tier Penalty—£80 for 16-year-olds and over (£40 for 10–15-year-olds)

Offence	Notice
Causing wasteful use of police time/wasting police time, Giving false report	Criminal Law Act 1967, s 5
Send false message/persistently use a public electronic communications network in order to cause annoyance, inconvenience, or needless anxiety	Communications Act 2003, s 127(2)
Knowingly give a false alarm to a person acting on behalf of a fire and rescue authority	Fire and Rescue Services Act 2004, s 49
Use words/conduct likely to cause fear of harassment, alarm, or distress	Public Order Act 1986, s 5
Fire/throw firework(s)	Explosives Act 1875, s 80
Drunk & disorderly in a public place	Criminal Justice Act 1967, s 91
Destroying or damaging property (under £300)	Criminal Damage Act 1971, s 1(1)
Theft from a shop (retail under £100)	Theft Act 1968, s 1
Breach of fireworks curfew (11 pm–7 am)	Fireworks Regulations 2004 under Fireworks Act 2003, s 11
Possession of a category 4 firework	Fireworks Regulations 2004 under Fireworks Act 2003, s 11
Possession by a person under 18 of an adult firework	Fireworks Regulations 2004 under Fireworks Act 2003, s 11
Sells or attempts to sell alcohol to a person who is drunk	Licensing Act 2003, s 141
Supply of alcohol by or on behalf of a club to a person aged under 18	Licensing Act 2003, s 146(3)
Sale of alcohol anywhere to a person under 18	Licensing Act 2003, s 146(1)
Buys or attempts to buy alcohol on behalf of person under 18	Licensing Act 2003, s 149(3)
Buys or attempts to buy alcohol for consumption on relevant premises by person under 18	Licensing Act 2003, s 149(4)
Delivery of alcohol to person under 18 or allowing such delivery	Licensing Act 2003, s 151
Possess a controlled drug of Class B—cannabis/cannabis resin	Misuse of Drugs Act 1971, s 5(2) and Sch 4

Lower Tier Penalty—£50 for 16-year-olds and over (£30 for 10–15-year-olds)

Offence	Notice
Trespass on a railway	British Transport Commission Act 1949, s 55
Throwing stones/matter/thing at a train	British Transport Commission Act 1949, s 56
Drunk in highway	Licensing Act 1872, s 12
Consume alcohol in designated public place, contrary to requirement by constable not to do so	Criminal Justice and Police Act 2001, s 12
Depositing and leave litter	Environmental Protection Act 1990, s 87(1) and (5)
Consumption of alcohol by a person under 18 on relevant premises	Licensing Act 2003, s 150(1)
Allowing consumption of alcohol by a person under 18 on relevant premises	Licensing Act 2003, s 150(2)
Buying or attempting to buy alcohol by a person under 18	Licensing Act 2003, s 149(1)

Decision to charge

The decision of whether to charge is one for the CPS in most cases (*Director of Public Prosecutions Guidance on Charging*), for which see:

www.cps.gov.uk/publications/directors_guidance/dpp_guidance.html

The Police may determine the charge in the following cases:

1.   Any offence under the Road Traffic Acts or any other offence arising from the presence of a motor vehicle, trailer, or pedal cycle on a road or other public place, **except where** (and the charge must therefore be determined by a Crown Prosecutor):

- The circumstances have resulted in the death of any person; or

- There is an allegation of dangerous driving; or

- The allegation is one of driving whilst disqualified and there has been no admission in a PACE interview to both the driving and the disqualification; or

- The statutory defence to being in charge of a motor vehicle (unfit through drink or drugs or excess alcohol) may be raised under Section 4(3) or 5(2) of the Road Traffic Act 1988; or

- There is an allegation of the unlawful taking of a motor vehicle or the aggravated unlawful taking of a motor vehicle (unless the case is suitable for disposal as an early guilty plea in the magistrates' court).

2. Any offence of absconding under the Bail Act 1976 and any offence contrary to Section 5 of the Public Order Act 1986 and any offence under the Town Police Clauses Act 1847, the Metropolitan Police Act 1839, the Vagrancy Act 1824, the Street Offences Act 1959, under Section 91 of the Criminal Justice Act 1967, Section 12 of the Licensing Act 1872, any offence under any bylaw and any summary offence punishable on conviction with a term of imprisonment of 3 months or less **except where** (and the charge must therefore be determined by a Crown Prosecutor):

- The Director of Public Prosecutions publishes other arrangements for the charging and prosecution of these offences.

Where the charges or joint charges to be preferred against one or more persons include a combination of offences, some of which may be determined by the police, and others that must be determined by a Crown Prosecutor, the Custody Officer shall refer all charges to a Crown Prosecutor for determination.

Special provisions apply when a person is charged for the purposes of retrial under the *CJA 2003* (ss. 87-91 *CJA 2003*).

Answer on charge

On charge the suspect must be cautioned (*Code C 16.2*), and a note made of any comment made (*Code C 16.8*).

Written charge and requisition

The CJA 2003 provides for a new method of charging which is currently being piloted. A suspect will be released without charge and will later receive a written charge along with a written requirement to attend at a magistrates' court. See ss. 29 -31 *CJA 2003*.

Complaints arising from police conduct

The Police Reform Act 2002 provides the regulatory framework in relation to complaints, and comprehensive information can be obtained from the Independent Police Complaints Commission (IPCC).

Complaints can be made by the person directly affected or a person acting on their behalf. Whilst complaints can be made to either the police direct or the IPCC, the IPCC only deals with the most serious complaints and therefore most matters are most appropriately dealt with at local level.

Many issues can be resolved outside of the formal complaint procedure and advisers can often achieve a quick informal resolution, whether that be an apology or rectification of the default reported by speaking to the custody sergeant or other senior police officer.

The timing of a complaint will be sensitive to its importance and any necessity to preserve evidence. If the complaint relates to the immediate investigation or treatment in custody then thought should be given to making the complaint either whilst the suspect is in custody or immediately upon his release.

A loss of temper by a person acting in a professional capacity is in itself a breakdown of professional standards and legal advisers are not exempt. Therefore some restraint should be shown before proceeding down the avenue of a complaint, at the very least until such point as the adviser himself can reflect on his own conduct. Legal advisers should also exercise the greatest care in the language used when lodging a complaint as this may in itself give rise to legal or regulatory proceedings in the future.

Most legal advisers attending at the police station will not be sufficiently versed in civil law to properly advise suspects, and rarely will an issue be so pressing that a complaint must be made there and then. Advisers would be best advised to refer their clients to a specialist solicitor.

Detention time limits

Introduction

There are strict limits on the time a person can be kept in custody prior to charge or release. Detention time limits are referenced from a starting time which is referred to as the *relevant time*. It is critical therefore to ensure that the *relevant time* is properly recorded as the accurate determination of the *relevant time* can depend on a number of relevant factors. See s. 42 *PACE 1984*.

What is the relevant time?

By default the relevant time is:

- The time the suspect arrived at the police station, or
- 24 hours after his arrest

whichever is earlier.

e.g. Suspect arrested by the police and 09.10 and conveyed to the police station. He arrives at the police station at 09.40. The relevant time is 09.40

If a person is under arrest for one offence and is then rearrested in relation to another offence, the original calculation of relevant time applies (s. 41(4) *PACE 1984*). In practice therefore an officer may wait until the release of a suspect in relation to matter 1 before arresting for matter 2 if the detention time limits might present a problem for the investigation.

Exceptions to the default time

Section 41 *PACE 1984* provides for the following exceptions:

- In the case of a person arrested outside England and Wales, shall be--
  (i) the time at which that person arrives at the first police station to which he is taken in the police area in England or Wales in which the offence for which he was arrested is being investigated; or
  (ii) the time 24 hours after the time of that person's entry into England and Wales, whichever is the earlier;

- In the case of a person who--
  (i) attends voluntarily at a police station; or
  (ii) accompanies a constable to a police station without having been arrested, and is arrested at the police station, the time of his arrest;

- In the case of a person who attends a police station to answer to bail granted under section 30A (street bail), the time when he arrives at the police station;
- Where a person is arrested in Police Area 1 (the first area) for an offence that he is wanted in connection with in another police area (the second area), and is then taken to Police Area 2, the relevant time is that persons arrival at the police station in Area 2, or 24 hours after his arrest, whichever is earlier. In the event that any questioning in relation to the arrest offence has taken place in Area 1 the normal rules will apply.
- If--

  (a) a person is in police detention in a police area in England and Wales ("the first area"); and

  (b) his arrest for an offence is sought in some other police area in England and Wales ("the second area"); and

  (c) he is taken to the second area for the purposes of investigating that offence, without being questioned in the first area in order to obtain evidence in relation to it,

  the relevant time shall be--

  (i) the time 24 hours after he leaves the place where he is detained in the first area; or

  (ii) the time at which he arrives at the first police station to which he is taken in the second area,

  whichever is the earlier.

- When a person who is in police detention is removed to hospital because he is in need of medical treatment, any time during which he is being questioned in hospital or on the way there or back by a police officer for the purpose of obtaining evidence relating to an offence shall be included in any period which falls to be calculated for the purposes of this Part of this Act, but any other time while he is in hospital or on his way there or back shall not be so included.
- If a person is bailed to return to the police station and is then rearrested for a new offence, a new relevant time will commence from that point (s. 47(7) *PACE 1984*).

Detention periods

Up to 24 hours	For all offences
24 – 36 hours (s. 42(1) *PACE 1984*)	Superintendent can authorise if: a) the detention of that person without charge is necessary to secure or preserve evidence relating to an offence for which he is under arrest or to

	obtain such evidence by questioning him;
	(b) an offence for which he is under arrest is an **indictable offence**; and
	(c) the investigation is being conducted diligently and expeditiously.
	[Note: indictable means triable on indictment only, or either-way]
	The extension does not have to be for the full 12 hours, but later extensions (up to a maximum detention time of 36 hours) can be authorised.
	Home Office Circular 60/2003 states that the power should be used sparingly.
36 – 96 hours	Application for warrant of further detention at a magistrates' court (see *Warrants of further detention*, later in text for this)
96 hours – 28 days	Terrorism cases only. See *Terrorism, suspects accused of*, later in the text. Note that at the time of writing powers to extend beyond 14 days detention had not been renewed by the government, therefore the current limit is 14 days detention.

Reviews of detention

The police must carry out periodic reviews of a suspect's detention in order to determine whether it is still justified. Note that review times stated below do not run from the relevant time, but instead from the time that the suspect's detention was first authorised by the custody sergeant (s. 37 *PACE 1984*). The review will be carried out by officer of inspector rank or above, who is not involved in the investigation.

- First review no later than 6 hours from time detention authorised;
- Reviews thereafter not exceeding 9 hourly intervals

Reviews may be postponed in limited circumstances (see s. 40 *PACE 1984*).

Duty Solicitor, rules relating to

Also see the related topic: *Legal aid funding.*

Retaining duty solicitor status

A duty solicitor must:

- Maintain CLAS membership (this includes undertaking 6 hours relevant CPD per year);

- Attend the magistrates' court at least once in every 4 month period (beginning 14th July 2010);

- Attend the police station at least 24 times per year, with at least 1 police station attendance each month (a month runs from the 14th day). "Attendance" is not defined.

There are other contractual requirements in addition to the above.

A duty solicitor compliance record can be found at:

www.crimeline.info/legal-resources/crimeline-documents/

Who can act in police station cases?

Duty Work	Duty Solicitor	Accredited representative	Probationary representative	Solicitors with PSQ	Solicitors without PSQ
*Accept initial call from the DSCC requesting duty solicitor	Yes	Yes	No	Yes	No
Provide initial telephone advice or attend in person	Yes	Yes	No	Yes	No
Own client work					
Accept initial call from the DSCC; Provide initial telephone advice or attend in person	Yes	Yes	Yes	Yes	Yes

*must be in full or part-time employment of, or a partner in the same organization as the Duty Solicitor

Financial interviews

Proceeds of Crime Act 2002

An interview in relation to the suspect's financial affairs may be conducted either prior to or post charge (*Code C 11.6*). Care should be taken in relation to interviews that take place prior to conviction as answers can be used in evidence during criminal proceedings. Given that there is no requirement to participate in these interviews unless a court orders otherwise, there is rarely any benefit to a suspect cooperating at that stage. If interviews takes place pursuant to court order (see s. 18 *POCA 2002* and Schedule 6) reference should be made to specialist texts.

Fingerprints

Fingerprints can be taken with consent (that consent to be in writing if the suspect is present at the police station), or without consent in appropriate cases. Section 61(7A) *PACE 1984* details what the police must say and record. A suspect under 14 years of age cannot consent – a parent or guardian will need to consent on his behalf. A juvenile aged 14-16 can consent, but the consent of a parent or guardian must also be obtained as well (see s. 65(1) *PACE 1984*). It should be noted that in some instances a speculative search for fingerprint matches cannot be made unless written consent has been given. If consent is given it cannot be withdrawn later (s. 63A *PACE 1984*).

Fingerprints can be taken without consent (and with the use of reasonable force if necessary) in the following circumstances (s. 61 *PACE 1984* – See *CODE D 4.3* for a definitive list):

(a) Suspect having been detained, charged or informed he will be reported for a recordable offence (whilst at the police station) and fingerprints not previously been taken during that investigation [if prints are incomplete or of too poor a quality then a new set can be taken].

(b) If a person answers bail at a court or a police station and an inspector has reasonable grounds to believe the person is not the same person from whom fingerprints were taken originally, or the person claims to be a different person from whom the fingerprints were originally taken.

(c) Following reprimand, warning, caution (provided that the suspect admitted the offence) or conviction for a recordable offence.

(d) If the person has not been detained at the police station but is reprimanded, cautioned (provided he admitted the offence), warned or convicted for/of a recordable offence, provided that fingerprints were not taken during the investigation or post-conviction. In this instance he can be required to go to the police station (s. 27(1) *PACE 1984*). A similar power exists if the prints are incomplete or of poor quality. The requirement to attend the police station must be made within one-month of the trigger event.

Sections 1 to 7 of the *Crime and Security Act 2010* and the *Serious Organised Crime and Police Act 2005* (s 117) will make amendments to the provisions above. These sections will come in to force on 7th March 2011.

Section 2(1) of the 2010 Act introduces a section 61(5A) in to *PACE 1984*, which provides:

The fingerprints of a person may be taken without the appropriate consent if (before or after the coming into force of this subsection) he has been arrested for a recordable offence and released and--

(a) in the case of a person who is on bail, he has not had his fingerprints taken in the course of the investigation of the offence by the police; or

(b) in any case, he has had his fingerprints taken in the course of that investigation but subsection (3A)(a) or (b) above applies [i.e. the set was incomplete or of poor quality].

Section 2(2) of the 2010 Act introduces a section 61(5B) in to *PACE 1984*, which provides:

The fingerprints of a person not detained at a police station may be taken without the appropriate consent if (before or after the coming into force of this subsection) he has been charged with a recordable offence or informed that he will be reported for such an offence and--

(a) he has not had his fingerprints taken in the course of the investigation of the offence by the police; or

(b) he has had his fingerprints taken in the course of that investigation but subsection (3A)(a) or (b) above applies [i.e. the set was incomplete or of poor quality].

Section 117(1), (2) *SOCPA 2005* amends section 61 of *PACE 1984*. The amendment gives a police constable the power to take a person's fingerprints without their consent where the person is unknown to the officer and their name cannot reasonably be ascertained, or where an officer has reasonable grounds for doubting the validity of the name given.

The *Counter Terrorism Act 2008* (s. 10) makes further amendments to the above. At the time of writing the relevant parts of this Act were not in force and no commencement date is anticipated.

Fingerprints, retention and destruction

Section 64 *PACE 1984* deals with retention and destruction of fingerprints. The retention and destruction of fingerprints is a complex topic and discussion goes far beyond s. 64 *PACE 1984*. Following legal challenges it is likely, during the life of this edition, that s. 14 of the *Crime and Security Act 2010* will come in to force.

It should be noted that as with many other provisions, different provisions apply to suspects detained for terrorism offences or in connection with immigration matters (see: *Terrorism, suspects accused of* and *Immigration matters, suspects detained in connection with*).

Identification

Code D of *PACE 1984* the latest version of which came in to force on 7th March 2011 can be found in Appendix 2. *Code D* regulates the conduct of identification procedures. There is no distinction in the code between procedures pre and post charge.

Types of procedure

There are 5 methods of identification:

- Video identification in relation to a known suspect who is available (*Code D 3.5*). This is carried out in accordance with *Code D Annex A*;

- Identification parade in relation to a known suspect who is available (*Code D 3.7*). This is carried out in accordance with *Code D Annex B*;

- Group identification in relation to a known suspect who is available (*Code D 3.9*). This is carried out in accordance with *Code D Annex C*;

- Confrontation (*Code D 3.23*). This is carried out in accordance with *Code D Annex D*;

- Photographic identification (*Code D 3.34*). This is carried out in accordance with *Code D Annex A* if the suspect is known, or *Annex E* if not known).

Voice identification

The code makes no particular provision for voice identification, but its absence does not preclude its use (*Code D 1.2*). For further reading in relation to voice identification see *R v Flynn* [2008] EWCA Crim 970 and *Home Office Circular* 57/2003:

www.homeoffice.gov.uk/about-us/home-office-circulars/circulars-2003/057-2003/

Refusal to participate in identification procedure

If a suspect refuses to participate in formal identification procedures there is a real risk that the police will resort to the confrontation procedure. However, it may also be the case that a refusal to participate may bring the investigation to an end, particularly in relation to less serious matters where the amount of time required to bring about a confrontation may be thought to be disproportionate, either by the officer or complainant. This remains therefore a tactical decision for the client to make on advice. There is no statutory basis for the drawing of inferences following a refusal to participate with identification procedures, but it would appear at least arguable that the prosecution are entitled, at common law, to make comment.

Immigration matters, suspects detained in connection with

Advising on immigration matters, contractual position

The crime contract makes a clear distinction between advice in relation to immigration offences, and general immigration advice. The starting point is that there is no duty to advise on general immigration matters unless you have the relevant expertise in this area. It should also be noted that even where a lawyer does have the expertise, the crime contract might not fund payment.

In many instances the investigation into criminal offences will overlap with pure immigration law issues and lawyers at the police station need to have a good working knowledge of immigration law issues in order to competently advise on the criminal aspects of the case.

Specialist immigration law firms can be located via: www.communitylegaladvice.org.uk or by calling 0845 345 4 345 (Mon-Friday 9am – 8pm; Saturday 9am – 12.30pm).

The contract provides as follows (*Specification Part B*):

Immigration Advice

9.63 Subject to Paragraph 9.68 below, where you give Police Station Advice and Assistance and it is apparent, or becomes apparent, that an immigration issue arises, you must give Advice and Assistance to the Client up until the point where the immigration authorities take over conduct of the investigation and it has been confirmed that no criminal offence or charge is being pursued. 9.64 You may continue to advise after this point if the Client remains in detention and requires advice in relation to a criminal offence (which may include an Immigration Offence).

9.65 In relation to any non-criminal immigration issue unless the Client chooses to instruct his/her Own Solicitor, you must either:

(a) refer the issue back to the DSCC (who will arrange for the provision of telephone advice by one of our civil Providers with a Contract to provide immigration advice to individuals detained at the Police Station); or

(b) consider whether it is practicable to refer the immigration issue to a Provider with a Contract in the immigration Category of Work in the local area (which may include your organisation).

9.66 Where the Client remains in detention and advice is required and it is not practicable to refer the Client to a Provider with a Contract in the immigration Category of Work, you may continue to provide Advice and Assistance. A full note of the relevant circumstances must be made on the file. The advice you may give includes any urgent advice required covering immigration status and procedure.

9.67 You must not give Police Station Advice and Assistance where: -

(a) an individual is detained after entry and is served with illegal entry papers or a notice of intention to deport; or

(b) an individual is detained by the immigration authorities on entry; or

(c) an individual is arrested by police on behalf of the immigration authorities where no criminal allegations are made and is detained under the immigration authorities© administrative powers.

9.68 You must treat an investigation as taken over by the immigration authority once you have verified (by confirmation from the Police or Immigration Officer) that:

(a) the immigration authorities will take over; and

(b) the police are not intending to interview until the immigration authorities take over; and

(c) there is no other criminal offence or other reason for detention; and

(d) the police have confirmed to you that they intend to do no more than simply hold the detainee until the arrival of the immigration authorities.

9.69 You must have a clear policy and procedure(s) for referral in accordance with Section 2 of this Specification. We expect organisations to build links with immigration Providers and document details of appropriate Providers to which you will refer Clients.

Fingerprints

Code D PACE Codes Applies. The main statutory power is to be found in section 141(and 142) of the 1999 Act. Other powers are to be found in Schedule 2 of the 1971 Act.

s 141 Fingerprinting.

(1) Fingerprints may be taken by an authorised person from a person to whom this section applies.

(2) Fingerprints may be taken under this section only during the relevant period.

(3) Fingerprints may not be taken under this section from a person under the age of sixteen ("the child") except in the presence of a person of full age who is--

(a) the child's parent or guardian; or

(b) a person who for the time being takes responsibility for the child.

(4) The person mentioned in subsection (3)(b) may not be--

(a) an officer of the Secretary of State who is not an authorised person;

(b) an authorised person.

(5) "Authorised person" means--

(a) a constable;

(b) an immigration officer;

(c) a prison officer;

(d) an officer of the Secretary of State authorised for the purpose; or

(e) a person who is employed by a contractor in connection with the discharge of the contractor's duties under a removal centre contract.

(6) In subsection (5)(e) "contractor" and "removal centre contract" have the same meaning as in Part VIII.

(7) This section applies to--

(a) any person ("A") who, on being required to do so by an immigration officer on his arrival in the United Kingdom, fails to produce a valid passport with photograph or some other document satisfactorily establishing his identity and nationality or citizenship;

(b) any person ("B") who has been refused leave to enter the United Kingdom but has been temporarily admitted under paragraph 21 of Schedule 2 to the 1971 Act if an immigration officer reasonably suspects that B might break any condition imposed on him relating to residence or as to reporting to the police or an immigration officer;

(c) any person ("C") in respect of whom a relevant immigration decision has been made;

(d) any person ("D") who has been detained under paragraph 16 of Schedule 2 to the 1971 Act or arrested under paragraph 17 of that Schedule;

(e) any person ("E") who has made a claim for asylum;

(f) any person ("F") who is a dependant of any of those persons, other than a dependant of a person who falls within paragraph (c) by reason of a relevant immigration decision within subsection (16)(b) having been made in respect of that person.

(8) "The relevant period" begins--

(a) for A, on his failure to produce the passport or other document;

(b) for B, on the decision to admit him temporarily;

(c) for C, on the service on him of notice of the relevant immigration decision by virtue of section 105 of the Nationality, Immigration and Asylum Act 2002 (c. 41);

(d) for D, on his detention or arrest;

(e) for E, on the making of his claim for asylum; and

(f) for F, at the same time as for the person whose dependant he is.

(9) "The relevant period" ends on the earliest of the following--

(a) the grant of leave to enter or remain in the United Kingdom;

(b) for A, B, C or D, his removal or deportation from the United Kingdom;

(c) for C-

(i) the time when the relevant immigration decision ceases to have effect, whether as a result of an appeal or otherwise, or

(ii) if a deportation order has been made against him, its revocation or its otherwise ceasing to have effect;

(d) for D, his release if he is no longer liable to the detained under paragraph 16 of Schedule 2 to the 1971 Act;

(e) for E, the final determination or abandonment of his claim for asylum; and

(f) for F, at the same time as for the person whose dependant he is

(10) No fingerprints may be taken from A if the immigration officer considers that A has a reasonable excuse for the failure concerned.

(11) No fingerprints may be taken from B unless the decision to take them has been confirmed by a chief immigration officer.

(12) An authorised person may not take fingerprints from a person under the age of sixteen unless his decision to take them has been confirmed--

(a) if he is a constable, by a person designated for the purpose by the chief constable of his police force;

(b) if he is a person mentioned in subsection (5)(b) or (e), by a chief immigration officer;

(c) if he is a prison officer, by a person designated for the purpose by the governor of the prison;

(d) if he is an officer of the Secretary of State, by a person designated for the purpose by the Secretary of State.

(13) Neither subsection (3) nor subsection (12) prevents an authorised person from taking fingerprints if he reasonably believes that the person from whom they are to be taken is aged sixteen or over.

(14) For the purposes of subsection (7)(f), a person is a dependant of another person if--

(a) he is that person's spouse or child under the age of eighteen; and

(b) he does not have a right of abode in the United Kingdom or indefinite leave to enter or remain in the United Kingdom.

(15) "Claim for asylum" has the same meaning as in Part VI.

Automatic deportation

Foreign nationals are liable for deportation if sentenced to 12 months or more imprisonment for an offence, or sentenced to any term of imprisonment for certain offences (s 32 *United Kingdom Borders Act 2007*). There are safeguards against deportation provided for in section 33 of the 2007 Act. It will not generally be appropriate to order deportation outside of the statutory scheme (*R v Kluxen* [2010] EWCA Crim 1081).

Legal issues

Illegal entrant

Section 33(1) *Immigration Act 1971*:

entrant" means a person entering or seeking to enter the United Kingdom and "illegal entrant" means a person--

(a) unlawfully entering or seeking to enter in breach of a deportation order or of the immigration laws, or

(b) entering or seeking to enter by means which include deception by another person,

and includes also a person who has entered as mentioned in paragraph (a) or (b) above;

Illegal entry and similar offences

Section 24 of the 1971 Act provides:

s 24 Illegal entry and similar offences.

(1) A person who is not a British citizen shall be guilty of an offence punishable on summary conviction with a fine of not more than level 5 on the standard scale or with imprisonment for not more than six months, or with both, in any of the following cases:--

(a) if contrary to this Act he knowingly enters the United Kingdom in breach of a deportation order or without leave;

(b) if, having only a limited leave to enter or remain in the United Kingdom, he knowingly either--

(i) remains beyond the time limited by the leave; or

(ii) fails to observe a condition of the leave;

(c) if, having lawfully entered the United Kingdom without leave by virtue of section 8(1) above, he remains without leave beyond the time allowed by section 8(1);

(d) if, without reasonable excuse, he fails to comply with any requirement imposed on him under Schedule 2 to this Act to report to a medical officer of health, or to attend, or submit to a test or examination, as required by such an officer;

(e) if, without reasonable excuse, he fails to observe any restriction imposed on him under Schedule 2 or 3 to this Act as to residence , as to his employment or occupation or as to reporting to the police, to an immigration officer or to the Secretary of State;

(f) if he disembarks in the United Kingdom from a ship or aircraft after being placed on board under Schedule 2 or 3 to this Act with a view to his removal from the United Kingdom;

(g) if he embarks in contravention of a restriction imposed by or under an Order in Council under section 3(7) of this Act.

(1A) A person commits an offence under subsection (1)(b)(i) above on the day when he first knows that the time limited by his leave has expired and continues to commit it throughout any period during which he is in the United Kingdom thereafter; but a person shall not be prosecuted under that provision more than once in respect of the same limited leave.

(3) The extended time limit for prosecutions which is provided for by section 28 below shall apply to offences under subsection (1)(a) and (c) above.

(4) In proceedings for an offence against subsection (1)(a) above of entering the United Kingdom without leave,--

(a) any stamp purporting to have been imprinted on a passport or other travel document by an immigration officer on a particular date for the purpose of giving leave shall be presumed to have been duly so imprinted, unless the contrary is proved;

(b) proof that a person had leave to enter the United Kingdom shall lie on the defence if, but only if, he is shown to have entered within six months before the date when the proceedings were commenced

Deception offences

Section 24A of the 1971 Act provides:

s 24A Deception.

(1) A person who is not a British citizen is guilty of an offence if, by means which include deception by him--

(a) he obtains or seeks to obtain leave to enter or remain in the United Kingdom; or

(b) he secures or seeks to secure the avoidance, postponement or revocation of enforcement action against him.

(2) "Enforcement action", in relation to a person, means--

(a) the giving of directions for his removal from the United Kingdom ("directions") under Schedule 2 to this Act or section 10 of the Immigration and Asylum Act 1999;

(b) the making of a deportation order against him under section 5 of this Act; or

(c) his removal from the United Kingdom in consequence of directions or a deportation order.

(3) A person guilty of an offence under this section is liable--

(a) on summary conviction, to imprisonment for a term not exceeding six months or to a fine not exceeding the statutory maximum, or to both; or

(b) on conviction on indictment, to imprisonment for a term not exceeding two years or to a fine, or to both.

Assisting unlawful immigration to member state

Section 25 of the 1971 Act provides:

s 25 Assisting unlawful immigration to member State

(1) A person commits an offence if he--

(a) does an act which facilitates the commission of a breach of immigration law by an individual who is not a citizen of the European Union,

(b) knows or has reasonable cause for believing that the act facilitates the commission of a breach of immigration law by the individual, and

(c) knows or has reasonable cause for believing that the individual is not a citizen of the European Union.

(2) In subsection (1) "immigration law" means a law which has effect in a member State and which controls, in respect of some or all persons who are not nationals of the State, entitlement to--

(a) enter the State,

(b) transit across the State, or

(c) be in the State.

(3) A document issued by the government of a member State certifying a matter of law in that State--

(a) shall be admissible in proceedings for an offence under this section, and

(b) shall be conclusive as to the matter certified.

(4) Subsection (1) applies to things done whether inside or outside the United Kingdom.

...

(6) A person guilty of an offence under this section shall be liable--

(a) on conviction on indictment, to imprisonment for a term not exceeding 14 years, to a fine or to both, or

(b) on summary conviction, to imprisonment for a term not exceeding six months, to a fine not exceeding the statutory maximum or to both.

(7) In this section-

(a) a reference to a member State includes a reference to a State on a list prescribed for the purposes of this section by order of the Secretary of State (to be known as the "Section 25 List of Schengen Acquis States"), and

(b) a reference to a citizen of the European Union includes a reference to a person who is a national of a State on that list.

Helping asylum seekers to enter the UK

Section 25A of the 1971 Act provides:

s 25A Helping asylum-seeker to enter United Kingdom

(1) A person commits an offence if--

(a) he knowingly and for gain facilitates the arrival in, or the entry into, the United Kingdom of an individual, and

(b) he knows or has reasonable cause to believe that the individual is an asylum-seeker.

(2) In this section "asylum-seeker" means a person who intends to claim that to remove him from or require him to leave the United Kingdom would be contrary to the United Kingdom's obligations under--

(a) the Refugee Convention (within the meaning given by section 167(1) of the Immigration and Asylum Act 1999 (c. 33) (interpretation)), or

(b) the Human Rights Convention (within the meaning given by that section).

(3) Subsection (1) does not apply to anything done by a person acting on behalf of an organisation which--

(a) aims to assist asylum-seekers, and

(b) does not charge for its services.

(4) subsections (4) and (6) of section 25 apply for the purpose of the offence in subsection (1) of this section as they apply for the purpose of the offence in subsection (1) of that section.

Assisting entry to United Kingdom in breach of deportation or exclusion order

Section 25B of the 1971 Act provides:

s 25B Assisting entry to United Kingdom in breach of deportation or exclusion order

(1) A person commits an offence if he--

(a) does an act which facilitates a breach of a deportation order in force against an individual who is a citizen of the European Union, and

(b) knows or has reasonable cause for believing that the act facilitates a breach of the deportation order.

(2) Subsection (3) applies where the Secretary of State personally directs that the exclusion from the United Kingdom of an individual who is a citizen of the European Union is conducive to the public good.

(3) A person commits an offence if he--

(a) does an act which assists the individual to arrive in, enter or remain in the United Kingdom,

(b) knows or has reasonable cause for believing that the act assists the individual to arrive in, enter or remain in the United Kingdom, and

(c) knows or has reasonable cause for believing that the Secretary of State has personally directed that the individual's exclusion from the United Kingdom is conducive to the public good.

(4) subsections (4) and (6) of section 25 apply for the purpose of an offence under this section as they apply for the purpose of an offence under that section.

General offences in connection with administration of Act

Section 26 of the 1971 Act provides:

s 26 General offences in connection with administration of Act.

(1) A person shall be guilty of an offence punishable on summary conviction with a fine of not more than level 5 on the standard scale or with imprisonment for not more than six months, or with both, in any of the following cases--

(a) if, without reasonable excuse, he refuses or fails to submit to examination under Schedule 2 to this Act;

(b) if, without reasonable excuse, he refuses to fails to furnish or produce any information in his possession, or any documents in his possession or control, which he is on an examination under that Schedule required to furnish or produce;

(c) if on any such examination or otherwise he makes or causes to be made to an immigration officer or other person lawfully acting in the execution of a relevant enactment a return, statement or representation which he knows to be false or does not believe to be true;

(d) if, without lawful authority, he alters any certificate of entitlement, entry clearance, work permit or other document issued or made under or for the purposes of this Act, or uses for the purposes of this Act, or has in his possession for such use, any passport, certificate of entitlement, entry clearance, work permit or other document which he knows or has reasonable cause to believe to be false;

(e) if, without reasonable excuse, he fails to complete and produce a landing or embarkation card in accordance with any order under Schedule 2 to this Act;

(f) if, without reasonable excuse, he fails to comply with any requirement of regulations under section 4(3) or of an order under section 4(4) above;

(g) if, without reasonable excuse, he obstructs an immigration officer or other person lawfully acting in the execution of this Act.

(2) The extended time limit for prosecutions which is provided for by section 28 below shall apply to offences under subsection (1)(c) and (d) above.

(3) "Relevant enactment" means--

(a) this Act;

(b) the Immigration Act 1988;

(c) the Asylum and Immigration Appeals Act 1993 (apart from section 4 or 5);

(d) the Immigration and Asylum Act 1999 (apart from Part VI); or

(e) the Nationality, Immigration and Asylum Act 2002 (apart from Part 5).

Registration card offences

Section 26A of the 1971 Act provides:

s 26A Registration card

(1) In this section "registration card" means a document which--

(a) carries information about a person (whether or not wholly or partly electronically), and

(b) is issued by the Secretary of State to the person wholly or partly in connection with--

(i) a claim for asylum (whether or not made by that person), or

(ii) a claim for support under section 4 of the Immigration and Asylum Act 1999 (whether or not made by that person).

(2) In subsection (1) "claim for asylum" has the meaning given by section 18 of the Nationality, Immigration and Asylum Act 2002.

(3) A person commits an offence if he--

(a) makes a false registration card,

(b) alters a registration card with intent to deceive or to enable another to deceive,

(c) has a false or altered registration card in his possession without reasonable excuse,

(d) uses or attempts to use a false registration card for a purpose for which a registration card is issued,

(e) uses or attempts to use an altered registration card with intent to deceive,

(f) makes an article designed to be used in making a false registration card,

(g) makes an article designed to be used in altering a registration card with intent to deceive or to enable another to deceive, or

(h) has an article within paragraph (f) or (g) in his possession without reasonable excuse.

(4) In subsection (3) "false registration card" means a document which is designed to appear to be a registration card.

(5) A person who is guilty of an offence under subsection (3)(a), (b), (d), (e), (f) or (g) shall be liable--

(a) on conviction on indictment, to imprisonment for a term not exceeding ten years, to a fine or to both, or

(b) on summary conviction, to imprisonment for a term not exceeding six months, to a fine not exceeding the statutory maximum or to both.

(6) A person who is guilty of an offence under subsection (3)(c) or (h) shall be liable--

(a) on conviction on indictment, to imprisonment for a term not exceeding two years, to a fine or to both, or

(b) on summary conviction, to imprisonment for a term not exceeding six months, to a fine not exceeding the statutory maximum or to both.

Possession of immigration stamp

Section 26B of the 1971 Act provides:

26B Possession of immigration stamp

(1) A person commits an offence if he has an immigration stamp in his possession without reasonable excuse.

(2) A person commits an offence if he has a replica immigration stamp in his possession without reasonable excuse.

(3) In this section--

(a) "immigration stamp" means a device which is designed for the purpose of stamping documents in the exercise of an immigration function,

(b) "replica immigration stamp" means a device which is designed for the purpose of stamping a document so that it appears to have been stamped in the exercise of an immigration function, and

(c) "immigration function" means a function of an immigration officer or the Secretary of State under the Immigration Acts.

(4) A person who is guilty of an offence under this section shall be liable--

(a) on conviction on indictment, to imprisonment for a term not exceeding two years, to a fine or to both, or

(b) on summary conviction, to imprisonment for a term not exceeding six months, to a fine not exceeding the statutory maximum or to both.

Time limits for proceedings

Section 28 of the 1971 Act provides:

s 28 Proceedings.

(1) Where the offence is one to which, under section 24 or 26 above, an extended time limit for prosecutions is to apply, then--

(a) an information relating to the offence may in England and Wales be tried by a magistrates' court if it is laid within six months after the commission of the offence, or if it is laid within three years after the commission of the offence and not more than two months after the date certified by an officer of police above the rank of chief superintendent to be the date on which evidence sufficient to justify proceedings came to the notice of an officer of the police force to which he belongs; and

(b) ...

(c) ...

(2) ...

(3) For the purposes of the trial of a person for an offence under this Part of this Act, the offence shall be deemed to have been committed either at the place at which it actually was committed or at any place at which he may be.

(4) Any powers exercisable under this Act in the case of any person may be exercised notwithstanding that proceedings for an offence under this Part of this Act have been taken against him.

Immigration officers, powers of arrest

Section 28A of the 1971 Act provides:

s 28A Arrest without warrant.

(1) An immigration officer may arrest without warrant a person--

(a) who has committed or attempted to commit an offence under section 24 or 24A; or

(b) whom he has reasonable grounds for suspecting has committed or attempted to commit such an offence.

(2) But subsection (1) does not apply in relation to an offence under section 24(1)(d).

(3) An immigration officer may arrest without warrant a person--

(a) who has committed an offence under section 25, 25A or 25B; or

(b) whom he has reasonable grounds for suspecting has committed that offence.

(5) An immigration officer may arrest without warrant a person ("the suspect") who, or whom he has reasonable grounds for suspecting--

(a) has committed or attempted to commit an offence under section 26(1)(g); or

(b) is committing or attempting to commit that offence.

(6) The power conferred by subsection (5) is exercisable only if either the first or the second condition is satisfied.

(7) The first condition is that it appears to the officer that service of a summons (or, in Scotland, a copy complaint) is impracticable or inappropriate because--

(a) he does not know, and cannot readily discover, the suspect's name;

(b) he has reasonable grounds for doubting whether a name given by the suspect as his name is his real name;

(c) the suspect has failed to give him a satisfactory address for service; or

(d) he has reasonable grounds for doubting whether an address given by the suspect is a satisfactory address for service.

(8) The second condition is that the officer has reasonable grounds for believing that arrest is necessary to prevent the suspect--

(a) causing physical injury to himself or another person;

(b) suffering physical injury; or

(c) causing loss of or damage to property.

(9) For the purposes of subsection (7), an address is a satisfactory address for service if it appears to the officer--

(a) that the suspect will be at that address for a sufficiently long period for it to be possible to serve him with a summons (or copy complaint); or

(b) that some other person specified by the suspect will accept service of a summons (or copy complaint) for the suspect at that address

(9A) An immigration officer may arrest without warrant a person--

(a) who has committed an offence under section 26A or 26B; or

(b) whom he has reasonable grounds for suspecting has committed an offence under section 26A or 26B.

(10) In relation to the exercise of the powers conferred by subsections (3)(b) and (5), it is immaterial that no offence has been committed.

(11) In Scotland the powers conferred by subsections (3) and (5) may also be exercised by a constable.

Section 14 of the Asylum and Immigration (Treatment of Claimants etc.) Act 2004 provides:

s 14 Immigration officer: power of arrest

(1) Where an immigration officer in the course of exercising a function under the Immigration Acts forms a reasonable suspicion that a person has committed or attempted to commit an offence listed in subsection (2), he may arrest the person without warrant.

(2) Those offences are-

(a) the offence of conspiracy at common law (in relation to conspiracy to defraud),

(b) at common law in Scotland, any of the following offences-

(i) fraud,

(ii) conspiracy to defraud,

(iii) uttering and fraud,

(iv) bigamy,

(v) theft, and

(vi) reset,

(c) an offence under section 57 of the Offences against the Person Act 1861 (c. 100) (bigamy),

(d) an offence under section 3 or 4 of the Perjury Act 1911 (c. 6) (false statements),

(e) an offence under section 7 of that Act (aiding, abetting &c.) if it relates to an offence under section 3 or 4 of that Act,

(f) an offence under section 53 of the Registration of Births, Deaths and Marriages (Scotland) Act 1965 (c. 49) (knowingly giving false information to district registrar, &c.),

(g) an offence under any of the following provisions of the Theft Act 1968 (c. 60)-

(i) section 1 (theft),

(iv) section 17 (false accounting), and

(v) section 22 (handling stolen goods),

(h) an offence under section 1, 17 or 21 of the Theft Act (Northern Ireland) 1969 (c. 16) (N.I.),

(ha) an offence under either of the following provisions of the Fraud Act 2006-

(i) section 1 (fraud);

(ii) section 11 (obtaining services dishonestly),

(k) an offence under Article 8 or 9 of the Perjury (Northern Ireland) Order 1979 (S.I. 1979/1714 (N.I. 19)),

(l) an offence under Article 12 of that Order if it relates to an offence under Article 8 or 9 of that Order,

(m) an offence under any of the following provisions of the Forgery and Counterfeiting Act 1981 (c. 45)-

(i) section 1 (forgery),

(ii) section 2 (copying false instrument),

(iii) section 3 (using false instrument),

(iv) section 4 (using copy of false instrument), and

(v) section 5(1) and (3) (false documents),

(n) an offence under any of sections 57 to 59 of the Sexual Offences Act 2003 (c. 42) (trafficking for sexual exploitation),

(o) an offence under section 22 of the Criminal Justice (Scotland) Act 2003 (asp 7) (trafficking in prostitution),

(p) an offence under section 4 of this Act,

(q) an offence under any of sections 4 to 6 of the Identity Documents Act 2010.

(3) The following provisions of the Immigration Act 1971 (c. 77) shall have effect for the purpose of making, or in connection with, an arrest under this section as they have effect for the purpose of making, or in connection with, arrests for offences under that Act-

(a) section 28C (entry and search before arrest),

(b) sections 28E and 28F (entry and search after arrest),

(c) sections 28G and 28H (search of arrested person), and

(d) section 28I (seized material).

Search and arrest powers, premises and persons

The main powers are contained in:

Sections 28B, 28C, 28CA, 28D, 28E, 28F, 28FA, 28FB, and 28G of the 1971 Act.

Searches whilst in police detention are covered by section 28H of the 1971 Act.

Detention powers

The main detention power can be found in Schedule 2 of the 1971 Act and section 10 of the 1999 Act.

Detention and Interview, fitness for

The following points emerge from *Code C and Code C Annex G*:

1. A fitness assessment should be carried out when the suspect arrives at the police station (*Code C 3.5*);

2. A risk assessment should be carried out in relation to harm to self or other (*Code C 3.6*);

3. See *Code C 1.4* for mentally disordered or vulnerable suspects;

4. Risk assessment should be an ongoing process (See: *Guidance on the Safer Detention and Handling of Persons in Police Custody* (2006), ACPO) (*Code C 3.10*);

5. Suspects should be visited hourly, or half-hourly if intoxicated or they otherwise present as a concern (*Code C 9.3 and 9.5B*);

6. A suspect who presents with symptoms listed in *Code C Annex H* should receive immediate medical attention;

7. Steps should be taken to protect police officers and other individuals if the suspect has an infectious disease (*Code C 9.7*);

8. *Code C Annex G* outlines the considerations in relation to assessing fitness for interview. Ultimately it is for the custody officer, relying on advice tendered by healthcare professionals, to decide on the issue of fitness;

9. A person who is otherwise unfit for interview may be interviewed in certain circumstances, see *Code C 11.1, 11.18-11.20.*

10. Physical injuries should be recorded and if necessary treated (*Code C 9.2, 9.5, 9.8*). Solicitors should consider taking their own photographic evidence.

Interpreters

General guidance

The Law Society has issued 2 practice notes in relation to use of interpreters in criminal cases, and sign language interpreters:

www.crimeline.info/legal-resources/law-society-practice-notes/

Entitlement to an interpreter

Code C 3.10 and *Note B* provide for interpreter services if a suspect cannot properly speak or understand the English language. There are limited circumstances where interpretation can be provided by a police officer or police employee (*Code C 13.9*).

Interpreters are provided at public expense. If a solicitor has doubts as to the competency of the interpretation services provided he is entitled to take steps to arrange for another interpreter to attend the police station, such services being a proper disbursement.

Contemporaneous notes must be made in the event that the interview is not audio and/or video recorded (*Code C 13.3*).

Exceptions

Code C 11.1, 11.18-19 prescribe the circumstances under which an interview can take place in the absence of interpretation services.

Confidentiality and Legal privilege

The interpreter is bound by the same rules as apply to a solicitor (*Bozkurt v Thames Magistrates' Court* [2001] EWHC Admin 400) and interpreters who are properly accredited fully understand this to be the case.

Interviews

Definition

An interview is the questioning of a person regarding their involvement or suspected involvement in a criminal offence or offences which must be carried out under caution. Whenever a person is interviewed they must be informed of the nature of the offence, or further offence. Procedures under the *Road Traffic Act 1988*, section 7 or the *Transport and Works Act* 1992, section 31 do not constitute interviewing for the purpose of *Code C*.

Protections

Following a decision to arrest a suspect, they must not be interviewed about the relevant offence except at a police station or other authorised place of detention, unless the consequent delay would be likely to:

(a)   lead to:

•   interference with, or harm to, evidence connected with an offence;

•   interference with, or physical harm to, other people; or

•   serious loss of, or damage to, property;

(b)   lead to alerting other people suspected of committing an offence but not yet arrested for it; or

(c)   hinder the recovery of property obtained in consequence of the commission of an offence.

Interviewing in any of these circumstances shall cease once the relevant risk has been averted or the necessary questions have been put in order to attempt to avert that risk.

Immediately prior to the commencement or re-commencement of any interview at a police station or other authorised place of detention, the interviewer should remind the suspect of their entitlement to free legal advice and that the interview can be delayed for legal advice to be obtained, unless one of the exceptions in *Code C 6.6* applies. It is the interviewer's responsibility to make sure all reminders are recorded in the interview record.

Juveniles and mentally disordered suspects

A juvenile or person who is mentally disordered or otherwise mentally vulnerable must not be interviewed regarding their involvement or suspected involvement in a criminal offence or offences, or asked to provide or sign a written statement under caution or record of interview, in the absence of the appropriate adult unless *Code C* 11.1, 11.18 to 11.20 apply.

Juveniles may only be interviewed at their place of education in exceptional circumstances and only when the principal or their nominee agrees. Every effort should be made to notify the parent(s) or other person responsible for the juvenile's welfare and the appropriate adult, if this is a different person, that the police want to interview the juvenile and reasonable time should be allowed to enable the appropriate adult to be present at the interview. If awaiting the appropriate adult would cause unreasonable delay, and unless the juvenile is suspected of an offence against the educational establishment, the principal or their nominee can act as the appropriate adult for the purposes of the interview.

In relation to urgent interviews see *Code C 11.18.*

Key points

- Cautioning – *Code C 10.1*

- Special warning – *Code C 10.10*

- Previous statements or silence - *Code C 11.4*

- Interview records - *Code C 11.7*

- Interpreters - *Code C 13.1*

- Special restriction - *Code C 14.1*

- Videotaped interviews – *Code F*

- Exclusion of solicitor – *Code C 6.9*

Oppression

No interviewer may try to obtain answers or elicit a statement by the use of oppression.

Except as in *Code C 10.9*, no interviewer shall indicate, except to answer a direct question, what action will be taken by the police if the person being questioned answers questions, makes a statement or refuses to do either. If the person asks directly what action will be taken if they answer questions, make a statement or refuse to do either, the interviewer may inform them what action the police propose to take provided that action is itself proper and warranted.

Ending the interview

The interview or further interview of a person about an offence with which that person has not been charged or for which they have not been informed they may be prosecuted, must cease when:

(a)   the officer in charge of the investigation is satisfied all the questions they consider relevant to obtaining accurate and reliable information about the offence have been put to the suspect, this includes allowing the suspect an opportunity to give an innocent explanation and asking questions to test if the explanation is accurate and reliable, e.g. to clear up ambiguities or clarify what the suspect said;

(b)   the officer in charge of the investigation has taken account of any other available evidence; and

(c)   the officer in charge of the investigation, or in the case of a detained suspect, the custody officer, see *Code C 16.1*, reasonably believes there is sufficient evidence to provide a realistic prospect of conviction for that offence. See Note 11B

This paragraph does not prevent officers in revenue cases or acting under the confiscation provisions of the Criminal Justice Act 1988 or the Drug Trafficking Act 1994 from inviting suspects to complete a formal question and answer record after the interview is concluded.

Juvenile detainees

Definition of

A suspect who appears to be under 17 years of age (s. 37(15) *PACE 1984*).

Purpose of detention

Detention will generally be for the purposes of investigating a criminal offence. There is no legal bar on arresting a juvenile under the age of criminal responsibility (although in most cases the necessity of doing so is questionable) in order to assist in determining whether a criminal offence has been committed and if so by whom.

In addition to normal powers to arrest in connection with criminal matters, juveniles can be taken into police custody for the following reasons:

- To keep them safe (s. 46 *Children Act 1989*);

- In compliance with a local child curfew (ss. 14,15 *CDA 1998*);

- Child absent from school (ss. 16(3), (3ZA) *CDA 1998*).

Key points

- There is a duty to notify those with a concern for the juvenile's welfare of the arrest (s. 34 *CYPA 1933, Code C 3.13*);

- Juvenile should not be held in a cell unless there is no other suitable and secure accommodation (*Code C 8.8*);

- There is a requirement for an appropriate adult (*Code C 3.18*);

- Juveniles should not be interviewed at their place of education, save in exceptional circumstances (*Code C 11.16*);

- If the juvenile is charged and refused bail he ought to be detained in local authority accommodation. In practice this rarely happens as secure accommodation is generally not available (see: s. 38(6) *PACE 1984, Code C 16.7*)

Appropriate adults

See *Code C 1.7*. It should be noted that appropriate adults are not bound by legal privilege.

Legal Aid Funding

Payment rates

A full list of payment rates, including police station fixed fees ("PSFF) can be found in *Appendix 4*.

2010 Contract, payment issues

A number of important changes to the remuneration of police station work were made in the July 2010 Standard Criminal Contract.

Witnesses

Before attending on witnesses at the police station some complicating factor must be identified, such as self-incrimination

DSCC reference number

The DSCC reference number must be obtained in all cases and recorded on file. A failure to record the number will result in nil assessment on audit.

In the event that a case generates more than one PSFF, a reference number must be obtained in relation to each and every fixed fee claimed.

e.g. You attend the police station to represent S who has been arrested for 2 offences. At the conclusion of the interview S is charged with one offence and bailed to return to the police station in respect to the other offence.

In this scenario your attendance at the bail to return for the second matter (provided it is justified under the contract) entitles you to a further PSFF; therefore you should contact the DSCC in order to obtain a second reference number. It should be noted that guidance issued in 2008 stated than only 1 number would be required – the LSC has confirmed that following the 2010 contract this guidance is no longer valid, and in January 2011 the LSC stated that it was changing the guidance to reflect the new obligation.

Telephone advice fixed fee

In order to trigger payment for a TAFF at least one call must be made to the client. Previously it only had to be a call on behalf of the client.

e.g. You are contacted by DSCC and as a result call the police station. You cannot speak to your client as he is drunk and asleep. In the morning you call back only to find out that he has been released already.

There would be no fee claimable in the above scenario.

Conflicts

The starting point is that you are paid one PSFF per client. However, under the 2010 contract if you have to withdraw from a case due to conflict of interest the following rule applies:

You always get a minimum of one fee, but never more fees than the number of suspects that you continue to represent.

E.g. You attend at the police station to represent Jack. On attending you find out that the complainant in the matter is an existing client of yours, and therefore you cannot act due to conflict.

In the above example one fee is payable.

e.g. You attend at the police station to represent 5 suspects. On attending you decide that you cannot act for 2 of the suspects due to conflict.

In this example you will be paid 3 x PSFF as this is the number of suspects that you continue to represent. You would however be entitled to claim TAFF's in relation to the 2 other suspects provided that you had spoken to them on the telephone (see above).

Note that it does not matter at what stage during the investigation stage the conflict arises.

Claiming more than one police station fixed fee

The following 4 rules dictate how many fees can be charged. Go through all 4 in relation to each case in order to determine how many fees arise.

Rule 1

An arrest for a new matter outside a continuous period of custody results in a new fee.

e.g. S is arrested and bailed to return to a future date. The day after he is released he is arrested for a new offence.

In the above example the second arrest triggers a new fee; this is irrespective of the new offence and applied even if the offences are linked.

Rule 2

With the sole exception of the case outlined in rule 1, there are no circumstances in which one single attendance at the police station might result in more than one fee. Attendance means during a continuous period of custody, so leaving the police station during a period when S is still in custody, to return later during that continuous detention period for a further attendance, does not count as a second attendance.

Rule 3

If S is charged with one or more offences AND is bailed to return for one or more other offences AND there is a contractually effective attendance on that second occasion, there will be at least 2 PSFF's claimable.

Notes:

1. In relation to the above rule no consideration needs to be given to the actual offences involved.
2. The word *charged* has a clear meaning. Therefore if one offence resulted in no further action or a caution, and another bailed to return, this would not trigger a new fee under this rule.
3. In order to achieve a contractually effective second attendance you must (a) take steps to ensure that the bail to return is effective before attending, (b) ensure that there is sufficient benefit in attending on the next occasion and making a note of the same on file, and (c) actually attend.
4. This rule will trigger at least 2 PSFF's. There may be more claimable under the principles outlined in rule 4.

Rule 4

If S is being investigated in relation to one or more offences AND there have been at least 2 contractually effective attendances, one fee will be payable for each and every matter which involve genuinely separate legal problems requiring separate advice.

As a starting point indictment rule principles should be applied, so if the offences are based on the same facts or form part of a series of offences then only 1 fee will be payable.

The LSC has issued some guidance that seeks to restrict the above. So for example, S is arrested for assault and when he arrives at the police station there are drugs found on him. This case at the moment is only 1 fee as there is only one attendance. It may become 2 fees due to rule 3 or 4. Let's say that S is bailed to return on both matters and that you properly attend that bail to return. In that instance rule 3 does not trigger, but does rule 4? You would have thought so as those 2 offences would not ordinarily be tried on the same indictment on the bare facts given, but the LSC guidance states that it is one fee.

An assault during arrest would certainly not be a separate matter, but consider criminal damage to a police cell, an assault during police detention or an offence of abstracting electricity discovered during a house search – all of those might depending on the exact circumstances.

The reality is that few cases will result in more than 1 fee and in all instances where you are seeking to claim more than 1 fee a clear justification for doing so must be recorded on your file.

Mentally disordered or otherwise mentally vulnerable suspects

Key points

- Defined in *Code C Note 1G*. The MHA 1983 has since been amended but the Code should be followed unless and until it is amended to reflect the legislative change;

- Vulnerable persons may be taken to the police station in order to provide a place of safety (s. 136 *MHA 1983*), it will be rare for a solicitor to become involved in the absence of any criminal investigation;

- An appropriate adult is required (*Code C 3.15*);

- Diversion from the criminal process should be considered in all cases and legal advisers need to be especially alert to ensure that vulnerable people are not unnecessarily brought into the criminal process.

Photographs, taking of

A photograph (which is defined to include video) can be taken with consent or without consent in appropriate cases if the person is detained at a police station (s. 64A *PACE 1984*). A photograph should only be obtained without consent if consent has been refused or it is not practicable to obtain consent.

For the power to take a photograph at a location other than a police station see s.64A(1A), (1B) *PACE 1984*.

A suspect under 14 years of age cannot consent – a parent or guardian will need to consent on his behalf. A juvenile aged 14-16 can consent, but the consent of a parent or guardian must also be obtained as well.

Police can require articles (e.g. hats, spectacles) to be removed (s. 64A(2) *PACE 1984*), if they obstruct the whole or part of head or face.

Police can use reasonable force to take a photograph and/or remove an article obstructing the whole or part of head or face, but only where it is not reasonable practicable to take the photograph covertly (*Code D 5.14*).

Post-charge interview, terrorism cases

Counter Terrorism Act 2008

Not in force at time of writing.

s.22 Post-charge questioning: England and Wales

(1) The following provisions apply in England and Wales.

(2) A judge of the Crown Court may authorise the questioning of a person about an offence--

(a) after the person has been charged with the offence or been officially informed that they may be prosecuted for it, or

(b) after the person has been sent for trial for the offence,

if the offence is a terrorism offence or it appears to the judge that the offence has a terrorist connection.

(3) The judge--

(a) must specify the period during which questioning is authorised, and

(b) may impose such conditions as appear to be necessary in the interests of justice, which may include conditions as to the place where the questioning is to be carried out.

(4) The period during which questioning is authorised--

(a) begins when questioning pursuant to the authorisation begins and runs continuously from that time (whether or not questioning continues), and

(b) must not exceed 48 hours.

This is without prejudice to any application for a further authorisation under this section.

(5) Where the person is in prison or otherwise lawfully detained, the judge may authorise the person's removal to another place and detention there for the purpose of being questioned.

(6) A judge must not authorise the questioning of a person under this section unless satisfied--

(a) that further questioning of the person is necessary in the interests of justice,

(b) that the investigation for the purposes of which the further questioning is proposed is being conducted diligently and expeditiously, and

(c) that what is authorised will not interfere unduly with the preparation of the person's defence to the charge in question or any other criminal charge.

(7) Codes of Practice under section 66 of the Police and Criminal Evidence Act 1984 (c. 60) must make provision about the questioning of a person by a constable in accordance with this section.

(8) Nothing in this section prevents Codes of Practice under that section making other provision for the questioning of a person by a constable about an offence--

(a) after the person has been charged with the offence or been officially informed that they may be prosecuted for it, or

(b) after the person has been sent for trial for the offence.

Inferences from silence

Section 34 CJPOA 1994 will, on commencement of this section, be amended to allow for inferences to be drawn from silence in appropriate cases.

Recordable offences

The following are recordable offences for the purposes of recording on the police national computer and the taking of fingerprints without consent (*SI 2000/1139; SI 2005/3106; SI 2007/2121*):

i. Any offence for which an adult could face imprisonment
ii. Offences specified under secondary legislation:

1. section 5 of the Children and Young Persons Act 1933 (offence of giving intoxicating liquor to children under five);

2. section 11 of the Children and Young Persons Act 1933 (offence of exposing children under twelve to risk of burning(2);

3. section 12 of the Children and Young Persons Act 1933 (offence of failing to provide for safety of children at entertainments);

4. section 91 of the Criminal Justice Act 1967(4) (offence of drunkenness in a public place);

5. section 167 of the Criminal Justice and Public Order Act 1994 (offence of touting for hire car services)

6. section 2 of the Crossbows Act 1987 (offence of purchasing or hiring a crossbow or part of a crossbow by person under the age of seventeen);

7. section 3 of the Crossbows Act 1987 (offence of possessing a crossbow or parts of a crossbow by unsupervised person under the age of seventeen);

8. section 5(6) of the Firearms Act 1968 (offence of failing to deliver up authority to possess prohibited weapon or ammunition);

9. section 22(3) of the Firearms Act 1968 (offence of possessing an assembled shotgun by unsupervised person under the age of fifteen);

10. section 22(4) of the Firearms Act 1968 (offence of possessing an air weapon or ammunition for an air weapon by unsupervised person under the age of fourteen);

11. section 22(5) of the Firearms Act 1968 (offence of possessing in a public place an air weapon by unsupervised person under the age of seventeen);

12. section 2 of the Football (Offences) Act 1991 (offence of throwing missiles);

13. section 3 of the Football (Offences) Act 1991 (offence of indecent or racialist chanting);

14. section 4 of the Football (Offences) Act 1991 (offence of unlawfully going on to the playing area);

15. section 30 of the Game Act 1831(offences of trespassing in daytime on land in search of game, etc.);

16. section 31 of the Game Act 1831 (offence of refusal of person trespassing in daytime on land in search of game to give his name and address);

17. section 32 of the Game Act 1831 (offence of five or more persons being found armed in daytime in search of game and using violence or refusal of such persons to give name and address);

18. section 12 of the Licensing Act 1872 (offence of being drunk in highway or public place);

19. section 59(5) of the Licensing Act 2003 (offence of obstructing an authorised person inspecting premises before the grant of a licence etc.);

20. section 82(6) of the Licensing Act 2003 (offence of failing to notify change of name or alteration of rules of club);

21. section 96(5) of the Licensing Act 2003 (offence of obstructing an authorised person inspecting premises before the grant of a certificate etc.);

22. section 108(3) of the Licensing Act 2003 (offence of obstructing an authorised person exercising a right of entry where a temporary event notice has been given);

23. section 123(2) of the Licensing Act 2003 (offence of failing to notify licensing authority of convictions during application period);

24. section 128(6) of the Licensing Act 2003 (offence of failing to notify court of personal licence);

24A. section 138(1) of the Licensing Act 2003 (offence of keeping alcohol on premises for unauthorised sale etc.);

24B. section 140(1) of the Licensing Act 2003 (offence of allowing disorderly conduct on licensed premises etc.);

24C. section 141(1) of the Licensing Act 2003 (offence of selling alcohol to a person who is drunk);

24D. section 142(1) of the Licensing Act 2003 (offence of obtaining alcohol for a person who is drunk);

24E. section 143(1) of the Licensing Act 2003 (offence of failing to leave licensed premises etc.);

24F. section 144(1) of the Licensing Act 2003 (offence of keeping smuggled goods);

24G. section 145(1) of the Licensing Act 2003 (offence of allowing unaccompanied children on certain premises);

24H. section 146(1) and (3) of the Licensing Act 2003 (offence of selling alcohol to children);

24I. section 147(1) of the Licensing Act 2003 (offence of allowing sale of alcohol to children);

24J. section 149(1), (3) and (4) of the Licensing Act 2003 (offence of purchasing alcohol by or on behalf of children);

24K. section 150(1) and (2) of the Licensing Act 2003 (offence of consumption of alcohol on relevant premises by children);

24L. section 151(1), (2) and (4) of the Licensing Act 2003 (offence of delivering alcohol to children);

24M. section 152 (1) of the Licensing Act 2003 (offence of send a child to obtain alcohol);

24N. section 153(1) of the Licensing Act 2003 (offence of allowing unsupervised sales by children);

24O. section 158(1) of the Licensing Act 2003 (offence of making false statements);

24P. section 160(4) of the Licensing Act 2003 (offence of allowing premises to remain open following a closure order);

24Q. section 179(4) of the Licensing Act 2003 (offence of obstructing authorised person exercising rights of entry to investigate licensable activities);

25. paragraph 21 of Schedule 3 to the Local Government (Miscellaneous Provisions) Act 1982(13) (offence of making false statement in connection with an application for a sex establishment licence);

26. ...

27. article 44 of the Nursing and Midwifery Order 2001(3) (offence of falsely claiming a professional qualification etc.);

28. section 1 of the Night Poaching Act 1828 (offence of taking or destroying game or rabbits by night, or entering any land for that purpose);

29. section 90(2) of the Police Act 1996 (offence of wearing police uniform with intent to deceive);

30. section 90(3) of the Police Act 1996 (offence of unlawful possession of article of police uniform);

31. section 5 of the Public Order Act 1986 (offence of causing harassment, alarm or distress);

32. section 11 of the Public Order Act 1986 (offence of failing to give advance notice of public procession);

33. section 12(5) of the Public Order Act 1986 (offence of failing to comply with conditions imposed on a public procession);

34. section 13(8) of the Public Order Act 1986 (offence of taking part in a prohibited public procession);

35. section 14(5) of the Public Order Act 1986 (offence of failing to comply with conditions imposed on a public assembly);

36. section 14B(2) of the Public Order Act 1986 (offence of taking part in a prohibited assembly);

37. section 14C(3) of the Public Order Act 1986 (offence of failing to comply with directions);

38. section 6 of the Road Traffic Act 1988(21) (offence of failing to provide specimen of breath);

39. section 25 of the Road Traffic Act 1988 (penalisation of tampering with vehicles);

40. section 1 of the Sexual Offences Act 1985 (offence of kerb crawling);

41. section 2 of the Sexual Offences Act 1985 (offence of persistently soliciting women for the purpose of prostitution);

42. section 1(2) of the Sporting Events (Control of Alcohol Etc.) Act 1985(23) (offence of allowing alcohol to be carried on public vehicles on journey to or from designated sporting event);

43. section 1(4) of the Sporting Events (Control of Alcohol Etc.) Act 1985 (offence of being drunk on public vehicles on journey to or from designated sporting event);

44. section 1A(2) of the Sporting Events (Control of Alcohol Etc.) Act 1985(24) (offence of allowing alcohol to be carried in vehicles on journey to or from designated sporting event);

45. section 2(2) of the Sporting Events (Control of Alcohol Etc.) Act 1985 (offence of trying to enter designated sports ground while drunk);

46. section 166(1) of the Criminal Justice and Public Order Act 1994 (offence of unauthorised sale or disposal of tickets for a designated football match);

47. section 19(6) of the Football Spectators Act 1989 (offence of an individual subject to a banning order failing to comply with the requirements determined by the enforcing authority and made of him by a police officer on the individual's initial reporting at the police station);

48. section 20(10) of the Football Spectators Act 1989 (offence of a person subject to a banning order knowingly or recklessly providing false or misleading information in support of his application for an exemption from a reporting requirement of his banning order)

49. ...

50. section 1 of the Street Offences Act 1959 (offence of loitering or soliciting for purposes of prostitution);

51. ...

52. section 12(5) of the Theft Act 1968 (offence of taking or riding a pedal cycle without owner's consent).

53. section 3 of the Vagrancy Act 1824 (offence of begging); and

54. section 4 of the Vagrancy Act 1824 (offence of persistent begging)

Rights, upon arrest

A suspect must be informed that he is under arrest at the time of arrest, or as soon as practicable afterwards (s. 28(1) *PACE 1984*), unless he escapes before that information can be given (s. 28(5) *PACE 1984*). It is irrelevant that the fact of arrest is obvious (e.g. suspect detained and handcuffed).

Similarly he must be informed of the grounds for his arrest. The arresting officer's minimum obligation is to inform the suspect sufficiently of the nature of the arrest, that is to say the act or acts which justify detention, to give him a sufficient opportunity to respond (*Wilson v Chief Constable of Lancashire Constabulary* (2001) 2 WLR 302).

The officer giving the information need not be the arresting officer (*Dhesi v Chief Constable of the West Midlands*, The Times 9 May 2000).

Failure to adhere to section 28 will render the arrest unlawful.

If the arrest takes place away from the police station he must either be bailed (s. 30A *PACE 1984*), or taken to a police station as soon as is practicable (see s. 30(10) *PACE 1984*). That police station ought generally to be a designated police station unless one of the exceptions applies (s. 30 *PACE 1984*).

Rights, when suspect arrives at the police station

Information on arrival at a police station

Upon arrival at the police station suspects will be advised as to the following (*Code C 3.1, 3.2*):

- The right to have someone informed of their arrest. If the first person named is not available, up to a further 2 individuals can be named, in practice however custody officers generally exercise their discretion to enable further attempts. This right may be delayed for up to 36 hours if detained for an indictable offence and an officer of at least the rank of Inspector believes one or more of the grounds specified in section 56(5) or 56(5A) *PACE 1984* are met. The suspect should be notified of the reasons for any delay in conferring this right and those reasons should be noted on the custody record.

- The right to consult a solicitor free of charge (for which see later)

- The right to consult the Codes of Practice

The suspect must also be given a written notice setting out:

- The above three rights

- The arrangements for securing legal advice

- The right to a copy of the custody record (see *Code C 2.4A*)

- The caution

- Entitlements while in custody

Certain foreign nationals must be informed as soon as practicable about their rights of communication with their High Commission, Embassy or Consulate (*Code C 7*).

Medical attention

Medical attention must be summonsed when the criteria under *Code C 9.5* is met. The suspect can also request a medical examination (*Code C 9.8*) and can instruct a doctor privately is he so wishes.

Rest

The suspect must be allowed at least 8 hours uninterrupted rest within each 24 hour period (*Code C 12.2*).

That rest period can be dispensed with at the request of the suspect (but note that the custody officer will still be the arbiter of whether the suspect is fit for interview), or if allowing rest would:

1. Risk harm to persons;

2. Risk serious loss of, or damage to, property;

3. Unnecessarily delay the suspect's release from custody; or

4. Prejudice the outcome of the investigation.

Letters and telephone calls

Suspects must be afforded access to writing materials and may speak with one person on the telephone for a 'reasonable' time. A custody officer does of course have the discretion to allow further calls. Communications can be read/listened to, provided that they are not privileged (*Code C 5.6-7*).

Miscellaneous rights

1. Assistance to blind or illiterate suspects (*Code C* 5.6);

2. Detention in single cell with adequate heating, lighting, ventilation and cleanliness (*Code C 8.1-2*);

3. Bedding to a reasonable standard (*Code C 8.3*);

4. Access to toilet and washing facilities (*Code C 8.4*);

5. Clothing (*Code C 8.5*);

6. Food and drink (*Code C 8.6*);

7. Exercise (*Code C 8.7*).

Samples

Intimate samples

- Defined under s. 65 *PACE 1984*;

- Modified provisions apply in relation to terrorism suspects (see later in this book);

- Can only be taken with consent (s. 62, 65 *PACE 1984*);

- Can only be taken if s.62(2) *PACE 1984* satisfied;

- S. 3 *CSA 2010* came in to force on 7th March 2011 and extended the range of conditions under which a sample could be requested (see ss. 62(2A), (2B) *PACE 1984*;

- Samples can be taken outside of a police station (s. 63A *PACE 1984*);

- Samples can only be taken in relation to recordable offences (for which see *Recordable offences* earlier in this book);

- An inference may lie from refusal to give an intimate sample (s. 62(10) *PACE 1984*);

The law on retention and destruction of samples is complex (see s. 64 *PACE 1984*). Section 14 *CSA* 2010 will substantially alter the present provisions but was not in force at the time of writing.

Non-intimate samples

- Defined under s. 65 *PACE 1984*;

- Modified provisions apply in relation to terrorism suspects (see later in this book);

- Can be taken with consent (see s. 65 *PACE 1984* for juveniles);

- Can be taken without consent provided criteria satisfied (s. 63 *PACE 1984*);

- Sections 2,3 and 4 *CSA 2010* came in to force on 7th March 2011 and made substantial amendments to the range of circumstances in which samples could be taken (see s 63 *PACE 1984*);

The law on retention and destruction of samples is complex (see s. 64 *PACE 1984*). Section 14 CSA 2010 will substantially alter the present provisions but was not in force at the time of writing.

Footwear impressions

- Can be taken with or without consent (s. 61A, 65 *PACE 1984*);

Handwriting samples

There is no legislative scheme covering such samples and in the absence of any positive reason to provide a sample (e.g. to exculpate a suspect) one must question the reason for cooperating. It is doubtful whether any inferences lie as a result of a refusal to give a handwriting sample but there appears to be no case law on the point.

Drugs, presence of

- Sample can be requested after charge;

- Sections 63B, 63C *PACE 1984* apply;

- Refusal without good cause is a criminal offence (3 months imprisonment/level 4);

- There must be a trigger offence (see below), or any other offence where an inspector has reasonable grounds for suspecting that the misuse by the suspect of a Class A drug has caused or contributed to that offence;

- The suspect must either be an adult, or aged between 14 and 17 years in a specified area.

Trigger offence

Sch. 6 *Criminal Justice and Court Services Act 2000*:

Offences under the following provisions of the Theft Act 1968 are trigger offences:

section 1 (theft)

section 8 (robbery)

section 9 (burglary)

section 10 (aggravated burglary)

section 12 (taking motor vehicle or other conveyance without authority)

section 12A (aggravated vehicle-taking)

section 22 (handling stolen goods)

section 25 (going equipped for stealing, etc.)

An offence under section 1(1) of the Criminal Attempts Act 1981 is a trigger offence, if committed in respect of an offence under:

(a) any of the following provisions of the Theft Act 1968:

section 1 (theft)

section 8 (robbery)

section 9 (burglary)

section 22 (handling stolen goods), or

(b) section 1 of the Fraud Act 2006 (fraud)

Offences under the following provisions of the Misuse of Drugs Act 1971 are trigger offences, if committed in respect of a specified Class A drug:

section 4 (restriction on production and supply of controlled drugs)

section 5(2) (possession of controlled drug)

section 5(3) (possession of controlled drug with intent to supply)

Offences under the following provisions of the Fraud Act 2006 are trigger offences-

section 1 (fraud)

section 6 (possession etc. of articles for use in frauds)

section 7 (making or supplying articles for use in frauds)

Offences under the following provisions of the Vagrancy Act 1824 are trigger offences:

section 3 (begging)

section 4 (persistent begging)

Search, of person or premises

Definitions

Premises, meaning of

Section 23 *PACE 1984*:

In this Act--

"premises" includes any place and, in particular, includes--

(a) any vehicle, vessel, aircraft or hovercraft;

(b) any offshore installation;

(ba) any renewable energy installation;

(c) any tent or movable structure;

"offshore installation" has the meaning given to it by section 1 of the Mineral Workings (Offshore Installations) Act 1971.

'renewable energy installation' has the same meaning as in Chapter 2 of Part 2 of the Energy Act 2004.

Note the use of the expression 'any place'. This is important in the context of searches in a public place, and premises should not be thought to be restricted simply to buildings and other structures.

Prohibited articles

Section 1(7) *PACE 1984*:

An article is prohibited for the purposes of this Part of this Act if it is--

(a) an offensive weapon; or

(b) an article--

(i) made or adapted for use in the course of or in connection with an offence to which this sub-paragraph applies; or

(ii) intended by the person having it with him for such use by him or by some other person.

(8) The offences to which subsection (7)(b)(i) above applies are--

(a) burglary;

(b) theft;

(c) offences under section 12 of the Theft Act 1968 (taking motor vehicle or other conveyance without authority);

(d) fraud (contrary to section 1 of the Fraud Act 2006); and

(e) offences under section 1 of the Criminal Damage Act 1971 (destroying or damaging property).

Overview of search powers

See *Code A Annex A* for a summary of the main search powers.

Pre-arrest

Person or premises	Purpose	Trigger	Power
Person or vehicle; anything which is in or on a vehicle. But note: A constable may exercise any power conferred by this section-- (a) in any place to which at the time when he proposes to exercise the power the public or any section of the public has access, on payment or otherwise, as of right or by virtue of express or implied permission; or	For stolen or prohibited articles or for any firework which a person possesses in contravention of a prohibition imposed by fireworks regulations.	Reasonable grounds to believe that he will find stolen or prohibited articles. Note that if the search is to take place in a yard or garden associated with a dwelling, the criteria in s. 1(4), (5) *PACE 1984* must be met.	s. 1 *PACE 1984*

(b) in any other place to which people have ready access at the time when he proposes to exercise the power but which is not a dwelling.			
Person or vehicle	For offensive weapons, bladed or sharply pointed instruments.	Reasonable grounds to believe that incidents involving serious violence or that the person is carrying such articles	s. 60 *CJPOA 1994*
Certain persons or vehicle	For the purpose of searching for articles of a kind which could be used in connection with terrorism	Authorisation under s. 44 *Terrorism Act 2000*	s. 45 *TA 2000*
Premises	To search for evidence in relation to the offence for which the suspect was arrested.	Must have been in the premises at the time of arrest of immediately before the arrest. Premises is defined under s. 23 *PACE 1984*.	s. 32 *PACE 1984*

An officer can only require the removal of an outer coat, jacket or gloves in public (s. 2(9) *PACE 1984*). If removal of other items of clothing is required an officer must conduct the search in private. For searches under s. 60 *CJPOA* 1994 see s.60(4A) *CJPOA 1994* for clothing removal powers. For searches under s. 45 *TA 2000* see s. 45(3) for additional powers authorizing officer to require removal of shoes and headgear.

Search of person, post arrest but prior to arrival at a police station

Person or premises	Purpose	Trigger	Power
Person	Seize articles	Reasonable grounds to suspect that the suspect may present a danger to himself or others, or for seizing evidence or an item that could be used to facilitate escape (there must be a reasonable belief that the suspect has such items).	s. 32 *PACE 1984*

Search of premises, post arrest

Person or premises	Purpose	Trigger	Power
Premises	Search for items linked to the offence for which the suspect was arrested, or any other indictable offence connected with or similar to that offence.	Arrest for an indictable offence. Premises must be in the occupation, or under the control, of the suspect. Inspector must authorise unless carried out before the suspect arrives at a police station.	s. 18 *PACE 1984*

Search of person, at a police station

Person or premises	Purpose	Trigger	Power
Person	In order to ascertain what the person has with him	Necessity, or to ascertain whether suspect has any item which may be used to cause injury, damage to	s. 54 *PACE 1984*

		property, interfere with evidence, or to assist with escape.	
Person	In order to ascertain identity; more specifically in order to search for any 'mark'.	Authority of Inspector. Suspect must either have refused to identify himself, or officer believes suspect not to be the person he claims to be.	s. 54A *PACE 1984*
Person – strip searches	In order to discover any item that the suspect is not allowed to have with him. Removal of outer clothing permitted.	Necessity.	s. 54(6) *PACE 1984* *Code C Annex A*
Person – intimate search		Authority of Inspector who believes items cannot be found without an intimate search.	s. 55 *PACE 1984*

Seizure of clothing and personal effects

Clothing and personal effects may be seized (s. 54 *PACE 1984*) as evidence or if the officer believes that the suspect may use them:

1. To cause physical harm (to himself or another);
2. To damage property
3. To interfere with evidence; or
4. To assist in an escape

Personal effects are defined in *Code C 4.3.*

Silence, right of

Common law

The right to remain silent when questioned by police remains intact, the issue is whether or not a court can draw inferences from silence.

At common law there if no question of an inference being drawn. For most practical purposes however the position is now regulated under statute.

There are some notable exceptions to the common law protection, namely:

- Silence in the face of an accusation made by a victim;

- Interviews in relation to companies, e.g. *Companies Act 2006, Insolvency Act 1986, Financial Services and Markets Act 2000, Insurance Companies Act 1982, Company Directors Disqualification Act 1986, Building Societies Act 1986, Banking Act 1987.* Note however that s.59 *Youth Justice and Criminal Evidence Act 1999* prevents answers given in such interviews from being used in criminal proceedings (save for perjury etc).

- Serious Fraud Office interviews under s.2 *Criminal Justice Act 1987*.

Criminal Justice and Public Order Act 1994

S.34 Effect of accused's failure to mention facts when questioned or charged.

(1) Where, in any proceedings against a person for an offence, evidence is given that the accused--

(a) at any time before he was charged with the offence, on being questioned under caution by a constable trying to discover whether or by whom the offence had been committed, failed to mention any fact relied on in his defence in those proceedings; or

(b) on being charged with the offence or officially informed that he might be prosecuted for it, failed to mention any such fact,

being a fact which in the circumstances existing at the time the accused could reasonably have been expected to mention when so questioned, charged or informed, as the case may be, subsection (2) below applies.

Where this section applies:

(a) a magistrates' court inquiring into the offence as examining justices;

(b) a judge, in deciding whether to grant an application made by the accused under paragraph 2 of Schedule 3 to the Crime and Disorder Act 1998;

(c) the court, in determining whether there is a case to answer; and

(d) the court or jury, in determining whether the accused is guilty of the offence charged,

may draw such inferences from the failure as appear proper.

When s.22(9) *Counter Terrorism Act 2008* comes in to force, post-charge questioning under the provisions of s.22 will fall under s.34 *CJPOA 1994* and therefore a suspect will be at risk of an inference being drawn.

Where the accused was at an authorised place of detention at the time of the failure, subsections (1) and (2) above do not apply if he had not been allowed an opportunity to consult a solicitor prior to being questioned, charged or informed as mentioned in subsection (1) above.

s.36 Effect of accused's failure or refusal to account for objects, substances or marks.

Where--

(a) a person is arrested by a constable, and there is--

(i) on his person; or

(ii) in or on his clothing or footwear; or

(iii) otherwise in his possession; or

(iv) in any place in which he is at the time of his arrest,

any object, substance or mark, or there is any mark on any such object; and

that or another constable investigating the case reasonably believes that the presence of the object, substance or mark may be attributable to the participation of the person arrested in the commission of an offence specified by the constable; and

(c) the constable informs the person arrested that he so believes, and requests him to account for the presence of the object, substance or mark; and

(d) the person fails or refuses to do so

A court may draw such inferences from the failure or refusal as appear proper.

s.37 Effect of accused's failure or refusal to account for presence at a particular place.

(1) Where--

(a) a person arrested by a constable was found by him at a place at or about the time the offence for which he was arrested is alleged to have been committed; and

(b) that or another constable investigating the offence reasonably believes that the presence of the person at that place and at that time may be attributable to his participation in the commission of the offence; and

(c) the constable informs the person that he so believes, and requests him to account for that presence; and

(d) the person fails or refuses to do so,

A court may draw such inferences from the failure or refusal as appear proper.

When inferences cannot be drawn

Code C Annex C deals with those instances where an inference will not arise from silence. A modified caution will be used, and the police must revert back to the appropriate caution should the suspect's status change.

Waiver of privilege

Nothing should be done by the adviser at the police station that might have the effect of waiving legal privilege. Under no circumstances should the reason(s) for a client declining to answer a question be given on tape as there is no possible advantage to be gained by that approach, and it is likely to lead to a waiver of privilege:

If, in the course of pre-trial questioning by the police, a suspect goes beyond saying that he declines to answer on legal advice and explains the basis on which he has been so advised, or if (as in the present case), his solicitor acting as his authorised representative gives such an explanation, a waiver of legal professional privilege is involved. (R v Bowden).

Whilst there is no advantage in saying anything at all to explain silence in interview, a mere assertion that the suspect is remaining silent on legal advice will not amount to a waiver of privilege (*R v Condron*).

The issue of waiver was considered in *R v Seaton* [2010] EWCA Crim 1980, and the following principles emerge:

a) Legal professional privilege is of paramount importance. There is no question of balancing privilege against other considerations of public interest: *R v Derby Justices ex p B*.

b) Therefore, in the absence of waiver, no question can be asked which intrudes upon privilege. That means, inter alia, that if a suggestion of recent fabrication is being pursued at trial, a witness, including the defendant, cannot, unless he has waived privilege, be asked whether he told his counsel or solicitor what he now says is the truth. Such a question would require him either to waive his privilege or suffer criticism for not doing so. If any such question is asked by an opposing party (whether the Crown or a co-accused) the judge must stop it, tell the witness directly that he does not need to answer it, and explain to the jury that no one can be asked about things which pass confidentially between him and his lawyer. For the same reasons, in the absence of waiver, the witness cannot be asked whether he is willing to waive.

c) However, the defendant is perfectly entitled to open up his communication with his lawyer, and it may sometimes be in his interest to do so. One example of when he may wish to do so is to rebut a suggestion of recent fabrication. Another may be to adduce in evidence the reasons he was advised not to answer questions. If he does so, there is no question of breach of privilege, because he cannot be in breach of his own privilege. What is happening is that he is waiving privilege.

d) If the defendant does give evidence of what passed between him and his solicitor he is not thereby waiving privilege entirely and generally, that is to say he does not automatically make available to all other parties everything that he said to his solicitor, or his solicitor to him, on every occasion. He may well not even be opening up everything said on the occasion of which he gives evidence, and not on topics unrelated to that of which he gives evidence. The test is fairness and/or the avoidance of a misleading impression. It is that the defendant should not, as it has been put in some of the cases, be able both to 'have his cake and eat it'.

e) If a defendant says that he gave his solicitor the account now offered at trial, that will ordinarily mean that he can be cross examined about exactly what he told the solicitor on that topic, and if the comment is fair another party can comment upon the fact that the solicitor has not been called to confirm something which, if it is true, he easily could confirm. If it is intended to pursue cross examination beyond what is evidently opened up, the proper extent of it can be discussed and the judge invited to rule.

f) A defendant who adduces evidence that he was advised by his lawyer not to answer questions but goes no further than that does not thereby waive privilege. This is the ratio of Bowden and is well established. After all, the mere fact of the advice can equally well be made evident by the solicitor announcing at the interview that he gives it then and there, and there is then no revelation whatever of any private conversation between him and the defendant.

g) But a defendant who adduces evidence of the content of, or reasons for, such advice, beyond the mere fact of it, does waive privilege at least to the extent of opening up questions which properly go to whether such reason can be the true explanation for his silence: Bowden. That will ordinarily include questions relating to recent fabrication, and thus to what he told his solicitor of the facts now relied upon at trial: *Bowden* and *Loizou*.

h) The rules as to privilege and waiver, and thus as to cross examination and comment, are the same whether it is the Crown or a co-accused who challenges the defendant.

The drawing of inferences

In R *v Argent* the court ruled that there are 6 formal conditions that must be met before an inference can be drawn:

(a) Proceedings for an offence must have been commenced
(b) A failure to account during an interview prior to charge. Note that failure to mention a fact on charge may also give rise to an inference (in R *v Dervish* [2001] EWCA Crim 2789) it was observed that a court must given separate consideration to the issue of whether an inference should be drawn in relation to each separate stage of the proceedings, i.e. during interview, and on charge).
(c) The questioning must be under caution. If an officer omits to caution the suspect the adviser should do nothing to rectify the error. Whilst this is unlikely to occur at the outset of an interview, it is more common when the police move questioning away from the original offence to a new matter (see for example *Charles v Crown Prosecution Service* [2009] EWHC 3521 (Admin)).
(d) The questioning must be directed to trying to discover whether or by whom the alleged offence had been committed. An officer is not obliged simply to charge when a prima facie case is established; he is entitled to give the suspect an opportunity to advance a defence. Only where a decision has been made to charge the suspect irrespective of any account he might give, will the questioning not be for the purpose of discovering whether or by whom the alleged offence had

been committed (see *R v Elliott* [2002] EWCA Crim 931). In practice this is now a largely academic point.

(e) the alleged failure by the defendant must be to mention any fact relied on in his defence in those proceedings. That raises two questions of fact: first, is there some fact which the defendant has relied on in his defence; and second, did the defendant fail to mention it to the constable when he was being questioned in accordance with the section? It is important to ensure that sufficient detail is given in interview, but it is sufficient to simply give a basic outline of a defence, e.g. I acted in self-defence, and then provide further detail during trial (e.g. he ran toward me with his fist clenched). Advisers will need to remember however that the level of detail required will be case specific. The oft-cited case of *R v McGarry* [1999] Crim L.R. 316 is poor authority for a blanket approach to outlining only the bones of a defence, adding the flesh later. It is sufficient to mention a fact by using a prepared statement (*R v Knight* [2003] EWCA Crim 1977) but care should be taken to ensure that all relevant facts are mentioned, a failure to do so may well expose the suspect to inferences later (see for example *R v Mohammed* [2009] EWCA Crim 1871).

(f) the appellant failed to mention a fact which in the circumstances existing at the time the accused could reasonably have been expected to mention when so questioned. The time referred to is the time of questioning, and account must be taken of all the relevant circumstances existing at that time. The courts should not construe the expression "in the circumstances" restrictively: matters such as time of day, the defendant's age, experience, mental capacity, state of health, sobriety, tiredness, knowledge, personality and legal advice are all part of the relevant circumstances; and those are only examples of things which may be relevant. When reference is made to "the accused" attention is directed not to some hypothetical, reasonable accused of ordinary phlegm and fortitude but to the actual accused with such qualities, apprehensions, knowledge and advice as he is shown to have had at the time. Good reason for failing to mention a fact later relied upon may well arise if, for example, the interviewing officer has disclosed to the solicitor little or nothing of the nature of the case against the defendant, so that the solicitor cannot usefully advise his client or, where the nature of the offence, or the material in the hands of the police is so complex, or relates to matters so long ago, that no sensible immediate response is feasible (*R v Roble*). Care should be taken when advising no comment due to lack of disclosure, in many instances a decision to make no comment will be a tactical decision as opposed to one supported by a protection from inferences (see *R v A*, unreported 12 November 2009, and R v Imran and Hussain [1997] Crim LR 754). . A simple reliance on legal advice will seldom be enough to avoid an inference (see *R v Roble* [1997] Crim L.R. 449: the evidence must generally go further and indicate the reason for that advice, for this must be relevant when the jury are assessing the reasonableness of the conduct in remaining silent).

In *R v Howell* the court held:

'This benign continuum from interview to trial, the public interest that inheres in reasonable disclosure by a suspected person of what he has to say when faced with a set of facts which accuse him, is thwarted if currency is given to the belief that if a suspect remains silent on legal advice he may systematically avoid adverse comment at his trial. And it may encourage solicitors to advise silence for other than good objective reasons. We do not consider, pace the reasoning in Betts & Hall, that once it is shown that the advice (of whatever quality) has genuinely been relied on as the reason for the suspect's remaining silent, adverse comment is thereby disallowed. The premise of such a position is that in such circumstances it is in principle not reasonable to expect the suspect to mention the facts in question. We do not believe that is so. What is reasonable depends on all the circumstances. We venture to say, recalling the circumstances of this present case, that we do not consider the absence of a written statement from the complainant to be good reason for silence (if adequate oral disclosure of the complaint has been given), and it does not become good reason merely because a solicitor has so advised. Nor is the possibility that the complainant may not pursue his complaint good reason, nor a belief by the solicitor that the suspect will be charged in any event whatever he says. The kind of circumstance which may most likely justify silence will be such matters as the suspect's condition (ill-health, in particular mental disability; confusion; intoxication; shock, and so forth – of course we are not laying down an authoritative list), or his inability genuinely to recollect events without reference to documents which are not to hand, or communication with other persons who may be able to assist his recollection. There must always be soundly based objective reasons for silence, sufficiently cogent and telling to weigh in the balance against the clear public interest in an account being given by the suspect to the police. Solicitors bearing the important responsibility of giving advice to suspects at police stations must always have that in mind.'

The court was even more robust in *R v Essa* [2009] EWCA Crim 43 and stated:

'The potential semantic complications of a section 34 direction are considerable. It is important to remember that the significance of section 34 does not lie in silence in interview, it lies in reliance at trial on something that should have been said in interview. Secondly, it is important to remember that the acid question in any section 34 case is not: was it reasonable to rely on the solicitor's advice? Rather it is: could the appellant reasonably have been expected to say what he now relies upon at trial? The first question must be answered en route to the second, but the second is the one that matters. We, for our part, are prepared to accept, at least for the purposes of argument, that there may sometimes be a case where an appellant may have good reason to rely on his solicitor's advice, even though he has in fact got an answer that could be given. A simple case, but a very long way from the present one, might be that of a vulnerable or disabled appellant who would have real difficulty getting across what he wanted to say, even though there was something there to be said. But there needs to be an element of realism in the approach to a subsequent analysis of what has been said in any particular case. In this case, as in many others, no evidence was given of what advice or why the solicitor gave the advice that he did, nor of the terms in which he gave it. The appellant can, of course, give such evidence if he chooses and he can call his solicitor if his evidence is not accepted. If he does not do that, privilege is not, as we have previously said, waived (see R v Bowden [1999] 2 Cr App R 176). But it nevertheless can be assumed, in the absence of evidence to the contrary, that the solicitor will have given proper advice and proper advice must include, first, the effect of section 34, and secondly, that an appellant exposes himself at least to the risk of criticism if he does not now say in interview what he later decides to say in court. It is with the benefit of that advice that an appellant himself makes the decision whether to answer questions or whether to decline to do so and take the risk which goes with it.'

Solicitor, right of access to

Statutory right

S. 58 *PACE 1984*:

Unless delay is authorised a person arrested and held in custody in a police station or other premises shall be entitled, if he so requests, to consult a solicitor privately at any time.

Instructions from third-party

A solicitor is entitled to receive instructions to act from a third-party. Ultimately however it remains a matter for the suspect as to whether he wishes to consult with a solicitor.

The solicitor should try and arrange telephone contact with the suspect, but on occasion this is not possible or is being thwarted by the police. The police should be reminded of *Code C 6.5* which speaks of a solicitor 'being requested'; *Para 6.5* is silent on whether that request must be from the suspect himself or from a third-party. It is submitted that a third-party request is sufficient to trigger the provision. If the solicitor believes that the suspect is not being informed of his communication the solicitor should attend the police station personally.

On attendance at a police station the police must inform the suspect of the solicitor's presence (*Code C 6.15*).

Solicitor, definition of

Code C 6.12 defines a solicitor as:

1. A solicitor who holds a current practicing certificate, or
2. An accredited or probationary police station representative.

Refusing to allow entry to a solicitor

Code C 6.12A – 6.14 and the guidance notes to part 6 detail the circumstances under which entry can be refused.

It should be noted that it is the suspect's right to have access to a solicitor, not the solicitors right to access the police station. This is important when it comes to consideration of rules of entry, for example surrender of mobile telephones and the like. The police are entitled at common law, subject to any administrative law challenge, to insist on reasonable safeguards so far as interference with an investigation, or safety of persons in a police station are concerned. The Criminal Law Committee of the Law Society is currently negotiating a protocol in relation to some of these issues, but it had not been finalized at the time of writing.

The Standard Criminal Contract requires persons carrying out duty solicitor work (but not own client work) under the contract to hold identification cards. There is however no requirement to produce such a document.

Statements under caution

A suspect can make a statement under caution as an alternative to answering questions in interview and is more often than not referred to as a prepared statement. Refer to *Silence, right of,* earlier in this book.

There are certain formalities for a statement under caution, see *Code C Annex D.*

Terrorism, suspects accused of

Introduction

The provisions of PACE 1984 apply to terrorism suspects, but they are in a number of respects modified to take account of the special considerations that apply in cases of this type. A thorough understanding of Sch 8 TA 2000 is required by all those advising suspects accused of terrorism matters (see *Appendix 6*).

Terrorism and terrorists, definition of

Section 1 *Terrorism Act 2000* provides:

(1) In this Act "terrorism" means the use or threat of action where-

(a) the action falls within subsection (2),

(b) the use or threat is designed to influence the government or an international govermental organisation or to intimidate the public or a section of the public, and

(c) the use or threat is made for the purpose of advancing a political, religious, racial or ideological cause.

(2) Action falls within this subsection if it-

(a) involves serious violence against a person,

(b) involves serious damage to property,

(c) endangers a person's life, other than that of the person committing the action,

(d) creates a serious risk to the health or safety of the public or a section of the public, or

(e) is designed seriously to interfere with or seriously to disrupt an electronic system.

(3) The use or threat of action falling within subsection (2) which involves the use of firearms or explosives is terrorism whether or not subsection (1)(b) is satisfied.

(4) In this section-

(a) "action" includes action outside the United Kingdom,

(b) a reference to any person or to property is a reference to any person, or to property, wherever situated,

(c) a reference to the public includes a reference to the public of a country other than the United Kingdom, and

(d) "the government" means the government of the United Kingdom, of a part of the United Kingdom or of a country other than the United Kingdom.

(5) In this Act a reference to action taken for the purposes of terrorism includes a reference to action taken for the benefit of a proscribed organisation.

Section 40 *Terrorism Act 2000* provides:

(1) In this Part "terrorist" means a person who-

(a) has committed an offence under any of sections 11, 12, 15 to 18, 54 and 56 to 63, or

(b) is or has been concerned in the commission, preparation or instigation of acts of terrorism.

(2) The reference in subsection (1)(b) to a person who has been concerned in the commission, preparation or instigation of acts of terrorism includes a reference to a person who has been, whether before or after the passing of this Act, concerned in the commission, preparation or instigation of acts of terrorism within the meaning given by section 1.

Proscribed organizations

Involvement with proscribed organizations is a criminal offence under the 2000 Act. Schedule 2 *Terrorism Act 2000* (last amended on 21 January 2011) provides that the following organizations are proscribed:

The Irish Republican Army.

Cumann na mBan.

Fianna na hEireann.

The Red Hand Commando.

Saor Eire.

The Ulster Freedom Fighters.

The Ulster Volunteer Force.

The Irish National Liberation Army.

The Irish People's Liberation Organisation.

The Ulster Defence Association.

The Loyalist Volunteer Force.

The Continuity Army Council.

The Orange Volunteers.

The Red Hand Defenders.

Al-Qa'ida

Egyptian Islamic Jihad

Al-Gama'at al-Islamiya

Armed Islamic Group (Groupe Islamique Armée) (GIA)

Salafist Group for Call and Combat (Groupe Salafiste pour la Prédication et le Combat) (GSPC)

Babbar Khalsa

International Sikh Youth Federation

Harakat Mujahideen

Jaish e Mohammed

Lashkar e Tayyaba

Liberation Tigers of Tamil Eelam (LTTE)

The military wing of Hizballah, including the Jihad Council and all units reporting to it (including the Hizballah External Security Organisation).

Hamas-Izz al-Din al-Qassem Brigades

Palestinian Islamic Jihad - Shaqaqi

Abu Nidal Organisation

Islamic Army of Aden

Kurdistan Workers' Party (Partiya Karkeren Kurdistan) (PKK)

Revolutionary Peoples' Liberation Party-Front (Devrimci Halk Kurtulus Partisi-Cephesi) (DHKP-C)

Basque Homeland and Liberty (Euskadi ta Askatasuna) (ETA)

17 November Revolutionary Organisation (N17)

Abu Sayyaf Group

Asbat Al-Ansar

Islamic Movement of Uzbekistan

Jemaah Islamiyah.

Al Ittihad Al Islamia

Ansar Al Islam

Ansar Al Sunna

Groupe Islamique Combattant Marocain

Harakat-ul-Jihad-ul-Islami

Harakat-ul-Jihad-ul-Islami (Bangladesh)

Harakat-ul-Mujahideen/Alami

Hezb-e Islami Gulbuddin

Islamic Jihad Union

Jamaat ul-Furquan

Jundallah

Khuddam ul-Islam

Lashkar-e Jhangvi

Libyan Islamic Fighting Group

Sipah-e Sahaba Pakistan.

Al-Ghurabaa

The Saved Sect

Baluchistan Liberation Army

Teyrebaz Azadiye Kurdistan.

Jammat-ul Mujahideen Bangladesh

Tehrik Nefaz-e Shari'at Muhammadi.

Al Shabaab

Tehrik-e Taliban Pakistan

Note

The entry for The Orange Volunteers refers to the organisation which uses that name and in the name of which a statement described as a press release was published on 14th October 1998.

The entry for Jemaah Islamiyah refers to the organisation using that name that is based in south-east Asia, members of which were arrested by the Singapore authorities in December 2001 in connection with a plot to attack US and other Western targets in Singapore.

Key points

- Detention and search powers at point of entry are governed by Sch. 7 *TA 2000*;
- There are additional stop, search and seizure powers, ss. 42-46 *TA 2000*;
- The arrest of a terrorist suspect will normally be under s. 41 *TA 2000*;
- Delayed right of access to a solicitor, see Sch 8 *TA 2000* para 8;
- Fingerprints and samples, see Sch 8 *TA 2000* para 6, 10, 11 and 13;
- The detention of suspects following arrest is subject to Sch. 8 *TA 2000* which is reproduced in full at *Appendix 6.*
- Section 25 Terrorism Act 2006 reduces the maximum period of pre-charge detention from 28 days to 14. That section has in the past been disapplied, most recently for a 6 month period beginning on 25th July 2010 (SI 2010/1909). In January 2011 the government stated its intention not to disapply section 25 so at the present time the maximum period of pre-charge detention remains at 14 days. Emergency powers to extend that to 28 days are, at the time of writing, before parliament: *Detention of Terrorist Suspects (Temporary Extension) Bill.*

Volunteers

A volunteer is a person at a police station who has not been arrested or charged with an offence. Save for some very exceptional instances (e.g. some terrorist matters) there is no obligation on a citizen to assist the police.

In many cases however the police take a pragmatic approach to a person's attendance at the police station and are happy to deal with suspects as volunteers rather than bring them formally into custody under arrest.

A volunteer must be afforded the same basic rights as a detained person, and is free to leave at any time (unless he is arrested). A volunteer of course has the right to access legal advice (*Code C* 3.21) and the Standard Criminal Contract 2010 provides for such advice to be remunerated as part of the police station attendance fixed fee, provided that he is assisting with an investigation and is not merely a witness, and that a constable is present.

Witnesses not under investigation may be entitled to freestanding advice and assistance (CDS 1 and 2) but there must be some 'complicating factor as set out in guidance'. Note that you cannot claim a police station fixed fee in relation to an attendance on a witness. Guidance issued in January 2011 mentioned only "self incrimination issues" as an example of a complicating factor, but the guidance made clear that this was not a definitive list of what might qualify.

If a volunteer is interviewed he should be cautioned in the usual way (*Code C 10.1*)

If a volunteer is subsequently arrested the relevant time will run from time of arrest, not time of arrival at the police station (*PACE 1984* s.41). Advisers need to be careful to ensure that police officers do not use volunteer status to extend the time a person is subject to police questioning.

Warrants of further detention

Introduction

If the police seek to detain someone for a period longer than 36 hours from the relevant time, authority must be sought from a magistrate. With the exception of terrorism cases detention up to a total of 96 hours can be granted. Sections 42 – 44 *PACE 1984* apply.

Key points

- The police can seek an extension of up to 36 hours in any single application;
- More than one application can be made, subject to the 96 hour detention limit not being exceeded;
- An application must be made before the expiry of the current detention period. An application is made when the police begin to give evidence before the court. If the court is unable to sit before expiry of the detention limit the suspect may be held in custody for a further 6 hours until such time as the court can be properly convened. Note s.43(7) *PACE 1984*.
- Argument can be raised as to whether the current detention of the suspect is lawful, in the event it is not lawful an extension to detention time cannot be authorised. Advisers should be careful to scrutinize the lawfulness of detention to date (*Re: Application for a warrant of further detention* [1988] Crim LR 296, a case where the initial extension to 36 hours was held unlawful as the suspect's solicitor had been denied the right to make representations);

Grounds for further detention

The court must be satisfied as to the following (s. 43(4) *PACE 1984*):

(a) his detention without charge is necessary to secure or preserve evidence relating to an offence for which he is under arrest or to obtain such evidence by questioning him;

(b) an offence for which he is under arrest is an indictable offence; and

(c) the investigation is being conducted diligently and expeditiously.

Appendix 1 Selected sections of PACE 1984

Police and Criminal Evidence Act 1984

Amendments to 7th March 2011

s 1 Power of constable to stop and search persons, vehicles etc.

(1) A constable may exercise any power conferred by this section--

(a) in any place to which at the time when he proposes to exercise the power the public or any section of the public has access, on payment or otherwise, as of right or by virtue of express or implied permission; or

(b) in any other place to which people have ready access at the time when he proposes to exercise the power but which is not a dwelling.

(2) Subject to subsection (3) to (5) below, a constable--

(a) may search--

(i) any person or vehicle;

(ii) anything which is in or on a vehicle,

for stolen or prohibited articles , any article to which subsection (8A) below applies or any firework to which subsection (8B) below applies; and

(b) may detain a person or vehicle for the purpose of such a search.

(3) This section does not give a constable power to search a person or vehicle or anything in or on a vehicle unless he has reasonable grounds for suspecting that he will find stolen or prohibited articles or, any article to which subsection (8A) below applies or any firework to which subsection (8B) below applies.

(4) If a person is in a garden or yard occupied with and used for the purposes of a dwelling or on other land so occupied and used, a constable may not search him in the exercise of the power conferred by this section unless the constable has reasonable grounds for believing--

(a) that he does not reside in the dwelling; and

(b) that he is not in the place in question with the express or implied permission of a person who resides in the dwelling.

(5) If a vehicle is in a garden or yard occupied with and used for the purposes of a dwelling or on other land so occupied and used, a constable may not search the vehicle or anything in or on it in the exercise of the power conferred by this section unless he has reasonable grounds for believing--

(a) that the person in charge of the vehicle does not reside in the dwelling; and

(b) that the vehicle is not in the place in question with the express or implied permission of a person who resides in the dwelling.

(6) If in the course of such a search a constable discovers an article which he has reasonable grounds for suspecting to be a stolen or prohibited article, an article to which subsection (8A) below applies or a firework to which subsection (8B) below applies, he may seize it.

(7) An article is prohibited for the purposes of this Part of this Act if it is--

(a) an offensive weapon; or

(b) an article--

(i) made or adapted for use in the course of or in connection with an offence to which this sub-paragraph applies; or

(ii) intended by the person having it with him for such use by him or by some other person.

(8) The offences to which subsection (7)(b)(i) above applies are--

(a) burglary;

(b) theft;

(c) offences under section 12 of the Theft Act 1968 (taking motor vehicle or other conveyance without authority);

(d) fraud (contrary to section 1 of the Fraud Act 2006); and

(e) offences under section 1 of the Criminal Damage Act 1971 (destroying or damaging property).

(8A) This subsection applies to any article in relation to which a person has committed, or is committing or is going to commit an offence under section 139 of the Criminal Justice Act 1988.

(8B) This subsection applies to any firework which a person possesses in contravention of a prohibition imposed by fireworks regulations.

(8C) In this section--

(a) "firework" shall be construed in accordance with the definition of "fireworks" in section 1(1) of the Fireworks Act 2003; and

(b) "fireworks regulations" has the same meaning as in that Act.

(9) In this Part of this Act "offensive weapon" means any article--

(a) made or adapted for use for causing injury to persons; or

(b) intended by the person having it with him for such use by him or by some other person.

s 2 Provisions relating to search under section 1 and other powers.

(1) A constable who detains a person or vehicle in the exercise--

(a) of the power conferred by section 1 above; or

(b) of any other power--

    (i) to search a person without first arresting him; or

    (ii) to search a vehicle without making an arrest,

need not conduct a search if it appears to him subsequently--

(i) that no search is required; or

(ii) that a search is impracticable.

(2) If a constable contemplates a search, other than a search of an unattended vehicle, in the exercise--

(a) of the power conferred by section 1 above; or

(b) of any other power, except the power conferred by section 6 below and the power conferred by section 27(2) of the Aviation Security Act 1982--

    (i) to search a person without first arresting him; or

    (ii) to search a vehicle without making an arrest,

it shall be his duty, subject to subsection (4) below, to take reasonable steps before he commences the search to bring to the attention of the appropriate person--

    (i) if the constable is not in uniform, documentary evidence that he is a constable; and

    (ii) whether he is in uniform or not, the matters specified in subsection (3) below;

and the constable shall not commence the search until he has performed that duty.

(3) The matters referred to in subsection (2)(ii) above are--

(a) the constable's name and the name of the police station to which he is attached;

(b) the object of the proposed search;

(c) the constable's grounds for proposing to make it; and

(d) the effect of section 3(7) or (8) below, as may be appropriate.

(4) A constable need not bring the effect of section 3(7) or (8) below to the attention of the

appropriate person if it appears to the constable that it will not be practicable to make the record in section 3(1) below.

(5) In this section "the appropriate person" means --

(a) if the constable proposes to search a person, that person; and

(b) if he proposes to search a vehicle, or anything in or on a vehicle, the person in charge of the vehicle.

(6) On completing a search of an unattended vehicle or anything in or on such a vehicle in the exercise of any such power as is mentioned in subsection (2) above a constable shall leave a notice--

(a) stating that he has searched it;

(b) giving the name of the police station to which he is attached;

(c) stating that an application for compensation for any damage caused by the search may be made to that police station; and

(d) stating the effect of section 3(8) below.

(7) The constable shall leave the notice inside the vehicle unless it is not reasonably practicable to do so without damaging the vehicle.

(8) The time for which a person or vehicle may be detained for the purposes of such a search is such time as is reasonably required to permit a search to be carried out either at the place where the person or vehicle was first detained or nearby.

(9) Neither the power conferred by section 1 above nor any other power to detain and search a person without first arresting him or to detain and search a vehicle without making an arrest is to be construed--

(a) as authorising a constable to require a person to remove any of his clothing in public other than an outer coat, jacket or gloves; or

(b) as authorising a constable not in uniform to stop a vehicle.

(10) This section and section 1 above apply to vessels, aircraft and hovercraft as they apply to vehicles.

s 4 Road checks.

(1) This section shall have effect in relation to the conduct of road checks by police officers for the purpose of ascertaining whether a vehicle is carrying--

(a) a person who has committed an offence other than a road traffic offence or a vehicle excise offence;

(b) a person who is a witness to such an offence;

(c) a person intending to commit such an offence; or

(d) a person who is unlawfully at large.

(2) For the purposes of this section a road check consists of the exercise in a locality of the power conferred by section 163 of the Road Traffic Act 1988 in such a way as to stop during the period for which its exercise in that way in that locality continues all vehicles or vehicles selected by any criterion.

(3) Subject to subsection (5) below, there may only be such a road check if a police officer of the rank of superintendent or above authorises it in writing.

(4) An officer may only authorise a road check under subsection (3) above--

(a) for the purpose specified in subsection (1)(a) above, if he has reasonable grounds--

(i) for believing that the offence is an indictable offence; and

(ii) for suspecting that the person is, or is about to be, in the locality in which vehicles would be stopped if the road check were authorised;

(b) for the purpose specified in subsection (1)(b) above, if he has reasonable grounds for believing that the offence is an indictable offence;

(c) for the purpose specified in subsection (1)(c) above, if he has reasonable grounds--

(i) for believing that the offence would be an indictable offence; and

(ii) for suspecting that the person is, or is about to be, in the locality in which vehicles would be stopped if the road check were authorised;

(d) for the purpose specified in subsection (1)(d) above, if he has reasonable grounds for suspecting that the person is, or is about to be, in that locality.

(5) An officer below the rank of superintendent may authorise such a road check if it appears to him that it is required as a matter of urgency for one of the purposes specified in subsection (1) above.

(6) If an authorisation is given under subsection (5) above, it shall be the duty of the officer who gives it--

(a) to make a written record of the time at which he gives it; and

(b) to cause an officer of the rank of superintendent or above to be informed that it has been given.

(7) The duties imposed by subsection (6) above shall be performed as soon as it is practicable to do so.

(8) An officer to whom a report is made under subsection (6) above may, in writing, authorise the road check to continue.

(9) If such an officer considers that the road check should not continue, he shall record in writing--

(a) the fact that it took place; and

(b) the purpose for which it took place.

(10) An officer giving an authorisation under this section shall specify the locality in which vehicles are to be stopped.

(11) An officer giving an authorisation under this section, other than an authorisation under subsection (5) above--

(a) shall specify a period, not exceeding seven days, during which the road check may continue; and

(b) may direct that the road check--

(i) shall be continuous; or

(ii) shall be conducted at specified times,

during that period.

(12) If it appears to an officer of the rank of superintendent or above that a road check ought to continue beyond the period for which it has been authorised he may, from time to time, in writing specify a further period, not exceeding seven days, during which it may continue.

(13) Every written authorisation shall specify--

(a) the name of the officer giving it;

(b) the purpose of the road check; and

(c) the locality in which vehicles are to be stopped.

(14) The duties to specify the purposes of a road check imposed by subsections (9) and (13) above include duties to specify any relevant indictable offence.

(15) Where a vehicle is stopped in a road check, the person in charge of the vehicle at the time when it is stopped shall be entitled to obtain a written statement of the purpose of the road check if he applies for such a statement not later than the end of the period of twelve months from the day on which the vehicle was stopped.

(16) Nothing in this section affects the exercise by police officers of any power to stop vehicles for purposes other than those specified in subsection (1) above.

s 8 Power of justice of the peace to authorise entry and search of premises.

(1) If on an application made by a constable a justice of the peace is satisfied that there are reasonable grounds for believing--

(a) that an indictable offence has been committed; and

(b) that there is material on premises mentioned in subsection (1A) below which is likely to be of substantial value (whether by itself or together with other material) to the investigation of the offence; and

(c) that the material is likely to be relevant evidence; and

(d) that it does not consist of or include items subject to legal privilege, excluded material or special procedure material; and

(e) that any of the conditions specified in subsection (3) below applies in relation to each set of premises specified in the application,

he may issue a warrant authorising a constable to enter and search the premises.

(1A) The premises referred to in subsection (1)(b) above are--

(a) one or more sets of premises specified in the application (in which case the application is for a "specific premises warrant"); or

(b) any premises occupied or controlled by a person specified in the application, including such sets of premises as are so specified (in which case the application is for an "all premises warrant").

(1B) If the application is for an all premises warrant, the justice of the peace must also be satisfied--

(a) that because of the particulars of the offence referred to in paragraph (a) of subsection (1) above, there are reasonable grounds for believing that it is necessary to search premises occupied or controlled by the person in question which are not specified in the application in order to find the material referred to in paragraph (b) of that subsection; and

(b) that it is not reasonably practicable to specify in the application all the premises which he occupies or controls and which might need to be searched.

(1C) The warrant may authorise entry to and search of premises on more than one occasion if, on the application, the justice of the peace is satisfied that it is necessary to authorise multiple entries in order to achieve the purpose for which he issues the warrant.

(1D) If it authorises multiple entries, the number of entries authorised may be unlimited, or limited to a maximum.

(2) A constable may seize and retain anything for which a search has been authorised under subsection (1) above.

(3) The conditions mentioned in subsection (1)(e) above are--

(a) that it is not practicable to communicate with any person entitled to grant entry to the premises;

(b) that it is practicable to communicate with a person entitled to grant entry to the premises but it is not practicable to communicate with any person entitled to grant access to the evidence;

(c) that entry to the premises will not be granted unless a warrant is produced;

(d) that the purpose of a search may be frustrated or seriously prejudiced unless a constable arriving at the premises can secure immediate entry to them.

(4) In this Act "relevant evidence", in relation to an offence, means anything that would be admissible in evidence at a trial for the offence.

(5) The power to issue a warrant conferred by this section is in addition to any such power otherwise conferred.

(6) This section applies in relation to a relevant offence (as defined in section 28D(4) of the Immigration Act 1971) as it applies in relation to an indictable offence.

(7) Section 4 of the Summary Jurisdiction (Process) Act 1881 (execution of process of English courts in Scotland) shall apply to a warrant issued on the application of an officer of Revenue and Customs under this section by virtue of section 114 below.

s 9 Special provisions as to access.

(1) A constable may obtain access to excluded material or special procedure material for the purposes of a criminal investigation by making an application under Schedule 1 below and in accordance with that Schedule.

(2) Any Act (including a local Act) passed before this Act under which a search of premises for the purposes of a criminal investigation could be authorised by the issue of a warrant to a constable shall cease to have effect so far as it relates to the authorisation of searches--

(a) for items subject to legal privilege; or

(b) for excluded material; or

(c) for special procedure material consisting of documents or records other than documents.

(2A) Section 4 of the Summary Jurisdiction (Process) Act 1881 (c. 24) (which includes provision for the execution of process of English courts in Scotland) and section 29 of the Petty Sessions (Ireland) Act 1851 (c. 93) (which makes equivalent provision for execution in Northern Ireland) shall each apply to any process issued by a circuit judge under Schedule 1 to this Act as it applies to process issued by a magistrates' court under the Magistrates' Courts Act 1980 (c. 43).

s 10 Meaning of "items subject to legal privilege".

(1) Subject to subsection (2) below, in this Act "items subject to legal privilege" means--

(a) communications between a professional legal adviser and his client or any person representing his client made in connection with the giving of legal advice to the client;

(b) communications between a professional legal adviser and his client or any person representing his client or between such an adviser or his client or any such representative and any other person made in connection with or in contemplation of legal proceedings and for the purposes of such proceedings; and

(c) items enclosed with or referred to in such communications and made--

(i) in connection with the giving of legal advice;

or

(ii) in connection with or in contemplation of legal proceedings and for the purposes of such proceedings,

when they are in the possession of a person who is entitled to possession of them.

(2) Items held with the intention of furthering a criminal purpose are not items subject to legal privilege.

s 11 Meaning of "excluded material".

(1) Subject to the following provisions of this section, in this Act "excluded material" means--

(a) personal records which a person has acquired or created in the course of any trade, business, profession or other occupation or for the purposes of any paid or unpaid office and which he holds in confidence;

(b) human tissue or tissue fluid which has been taken for the purposes of diagnosis or medical treatment and which a person holds in confidence;

(c) journalistic material which a person holds in confidence and which consists--

(i) of documents; or

(ii) of records other than documents.

(2) A person holds material other than journalistic material in confidence for the purposes of this section if he holds it subject--

(a) to an express or implied undertaking to hold it in confidence; or

(b) to a restriction on disclosure or an obligation of secrecy contained in any enactment, including an enactment contained in an Act passed after this Act.

(3) A person holds journalistic material in confidence for the purposes of this section if--

(a) he holds it subject to such an undertaking, restriction or obligation; and

(b) it has been continuously held (by one or more persons) subject to such an undertaking, restriction or obligation since it was first acquired or created for the purposes of journalism.

s 12 Meaning of "personal records".

In this Part of this Act "personal records" means documentary and other records concerning an individual (whether living or dead) who can be identified from them and relating--

(a) to his physical or mental health;

(b) to spiritual counselling or assistance given or to be given to him; or

(c) to counselling or assistance given or to be given to him, for the purposes of his personal welfare, by any voluntary organisation or by any individual who--

(i) by reason of his office or occupation has responsibilities for his personal welfare; or

(ii) by reason of an order of a court has responsibilities for his supervision.

s 13 Meaning of "journalistic material".

(1) Subject to subsection (2) below, in this Act "journalistic material" means material acquired or created for the purposes of journalism.

(2) Material is only journalistic material for the purposes of this Act if it is in the possession of a person who acquired or created it for the purposes of journalism.

(3) A person who receives material from someone who intends that the recipient shall use it for the purposes of journalism is to be taken to have acquired it for those purposes.

s 14 Meaning of "special procedure material".

(1) In this Act "special procedure material" means --

(a) material to which subsection (2) below applies; and

(b) journalistic material, other than excluded material.

(2) Subject to the following provisions of this section, this subsection applies to material, other than items subject to legal privilege and excluded material, in the possession of a person who--

(a) acquired or created it in the course of any trade, business, profession or other occupation or for the purpose of any paid or unpaid office; and

(b) holds it subject--

(i) to an express or implied undertaking to hold it in confidence; or

(ii) to a restriction or obligation such as is mentioned in section 11(2)(b) above.

(3) Where material is acquired--

(a) by an employee from his employer and in the course of his employment; or

(b) by a company from an associated company,

it is only special procedure material if it was special procedure material immediately before the acquisition.

(4) Where material is created by an employee in the course of his employment, it is only special procedure material if it would have been special procedure material had his employer created it.

(5) Where material is created by a company on behalf of an associated company, it is only special procedure material if it would have been special procedure material had the associated company created it.

(6) A company is to be treated as another's associated company for the purposes of this section if it would be so treated under section 449 of the Corporation Tax Act 2010.

s 15 Search warrants--safeguards.

(1) This section and section 16 below have effect in relation to the issue to constables under any enactment, including an enactment contained in an Act passed after this Act, of warrants to enter and search premises; and an entry on or search of premises under a warrant is unlawful unless it complies with this section and section 16 below.

(2) Where a constable applies for any such warrant, it shall be his duty--

(a) to state--

(i) the ground on which he makes the application;

(ii) the enactment under which the warrant would be issued; and

(iii) if the application is for a warrant authorising entry and search on more than one occasion, the ground on which he applies for such a warrant, and whether he seeks a warrant authorising an unlimited number of entries, or (if not) the maximum number of entries desired;

(b) to specify the matters set out in subsection (2A) below; and

(c) to identify, so far as is practicable, the articles or persons to be sought.

(2A) The matters which must be specified pursuant to subsection (2)(b) above are--

(a) if the application relates to one or more sets of premises specified in the application, each set of premises which it is desired to enter and search;

(b) if the application relates to any premises occupied or controlled by a person specified in the application-

(i) as many sets of premises which it is desired to enter and search as it is reasonably practicable to specify;

(ii) the person who is in occupation or control of those premises and any others which it is desired to enter and search;

(iii) why it is necessary to search more premises than those specified under sub-paragraph (i); and

(iv) why it is not reasonably practicable to specify all the premises which it is desired to enter and search.

(3) An application for such a warrant shall be made ex parte and supported by an information in writing.

(4) The constable shall answer on oath any question that the justice of the peace or judge hearing the application asks him.

(5) A warrant shall authorise an entry on one occasion only unless it specifies that it authorises multiple entries.

(5A) If it specifies that it authorises multiple entries, it must also specify whether the number of entries authorised is unlimited, or limited to a specified maximum.

(6) A warrant--

(a) shall specify--

(i) the name of the person who applies for it;

(ii) the date on which it is issued;

(iii) the enactment under which it is issued; and

(iv) each set of premises to be searched, or (in the case of an all premises warrant) the person who is in occupation or control of premises to be searched, together with any premises under his occupation or control which can be specified and which are to be searched; and

(b) shall identify, so far as is practicable, the articles or persons to be sought.

(7) Two copies shall be made of a warrant which specifies only one set of premises and does not authorise multiple entries; and as many copies as are reasonably required may be made of any other

kind of warrant.

(8) The copies shall be clearly certified as copies.

s 16 Execution of warrants.

(1) A warrant to enter and search premises may be executed by any constable.

(2) Such a warrant may authorise persons to accompany any constable who is executing it.

(2A) A person so authorised has the same powers as the constable whom he accompanies in respect of--

(a) the execution of the warrant, and

(b) the seizure of anything to which the warrant relates.

(2B) But he may exercise those powers only in the company, and under the supervision, of a constable.

(3) Entry and search under a warrant must be within three months from the date of its issue.

(3A) If the warrant is an all premises warrant, no premises which are not specified in it may be entered or searched unless a police officer of at least the rank of inspector has in writing authorised them to be entered.

(3B) No premises may be entered or searched for the second or any subsequent time under a warrant which authorises multiple entries unless a police officer of at least the rank of inspector has in writing authorised that entry to those premises.

(4) Entry and search under a warrant must be at a reasonable hour unless it appears to the constable executing it that the purpose of a search may be frustrated on an entry at a reasonable hour.

(5) Where the occupier of premises which are to be entered and searched is present at the time when a constable seeks to execute a warrant to enter and search them, the constable--

(a) shall identify himself to the occupier and, if not in uniform, shall produce to him documentary evidence that he is a constable;

(b) shall produce the warrant to him; and

(c) shall supply him with a copy of it.

(6) Where--

(a) the occupier of such premises is not present at the time when a constable seeks to execute such a warrant; but

(b) some other person who appears to the constable to be in charge of the premises is present,

subsection (5) above shall have effect as if any reference to the occupier were a reference to that other person.

(7) If there is no person present who appears to the constable to be in charge of the premises, he shall leave a copy of the warrant in a prominent place on the premises.

(8) A search under a warrant may only be a search to the extent required for the purpose for which the warrant was issued.

(9) A constable executing a warrant shall make an endorsement on it stating--

(a) whether the articles or persons sought were found; and

(b) whether any articles were seized, other than articles which were sought,

and, unless the warrant is a warrant specifying one set of premises only, he shall do so separately in respect of each set of premises entered and searched, which he shall in each case state in the endorsement.

(10) A warrant shall be returned to the appropriate person mentioned in subsection (10A) below--

(a) when it has been executed; or

(b) in the case of a specific premises warrant which has not been executed, or an all premises warrant, or any warrant authorising multiple entries, upon the expiry of the period of three months referred to in subsection (3) above or sooner.

(10A) The appropriate person is--

(a) if the warrant was issued by a justice of the peace, the designated officer for the local justice area in which the justice was acting when he issued the warrant;

(b) if it was issued by a judge, the appropriate officer of the court from which he issued it.

(11) A warrant which is returned under subsection (10) above shall be retained for 12 months from its return--

(a) by the designated officer for the local justice area, if it was returned under paragraph (i) of that subsection; and

(b) by the appropriate officer, if it was returned under paragraph (ii).

(12) If during the period for which a warrant is to be retained the occupier of premises to which it relates asks to inspect it, he shall be allowed to do so.

s 17 Entry for purpose of arrest etc.

(1) Subject to the following provisions of this section, and without prejudice to any other enactment, a constable may enter and search any premises for the purpose--

(a) of executing--

(i) a warrant of arrest issued in connection with or arising out of criminal proceedings; or

(ii) a warrant of commitment issued under section 76 of the Magistrates' Courts Act 1980;

(b) of arresting a person for an indictable offence;

(c) of arresting a person for an offence under--

(i) section 1 (prohibition of uniforms in connection with political objects) of the Public Order Act 1936;

(ii) any enactment contained in sections 6 to 8 or 10 of the Criminal Law Act 1977 (offences relating to entering and remaining on property);

(iii) section 4 of the Public Order Act 1986 (fear or provocation of violence);

(iiia) section 4 (driving etc. when under influence of drink or drugs) or 163 (failure to stop when required to do so by constable in uniform) of the Road Traffic Act 1988;

(iiib) section 27 of the Transport and Works Act 1992 (which relates to offences involving drink or drugs);

(iv) section 76 of the Criminal Justice and Public Order Act 1994 (failure to comply with interim possession order);

(v) any of sections 4, 5, 6(1) and (2), 7 and 8(1) and (2) of the Animal Welfare Act 2006 (offences relating to the prevention of harm to animals);".

(ca) of arresting, in pursuance of section 32(1A) of the Children and Young Persons Act 1969, any child or young person who has been remanded or committed to local authority accommodation under section 23(1) of that Act;

(caa) of arresting a person for an offence to which section 61 of the Animal Health Act 1981 applies;

(cb) of recapturing any person who is, or is deemed for any purpose to be, unlawfully at large while liable to be detained--

(i) in a prison, remand centre, young offender institution or secure training centre, or

(ii) in pursuance of section 92 of the Powers of Criminal Courts (Sentencing) Act 2000 (dealing with children and young persons guilty of grave crimes), in any other place;

(d) of recapturing any person whatever who is unlawfully at large and whom he is pursuing; or

(e) of saving life or limb or preventing serious damage to property.

(2) Except for the purpose specified in paragraph (e) of subsection (1) above, the powers of entry and search conferred by this section--

(a) are only exercisable if the constable has reasonable grounds for believing that the person whom he is seeking is on the premises; and

(b) are limited, in relation to premises consisting of two or more separate dwellings, to powers to enter and search--

(i) any parts of the premises which the occupiers of any dwelling comprised in the premises use in common with the occupiers of any other such dwelling; and

(ii) any such dwelling in which the constable has reasonable grounds for believing that the person whom he is seeking may be.

(3) The powers of entry and search conferred by this section are only exercisable for the purposes specified in subsection (1)(c)(ii) or (iv) above by a constable in uniform.

(4) The power of search conferred by this section is only a power to search to the extent that is reasonably required for the purpose for which the power of entry is exercised.

(5) Subject to subsection (6) below, all the rules of common law under which a constable has power to enter premises without a warrant are hereby abolished.

(6) Nothing in subsection (5) above affects any power of entry to deal with or prevent a breach of the peace.

s 18 Entry and search after arrest.

(1) Subject to the following provisions of this section, a constable may enter and search any premises occupied or controlled by a person who is under arrest for an indictable offence, if he has reasonable grounds for suspecting that there is on the premises evidence, other than items subject to legal privilege, that relates--

(a) to that offence; or

(b) to some other indictable offence which is connected with or similar to that offence.

(2) A constable may seize and retain anything for which he may search under subsection (1) above.

(3) The power to search conferred by subsection (1) above is only a power to search to the extent that is reasonably required for the purpose of discovering such evidence.

(4) Subject to subsection (5) below, the powers conferred by this section may not be exercised unless an officer of the rank of inspector or above has authorised them in writing.

(5) A constable may conduct a search under subsection (1)--

(a) before the person is taken to a police station or released on bail under section 30A, and

(b) without obtaining an authorisation under subsection (4),

if the condition in subsection (5A) is satisfied.

(5A) The condition is that the presence of the person at a place (other than a police station) is necessary for the effective investigation of the offence.

(6) If a constable conducts a search by virtue of subsection (5) above, he shall inform an officer of the rank of inspector or above that he has made the search as soon as practicable after he has made it.

(7) An officer who--

    (a) authorises a search; or

    (b) is informed of a search under subsection (6) above, shall make a record in writing--

        (i) of the grounds for the search; and

        (ii) of the nature of the evidence that was sought.

(8) If the person who was in occupation or control of the premises at the time of the search is in police detention at the time the record is to be made, the officer shall make the record as part of his custody record.

s 19 General power of seizure etc.

(1) The powers conferred by subsections (2), (3) and (4) below are exercisable by a constable who is lawfully on any premises.

(2) The constable may seize anything which is on the premises if he has reasonable grounds for believing--

(a) that it has been obtained in consequence of the commission of an offence; and

(b) that it is necessary to seize it in order to prevent it being concealed, lost, damaged, altered or destroyed.

(3) The constable may seize anything which is on the premises if he has reasonable grounds for believing--

(a) that it is evidence in relation to an offence which he is investigating or any other offence; and

(b) that it is necessary to seize it in order to prevent the evidence being concealed, lost, altered or destroyed.

(4) The constable may require any information which is stored in any electronic form and is accessible from the premises to be produced in a form in which it can be taken away and in which it is visible and legible or from which it can readily be produced in a visible and legible form if he has reasonable grounds for believing--

(a) that--

    (i) it is evidence in relation to an offence which he is investigating or any other offence; or

    (ii) it has been obtained in consequence of the commission of an offence; and

(b) that it is necessary to do so in order to prevent it being concealed, lost, tampered with or destroyed.

(5) The powers conferred by this section are in addition to any power otherwise conferred.

(6) No power of seizure conferred on a constable under any enactment (including an enactment contained in an Act passed after this Act) is to be taken to authorise the seizure of an item which the constable exercising the power has reasonable grounds for believing to be subject to legal privilege.

s 20 Extension of powers of seizure to computerised information.

(1) Every power of seizure which is conferred by an enactment to which this section applies on a constable who has entered premises in the exercise of a power conferred by an enactment shall be construed as including a power to require any information stored in any electronic form and accessible from the premises to be produced in a form in which it can be taken away and in which it is visible and legible or from which it can readily be produced in a visible and legible form.

(2) This section applies--

(a) to any enactment contained in an Act passed before this Act;

(b) to sections 8 and 18 above;

(c) to paragraph 13 of Schedule 1 to this Act; and

(d) to any enactment contained in an Act passed after this Act.

s 21 Access and copying.

(1) A constable who seizes anything in the exercise of a power conferred by any enactment, including an enactment contained in an Act passed after this Act, shall, if so requested by a person showing himself--

(a) to be the occupier of premises on which it was seized; or

(b) to have had custody or control of it immediately before the seizure,

provide that person with a record of what he seized.

(2) The officer shall provide the record within a reasonable time from the making of the request for it.

(3) Subject to subsection (8) below, if a request for permission to be granted access to anything which--

(a) has been seized by a constable; and

(b) is retained by the police for the purpose of investigating an offence,

is made to the officer in charge of the investigation by a person who had custody or control of the thing immediately before it was so seized or by someone acting on behalf of such a person, the officer shall allow the person who made the request access to it under the supervision of a constable.

(4) Subject to subsection (8) below, if a request for a photograph or copy of any such thing is made to the officer in charge of the investigation by a person who had custody or control of the thing immediately before it was so seized, or by someone acting on behalf of such a person, the officer shall--

(a) allow the person who made the request access to it under the supervision of a constable for the purpose of photographing or copying it; or

(b) photograph or copy it, or cause it to be photographed or copied.

(5) A constable may also photograph or copy, or have photographed or copied, anything which he has power to seize, without a request being made under subsection (4) above.

(6) Where anything is photographed or copied under subsection (4)(b) above, the photograph or copy shall be supplied to the person who made the request.

(7) The photograph or copy shall be so supplied within a reasonable time from the making of the request.

(8) There is no duty under this section to grant access to, or to supply a photograph or copy of, anything if the officer in charge of the investigation for the purposes of which it was seized has reasonable grounds for believing that to do so would prejudice--

(a) that investigation;

(b) the investigation of an offence other than the offence for the purposes of investigating which the thing was seized; or

(c) any criminal proceedings which may be brought as a result of--

(i) the investigation of which he is in charge; or

(ii) any such investigation as is mentioned in paragraph (b) above.

(9) The references to a constable in subsections (1), (2), (3)(a) and (5) include a person authorised under section 16(2) to accompany a constable executing a warrant.

s 22 Retention.

(1) Subject to subsection (4) below, anything which has been seized by a constable or taken away by a constable following a requirement made by virtue of section 19 or 20 above may be retained so long as is necessary in all the circumstances.

(2) Without prejudice to the generality of subsection (1) above--

(a) anything seized for the purposes of a criminal investigation may be retained, except as provided by subsection (4) below--

(i) for use as evidence at a trial for an offence; or

(ii) for forensic examination or for investigation in connection with an offence; and

(b) anything may be retained in order to establish its lawful owner, where there are reasonable grounds for believing that it has been obtained in consequence of the commission of an offence.

(3) Nothing seized on the ground that it may be used--

(a) to cause physical injury to any person;

(b) to damage property;

(c) to interfere with evidence; or

(d) to assist in escape from police detention or lawful custody,

may be retained when the person from whom it was seized is no longer in police detention or the custody of a court or is in the custody of a court but has been released on bail.

(4) Nothing may be retained for either of the purposes mentioned in subsection (2)(a) above if a photograph or copy would be sufficient for that purpose.

(5) Nothing in this section affects any power of a court to make an order under section 1 of the Police (Property) Act 1897.

(6) This section also applies to anything retained by the police under section 28H(5) of the Immigration Act 1971.

(7) The reference in subsection (1) to anything seized by a constable includes anything seized by a person authorised under section 16(2) to accompany a constable executing a warrant.

s 23 Meaning of "premises" etc.

In this Act--

"premises" includes any place and, in particular, includes--

(a) any vehicle, vessel, aircraft or hovercraft;

(b) any offshore installation;

(ba) any renewable energy installation;

(c) any tent or movable structure;

"offshore installation" has the meaning given to it by section 1 of the Mineral Workings (Offshore Installations) Act 1971.

'renewable energy installation' has the same meaning as in Chapter 2 of Part 2 of the Energy Act 2004.

s 24 Arrest without warrant: constables

24 Arrest without warrant: constables

(1) A constable may arrest without a warrant--

(a) anyone who is about to commit an offence;

(b) anyone who is in the act of committing an offence;

(c) anyone whom he has reasonable grounds for suspecting to be about to commit an offence;

(d) anyone whom he has reasonable grounds for suspecting to be committing an offence.

(2) If a constable has reasonable grounds for suspecting that an offence has been committed, he may arrest without a warrant anyone whom he has reasonable grounds to suspect of being guilty of it.

(3) If an offence has been committed, a constable may arrest without a warrant--

(a) anyone who is guilty of the offence;

(b) anyone whom he has reasonable grounds for suspecting to be guilty of it.

(4) But the power of summary arrest conferred by subsection (1), (2) or (3) is exercisable only if the constable has reasonable grounds for believing that for any of the reasons mentioned in subsection (5) it is necessary to arrest the person in question.

(5) The reasons are--

(a) to enable the name of the person in question to be ascertained (in the case where the constable does not know, and cannot readily ascertain, the person's name, or has reasonable grounds for doubting whether a name given by the person as his name is his real name);

(b) correspondingly as regards the person's address;

(c) to prevent the person in question--

(i) causing physical injury to himself or any other person;

(ii) suffering physical injury;

(iii) causing loss of or damage to property;

(iv) committing an offence against public decency (subject to subsection (6)); or

(v) causing an unlawful obstruction of the highway;

(d) to protect a child or other vulnerable person from the person in question;

(e) to allow the prompt and effective investigation of the offence or of the conduct of the person in question;

(f) to prevent any prosecution for the offence from being hindered by the disappearance of the person in question.

(6) Subsection (5)(c)(iv) applies only where members of the public going about their normal business cannot reasonably be expected to avoid the person in question.

s 24A Arrest without warrant: other persons

(1) A person other than a constable may arrest without a warrant--

(a) anyone who is in the act of committing an indictable offence;

(b) anyone whom he has reasonable grounds for suspecting to be committing an indictable offence.

(2) Where an indictable offence has been committed, a person other than a constable may arrest without a warrant--

(a) anyone who is guilty of the offence;

(b) anyone whom he has reasonable grounds for suspecting to be guilty of it.

(3) But the power of summary arrest conferred by subsection (1) or (2) is exercisable only if--

(a) the person making the arrest has reasonable grounds for believing that for any of the reasons mentioned in subsection (4) it is necessary to arrest the person in question; and

(b) it appears to the person making the arrest that it is not reasonably practicable for a constable to make it instead.

(4) The reasons are to prevent the person in question--

(a) causing physical injury to himself or any other person;

(b) suffering physical injury;

(c) causing loss of or damage to property; or

(d) making off before a constable can assume responsibility for him.

(5) This section does not apply in relation to an offence under Part 3 or 3A of the Public Order Act 1986.

s 27 Fingerprinting of certain offenders.

(4) The Secretary of State may by regulations make provision for recording in national police records convictions for such offences as are specified in the regulations.

(5) Regulations under this section shall be made by statutory instrument and shall be subject to annulment in pursuance of a resolution of either House of Parliament.

s 28 Information to be given on arrest.

(1) Subject to subsection (5) below, where a person is arrested, otherwise than by being informed that he is under arrest, the arrest is not lawful unless the person arrested is informed that he is under arrest as soon as is practicable after his arrest.

(2) Where a person is arrested by a constable, subsection (1) above applies regardless of whether the fact of the arrest is obvious.

(3) Subject to subsection (5) below, no arrest is lawful unless the person arrested is informed of the ground for the arrest at the time of, or as soon as is practicable after, the arrest.

(4) Where a person is arrested by a constable, subsection (3) above applies regardless of whether the ground for the arrest is obvious.

(5) Nothing in this section is to be taken to require a person to be informed--

(a) that he is under arrest; or

(b) of the ground for the arrest,

if it was not reasonably practicable for him to be so informed by reason of his having escaped from arrest before the information could be given.

s 29 Voluntary attendance at police station etc.

Where for the purpose of assisting with an investigation a person attends voluntarily at a police station or at any other place where a constable is present or accompanies a constable to a police station or any such other place without having been arrested--

(a) he shall be entitled to leave at will unless he is placed under arrest;

(b) he shall be informed at once that he is under arrest if a decision is taken by a constable to prevent him from leaving at will.

s 30 Arrest elsewhere than at police station.

(1) Subsection (1A) applies where a person is, at any place other than a police station--

(a) arrested by a constable for an offence, or

(b) taken into custody by a constable after being arrested for an offence by a person other than a constable.

(1A) The person must be taken by a constable to a police station as soon as practicable after the arrest.

(1B) Subsection (1A) has effect subject to section 30A (release on bail) and subsection (7) (release without bail).

(2) Subject to subsections (3) and (5) below, the police station to which an arrested person is taken under subsection (1A) above shall be a designated police station.

(3) A constable to whom this subsection applies may take an arrested person to any police station unless it appears to the constable that it may be necessary to keep the arrested person in police detention for more than six hours.

(4) Subsection (3) above applies--

(a) to a constable who is working in a locality covered by a police station which is not a designated police station; and

(b) to a constable belonging to a body of constables maintained by an authority other than a police authority.

(5) Any constable may take an arrested person to any police station if--

(a) either of the following conditions is satisfied--

    (i) the constable has arrested him without the assistance of any other constable and no other constable is available to assist him;

    (ii) the constable has taken him into custody from a person other than a constable without the assistance of any other constable and no other constable is available to assist him; and

(b) it appears to the constable that he will be unable to take the arrested person to a designated police station without the arrested person injuring himself, the constable or some other person.

(6) If the first police station to which an arrested person is taken after his arrest is not a designated police station, he shall be taken to a designated police station not more than six hours after his arrival at the first police station unless he is released previously.

(7) A person arrested by a constable at any place other than a police station must be released without bail if the condition in subsection (7A) is satisfied.

(7A) The condition is that, at any time before the person arrested reaches a police station, a constable is satisfied that there are no grounds for keeping him under arrest or releasing him on bail under section 30A.

(8) A constable who releases a person under subsection (7) above shall record the fact that he has done so.

(9) The constable shall make the record as soon as is practicable after the release.

(10) Nothing in subsection (1A) or in section 30A prevents a constable delaying taking a person to a police station or releasing him on bail if the condition in subsection (10A) is satisfied.

(10A) The condition is that the presence of the person at a place (other than a police station) is necessary in order to carry out such investigations as it is reasonable to carry out immediately.

(11) Where there is any such delay the reasons for the delay must be recorded when the person first arrives at the police station or (as the case may be) is released on bail.

(12) Nothing in subsection (1A) or section 30A above shall be taken to affect--

(a) paragraphs 16(3) or 18(1) of Schedule 2 to the Immigration Act 1971;

(b) section 34(1) of the Criminal Justice Act 1972; or

(c) any provision of the Terrorism Act 2000.

(13) Nothing in subsection (10) above shall be taken to affect paragraph 18(3) of Schedule 2 to the Immigration Act 1971.

s 30A Bail elsewhere than at police station

(1) A constable may release on bail a person who is arrested or taken into custody in the circumstances mentioned in section 30(1).

(2) A person may be released on bail under subsection (1) at any time before he arrives at a police station.

(3) A person released on bail under subsection (1) must be required to attend a police station.

(3A) Where a constable releases a person on bail under subsection (1)-

(a) no recognizance for the person's surrender to custody shall be taken from the person,

(b) no security for the person's surrender to custody shall be taken from the person or from anyone else on the person's behalf,

(c) the person shall not be required to provide a surety or sureties for his surrender to custody, and

(d) no requirement to reside in a bail hostel may be imposed as a condition of bail.

(3B) Subject to subsection (3A), where a constable releases a person on bail under subsection (1) the constable may impose, as conditions of the bail, such requirements as appear to the constable to be necessary-

(a) to secure that the person surrenders to custody,

(b) to secure that the person does not commit an offence while on bail,

(c) to secure that the person does not interfere with witnesses or otherwise obstruct the course of justice, whether in relation to himself or any other person, or

(d) for the person's own protection or, if the person is under the age of 17, for the person's own welfare or in the person's own interests.

(4) Where a person is released on bail under subsection (1), a requirement may be imposed on the person as a condition of bail only under the preceding provisions of this section.

(5) The police station which the person is required to attend may be any police station.

s 30B Bail under section 30A: notices

(1) Where a constable grants bail to a person under section 30A, he must give that person a notice in writing before he is released.

(2) The notice must state--

(a) the offence for which he was arrested, and

(b) the ground on which he was arrested.

(3) The notice must inform him that he is required to attend a police station.

(4) It may also specify the police station which he is required to attend and the time when he is required to attend.

(4A) If the person is granted bail subject to conditions under section 30A(3B), the notice also-

(a) must specify the requirements imposed by those conditions,

(b) must explain the opportunities under sections 30CA(1) and 30CB(1) for variation of those conditions, and

(c) if it does not specify the police station at which the person is required to attend, must specify a police station at which the person may make a request under section 30CA(1)(b).

(5) If the notice does not include the information mentioned in subsection (4), the person must subsequently be given a further notice in writing which contains that information.

(6) The person may be required to attend a different police station from that specified in the notice under subsection (1) or (5) or to attend at a different time.

(7) He must be given notice in writing of any such change as is mentioned in subsection (6) but more than one such notice may be given to him.

s 30C Bail under section 30A: supplemental

30C Bail under section 30A: supplemental

(1) A person who has been required to attend a police station is not required to do so if he is given notice in writing that his attendance is no longer required.

(2) If a person is required to attend a police station which is not a designated police station he must be--

(a) released, or

(b) taken to a designated police station,

not more than six hours after his arrival.

(3) Nothing in the Bail Act 1976 applies in relation to bail under section 30A.

(4) Nothing in section 30A or 30B or in this section prevents the re-arrest without a warrant of a person released on bail under section 30A if new evidence justifying a further arrest has come to light since his release.

s 30CA Bail under section 30A: variation of conditions by police

(1) Where a person released on bail under section 30A(1) is on bail subject to conditions-

(a) a relevant officer at the police station at which the person is required to attend, or

(b) where no notice under section 30B specifying that police station has been given to the person, a relevant officer at the police station specified under section 30B(4A)(c),

may, at the request of the person but subject to subsection (2), vary the conditions.

(2) On any subsequent request made in respect of the same grant of bail, subsection (1) confers power to vary the conditions of the bail only if the request is based on information that, in the case of the previous request or each previous request, was not available to the relevant officer considering that previous request when he was considering it.

(3) Where conditions of bail granted to a person under section 30A(1) are varied under subsection (1)-

(a) paragraphs (a) to (d) of section 30A(3A) apply,

(b) requirements imposed by the conditions as so varied must be requirements that appear to the relevant officer varying the conditions to be necessary for any of the purposes mentioned in paragraphs (a) to (d) of section 30A(3B), and

(c) the relevant officer who varies the conditions must give the person notice in writing of the variation.

(4) Power under subsection (1) to vary conditions is, subject to subsection (3)(a) and (b), power-

(a) to vary or rescind any of the conditions, and

(b) to impose further conditions.

(5) In this section "relevant officer", in relation to a designated police station, means a custody officer but, in relation to any other police station-

(a) means a constable who is not involved in the investigation of the offence for which the person making the request under subsection (1) was under arrest when granted bail under section 30A(1), if such a constable is readily available, and

(b) if no such constable is readily available-

(i) means a constable other than the one who granted bail to the person, if such a constable is readily available, and

(ii) if no such constable is readily available, means the constable who granted bail.

s 30CB Bail under section 30A: variation of conditions by court

30CB Bail under section 30A: variation of conditions by court

(1) Where a person released on bail under section 30A(1) is on bail subject to conditions, a magistrates' court may, on an application by or on behalf of the person, vary the conditions if-

(a) the conditions have been varied under section 30CA(1) since being imposed under section 30A(3B),

(b) a request for variation under section 30CA(1) of the conditions has been made and refused, or

(c) a request for variation under section 30CA(1) of the conditions has been made and the period of 48 hours beginning with the day when the request was made has expired without the request having been withdrawn or the conditions having been varied in response to the request.

(2) In proceedings on an application for a variation under subsection (1), a ground may not be relied upon unless-

(a) in a case falling within subsection (1)(a), the ground was relied upon in the request in response to which the conditions were varied under section 30CA(1), or

(b) in a case falling within paragraph (b) or (c) of subsection (1), the ground was relied upon in the request mentioned in that paragraph,

but this does not prevent the court, when deciding the application, from considering different grounds arising out of a change in circumstances that has occurred since the making of the application.

(3) Where conditions of bail granted to a person under section 30A(1) are varied under subsection (1)-

(a) paragraphs (a) to (d) of section 30A(3A) apply,

(b) requirements imposed by the conditions as so varied must be requirements that appear to the court varying the conditions to be necessary for any of the purposes mentioned in paragraphs (a) to (d) of section 30A(3B), and

(c) that bail shall not lapse but shall continue subject to the conditions as so varied.

(4) Power under subsection (1) to vary conditions is, subject to subsection (3)(a) and (b), power-

(a) to vary or rescind any of the conditions, and

(b) to impose further conditions.

s 30D Failure to answer to bail under section 30A

(1) A constable may arrest without a warrant a person who--

(a) has been released on bail under section 30A subject to a requirement to attend a specified police station, but

(b) fails to attend the police station at the specified time.

(2) A person arrested under subsection (1) must be taken to a police station (which may be the specified police station or any other police station) as soon as practicable after the arrest.

(2A) A person who has been released on bail under section 30A may be arrested without a warrant by a constable if the constable has reasonable grounds for suspecting that the person has broken any of the conditions of bail.

(2B) A person arrested under subsection (2A) must be taken to a police station (which may be the specified police station mentioned in subsection (1) or any other police station) as soon as practicable after the arrest.

(3) In subsection (1), "specified" means specified in a notice under subsection (1) or (5) of section 30B or, if notice of change has been given under subsection (7) of that section, in that notice.

(4) For the purposes of--

(a) section 30 (subject to the obligations in subsections (2) and (2B)), and

(b) section 31,

an arrest under this section is to be treated as an arrest for an offence.

s 31 Arrest for further offence.

Where--

(a) a person--

    (i) has been arrested for an offence; and

    (ii) is at a police station in consequence of that arrest; and

(b) it appears to a constable that, if he were released from that arrest, he would be liable to arrest for some other offence,

he shall be arrested for that other offence.

s 32 Search upon arrest.

(1) A constable may search an arrested person, in any case where the person to be searched has been arrested at a place other than a police station, if the constable has reasonable grounds for believing that the arrested person may present a danger to himself or others.

(2) Subject to subsections (3) to (5) below, a constable shall also have power in any such case--

    (a) to search the arrested person for anything--

        (i) which he might use to assist him to escape from lawful custody; or

        (ii) which might be evidence relating to an offence; and

    (b) if the offence for which he has been arrested is an indictable offence, to enter and search any premises in which he was when arrested or immediately before he was arrested for evidence relating to the offence.

(3) The power to search conferred by subsection (2) above is only a power to search to the extent that is reasonably required for the purpose of discovering any such thing or any such evidence.

(4) The powers conferred by this section to search a person are not to be construed as authorising a constable to require a person to remove any of his clothing in public other than an outer coat, jacket or gloves but they do authorise a search of a person's mouth.

(5) A constable may not search a person in the exercise of the power conferred by subsection (2)(a) above unless he has reasonable grounds for believing that the person to be searched may have concealed on him anything for which a search is permitted under that paragraph.

(6) A constable may not search premises in the exercise of the power conferred by subsection (2)(b) above unless he has reasonable grounds for believing that there is evidence for which a search is permitted under that paragraph on the premises.

(7) In so far as the power of search conferred by subsection (2)(b) above relates to premises

consisting of two or more separate dwellings, it is limited to a power to search--

(a) any dwelling in which the arrest took place or in which the person arrested was immediately before his arrest; and

(b) any parts of the premises which the occupier of any such dwelling uses in common with the occupiers of any other dwellings comprised in the premises.

(8) A constable searching a person in the exercise of the power conferred by subsection (1) above may seize and retain anything he finds, if he has reasonable grounds for believing that the person searched might use it to cause physical injury to himself or to any other person.

(9) A constable searching a person in the exercise of the power conferred by subsection (2)(a) above may seize and retain anything he finds, other than an item subject to legal privilege, if he has reasonable grounds for believing--

(a) that he might use it to assist him to escape from lawful custody; or

(b) that it is evidence of an offence or has been obtained in consequence of the commission of an offence.

(10) Nothing in this section shall be taken to affect the power conferred by section 43 of the Terrorism Act 2000.

s 34 Limitations on police detention.

(1) A person arrested for an offence shall not be kept in police detention except in accordance with the provisions of this Part of this Act.

(2) Subject to subsection (3) below, if at any time a custody officer--

(a) becomes aware, in relation to any person in police detention, that the grounds for the detention of that person have ceased to apply; and

(b) is not aware of any other grounds on which the continued detention of that person could be justified under the provisions of this Part of this Act,

it shall be the duty of the custody officer, subject to subsection (4) below, to order his immediate release from custody.

(3) No person in police detention shall be released except on the authority of a custody officer at the police station where his detention was authorised or, if it was authorised at more than one station, a custody officer at the station where it was last authorised.

(4) A person who appears to the custody officer to have been unlawfully at large when he was arrested is not to be released under subsection (2) above.

(5) A person whose release is ordered under subsection (2) above shall be released without bail unless it appears to the custody officer--

(a) that there is need for further investigation of any matter in connection with which he was detained at any time during the period of his detention; or

(b) that, in respect of any such matter, proceedings may be taken against him or he may be reprimanded or warned under section 65 of the Crime and Disorder Act 1998

and, if it so appears, he shall be released on bail.

(6) For the purposes of this Part of this Act a person arrested under section 6D of the Road Traffic Act 1988 or section 30(2) of the Transport and Works Act 1992 (c. 42) is arrested for an offence.

(7) For the purposes of this Part a person who--

(a) attends a police station to answer to bail granted under section 30A,

(b) returns to a police station to answer to bail granted under this Part, or

(c) is arrested under section 30D or 46A,

is to be treated as arrested for an offence and that offence is the offence in connection with which he was granted bail.

(8) Subsection (7) does not apply in relation to a person who is granted bail subject to the duty mentioned in section 47(3)(b) and who either-

(a) attends a police station to answer to such bail, or

(b) is arrested under section 46A for failing to do so,

(provision as to the treatment of such persons for the purposes of this Part being made by section 46ZA).

s 35 Designated police stations.

(1) The chief officer of police for each police area shall designate the police stations in his area which, subject to sections 30(3) and (5), 30A(5) and 30D(2)], are to be the stations in that area to be used for the purpose of detaining arrested persons.

(2) A chief officer's duty under subsection (1) above is to designate police stations appearing to him to provide enough accommodation for that purpose.

(2A) The Chief Constable of the British Transport Police Force may designate police stations which (in addition to those designated under subsection (1) above) may be used for the purpose of detaining arrested persons.

(3) Without prejudice to section 12 of the Interpretation Act 1978 (continuity of duties) a chief officer--

(a) may designate a station which was not previously designated; and

(b) may direct that a designation of a station previously made shall cease to operate.

(4) In this Act "designated police station" means a police station for the time being designated under this section.

s 36 Custody officers at police stations.

(1) One or more custody officers shall be appointed for each designated police station.

(2) A custody officer for a police station designated under section 35(1) above shall be appointed-

(a) by the chief officer of police for the area in which the designated police station is situated; or

(b) by such other police officer as the chief officer of police for that area may direct.

(2A) A custody officer for a police station designated under section 35(2A) above shall be appointed--

(a) by the Chief Constable of the British Transport Police Force; or

(b) by such other member of that Force as that Chief Constable may direct.

(3) No officer may be appointed a custody officer unless the officer is of at least the rank of sergeant.

(4) An officer of any rank may perform the functions of a custody officer at a designated police station if a custody officer is not readily available to perform them.

(5) Subject to the following provisions of this section and to section 39(2) below, none of the functions of a custody officer in relation to a person shall be performed by an officer who at the time when the function falls to be performed is involved in the investigation of an offence for which that person is in police detention at that time.

(6) Nothing in subsection (5) above is to be taken to prevent a custody officer--

(a) performing any function assigned to custody officers--

(i) by this Act; or

(ii) by a code of practice issued under this Act;

(b) carrying out the duty imposed on custody officers by section 39 below;

(c) doing anything in connection with the identification of a suspect; or

(d) doing anything under sections 7 and 8 of the Road Traffic Act 1988.

(7) Where an arrested person is taken to a police station which is not a designated police station, the functions in relation to him which at a designated police station would be the functions of a custody officer shall be performed--

(a) by an officer who is not involved in the investigation of an offence for which he is in police detention, if such an officer is readily available; and

(b) if no such officer is readily available, by the officer who took him to the station or any other officer.

(7A) Subject to subsection (7B), subsection (7) applies where a person attends a police station which is not a designated station to answer to bail granted under section 30A as it applies where a person is taken to such a station.

(7B) Where subsection (7) applies because of subsection (7A), the reference in subsection (7)(b) to the officer who took him to the station is to be read as a reference to the officer who granted him bail.

(8) References to a custody officer in section 34 above or in the following provisions of this Act include references to an officer other than a custody officer who is performing the functions of a custody officer by virtue of subsection (4) or (7) above.

(9) Where by virtue of subsection (7) above an officer of a force maintained by a police authority who took an arrested person to a police station is to perform the functions of a custody officer in relation to him, the officer shall inform an officer who--

(a) is attached to a designated police station; and

(b) is of at least the rank of inspector,

that he is to do so.

(10) The duty imposed by subsection (9) above shall be performed as soon as it is practicable to perform it.

s 37 Duties of custody officer before charge.

(1) Where--

(a) a person is arrested for an offence--

(i) without a warrant; or

(ii) under a warrant not endorsed for bail,

the custody officer at each police station where he is detained after his arrest shall determine whether he has before him sufficient evidence to charge that person with the offence for which he was arrested and may detain him at the police station for such period as is necessary to enable him to do so.

(2) If the custody officer determines that he does not have such evidence before him, the person arrested shall be released either on bail or without bail, unless the custody officer has reasonable grounds for believing that his detention without being charged is necessary to secure or preserve evidence relating to an offence for which he is under arrest or to obtain such evidence by questioning him.

(3) If the custody officer has reasonable grounds for so believing, he may authorise the person arrested to be kept in police detention.

(4) Where a custody officer authorises a person who has not been charged to be kept in police detention, he shall, as soon as is practicable, make a written record of the grounds for the detention.

(5) Subject to subsection (6) below, the written record shall be made in the presence of the person arrested who shall at that time be informed by the custody officer of the grounds for his detention.

(6) Subsection (5) above shall not apply where the person arrested is, at the time when the written record is made--

(a) incapable of understanding what is said to him;

(b) violent or likely to become violent; or

(c) in urgent need of medical attention.

(7) Subject to section 41(7) below, if the custody officer determines that he has before him sufficient evidence to charge the person arrested with the offence for which he was arrested, the person arrested--

(a) shall be-

(i) released without charge and on bail, or

(ii) kept in police detention,

for the purpose of enabling the Director of Public Prosecutions to make a decision under section 37B below,

(b) shall be released without charge and on bail but not for that purpose,

(c) shall be released without charge and without bail, or

(d) shall be charged.

(7A) The decision as to how a person is to be dealt with under subsection (7) above shall be that of the custody officer.

(7B) Where a person is dealt with under subsection (7)(a) above, it shall be the duty of the custody officer to inform him that he is being released, or (as the case may be) detained, to enable the Director of Public Prosecutions to make a decision under section 37B below.

(8) Where--

(a) a person is released under subsection (7)(b) or (c) above; and

(b) at the time of his release a decision whether he should be prosecuted for the offence for which he was arrested has not been taken,

it shall be the duty of the custody officer so to inform him.

(8A) Subsection (8B) applies if the offence for which the person is arrested is one in relation to which a sample could be taken under section 63B below and the custody officer-

(a) is required in pursuance of subsection (2) above to release the person arrested and decides to release him on bail, or

(b) decides in pursuance of subsection (7)(a) or (b) above to release the person without charge and on bail.

(8B) The detention of the person may be continued to enable a sample to be taken under section 63B, but this subsection does not permit a person to be detained for a period of more than 24 hours after the relevant time.

(9) If the person arrested is not in a fit state to be dealt with under subsection (7) above, he may be kept in police detention until he is.

(10) The duty imposed on the custody officer under subsection (1) above shall be carried out by him as soon as practicable after the person arrested arrives at the police station or, in the case of a person arrested at the police station, as soon as practicable after the arrest.

(15) In this Part of this Act--

"arrested juvenile" means a person arrested with or without a warrant who appears to be under the age of 17;

"endorsed for bail" means endorsed with a direction for bail in accordance with section 117(2) of the Magistrates' Courts Act 1980.

s 37A Guidance

(1) The Director of Public Prosecutions may issue guidance--

(a) for the purpose of enabling custody officers to decide how persons should be dealt with under section 37(7) above or 37C(2) or 37CA(2) below, and

(b) as to the information to be sent to the Director of Public Prosecutions under section 37B(1) below.

(2) The Director of Public Prosecutions may from time to time revise guidance issued under this section.

(3) Custody officers are to have regard to guidance under this section in deciding how persons should be dealt with under section 37(7) above or 37C(2) or 37CA(2) below.

(4) A report under section 9 of the Prosecution of Offences Act 1985 (report by DPP to Attorney General) must set out the provisions of any guidance issued, and any revisions to guidance made, in the year to which the report relates.

(5) The Director of Public Prosecutions must publish in such manner as he thinks fit--

(a) any guidance issued under this section, and

(b) any revisions made to such guidance.

(6) Guidance under this section may make different provision for different cases, circumstances or areas.

s 37B Consultation with the Director of Public Prosecutions

(1) Where a person is dealt with under section 37(7)(a) above, an officer involved in the investigation of the offence shall, as soon as is practicable, send to the Director of Public Prosecutions such information as may be specified in guidance under section 37A above.

(2) The Director of Public Prosecutions shall decide whether there is sufficient evidence to charge the person with an offence.

(3) If he decides that there is sufficient evidence to charge the person with an offence, he shall decide--

(a) whether or not the person should be charged and, if so, the offence with which he should be charged, and

(b) whether or not the person should be given a caution and, if so, the offence in respect of which he should be given a caution.

(4) The Director of Public Prosecutions shall give notice of his decision to an officer involved in the investigation of the offence.

(4A) Notice under subsection (4) above shall be in writing, but in the case of a person kept in police detention under section 37(7)(a) above it may be given orally in the first instance and confirmed in writing subsequently.

(5) If his decision is--

(a) that there is not sufficient evidence to charge the person with an offence, or

(b) that there is sufficient evidence to charge the person with an offence but that the person should not be charged with an offence or given a caution in respect of an offence,

a custody officer shall give the person notice in writing that he is not to be prosecuted.

(6) If the decision of the Director of Public Prosecutions is that the person should be charged with an offence, or given a caution in respect of an offence, the person shall be charged or cautioned accordingly.

(7) But if his decision is that the person should be given a caution in respect of the offence and it proves not to be possible to give the person such a caution, he shall instead be charged with the offence.

(8) For the purposes of this section, a person is to be charged with an offence either--

(a) when he is in police detention at a police station (whether because he has returned to answer bail, because he is detained under section 37(7)(a) above or for some other reason), or

(b) in accordance with section 29 of the Criminal Justice Act 2003.

(9) In this section "caution" includes--

(a) a conditional caution within the meaning of Part 3 of the Criminal Justice Act 2003,

(aa) a youth conditional caution within the meaning of Chapter 1 of Part 4 of the Crime and Disorder Act 1998, and

(b) a warning or reprimand under section 65 of that Act.

s 37C Breach of bail following release under section 37(7)(a)

37C Breach of bail following release under section 37(7)(a)

(1) This section applies where--

(a) a person released on bail under section 37(7)(a) above or subsection (2)(b) below is arrested under section 46A below in respect of that bail, and

(b) at the time of his detention following that arrest at the police station mentioned in section 46A(2) below, notice under section 37B(4) above has not been given.

(2) The person arrested--

(a) shall be charged, or

(b) shall be released without charge, either on bail or without bail.

(3) The decision as to how a person is to be dealt with under subsection (2) above shall be that of a custody officer.

(4) A person released on bail under subsection (2)(b) above shall be released on bail subject to the same conditions (if any) which applied immediately before his arrest.

s 37CA Breach of bail following release under section 37(7)(b)

37CA Breach of bail following release under section 37(7)(b)

(1) This section applies where a person released on bail under section 37(7)(b) above or subsection (2)(b) below-

(a) is arrested under section 46A below in respect of that bail, and

(b) is being detained following that arrest at the police station mentioned in section

46A(2) below.

(2) The person arrested-

(a) shall be charged, or

(b) shall be released without charge, either on bail or without bail.

(3) The decision as to how a person is to be dealt with under subsection (2) above shall be that of a custody officer.

(4) A person released on bail under subsection (2)(b) above shall be released on bail subject to the same conditions (if any) which applied immediately before his arrest.

s 37D Release on bail under section 37: further provision

(1) Where a person is released on bail under 37, 37C(2)(b) or 37CA(2)(b) above, a custody officer may subsequently appoint a different time, or an additional time, at which the person is to attend at the police station to answer bail.

(2) The custody officer shall give the person notice in writing of the exercise of the power under subsection (1).

(3) The exercise of the power under subsection (1) shall not affect the conditions (if any) to which bail is subject.

(4) Where a person released on bail under section 37(7)(a) or 37C(2)(b) above returns to a police station to answer bail or is otherwise in police detention at a police station, he may be kept in police detention to enable him to be dealt with in accordance with section 37B or 37C above or to enable the power under subsection (1) above to be exercised.

(4A) Where a person released on bail under section 37(7)(b) or 37CA(2)(b) above returns to a police station to answer bail or is otherwise in police detention at a police station, he may be kept in police detention to enable him to be dealt with in accordance with section 37CA above or to enable the power under subsection (1) above to be exercised.

(5) If the person mentioned in subsection (4) or (4A) above is not in a fit state to enable him to be dealt with as mentioned in that subsection or to enable the power under subsection (1) above to be exercised, he may be kept in police detention until he is.

(6) Where a person is kept in police detention by virtue of subsection (4), (4A) or (5) above, section 37(1) to (3) and (7) above (and section 40(8) below so far as it relates to section 37(1) to (3)) shall not apply to the offence in connection with which he was released on bail under section 37(7), 37C(2)(b) or 37CA(2)(b) above.

s 38 Duties of custody officer after charge.

(1) Where a person arrested for an offence otherwise than under a warrant endorsed for bail is charged with an offence, the custody officer shall, subject to section 25 of the Criminal Justice and Public Order Act 1994, order his release from police detention, either on bail or without bail,

unless--

    (a) if the person arrested is not an arrested juvenile--

        (i) his name or address cannot be ascertained or the custody officer has reasonable grounds for doubting whether a name or address furnished by him as his name or address is his real name or address;

        (ii) the custody officer has reasonable grounds for believing that the person arrested will fail to appear in court to answer to bail;

        (iii) in the case of a person arrested for an imprisonable offence, the custody officer has reasonable grounds for believing that the detention of the person arrested is necessary to prevent him from committing an offence;

        (iiia) in a case where a sample may be taken from the person under section 63B below, the custody officer has reasonable grounds for believing that the detention of the person is necessary to enable the sample to be taken from him;

        (iv) in the case of a person arrested for an offence which is not an imprisonable offence, the custody officer has reasonable grounds for believing that the detention of the person arrested is necessary to prevent him from causing physical injury to any other person or from causing loss of or damage to property;

        (v) the custody officer has reasonable grounds for believing that the detention of the person arrested is necessary to prevent him from interfering with the administration of justice or with the investigation of offences or of a particular offence; or

        (vi) the custody officer has reasonable grounds for believing that the detention of the person arrested is necessary for his own protection;

    (b) if he is an arrested juvenile--

        (i) any of the requirements of paragraph (a) above is satisfied (but, in the case of paragraph (a)(iiia) above, only if the arrested juvenile has attained the minimum age); or

        (ii) the custody officer has reasonable grounds for believing that he ought to be detained in his own interests;

    (c) the offence with which the person is charged is murder.

(2) If the release of a person arrested is not required by subsection (1) above, the custody officer may authorise him to be kept in police detention but may not authorise a person to be kept in police detention by virtue of subsection (1)(a)(iiia) after the end of the period of six hours beginning when he was charged with the offence.

(2A) The custody officer, in taking the decisions required by subsection (1)(a) and (b) above (except (a)(i) and (vi) and (b)(ii)), shall have regard to the same considerations as those which a court is required to have regard to in taking the corresponding decisions under paragraph 2(1) of Part I of Schedule 1 to the Bail Act 1976 (disregarding paragraph 2(2) of that Part).

(3) Where a custody officer authorises a person who has been charged to be kept in police detention, he shall, as soon as practicable, make a written record of the grounds for the detention.

(4) Subject to subsection (5) below, the written record shall be made in the presence of the person charged who shall at that time be informed by the custody officer of the grounds for his detention.

(5) Subsection (4) above shall not apply where the person charged is, at the time when the written record is made--

(a) incapable of understanding what is said to him;

(b) violent or likely to become violent; or

(c) in urgent need of medical attention.

(6) Where a custody officer authorises an arrested juvenile to be kept in police detention under subsection (1) above, the custody officer shall, unless he certifies--

(a) that, by reason of such circumstances as are specified in the certificate, it is impracticable for him to do so; or

(b) in the case of an arrested juvenile who has attained the age of 12 years, that no secure accommodation is available and that keeping him in other local authority accommodation would not be adequate to protect the public from serious harm from him,

secure that the arrested juvenile is moved to local authority accommodation.

(6A) In this section--

'local authority accommodation' means accommodation provided by or on behalf of a local authority (within the meaning of the Children Act 1989);

"minimum age" means the age specified in section 63B(3)(b) below;

'secure accommodation' means accommodation provided for the purpose of restricting liberty;

"sexual offence" means an offence specified in Part 2 of Schedule 15 to the Criminal Justice Act 2003;

"violent offence" means murder or an offence specified in Part 1 of that Schedule;

and any reference, in relation to an arrested juvenile charged with a violent or sexual offence, to protecting the public from serious harm from him shall be construed as a reference to protecting members of the public from death or serious personal injury, whether physical or psychological, occasioned by further such offences committed by him.

(6B) Where an arrested juvenile is moved to local authority accommodation under subsection (6) above, it shall be lawful for any person acting on behalf of the authority to detain him.

(7) A certificate made under subsection (6) above in respect of an arrested juvenile shall be produced to the court before which he is first brought thereafter.

(7A) In this section "imprisonable offence" has the same meaning as in Schedule 1 to the Bail Act 1976.

(8) In this Part of this Act "local authority" has the same meaning as in the Children Act 1989.

s 39 Responsibilities in relation to persons detained.

(1) Subject to subsections (2) and (4) below, it shall be the duty of the custody officer at a police station to ensure--

(a) that all persons in police detention at that station are treated in accordance with this Act and any code of practice issued under it and relating to the treatment of persons in police detention; and

(b) that all matters relating to such persons which are required by this Act or by such Codes of Practice to be recorded are recorded in the custody records relating to such persons.

(2) If the custody officer, in accordance with any code of practice issued under this Act, transfers or permits the transfer of a person in police detention--

(a) to the custody of a police officer investigating an offence for which that person is in police detention; or

(b) to the custody of an officer who has charge of that person outside the police station,

the custody officer shall cease in relation to that person to be subject to the duty imposed on him by subsection (1)(a) above; and it shall be the duty of the officer to whom the transfer is made to ensure that he is treated in accordance with the provisions of this Act and of any such Codes of Practice as are mentioned in subsection (1) above.

(3) If the person detained is subsequently returned to the custody of the custody officer, it shall be the duty of the officer investigating the offence to report to the custody officer as to the manner in which this section and the Codes of Practice have been complied with while that person was in his custody.

(4) If an arrested juvenile is moved to local authority accommodation under section 38(6) above, the custody officer shall cease in relation to that person to be subject to the duty imposed on him by subsection (1) above.

(6) Where--

(a) an officer of higher rank than the custody officer gives directions relating to a person in police detention; and

(b) the directions are at variance--

(i) with any decision made or action taken by the custody officer in the performance of a duty imposed on him under this Part of this Act; or

(ii) with any decision or action which would but for the directions have been made or taken by him in the performance of such a duty,

the custody officer shall refer the matter at once to an officer of the rank of superintendent or above who is responsible for the police station for which the custody officer is acting as custody officer.

s 40 Review of police detention.

(1) Reviews of the detention of each person in police detention in connection with the investigation of an offence shall be carried out periodically in accordance with the following provisions of this section--

(a) in the case of a person who has been arrested and charged, by the custody officer; and

(b) in the case of a person who has been arrested but not charged, by an officer of at least the rank of inspector who has not been directly involved in the investigation.

(2) The officer to whom it falls to carry out a review is referred to in this section as a "review officer".

(3) Subject to subsection (4) below--

(a) the first review shall be not later than six hours after the detention was first authorised;

(b) the second review shall be not later than nine hours after the first;

(c) subsequent reviews shall be at intervals of not more than nine hours.

(4) A review may be postponed--

(a) if, having regard to all the circumstances prevailing at the latest time for it specified in subsection (3) above, it is not practicable to carry out the review at that time;

(b) without prejudice to the generality of paragraph (a) above--

(i) if at that time the person in detention is being questioned by a police officer and the review officer is satisfied that an interruption of the questioning for the purpose of carrying out the review would prejudice the investigation in connection with which he is being questioned; or

(ii) if at that time no review officer is readily available.

(5) If a review is postponed under subsection (4) above it shall be carried out as soon as practicable after the latest time specified for it in subsection (3) above.

(6) If a review is carried out after postponement under subsection (4) above, the fact that it was so carried out shall not affect any requirement of this section as to the time at which any subsequent review is to be carried out.

(7) The review officer shall record the reasons for any postponement of a review in the custody record.

(8) Subject to subsection (9) below, where the person whose detention is under review has not been charged before the time of the review, section 37(1) to (6) above shall have effect in relation to him, but with the modifications specified in subsection (8A).

(8A) The modifications are--

(a) the substitution of references to the person whose detention is under review for references to the person arrested;

(b) the substitution of references to the review officer for references to the custody officer; and

(c) in subsection (6), the insertion of the following paragraph after paragraph (a)--

'(aa) asleep;'.

(9) Where a person has been kept in police detention by virtue of section 37(9) or 37D(5) above, section 37(1) to (6) shall not have effect in relation to him but it shall be the duty of the review officer to determine whether he is yet in a fit state.

(10) Where the person whose detention is under review has been charged before the time of the review, section 38(1) to (6B) above shall have effect in relation to him, but with the modifications specified in subsection (10A).

(10A) The modifications are--

(a) the substitution of a reference to the person whose detention is under review for any reference to the person arrested or to the person charged; and

(b) in subsection (5), the insertion of the following paragraph after paragraph (a)--

'(aa) asleep;'.

(11) Where--

(a) an officer of higher rank than the review officer gives directions relating to a person in police detention; and

(b) the directions are at variance--

(i) with any decision made or action taken by the review officer in the performance of a duty imposed on him under this Part of this Act; or

(ii) with any decision or action which would but for the directions have been made or taken by him in the performance of such a duty,

the review officer shall refer the matter at once to an officer of the rank of superintendent or above who is responsible for the police station for which the review officer is acting as review officer in connection with the detention.

(12) Before determining whether to authorise a person's continued detention the review officer shall give--

(a) that person (unless he is asleep); or

(b) any solicitor representing him who is available at the time of the review, an opportunity to make representations to him about the detention.

(13) Subject to subsection (14) below, the person whose detention is under review or his solicitor may make representations under subsection (12) above either orally or in writing.

(14) The review officer may refuse to hear oral representations from the person whose detention is under review if he considers that he is unfit to make such representations by reason of his condition or behaviour.

s 40A Use of telephone for review under s. 40

(1) A review under section 40(1)(b) may be carried out by means of a discussion, conducted by telephone, with one or more persons at the police station where the arrested person is held.

(2) But subsection (1) does not apply if--

(a) the review is of a kind authorised by regulations under section 45A to be carried out using video-conferencing facilities; and

(b) it is reasonably practicable to carry it out in accordance with those regulations.

(3) Where any review is carried out under this section by an officer who is not present at the station where the arrested person is held-

(a) any obligation of that officer to make a record in connection with the carrying out of the review shall have effect as an obligation to cause another officer to make the record;

(b) any requirement for the record to be made in the presence of the arrested person shall apply to the making of that record by that other officer; and

(c) the requirements under section 40(12) and (13) above for-

(i) the arrested person, or

(ii) a solicitor representing him,

to be given any opportunity to make representations (whether in writing or orally) to that officer shall have effect as a requirement for that person, or such a solicitor, to be given an opportunity to make representations in a manner authorised by subsection (4) below.

(4) Representations are made in a manner authorised by this subsection-

(a) in a case where facilities exist for the immediate transmission of written representations to the officer carrying out the review, if they are made either-

(i) orally by telephone to that officer; or

(ii) in writing to that officer by means of those facilities;

and

(b) in any other case, if they are made orally by telephone to that officer.

(5) In this section 'video-conferencing facilities' has the same meaning as in section 45A below.

s 41 Limits on period of detention without charge.

(1) Subject to the following provisions of this section and to sections 42 and 43 below, a person shall not be kept in police detention for more than 24 hours without being charged.

(2) The time from which the period of detention of a person is to be calculated (in this Act referred to as "the relevant time")--

(a) in the case of a person to whom this paragraph applies, shall be--

(i) the time at which that person arrives at the relevant police station; or

(ii) the time 24 hours after the time of that person's arrest,

whichever is the earlier;

(b) in the case of a person arrested outside England and Wales, shall be--

(i) the time at which that person arrives at the first police station to which he is taken in the police area in England or Wales in which the offence for which he was arrested is being investigated; or

(ii) the time 24 hours after the time of that person's entry into England and Wales,

whichever is the earlier;

(c) in the case of a person who--

(i) attends voluntarily at a police station; or

(ii) accompanies a constable to a police station without having been arrested,

and is arrested at the police station, the time of his arrest;

(ca) in the case of a person who attends a police station to answer to bail granted under section 30A, the time when he arrives at the police station;

(d) in any other case, except where subsection (5) below applies, shall be the time at which the person arrested arrives at the first police station to which he is taken after his arrest.

(3) Subsection (2)(a) above applies to a person if--

(a) his arrest is sought in one police area in England and Wales;

(b) he is arrested in another police area; and

(c) he is not questioned in the area in which he is arrested in order to obtain evidence in relation to an offence for which he is arrested;

and in sub-paragraph (i) of that paragraph "the relevant police station" means the first police station to which he is taken in the police area in which his arrest was sought.

(4) Subsection (2) above shall have effect in relation to a person arrested under section 31 above as if every reference in it to his arrest or his being arrested were a reference to his arrest or his being arrested for the offence for which he was originally arrested.

(5) If--

(a) a person is in police detention in a police area in England and Wales ("the first area"); and

(b) his arrest for an offence is sought in some other police area in England and Wales ("the second area"); and

(c) he is taken to the second area for the purposes of investigating that offence, without being questioned in the first area in order to obtain evidence in relation to it,

the relevant time shall be--

(i) the time 24 hours after he leaves the place where he is detained in the first area; or

(ii) the time at which he arrives at the first police station to which he is taken in the second area,

whichever is the earlier.

(6) When a person who is in police detention is removed to hospital because he is in need of medical treatment, any time during which he is being questioned in hospital or on the way there or back by a police officer for the purpose of obtaining evidence relating to an offence shall be included in any period which falls to be calculated for the purposes of this Part of this Act, but any other time while he is in hospital or on his way there or back shall not be so included.

(7) Subject to subsection (8) below, a person who at the expiry of 24 hours after the relevant time is in police detention and has not been charged shall be released at that time either on bail or without bail.

(8) Subsection (7) above does not apply to a person whose detention for more than 24 hours after the relevant time has been authorised or is otherwise permitted in accordance with section 42 or 43 below.

(9) A person released under subsection (7) above shall not be re-arrested without a warrant for the offence for which he was previously arrested unless new evidence justifying a further arrest has come to light since his release; but this subsection does not prevent an arrest under section 46A below.

s 42 Authorisation of continued detention.

(1) Where a police officer of the rank of superintendent or above who is responsible for the police station at which a person is detained has reasonable grounds for believing that--

(a) the detention of that person without charge is necessary to secure or preserve evidence relating to an offence for which he is under arrest or to obtain such evidence by questioning him;

(b) an offence for which he is under arrest is an indictable offence; and

(c) the investigation is being conducted diligently and expeditiously,

he may authorise the keeping of that person in police detention for a period expiring at or before 36 hours after the relevant time.

(2) Where an officer such as is mentioned in subsection (1) above has authorised the keeping of a person in police detention for a period expiring less than 36 hours after the relevant time, such an officer may authorise the keeping of that person in police detention for a further period expiring not more than 36 hours after that time if the conditions specified in subsection (1) above are still satisfied when he gives the authorisation.

(3) If it is proposed to transfer a person in police detention to another police area, the officer determining whether or not to authorise keeping him in detention under subsection (1) above shall have regard to the distance and the time the journey would take.

(4) No authorisation under subsection (1) above shall be given in respect of any person--

(a) more than 24 hours after the relevant time; or

(b) before the second review of his detention under section 40 above has been carried out.

(5) Where an officer authorises the keeping of a person in police detention under subsection (1) above, it shall be his duty--

(a) to inform that person of the grounds for his continued detention; and

(b) to record the grounds in that person's custody record.

(6) Before determining whether to authorise the keeping of a person in detention under subsection (1) or (2) above, an officer shall give--

(a) that person; or

(b) any solicitor representing him who is available at the time when it falls to the officer to determine whether to give the authorisation,

an opportunity to make representations to him about the detention.

(7) Subject to subsection (8) below, the person in detention or his solicitor may make representations under subsection (6) above either orally or in writing.

(8) The officer to whom it falls to determine whether to give the authorisation may refuse to hear oral representations from the person in detention if he considers that he is unfit to make such representations by reason of his condition or behaviour.

(9) Where--

(a) an officer authorises the keeping of a person in detention under subsection (1) above; and

(b) at the time of the authorisation he has not yet exercised a right conferred on him by section 56 or 58 below,

the officer--

(i) shall inform him of that right;

(ii) shall decide whether he should be permitted to exercise it;

(iii) shall record the decision in his custody record; and

(iv) if the decision is to refuse to permit the exercise of the right, shall also record the grounds for the decision in that record.

(10) Where an officer has authorised the keeping of a person who has not been charged in detention under subsection (1) or (2) above, he shall be released from detention, either on bail or without bail, not later than 36 hours after the relevant time, unless--

(a) he has been charged with an offence; or

(b) his continued detention is authorised or otherwise permitted in accordance with section 43 below.

(11) A person released under subsection (10) above shall not be re-arrested without a warrant for the offence for which he was previously arrested unless new evidence justifying a further arrest has come to light since his release; but this subsection does not prevent an arrest under section 46A below.

s 43 Warrants of further detention.

(1) Where, on an application on oath made by a constable and supported by an information, a magistrates' court is satisfied that there are reasonable grounds for believing that the further detention of the person to whom the application relates is justified, it may issue a warrant of further detention authorising the keeping of that person in police detention.

(2) A court may not hear an application for a warrant of further detention unless the person to whom the application relates--

(a) has been furnished with a copy of the information; and

(b) has been brought before the court for the hearing.

(3) The person to whom the application relates shall be entitled to be legally represented at the hearing and, if he is not so represented but wishes to be so represented--

(a) the court shall adjourn the hearing to enable him to obtain representation; and

(b) he may be kept in police detention during the adjournment.

(4) A person's further detention is only justified for the purposes of this section or section 44

below if--

(a) his detention without charge is necessary to secure or preserve evidence relating to an offence for which he is under arrest or to obtain such evidence by questioning him;

(b) an offence for which he is under arrest is an indictable offence; and

(c) the investigation is being conducted diligently and expeditiously.

(5) Subject to subsection (7) below, an application for a warrant of further detention may be made--

(a) at any time before the expiry of 36 hours after the relevant time; or

(b) in a case where--

(i) it is not practicable for the magistrates' court to which the application will be made to sit at the expiry of 36 hours after the relevant time; but

(ii) the court will sit during the 6 hours following the end of that period,

at any time before the expiry of the said 6 hours.

(6) In a case to which subsection (5)(b) above applies--

(a) the person to whom the application relates may be kept in police detention until the application is heard; and

(b) the custody officer shall make a note in that person's custody record--

(i) of the fact that he was kept in police detention for more than 36 hours after the relevant time; and

(ii) of the reason why he was so kept.

(7) If--

(a) an application for a warrant of further detention is made after the expiry of 36 hours after the relevant time; and

(b) it appears to the magistrates' court that it would have been reasonable for the police to make it before the expiry of that period,

the court shall dismiss the application.

(8) Where on an application such as is mentioned in subsection (1) above a magistrates' court is not satisfied that there are reasonable grounds for believing that the further detention of the person to whom the application relates is justified, it shall be its duty--

(a) to refuse the application; or

(b) to adjourn the hearing of it until a time not later than 36 hours after the relevant time.

(9) The person to whom the application relates may be kept in police detention during the adjournment.

(10) A warrant of further detention shall--

(a) state the time at which it is issued;

(b) authorise the keeping in police detention of the person to whom it relates for the period stated in it.

(11) Subject to subsection (12) below, the period stated in a warrant of further detention shall be such period as the magistrates' court thinks fit, having regard to the evidence before it.

(12) The period shall not be longer than 36 hours.

(13) If it is proposed to transfer a person in police detention to a police area other than that in which he is detained when the application for a warrant of further detention is made, the court hearing the application shall have regard to the distance and the time the journey would take.

(14) Any information submitted in support of an application under this section shall state--

(a) the nature of the offence for which the person to whom the application relates has been arrested;

(b) the general nature of the evidence on which that person was arrested;

(c) what inquiries relating to the offence have been made by the police and what further inquiries are proposed by them;

(d) the reasons for believing the continued detention of that person to be necessary for the purposes of such further inquiries.

(15) Where an application under this section is refused, the person to whom the application relates shall forthwith be charged or, subject to subsection (16) below, released, either on bail or without bail.

(16) A person need not be released under subsection (15) above--

(a) before the expiry of 24 hours after the relevant time; or

(b) before the expiry of any longer period for which his continued detention is or has been authorised under section 42 above.

(17) Where an application under this section is refused, no further application shall be made under this section in respect of the person to whom the refusal relates, unless supported by evidence which has come to light since the refusal.

(18) Where a warrant of further detention is issued, the person to whom it relates shall be released from police detention, either on bail or without bail, upon or before the expiry of the warrant unless he is charged.

(19) A person released under subsection (18) above shall not be re-arrested without a warrant for the offence for which he was previously arrested unless new evidence justifying a further arrest has

come to light since his release; but this subsection does not prevent an arrest under section 46A below.

s 44 Extension of warrants of further detention.

(1) On an application on oath made by a constable and supported by an information a magistrates' court may extend a warrant of further detention issued under section 43 above if it is satisfied that there are reasonable grounds for believing that the further detention of the person to whom the application relates is justified.

(2) Subject to subsection (3) below, the period for which a warrant of further detention may be extended shall be such period as the court thinks fit, having regard to the evidence before it.

(3) The period shall not--

(a) be longer than 36 hours; or

(b) end later than 96 hours after the relevant time.

(4) Where a warrant of further detention has been extended under subsection (1) above, or further extended under this subsection, for a period ending before 96 hours after the relevant time, on an application such as is mentioned in that subsection a magistrates' court may further extend the warrant if it is satisfied as there mentioned; and subsections (2) and (3) above apply to such further extensions as they apply to extensions under subsection (1) above.

(5) A warrant of further detention shall, if extended or further extended under this section, be endorsed with a note of the period of the extension.

(6) Subsections (2), (3) and (14) of section 43 above shall apply to an application made under this section as they apply to an application made under that section.

(7) Where an application under this section is refused, the person to whom the application relates shall forthwith be charged or, subject to subsection (8) below, released, either on bail or without bail.

(8) A person need not be released under subsection (7) above before the expiry of any period for which a warrant of further detention issued in relation to him has been extended or further extended on an earlier application made under this section.

s 45 Detention before charge--supplementary.

(1) In sections 43 and 44 of this Act "magistrates' court" means a court consisting of two or more justices of the peace sitting otherwise than in open court.

(2) Any reference in this Part of this Act to a period of time or a time of day is to be treated as approximate only.

s 45A Use of video-conferencing facilities for decisions about detention

(1) Subject to the following provisions of this section, the Secretary of State may by regulations provide that, in the case of an arrested person who is held in a police station, some or all of the functions mentioned in subsection (2) may be performed (notwithstanding anything in the preceding provisions of this Part) by an officer who-

(a) is not present in that police station; but

(b) has access to the use of video-conferencing facilities that enable him to communicate with persons in that station.

(2) Those functions are-

(a) the functions in relation to an arrested person taken to, or answering to bail at, a police station that is not a designated police station which, in the case of an arrested person taken to a station that is a designated police station, are functions of a custody officer under section 37, 38 or 40 above; and

(b) the function of carrying out a review under section 40(1)(b) above (review, by an officer of at least the rank of inspector, of the detention of person arrested but not charged).

(3) Regulations under this section shall specify the use to be made in the performance of the functions mentioned in subsection (2) above of the facilities mentioned in subsection (1) above.

(4) Regulations under this section shall not authorise the performance of any of the functions mentioned in subsection (2)(a) above by such an officer as is mentioned in subsection (1) above unless he is a custody officer for a designated police station.

(5) Where any functions mentioned in subsection (2) above are performed in a manner authorised by regulations under this section-

(a) any obligation of the officer performing those functions to make a record in connection with the performance of those functions shall have effect as an obligation to cause another officer to make the record; and

(b) any requirement for the record to be made in the presence of the arrested person shall apply to the making of that record by that other officer.

(6) Where the functions mentioned in subsection (2)(b) are performed in a manner authorised by regulations under this section, the requirements under section 40(12) and (13) above for-

(a) the arrested person, or

(b) a solicitor representing him,

to be given any opportunity to make representations (whether in writing or orally) to the person performing those functions shall have effect as a requirement for that person, or such a solicitor, to be given an opportunity to make representations in a manner authorised by subsection (7) below.

(7) Representations are made in a manner authorised by this subsection-

(a) in a case where facilities exist for the immediate transmission of written representations to the officer performing the functions, if they are made either-

(i) orally to that officer by means of the video-conferencing facilities used by him for performing those functions; or

(ii) in writing to that officer by means of the facilities available for the immediate transmission of the representations;

and

(b) in any other case if they are made orally to that officer by means of the video-conferencing facilities used by him for performing the functions.

(8) Regulations under this section may make different provision for different cases and may be made so as to have effect in relation only to the police stations specified or described in the regulations.

(9) Regulations under this section shall be made by statutory instrument and shall be subject to annulment in pursuance of a resolution of either House of Parliament.

(10) Any reference in this section to video-conferencing facilities, in relation to any functions, is a reference to any facilities (whether a live television link or other facilities) by means of which the functions may be performed with the officer performing them, the person in relation to whom they are performed and any legal representative of that person all able to both see and to hear each other.

s 46 Detention after charge.

(1) Where a person--

(a) is charged with an offence; and

(b) after being charged--

(i) is kept in police detention; or

(ii) is detained by a local authority in pursuance of arrangements made under section 38(6) above,

he shall be brought before a magistrates' court in accordance with the provisions of this section.

(2) If he is to be brought before a magistrates' court in the local justice area in which the police station at which he was charged is situated, he shall be brought before such a court as soon as is practicable and in any event not later than the first sitting after he is charged with the offence.

(3) If no magistrates' court in that area is due to sit either on the day on which he is charged or on the next day, the custody officer for the police station at which he was charged shall inform the designated officer for the area that there is a person in the area to whom subsection (2) above applies.

(4) If the person charged is to be brought before a magistrates' court in a local justice area other than that in which the police station at which he was charged is situated, he shall be removed to that area as soon as is practicable and brought before such a court as soon as is practicable after his arrival in the area and in any event not later than the first sitting of a magistrates' court in that area after his arrival in the area.

(5) If no magistrates' court in that area is due to sit either on the day on which he arrives in the area or on the next day--

(a) he shall be taken to a police station in the area; and

(b) the custody officer at that station shall inform the designated officer for the area that there is a person in the area to whom subsection (4) applies.

(6) Subject to subsection (8) below, where the designated officer for a local justice area has been informed--

(a) under subsection (3) above that there is a person in the area to whom subsection (2) above applies; or

(b) under subsection (5) above that there is a person in the area to whom subsection (4) above applies,

the designated officer shall arrange for a magistrates' court to sit not later than the day next following the relevant day.

(7) In this section "the relevant day"--

(a) in relation to a person who is to be brought before a magistrates' court in the local justice area in which the police station at which he was charged is situated, means the day on which he was charged; and

(b) in relation to a person who is to be brought before a magistrates' court in any other local justice area, means the day on which he arrives in the area.

(8) Where the day next following the relevant day is Christmas Day, Good Friday or a Sunday, the duty of the designated officer under subsection (6) above is a duty to arrange for a magistrates' court to sit not later than the first day after the relevant day which is not one of those days.

(9) Nothing in this section requires a person who is in hospital to be brought before a court if he is not well enough.

s 46ZA Persons granted live link bail

(1) This section applies in relation to bail granted under this Part subject to the duty mentioned in section 47(3)(b) ("live link bail").

(2) An accused person who attends a police station to answer to live link bail is not to be treated as in police detention for the purposes of this Act.

(3) Subsection (2) does not apply in relation to an accused person if-

(b) at any time before the beginning of proceedings in relation to a live link direction under section 57C of the Crime and Disorder Act 1998 in relation to the accused person, a constable informs him that a live link will not be available for his use for the purposes of that section; or

(d) the court determines for any reason not to give such a direction.

(4) If paragraph (b) or (d) of subsection (3) applies in relation to a person, he is to be treated for the purposes of this Part-

(a) as if he had been arrested for and charged with the offence in connection with which he was granted bail, and

(b) as if he had been so charged at the time when that paragraph first applied in relation to him.

(5) An accused person who is arrested under section 46A for failing to attend at a police station to answer to live link bail, and who is brought to a police station in accordance with that section, is to be treated for the purposes of this Part-

(a) as if he had been arrested for and charged with the offence in connection with which he was granted bail, and

(b) as if he had been so charged at the time when he is brought to the station.

(6) Nothing in subsection (4) or (5) affects the operation of section 47(6).

s 46A Power of arrest for failure to answer to

(1) A constable may arrest without a warrant any person who, having been released on bail under this Part of this Act subject to a duty to attend at a police station, fails to attend at that police station at the time appointed for him to do so.

(1ZA) The reference in subsection (1) to a person who fails to attend at a police station at the time appointed for him to do so includes a reference to a person who-

(a) attends at a police station to answer to bail granted subject to the duty mentioned in section 47(3)(b), but

(b) leaves the police station at any time before the beginning of proceedings in relation to a live link direction under section 57C of the Crime and Disorder Act 1998 in relation to him.

(1ZB) The reference in subsection (1) to a person who fails to attend at a police station at the time appointed for the person to do so includes a reference to a person who--

(a) attends at a police station to answer to bail granted subject to the duty mentioned in section 47(3)(b), but

(b) refuses to be searched under section 54B.

(1A) A person who has been released on bail under section 37, 37C(2)(b) or 37CA(2)(b) above may be arrested without warrant by a constable if the constable has reasonable grounds for suspecting that the person has broken any of the conditions of bail.

(2) A person who is arrested under this section shall be taken to the police station appointed as the place at which he is to surrender to custody as soon as practicable after the arrest.

(3) For the purposes of--

(a) section 30 above (subject to the obligation in subsection (2) above), and

(b) section 31 above,

an arrest under this section shall be treated as an arrest for an offence.

s 47 Bail after arrest.

(1) Subject to the following provisions of this section, a release on bail of a person under this Part of this Act shall be a release on bail granted in accordance with sections 3, 3A, 5 and 5A of the Bail Act 1976 as they apply to bail granted by a constable.

(1A) The normal powers to impose conditions of bail shall be available to him where a custody officer releases a person on bail under section 37 above or section 38(1) above (including that subsection as applied by section 40(10) above) but not in any other cases.

In this subsection, "the normal powers to impose conditions of bail" has the meaning given in section 3(6) of the Bail Act 1976.

(1B) No application may be made under section 5B of the Bail Act 1976 if a person is released on bail under 37, 37C(2)(b), or 37CA(2)(b) above.

(1C) Subsections (1D) to (1F) below apply where a person released on bail under section 37, 37C(2)(b) or 37CA(2)(b) above is on bail subject to conditions.

(1D) The person shall not be entitled to make an application under section 43B of the Magistrates' Courts Act 1980.

(1E) A magistrates' court may, on an application by or on behalf of the person, vary the conditions of bail; and in this subsection "vary" has the same meaning as in the Bail Act 1976.

(1F) Where a magistrates' court varies the conditions of bail under subsection (1E) above, that bail shall not lapse but shall continue subject to the conditions as so varied.

(2) Nothing in the Bail Act 1976 shall prevent the re-arrest without warrant of a person released on bail subject to a duty to attend at a police station if new evidence justifying a further arrest has come to light since his release.

(3) Subject to subsections (3A) and (4) below, in this Part of this Act references to "bail" are references to bail subject to a duty--

(a) to appear before a magistrates' court at such time and such place as the custody officer may appoint;

(b) to attend at such police station as the custody officer may appoint at such time as he may appoint for the purposes of-

(i) proceedings in relation to a live link direction under section 57C of the Crime and Disorder Act 1998 (use of live link direction at preliminary hearings where accused is at police station); and

(ii) any preliminary hearing in relation to which such a direction is given; or

(c) to attend at such police station as the custody officer may appoint at such time as he may appoint for purposes other than those mentioned in paragraph (b).

(3A) Where a custody officer grants bail to a person subject to a duty to appear before a magistrates' court, he shall appoint for the appearance--

(a) a date which is not later than the first sitting of the court after the person is charged with the offence; or

(b) where he is informed by the designated officer for the relevant local justice area that the appearance cannot be accommodated until a later date, that later date.

(4) Where a custody officer has granted bail to a person subject to a duty to appear at a police station, the custody officer may give notice in writing to that person that his attendance at the police station is not required.

(6) Where a person who has been granted bail under this Part and either has attended at the police station in accordance with the grant of bail or has been arrested under section 46A above is detained at a police station, any time during which he was in police detention prior to being granted bail shall be included as part of any period which falls to be calculated under this Part of this Act.

(7) Where a person who was released on bail under this Part subject to a duty to attend at a police station is re-arrested, the provisions of this Part of this Act shall apply to him as they apply to a person arrested for the first time; but this subsection does not apply to a person who is arrested under section 46A above or has attended a police station in accordance with the grant of bail (and who accordingly is deemed by section 34(7) above to have been arrested for an offence) or to a person to whom section 46ZA(4) or (5) applies.

s 47A Early administrative hearings conducted by justices' clerks.

Where a person has been charged with an offence at a police station, any requirement imposed under this Part for the person to appear or be brought before a magistrates' court shall be taken to be satisfied if the person appears or is brought before a justices' clerk in order for the clerk to conduct a hearing under section 50 of the Crime and Disorder Act 1998 (early administrative hearings).

s 48 Remands to police detention.

In section 128 of the Magistrates' Courts Act 1980--

(a) in subsection (7) for the words "the custody of a constable" there shall be substituted the words "detention at a police station";

(b) after subsection (7) there shall be inserted the following subsection--

"(8) Where a person is committed to detention at a police station under subsection (7) above--

(a) he shall not be kept in such detention unless there is a need for him to be so detained for the purposes of inquiries into other offences;

(b) if kept in such detention, he shall be brought back before the magistrates' court which committed him as soon as that need ceases;

(c) he shall be treated as a person in police detention to whom the duties under section 39 of the Police and Criminal Evidence Act 1984 (responsibilities in relation to persons detained) relate;

(d) his detention shall be subject to periodic review at the times set out in section 40 of that Act (review of police detention).".

s 54 Searches of detained persons.

(1) The custody officer at a police station shall ascertain everything which a person has with him when he is--

(a) brought to the station after being arrested elsewhere or after being committed to custody by an order or sentence of a court; or

(b) arrested at the station or detained there , as a person falling within section 34(7), under section 37 above or as a person to whom section 46ZA(4) or (5) applies.

(2) The custody officer may record or cause to be recorded all or any of the things which he ascertains under subsection (1).

(2A) In the case of an arrested person, any such record may be made as part of his custody record.

(3) Subject to subsection (4) below, a custody officer may seize and retain any such thing or cause any such thing to be seized and retained.

(4) Clothes and personal effects may only be seized if the custody officer--

(a) believes that the person from whom they are seized may use them--

(i) to cause physical injury to himself or any other person;

(ii) to damage property;

(iii) to interfere with evidence; or

(iv) to assist him to escape; or

(b) has reasonable grounds for believing that they may be evidence relating to an offence.

(5) Where anything is seized, the person from whom it is seized shall be told the reason for the seizure unless he is--

(a) violent or likely to become violent; or

(b) incapable of understanding what is said to him.

(6) Subject to subsection (7) below, a person may be searched if the custody officer considers it necessary to enable him to carry out his duty under subsection (1) above and to the extent that the custody officer considers necessary for that purpose.

(6A) A person who is in custody at a police station or is in police detention otherwise than at a police station may at any time be searched in order to ascertain whether he has with him anything which he could use for any of the purposes specified in subsection (4)(a) above.

(6B) Subject to subsection (6C) below, a constable may seize and retain, or cause to be seized and retained, anything found on such a search.

(6C) A constable may only seize clothes and personal effects in the circumstances specified in subsection (4) above.

(7) An intimate search may not be conducted under this section.

(8) A search under this section shall be carried out by a constable.

(9) The constable carrying out a search shall be of the same sex as the person searched.

s 54A Searches and examination to ascertain identity

(1) If an officer of at least the rank of inspector authorises it, a person who is detained in a police station may be searched or examined, or both--

(a) for the purpose of ascertaining whether he has any mark that would tend to identify him as a person involved in the commission of an offence; or

(b) for the purpose of facilitating the ascertainment of his identity.

(2) An officer may only give an authorisation under subsection (1) for the purpose mentioned in paragraph (a) of that subsection if--

(a) the appropriate consent to a search or examination that would reveal whether the mark in question exists has been withheld; or

(b) it is not practicable to obtain such consent.

(3) An officer may only give an authorisation under subsection (1) in a case in which subsection (2) does not apply if--

(a) the person in question has refused to identify himself; or

(b) the officer has reasonable grounds for suspecting that that person is not who he claims to be.

(4) An officer may give an authorisation under subsection (1) orally or in writing but, if he gives it orally, he shall confirm it in writing as soon as is practicable.

(5) Any identifying mark found on a search or examination under this section may be photographed--

(a) with the appropriate consent; or

(b) if the appropriate consent is withheld or it is not practicable to obtain it, without it.

(6) Where a search or examination may be carried out under this section, or a photograph may be taken under this section, the only persons entitled to carry out the search or examination, or to take the photograph, are constables.

(7) A person may not under this section carry out a search or examination of a person of the opposite sex or take a photograph of any part of the body of a person of the opposite sex.

(8) An intimate search may not be carried out under this section.

(9) A photograph taken under this section--

(a) may be used by, or disclosed to, any person for any purpose related to the prevention or detection of crime, the investigation of an offence or the conduct of a prosecution; and

(b) after being so used or disclosed, may be retained but may not be used or disclosed except for a purpose so related.

(10) In subsection (9)--

(a) the reference to crime includes a reference to any conduct which--

(i) constitutes one or more criminal offences (whether under the law of a part of the United Kingdom or of a country or territory outside the United Kingdom); or

(ii) is, or corresponds to, any conduct which, if it all took place in any one part of the United Kingdom, would constitute one or more criminal offences;

and

(b) the references to an investigation and to a prosecution include references, respectively, to any investigation outside the United Kingdom of any crime or suspected crime and to a prosecution brought in respect of any crime in a country or territory outside the United Kingdom.

(11) In this section--

(a) references to ascertaining a person's identity include references to showing that he is not a particular person; and

(b) references to taking a photograph include references to using any process by means of which a visual image may be produced, and references to photographing a person shall be construed accordingly.

(12) In this section 'mark' includes features and injuries; and a mark is an identifying mark for the purposes of this section if its existence in any person's case facilitates the ascertainment of his identity or his identification as a person involved in the commission of an offence.

(13) Nothing in this section applies to a person arrested under an extradition arrest power.

s 54B Searches of persons answering to live link bail

54B Searches of persons answering to live link bail

(1) A constable may search at any time--

(a) any person who is at a police station to answer to live link bail; and

(b) any article in the possession of such a person.

(2) If the constable reasonably believes a thing in the possession of the person ought to be seized on any of the grounds mentioned in subsection (3), the constable may seize and retain it or cause it to be seized and retained.

(3) The grounds are that the thing--

(a) may jeopardise the maintenance of order in the police station;

(b) may put the safety of any person in the police station at risk; or

(c) may be evidence of, or in relation to, an offence.

(4) The constable may record or cause to be recorded all or any of the things seized and retained pursuant to subsection (2).

(5) An intimate search may not be carried out under this section.

(6) The constable carrying out a search under subsection (1) must be of the same sex as the person being searched.

(7) In this section "live link bail" means bail granted under Part 4 of this Act subject to the duty mentioned in section 47(3)(b).

s 54C Power to retain articles seized

54C Power to retain articles seized

(1) Except as provided by subsections (2) and (3), a constable may retain a thing seized

under section 54B until the time when the person from whom it was seized leaves the police station.

(2) A constable may retain a thing seized under section 54B in order to establish its lawful owner, where there are reasonable grounds for believing that it has been obtained in consequence of the commission of an offence.

(3) If a thing seized under section 54B may be evidence of, or in relation to, an offence, a constable may retain it--

(a) for use as evidence at a trial for an offence; or

(b) for forensic examination or for investigation in connection with an offence.

(4) Nothing may be retained for either of the purposes mentioned in subsection (3) if a photograph or copy would be sufficient for that purpose.

(5) Nothing in this section affects any power of a court to make an order under section 1 of the Police (Property) Act 1897.

(6) The references in this section to anything seized under section 54B include anything seized by a person to whom paragraph 27A of Schedule 4 to the Police Reform Act 2002 applies.

s 55 Intimate searches.

(1) Subject to the following provisions of this section, if an officer of at least the rank of inspector has reasonable grounds for believing--

(a) that a person who has been arrested and is in police detention may have concealed on him anything which--

(i) he could use to cause physical injury to himself or others; and

(ii) he might so use while he is in police detention or in the custody of a court; or

(b) that such a person--

(i) may have a Class A drug concealed on him; and

(ii) was in possession of it with the appropriate criminal intent before his arrest,

he may authorise an intimate search of that person.

(2) An officer may not authorise an intimate search of a person for anything unless he has reasonable grounds for believing that it cannot be found without his being intimately searched.

(3) An officer may give an authorisation under subsection (1) above orally or in writing but, if he gives it orally, he shall confirm it in writing as soon as is practicable.

(3A) A drug offence search shall not be carried out unless the appropriate consent has been given in writing.

(3B) Where it is proposed that a drug offence search be carried out, an appropriate officer shall inform the person who is to be subject to it-

(a) of the giving of the authorisation for it; and

(b) of the grounds for giving the authorisation.

(4) An intimate search which is only a drug offence search shall be by way of examination by a suitably qualified person.

(5) Except as provided by subsection (4) above, an intimate search shall be by way of examination by a suitably qualified person unless an officer of at least the rank of inspector considers that this is not practicable.

(6) An intimate search which is not carried out as mentioned in subsection (5) above shall be carried out by a constable.

(7) A constable may not carry out an intimate search of a person of the opposite sex.

(8) No intimate search may be carried out except--

(a) at a police station;

(b) at a hospital;

(c) at a registered medical practitioner's surgery; or

(d) at some other place used for medical purposes.

(9) An intimate search which is only a drug offence search may not be carried out at a police station.

(10) If an intimate search of a person is carried out, the custody record relating to him shall state--

(a) which parts of his body were searched; and

(b) why they were searched.

(10A) If the intimate search is a drug offence search, the custody record relating to that person shall also state-

(a) the authorisation by virtue of which the search was carried out;

(b) the grounds for giving the authorisation; and

(c) the fact that the appropriate consent was given.

(11) The information required to be recorded by subsections (10) and (10A) above shall be recorded as soon as practicable after the completion of the search.

(12) The custody officer at a police station may seize and retain anything which is found on an intimate search of a person, or cause any such thing to be seized and retained--

(a) if he believes that the person from whom it is seized may use it--

(i) to cause physical injury to himself or any other person;

(ii) to damage property;

(iii) to interfere with evidence; or

(iv) to assist him to escape; or

(b) if he has reasonable grounds for believing that it may be evidence relating to an offence.

(13) Where anything is seized under this section, the person from whom it is seized shall be told the reason for the seizure unless he is--

(a) violent or likely to become violent; or

(b) incapable of understanding what is said to him.

(13A) Where the appropriate consent to a drug offence search of any person was refused without good cause, in any proceedings against that person for an offence-

(a) the court, in determining whether there is a case to answer;

(b) a judge, in deciding whether to grant an application made by the accused under paragraph 2 of Schedule 3 to the Crime and Disorder Act 1998 (applications for dismissal); and

(c) the court or jury, in determining whether that person is guilty of the offence charged,

may draw such inferences from the refusal as appear proper.

(14) Every annual report--

(a) under section 22 of the Police Act 1996; or

(b) made by the Commissioner of Police of the Metropolis,

shall contain information about searches under this section which have been carried out in the area to which the report relates during the period to which it relates.

(15) The information about such searches shall include--

(a) the total number of searches;

(b) the number of searches conducted by way of examination by a suitably qualified person;

(c) the number of searches not so conducted but conducted in the presence of such a person; and

(d) the result of the searches carried out.

(16) The information shall also include, as separate items--

(a) the total number of drug offence searches; and

(b) the result of those searches.

(17) In this section--

"the appropriate criminal intent" means an intent to commit an offence under--

(a) section 5(3) of the Misuse of Drugs Act 1971 (possession of controlled drug with intent to supply to another); or

(b) section 68(2) of the Customs and Excise Management Act 1979 (exportation etc. with intent to evade a prohibition or restriction);

"appropriate officer" means-

(a) a constable,

(b) a person who is designated as a detention officer in pursuance of section 38 of the Police Reform Act 2002 if his designation applies paragraph 33D of Schedule 4 to that Act;

...

"Class A drug" has the meaning assigned to it by section 2(1)(b) of the Misuse of Drugs Act 1971;

"drug offence search" means an intimate search for a Class A drug which an officer has authorised by virtue of subsection (1)(b) above; and

"suitably qualified person" means --

(a) a registered medical practitioner; or

(b) a registered nurse.

s 55A X-rays and ultrasound scans

55A X-rays and ultrasound scans

(1) If an officer of at least the rank of inspector has reasonable grounds for believing that a person who has been arrested for an offence and is in police detention-

(a) may have swallowed a Class A drug, and

(b) was in possession of it with the appropriate criminal intent before his arrest,

the officer may authorise that an x-ray is taken of the person or an ultrasound scan is carried out on the person (or both).

(2) An x-ray must not be taken of a person and an ultrasound scan must not be carried out on him unless the appropriate consent has been given in writing.

(3) If it is proposed that an x-ray is taken or an ultrasound scan is carried out, an appropriate officer must inform the person who is to be subject to it-

(a) of the giving of the authorisation for it, and

(b) of the grounds for giving the authorisation.

(4) An x-ray may be taken or an ultrasound scan carried out only by a suitably qualified person and only at-

(a) a hospital,

(b) a registered medical practitioner's surgery, or

(c) some other place used for medical purposes.

(5) The custody record of the person must also state-

(a) the authorisation by virtue of which the x-ray was taken or the ultrasound scan was carried out,

(b) the grounds for giving the authorisation, and

(c) the fact that the appropriate consent was given.

(6) The information required to be recorded by subsection (5) must be recorded as soon as practicable after the x-ray has been taken or ultrasound scan carried out (as the case may be).

(7) Every annual report-

(a) under section 22 of the Police Act 1996, or

(b) made by the Commissioner of Police of the Metropolis,

must contain information about x-rays which have been taken and ultrasound scans which have been carried out under this section in the area to which the report relates during the period to which it relates.

(8) The information about such x-rays and ultrasound scans must be presented separately and must include-

(a) the total number of x-rays;

(b) the total number of ultrasound scans;

(c) the results of the x-rays;

(d) the results of the ultrasound scans.

(9) If the appropriate consent to an x-ray or ultrasound scan of any person is refused without good cause, in any proceedings against that person for an offence-

(a) the court, in determining whether there is a case to answer,

(b) a judge, in deciding whether to grant an application made by the accused under paragraph 2 of Schedule 3 to the Crime and Disorder Act 1998 (applications for dismissal), and

(c) the court or jury, in determining whether that person is guilty of the offence charged,

may draw such inferences from the refusal as appear proper.

(10) In this section "the appropriate criminal intent", "appropriate officer", "Class A drug" and "suitably qualified person" have the same meanings as in section 55 above.

s 56 Right to have someone informed when arrested.

(1) Where a person has been arrested and is being held in custody in a police station or other premises, he shall be entitled, if he so requests, to have one friend or relative or other person who is known to him or who is likely to take an interest in his welfare told, as soon as is practicable except to the extent that delay is permitted by this section, that he has been arrested and is being detained there.

(2) Delay is only permitted--

(a) in the case of a person who is in police detention for an indictable offence; and

(b) if an officer of at least the rank of inspector authorises it.

(3) In any case the person in custody must be permitted to exercise the right conferred by subsection (1) above within 36 hours from the relevant time, as defined in section 41(2) above.

(4) An officer may give an authorisation under subsection (2) above orally or in writing but, if he gives it orally, he shall confirm it in writing as soon as is practicable.

(5) Subject to sub-section (5A) below an officer may only authorise delay where he has reasonable grounds for believing that telling the named person of the arrest--

(a) will lead to interference with or harm to evidence connected with an indictable offence or interference with or physical injury to other persons; or

(b) will lead to the alerting of other persons suspected of having committed such an offence but not yet arrested for it; or

(c) will hinder the recovery of any property obtained as a result of such an offence.

(5A) An officer may also authorise delay where he has reasonable grounds for believing that--

(a) the person detained for the indictable offence has benefited from his criminal conduct, and

(b) the recovery of the value of the property constituting the benefit will be hindered by telling the named person of the arrest.

(5B) For the purposes of subsection (5A) above the question whether a person has benefited from his criminal conduct is to be decided in accordance with Part 2 of the Proceeds of Crime Act 2002.

(6) If a delay is authorised--

(a) the detained person shall be told the reason for it; and

(b) the reason shall be noted on his custody record.

(7) The duties imposed by subsection (6) above shall be performed as soon as is practicable.

(8) The rights conferred by this section on a person detained at a police station or other premises are exercisable whenever he is transferred from one place to another; and this section applies to each subsequent occasion on which they are exercisable as it applies to the first such occasion.

(9) There may be no further delay in permitting the exercise of the right conferred by subsection (1) above once the reason for authorising delay ceases to subsist.

(10) Nothing in this section applies to a person arrested or detained under the terrorism provisions.

s 57 Additional rights of children and young persons.

The following subsections shall be substituted for section 34(2) of the Children and Young Persons Act 1933

"(2) Where a child or young person is in police detention, such steps as are practicable shall be taken to ascertain the identity of a person responsible for his welfare.

(3) If it is practicable to ascertain the identity of a person responsible for the welfare of the child or young person, that person shall be informed, unless it is not practicable to do so--

(a) that the child or young person has been arrested;

(b) why he has been arrested; and

(c) where he is being detained.

(4) Where information falls to be given under subsection (3) above, it shall be given as soon as it is practicable to do so.

(5) For the purposes of this section the persons who may be responsible for the welfare of a

child or young person are--

(a) his parent or guardian; or

(b) any other person who has for the time being assumed responsibility for his welfare.

(6) If it is practicable to give a person responsible for the welfare of the child or young person the information required by subsection (3) above, that person shall be given it as soon as it is practicable to do so.

(7) If it appears that at the time of his arrest a supervision order, as defined in section 11 of the Children and Young Persons Act 1969, is in force in respect of him, the person responsible for his supervision shall also be informed as described in subsection (3) above as soon as it is reasonably practicable to do so.

(8) The reference to a parent or guardian in subsection (5) above is--

(a) in the case of a child or young person in the care of a local authority, a reference to that authority; and

(b) in the case of a child or young person in the care of a voluntary organisation in which parental rights and duties with respect to him are vested by virtue of a resolution under section 64(1) of the Child Care Act 1980, a reference to that organisation.

(9) The rights conferred on a child or young person by subsections (2) to (8) above are in addition to his rights under section 56 of the Police and Criminal Evidence Act 1984.

(10) The reference in subsection (2) above to a child or young person who is in police detention includes a reference to a child or young person who has been detained under the terrorism provisions; and in subsection (3) above "arrest" includes such detention.

(11) In subsection (10) above "the terrorism provisions" has the meaning assigned to it by section 65 of the Police and Criminal Evidence Act 1984".

s 58 Access to legal advice.

(1) A person arrested and held in custody in a police station or other premises shall be entitled, if he so requests, to consult a solicitor privately at any time.

(2) Subject to subsection (3) below, a request under subsection (1) above and the time at which it was made shall be recorded in the custody record.

(3) Such a request need not be recorded in the custody record of a person who makes it at a time while he is at a court after being charged with an offence.

(4) If a person makes such a request, he must be permitted to consult a solicitor as soon as is practicable except to the extent that delay is permitted by this section.

(5) In any case he must be permitted to consult a solicitor within 36 hours from the relevant time, as defined in section 41(2) above.

(6) Delay in compliance with a request is only permitted--

(a) in the case of a person who is in police detention for an indictable offence; and

(b) if an officer of at least the rank of superintendent authorises it.

(7) An officer may give an authorisation under subsection (6) above orally or in writing but, if he gives it orally, he shall confirm it in writing as soon as is practicable.

(8) Subject to sub-section (8A) below an officer may only authorise delay where he has reasonable grounds for believing that the exercise of the right conferred by subsection (1) above at the time when the person detained desires to exercise it--

(a) will lead to interference with or harm to evidence connected with an indictable offence or interference with or physical injury to other persons; or

(b) will lead to the alerting of other persons suspected of having committed such an offence but not yet arrested for it; or

(c) will hinder the recovery of any property obtained as a result of such an offence.

(8A) An officer may also authorise delay where he has reasonable grounds for believing that--

(a) the person detained for the indictable offence has benefited from his criminal conduct, and

(b) the recovery of the value of the property constituting the benefit will be hindered by the exercise of the right conferred by subsection (1) above.

(8B) For the purposes of subsection (8A) above the question whether a person has benefited from his criminal conduct is to be decided in accordance with Part 2 of the Proceeds of Crime Act 2002.

(9) If delay is authorised--

(a) the detained person shall be told the reason for it; and

(b) the reason shall be noted on his custody record.

(10) The duties imposed by subsection (9) above shall be performed as soon as is practicable.

(11) There may be no further delay in permitting the exercise of the right conferred by subsection (1) above once the reason for authorising delay ceases to subsist.

(12) Nothing in this section applies to a person arrested or detained under the terrorism provisions.

s 60 Tape-recording of interviews.

(1) It shall be the duty of the Secretary of State--

(a) to issue a code of practice in connection with the tape-recording of interviews of persons suspected of the commission of criminal offences which are held by police officers at police stations; and

(b) to make an order requiring the tape-recording of interviews of persons suspected of the commission of criminal offences, or of such descriptions of criminal offences as may be specified in the order, which are so held, in accordance with the code as it has effect for the time being.

(2) An order under subsection (1) above shall be made by statutory instrument and shall be subject to annulment in pursuance of a resolution of either House of Parliament.

s 60A Visual recording of interviews

60A Visual recording of interviews

(1) The Secretary of State shall have power-

(a) to issue a code of practice for the visual recording of interviews held by police officers at police stations; and

(b) to make an order requiring the visual recording of interviews so held, and requiring the visual recording to be in accordance with the code for the time being in force under this section.

(2) A requirement imposed by an order under this section may be imposed in relation to such cases or police stations in such areas, or both, as may be specified or described in the order.

(3) An order under subsection (1) above shall be made by statutory instrument and shall be subject to annulment in pursuance of a resolution of either House of Parliament.

(4) In this section-

(a) references to any interview are references to an interview of a person suspected of a criminal offence; and

(b) references to a visual recording include references to a visual recording in which an audio recording is comprised.

s 61 Finger-printing.

(1) Except as provided by this section no person's fingerprints may be taken without the appropriate consent.

(2) Consent to the taking of a person's fingerprints must be in writing if it is given at a time when he is at a police station.

(3) The fingerprints of a person detained at a police station may be taken without the appropriate consent if--

(a) he is detained in consequence of his arrest for a recordable offence; and

(b) he has not had his fingerprints taken in the course of the investigation of the offence by the police.

(3A) Where a person mentioned in paragraph (a) of subsection (3) or (4) has already had his fingerprints taken in the course of the investigation of the offence by the police, that fact shall be disregarded for the purposes of that subsection if-

(a) the fingerprints taken on the previous occasion do not constitute a complete set of his fingerprints; or

(b) some or all of the fingerprints taken on the previous occasion are not of sufficient quality to allow satisfactory analysis, comparison or matching (whether in the case in question or generally).

(4) The fingerprints of a person detained at a police station may be taken without the appropriate consent if--

(a) he has been charged with a recordable offence or informed that he will be reported for such an offence; and

(b) he has not had his fingerprints taken in the course of the investigation of the offence by the police.

(4A) The fingerprints of a person who has answered to bail at a court or police station may be taken without the appropriate consent at the court or station if-

(a) the court, or

(b) an officer of at least the rank of inspector,

authorises them to be taken.

(4B) A court or officer may only give an authorisation under subsection (4A) if-

(a) the person who has answered to bail has answered to it for a person whose fingerprints were taken on a previous occasion and there are reasonable grounds for believing that he is not the same person; or

(b) the person who has answered to bail claims to be a different person from a person whose fingerprints were taken on a previous occasion.

(5) An officer may give an authorisation under subsection (4A) above orally or in writing but, if he gives it orally, he shall confirm it in writing as soon as is practicable.

(5A) The fingerprints of a person may be taken without the appropriate consent if (before or after the coming into force of this subsection) he has been arrested for a recordable offence and released and--
(a) in the case of a person who is on bail, he has not had his fingerprints taken in the course of the investigation of the offence by the police; or
(b) in any case, he has had his fingerprints taken in the course of that investigation but subsection (3A)(a) or (b) above applies.

(5B) The fingerprints of a person not detained at a police station may be taken without the appropriate consent if (before or after the coming into force of this subsection) he has been charged with a recordable offence or informed that he will be reported for such an offence and--

(a) he has not had his fingerprints taken in the course of the investigation of the offence by the police; or

(b) he has had his fingerprints taken in the course of that investigation but subsection (3A)(a) or (b) above applies.

(6) Subject to this section, the fingerprints of a person may be taken without the appropriate consent if (before or after the coming into force of this subsection)--

(a) he has been convicted of a recordable offence,

(b) he has been given a caution in respect of a recordable offence which, at the time of the caution, he has admitted, or

(c) he has been warned or reprimanded under section 65 of the Crime and Disorder Act 1998 for a recordable offence, and

either of the conditions mentioned in subsection (6ZA) below is met.

(6A) A constable may take a person's fingerprints without the appropriate consent if--

(a) the constable reasonably suspects that the person is committing or attempting to commit an offence, or has committed or attempted to commit an offence; and

(b) either of the two conditions mentioned in subsection (6B) is met.

(6B) The conditions are that--

(a) the name of the person is unknown to, and cannot be readily ascertained by, the constable;

(b) the constable has reasonable grounds for doubting whether a name furnished by the person as his name is his real name.

(6C) The taking of fingerprints by virtue of subsection (6A) does not count for any of the purposes of this Act as taking them in the course of the investigation of an offence by the police.

(6D) Subject to this section, the fingerprints of a person may be taken without the appropriate consent if--

(a) under the law in force in a country or territory outside England and Wales the person has been convicted of an offence under that law (whether before or after the coming into force of this subsection and whether or not he has been punished for it);

(b) the act constituting the offence would constitute a qualifying offence if done in England and Wales (whether or not it constituted such an offence when the person was convicted); and

(c) either of the conditions mentioned in subsection (6E) below is met.

(6E) The conditions referred to in subsection (6D)(c) above are--

(a) the person has not had his fingerprints taken on a previous occasion under subsection (6D) above;

(b) he has had his fingerprints taken on a previous occasion under that subsection but subsection (3A)(a) or (b) above applies.

(6F) Fingerprints may only be taken as specified in subsection (6D) above with the authorisation of an officer of at least the rank of inspector.

(6G) An officer may only give an authorisation under subsection (6F) above if the officer is satisfied that taking the fingerprints is necessary to assist in the prevention or detection of crime.

(6ZA) The conditions referred to in subsection (6) above are--

(a) the person has not had his fingerprints taken since he was convicted, cautioned or warned or reprimanded;

(b) he has had his fingerprints taken since then but subsection (3A)(a) or (b) above applies.

(6ZB) Fingerprints may only be taken as specified in subsection (6) above with the authorisation of an officer of at least the rank of inspector.

(6ZC) An officer may only give an authorisation under subsection (6ZB) above if the officer is satisfied that taking the fingerprints is necessary to assist in the prevention or detection of crime.

(7) In a case where by virtue of subsection (3), (4), or (6) above a person's fingerprints are taken without the appropriate consent--

(a) he shall be told the reason before his fingerprints are taken; and

(b) the reason shall be recorded as soon as is practicable after the fingerprints are taken.

(7A) If a person's fingerprints are taken at a police station or by virtue of subsection (4A) or (6A) at a place other than a police station, whether with or without the appropriate consent--

(a) before the fingerprints are taken, an officer shall inform him that they may be the subject of a speculative search; and

(b) the fact that the person has been informed of this possibility shall be recorded as soon as is practicable after the fingerprints have been taken.

(8) If he is detained at a police station when the fingerprints are taken, the matters referred to in subsection (7)(a)(i) to (iii) above and, in the case falling within subsection (7A) above, the fact referred to in paragraph (b) of that subsection shall be recorded on his custody record.

(8B) Any power under this section to take the fingerprints of a person without the appropriate consent, if not otherwise specified to be exercisable by a constable, shall be exercisable by a constable.

(9) Nothing in this section--

(a) affects any power conferred by paragraph 18(2) of Schedule 2 to the Immigration Act 1971; or

(b) applies to a person arrested or detained under the terrorism provisions.

(10) Nothing in this section applies to a person arrested under an extradition arrest power.

s 61A Impressions of footwear

61A Impressions of footwear

(1) Except as provided by this section, no impression of a person's footwear may be taken without the appropriate consent.

(2) Consent to the taking of an impression of a person's footwear must be in writing if it is given at a time when he is at a police station.

(3) Where a person is detained at a police station, an impression of his footwear may be taken without the appropriate consent if--

(a) he is detained in consequence of his arrest for a recordable offence, or has been charged with a recordable offence, or informed that he will be reported for a recordable offence; and

(b) he has not had an impression taken of his footwear in the course of the investigation of the offence by the police.

(4) Where a person mentioned in paragraph (a) of subsection (3) above has already had an impression taken of his footwear in the course of the investigation of the offence by the police, that fact shall be disregarded for the purposes of that subsection if the impression of his footwear taken previously is--

(a) incomplete; or

(b) is not of sufficient quality to allow satisfactory analysis, comparison or matching (whether in the case in question or generally).

(5) If an impression of a person's footwear is taken at a police station, whether with or without the appropriate consent--

(a) before it is taken, an officer shall inform him that it may be the subject of a speculative search; and

(b) the fact that the person has been informed of this possibility shall be recorded as soon as is practicable after the impression has been taken, and if he is detained at a police station, the record shall be made on his custody record.

(6) In a case where, by virtue of subsection (3) above, an impression of a person's footwear is taken without the appropriate consent--

(a) he shall be told the reason before it is taken; and

(b) the reason shall be recorded on his custody record as soon as is practicable after the impression is taken.

(7) The power to take an impression of the footwear of a person detained at a police station without the appropriate consent shall be exercisable by any constable.

(8) Nothing in this section applies to any person--

(a) arrested or detained under the terrorism provisions;

(b) arrested under an extradition arrest power.

s 62 Intimate samples

(1) Subject to section 63B below an intimate sample may be taken from a person in police detention only--

(a) if a police officer of at least the rank of inspector authorises it to be taken; and

(b) if the appropriate consent is given.

(1A) An intimate sample may be taken from a person who is not in police detention but from whom, in the course of the investigation of an offence, two or more non-intimate samples suitable for the same means of analysis have been taken which have proved insufficient--

(a) if a police officer of at least the rank of inspector authorises it to be taken; and

(b) if the appropriate consent is given.

(2) An officer may only give an authorisation under subsection (1) or (1A) above if he has reasonable grounds--

(a) for suspecting the involvement of the person from whom the sample is to be taken in a recordable offence; and

(b) for believing that the sample will tend to confirm or disprove his involvement.

(2A) An intimate sample may be taken from a person where--
(a) two or more non-intimate samples suitable for the same means of analysis have been taken from the person under section 63(3E) below (persons convicted of offences outside England and Wales etc) but have proved insufficient;
(b) a police officer of at least the rank of inspector authorises it to be taken; and
(c) the appropriate consent is given.

(2B) An officer may only give an authorisation under subsection (2A) above if the officer is satisfied that taking the sample is necessary to assist in the prevention or detection of crime.

(3) An officer may give an authorisation under subsection (1) or (1A), or (2A) above orally or in writing but, if he gives it orally, he shall confirm it in writing as soon as is practicable.

(4) The appropriate consent must be given in writing.

(5) Before an intimate sample is taken from a person, an officer shall inform him of the following--
(a) the reason for taking the sample;
(b) the fact that authorisation has been given and the provision of this section under which it has been given; and
(c) if the sample was taken at a police station, the fact that the sample may be the subject of a speculative search.
(6) The reason referred to in subsection (5)(a) above must include, except in a case where the sample is taken under subsection (2A) above, a statement of the nature of the offence in which it is suspected that the person has been involved.
(7) After an intimate sample has been taken from a person, the following shall be recorded as soon as practicable--
(a) the matters referred to in subsection (5)(a) and (b) above;
(b) if the sample was taken at a police station, the fact that the person has been informed as specified in subsection (5)(c) above; and
(c) the fact that the appropriate consent was given.

(8) If an intimate sample is taken from a person detained at a police station, the matters required to be recorded by subsection (7) above shall be recorded in his custody record.

(9) In the case of an intimate sample which is a dental impression, the sample may be taken from a person only by a registered dentist.

(9A) In the case of any other form of intimate sample, except in the case of a sample of urine, the sample may be taken from a person only by--

(a) a registered medical practitioner; or

(b) a registered health care professional.

(10) Where the appropriate consent to the taking of an intimate sample from a person was refused without good cause, in any proceedings against that person for an offence--

(a) the court, in determining--

(i) whether to commit that person for trial; or

(ii) whether there is a case to answer; and

(aa) a judge, in deciding whether to grant an application made by the accused under paragraph 2 of Schedule 3 to the Crime and Disorder Act 1998 (applications for dismissal); and

(b) the court or jury, in determining whether that person is guilty of the offence charged,

may draw such inferences from the refusal as appear proper.

(11) Nothing in this section applies to the taking of a specimen for the purposes of any of the provisions of sections 4 to 11 of the Road Traffic Act 1988 or of sections 26 to 38 of the Transport and Works Act 1992.

(12) Nothing in this section applies to a person arrested or detained under the terrorism provisions; and subsection (1A) shall not apply where the non-intimate samples mentioned in that subsection were taken under paragraph 10 of Schedule 8 to the Terrorism Act 2000.

s 63 Other samples.

(1) Except as provided by this section, a non-intimate sample may not be taken from a person without the appropriate consent.

(2) Consent to the taking of a non-intimate sample must be given in writing.

(2A) A non-intimate sample may be taken from a person without the appropriate consent if two conditions are satisfied.

(2B) The first is that the person is in police detention in consequence of his arrest for a recordable offence.

(2C) The second is that--

(a) he has not had a non-intimate sample of the same type and from the same part of the body taken in the course of the investigation of the offence by the police, or

(b) he has had such a sample taken but it proved insufficient.

(3) A non-intimate sample may be taken from a person without the appropriate consent if--

(a) he is being held in custody by the police on the authority of a court; and

(b) an officer of at least the rank of inspector authorises it to be taken without the appropriate consent.

(3ZA) A non-intimate sample may be taken from a person without the appropriate consent if (before or after the coming into force of this subsection) he has been arrested for a recordable offence and released and--
(a) in the case of a person who is on bail, he has not had a non intimate sample of the same type and from the same part of the body taken from him in the course of the investigation of the offence by the police; or
(b) in any case, he has had a non-intimate sample taken from him in the course of that investigation but--
(i) it was not suitable for the same means of analysis, or
(ii) it proved insufficient.

(3A) A non-intimate sample may be taken from a person (whether or not he is in police detention or held in custody by the police on the authority of a court) without the appropriate consent if he has been charged with a recordable offence or informed that he will be reported for such an offence and--
(a) he has not had a non-intimate sample taken from him in the course of the investigation of the offence by the police; or
(b) he has had a non-intimate sample taken from him in the course of that investigation but--
(i) it was not suitable for the same means of analysis, or
(ii) it proved insufficient; or
(c) he has had a non-intimate sample taken from him in the course of that investigation and--
(i) the sample has been destroyed pursuant to section 64ZA below or any other enactment, and
(ii) it is disputed, in relation to any proceedings relating to the offence, whether a DNA profile relevant to the proceedings is derived from the sample.

(3B) Subject to this section, a non-intimate sample may be taken from a person without the appropriate consent if (before or after the coming into force of this subsection)--

(a) he has been convicted of a recordable offence,
(b) he has been given a caution in respect of a recordable offence which, at the time of the caution, he has admitted, or
(c) he has been warned or reprimanded under section 65 of the Crime and Disorder Act 1998 for a recordable offence, and
either of the conditions mentioned in subsection (3BA) below is met.
(3BA) The conditions referred to in subsection (3B) above are--
(a) a non-intimate sample has not been taken from the person since he was convicted, cautioned or warned or reprimanded;
(b) such a sample has been taken from him since then but--
(i) it was not suitable for the same means of analysis, or
(ii) it proved insufficient.
(3BB) A non-intimate sample may only be taken as specified in subsection (3B) above with the authorisation of an officer of at least the rank of inspector.
(3BC) An officer may only give an authorisation under subsection (3BB) above if the officer is satisfied that taking the sample is necessary to assist in the prevention or detection of crime.

(3C) A non-intimate sample may also be taken from a person without the appropriate consent if he is a person to whom section 2 of the Criminal Evidence (Amendment) Act 1997 applies (persons detained following acquittal on grounds of insanity or finding of unfitness to plead).

(3E) Subject to this section, a non-intimate sample may be taken without the appropriate consent from a person if--
(a) under the law in force in a country or territory outside England and Wales the person has been convicted of an offence under that law (whether before or after the coming into force of this subsection and whether or not he has been punished for it);
(b) the act constituting the offence would constitute a qualifying offence if done in England and Wales (whether or not it constituted such an offence when the person was convicted); and
(c) either of the conditions mentioned in subsection (3F) below is met.
(3F) The conditions referred to in subsection (3E)(c) above are--
(a) the person has not had a non-intimate sample taken from him on a previous occasion under subsection (3E) above;
(b) he has had such a sample taken from him on a previous occasion under that subsection but--
(i) the sample was not suitable for the same means of analysis, or
(ii) it proved insufficient.
(3G) A non-intimate sample may only be taken as specified in subsection (3E) above with the authorisation of an officer of at least the rank of inspector.
(3H) An officer may only give an authorisation under subsection (3G) above if the officer is satisfied that taking the sample is necessary to assist in the prevention or detection of crime.

(4) An officer may only give an authorisation under subsection (3) above if he has reasonable grounds--

(a) for suspecting the involvement of the person from whom the sample is to be taken in a recordable offence; and

(b) for believing that the sample will tend to confirm or disprove his involvement.

(5) An officer may give an authorisation under subsection (3) above orally or in writing but, if he gives it orally, he shall confirm it in writing as soon as is practicable.

(5A) An officer shall not give an authorisation under subsection (3) above for the taking from any person of a non-intimate sample consisting of a skin impression if-

(a) a skin impression of the same part of the body has already been taken from that person in the course of the investigation of the offence; and

(b) the impression previously taken is not one that has proved insufficient.

(6) Where a non-intimate sample is taken from a person without the appropriate consent by virtue of any power conferred by this section--
(a) before the sample is taken, an officer shall inform him of--
(i) the reason for taking the sample;
(ii) the power by virtue of which it is taken; and
(iii) in a case where the authorisation of an officer is required for the exercise of the power, the fact that the authorisation has been given; and
(b) those matters shall be recorded as soon as practicable after the sample is taken.
(7) The reason referred to in subsection (6)(a)(i) above must include, except in a case where the non-intimate sample is taken under subsection (3B) or (3E) above, a statement of the nature of the offence in which it is suspected that the person has been involved.

(8B) If a non-intimate sample is taken from a person at a police station, whether with or without the appropriate consent--

(a) before the sample is taken, an officer shall inform him that it may be the subject of a speculative search; and

(b) the fact that the person has been informed of this possibility shall be recorded as soon as practicable after the sample has been taken.

(9) If a non-intimate sample is taken from a person detained at a police station, the matters required to be recorded by subsection (6) or (8B) above shall be recorded in his custody record.

(9ZA) The power to take a non-intimate sample from a person without the appropriate consent shall be exercisable by any constable.

(9A) Subsection (3B) above shall not apply to

(a)   any person convicted before 10th April 1995 unless he is a person to whom section 1 of the Criminal Evidence (Amendment) Act 1997 applies (persons imprisoned or detained by virtue of pre-existing conviction for sexual offence etc.); or

(b)   a person given a caution before 10th April 1995.

(10) Nothing in this section applies to a person arrested or detained under the terrorism provisions.

(11) Nothing in this section applies to a person arrested under an extradition arrest power.

s 63A Fingerprints and samples: supplementary provisions.

(1) Where a person has been arrested on suspicion of being involved in a recordable offence or has been charged with such an offence or has been informed that he will be reported for such an offence, fingerprints, impressions of footwear or samples or the information derived from samples taken under any power conferred by this Part of this Act from the person may be checked against--

(a) other fingerprints, impressions of footwear or samples to which the person seeking to check has access and which are held by or on behalf of any one or more relevant law-enforcement authorities or which are held in connection with or as a result of an investigation of an offence;

(b) information derived from other samples if the information is contained in records to which the person seeking to check has access and which are held as mentioned in paragraph (a) above.

(1ZA) Fingerprints taken by virtue of section 61(6A) above may be checked against other fingerprints to which the person seeking to check has access and which are held by or on behalf of any one or more relevant law-enforcement authorities or which are held in connection with or as a result of an investigation of an offence.

(1A) In subsection (1) and (1ZA) above 'relevant law-enforcement authority' means-

(a) a police force;

(b) the Serious Organised Crime Agency;

(d) a public authority (not falling within paragraphs (a) to (c)) with functions in any part of the British Islands which consist of or include the investigation of crimes or the charging of offenders;

(e) any person with functions in any country or territory outside the United Kingdom which-

(i) correspond to those of a police force; or

(ii) otherwise consist of or include the investigation of conduct contrary to the law of that country or territory, or the apprehension of persons guilty of such conduct;

(f) any person with functions under any international agreement which consist of or include the investigation of conduct which is-

(i) unlawful under the law of one or more places,

(ii) prohibited by such an agreement, or

(iii) contrary to international law,

or the apprehension of persons guilty of such conduct.

(1B) The reference in subsection (1A) above to a police force is a reference to any of the following-

(a) any police force maintained under section 2 of the Police Act 1996 (c. 16) (police forces in England and Wales outside London);

(b) the metropolitan police force;

(c) the City of London police force;

(d) any police force maintained under or by virtue of section 1 of the Police (Scotland) Act 1967 (c. 77);

(e) the Police Service of Northern Ireland;

(f) the Police Service of Northern Ireland Reserve;

(g) the Ministry of Defence Police;

(h) the Royal Navy Police;

(i) the Royal Military Police;

(j) the Royal Air Force Police;

(l) the British Transport Police;

(m) the States of Jersey Police Force;

(n) the salaried police force of the Island of Guernsey;

(o) the Isle of Man Constabulary.

(1C) Where-

(a) fingerprints, impressions of footwear or samples have been taken from any person in connection with the investigation of an offence but otherwise than in circumstances to which subsection (1) above applies, and

(b) that person has given his consent in writing to the use in a speculative search of the fingerprints, of the impressions of footwear or of the samples and of information derived from them,

the fingerprints or impressions of footwear or, as the case may be, those samples and that information may be checked against any of the fingerprints, impressions of footwear, samples or information mentioned in paragraph (a) or (b) of that subsection.

(1D) A consent given for the purposes of subsection (1C) above shall not be capable of being withdrawn.

(1E) Where fingerprints or samples have been taken from any person under section 61(6) or 63(3B) above (persons convicted etc), the fingerprints or samples, or information derived from the samples, may be checked against any of the fingerprints, samples or information mentioned in subsection (1)(a) or (b) above.
(1F) Where fingerprints or samples have been taken from any person under section 61(6D), 62(2A) or 63(3E) above (offences outside England and Wales etc), the fingerprints or samples, or information derived from the samples, may be checked against any of the fingerprints, samples or information mentioned in subsection (1)(a) or (b) above.

(2) Where a sample of hair other than pubic hair is to be taken the sample may be taken either by cutting hairs or by plucking hairs with their roots so long as no more are plucked than the person taking the sample reasonably considers to be necessary for a sufficient sample.

(3) Where any power to take a sample is exercisable in relation to a person the sample may be taken in a prison or other institution to which the Prison Act 1952 applies.

(3A) Where--

(a) the power to take a non-intimate sample under section 63(3B) above is exercisable in relation to any person who is detained under Part III of the Mental Health Act 1983 in pursuance of--

(i) a hospital order or interim hospital order made following his conviction for the recordable offence in question, or

(ii) a transfer direction given at a time when he was detained in pursuance of any sentence or order imposed following that conviction, or

(b) the power to take a non-intimate sample under section 63(3C) above is exercisable in relation to any person,

the sample may be taken in the hospital in which he is detained under that Part of that Act.

Expressions used in this subsection and in the Mental Health Act 1983 have the same meaning as in that Act.

(3B) Where the power to take a non-intimate sample under section 63(3B) above is exercisable in relation to a person detained in pursuance of directions of the Secretary of State under section 92 of the Powers of Criminal Courts (Sentencing) Act 2000 the sample may be taken at the place where he is so detained.

(4) Schedule 2A (fingerprinting and samples: power to require attendance at police station) shall have effect.

s 63B Testing for presence of Class A drugs.

(1) A sample of urine or a non-intimate sample may be taken from a person in police detention for the purpose of ascertaining whether he has any specified Class A drug in his body if--

(a) either the arrest condition or the charge condition is met;

(b) both the age condition and the request condition are met; and

(c) the notification condition is met in relation to the arrest condition, the charge condition or the age condition (as the case may be).

(1A) The arrest condition is that the person concerned has been arrested for an offence but has not been charged with that offence and either-

(a) the offence is a trigger offence; or

(b) a police officer of at least the rank of inspector has reasonable grounds for suspecting that the misuse by that person of a specified Class A drug caused or contributed to the offence and has authorised the sample to be taken.

(2) The charge condition is either--

(a) that the person concerned has been charged with a trigger offence; or

(b) that the person concerned has been charged with an offence and a police officer of at least the rank of inspector, who has reasonable grounds for suspecting that the misuse by that person of any specified Class A drug caused or contributed to the offence, has authorised the sample to be taken.

(3) The age condition is-

(a) if the arrest condition is met, that the person concerned has attained the age of 18;

(b) if the charge condition is met, that he has attained the age of 14.

(4) The request condition is that a police officer has requested the person concerned to give the sample.

(4A) The notification condition is that-

(a) the relevant chief officer has been notified by the Secretary of State that appropriate arrangements have been made for the police area as a whole, or for the particular police station, in which the person is in police detention, and

(b) the notice has not been withdrawn.

(4B) For the purposes of subsection (4A) above, appropriate arrangements are arrangements for the taking of samples under this section from whichever of the following is specified in the notification-

(a) persons in respect of whom the arrest condition is met;

(b) persons in respect of whom the charge condition is met;

(c) persons who have not attained the age of 18.

(5) Before requesting the person concerned to give a sample, an officer must--

(a) warn him that if, when so requested, he fails without good cause to do so he may be liable to prosecution, and

(b) in a case within subsection (1A)(b) or (2)(b) above, inform him of the giving of the authorisation and of the grounds in question.

(5A) In the case of a person who has not attained the age of 17--

(a) the making of the request under subsection (4) above;

(b) the giving of the warning and (where applicable) the information under subsection (5) above; and

(c) the taking of the sample,

may not take place except in the presence of an appropriate adult.

(5B) If a sample is taken under this section from a person in respect of whom the arrest condition is met no other sample may be taken from him under this section during the same continuous period of detention but-

(a) if the charge condition is also met in respect of him at any time during that period, the sample must be treated as a sample taken by virtue of the fact that the charge condition is met;

(b) the fact that the sample is to be so treated must be recorded in the person's custody record.

(5C) Despite subsection (1)(a) above, a sample may be taken from a person under this section if-

(a) he was arrested for an offence (the first offence),

(b) the arrest condition is met but the charge condition is not met,

(c) before a sample is taken by virtue of subsection (1) above he would (but for his arrest as mentioned in paragraph (d) below) be required to be released from police detention,

(d) he continues to be in police detention by virtue of his having been arrested for an offence not falling within subsection (1A) above, and

(e) the sample is taken before the end of the period of 24 hours starting with the time when his detention by virtue of his arrest for the first offence began.

(5D) A sample must not be taken from a person under this section if he is detained in a police station unless he has been brought before the custody officer.

(6) A sample may be taken under this section only by a person prescribed by regulations made by the Secretary of State by statutory instrument.

No regulations shall be made under this subsection unless a draft has been laid before, and approved by resolution of, each House of Parliament.

(6A) The Secretary of State may by order made by statutory instrument amend-

(a) paragraph (a) of subsection (3) above, by substituting for the age for the time being specified a different age specified in the order, or different ages so specified for different police areas so specified;

(b) paragraph (b) of that subsection, by substituting for the age for the time being specified a different age specified in the order.

(6B) A statutory instrument containing an order under subsection (6A) above shall not be made unless a draft of the instrument has been laid before, and approved by a resolution of, each House of Parliament.

(7) Information obtained from a sample taken under this section may be disclosed--

(a) for the purpose of informing any decision about granting bail in criminal proceedings (within the meaning of the Bail Act 1976) to the person concerned;

(aa) for the purpose of informing any decision about the giving of a conditional caution under Part 3 of the Criminal Justice Act 2003 or a youth conditional caution under Chapter 1 of Part 4 of the Crime and Disorder Act 1998 to the person concerned;

(b) where the person concerned is in police detention or is remanded in or committed to custody by an order of a court or has been granted such bail, for the purpose of informing any decision about his supervision;

(c) where the person concerned is convicted of an offence, for the purpose of informing any decision about the appropriate sentence to be passed by a court and any decision about his supervision or release;

(ca) for the purpose of an assessment which the person concerned is required to attend by virtue of section 9(2) or 10(2) of the Drugs Act 2005;

(cb) for the purpose of proceedings against the person concerned for an offence under section 12(3) or 14(3) of that Act;

(d) for the purpose of ensuring that appropriate advice and treatment is made available to the person concerned.

(8) A person who fails without good cause to give any sample which may be taken from him under this section shall be guilty of an offence.

(10) In this section--

"appropriate adult", in relation to a person who has not attained the age of 17, means--

(a) his parent or guardian or, if he is in the care of a local authority or voluntary organisation, a person representing that authority or organisation; or

(b) a social worker of a local authority; or

(c) if no person falling within paragraph (a) or (b) is available, any responsible person aged 18 or over who is not a police officer or a person employed by the police;

"relevant chief officer" means--

(a) in relation to a police area, the chief officer of police of the police force for that police area; or

(b) in relation to a police station, the chief officer of police of the police force for the police area in which the police station is situated.

s 63C Testing for presence of Class A drugs: supplementary.

63C.-- Testing for presence of Class A drugs: supplementary.

(1) A person guilty of an offence under section 63B above shall be liable on summary conviction to imprisonment for a term not exceeding three months, or to a fine not exceeding level 4 on the standard scale, or to both.

(2) A police officer may give an authorisation under section 63B above orally or in writing but, if he gives it orally, he shall confirm it in writing as soon as is practicable.

(3) If a sample is taken under section 63B above by virtue of an authorisation, the authorisation and the grounds for the suspicion shall be recorded as soon as is practicable after the sample is taken.

(4) If the sample is taken from a person detained at a police station, the matters required to be recorded by subsection (3) above shall be recorded in his custody record.

(5) Subsections (11) and (12) of section 62 above apply for the purposes of section 63B above as they do for the purposes of that section; and section 63B above does not prejudice the generality of sections 62 and 63 above.

(6) In section 63B above--

"Class A drug" and "misuse" have the same meanings as in the Misuse of Drugs Act 1971;

"specified" (in relation to a Class A drug) and "trigger offence" have the same meanings as in Part III of the Criminal Justice and Court Services Act 2000.

s 64 Destruction of fingerprints and samples.

(1A) Where-

(a) fingerprints, impressions of footwear or samples are taken from a person in connection with the investigation of an offence, and

(b) subsection (3) below does not require them to be destroyed,

the fingerprints, impressions of footwear or samples may be retained after they have fulfilled the purposes for which they were taken but shall not be used by any person except for purposes related to the prevention or detection of crime, the investigation of an offence, the conduct of a prosecution or the identification of a deceased person or of the person from whom a body part came or the identification of a deceased person or of the person from whom a body part came.

(1B) In subsection (1A) above-

(a) the reference to using a fingerprint or an impression of footwear includes a reference to allowing any check to be made against it under section 63A(1) or (1C) above and to disclosing it to any person;

(b) the reference to using a sample includes a reference to allowing any check to be made under section 63A(1) or (1C) above against it or against information derived from it and to disclosing it or any such information to any person;

(c) the reference to crime includes a reference to any conduct which-

(i) constitutes one or more criminal offences (whether under the law of a part of the United Kingdom or of a country or territory outside the United Kingdom); or

(ii) is, or corresponds to, any conduct which, if it all took place in any one part of the United Kingdom, would constitute one or more criminal offences;

and

(d) the references to an investigation and to a prosecution include references, respectively, to any investigation outside the United Kingdom of any crime or suspected crime and to a prosecution brought in respect of any crime in a country or territory outside the United Kingdom.

(3) If--

(a) fingerprints, impressions of footwear or samples are taken from a person in connection with the investigation of an offence; and

(b) that person is not suspected of having committed the offence,

they must, except as provided in the following provisions of this section, be destroyed as soon as they have fulfilled the purpose for which they were taken.

(1BA) Fingerprints taken from a person by virtue of section 61(6A) above must be destroyed as soon as they have fulfilled the purpose for which they were taken.

(3AA) Samples, fingerprints and impressions of footwear are not required to be destroyed under subsection (3) above if-

(a) they were taken for the purposes of the investigation of an offence of which a person has been convicted; and

(b) a sample, fingerprint, (or as the case may be) an impression of footwear was also taken from the convicted person for the purposes of that investigation.

(3AB) Subject to subsection (3AC) below, where a person is entitled under subsection (1BA) or (3) above to the destruction of any fingerprint, impression of footwear or sample taken from him (or would be but for subsection (3AA) above), neither the fingerprint, nor the impression of footwear, nor the sample, nor any information derived from the sample, shall be used-

(a) in evidence against the person who is or would be entitled to the destruction of that fingerprint, impression of footwear or sample; or

(b) for the purposes of the investigation of any offence;

and subsection (1B) above applies for the purposes of this subsection as it applies for the purposes of subsection (1A) above.

(3AC) Where a person from whom a fingerprint, impression of footwear or sample has been taken consents in writing to its retention-

(a) that fingerprint or sample need not be destroyed under subsection (3) above;

(b) subsection (3AB) above shall not restrict the use that may be made of the fingerprint, impression of footwear or sample or, in the case of a sample, of any information derived from it; and

(c) that consent shall be treated as comprising a consent for the purposes of section 63A(1C) above;

and a consent given for the purpose of this subsection shall not be capable of being withdrawn.

This subsection does not apply to fingerprints taken from a person by virtue of section 61(6A) above.

(3AD) For the purposes of subsection (3AC) above it shall be immaterial whether the consent is given at, before or after the time when the entitlement to the destruction of the fingerprint, impression of footwear or sample arises.

(5) If fingerprints or impressions of footwear are destroyed--

(a) any copies of the fingerprints or impressions of footwear shall also be destroyed; and

(b) any chief officer of police controlling access to computer data relating to the fingerprints or impressions of footwear shall make access to the data impossible, as soon as it is practicable to do so.

(6) A person who asks to be allowed to witness the destruction of his fingerprints or impressions of footwear or copies of them shall have a right to witness it.

(6A) If--

(a) subsection (5)(b) above falls to be complied with; and

(b) the person to whose fingerprints or impressions of footwear the data relate asks for a certificate that it has been complied with,

such a certificate shall be issued to him, not later than the end of the period of three months beginning with the day on which he asks for it, by the responsible chief officer of police or a person authorised by him or on his behalf for the purposes of this section.

(6B) In this section--

"the responsible chief officer of police" means the chief officer of police in whose police area the computer data were put on to the computer.

(7) Nothing in this section--

(a) affects any power conferred by paragraph 18(2) of Schedule 2 to the Immigration Act 1971 or section 20 of the Immigration and Asylum Act 1999 (c. 33) (disclosure of police information to the Secretary of State for use for immigration purposes); or

(b) applies to a person arrested or detained under the terrorism provisions.

s 64A Photographing of suspects etc.

(1) A person who is detained at a police station may be photographed--

(a) with the appropriate consent; or

(b) if the appropriate consent is withheld or it is not practicable to obtain it, without it.

(1A) A person falling within subsection (1B) below may, on the occasion of the relevant event referred to in subsection (1B), be photographed elsewhere than at a police station--

(a) with the appropriate consent; or

(b) if the appropriate consent is withheld or it is not practicable to obtain it, without it.

(1B) A person falls within this subsection if he has been--

(a) arrested by a constable for an offence;

(b) taken into custody by a constable after being arrested for an offence by a person other than a constable;

(c) made subject to a requirement to wait with a community support officer under paragraph 2(3) or (3B) of Schedule 4 to the Police Reform Act 2002 ("the 2002 Act");

(ca) given a direction by a constable under section 27 of the Violent Crime Reduction Act 2006;

(d) given a penalty notice by a constable in uniform under Chapter 1 of Part 1 of the Criminal Justice and Police Act 2001, a penalty notice by a constable under section 444A of the Education Act 1996, or a fixed penalty notice by a constable in uniform under section 54 of the Road Traffic Offenders Act 1988;

(e) given a notice in relation to a relevant fixed penalty offence (within the meaning of paragraph 1 of Schedule 4 to the 2002 Act) by a community support officer by virtue of a designation applying that paragraph to him;

(f) given a notice in relation to a relevant fixed penalty offence (within the meaning of paragraph 1 of Schedule 5 to the 2002 Act) by an accredited person by virtue of accreditation specifying that that paragraph applies to him; or

(g) given a notice in relation to a relevant fixed penalty offence (within the meaning of Schedule 5A to the 2002 Act) by an accredited inspector by virtue of accreditation specifying that paragraph 1 of Schedule 5A to the 2002 Act applies to him.

(2) A person proposing to take a photograph of any person under this section--

(a) may, for the purpose of doing so, require the removal of any item or substance worn on or over the whole or any part of the head or face of the person to be photographed; and

(b) if the requirement is not complied with, may remove the item or substance himself.

(3) Where a photograph may be taken under this section, the only persons entitled to take the photograph are constables.

(4) A photograph taken under this section--

(a) may be used by, or disclosed to, any person for any purpose related to the prevention or detection of crime, the investigation of an offence or the conduct of a prosecution or to the enforcement of a sentence; and

(b) after being so used or disclosed, may be retained but may not be used or disclosed except for a purpose so related.

(5) In subsection (4)--

(a) the reference to crime includes a reference to any conduct which--

(i) constitutes one or more criminal offences (whether under the law of a part of the United Kingdom or of a country or territory outside the United Kingdom); or

(ii) is, or corresponds to, any conduct which, if it all took place in any one part of the United Kingdom, would constitute one or more criminal offences;

and

(b) the references to an investigation and to a prosecution include references, respectively, to any investigation outside the United Kingdom of any crime or suspected crime and to a prosecution brought in respect of any crime in a country or territory outside the United Kingdom; and

(c) "sentence" includes any order made by a court in England and Wales when dealing with an offender in respect of his offence.

(6) References in this section to taking a photograph include references to using any process by means of which a visual image may be produced; and references to photographing a person shall be construed accordingly.

(6A) In this section, a "photograph" includes a moving image, and corresponding expressions shall be construed accordingly.

(7) Nothing in this section applies to a person arrested under an extradition arrest power.

s 65 Part V supplementary.

(1) In this Part of this Act--

"analysis", in relation to a skin impression, includes comparison and matching;

"appropriate consent" means --

(a) in relation to a person who has attained the age of 17 years, the consent of that person;

(b) in relation to a person who has not attained that age but has attained the age of 14 years, the consent of that person and his parent or guardian; and

(c) in relation to a person who has not attained the age of 14 years, the consent of his parent or guardian;

"extradition arrest power" means any of the following--

(a) a Part 1 warrant (within the meaning given by the Extradition Act 2003) in respect of which a certificate under section 2 of that Act has been issued;

(b) section 5 of that Act;

(c) a warrant issued under section 71 of that Act;

(d) a provisional warrant (within the meaning given by that Act);

"fingerprints", in relation to any person, means a record (in any form and produced by any method) of the skin pattern and other physical characteristics or features of-

(a) any of that person's fingers; or

(b) either of his palms;

"intimate sample" means--

(a) a sample of blood, semen or any other tissue fluid, urine or pubic hair;

(b) a dental impression;

(c) a swab taken from any part of a person's genitals (including pubic hair) or from a person's body orifice other than the mouth;

"intimate search" means a search which consists of the physical examination of a person's body orifices other than the mouth;

"non-intimate sample" means--

(a) a sample of hair other than pubic hair;

(b) a sample taken from a nail on from under a nail;

(c) a swab taken from any part of a person's body other than a part from which a swab taken would be an intimate sample;

(d) saliva;

(e) a skin impression;

"offence", in relation to any country or territory outside England and Wales, includes an act punishable under the law of that country or territory, however it is described;

"registered dentist" has the same meaning as in the Dentists Act 1984;

"skin impression", in relation to any person, means any record (other than a fingerprint) which is a record (in any form and produced by any method) of the skin pattern and other physical characteristics or features of the whole or any part of his foot or of any other part of his body;

"registered health care professional" means a person (other than a medical practitioner) who is--

(a) a registered nurse; or

(b) a registered member of a health care profession which is designated for the purposes of this paragraph by an order made by the Secretary of State;

"speculative search", in relation to a person's fingerprints or samples, means such a check against other fingerprints or samples or against information derived from other samples as is referred to in section 63A(1) above;

"sufficient" and "insufficient", in relation to a sample, means (subject to subsection (2) below) sufficient or insufficient (in point of quantity or quality) for the purpose of enabling information to be produced by the means of analysis used or to be used in relation to the sample.

"the terrorism provisions" means section 41 of the Terrorism Act 2000, and any provision of Schedule 7 to that Act conferring a power of detention; and

"terrorism" has the meaning given in section 1 of that Act.

(1A) A health care profession is any profession mentioned in section 60(2) of the Health Act 1999 (c. 8) other than the profession of practising medicine and the profession of nursing.

(1B) An order under subsection (1) shall be made by statutory instrument and shall be subject to annulment in pursuance of a resolution of either House of Parliament.

(2) References in this Part of this Act to a sample's proving insufficient include references to where, as a consequence of-

(a) the loss, destruction or contamination of the whole or any part of the sample,

(b) any damage to the whole or a part of the sample, or

(c) the use of the whole or a part of the sample for an analysis which produced no results or which produced results some or all of which must be regarded, in the circumstances, as unreliable,

the sample has become unavailable or insufficient for the purpose of enabling information, or information of a particular description, to be obtained by means of analysis of the sample.

(3) For the purposes of this Part, a person has in particular been convicted of an offence under the law of a country or territory outside England and Wales if--
(a) a court exercising jurisdiction under the law of that country or territory has made in respect of such an offence a finding equivalent to a finding that the person is not guilty by reason of insanity; or
(b) such a court has made in respect of such an offence a finding equivalent to a finding that the person is under a disability and did the act charged against him in respect of the offence.

65A "Qualifying Offence"

(1) In this Part, "qualifying offence" means--
(a) an offence specified in subsection (2) below, or
(b) an ancillary offence relating to such an offence.
(2) The offences referred to in subsection (1)(a) above are--
(a) murder;
(b) manslaughter;
(c) false imprisonment;
(d) kidnapping;

(e) an offence under section 4, 16, 18, 20 to 24 or 47 of the Offences Against the Person Act 1861;

(f) an offence under section 2 or 3 of the Explosive Substances Act 1883;

(g) an offence under section 1 of the Children and Young Persons Act 1933;

(h) an offence under section 4(1) of the Criminal Law Act 1967 committed in relation to murder;

(i) an offence under sections 16 to 18 of the Firearms Act 1968;

(j) an offence under section 9 or 10 of the Theft Act 1968 or an offence under section 12A of that Act involving an accident which caused a person's death;

(k) an offence under section 1 of the Criminal Damage Act 1971 required to be charged as arson;

(l) an offence under section 1 of the Protection of Children Act 1978;

(m) an offence under section 1 of the Aviation Security Act 1982;

(n) an offence under section 2 of the Child Abduction Act 1984;

(o) an offence under section 9 of the Aviation and Maritime Security Act 1990;

(p) an offence under any of sections 1 to 19, 25, 26, 30 to 41, 47 to 50, 52, 53, 57 to 59, 61 to 67, 69 and 70 of the Sexual Offences Act 2003;

(q) an offence under section 5 of the Domestic Violence, Crime and Victims Act 2004;

(r) an offence for the time being listed in section 41(1) of the Counter-Terrorism Act 2008.

(3) The Secretary of State may by order made by statutory instrument amend subsection (2) above.

(4) A statutory instrument containing an order under subsection (3) above shall not be made unless a draft of the instrument has been laid before, and approved by resolution of, each House of Parliament.

(5) In subsection (1)(b) above "ancillary offence", in relation to an offence, means--

(a) aiding, abetting, counselling or procuring the commission of the offence;

(b) an offence under Part 2 of the Serious Crime Act 2007 (encouraging or assisting crime) in relation to the offence (including, in relation to times before the commencement of that Part, an offence of incitement);

(c) attempting or conspiring to commit the offence.

s 76 Confessions.

(1) In any proceedings a confession made by an accused person may be given in evidence against him in so far as it is relevant to any matter in issue in the proceedings and is not excluded by the court in pursuance of this section.

(2) If, in any proceedings where the prosecution proposes to give in evidence a confession made by an accused person, it is represented to the court that the confession was or may have been obtained--

(a) by oppression of the person who made it; or

(b) in consequence of anything said or done which was likely, in the circumstances existing at the time, to render unreliable any confession which might be made by him in consequence thereof,

the court shall not allow the confession to be given in evidence against him except in so far as the prosecution proves to the court beyond reasonable doubt that the confession (notwithstanding that it may be true) was not obtained as aforesaid.

(3) In any proceedings where the prosecution proposes to give in evidence a confession made by an accused person, the court may of its own motion require the prosecution, as a condition of allowing it to do so, to prove that the confession was not obtained as mentioned in subsection (2) above.

(4) The fact that a confession is wholly or partly excluded in pursuance of this section shall not

affect the admissibility in evidence--

(a) of any facts discovered as a result of the confession; or

(b) where the confession is relevant as showing that the accused speaks, writes or expresses himself in a particular way, of so much of the confession as is necessary to show that he does so.

(5) Evidence that a fact to which this subsection applies was discovered as a result of a statement made by an accused person shall not be admissible unless evidence of how it was discovered is given by him or on his behalf.

(6) Subsection (5) above applies--

(a) to any fact discovered as a result of a confession which is wholly excluded in pursuance of this section; and

(b) to any fact discovered as a result of a confession which is partly so excluded, if the fact is discovered as a result of the excluded part of the confession.

(7) Nothing in Part VII of this Act shall prejudice the admissibility of a confession made by an accused person.

(8) In this section "oppression" includes torture, inhuman or degrading treatment, and the use or threat of violence (whether or not amounting to torture).

(9) Where the proceedings mentioned in subsection (1) above are proceedings before a magistrates' court inquiring into an offence as examining justices this section shall have effect with the omission of--

(a) in subsection (1) the words "and is not excluded by the court in pursuance of this section", and

(b) subsections (2) to (6) and (8).

s 76A Confessions may be given in evidence for co-accused

76A Confessions may be given in evidence for co-accused

(1) In any proceedings a confession made by an accused person may be given in evidence for another person charged in the same proceedings (a co-accused) in so far as it is relevant to any matter in issue in the proceedings and is not excluded by the court in pursuance of this section.

(2) If, in any proceedings where a co-accused proposes to give in evidence a confession made by an accused person, it is represented to the court that the confession was or may have been obtained--

(a) by oppression of the person who made it; or

(b) in consequence of anything said or done which was likely, in the circumstances existing at the time, to render unreliable any confession which might be made by him in consequence thereof,

the court shall not allow the confession to be given in evidence for the co-accused except in so far as it is proved to the court on the balance of probabilities that the confession (notwithstanding that it may be true) was not so obtained.

(3) Before allowing a confession made by an accused person to be given in evidence for a co-accused in any proceedings, the court may of its own motion require the fact that the confession was not obtained as mentioned in subsection (2) above to be proved in the proceedings on the balance of probabilities.

(4) The fact that a confession is wholly or partly excluded in pursuance of this section shall not affect the admissibility in evidence--

(a) of any facts discovered as a result of the confession; or

(b) where the confession is relevant as showing that the accused speaks, writes or expresses himself in a particular way, of so much of the confession as is necessary to show that he does so.

(5) Evidence that a fact to which this subsection applies was discovered as a result of a statement made by an accused person shall not be admissible unless evidence of how it was discovered is given by him or on his behalf.

(6) Subsection (5) above applies--

(a) to any fact discovered as a result of a confession which is wholly excluded in pursuance of this section; and

(b) to any fact discovered as a result of a confession which is partly so excluded, if the fact is discovered as a result of the excluded part of the confession.

(7) In this section "oppression" includes torture, inhuman or degrading treatment, and the use or threat of violence (whether or not amounting to torture).

s 77 Confessions by mentally handicapped persons.

(1) Without prejudice to the general duty of the court at a trial on indictment with a jury to direct the jury on any matter on which it appears to the court appropriate to do so, where at such a trial--

(a) the case against the accused depends wholly or substantially on a confession by him; and

(b) the court is satisfied--

(i) that he is mentally handicapped; and

(ii) that the confession was not made in the presence of an independent person, the court shall warn the jury that there is special need for caution before convicting the accused in reliance on the confession, and shall explain that the need arises because of the circumstances mentioned in paragraphs (a) and (b) above.

(2) In any case where at the summary trial of a person for an offence it appears to the court that a warning under subsection (1) above would be required if the trial were on indictment with a jury, the court shall treat the case as one in which there is a special need for caution before convicting the accused on his confession.

(2A) In any case where at the trial on indictment without a jury of a person for an offence it appears to the court that a warning under subsection (1) above would be required if the trial were with a jury, the court shall treat the case as one in which there is a special need for caution before convicting the accused on his confession.

(3) In this section--

"independent person" does not include a police officer or a person employed for, or engaged on, police purposes;

"mentally handicapped", in relation to a person, means that he is in a state of arrested or incomplete development of mind which includes significant impairment of intelligence and social functioning; and

"police purposes" has the meaning assigned to it by section 101(2) of the Police Act 1996.

s 78 Exclusion of unfair evidence.

(1) In any proceedings the court may refuse to allow evidence on which the prosecution proposes to rely to be given if it appears to the court that, having regard to all the circumstances, including the circumstances in which the evidence was obtained, the admission of the evidence would have such an adverse effect on the fairness of the proceedings that the court ought not to admit it.

(2) Nothing in this section shall prejudice any rule of law requiring a court to exclude evidence.

(3) This section shall not apply in the case of proceedings before a magistrates' court inquiring into an offences as examining justices.

Schedule 2A

SCHEDULE 2A FINGERPRINTING AND SAMPLES: POWER TO REQUIRE ATTENDANCE AT POLICE STATION
Section 63A (4) PART 1 FINGERPRINTING
1 Persons arrested and released
(1) A constable may require a person to attend a police station for the purpose of taking his fingerprints under section 61(5A).
(2) The power under sub-paragraph (1) above may not be exercised in a case falling within section 61(5A)(b) (fingerprints taken on previous occasion insufficient etc) after the end of the period of six months beginning with the day on which the appropriate officer was informed that section 61(3A)(a) or (b) applied.

(3) In sub-paragraph (2) above "appropriate officer" means the officer investigating the offence for which the person was arrested.

2 Persons charged etc

(1) A constable may require a person to attend a police station for the purpose of taking his fingerprints under section 61(5B).

(2) The power under sub-paragraph (1) above may not be exercised after the end of the period of six months beginning with--

(a) in a case falling within section 61(5B) (a) (fingerprints not taken previously), the day on which the person was charged or informed that he would be reported, or

(b) in a case falling within section 61(5B) (b) (fingerprints taken on previous occasion insufficient etc), the day on which the appropriate officer was informed that section 61(3A) (a) or (b) applied.

(3) In sub-paragraph (2) (b) above "appropriate officer" means the officer investigating the offence for which the person was charged or informed that he would be reported.

3 Persons convicted etc of an offence in England and Wales

(1) A constable may require a person to attend a police station for the purpose of taking his fingerprints under section 61(6).

(2) Where the condition in section 61(6ZA) (a) is satisfied (fingerprints not taken previously), the power under sub-paragraph (1) above may not be exercised after the end of the period of two years beginning with--

(a) the day on which the person was convicted, cautioned or warned or reprimanded, or

(b) if later, the day on which this Schedule comes into force.

(3) Where the condition in section 61(6ZA) (b) is satisfied (fingerprints taken on previous occasion insufficient etc), the power under sub-paragraph (1) above may not be exercised after the end of the period of two years beginning with--

(a) the day on which an appropriate officer was informed that section 61(3A) (a) or (b) applied, or

(b) if later, the day on which this Schedule comes into force.

(4) In sub-paragraph (3) (a) above "appropriate officer" means an officer of the police force which investigated the offence in question.

(5) Sub-paragraphs (2) and (3) above do not apply where the offence is a qualifying offence (whether or not it was such an offence at the time of the conviction, caution or warning or reprimand).

4 Persons subject to a control order

[not in force]

5 Persons convicted etc of an offence outside England and Wales

A constable may require a person to attend a police station for the purpose of taking his fingerprints under section 61(6D).

6 Multiple attendance

(1) Where a person's fingerprints have been taken under section 61 on two occasions in relation to any offence, he may not under this Schedule be required to attend a police station to have his fingerprints taken under that section in relation to that offence on a subsequent occasion without the authorisation of an officer of at least the rank of inspector.

(2) Where an authorisation is given under sub-paragraph (1) above--

(a) the fact of the authorisation, and

(b) the reasons for giving it,

shall be recorded as soon as practicable after it has been given.

PART 2 INTIMATE SAMPLES

7 Persons suspected to be involved in an offence

A constable may require a person to attend a police station for the purpose of taking an intimate sample from him under section 62(1A) if, in the course of the investigation of an offence, two or more non intimate samples suitable for the same means of analysis have been taken from him but have proved insufficient.

8 Persons convicted etc of an offence outside England and Wales

A constable may require a person to attend a police station for the purpose of taking a sample from him under section 62(2A) if two or more non-intimate samples suitable for the same means of analysis have been taken from him under section 63(3E) but have proved insufficient.

PART 3 NON-INTIMATE SAMPLES
9 Persons arrested and released
(1) A constable may require a person to attend a police station for the purpose of taking a non-intimate sample from him under section 63(3ZA).
(2) The power under sub-paragraph (1) above may not be exercised in a case falling within section 63(3ZA) (b) (sample taken on a previous occasion not suitable etc) after the end of the period of six months beginning with the day on which the appropriate officer was informed of the matters specified in section 63(3ZA) (b) (i) or (ii).
(3) In sub-paragraph (2) above, "appropriate officer" means the officer investigating the offence for which the person was arrested.
10 Persons charged etc
(1) A constable may require a person to attend a police station for the purpose of taking a non-intimate sample from him under section 63(3A).
(2) The power under sub-paragraph (1) above may not be exercised in a case falling within section 63(3A)(a) (sample not taken previously) after the end of the period of six months beginning with the day on which he was charged or informed that he would be reported.
(3) The power under sub-paragraph (1) above may not be exercised in a case falling within section 63(3A) (b) (sample taken on a previous occasion not suitable etc) after the end of the period of six months beginning with the day on which the appropriate officer was informed of the matters specified in section 63(3A) (b) (i) or (ii).
(4) In sub-paragraph (3) above "appropriate officer" means the officer investigating the offence for which the person was charged or informed that he would be reported.
11 Persons convicted etc of an offence in England and Wales
(1) A constable may require a person to attend a police station for the purpose of taking a non-intimate sample from him under section 63(3B).
(2) Where the condition in section 63(3BA)(a) is satisfied (sample not taken previously), the power under sub-paragraph (1) above may not be exercised after the end of the period of two years beginning with--
(a) the day on which the person was convicted, cautioned or warned or reprimanded, or
(b) if later, the day on which this Schedule comes into force.
(3) Where the condition in section 63(3BA)(b) is satisfied (sample taken on a previous occasion not suitable etc), the power under sub-paragraph (1) above may not be exercised after the end of the period of two years beginning with--
(a) the day on which an appropriate officer was informed of the matters specified in section 63(3BA)(b)(i) or (ii), or
(b) if later, the day on which this Schedule comes into force.
(4) In sub-paragraph (3)(a) above "appropriate officer" means an officer of the police force which investigated the offence in question.
(5) Sub-paragraphs (2) and (3) above do not apply where--
(a) the offence is a qualifying offence (whether or not it was such an offence at the time of the conviction, caution or warning or reprimand), or
(b) he was convicted before 10th April 1995 and is a person to whom section 1 of the Criminal Evidence (Amendment) Act 1997 applies.
12 Persons subject to a control order
[Not in force]
13 Persons convicted etc of an offence outside England and Wales
A constable may require a person to attend a police station for the purpose of taking a non-intimate sample from him under section 63(3E).
14 Multiple exercise of power
(1) Where a non-intimate sample has been taken from a person under section 63 on two occasions in relation to any offence, he may not under this Schedule be required to attend a police station to have another such sample taken from him under that section in relation to that offence on a subsequent occasion without the authorisation of an officer of at least the rank of inspector.
(2) Where an authorisation is given under sub-paragraph (1) above--
(a) the fact of the authorisation, and

(b) the reasons for giving it,

shall be recorded as soon as practicable after it has been given.

PART 4 GENERAL AND SUPPLEMENTARY

15 Requirement to have power to take fingerprints or sample

A power conferred by this Schedule to require a person to attend a police station for the purposes of taking fingerprints or a sample under any provision of this Act may be exercised only in a case where the fingerprints or sample may be taken from the person under that provision (and, in particular, if any necessary authorisation for taking the fingerprints or sample under that provision has been obtained).

16 Date and time of attendance

(1) A requirement under this Schedule--

(a) shall give the person a period of at least seven days within which he must attend the police station; and

(b) may direct him so to attend at a specified time of day or between specified times of day.

(2) In specifying a period or time or times of day for the purposes of sub-paragraph (1) above, the constable shall consider whether the fingerprints or sample could reasonably be taken at a time when the person is for any other reason required to attend the police station.

(3) A requirement under this Schedule may specify a period shorter than seven days if--

(a) there is an urgent need for the fingerprints or sample for the purposes of the investigation of an offence; and

(b) the shorter period is authorised by an officer of at least the rank of inspector.

(4) Where an authorisation is given under sub-paragraph (3)(b) above--

(a) the fact of the authorisation, and

(b) the reasons for giving it,

shall be recorded as soon as practicable after it has been given.

(5) If the constable giving a requirement under this Schedule and the person to whom it is given so agree, it may be varied so as to specify any period within which, or date or time at which, the person must attend; but a variation shall not have effect unless confirmed by the constable in writing.

17 Enforcement

A constable may arrest without warrant a person who has failed to comply with a requirement under this Schedule.

Appendix 2 – PACE Codes of Practice

Codes of Practice - Code A Exercise by police officers of statutory powers of stop and search

General

This code of practice must be readily available at all police stations for consultation by police officers, police staff, detained persons and members of the public.

The notes for guidance included are not provisions of this code, but are guidance to police officers and others about its application and interpretation. Provisions in the annexes to the code are provisions of this code.

This code governs the exercise by police officers of statutory powers to search a person or a vehicle without first making an arrest. The main stop and search powers to which this code applies are set out in Annex A, but that list should not be regarded as definitive. [See Note 1] In addition, it covers requirements on police officers and police staff to record encounters not governed by statutory powers. This code does not apply to:

(a)   the powers of stop and search under;

(i)   Aviation Security Act 1982, section 27(2);

(ii)   Police and Criminal Evidence Act 1984, section 6(1) (which relates specifically to powers of constables employed by statutory undertakers on the premises of the statutory undertakers).

(b)   searches carried out for the purposes of examination under Schedule 7 to the Terrorism Act 2000 and to which the Code of Practice issued under paragraph 6 of Schedule 14 to the Terrorism Act 2000 applies.

1   Principles governing stop and search

1.1   Powers to stop and search must be used fairly, responsibly, with respect for people being searched and without unlawful discrimination. The Equality Act 2010 makes it unlawful for police officers to discriminate against, harass or victimise any person on the grounds of the 'protected characteristics' of age, disability, gender reassignment, race, religion or belief, sex and sexual orientation, marriage and civil partnership, pregnancy and maternity when using their powers. When police forces are carrying out their functions they also have a duty to have regard to the need to eliminate unlawful discrimination, harassment and victimisation and to take steps to foster good relations.

1.2   The intrusion on the liberty of the person stopped or searched must be brief and detention for the purposes of a search must take place at or near the location of the stop.

1.3   If these fundamental principles are not observed the use of powers to stop and search may be drawn into question. Failure to use the powers in the proper manner reduces their effectiveness. Stop and search can play an important role in the detection and prevention of crime, and using the powers fairly makes them more effective.

1.4   The primary purpose of stop and search powers is to enable officers to allay or confirm suspicions about individuals without exercising their power of arrest. Officers may be required to justify the use or authorisation of such powers, in relation both to individual searches and the overall pattern of their activity in this regard, to their supervisory officers or in court. Any misuse of the powers is likely to be harmful to policing and lead to mistrust of the police. Officers must also be able to explain their actions to the member of the public searched. The misuse of these powers can lead to disciplinary action.

1.5   An officer must not search a person, even with his or her consent, where no power to search is applicable. Even where a person is prepared to submit to a search voluntarily, the person must not be searched unless the necessary legal power exists, and the search must be in accordance with the relevant power and the provisions of this Code. The only exception, where an officer does not require a specific power, applies to searches of persons entering sports grounds or other premises carried out with their consent given as a condition of entry.

2   Explanation of powers to stop and search

2.1   This code applies to powers of stop and search as follows:

(a)   powers which require reasonable grounds for suspicion, before they may be exercised; that articles unlawfully obtained or possessed are being carried, or under Section 43 of the Terrorism Act 2000 that a person is a terrorist;

(b)   authorised under section 60 of the Criminal Justice and Public Order Act

1994, based upon a reasonable belief that incidents involving serious violence may take place or that people are carrying dangerous instruments or offensive weapons within any locality in the police area or that it is expedient to use the powers to find such instruments or weapons that have been used in incidents of serious violence;

(c)   authorised under section 44(1) of the Terrorism Act 2000 based upon a consideration that the exercise of the power is necessary for the prevention of acts of terrorism (see paragraph 2.18A), and

(d)   powers to search a person who has not been arrested in the exercise of a power to search premises (see Code B paragraph 2.4).

Searches requiring reasonable grounds for suspicion

2.2   Reasonable grounds for suspicion depend on the circumstances in each case. There must be an objective basis for that suspicion based on facts, information, and/or intelligence which are relevant to the likelihood of finding an article of a certain kind or, in the case of searches under section 43 of the Terrorism Act 2000, to the likelihood that the person is a terrorist. Reasonable suspicion can never be supported on the basis of personal factors.It must rely on intelligence or information about, or some specific behaviour by, the person concerned.   For example, unless the police have a description of a suspect, a person's physical appearance (including any of the 'protected characteristics' set out in the Equality Act 2010 (see paragraph 1.1), or the fact that the person is known to have a previous conviction, cannot be used alone or in combination with each other, or in combination with any other factor, as the reason for searching that person. Reasonable suspicion cannot be based on generalisations or stereotypical images of certain groups or categories of people as more likely to be involved in criminal activity.

2.3   Reasonable suspicion may also exist without specific information or intelligence and on the basis of the behaviour of a person. For example, if an officer encounters someone on the street at night who is obviously trying to hide something, the officer may (depending on the other surrounding circumstances) base such suspicion on the fact that this kind of behaviour is often linked to stolen or prohibited articles being carried. Similarly, for the purposes of section 43 of the Terrorism Act 2000, suspicion that a person is a terrorist may arise from the person's behaviour at or near a location which has been identified as a potential target for terrorists.

2.4   However, reasonable suspicion should normally be linked to accurate and current intelligence or information, such as information describing an article being carried, a suspected offender, or a person who has been seen carrying a type of article known to have been stolen recently from premises in the area. Searches based on accurate and current intelligence or information are more likely to be effective. Targeting searches in a particular area at specified crime problems increases their effectiveness and minimises inconvenience to law-abiding members of the public. It also helps in justifying the use of searches both to those who are searched and to the public. This does not however prevent stop and search powers being exercised in other locations where such powers may be exercised and reasonable suspicion exists.

2.5   Searches are more likely to be effective, legitimate, and secure public confidence when reasonable suspicion is based on a range of factors. The overall use of these powers is more likely to be effective when up to date and accurate intelligence or information is communicated to officers and they are well-informed about local crime patterns.

2.6   Where there is reliable information or intelligence that members of a group or gang habitually carry knives unlawfully or weapons or controlled drugs, and wear a distinctive item of clothing or other means of identification to indicate their membership of the group or gang, that distinctive item of clothing or other means of identification may provide reasonable grounds to stop and search a person. [See Note 9]

2.7   A police officer may have reasonable grounds to suspect that a person is in innocent possession of a stolen or prohibited article or other item for which he or she is empowered to search. In that case the officer may stop and search the person even though there would be no power of arrest.

2.8   Under section 43(1) of the Terrorism Act 2000 a constable may stop and search a person whom the officer reasonably suspects to be a terrorist to discover whether the person is in possession of anything which may constitute evidence that the person is a terrorist. These searches may only be carried out by an officer of the same sex as the person searched (see Annex F). An authorisation under section

44(1) of the Terrorism Act 2000 allows vehicles to be stopped and searched by a constable in uniform who reasonably suspects that articles which could be used in connection with terrorism will be found in the vehicle or in anything in or on that vehicle. See paragraph 2.18A below.

2.9   An officer who has reasonable grounds for suspicion may detain the person concerned in order to carry out a search. Before carrying out a search the officer may ask questions about the person's behaviour or presence in circumstances which gave rise to the suspicion. As a result of questioning the detained person, the reasonable grounds for suspicion necessary to detain that person may be confirmed or, because of a satisfactory explanation, be eliminated.   [See Notes 2 and 3] Questioning may also reveal reasonable grounds to suspect the possession of a different kind of unlawful article from that originally suspected. Reasonable   grounds   for suspicion however cannot be provided retrospectively by such questioning during a person's detention or by refusal to answer any questions put.

2.10   If, as a result of questioning before a search, or other circumstances which come to the attention of the officer, there cease to be reasonable grounds for suspecting that an article is being carried of a kind for which there is a power to stop and search, no search may take place. [See Note 3] In the absence of any other lawful power to detain, the person is free to leave at will and must be so informed.

2.11   There is no power to stop or detain a person in order to find grounds for a search.

Police officers have many encounters with members of the public which do not involve detaining people against their will. If reasonable grounds for suspicion emerge during such an encounter, the officer may search the person, even though no grounds existed when the encounter began. If an officer is detaining someone for the purpose of a search, he or she should inform the person as soon as detention begins.

Searches authorised under section 60 of the Criminal Justice and Public Order Act 1994

2.12   Authority for a constable in uniform to stop and search under section 60 of the Criminal Justice and Public Order Act 1994 may be given if the authorising officer reasonably believes:

(a)   that incidents involving serious violence may take place in any locality in the officer's police area, and it is expedient to use these powers to prevent their occurrence;

(b)   that persons are carrying dangerous instruments or offensive weapons without good reason in any locality in the officer's police area or

(c)   that an incident involving serious violence has taken place in the officer's police area, a dangerous instrument or offensive weapon used in the incident is being carried by a person in any locality in that police area, and it is expedient to use these powers to find that instrument or weapon.

2.13   An authorisation under section 60 may only be given by an officer of the rank of inspector or above and in writing, or orally if paragraph 2.12(c) applies and it is not practicable to give the authorisation in writing. The authorisation (whether written or oral) must specify the grounds on which it was given, the locality in which the powers may be exercised and the period of time for which they are in force. The period authorised shall be no longer than appears reasonably necessary to prevent, or seek to prevent incidents of serious violence, or to deal with the problem of carrying dangerous instruments or offensive weapons or to find a dangerous instrument or offensive weapon that has been used. It may not exceed 24 hours. An oral authorisation given where paragraph 2.12(c) applies must be recorded in writing as soon as practicable. [See Notes 10-13]

2.14   An inspector who gives an authorisation must, as soon as practicable, inform an officer of or above the rank of superintendent. This officer may direct that the authorisation shall be extended for a further 24 hours, if violence or the carrying of dangerous instruments or offensive weapons has occurred, or is suspected to have occurred, and the continued use of the powers is considered necessary to prevent or deal with further such activity or to find a dangerous instrument or offensive weapon used that has been used. That direction must be given in writing unless it is not practicable to do so, in which case it must be recorded in writing as soon as practicable afterwards. [See Note 12]

2.14A The selection of persons and vehicles under section 60 to be stopped and, if appropriate, searched should reflect an objective assessment of the nature of the incident or weapon in question and the individuals and vehicles thought likely to be associated with that incident or those weapons (see Notes 10 and 11). The powers must not be used to stop and search persons and vehicles for reasons unconnected with the purpose of the authorisation. When selecting persons and vehicles to be stopped in response to a specific threat or incident, officers must take care not to discriminate unlawfully against anyone on the grounds of any of the protected characteristics set out in the Equality Act 2010 (see paragraph 1.1).

2.14B   The driver of a vehicle which is stopped under section 60 and any person who is searched under section 60 are entitled to a written statement to that effect if they apply within twelve months from the day the vehicle was stopped or the person was searched. This statement is a record which states that the vehicle was stopped or (as the case may be) that the person was searched under section 60 and it may form part of the search record or be supplied as a separate record.

Powers to require removal of face coverings

2.15   Section 60AA of the Criminal Justice and Public Order Act 1994 also provides a power to demand the removal of disguises. The officer exercising the power must reasonably believe that someone is wearing an item wholly or mainly for the purpose of concealing identity. There is also a power to seize such items where the officer believes that a person intends to wear them for this purpose. There is no power to stop and search for disguises. An officer may seize any such item which is discovered when exercising a power of search for something else, or which is being carried, and which the officer reasonably believes is intended to be used for concealing anyone's identity. This power can only be used if an authorisation given under section 60 or under section 60AA, is in force. [See Note 4]

2.16   Authority under section 60AA for a constable in uniform to require the removal of disguises and to seize them may be given if the authorising officer reasonably believes that activities may take place in any locality in the officer's police area that are likely to involve the commission of offences and it is expedient to use these powers to prevent or control these activities.

2.17   An authorisation under section 60AA may only be given by an officer of the rank of inspector or above, in writing, specifying the grounds on which it was given, the locality in which the powers may be exercised and the period of time for which they are in force. The period authorised shall be no longer than appears reasonably necessary to prevent, or seek to prevent the commission of offences. It may not exceed 24 hours. [See Notes 10-13]

2.18   An inspector who gives an authorisation must, as soon as practicable, inform an officer of or above the rank of superintendent. This officer may direct that the authorisation shall be extended for a further 24 hours, if crimes have been committed, or are suspected to have been committed, and the continued use of the powers is considered necessary to prevent or deal with further such activity. This direction must also be given in writing at the time or as soon as practicable afterwards. [See Note 12]

Searches authorised under section 44 of the Terrorism Act 2000

2.18A   The European Court of Human Rights has ruled that the stop and search powers under sections 44 to 47 of the Terrorism Act 2000 are not compatible with the right to a private life under Article 8 of the European Convention on Human Rights. Neither the European Court ruling nor the provisions of this Code can amend these statutory provisions. However, in an oral statement made by the Home Secretary in the House of Commons on 8 July 2010, interim guidelines were announced pending a review (with a view to legislative amendment) of these provisions to ensure that police do not exercise any powers under section 44 in a way which would be incompatible with Convention rights. Under these guidelines:

(i)   Authorisations under section 44(1) should be given, and may be confirmed by the Secretary of State, only:

• in relation to searches of vehicles and anything in or on vehicles, but not searches of drivers or passengers or anything being carried by a driver or passenger; and

• if such searches are considered necessary for the prevention of acts of terrorism.

Note: Section 44(3) provides that an authorising officer may give an authorisation when they consider it is 'expedient' for the prevention of acts of terrorism, but the test now to be applied is that of necessity – taking account of all of the circumstances.

(ii) A search of a vehicle or of anything in or on a vehicle under section 44(1) should only be carried out if it is reasonably suspected that articles which could be used in connection with terrorism will be found in the vehicle or in anything in or on that vehicle.

Note: This now applies despite the provision in section 45(1)(b) which allows the power to be exercised whether or not the constable has grounds for suspecting the presence of such articles.

(iii) Authorisations to search pedestrians, drivers of vehicles and passengers in vehicles and anything carried by a driver or passenger, are not to be given under section 44(1) or (2) and if given, will not be confirmed. For these searches police must rely on the power under section 43 which requires the person who may be searched to be reasonably suspected of being a terrorist, but does not authorise the removal of headgear or footwear in public.

The provisions of paragraphs 2.1, 2.8, 2.19 to 2.26, 3.5, Annex A paragraphs 15 and

16 and Annex C paragraph 1 are amended by this Code to reflect these guidelines:

2.19 An officer of the rank of assistant chief constable (or equivalent) or above, may give authority under section 44(1) of the Terrorism Act 2000 for a constable in uniform to exercise the power to stop and search any vehicle and anything in or on any vehicle, in the whole or any part or parts of the authorising officer's police area. An authorisation may only be given if the officer considers it is necessary for the prevention of acts of terrorism.

2.20 If an authorisation is given orally at first, it must be confirmed in writing by the officer who gave it as soon as reasonably practicable.

2.21 When giving an authorisation, the officer must specify the geographical area in which the power may be used, and the time and date that the authorisation ends (up to a maximum of 28 days from the time the authorisation was given). [See Notes 12 and 13]

2.22 The officer giving an authorisation under section 44(1) must cause the Secretary of State to be informed, as soon as reasonably practicable, that such an authorisation has been given. An authorisation which is not confirmed by the Secretary of State within 48 hours of its having been given, shall have effect up until the end of that 48 hour period or the end of the period specified in the authorisation (whichever is the earlier). [See Note 14]

2.23 Following notification of the authorisation, the Secretary of State may:

(i) cancel the authorisation with immediate effect or with effect from such other time as he or she may direct;

(ii) confirm it but for a shorter period than that specified in the authorisation;

or

(iii)   confirm the authorisation as given.

2.24   When an authorisation under section 44(1) is given, a constable in uniform may exercise the power:

(a)   only for the purpose of stopping and searching a vehicle and anything in or on a vehicle for articles of a kind which could be used in connection with terrorism (see paragraph 2.25); and

(b)   only if there are reasonable grounds for suspecting the presence of such articles.   See paragraphs 2.2 to 2.11, "Searches requiring reasonable grounds for suspicion"

2.24A   When a Community Support Officer on duty and in uniform has been conferred powers under Section 44(1) of the Terrorism Act 2000 by a Chief Officer of their force, the exercise of this power must comply with the requirements of this Code of Practice, including the recording requirements.

2.25   Paragraphs 2.2 to 2.11 above ("Searches requiring reasonable grounds for suspicion") are to be applied to the stopping and searching of vehicles when an authorisation under section 44(1) is given.

2.26   The powers under sections 43 and 44(1) of the Terrorism Act 2000 allow a constable to search only for articles which could be used for terrorist purposes. However, this would not prevent a search being carried out under other powers if, in the course of exercising these powers, the officer formed reasonable grounds for suspicion.

Powers to search in the exercise of a power to search premises

2.27   The following powers to search premises also authorise the search of a person, not under arrest, who is found on the premises during the course of the search:

(a)   section 139B of the Criminal Justice Act 1988 under which a constable may enter school premises and search the premises and any person on those premises for any bladed or pointed article or offensive weapon;

(b)   under a warrant issued under section 23(3) of the Misuse of Drugs Act 1971 to search premises for drugs or documents but only if the warrant specifically authorises the search of persons found on the premises; and

(c)   under a search warrant or order issued under paragraph 1, 3 or 11 of Schedule 5 to the Terrorism Act 2000 to search premises and any person found there for material likely to be of substantial value to a terrorist investigation.

2.28   Before the power under section 139B of the Criminal Justice Act 1988 may be exercised, the constable must have reasonable grounds to believe that an offence under section 139A of the Criminal Justice Act 1988 (having a bladed or pointed article or offensive weapon on school premises) has been or is being committed. A warrant to search premises and persons found therein may be issued under section

23(3) of the Misuse of Drugs Act 1971 if there are reasonable grounds to suspect that controlled drugs or certain documents are in the possession of a person on the premises.

2.29   The powers in paragraph 2.27 do not require prior specific grounds to suspect that the person to be searched is in possession of an item for which there is an existing power to search. However, it is still necessary to ensure that the selection and treatment of those searched under these powers is based upon objective factors connected with the search of the premises, and not upon personal prejudice.

3   Conduct of searches

3.1   All stops and searches must be carried out with courtesy, consideration and respect for the person concerned.   This has a significant impact on public confidence in the police. Every reasonable effort must be made to minimise the embarrassment that a person being searched may experience. [See Note 4]

3.2   The co-operation of the person to be searched must be sought in every case, even if the person initially objects to the search. A forcible search may be made only if it has been established that the person is unwilling to co-operate or resists. Reasonable force may be used as a last resort if necessary to conduct a search or to detain a person or vehicle for the purposes of a search.

3.3   The length of time for which a person or vehicle may be detained must be reasonable and kept to a minimum.   Where the exercise of the power requires reasonable suspicion, the thoroughness and extent of a search must depend on what is suspected of being carried, and by whom.   If the suspicion relates to a particular article which is seen to be slipped into a person's pocket, then, in the absence of other grounds for suspicion or an opportunity for the article to be moved elsewhere, the search must be confined to that pocket.   In the case of a small article which can readily be concealed, such as a drug, and which might be concealed anywhere on the person, a more extensive search may be necessary.   In the case of searches mentioned in paragraph 2.1(b), (c), and (d), which do not require reasonable grounds for suspicion, officers may make any reasonable search to look for items for which they are empowered to search. [See Note 5]

3.4   The search must be carried out at or near the place where the person or vehicle was first detained. [See Note 6]

3.5   There is no power to require a person to remove any clothing in public other than an outer coat, jacket or gloves, except under section 60AA of the Criminal Justice and Public Order Act 1994 (which empowers a constable to require a person to remove any item worn to conceal identity).   [See Notes 4 and 6]   A search in public of a person's clothing which has not been removed must be restricted to superficial examination of outer garments.   This does not, however, prevent an officer from placing his or her hand inside the pockets of the outer clothing, or feeling round the inside of collars, socks and shoes if this is reasonably necessary in the circumstances to look for the object of the search or to remove and examine any item reasonably suspected to be the object of the search.   For the same reasons, subject to the restrictions on the removal of headgear, a person's hair may also be searched in public (see paragraphs 3.1 and 3.3).

3.6   Where on reasonable grounds it is considered necessary to conduct a more thorough search (e.g. by requiring a person to take off a T-shirt), this must be done out of public view, for example, in a police van unless paragraph 3.7 applies, or police station if there is one nearby.   [See Note 6]   Any search involving the removal of more than an outer coat, jacket, gloves, headgear or footwear, or any other item concealing identity, may only be made by an officer of the same sex as the person searched and may not be made in the presence of anyone of the opposite sex unless the person being searched specifically requests it.   [See Annex F and Notes 4, 7 and 8]

3.7   Searches involving exposure of intimate parts of the body must not be conducted as a routine extension of a less thorough search, simply because nothing is found in the course of the initial search. Searches involving exposure of intimate parts of the body may be carried out only at a nearby police station or other nearby location which is out of public view (but not a police vehicle). These searches must be conducted in accordance with paragraph 11 of Annex A to Code C except that an intimate search mentioned in paragraph 11(f) of Annex A to Code C may not be authorised or carried out under any stop and search powers. The other provisions of Code C do not apply to the conduct and recording of searches of persons detained at police stations in the exercise of stop and search powers. [See Note 7]

Steps to be taken prior to a search

3.8   Before any search of a detained person or attended vehicle takes place the officer must take reasonable steps, if not in uniform (see paragraph 3.9), to show their warrant card to the person to be searched or in charge of the vehicle to be searched and whether or not in uniform, to give that person the following information:

(a)   that they are being detained for the purposes of a search

(b)   the officer's name (except in the case of enquiries linked to the investigation of terrorism, or otherwise where the officer reasonably believes that giving his or her name might put him or her in danger, in which case a warrant or other identification number shall be given) and the name of the police station to which the officer is attached;

(c)   the legal search power which is being exercised; and

(d)   a clear explanation of:

(i)   the object of the search in terms of the article or articles for which there is a power to search; and

(ii)   in the case of:

•   the power under section 60 of the Criminal Justice and Public Order Act 1994 (see paragraph 2.1(b)), the nature of the power, the authorisation and the fact that it has been given;

•   the power under section 44 of the Terrorism Act 2000, the nature of the power, the authorisation and the fact that it has been given and the grounds for suspicion; (see paragraph 2.1(c) and 2.18A.

•   all other powers requiring reasonable suspicion (see paragraph

2.1(a)), the grounds for that suspicion.

(e)   that they are entitled to a copy of the record of the search if one is made (see section 4 below) if they ask within 3 months from the date of the search and:

(i)   if they are not arrested and taken to a police station as a result of the search and it is practicable to make the record on the spot, that immediately after the search is completed they will be given, if they request, either:

•   a copy of the record, or

•   a receipt which explains how they can obtain a copy of the full record or access to an electronic copy of the record, or

(ii)   if they are arrested and taken to a police station as a result of the search, that the record will be made at the station as part of their custody record and they will be given, if they request, a copy of their custody record which includes a record of the search as soon as practicable whilst they are at the station. [See Note 16]

3.9   Stops and searches under the powers mentioned in paragraphs 2.1(b), and (c) may be undertaken only by a constable in uniform.

3.10   The person should also be given information about police powers to stop and search and the individual's rights in these circumstances.

3.11   If the person to be searched, or in charge of a vehicle to be searched, does not appear to understand what is being said, or there is any doubt about the person's ability to understand English, the officer must take reasonable steps to bring information regarding the person's rights and any relevant provisions of this Code to his or her attention.   If the person is deaf or cannot understand English and is accompanied by someone, then the officer must try to establish whether that person can interpret or otherwise help the officer to give the required information.

4   Recording requirements

(a)   Searches which do not result in an arrest

4.1   When an officer carries out a search in the exercise of any power to which this Code applies and the search does not result in the person searched or person in charge of the vehicle searched being arrested and taken to a police station, a record must be made of it, electronically or on paper, unless there are exceptional circumstances which make this wholly impracticable (e.g. in situations involving public disorder or when the recording officer's presence is urgently required elsewhere).   If a record is to be made, the officer carrying out the search must make the record on the spot unless this is not practicable, in which case, the officer must make the record as soon as practicable after the search is completed. [See Note 16.]

4.2   If the record is made at the time, the person who has been searched or who is in charge of the vehicle that has been searched must be asked if they want a copy and if they do, they must be given immediately, either:

•   a copy of the record, or

•   a receipt which explains how they can obtain a copy of the full record or access to an electronic copy of the record

4.2A   An officer is not required to provide a copy of the full record or a receipt at the time if they are called to an incident of higher priority. [See Note 21]

(b)   Searches which result in an arrest

4.2B   If a search in the exercise of any power to which this Code applies results in a person being arrested and taken to a police station, the officer carrying out the search is responsible for ensuring that a record of the search is made as part of their custody record. The custody officer must then ensure that the person is asked if they want a copy of the record and if they do, that they are given a copy as soon as practicable. [See Note 16].

(c)   Record of search

4.3   The record of a search must always include the following information:

(a)   A note of the self defined ethnicity, and if different, the ethnicity as perceived by the officer making the search, of the person searched or of the person in charge of the vehicle searched (as the case may be); [See Note 18]

(b)   The date, time and place the person or vehicle was searched [See Note 6];

(c)   The object of the search in terms of the article or articles for which there is a power to search;

(d)   In the case of:

•   the power under section 60 of the Criminal Justice and Public Order Act

1994 (see paragraph 2.1(b)), the nature of the power, the authorisation and the fact that it has been given; [See Note 17]

•   the power under section 44 of the Terrorism Act 2000, the nature of the power, the authorisation and the fact that it has been given and the grounds for suspicion; [see paragraphs 2.1(c) and 2.18A and Note 17].

•   all other powers requiring reasonable suspicion (see paragraph 2.1(a)), the grounds for that suspicion.

(e)   subject to paragraph 3.8(b), the identity of the officer carrying out the search. [See Note 15]

4.3A   For the purposes of completing the search record, there is no requirement to record the name, address and date of birth of the person searched or the person in charge of a vehicle which is searched and the person is under no obligation to provide this information.

4.4   Nothing in paragraph 4.3 requires the names of police officers to be shown on the search record or any other record required to be made under this code in the case of enquiries linked to the investigation of terrorism or otherwise where an officer reasonably believes that recording names might endanger the officers.   In such cases the record must show the officers' warrant or other identification number and duty station.

4.5   A record is required for each person and each vehicle searched. However, if a person is in a vehicle and both are searched, and the object and grounds of the search are the same, only one record need be completed. If more than one person in a vehicle is searched, separate records for each search of a person must be made.   If only a vehicle is searched, the self-defined ethnic background of the person in charge of the vehicle must be recorded, unless the vehicle is unattended.

4.6   The record of the grounds for making a search must, briefly but informatively, explain the reason for suspecting the person concerned, by reference to the person's behaviour and/or other circumstances.

4.7   Where officers detain an individual with a view to performing a search, but the need to search is eliminated as a result of questioning the person detained, a search should not be carried out and a record is not required. [See paragraph 2.10, Notes 3 and 22A]

4.8   After searching an unattended vehicle, or anything in or on it, an officer must leave a notice in it (or on it, if things on it have been searched without opening it) recording the fact that it has been searched.

4.9   The notice must include the name of the police station to which the officer concerned is attached and state where a copy of the record of the search may be obtained and how (if applicable) an electronic copy may be accessed and where any application for compensation should be directed.

4.10   The vehicle must if practicable be left secure.

4.10A   Not used

4.10B   Not used

Recording of encounters not governed by statutory powers

4.11   Not used.

4.12   There is no national requirement for an officer who requests a person in a public place to account for themselves, i.e. their actions, behaviour, presence in an area or possession of anything, to make any record of the encounter or to give the person a receipt. [See Notes 22A and 22B]

4.12A   Not used

4.13   Not used

4.14   Not used

4.15   Not used

4.16   Not used

4.17   Not used .

4.18   Not used

4.19   Not used

4.20   Not used

5   Monitoring and supervising the use of stop and search powers

5.1   Supervising officers must monitor the use of stop and search powers and should consider in particular whether there is any evidence that they are being exercised on the basis of stereotyped images or inappropriate generalisations.   Supervising officers should satisfy themselves that the practice of officers under their supervision in stopping, searching and recording is fully in accordance with this Code.   Supervisors must also examine whether the records reveal any trends or patterns which give cause for concern, and if so take appropriate action to address this.

5.2   Senior officers with area or force-wide responsibilities must also monitor the broader use of stop and search powers and, where necessary, take action at the relevant level.

5.3   Supervision and monitoring must be supported by the compilation of comprehensive statistical records of stops and searches at force, area and local level. Any   apparently disproportionate use of the powers by particular officers or groups of officers or in relation to specific sections of the community should be identified and investigated.

5.4   In order to promote public confidence in the use of the powers, forces in consultation with police authorities must make arrangements for the records to be scrutinised by representatives of the community, and to explain the use of the powers at a local level. [See Note 19].

Notes for Guidance   Officers exercising stop and search powers

1   This code does not affect the ability of an officer to speak to or question a person

in the ordinary course of the officer's duties without detaining the person or exercising any element of compulsion. It is not the purpose of the code to prohibit

such encounters between the police and the community with the co-operation of

the person concerned and neither does it affect the principle that all citizens have a duty to help police officers to prevent crime and discover offenders. This is a civic rather than a legal duty; but when a police officer is trying to discover whether, or by whom, an offence has been committed he or she may question any person from whom useful information might be obtained, subject to the restrictions imposed by Code C. A person's unwillingness to reply does not alter this entitlement, but in the absence of a power to arrest, or to detain in order to search, the person is free to leave at will and cannot be compelled to remain with the officer.

2   In some circumstances preparatory questioning may be unnecessary, but in general a brief conversation or exchange will be desirable not only as a means of avoiding unsuccessful searches, but to explain the grounds for the stop/search, to gain co- operation and reduce any tension there might be surrounding the stop/search.

3   Where a person is lawfully detained for the purpose of a search, but no search in the event takes place, the detention will not thereby have been rendered unlawful.

4   Many people customarily cover their heads or faces for religious reasons - for example, Muslim women, Sikh men, Sikh or Hindu women, or Rastafarian men or women. A   police officer cannot order the removal of a head or face covering except where there is reason to believe that the item is being worn by the individual wholly or mainly for the purpose of disguising identity, not simply because it disguises identity.   Where there may be religious sensitivities about ordering the removal of such an item, the officer should permit the item to be removed out of public view. Where practicable, the item should be removed in the presence of an officer of the same sex as the person and out of sight of anyone of the opposite sex [see Annex F].

5   A search of a person in public should be completed as soon as possible.

6   A person may be detained under a stop and search power at a place other than where the person was first detained, only if that place, be it a police station or elsewhere, is nearby.   Such a place should be located within a reasonable travelling distance using whatever mode of travel (on foot or by car) is appropriate. This applies to all searches under stop and search powers, whether or not they involve the removal of clothing or exposure of intimate parts of the

body (see paragraphs 3.6 and 3.7) or take place in or out of public view. It means, for example, that a search under the stop and search power in section 23 of the Misuse of Drugs Act 1971 which involves the compulsory removal of more than a person's outer coat, jacket or gloves cannot be carried out unless a place which is both nearby the place they were first detained and out of public view, is available. If a search involves exposure of intimate parts of the body and a police station is not nearby, particular care must be taken to ensure that the location is suitable in that it enables the search to be conducted in accordance with the requirements of paragraph 11 of Annex A to Code C.

7   A search in the street itself should be regarded as being in public for the purposes of paragraphs 3.6 and 3.7 above, even though it may be empty at the time a search begins. Although there is no power to require a person to do so, there is nothing to prevent an officer from asking a person voluntarily to remove more than an outer coat, jacket or gloves in public.

8   Not used

9   Other means of identification might include jewellery, insignias, tattoos or other features which are known to identify members of the particular gang or group.

Authorising officers

10   The powers under section 60 are separate from and additional to the normal stop and search powers which require reasonable grounds to suspect an individual of carrying an offensive weapon (or other article).   Their overall purpose is to prevent serious violence and the widespread carrying of weapons which might lead to persons being seriously injured by disarming potential offenders or finding weapons that have been used in circumstances where other powers would not be sufficient. They should not therefore be used to replace or circumvent the normal powers for dealing with routine crime problems. A particular example might be an authorisation to prevent serious violence or the carrying of offensive weapons at a sports event by rival team supporters when the expected general appearance and age range of those likely to be responsible, alone, would not be sufficiently distinctive to support reasonable suspicion (see paragraph 2.6). The purpose of the powers under section 60AA is to prevent those involved in intimidatory or violent protests using face coverings to disguise identity.

11   Authorisations under section 60 require a reasonable belief on the part of the authorising officer. This must have an objective basis, for example: intelligence or relevant information such as a history of antagonism and violence between particular groups; previous incidents of violence at, or connected with, particular events or locations; a significant increase in knife-point robberies in a limited area; reports that individuals are regularly carrying weapons in a particular locality; information following an incident in which weapons were used about where the weapons might be found or in the case of section 60AA previous incidents of crimes being committed while wearing face coverings to conceal identity.

12   It is for the authorising officer to determine the period of time during which the powers mentioned in paragraph 2.1(b) and (c) may be exercised. The officer should set the minimum period he or she considers necessary to deal with the risk of violence, the carrying of knives or offensive weapons, or terrorism or to find dangerous instruments or weapons that have been used. A direction to extend the period authorised under the powers mentioned in paragraph 2.1(b) may be given only once. Thereafter further use of the powers requires a new authorisation. There is no provision to extend an authorisation of the powers mentioned in paragraph 2.1(c); further use of the powers requires a new authorisation.

13   It is for the authorising officer to determine the geographical area in which the use of the powers is to be authorised. In doing so the officer may wish to take into account factors such as the

nature and venue of the anticipated incident or the incident which has taken place, the number of people who may be in the immediate area of that incident, their access to surrounding areas and the anticipated or actual level of violence. The officer should not set a geographical area which is wider than that he or she believes necessary for the purpose of preventing anticipated violence, the carrying of knives or offensive weapons, acts of terrorism, finding a dangerous instrument or weapon that has been used or, in the case of section 60AA, the prevention of commission of offences. It is particularly important to ensure that constables exercising such powers are fully aware of where they may be used. If the area specified is smaller than the whole force area, the officer giving the authorisation should specify either the streets which form the boundary of the area or a divisional boundary within the force area. If the power is to be used in response to a threat or incident that straddles police force areas, an officer from each of the forces concerned will need to give an authorisation.

14   An officer who has authorised the use of powers under section 44(1) of the Terrorism Act 2000 must take immediate steps to send a copy of the authorisation to the National Joint Unit, Metropolitan Police Special Branch, who will forward it to the Secretary of State. The Secretary of State should be informed of the reasons for the authorisation. The National Joint Unit will inform the force concerned, within 48 hours of the authorisation being made, whether the Secretary of State has confirmed or cancelled or altered the authorisation. See paragraph 2.18A.

Recording

15   Where a stop and search is conducted by more than one officer the identity of all the officers engaged in the search must be recorded on the record. Nothing prevents an officer who is present but not directly involved in searching from completing the record during the course of the encounter.

16   When the search results in the person searched or in charge of a vehicle which is searched being arrested, the requirement to make the record of the search as part of the person's custody record does not apply if the person is granted "street bail" after arrest (see section 30A of PACE) to attend a police station and is not taken in custody to the police station An arrested person's entitlement to a copy of the search record which is made as part of their custody record does not affect, their entitlement to a copy of their custody record or any other provisions of PACE Code C section 2 (Custody records).

17   It is important for monitoring purposes to specify whether the authority for exercising a stop and search power was given under section 60 of the Criminal Justice and Public Order Act 1994, or under section 44(1) of the Terrorism Act 2000.

18   Officers should record the self-defined ethnicity of every person stopped according to the categories used in the 2001 census question listed in Annex B. The person should be asked to select one of the five main categories representing broad ethnic groups and then a more specific cultural background from within this group. The ethnic classification should be coded for recording purposes using the coding system in Annex B. An additional "Not stated" box is available but should not be offered to respondents explicitly. Officers should be aware and explain to members of the public, especially where concerns are raised, that this information is required to obtain a true picture of stop and search activity and to help improve ethnic monitoring, tackle discriminatory practice, and promote effective use of the powers. If the person gives what appears to the officer to be an "incorrect" answer (e.g. a person who appears to be white states that they are black), the officer should record the response that has been given and then record their own perception of the person's ethnic background by using the PNC classification system. If the "Not stated" category is used the reason for this must be recorded on the form.

19   Arrangements for public scrutiny of records should take account of the right to confidentiality of those stopped and searched. Anonymised forms and/or statistics generated from records should be the focus of the examinations by members of the public.

20   Not used

21   In situations where it is not practicable to provide a written copy of the record or immediate access to an electronic copy of the record or a receipt of the search at the time (see paragraph 4.2A above), the officer should consider giving the person details of the station which they may attend for a copy of the record. A receipt may take the form of a simple business card which includes sufficient information to locate the record should the person ask for copy, for example, the date and place of the search, a reference number or the name of the officer who carried out the search (unless paragraph 4.4 applies).

22   Not used

22A   Where there are concerns which make it necessary to monitor any local disproportionality, forces have discretion to direct officers to record the self- defined ethnicity of persons they request to account for themselves in a public place or who they detain with a view to searching but do not search. Guidance should be provided locally and efforts made to minimise the bureaucracy involved. Records should be closely monitored and supervised in line with paragraphs 5.1 to

5.4 and forces can suspend or re-instate recording of these encounters as appropriate.

22B   A person who is asked to account for themselves should, if they request, be given information about how they can report their dissatisfaction about how they have been treated.

Definition of Offensive Weapon

23   'Offensive weapon' is defined as any article made or adapted for use for causing injury to the person, or intended by the person having it with him for such use or by someone else. There are three categories of offensive weapons: those made for causing injury to the person; those adapted for such a purpose; and those not so made or adapted, but carried with the intention of causing injury to the person. A firearm, as defined by section 57 of the Firearms Act 1968, would fall within the definition of offensive weapon if any of the criteria above apply.

24   Not used

25   Not used

ANNEX A SUMMARY OF MAIN STOP AND SEARCH POWERS

THIS TABLE RELATES TO STOP AND SEARCH POWERS ONLY. INDIVIDUAL STATUTES BELOW MAY CONTAIN OTHER POLICE POWERS OF ENTRY, SEARCH AND SEIZURE

POWER	OBJECT OF SEARCH	EXTENT OF SEARCH	WHERE EXERCISABLE
Unlawful articles			
1. Public Stores Act 1875, s6	HM Stores stolen or unlawfully obtained	Persons, vehicles and vessels	Anywhere where the constabulary powers are exercisable
2. Firearms Act 1968, s47	Firearms	Persons and vehicles	A public place, or anywhere in the case of reasonable suspicion of offences of carrying
3. Misuse of Drugs Act	Controlled drugs	Persons and vehicles	Anywhere
4. Customs and Excise Management Act 1979, s163	Goods: (a) on which duty has not been paid; (b) being unlawfully removed, imported or exported; (c) otherwise liable to forfeiture to HM Revenue and Customs	Vehicles and vessels only	Anywhere
5. Aviation Security Act 1982, s27(1)	Stolen or unlawfully obtained goods	Airport employees and vehicles carrying airport employees or aircraft or any vehicle in a cargo area whether or not carrying an employee	Any designated airport

| 6. Police and Criminal Evidence Act 1984, s1 | Stolen goods; articles for use in certain Theft Act offences; offensive weapons, including bladed or sharply- pointed articles (except folding pocket knives with a bladed cutting edge not exceeding 3 inches); prohibited possession of a category

4 (display grade) firework, any person under 18 in possession

of an adult firework in a public place. | Persons and vehicles | Where there is public access |
|---|---|---|---|

7. Sporting events (Control of Alcohol etc.) Act 1985, s7	Intoxicating liquor	Persons, coaches and trains	Designated sports grounds or coaches and trains travelling to or from a designated
8. Crossbows Act 1987, s4	Crossbows or parts of crossbows (except crossbows with a draw weight of less than 1.4 kilograms)	Persons and vehicles	Anywhere except dwellings
9. Criminal Justice Act 1988 s139B	Offensive weapons, bladed or sharply pointed article	Persons	School premises
Evidence of game and wildlife			
10. Poaching Prevention Act 1862, s2	Game or poaching equipment	Persons and vehicles	A public place

11. Deer Act 1991, s12	Evidence of offences under the Act	Persons and vehicles	Anywhere except dwellings
12. Conservation of Seals Act 1970, s4	Seals or hunting equipment	Vehicles only	Anywhere
13. Protection of Badgers Act 1992, s11	Evidence of offences under the Act	Persons and vehicles	Anywhere
14. Wildlife and Countryside Act	Evidence of wildlife offences	Persons and vehicles	Anywhere except dwellings
Other			
15. Terrorism Act 2000, s.43(1)	Anything which may constitute evidence that the person is a terrorist	Persons	Anywhere
16. Terrorism Act 2000, s.44(1)	Articles of a kind which could be used in connection with terrorism	Vehicles, and anything in or on vehicles (See *paragraph 2.18A*)	Anywhere within the area or locality authorised under subsection (1)
17. *Not used*			
18. Paragraphs 7 and 8 of Schedule 7 to the Terrorism Act 2000	Anything relevant to determining if a person being examined falls within section 40(1)(b)	Persons, vehicles, vessels etc. *(Note: These searches are subject to the Code of Practice issued under paragraph 6 of Schedule 14 to the*	Ports and airports
19. Section 60 Criminal Justice and Public Order Act 1994	Offensive weapons or dangerous instruments to prevent incidents of serious violence or to deal with the carrying of such items or find such items which have been used in incidents of serious violence	Persons and vehicles	Anywhere within a locality authorised under subsection (1)

ANNEX B   SELF-DEFINED ETHNIC CLASSIFICATION CATEGORIES

White   W

A.   White - British   W1

B.   White - Irish   W2

C.   Any other White background   W9

Mixed   M

D.   White and Black Caribbean   M1

E.   White and Black African M2

F.   White and Asian M3

G.   Any other Mixed Background   M9

Asian / Asian - British   A

H.   Asian - Indian   A1

I.   Asian - Pakistani A2

J.   Asian - Bangladeshi   A3

K.   Any other Asian background   A9

Black / Black - British   B

L.   Black - Caribbean   B1

M.   Black African   B2

N.   Any other Black background   B9

Other   O

O.   Chinese 01

P.   Any other   09

Not Stated   NS

ANNEX C   SUMMARY OF POWERS OF COMMUNITY SUPPORT OFFICERS TO SEARCH AND SEIZE

The following is a summary of the search and seizure powers that may be exercised by a community support officer (CSO) who has been designated with the relevant powers in accordance with Part 4 of the Police Reform Act 2002.

When exercising any of these powers, a CSO must have regard to any relevant provisions of this Code, including section 3 governing the conduct of searches and the steps to be taken prior to a search.

A CSO may detain a person using reasonable force where necessary as set out in Part 1 of Schedule 4 to the Police Reform Act 2002. If the person has been lawfully detained, the CSO may search the person provided that person gives consent to such a search in relation to the following:

Designation	Powers conferred	Object of search	Extent of search	Where exercisable
1. Police Reform Act 2002, Schedule 4, paragraph 15	Terrorism Act 2000, s44(1)(a) and (d) and 45(2); (See *paragraph* *2.18A*)	Items intended to be used in connection with terrorism.	a) Vehicles or anything carried in or on the vehicle	Anywhere within area of locality authorised and in the company and under the supervision of a constable.

2.   Powers to search requiring the consent of the person and seizure

A CSO may detain a person using reasonable force where necessary as set out in Part 1 of Schedule 4 to the Police Reform Act 2002. If the person has been lawfully detained, the CSO may search the person provided that person gives consent to such a search in relation to the following:

Designation	Powers conferred	Object of search	Extent of search	Where exercisable
1. Police Reform Act 2002, Schedule 4, paragraph 7A	(a) Criminal Justice and Police Act 2001, s12(2)	(a) Alcohol or a container for alcohol	(a) Persons	(a) Designated public place
				(b) Public place
	(b) Confiscation of Alcohol (Young Persons) Act 1997, s1	(b) Alcohol	(b) Persons under 18 years old	
	(c) Children and Young Persons Act 1933, section 7(3)	(c) Tobacco or cigarette papers	(c) Persons under 16 years old found smoking	(c) Public place

3.   Powers to search not requiring the consent of the person and seizure

A CSO may detain a person using reasonable force where necessary as set out in Part 1 of Schedule 4 to the Police Reform Act 2002. If the person has been lawfully detained, the CSO may search the person without the need for that person's consent in relation to the following:

Designation	Powers conferred	Object of search	Extent of search	Where exercisable
Police Reform Act 2002, Schedule 4, paragraph 2A	Police and Criminal Evidence Act 1984, s.32	a) Objects that might be used to cause physical injury to the person or the CSO.	Persons made subject to a requirement to wait.	Any place where the requirement to wait has been made.
		b) Items that might be used to assist escape.		

4.   Powers to seize without consent

This power applies when drugs are found in the course of any search mentioned above.

Designation	Powers conferred	Object of seizure	Where exercisable
Police Reform Act 2002, Schedule 4, paragraph 7B	*Police Reform Act 2002, Schedule 4, paragraph 7B*	Controlled drugs in a person's possession.	Any place where the person is in possession of the drug.

ANNEX D – Deleted.

ANNEX E – Deleted.

ANNEX F   ESTABLISHING GENDER OF PERSONS FOR THE PURPOSE OF SEARCHING

1.   Certain provisions of this and other Codes explicitly state that searches and other procedures may only be carried out by, or in the presence of, persons of the same sex as the person subject to the search or other procedure. (See paragraphs 2.8 and 3.6 and Note 4 of this Code, Code C paragraph 4.1 and Annex A paragraphs 5,

6, 11 and 12 (searches, strip and intimate searches of detainees under sections 54 and 55 of PACE), Code D paragraph 5.5 and Note 5F (searches, examinations and photographing of detainees under section 54A of PACE) and 6.9 (taking samples) and Code H paragraph 4.1 and Annex A paragraphs 6, 7 and 12 (searches, strip and intimate searches under sections 54 and 55 of PACE and 43(2) of the Terrorism Act of persons arrested under section 41 of the Terrorism Act 2000).

2.   All searches should be carried out with courtesy, consideration and respect for the person concerned. Police officers should show particular sensitivity when dealing with transsexual or transvestite persons (see Notes F1 and F2). The following approach is designed to minimise embarrassment and secure the co-operation of the person subject to the search.

(a)   Consideration

3.   At law, the gender of an individual is their gender as registered at birth unless they possess a gender recognition certificate as issued under section 9 of the Gender Recognition Act 2004, in which case the person's gender is the acquired gender.

(a)   If there is no doubt as to the sex of a person, or there is no reason to suspect that the person is not the sex that they appear to be, they should be dealt with as that sex.

(b)   A person who possesses a gender recognition certificate must be treated as their acquired gender.

(c)   If the police are not satisfied that the person possesses a gender recognition certificate and there is doubt as to a person's gender, the person should be asked what gender they consider themselves to be. If the person expresses a preference to be dealt with as a particular gender, they should be asked to sign the search record, the officer's notebook or, if applicable, their custody record, to indicate and confirm their preference. If appropriate, the person should be treated as being that gender.

(d)   If a person is unwilling to make such an election, efforts should be made to determine the predominant lifestyle of the person. For example, if they appear to live predominantly as a woman, they should be treated as such.

(e)   If there is still doubt, the person should be dealt with according to the sex that they were born.

5.   Once a decision has been made about which gender an individual is to be treated as, where possible before an officer searches that person, the officer should be advised of the doubt as to the person's gender. This is important so as to maintain the dignity of the officer(s) concerned.

(b)   Documentation

6.   Where the gender of the detainee is established under paragraphs 2(b) to (e) above the decision should be recorded either on the search record, in the officer's notebook or, if applicable, in the person's custody record.

7.   Where the person elects which gender they consider themselves to be under paragraph 2(c) but is not treated as their elected gender, the reason must be recorded in the search record, in the officer's notebook or, if applicable, in the person's custody record..

Note for Guidance

F1   Transsexual means a person who is proposing to undergo, is undergoing or has undergone a process (or part of a process) for the purpose of gender reassignment which is a protected characteristic under the Equality Act 2010 (see paragraph 1.1) by changing physiological or other attributes of their sex. It would apply to a woman making the transition to being a man and a man making the transition to being a woman as well as to a person who has only just started out on the process of gender reassignment and to a person who has completed the process. Both would share the characteristic of gender reassignment with each having the characteristics of one sex, but with certain characteristics of the other sex.

F2   Transvestite means a person of one gender who dresses in the clothes of a person of the opposite gender.

F3   Similar principles will apply to police officers and police staff whose duties involve carrying out, or being present at, any of the searches and other procedures mentioned in paragraph 1. Chief officers are responsible for providing corresponding operational guidance and instructions for the deployment of any transsexual officers and staff under their direction and control.

Codes of Practice - Code B Searching premises and seizing property

1   Introduction

1.1   This Code of Practice deals with police powers to:

* search premises

* seize and retain property found on premises and persons

1.1A   These powers may be used to find:

* property and material relating to a crime

* wanted persons

* children who abscond from local authority accommodation where they have been remanded or committed by a court

1.2   A justice of the peace may issue a search warrant granting powers of entry, search and seizure, e.g. warrants to search for stolen property, drugs, firearms and evidence of serious offences. Police also have powers without a search warrant. The main ones provided by the Police and Criminal Evidence Act 1984 (PACE) include powers to search premises:

* to make an arrest

* after an arrest

1.3   The right to privacy and respect for personal property are key principles of the Human Rights Act 1998. Powers of entry, search and seizure should be fully and clearly justified before use because they may significantly interfere with the occupier's privacy. Officers should consider if the necessary objectives can be met by less intrusive means.

1.3A   Powers to search and seize must be used fairly, responsibly, with respect for people who occupy premises being searched or are in charge of property being seized and without unlawful discrimination. The Equality Act 2010 makes it unlawful for police officers to discriminate against, harass or victimise any person on the grounds of the 'protected characteristics' of age, disability, gender reassignment, race, religion or belief, sex and sexual orientation, marriage and civil partnership, pregnancy and maternity when using their powers. When police forces are carrying out their functions they also have a duty to have regard to the need to eliminate unlawful discrimination, harassment and victimisation and to take steps to foster good relations.

1.4   In all cases, police should therefore:

* exercise their powers courteously and with respect for persons and property

* only use reasonable force when this is considered necessary and proportionate to the circumstances

1.5   If the provisions of PACE and this Code are not observed, evidence obtained from a search may be open to question.

2   General

2.1   This Code must be readily available at all police stations for consultation by:

• police officers

• police staff

• detained persons

• members of the public

2.2   The Notes for Guidance included are not provisions of this Code.

2.3   This Code applies to searches of premises:

(a) by police for the purposes of an investigation into an alleged offence, with the occupier's consent, other than:

• routine scene of crime searches;

•   calls to a fire or burglary made by or on behalf of an occupier or searches following the activation of fire or burglar alarms or discovery of insecure premises;

• searches when paragraph 5.4 applies;

• bomb threat calls;

(b) under powers conferred on police officers by PACE, sections 17, 18 and 32;

(c) undertaken in pursuance of search warrants issued to and executed by constables in accordance with PACE, sections 15 and 16. See Note 2A;

(d) subject to paragraph 2.6, under any other power given to police to enter premises with or without a search warrant for any purpose connected with the investigation into an alleged or suspected offence. See Note 2B.

For the purposes of this Code, 'premises' as defined in PACE, section 23, includes any place, vehicle, vessel, aircraft, hovercraft, tent or movable structure and any offshore installation as defined in the Mineral Workings (Offshore Installations) Act 1971, section 1. See Note 2D

2.4   A person who has not been arrested but is searched during a search of premises should be searched in accordance with Code A. See Note 2C

2.5   This Code does not apply to the exercise of a statutory power to enter premises or to inspect goods, equipment or procedures if the exercise of that power is not dependent on the existence of grounds for suspecting that an offence may have been committed and the person exercising the power has no reasonable grounds for such suspicion.

2.6   This Code does not affect any directions or requirements of a search warrant, order or other power to search and seize lawfully exercised in England or Wales that any item or evidence seized under that warrant, order or power be handed over to a police force, court, tribunal, or other authority outside England or Wales. For example, warrants and orders issued in Scotland or Northern Ireland, see Note 2B(f) and search warrants and powers provided for in sections 14 to 17 of the Crime (International Co-operation) Act 2003.

2.7   When this Code requires the prior authority or agreement of an officer of at least inspector or superintendent rank, that authority may be given by a sergeant or chief inspector authorised to perform the functions of the higher rank under PACE, section 107.

2.8   Written records required under this Code not made in the search record shall, unless otherwise specified, be made:

• in the recording officer's pocket book ('pocket book' includes any official report book issued to police officers) or

• on forms provided for the purpose

2.9   Nothing in this Code requires the identity of officers, or anyone accompanying them during a search of premises, to be recorded or disclosed:

(a) in the case of enquiries linked to the investigation of terrorism; or

(b) if officers reasonably believe recording or disclosing their names might put them in danger.

In these cases officers should use warrant or other identification numbers and the name of their police station. Police staff should use any identification number provided to them by the police force. See Note 2E

2.10   The 'officer in charge of the search' means the officer assigned specific duties and responsibilities under this Code. Whenever there is a search of premises to which this Code applies one officer must act as the officer in charge of the search. See Note 2F

2.11   In this Code:

(a) 'designated person' means a person other than a police officer, designated under the Police Reform Act 2002, Part 4 who has specified powers and duties of police officers conferred or imposed on them. See Note 2G.

(b) any reference to a police officer includes a designated person acting in the exercise or performance of the powers and duties conferred or imposed on them by their designation.

(c) a person authorised to accompany police officers or designated persons in the execution of a warrant has the same powers as a constable in the execution of the warrant and the search and seizure of anything related to the warrant. These powers must be exercised in the company and under the supervision of a police officer. See Note 3C.

2.12   If a power conferred on a designated person:

(a) allows reasonable force to be used when exercised by a police officer, a designated person exercising that power has the same entitlement to use force;

(b) includes power to use force to enter any premises, that power is not exercisable by that designated person except:

(i) in the company and under the supervision of a police officer; or

(ii) for the purpose of:

• saving life or limb; or

• preventing serious damage to property.

2.13   Designated persons must have regard to any relevant provisions of the Codes of Practice.

Notes for guidance

2A   PACE sections 15 and 16 apply to all search warrants issued to and executed by constables under any enactment, e.g. search warrants issued by a:

(a) justice of the peace under the:

•   Theft Act 1968, section 26 - stolen property;

•   Misuse of Drugs Act 1971, section 23 - controlled drugs;

•   PACE, section 8 - evidence of an indictable offence;

•   Terrorism Act 2000, Schedule 5, paragraph 1;

•   Prevention of Terrorism Act 2005, section 7C – monitoring compliance with control order (see paragraph 10.1).

(b) Circuit judge under:

•   PACE, Schedule 1;

•   Terrorism Act 2000, Schedule 5, paragraph 11.

2B   Examples of the other powers in paragraph 2.3(d) include:

(a) Road Traffic Act 1988, section 6E(1) giving police power to enter premises under section 6E(1) to:

•   require a person to provide a specimen of breath; or

•   arrest a person following:

~a positive breath test;

~ failure to provide a specimen of breath;

(b) Transport and Works Act 1992, section 30(4) giving police powers to enter premises mirroring the powers in (a) in relation to specified persons working on transport systems to which the Act applies;

(c) Criminal Justice Act 1988, section 139B giving police power to enter and search school premises for offensive weapons, bladed or pointed articles;

(d) Terrorism Act 2000, Schedule 5, paragraphs 3 and 15 empowering a superintendent in urgent cases to give written authority for police to enter and search premises for the purposes of a terrorist investigation;

(e) Explosives Act 1875, section 73(b) empowering a superintendent to give written authority for police to enter premises, examine and search them for explosives;

(f) search warrants and production orders or the equivalent issued in Scotland or Northern Ireland endorsed under the Summary Jurisdiction (Process) Act 1881 or the Petty Sessions (Ireland) Act 1851 respectively for execution in England and Wales.

(g) Sections 7A and 7B of the Prevention of Terrorism Act 2005, searches connected with the enforcement of control orders (see paragraph 10.1).

2C   The Criminal Justice Act 1988, section 139B provides that a constable who has reasonable grounds to believe an offence under the Criminal Justice Act 1988, section

139A has or is being committed may enter school premises and search the premises and any persons on the premises for any bladed or pointed article or offensive weapon. Persons may be searched under a warrant issued under the Misuse of Drugs Act 1971, section 23(3) to search premises for drugs or documents only if the warrant specifically authorises the search of persons on the premises. Powers to search premises under certain terrorism provisions also authorise the search of persons on the premises, for example, under paragraphs 1, 2, 11 and 15 of Schedule 5 to the Terrorism Act 2000 and section 52 of the Anti-terrorism, Crime and Security Act 2001.

2D   The Immigration Act 1971, Part III and Schedule 2 gives immigration officers powers to enter and search premises, seize and retain property, with and without a search warrant. These are similar to the powers available to police under search warrants issued by a justice of the peace and without a warrant under PACE, sections 17, 18, 19 and 32 except they only apply to specified offences under the Immigration Act 1971 and immigration control powers. For certain types of investigations and enquiries these powers avoid the need for the Immigration Service to rely on police officers becoming directly involved. When exercising these powers, immigration officers are required by the Immigration and Asylum Act 1999, section 145 to have regard to this Code's corresponding provisions. When immigration officers are dealing with persons or property at police stations, police officers should give appropriate assistance to help them discharge their specific duties and responsibilities.

2E   The purpose of paragraph 2.9(b) is to protect those involved in serious organised crime investigations or arrests of particularly violent suspects when there is reliable information that those arrested or their associates may threaten or cause harm to the officers or anyone accompanying them during a search of premises. In cases of doubt, an officer of inspector rank or above should be consulted.

2F   For the purposes of paragraph 2.10, the officer in charge of the search should normally be the most senior officer present. Some exceptions are:

(a) a supervising officer who attends or assists at the scene of a premises search may appoint an officer of lower rank as officer in charge of the search if that officer is:

- more conversant with the facts;

- a more appropriate officer to be in charge of the search;

(b) when all officers in a premises search are the same rank. The supervising officer if available must make sure one of them is appointed officer in charge of the search, otherwise the officers themselves must nominate one of their number as the officer in charge;

(c) a senior officer assisting in a specialist role. This officer need not be regarded as having a general supervisory role over the conduct of the search or be appointed or expected to act as the officer in charge of the search.

Except in (c), nothing in this Note diminishes the role and responsibilities of a supervisory officer who is present at the search or knows of a search taking place.

2G   An officer of the rank of inspector or above may direct a designated investigating officer not to wear a uniform for the purposes of a specific operation.

3   Search warrants and production orders

(a) Before making an application

3.1   When information appears to justify an application, the officer must take reasonable steps to check the information is accurate, recent and not provided maliciously or irresponsibly. An application may not be made on the basis of information from an anonymous source if corroboration has not been sought. See Note 3A

3.2   The officer shall ascertain as specifically as possible the nature of the articles concerned and their location.

3.3   The officer shall make reasonable enquiries to: (i)   establish if:

- anything is known about the likely occupier of the premises and the nature of

the premises themselves;

- the premises have been searched previously and how recently; (ii) obtain any other relevant information.

3.4   An application:

(a) to a justice of the peace for a search warrant or to a Circuit judge for a search warrant or production order under PACE, Schedule 1 must be supported by a signed written authority from an officer of inspector rank or above:

Note: If the case is an urgent application to a justice of the peace and an inspector or above is not readily available, the next most senior officer on duty can give the written authority.

(b) to a circuit judge under the Terrorism Act 2000, Schedule 5 for

- a production order;

- search warrant; or

- an order requiring an explanation of material seized or produced under such a warrant or production order must be supported by a signed written authority from an officer of superintendent rank or above.

3.5   Except in a case of urgency, if there is reason to believe a search might have an adverse effect on relations between the police and the community, the officer in charge shall consult the local police/community liaison officer:

- before the search; or

- in urgent cases, as soon as practicable after the search

(b) Making an application

3.6   A search warrant application must be supported in writing, specifying: (a) the enactment under which the application is made, see Note 2A; (b) (i) whether the warrant is to authorise entry and search of:

- one set of premises; or

- if the application is under PACE section 8, or Schedule 1, paragraph 12, more than one set of specified premises or all premises occupied or controlled by a specified person, and

(ii) the premises to be searched;

(c) the object of the search, see Note 3B;

(d) the grounds for the application, including, when the purpose of the proposed search is to find evidence of an alleged offence, an indication of how the evidence relates to the investigation;

(da)Where the application is under PACE section 8, or Schedule 1, paragraph 12 for a single warrant to enter and search:

(i)   more than one set of specified premises, the officer must specify each set of premises which it is desired to enter and search

(ii)   all premises occupied or controlled by a specified person, the officer must specify;

- as many sets of premises which it is desired to enter and search as it is reasonably practicable to specify

- the person who is in occupation or control of those premises and any others which it is desired to search

- why it is necessary to search more premises than those which can be specified

- why it is not reasonably practicable to specify all the premises which it is desired to enter and search

(db)Whether an application under PACE section 8 is for a warrant authorising entry and search on more than one occasion, and if so, the officer must state the grounds for this and whether the desired number of entries authorised is unlimited or a specified maximum.

(e) there are no reasonable grounds to believe the material to be sought, when making application to a:

(i) justice of the peace or a Circuit judge consists of or includes items subject to legal privilege;

(ii) justice of the peace, consists of or includes excluded material or special procedure material;

Note: this does not affect the additional powers of seizure in the Criminal Justice and Police Act 2001, Part 2 covered in paragraph 7.7, see Note 3B;

(f) if applicable, a request for the warrant to authorise a person or persons to accompany the officer who executes the warrant, see Note 3C.

3.7   A search warrant application under PACE, Schedule 1, paragraph 12(a), shall if appropriate indicate why it is believed service of notice of an application for a production order may seriously prejudice the investigation. Applications for search warrants under the Terrorism Act 2000, Schedule 5, paragraph 11 must indicate why a production order would not be appropriate.

3.8   If a search warrant application is refused, a further application may not be made for those premises unless supported by additional grounds.

Notes for guidance

3A   The identity of an informant need not be disclosed when making an application, but the officer should be prepared to answer any questions the magistrate or judge may have about:

- the accuracy of previous information from that source

- any other related matters

3B   The information supporting a search warrant application should be as specific as

possible, particularly in relation to the articles or persons being sought and where in the premises it is suspected they may be found. The meaning of 'items subject to legal privilege', 'excluded material' and 'special procedure material' are defined by PACE, sections 10, 11 and 14 respectively.

3C   Under PACE, section 16(2), a search warrant may authorise persons other than police officers to accompany the constable who executes the warrant. This includes, e.g. any suitably qualified or skilled person or an expert in a particular field whose presence is needed to help accurately identify the material sought or to advise where certain evidence is most likely to be found and how it should be dealt with. It does not give them any right to force entry, but it gives them the right to be on the premises during the search and to search for or seize property without the occupier's permission.

4   Entry without warrant - particular powers

(a) Making an arrest etc

4.1   The conditions under which an officer may enter and search premises without a warrant are set out in PACE, section 17. It should be noted that this section does not create or confer any powers of arrest. See other powers in Note 2B(a).

(b) Search of premises where arrest takes place or the arrested person was immediately before arrest

4.2   When a person has been arrested for an indictable offence, a police officer has power under PACE, section 32 to search the premises where the person was arrested or where the person was immediately before being arrested.

(c) Search of premises occupied or controlled by the arrested person

4.3   The specific powers to search premises which are occupied or controlled by a person arrested for an indictable offence are set out in PACE, section 18. They may not be exercised, except if section 18(5) applies, unless an officer of inspector rank or above has given written authority. That authority should only be given when the authorising officer is satisfied that the premises are occupied or controlled by the arrested person and that the necessary grounds exist. If possible the authorising officer should record the authority on the Notice of Powers and Rights and, subject to paragraph 2.9, sign the Notice. The record of the grounds for the search and the nature of the evidence sought as required by section 18(7) of the Act should be made in:

•   the custody record if there is one, otherwise

•   the officer's pocket book, or

•   the search record

5   Search with consent

5.1   Subject to paragraph 5.4, if it is proposed to search premises with the consent of a person entitled to grant entry the consent must, if practicable, be given in writing on the Notice of Powers and Rights before the search. The officer must make any necessary enquiries to be satisfied the person is in a position to give such consent. See Notes 5A and 5B

5.2   Before seeking consent the officer in charge of the search shall state the purpose of the proposed search and its extent. This information must be as specific as possible, particularly regarding the articles or persons being sought and the parts of the premises to be searched. The person concerned must be clearly informed they are not obliged to consent, that any consent given can be withdrawn at any time, including before the search starts or while it is underway and anything seized may be produced in evidence. If at the time the person is not suspected of an offence, the officer shall say this when stating the purpose of the search.

5.3   An officer cannot enter and search or continue to search premises under paragraph 5.1 if consent is given under duress or withdrawn before the search is completed.

5.4   It is unnecessary to seek consent under paragraphs 5.1 and 5.2 if this would cause disproportionate inconvenience to the person concerned. See Note 5C

Notes for guidance

5A   In a lodging house, hostel or similar accommodation, every reasonable effort should be made to obtain the consent of the tenant, lodger or occupier. A search should not be made solely on the basis of the landlord's consent.

5B   If the intention is to search premises under the authority of a warrant or a power of entry and search without warrant, and the occupier of the premises co-operates in accordance with paragraph 6.4, there is no need to obtain written consent.

5C   Paragraph 5.4 is intended to apply when it is reasonable to assume innocent occupiers would agree to, and expect, police to take the proposed action, e.g. if:

•   a suspect has fled the scene of a crime or to evade arrest and it is necessary quickly to check surrounding gardens and readily accessible places to see if the suspect is hiding

•   police have arrested someone in the night after a pursuit and it is necessary to make a brief check of gardens along the pursuit route to see if stolen or incriminating articles have been discarded

6   Searching premises - general considerations

(a) Time of searches

6.1   Searches made under warrant must be made within three calendar months of the date of the warrant's issue.

6.2   Searches must be made at a reasonable hour unless this might frustrate the purpose of the search.

6.3   When the extent or complexity of a search mean it is likely to take a long time, the officer in charge of the search may consider using the seize and sift powers referred to in section 7.

6.3A   A warrant under PACE, section 8 may authorise entry to and search of premises on more than one occasion if, on the application, the justice of the peace is satisfied that it is necessary to authorise multiple entries in order to achieve the purpose for which the warrant is issued. No premises may be entered or searched on any subsequent occasions without the prior written authority of an officer of the rank of inspector who is not involved in the investigation. All other warrants authorise entry on one occasion only.

6.3B   Where a warrant under PACE section 8, or Schedule 1, paragraph 12 authorises entry to and search of all premises occupied or controlled by a specified person, no premises which are not specified in the warrant may be entered and searched without the prior written authority of an officer of the rank of inspector who is not involved in the investigation.

(b) Entry other than with consent

6.4   The officer in charge of the search shall first try to communicate with the occupier, or any other person entitled to grant access to the premises, explain the authority under which entry is sought and ask the occupier to allow entry, unless:

(i) the search premises are unoccupied;

(ii) the occupier and any other person entitled to grant access are absent;

(iii) there are reasonable grounds for believing that alerting the occupier or any other person entitled to grant access would frustrate the object of the search or endanger officers or other people.

6.5   Unless sub-paragraph 6.4(iii) applies, if the premises are occupied the officer, subject to

paragraph 2.9, shall, before the search begins:

(i)   identify him or herself, show their warrant card (if not in uniform) and state the purpose of and grounds for the search;

(ii)   identify and introduce any person accompanying the officer on the search (such persons should carry identification for production on request) and briefly describe that person's role in the process.

6.6   Reasonable and proportionate force may be used if necessary to enter premises if the officer in charge of the search is satisfied the premises are those specified in any warrant, or in exercise of the powers described in paragraphs 4.1 to 4.3, and if:
(i) the occupier or any other person entitled to grant access has refused entry;

(ii) it is impossible to communicate with the occupier or any other person entitled to grant access; or

(iii) any of the provisions of paragraph 6.4 apply.

(c) Notice of Powers and Rights

6.7   If an officer conducts a search to which this Code applies the officer shall, unless it is impracticable to do so, provide the occupier with a copy of a Notice in a standard format:

(i) specifying if the search is made under warrant, with consent, or in the exercise of the powers described in paragraphs 4.1 to 4.3. Note: the notice format shall provide for authority or consent to be indicated, see paragraphs 4.3 and 5.1;

(ii) summarising the extent of the powers of search and seizure conferred by PACE and other relevant legislation as appropriate;

(iii)   explaining the rights of the occupier, and the owner of the property seized;

(iv)   explaining compensation may be payable in appropriate cases for damages caused entering and searching premises, and giving the address to send a compensation application, see Note 6A;

(v)   stating this Code is available at any police station.

6.8   If the occupier is:

• present, copies of the Notice and warrant shall, if practicable, be given to them before the search begins, unless the officer in charge of the search reasonably believes this would frustrate the object of the search or endanger officers or other people

• not present, copies of the Notice and warrant shall be left in a prominent place on the premises or appropriate part of the premises and endorsed, subject to paragraph 2.9 with the name of the officer in charge of the search, the date and time of the search

The warrant shall be endorsed to show this has been done.

(d) Conduct of searches

6.9   Premises may be searched only to the extent necessary to achieve the purpose of the search, having regard to the size and nature of whatever is sought.

6.9A   A search may not continue under:

• a warrant's authority once all the things specified in that warrant have been found;

• any other power once the object of that search has been achieved.

6.9B   No search may continue once the officer in charge of the search is satisfied whatever is being sought is not on the premises. See Note 6B. This does not prevent a further search of the same premises if additional grounds come to light supporting a further application for a search warrant or exercise or further exercise of another power. For example, when, as a result of new information, it is believed articles previously not found or additional articles are on the premises.

6.10   Searches must be conducted with due consideration for the property and privacy of the occupier and with no more disturbance than necessary. Reasonable force may be used only when necessary and proportionate because the co-operation of the occupier cannot be obtained or is insufficient for the purpose. See Note 6C

6.11   A friend, neighbour or other person must be allowed to witness the search if the occupier wishes unless the officer in charge of the search has reasonable grounds for believing the presence of the person asked for would seriously hinder the investigation or endanger officers or other people. A search need not be unreasonably delayed for this purpose. A record of the action taken should be made on the premises search record including the grounds for refusing the occupier's request.

6.12   A person is not required to be cautioned prior to being asked questions that are solely necessary for the purpose of furthering the proper and effective conduct of a search, see Code C, paragraph 10.1(c). For example, questions to discover the occupier of specified premises, to find a key to open a locked drawer or cupboard or to otherwise seek co- operation during the search or to determine if a particular item is liable to be seized.

6.12A   If questioning goes beyond what is necessary for the purpose of the exemption in Code C, the exchange is likely to constitute an interview as defined by Code C, paragraph 11.1A and would require the associated safeguards included in Code C, section 10.

(e) Leaving premises

6.13   If premises have been entered by force, before leaving the officer in charge of the search must make sure they are secure by:

• arranging for the occupier or their agent to be present

• any other appropriate means

(f) Searches under PACE Schedule 1 or the Terrorism Act 2000, Schedule 5

6.14   An officer shall be appointed as the officer in charge of the search, see paragraph 2.10, in respect of any search made under a warrant issued under PACE Act 1984, Schedule 1 or the Terrorism Act 2000, Schedule 5. They are responsible for making sure the search is conducted with discretion and in a manner that causes the least possible disruption to

any business or other activities carried out on the premises.

6.15   Once the officer in charge of the search is satisfied material may not be taken from the premises without their knowledge, they shall ask for the documents or other records concerned. The officer in charge of the search may also ask to see the index to files held on the premises, and the officers conducting the search may inspect any files which, according to the index, appear to contain the material sought. A more extensive search

of the premises may be made only if:

- the person responsible for them refuses to:

~ produce the material sought, or

~ allow access to the index

- it appears the index is:

~ inaccurate, or

~ incomplete

- for any other reason the officer in charge of the search has reasonable grounds for believing such a search is necessary in order to find the material sought

Notes for guidance

6A   Whether compensation is appropriate depends on the circumstances in each case.

Compensation for damage caused when effecting entry is unlikely to be appropriate if the search was lawful, and the force used can be shown to be reasonable, proportionate and necessary to effect entry. If the wrong premises are searched by mistake everything possible should be done at the earliest opportunity to allay any sense of grievance and there should normally be a strong presumption in favour of paying compensation.

6B   It is important that, when possible, all those involved in a search are fully briefed about any powers to be exercised and the extent and limits within which it should be conducted.

6C   In all cases the number of officers and other persons involved in executing the warrant should be determined by what is reasonable and necessary according to the particular circumstances.

7   Seizure and retention of property

(a) Seizure

7.1   Subject to paragraph 7.2, an officer who is searching any person or premises under any statutory power or with the consent of the occupier may seize anything:

(a) covered by a warrant

(b) the officer has reasonable grounds for believing is evidence of an offence or has been obtained in consequence of the commission of an offence but only if seizure is necessary to prevent the items being concealed, lost, disposed of, altered, damaged, destroyed or tampered with

(c) covered by the powers in the Criminal Justice and Police Act 2001, Part 2 allowing an officer to seize property from persons or premises and retain it for sifting or examination elsewhere See Note 7B

7.2   No item may be seized which an officer has reasonable grounds for believing to be subject to legal privilege, as defined in PACE, section 10, other than under the Criminal Justice and Police Act 2001, Part 2.

7.3   Officers must be aware of the provisions in the Criminal Justice and Police Act 2001, section 59, allowing for applications to a judicial authority for the return of property seized and the subsequent duty to secure in section 60, see paragraph 7.12(iii).

7.4   An officer may decide it is not appropriate to seize property because of an explanation from the person holding it but may nevertheless have reasonable grounds for believing it was obtained in consequence of an offence by some person. In these circumstances, the officer should identify the property to the holder, inform the holder of their suspicions and explain the holder may be liable to civil or criminal proceedings if they dispose of, alter or destroy the property.

7.5   An officer may arrange to photograph, image or copy, any document or other article they have the power to seize in accordance with paragraph 7.1. This is subject to specific restrictions on the examination, imaging or copying of certain property seized under the Criminal Justice and Police Act 2001, Part 2. An officer must have regard to their statutory obligation to retain an original document or other article only when a photograph or copy is not sufficient.

7.6   If an officer considers information stored in any electronic form and accessible from the premises could be used in evidence, they may require the information to be produced in a form:

• which can be taken away and in which it is visible and legible; or

• from which it can readily be produced in a visible and legible form

(b) Criminal Justice and Police Act 2001: Specific procedures for seize and sift powers

7.7   The Criminal Justice and Police Act 2001, Part 2 gives officers limited powers to seize property from premises or persons so they can sift or examine it elsewhere. Officers must be careful they only exercise these powers when it is essential and they do not remove any more material than necessary. The removal of large volumes of material, much of which may not ultimately be retainable, may have serious implications for the owners, particularly when they are involved in business or activities such as journalism or the provision of medical services. Officers must carefully consider if removing copies or images of relevant material or data would be a satisfactory alternative to removing originals. When originals are taken, officers must be prepared to facilitate the provision of copies or images for the owners when reasonably practicable. See Note 7C

7.8   Property seized under the Criminal Justice and Police Act 2001, sections 50 or 51 must be kept securely and separately from any material seized under other powers. An examination under section 53 to determine which elements may be retained must be carried out at the earliest practicable time, having due regard to the desirability of allowing the person from whom the property was seized, or a person with an interest in the property, an opportunity of being present or represented at the examination.

7.8A   All reasonable steps should be taken to accommodate an interested person's request to be present, provided the request is reasonable and subject to the need to prevent harm to, interference with, or unreasonable delay to the investigatory process. If an examination proceeds in the absence of an interested person who asked to attend or

their representative, the officer who exercised the relevant seizure power must give that person a written notice of why the examination was carried out in those circumstances.

If it is necessary for security reasons or to maintain confidentiality officers may exclude interested persons from decryption or other processes which facilitate the examination but do not form part of it. See Note 7D

7.9   It is the responsibility of the officer in charge of the investigation to make sure property is returned in accordance with sections 53 to 55. Material which there is no power to retain must be:

• separated from the rest of the seized property

• returned as soon as reasonably practicable after examination of all the seized property

7.9A   Delay is only warranted if very clear and compelling reasons exist, e.g. the:

• unavailability of the person to whom the material is to be returned

• need to agree a convenient time to return a large volume of material

7.9B   Legally privileged, excluded or special procedure material which cannot be retained must be returned:

• as soon as reasonably practicable

• without waiting for the whole examination

7.9C   As set out in section 58, material must be returned to the person from whom it was seized, except when it is clear some other person has a better right to it. See Note 7E

7.10   When an officer involved in the investigation has reasonable grounds to believe a person with a relevant interest in property seized under section 50 or 51 intends to make an application under section 59 for the return of any legally privileged, special procedure or excluded material, the officer in charge of the investigation should be informed as soon as practicable and the material seized should be kept secure in accordance with section 61. See Note 7C

7.11   The officer in charge of the investigation is responsible for making sure property is properly secured. Securing involves making sure the property is not examined, copied, imaged or put to any other use except at the request, or with the consent, of the applicant or in accordance with the directions of the appropriate judicial authority. Any request, consent or directions must be recorded in writing and signed by both the initiator and the officer in charge of the investigation. See Notes 7F and 7G

7.12   When an officer exercises a power of seizure conferred by sections 50 or 51 they shall provide the occupier of the premises or the person from whom the property is being seized with a written notice:

(i) specifying what has been seized under the powers conferred by that section; (ii) specifying the grounds for those powers;

(iii) setting out the effect of sections 59 to 61 covering the grounds for a person with a relevant interest in seized property to apply to a judicial authority for its return and the duty of officers to secure property in certain circumstances when an application is made;

(iv) specifying the name and address of the person to whom:

•   notice of an application to the appropriate judicial authority in respect of any of the seized property must be given;

•   an application may be made to allow attendance at the initial examination of the property.

7.13   If the occupier is not present but there is someone in charge of the premises, the notice shall be given to them. If no suitable person is available, so the notice will easily be found it should either be:

• left in a prominent place on the premises

• attached to the exterior of the premises

(c) Retention

7.14   Subject to paragraph 7.15, anything seized in accordance with the above provisions may be retained only for as long as is necessary. It may be retained, among other purposes:

(i) for use as evidence at a trial for an offence;

(ii) to facilitate the use in any investigation or proceedings of anything to which it is inextricably linked, see Note 7H;

(iii) for forensic examination or other investigation in connection with an offence;

(iv) in order to establish its lawful owner when there are reasonable grounds for believing it has been stolen or obtained by the commission of an offence.

7.15   Property shall not be retained under paragraph 7.14(i), (ii) or (iii) if a copy or image would be sufficient.

(d) Rights of owners etc

7.16   If property is retained, the person who had custody or control of it immediately before seizure must, on request, be provided with a list or description of the property within a reasonable time.

7.17   That person or their representative must be allowed supervised access to the property to examine it or have it photographed or copied, or must be provided with a photograph or copy, in either case within a reasonable time of any request and at their own expense, unless the officer in charge of an investigation has reasonable grounds for believing this would:

(i) prejudice the investigation of any offence or criminal proceedings; or

(ii) lead to the commission of an offence by providing access to unlawful material such as pornography;

A record of the grounds shall be made when access is denied.

Notes for guidance

7A   Any person claiming property seized by the police may apply to a magistrates' court under the Police (Property) Act 1897 for its possession and should, if appropriate, be advised of this procedure.

7B   The powers of seizure conferred by PACE, sections 18(2) and 19(3) extend to the seizure of the whole premises when it is physically possible to seize and retain the premises in their totality and practical considerations make seizure desirable. For example, police may remove premises such as tents, vehicles or caravans to a police station for the purpose of preserving evidence.

7C   Officers should consider reaching agreement with owners and/or other interested parties on the procedures for examining a specific set of property, rather than awaiting the judicial authority's determination. Agreement can sometimes give a quicker and more satisfactory route for all concerned and minimise costs and legal complexities.

7D   What constitutes a relevant interest in specific material may depend on the nature of that material and the circumstances in which it is seized. Anyone with a reasonable claim to ownership of the material and anyone entrusted with its safe keeping by the owner should be considered.

7E   Requirements to secure and return property apply equally to all copies, images or other material created because of seizure of the original property.

7F   The mechanics of securing property vary according to the circumstances; "bagging up", i.e. placing material in sealed bags or containers and strict subsequent control of access is the appropriate procedure in many cases.

7G   When material is seized under the powers of seizure conferred by PACE, the duty to retain it under the Code of Practice issued under the Criminal Procedure and Investigations Act 1996 is subject to the provisions on retention of seized material in PACE, section 22.

7H   Paragraph 7.14 (ii) applies if inextricably linked material is seized under the Criminal Justice and Police Act 2001, sections 50 or 51. Inextricably linked material is material it is not reasonably practicable to separate from other linked material without prejudicing the use of that other material in any investigation or proceedings. For example, it may not be possible to separate items of data held on computer disk without damaging their evidential integrity. Inextricably linked material must not be examined, imaged, copied or used for any purpose other than for proving the source and/or integrity of the linked material.

8   Action after searches

8.1   If premises are searched in circumstances where this Code applies, unless the exceptions in paragraph 2.3(a) apply, on arrival at a police station the officer in charge of the search shall make or have made a record of the search, to include:

(i)   the address of the searched premises;

(ii)   the date, time and duration of the search; (iii)   the authority used for the search:

•   if the search was made in exercise of a statutory power to search premises without warrant, the power which was used for the search:

•   if the search was made under a warrant or with written consent;

~ a copy of the warrant and the written authority to apply for it, see paragraph

3.4; or

~ the written consent;

shall be appended to the record or the record shall show the location of the copy warrant or consent.

(iv)   subject to paragraph 2.9, the names of:

•   the officer(s) in charge of the search;

•   all other officers and authorised persons who conducted the search; (v)   the names of any people on the premises if they are known;

(vi)   any grounds for refusing the occupier's request to have someone present during the search, see paragraph 6.11;

(vii) a list of any articles seized or the location of a list and, if not covered by a warrant, the grounds for their seizure;

(viii) whether force was used, and the reason;

(ix)   details of any damage caused during the search, and the circumstances; (x)   if   applicable, the reason it was not practicable;

(a) to give the occupier a copy of the Notice of Powers and Rights, see paragraph 6.7;

(b) before the search to give the occupier a copy of the Notice, see paragraph 6.8;

(xi)   when the occupier was not present, the place where copies of the Notice of Powers and Rights and search warrant were left on the premises, see paragraph 6.8.

8.2   On each occasion when premises are searched under warrant, the warrant authorising the search on that occasion shall be endorsed to show:

(i) if any articles specified in the warrant were found and the address where found; (ii) if any other articles were seized;

(iii) the date and time it was executed and if present, the name of the occupier or if the occupier is not present the name of the person in charge of the premises;

(iv) subject to paragraph 2.9, the names of the officers who executed it and any authorised persons who accompanied them;

(v) if a copy, together with a copy of the Notice of Powers and Rights was:

• handed to the occupier; or

• endorsed as required by paragraph 6.8; and left on the premises and where.

8.3   Any warrant shall be returned within three calendar months of its issue or sooner on completion of the search(es) authorised by that warrant, if it was issued by a:

• justice of the peace, to the designated officer for the local justice area in which the justice was acting when issuing the warrant; or

• judge, to the appropriate officer of the court concerned,

9   Search registers

9.1   A search register will be maintained at each sub-divisional or equivalent police station.

All search records required under paragraph 8.1 shall be made, copied, or referred to in the register. See Note 9A

Note for guidance

9A   Paragraph 9.1 also applies to search records made by immigration officers. In these cases, a search register must also be maintained at an immigration office. See also Note 2D

10   Searches under sections 7A, 7B and 7C of the Prevention of Terrorism Act 2005 in connection with control orders

10.1   This Code applies to the powers under sections 7A, 7B and 7C of the Prevention of Terrorism Act 2005 to enter and search premises subject to the modifications in the following paragraphs.

10.2   In paragraph 2.3(d), the reference to the investigation into an alleged or suspected offence include the enforcement of obligations imposed by or under a control order made under the Prevention of Terrorism Act 2005.

10.3   References to the purpose and object of the search, the nature of articles sought and what may be seized and retained include (as appropriate):

• in relation section 7A (absconding), determining whether the controlled person has absconded and if it appears so, any material or information that may assist in the pursuit and arrest of the controlled person.

• in relation to section 7B (failure to grant access to premises), determining whether any control order obligations have been contravened and if it appears so, any material or information that may assist in determining whether the controlled person is complying with the obligations imposed by the control order or in investigating any apparent contravention of those obligations.

• in relation to section 7C (monitoring compliance), determining whether the controlled person is complying with their control order obligations, and any material that may assist in that determination.

• evidence in relation to an offence under section 9 of the Prevention of Terrorism Act 2005 (offences relating to control orders).

Codes of Practice – Code C Detention, treatment and questioning of persons by police officers

1 **General**

1.1   All persons in custody must be dealt with expeditiously, and released as soon as the need for detention no longer applies.

1.1A   A custody officer must perform the functions in this Code as soon as practicable. A custody officer will not be in breach of this Code if delay is justifiable and reasonable steps are taken to prevent unnecessary delay. The custody record shall show when a delay has occurred and the reason. See Note 1H

1.2   This Code of Practice must be readily available at all police stations for consultation by:

•   police officers

•   police staff

•   detained persons

•   members of the public.

1.3   The provisions of this Code:

•   include the Annexes

•   do not include the Notes for Guidance.

1.4   If an officer has any suspicion, or is told in good faith, that a person of any age may be mentally disordered or otherwise mentally vulnerable, in the absence of clear evidence to dispel that suspicion, the person shall be treated as such for the purposes of this Code. See Note 1G

1.5   If anyone appears to be under 17, they shall be treated as a juvenile for the purposes of this Code in the absence of clear evidence that they are older.

1.6   If a person appears to be blind, seriously visually impaired, deaf, unable to read or speak or has difficulty orally because of a speech impediment, they shall be treated as such for the purposes of this Code in the absence of clear evidence to the contrary.

1.7   'The appropriate adult' means, in the case of a:

(a)   juvenile:

(i)   the parent, guardian or, if the juvenile is in local authority or voluntary organisation care, or is otherwise being looked after under the Children Act 1989, a person representing that authority or organisation;

(ii)   a social worker of a local authority;

(iii)   failing these, some other responsible adult aged 18 or over who is not a police officer or employed by the police.

(b)   person who is mentally disordered or mentally vulnerable: See Note 1D

(iv)   a relative, guardian or other person responsible for their care or custody;

(v)   someone experienced in dealing with mentally disordered or mentally vulnerable people but who is not a police officer or employed by the police;

(vi)   failing these, some other responsible adult aged 18 or over who is not a police officer or employed by the police.

1.8   If this Code requires a person be given certain information, they do not have to be given it if at the time they are incapable of understanding what is said, are violent or may become violent or in urgent need of medical attention, but they must be given it as soon as practicable.

1.9   References to a custody officer include any:-

•   police officer; or

•   designated staff custody officer acting in the exercise or performance of the

powers and duties conferred or imposed on them by their designation, performing the functions of a custody officer. See Note 1J.

1.9A   When this Code requires the prior authority or agreement of an officer of at least inspector or superintendent rank, that authority may be given by a sergeant or chief inspector authorised to perform the functions of the higher rank under the Police and Criminal Evidence Act 1984 (PACE), section 107.

1.10   Subject to paragraph 1.12, this Code applies to people in custody at police stations in England and Wales, whether or not they have been arrested, and to those removed to a police station as a place of safety under the Mental Health Act 1983, sections 135 and 136. Section 15 applies solely to people in police detention, e.g. those brought to a police station under arrest or arrested at a police station for an offence after going there voluntarily.

1.11   People detained under the Terrorism Act 2000, Schedule 8 and section 41 and other provisions of that Act are not subject to any part of this Code. Such persons are subject to the Code of Practice for detention, treatment and questioning of persons by police officers detained under that Act.

1.12   This Code's provisions do not apply to people in custody:

(i)   arrested on warrants issued in Scotland by officers under the Criminal Justice and Public Order Act 1994, section 136(2), or arrested or detained without warrant by officers from a police force in Scotland under section 137(2). In these cases, police powers and duties and the person's rights and entitlements whilst at a police station in England or Wales are the same as those in Scotland;

(ii)   arrested under the Immigration and Asylum Act 1999, section 142(3) in order to have their fingerprints taken;

(iii)   whose detention is authorised by an immigration officer under the Immigration

Act 1971;

(iv)   who are convicted or remanded prisoners held in police cells on behalf of the

Prison Service under the Imprisonment (Temporary Provisions) Act 1980;

(v)   not used

(vi)   detained for searches under stop and search powers except as required by Code A.

The provisions on conditions of detention and treatment in sections 8 and 9 must be considered as the minimum standards of treatment for such detainees.

1.13   In this Code:

(a)   'designated person' means a person other than a police officer, designated under the Police Reform Act 2002, Part 4 who has specified powers and duties of police officers conferred or imposed on them;

(b)   reference to a police officer includes a designated person acting in the exercise or performance of the powers and duties conferred or imposed on them by their designation.

1.14   Designated persons are entitled to use reasonable force as follows:-

(a)   when exercising a power conferred on them which allows a police officer exercising that power to use reasonable force, a designated person has the same entitlement to use force; and

(b)   at other times when carrying out duties conferred or imposed on them that also entitle them to use reasonable force, for example:

•   when at a police station carrying out the duty to keep detainees for whom they

are responsible under control and to assist any other police officer or designated person to keep any detainee under control and to prevent their escape.

•   when securing, or assisting any other police officer or designated person in

securing, the detention of a person at a police station.

•   when escorting, or assisting any other police officer or designated person in

escorting, a detainee within a police station.

•   for the purpose of saving life or limb; or

•   preventing serious damage to property.

1.15   Nothing in this Code prevents the custody officer, or other officer given custody of the detainee, from allowing police staff who are not designated persons to carry out individual procedures or tasks at the police station if the law allows. However, the officer remains responsible for making sure the procedures and tasks are carried out correctly in accordance with the Codes of Practice. Any such person must be:

(a)   a person employed by a police authority maintaining a police force and under the control and direction of the Chief Officer of that force;

(b)   employed by a person with whom a police authority has a contract for the provision of services relating to persons arrested or otherwise in custody.

1.16 Designated persons and other police staff must have regard to any relevant provisions of the Codes of Practice.

1.17 References to pocket books include any official report book issued to police officers or other police staff.

Notes for guidance

1A   Although certain sections of this Code apply specifically to people in custody at police stations, those there voluntarily to assist with an investigation should be treated with no less consideration, e.g. offered refreshments at appropriate times, and enjoy an absolute right to obtain legal advice or communicate with anyone outside the police station.

1B   A person, including a parent or guardian, should not be an appropriate adult if they:

•   are

–   suspected of involvement in the offence

–   the victim

–   a witness

–   involved in the investigation

•   received admissions prior to attending to act as the appropriate adult.

Note: If a juvenile's parent is estranged from the juvenile, they should not be asked to act as the appropriate adult if the juvenile expressly and specifically objects to their presence.

1C   If a juvenile admits an offence to, or in the presence of, a social worker or member of a youth offending team other than during the time that person is acting as the juvenile's appropriate adult, another appropriate adult should be appointed in the interest of fairness.

1D   In the case of people who are mentally disordered or otherwise mentally vulnerable, it may be more satisfactory if the appropriate adult is someone experienced or trained in their care rather than a relative lacking such qualifications. But if the detainee prefers a relative to a better qualified stranger or objects to a particular person their wishes should, if practicable, be respected.

1E   A detainee should always be given an opportunity, when an appropriate adult is called to the police station, to consult privately with a solicitor in the appropriate adult's absence if they want. An appropriate adult is not subject to legal privilege.

1F   A solicitor or independent custody visitor (formerly a lay visitor) present at the police station in that capacity may not be the appropriate adult.

1G   'Mentally vulnerable' applies to any detainee who, because of their mental state or capacity, may not understand the significance of what is said, of questions or of their replies. 'Mental disorder' is defined in the Mental Health Act 1983, section 1(2) as

'mental illness, arrested or incomplete development of mind, psychopathic disorder and any other disorder or disability of mind'. When the custody officer has any doubt about the mental state or capacity of a detainee, that detainee should be treated as mentally vulnerable and an appropriate adult called.

1H   Paragraph 1.1A is intended to cover delays which may occur in processing detainees e.g. if:

•   a large number of suspects are brought into the station simultaneously to be

placed in custody;

•   interview rooms are all being used;

•   there are difficulties contacting an appropriate adult, solicitor or interpreter.

1I   The custody officer must remind the appropriate adult and detainee about the right to

legal advice and record any reasons for waiving it in accordance with section 6.

1J   The designation of police staff custody officers applies only in police areas where an order commencing the provisions of the Police Reform Act 2002, section 38 and Schedule 4A, for designating police staff custody officers is in effect.

1K   This Code does not affect the principle that all citizens have a duty to help police officers to prevent crime and discover offenders. This is a civic rather than a legal duty; but when a police officer is trying to discover whether, or by whom, an offence has been committed he is entitled to question any person from whom he thinks useful information can be obtained, subject to the restrictions imposed by this Code. A person's declaration that he is unwilling to reply does not alter this entitlement.

2   Custody records

2.1A When a person is brought to a police station:

•   under arrest

•   is arrested at the police station having attended there voluntarily or

•   attends a police station to answer bail

they should be brought before the custody officer as soon as practicable after their arrival at the station or, if appropriate, following arrest after attending the police station voluntarily. This applies to designated and non-designated police stations. A person is deemed to be "at a police station" for these purposes if they are within the boundary of any building or enclosed yard which forms part of that police station.

2.1   A separate custody record must be opened as soon as practicable for each person brought to a police station under arrest or arrested at the station having gone there voluntarily or attending a police station in answer to street bail. All information recorded under this Code must be recorded as soon as practicable in the custody record unless otherwise specified. Any audio or video recording made in the custody area is not part of the custody record.

2.2   If any action requires the authority of an officer of a specified rank, subject to paragraph

2.6A, their name and rank must be noted in the custody record.

2.3   The custody officer is responsible for the custody record's accuracy and completeness and for making sure the record or copy of the record accompanies a detainee if they are transferred to another police station. The record shall show the:

•   time and reason for transfer;

•   time a person is released from detention.

2.4   A solicitor or appropriate adult must be permitted to consult a detainee's custody record as soon as practicable after their arrival at the station and at any other time whilst the person is detained. Arrangements for this access must be agreed with the custody officer and may not unreasonably interfere with the custody officer's duties.

2.4A   When a detainee leaves police detention or is taken before a   court they, their legal representative or appropriate adult shall be given, on request, a copy of the custody record as soon as practicable. This entitlement lasts for 12 months after release.

2.5   The detainee, appropriate adult or legal representative shall be permitted to inspect the original custody record after the detainee has left police detention provided they give reasonable notice of their request. Any such inspection shall be noted in the custody record.

2.6   Subject to paragraph 2.6A, all entries in custody records must be timed and signed by the maker. Records entered on computer shall be timed and contain the operator's identification.

2.6A   Nothing in this Code requires the identity of officers or other police staff to be recorded or disclosed:

(a)   not used;

(b)   if the officer or police staff reasonably believe recording or disclosing their name might put them in danger.

In these cases, they shall use their warrant or other identification numbers and the name of their police station. See Note 2A

2.7   The fact and time of any detainee's refusal to sign a custody record, when asked in accordance with this Code, must be recorded.

Note for guidance

2A   The purpose of paragraph 2.6A(b) is to protect those involved in serious organised crime investigations or arrests of particularly violent suspects when there is reliable information that those arrested or their associates may threaten or cause harm to those involved. In cases of doubt, an officer of inspector rank or above should be consulted.

3   Initial action

(a)   Detained persons – normal procedure

3.1   When a person is brought to a police station under arrest or arrested at the station having gone there voluntarily, the custody officer must make sure the person is told clearly about the following continuing rights which may be exercised at any stage during the period in custody:

(i)   the right to have someone informed of their arrest as in section 5;

(ii)   the right to consult privately with a solicitor and that free independent legal advice is available;

(iii)   the right to consult these Codes of Practice. See Note 3D

3.2   The detainee must also be given:

•   a written notice setting out:

–   the above three rights;

–   the arrangements for obtaining legal advice;

–   the right to a copy of the custody record as in paragraph 2.4A;

–   the caution in the terms prescribed in section 10.

•   an additional written notice briefly setting out their entitlements while in custody,

see Notes 3A and 3B.

Note: The detainee shall be asked to sign the custody record to acknowledge receipt of these notices. Any refusal must be recorded on the custody record.

3.3   A citizen of an independent Commonwealth country or a national of a foreign country, including the Republic of Ireland, must be informed as soon as practicable about their rights of communication with their High Commission, Embassy or Consulate. See section 7

3.4   The custody officer shall:

•   record the offence(s) that the detainee has been arrested for and the reason(s) for

the arrest on the custody record. See paragraph 10.3 and Code G paragraphs 2.2 and 4.3.

•   note on the custody record any comment the detainee makes in relation to the arresting officer's account but shall not invite comment. If the arresting officer is not physically present when the detainee is brought to a police station, the arresting officer's account must be made available to the custody officer remotely or by a third party on the arresting officer's behalf. If the custody officer authorises a person's detention the detainee must be informed of the grounds as soon as practicable and before they are questioned about any offence;

• note any comment the detainee makes in respect of the decision to detain them but shall not invite comment;

• not put specific questions to the detainee regarding their involvement in any offence, nor in respect of any comments they may make in response to the arresting officer's account or the decision to place them in detention. Such an exchange is likely to constitute an interview as in paragraph 11.1A and require the associated safeguards in section 11.

See paragraph 11.13 in respect of unsolicited comments.

3.5   The custody officer shall:

(a)   ask the detainee, whether at this time, they:

(i)   would like legal advice, see paragraph 6.5;

(iii)   want someone informed of their detention, see section 5;

(b)   ask the detainee to sign the custody record to confirm their decisions in respect of (a);

(c)   determine whether the detainee:

(iii)   is, or might be, in need of medical treatment or attention, see section 9; (iv) requires:

•   an appropriate adult;

•   help to check documentation;

•   an interpreter;

(d)   record the decision in respect of (c).

3.6   When determining these needs the custody officer is responsible for initiating an assessment to consider whether the detainee is likely to present specific risks to custody staff or themselves. Such assessments should always include a check on the Police National Computer, to be carried out as soon as practicable, to identify any risks highlighted in relation to the detainee. Although such assessments are primarily the custody officer's responsibility, it may be necessary for them to consult and involve others,

e.g. the arresting officer or an appropriate health care professional, see paragraph 9.13. Reasons for delaying the initiation or completion of the assessment must be recorded.

3.7   Chief Officers should ensure that arrangements for proper and effective risk assessments required by paragraph 3.6 are implemented in respect of all detainees at police stations in their area.

3.8   Risk assessments must follow a structured process which clearly defines the categories of risk to be considered and the results must be incorporated in the detainee's custody record. The custody officer is responsible for making sure those responsible for the detainee's custody are appropriately briefed about the risks. If no specific risks are identified by the assessment, that should be noted in the custody record. See Note 3E and paragraph 9.14

3.9   The custody officer is responsible for implementing the response to any specific risk assessment, e.g.:

- reducing opportunities for self harm;

- calling a health care professional;

- increasing levels of monitoring or observation.

3.10   Risk assessment is an ongoing process and assessments must always be subject to review if circumstances change.

3.11   If video cameras are installed in the custody area, notices shall be prominently displayed showing cameras are in use. Any request to have video cameras switched off shall be refused.

(b)   Detained persons – special groups

3.12   If the detainee appears deaf or there is doubt about their hearing or speaking ability or ability to understand English, and the custody officer cannot establish effective communication, the custody officer must, as soon as practicable, call an interpreter for assistance in the action under paragraphs 3.1–3.5. See section 13

3.13   If the detainee is a juvenile, the custody officer must, if it is practicable, ascertain the identity of a person responsible for their welfare. That person:

- may be:

–   the parent or guardian;

–   if the juvenile is in local authority or voluntary organisation care, or is otherwise being looked after under the Children Act 1989, a person appointed by that authority or organisation to have responsibility for the juvenile's welfare;

–   any other person who has, for the time being, assumed responsibility for the juvenile's welfare.

- must be informed as soon as practicable that the juvenile has been arrested, why they have been arrested and where they are detained. This right is in addition to the juvenile's right in section 5 not to be held incommunicado. See Note 3C

3.14   If a juvenile is known to be subject to a court order under which a person or organisation is given any degree of statutory responsibility to supervise or otherwise monitor them, reasonable steps must also be taken to notify that person or organisation (the 'responsible officer'). The responsible officer will normally be a member of a Youth Offending Team, except for a curfew order which involves electronic monitoring when the contractor providing the monitoring will normally be the responsible officer.

3.15   If the detainee is a juvenile, mentally disordered or otherwise mentally vulnerable, the custody officer must, as soon as practicable:

- inform the appropriate adult, who in the case of a juvenile may or may not be a

person responsible for their welfare, as in paragraph 3.13, of:

– the grounds for their detention;

– their whereabouts.

- ask the adult to come to the police station to see the detainee.

3.16   It is imperative that a mentally disordered or otherwise mentally vulnerable person, detained under the Mental Health Act 1983, section 136, be assessed as soon as possible. If that assessment is to take place at the police station, an approved social worker and a registered medical practitioner shall be called to the station as soon as possible in order to interview and examine the detainee. Once the detainee has been interviewed, examined and suitable arrangements made for their treatment or care, they can no longer be detained under section 136. A detainee must be immediately discharged from detention under section 136 if a registered medical practitioner, having examined them, concludes they are not mentally disordered within the meaning of the Act.

3.17   If the appropriate adult is:

- already at the police station, the provisions of paragraphs 3.1 to 3.5 must be complied with in the appropriate adult's presence;

- not at the station when these provisions are complied with, they must be complied with again in the presence of the appropriate adult when they arrive.

3.18   The detainee shall be advised that:

- the duties of the appropriate adult include giving advice and assistance;

- they can consult privately with the appropriate adult at any time.

3.19   If the detainee, or appropriate adult on the detainee's behalf, asks for a solicitor to be called to give legal advice, the provisions of section 6 apply.

3.20   If the detainee is blind, seriously visually impaired or unable to read, the custody officer shall make sure their solicitor, relative, appropriate adult or some other person likely to take an interest in them and not involved in the investigation is available to help check any documentation. When this Code requires written consent or signing the person assisting may be asked to sign instead, if the detainee prefers. This paragraph does not require an appropriate adult to be called solely to assist in checking and signing documentation for a person who is not a juvenile, or mentally disordered or otherwise mentally vulnerable (see paragraph 3.15).

(c)   Persons attending a police station voluntarily

3.21   Anybody attending a police station voluntarily to assist with an investigation may leave at will unless arrested. See Note 1K. If it is decided they shall not be allowed to leave, they must be informed at once that they are under arrest and brought before the custody officer, who is responsible for making sure they are notified of their rights in the same way as other detainees. If they are not arrested but are cautioned as in section 10, the person who gives the caution must, at the same time, inform them they are not under arrest, they are not obliged to remain at the station but if they remain at the station they may obtain free and independent legal advice if they want.

They shall be told the right to legal advice includes the right to speak with a solicitor on the telephone and be asked if they want to do so.

3.22 If a person attending the police station voluntarily asks about their entitlement to legal advice, they shall be given a copy of the notice explaining the arrangements for obtaining legal advice. See paragraph 3.2

(d) Documentation

3.23 The grounds for a person's detention shall be recorded, in the person's presence if practicable.

3.24 Action taken under paragraphs 3.12 to 3.20 shall be recorded.

(e) Persons answering street bail

3.25 When a person is answering street bail, the custody officer should link any documentation held in relation to arrest with the custody record. Any further action shall be recorded on the custody record in accordance with paragraphs 3.23 and 3.24 above.

Notes for guidance

3A The notice of entitlements should:

• list the entitlements in this Code, including:

– visits and contact with outside parties, including special provisions for

Commonwealth citizens and foreign nationals;

– reasonable standards of physical comfort;

– adequate food and drink;

– access to toilets and washing facilities, clothing, medical attention, and exercise when practicable.

• mention the:

– provisions relating to the conduct of interviews;

– circumstances in which an appropriate adult should be available to assist the detainee and their statutory rights to make representation whenever the period of their detention is reviewed.

3B In addition to notices in English, translations should be available in Welsh, the main minority ethnic languages and the principal European languages, whenever they are likely to be helpful. Audio versions of the notice should also be made available.

3C If the juvenile is in local authority or voluntary organisation care but living with their parents or other adults responsible for their welfare, although there is no legal obligation to inform them, they should normally be contacted, as well as the authority or organisation unless suspected of involvement in the offence concerned. Even if the juvenile is not living with their parents, consideration should be given to informing them.

3D   The right to consult the Codes of Practice does not entitle the person concerned to delay unreasonably any necessary investigative or administrative action whilst they do so. Examples of action which need not be delayed unreasonably include:

•   procedures requiring the provision of breath, blood or urine specimens under the

Road Traffic Act 1988 or the Transport and Works Act 1992;

•   searching detainees at the police station;

•   taking fingerprints, footwear impressions or non-intimate samples without consent for evidential purposes.

3E   Home Office Circular 32/2000 provides more detailed guidance on risk assessments and identifies key risk areas which should always be considered.

4   Detainee's property

(a)   Action

4.1   The custody officer is responsible for:

(a)   ascertaining what property a detainee:

(i)   has with them when they come to the police station, whether on:

•   arrest or re-detention on answering to bail;

•   commitment to prison custody on the order or sentence of a court;

•   lodgement at the police station with a view to their production in

court from prison custody;

•   transfer from detention at another station or hospital;

•   detention under the Mental Health Act 1983, section 135 or 136;

•   remand into police custody on the authority of a court

(ii)   might have acquired for an unlawful or harmful purpose while in custody;

(b)   the safekeeping of any property taken from a detainee which remains at the police station.

The custody officer may search the detainee or authorise their being searched to the extent they consider necessary, provided a search of intimate parts of the body or involving the removal of more than outer clothing is only made as in Annex A. A search may only be carried out by an officer of the same sex as the detainee. See Note 4A

4.2   Detainees may retain clothing and personal effects at their own risk unless the custody officer considers they may use them to cause harm to themselves or others, interfere with evidence, damage property, effect an escape or they are needed as evidence. In this event the custody officer may withhold such articles as they consider necessary and must tell the detainee why.

4.3   Personal effects are those items a detainee may lawfully need, use or refer to while in detention but do not include cash and other items of value.

(b)   Documentation

4.4   It is a matter for the custody officer to determine whether a record should be made of the property a detained person has with him or had taken from him on arrest. Any record made is not required to be kept as part of the custody record but the custody record should be noted as to where such a record exists. Whenever a record is made the detainee shall be allowed to check and sign the record of property as correct. Any refusal to sign shall be recorded.

4.5   If a detainee is not allowed to keep any article of clothing or personal effects, the reason must be recorded.

Notes for guidance

4A   PACE, Section 54(1) and paragraph 4.1 require a detainee to be searched when it is clear the custody officer will have continuing duties in relation to that detainee or when that detainee's behaviour or offence makes an inventory appropriate. They do not require every detainee to be searched, e.g. if it is clear a person will only be detained for a short period and is not to be placed in a cell, the custody officer may decide not to search them. In such a case the custody record will be endorsed 'not searched', paragraph 4.4 will not apply, and the detainee will be invited to sign the entry. If the detainee refuses, the custody officer will be obliged to ascertain what property they have in accordance with paragraph 4.1.

4B   Paragraph 4.4 does not require the custody officer to record on the custody record property in the detainee's possession on arrest if, by virtue of its nature, quantity or size, it is not practicable to remove it to the police station.

4C   Paragraph 4.4 does not require items of clothing worn by the person be recorded unless withheld by the custody officer as in paragraph 4.2.

5   Right not to be held incommunicado

(a)   Action

5.1   Any person arrested and held in custody at a police station or other premises may, on request, have one person known to them or likely to take an interest in their welfare informed at public expense of their whereabouts as soon as practicable. If the person cannot be contacted the detainee may choose up to two alternatives. If they cannot be contacted, the person in charge of detention or the investigation has discretion to allow further attempts until the information has been conveyed. See Notes 5C and 5D

5.2   The exercise of the above right in respect of each person nominated may be delayed only in accordance with Annex B.

5.3   The above right may be exercised each time a detainee is taken to another police station.

5.4   The detainee may receive visits at the custody officer's discretion. See Note 5B

5.5   If a friend, relative or person with an interest in the detainee's welfare enquires about their whereabouts, this information shall be given if the suspect agrees and Annex B does not apply. See Note 5D

5.6   The detainee shall be given writing materials, on request, and allowed to telephone one person for a reasonable time, see Notes 5A and 5E. Either or both these privileges may be denied or delayed if an officer of inspector rank or above considers sending a letter or making a telephone call may result in any of the consequences in:

(a)   Annex B paragraphs 1 and 2 and the person is detained in connection with an indictable offence;

(b)   Not used

Nothing in this paragraph permits the restriction or denial of the rights in paragraphs 5.1 and 6.1.

5.7   Before any letter or message is sent, or telephone call made, the detainee shall be informed that what they say in any letter, call or message (other than in a communication to a solicitor) may be read or listened to and may be given in evidence. A telephone call may be terminated if it is being abused. The costs can be at public expense at the custody officer's discretion.

5.7A Any delay or denial of the rights in this section should be proportionate and should last no longer than necessary.

(b)   Documentation

5.8   A record must be kept of any:

(a)   request made under this section and the action taken;

(b)   letters, messages or telephone calls made or received or visit received;

(c)   refusal by the detainee to have information about them given to an outside enquirer. The detainee must be asked to countersign the record accordingly and any refusal recorded.

Notes for guidance

5A   A person may request an interpreter to interpret a telephone call or translate a letter.

5B   At the custody officer's discretion, visits should be allowed when possible, subject to having sufficient personnel to supervise a visit and any possible hindrance to the investigation.

5C   If the detainee does not know anyone to contact for advice or support or cannot contact a friend or relative, the custody officer should bear in mind any local voluntary bodies or other organisations who might be able to help. Paragraph 6.1 applies if legal advice is required.

5D   In some circumstances it may not be appropriate to use the telephone to disclose information under paragraphs 5.1 and 5.5.

5E   The telephone call at paragraph 5.6 is in addition to any communication under paragraphs

5.1 and 6.1.

6   Right to legal advice

(a)   Action

6.1   Unless Annex B applies, all detainees must be informed that they may at any time consult and communicate privately with a solicitor, whether in person, in writing or by telephone, and that free independent legal advice is available. See paragraph 3.1, Note 6B, 6B1, 6B2 and Note 6J

6.2   Not Used

6.3   A poster advertising the right to legal advice must be prominently displayed in the charging area of every police station. See Note 6H

6.4   No police officer should, at any time, do or say anything with the intention of dissuading

a detainee from obtaining legal advice.

6.5   The exercise of the right of access to legal advice may be delayed only as in Annex B.

Whenever legal advice is requested, and unless Annex B applies, the custody officer must act without delay to secure the provision of such advice. If, on being informed or reminded of this right, the detainee declines to speak to a solicitor in person, the officer should point out that the right includes the right to speak with a solicitor on the telephone. If the detainee continues to waive this right the officer should ask them why and any reasons should be recorded on the custody record or the interview record as appropriate. Reminders of the right to legal advice must be given as in paragraphs 3.5, 11.2, 15.4, 16.4, 2B of Annex A, 3 of Annex K and 16.5 and Code D, paragraphs 3.17(ii) and 6.3. Once it is clear a detainee does not want to speak to a solicitor in person or by telephone they should cease to be asked their reasons. See Note 6K

6.5A   In the case of a juvenile, an appropriate adult should consider whether legal advice from a solicitor is required. If the juvenile indicates that they do not want legal advice, the appropriate adult has the right to ask for a solicitor to attend if this would be in the best interests of the person. However, the detained person cannot be forced to see the solicitor if he is adamant that he does not wish to do so.

6.6   A detainee who wants legal advice may not be interviewed or continue to be interviewed until they have received such advice unless:

(a)   Annex B applies, when the restriction on drawing adverse inferences from silence in Annex C will apply because the detainee is not allowed an opportunity to consult a solicitor; or

(b)   an officer of superintendent rank or above has reasonable grounds for believing that:

(i)   the consequent delay might:

•   lead to interference with, or harm to, evidence connected with an offence;

•   lead to interference with, or physical harm to, other people;

•   lead to serious loss of, or damage to, property;

•   lead to alerting other people suspected of having committed an offence but not yet arrested for it;

• hinder the recovery of property obtained in consequence of the commission of an offence.

(ii) when a solicitor, including a duty solicitor, has been contacted and has agreed to attend, awaiting their arrival would cause unreasonable delay to the process of investigation.

Note: In these cases the restriction on drawing adverse inferences from silence in Annex C will apply because the detainee is not allowed an opportunity to consult a solicitor.

(c) the solicitor the detainee has nominated or selected from a list: (i) cannot be contacted;

(ii) has previously indicated they do not wish to be contacted; or

(iii) having been contacted, has declined to attend; and

the detainee has been advised of the Duty Solicitor Scheme but has declined to ask for the duty solicitor.

In these circumstances the interview may be started or continued without further delay provided an officer of inspector rank or above has agreed to the interview proceeding.

Note: The restriction on drawing adverse inferences from silence in Annex C will not apply because the detainee is allowed an opportunity to consult the duty solicitor;

(d) the detainee changes their mind, about wanting legal advice.

In these circumstances the interview may be started or continued without delay provided that:

(i) the detainee agrees to do so , in writing or on the interview record made in accordance with Code E or F; and

(ii) an officer of inspector rank or above has inquired about the detainee's reasons for their change of mind and gives authority for the interview to proceed.

Confirmation of the detainee's agreement, their change of mind, the reasons for it if given and, subject to paragraph 2.6A, the name of the authorising officer shall be recorded in the written interview record or the interview record made in accordance with Code E or F. See Note 6I. Note: In these circumstances the restriction on drawing adverse inferences from silence in Annex C will not apply because the detainee is allowed an opportunity to consult a solicitor if they wish.

6.7 If paragraph 6.6(b)(i) applies, once sufficient information has been obtained to avert the risk, questioning must cease until the detainee has received legal advice unless paragraph 6.6(a), (b)(ii), (c) or (d) applies.

6.8 A detainee who has been permitted to consult a solicitor shall be entitled on request to have the solicitor present when they are interviewed unless one of the exceptions in paragraph 6.6 applies.

6.9 The solicitor may only be required to leave the interview if their conduct is such that the interviewer is unable properly to put questions to the suspect. See Notes 6D and 6E

6.10 If the interviewer considers a solicitor is acting in such a way, they will stop the interview and consult an officer not below superintendent rank, if one is readily available, and otherwise an officer not below inspector rank not connected with the investigation. After speaking to the solicitor, the officer consulted will decide if the interview should continue in the presence of that solicitor. If they decide it should not, the suspect will be given the opportunity to consult another solicitor before the interview continues and that solicitor given an opportunity to be present at the interview. See Note 6E

6.11 The removal of a solicitor from an interview is a serious step and, if it occurs, the officer of superintendent rank or above who took the decision will consider if the incident should be reported to the Law Society. If the decision to remove the solicitor has been taken by an officer below superintendent rank, the facts must be reported to an officer of superintendent rank or above who will similarly consider whether a report to the Law Society would be appropriate. When the solicitor concerned is a duty solicitor, the report should be both to the Law Society and to the Legal Services Commission.

6.12 'Solicitor' in this Code means:

•   a solicitor who holds a current practising certificate

•   an accredited or probationary representative included on the register of representatives maintained by the Legal Services Commission.

6.12A An accredited or probationary representative sent to provide advice by, and on behalf of, a solicitor shall be admitted to the police station for this purpose unless an officer of inspector rank or above considers such a visit will hinder the investigation and directs otherwise. Hindering the investigation does not include giving proper legal advice to a detainee as in Note 6D. Once admitted to the police station, paragraphs 6.6 to 6.10 apply.

6.13 In exercising their discretion under paragraph 6.12A, the officer should take into account in particular:

•   whether:

–   the identity and status of an accredited or probationary representative have been satisfactorily established;

–   they are of suitable character to provide legal advice, e.g. a person with a criminal record is unlikely to be suitable unless the conviction was for a minor offence and not recent.

•   any other matters in any written letter of authorisation provided by the solicitor on whose behalf the person is attending the police station. See Note 6F

6.14 If the inspector refuses access to an accredited or probationary representative or a decision is taken that such a person should not be permitted to remain at an interview, the inspector must notify the solicitor on whose behalf the representative was acting and give them an opportunity to make alternative arrangements. The detainee must be informed and the custody record noted.

6.15 If a solicitor arrives at the station to see a particular person, that person must, unless Annex B applies, be so informed whether or not they are being interviewed and asked if they would like to see the solicitor. This applies even if the detainee has declined legal advice or, having requested it, subsequently agreed to be interviewed without receiving advice. The solicitor's attendance and the detainee's decision must be noted in the custody record.

(b)   Documentation

6.16 Any request for legal advice and the action taken shall be recorded.

6.17 A record shall be made in the interview record if a detainee asks for legal advice and an interview is begun either in the absence of a solicitor or their representative, or they have been required to leave an interview.

Notes for guidance

6A   In considering if paragraph 6.6(b) applies, the officer should, if practicable, ask the solicitor for an estimate of how long it will take to come to the station and relate this to the time detention is permitted, the time of day (i.e. whether the rest period under paragraph 12.2 is imminent) and the requirements of other investigations. If the solicitor is on their way or is to set off immediately, it will not normally be appropriate to begin an interview before they arrive. If it appears necessary to begin an interview before the solicitor's arrival, they should be given an indication of how long the police would be able to wait before 6.6(b) applies so there is an opportunity to make arrangements for someone else to provide legal advice.

6B   A detainee who asks for legal advice should be given an opportunity to consult a specific solicitor or another solicitor from that solicitor's firm or the duty solicitor. If advice is not available by these means, or they do not want to consult the duty solicitor, the detainee should be given an opportunity to choose a solicitor from a list of those willing to provide legal advice. If this solicitor is unavailable, they may choose up to two alternatives. If these attempts are unsuccessful, the custody officer has discretion to allow further attempts until a solicitor has been contacted and agrees to provide legal advice. Apart from carrying out these duties, an officer must not advise the suspect about any particular firm of solicitors. See Notes for Guidance 6B1 and 6B2 below.

6B1   With effect from 1 February 2008, Note for Guidance 6B above will cease to apply in the following forces areas:

Greater Manchester Police

West Midlands Police

West Yorkshire Police

and the following provisions will apply to those force areas: a detainee who asks for legal advice to be paid for by himself should be given an opportunity to consult a specific solicitor or another solicitor from that solicitor's firm. If this solicitor is unavailable by these means, they may choose up to two alternatives. If these attempts are unsuccessful, the custody officer has discretion to allow further attempts until a solicitor has been contacted and agrees to provide legal advice. Otherwise, publicly funded legal advice shall in the first instance be accessed by telephoning a call centre authorised by the Legal Services Commission (LSC) to deal with calls from the police station. The Defence Solicitor Call Centre will determine whether legal advice should be limited to telephone advice or whether a solicitor should attend. Legal advice will be by telephone if a detainee is:

- detained for a non-imprisonable offence,

- arrested on a bench warrant for failing to appear and being held for production before the court (except where the solicitor has clear documentary evidence available that would result in the client being released from custody),

- arrested on suspicion of driving with excess alcohol (failure to provide a specimen, driving whilst unfit/drunk in charge of a motor vehicle), or

- detained in relation to breach of police or court bail conditions.

An attendance by a solicitor for an offence suitable for telephone advice will depend on whether limited exceptions apply, such as:

- whether the police are going to carry out an interview or an identification parade,

- whether the detainee is eligible for assistance from an appropriate adult,

- whether the detainee is unable to communicate over the telephone,

- whether the detainee alleges serious maltreatment by the police.

Apart from carrying out these duties, an officer must not advise the suspect about any particular firm of solicitors. See Note for Guidance 6B2 below.

6B2 With effect from 21 April 2008, the contents of Notes for Guidance 6B and 6B1 above will be superseded by this paragraph in all police forces areas in England and Wales by the following. A detainee who asks for legal advice to be paid for by himself should be given an opportunity to consult a specific solicitor or another solicitor from that solicitor's firm. If this solicitor is unavailable by these means, they may choose up to two alternatives. If these attempts are unsuccessful, the custody officer has discretion to allow further attempts until a solicitor has been contacted and agrees to provide legal advice. Otherwise, publicly funded legal advice shall in the first instance be accessed by telephoning a call centre authorised by the Legal Services Commission (LSC) to deal with calls from the police station. The Defence Solicitor Call Centre will determine whether legal advice should be limited to telephone advice or whether a solicitor should attend. Legal advice will be by telephone if a detainee is:

- detained for a non-imprisonable offence,

- arrested on a bench warrant for failing to appear and being held for production before the court (except where the solicitor has clear documentary evidence available that would result in the client being released from custody),

- arrested on suspicion of driving with excess alcohol (failure to provide a specimen, driving whilst unfit/drunk in charge of a motor vehicle), or

- detained in relation to breach of police or court bail conditions.

An attendance by a solicitor for an offence suitable for telephone advice will depend on whether limited exceptions apply, such as:

- whether the police are going to carry out an interview or an identification parade,

- whether the detainee is eligible for assistance from an appropriate adult,

- whether the detainee is unable to communicate over the telephone,

- whether the detainee alleges serious maltreatment by the police.

Apart from carrying out these duties, an officer must not advise the suspect about any particular firm of solicitors.

6C   Not Used

6D   A detainee has a right to free legal advice and to be represented by a solicitor. Legal advice by telephone advice may be provided in respect of those offences listed in Note for Guidance 6B1 and 6B2 above. The Defence Solicitor Call Centre will determine whether attendance is required by a solicitor. The solicitor's only role in the police station is to protect and advance the legal rights of their client. On occasions this may require the solicitor to give advice which has t he effect of the client avoiding giving evidence which strengthens a prosecution case. The solicitor may intervene in order to seek clarification, challenge an improper question to their client or the manner in which it is put, advise their client not to reply to particular questions, or if they wish to give their client further legal advice. Paragraph 6.9 only applies if the solicitor's approach or conduct prevents or unreasonably obstructs proper questions being put to the suspect or the suspect's response being recorded. Examples of unacceptable conduct include answering questions on a suspect's behalf or providing written replies for the suspect to quote.

6E   An officer who takes the decision to exclude a solicitor must be in a position to satisfy the court the decision was properly made. In order to do this they may need to witness what is happening.

6F   If an officer of at least inspector rank considers a particular solicitor or firm of solicitors is persistently sending probationary representatives who are unsuited to provide legal advice, they should inform an officer of at least superintendent rank, who may wish to take the matter up with the Law Society.

6G   Subject to the constraints of Annex B, a solicitor may advise more than one client in an investigation if they wish. Any question of a conflict of interest is for the solicitor under their professional code of conduct. If, however, waiting for a solicitor to give advice to one client may lead to unreasonable delay to the interview with another, the provisions of paragraph 6.6(b) may apply.

6H   In addition to a poster in English, a poster or posters containing translations into Welsh, the main minority ethnic languages and the principal European languages should be displayed wherever they are likely to be helpful and it is practicable to do so.

6I   Paragraph 6.6(d) requires the authorisation of an officer of inspector rank or above to the continuation of an interview when a detainee who wanted legal advice changes their mind. It is permissible for such authorisation to be given over the telephone, if the authorising officer is able to satisfy themselves about the reason for the detainee's change of mind and is satisfied it is proper to continue the interview in those circumstances.

6J   Whenever a detainee exercises their right to legal advice by consulting or communicating with a solicitor, they must be allowed to do so in private. This right to consult or communicate in private is fundamental. If the requirement for privacy is compromised because what is said or written by the detainee or solicitor for the purpose of giving and receiving legal advice is overheard, listened to, or read by others without the informed consent of the detainee, the right will effectively have been denied. When a detainee chooses to speak to a solicitor on the telephone, they should be allowed to do so in private unless this is impractical because of the design and layout of the custody area or the location of telephones. However, the normal expectation should be that facilities will be available, unless they are being used, at all police stations to enable detainees to speak in private to a solicitor either face to face or over the telephone.

6K   A detainee is not obliged to give reasons for declining legal advice and should not be pressed to do so.

7   Citizens of independent Commonwealth countries or foreign nationals

(a)   Action

7.1   Any citizen of an independent Commonwealth country or a national of a foreign country, including the Republic of Ireland, may communicate at any time with the appropriate High Commission, Embassy or Consulate. The detainee must be informed as soon as practicable of:

•   this right;

•   their right, upon request, to have their High Commission, Embassy or Consulate told of their whereabouts and the grounds for their detention. Such a request should be acted upon as soon as practicable.

7.2   If a detainee is a citizen of a country with which a bilateral consular convention or agreement is in force requiring notification of arrest, the appropriate High Commission, Embassy or Consulate shall be informed as soon as practicable, subject to paragraph

7.4. The countries to which this applies as at 1 April 2003 are listed in Annex F.

7.3   Consular officers may visit one of their nationals in police detention to talk to them and, if required, to arrange for legal advice. Such visits shall take place out of the hearing of a police officer.

7.4   Notwithstanding the provisions of consular conventions, if the detainee is a political refugee whether for reasons of race, nationality, political opinion or religion, or is seeking political asylum, consular officers shall not be informed of the arrest of one of their nationals or given access or information about them except at the detainee's express request.

(b)   Documentation

7.5   A record shall be made when a detainee is informed of their rights under this section and of any communications with a High Commission, Embassy or Consulate.

Note for guidance

7A   The exercise of the rights in this section may not be interfered with even though Annex

B applies.

8   Conditions of detention

(a)   Action

8.1   So far as it is practicable, not more than one detainee should be detained in each cell.

8.2   Cells in use must be adequately heated, cleaned and ventilated. They must be adequately lit, subject to such dimming as is compatible with safety and security to allow people detained overnight to sleep. No additional restraints shall be used within a locked cell unless absolutely necessary and then only restraint equipment, approved for use in that force by the Chief Officer, which is reasonable and necessary in the circumstances having regard to the detainee's demeanour and with a view to ensuring their safety and the safety of others. If a detainee is deaf, mentally disordered or otherwise mentally vulnerable, particular care must be taken when deciding whether to use any form of approved restraints.

8.3   Blankets, mattresses, pillows and other bedding supplied shall be of a reasonable standard and in a clean and sanitary condition. See Note 8A

8.4   Access to toilet and washing facilities must be provided.

8.5   If it is necessary to remove a detainee's clothes for the purposes of investigation, for hygiene, health reasons or cleaning, replacement clothing of a reasonable standard of comfort and cleanliness shall be provided. A detainee may not be interviewed unless adequate clothing has been offered.

8.6   At least two light meals and one main meal should be offered in any 24 hour period.

See Note 8B. Drinks should be provided at meal times and upon reasonable request between meals. Whenever necessary, advice shall be sought from the appropriate health care professional, see Note 9A, on medical and dietary matters. As far as practicable, meals provided shall offer a varied diet and meet any specific dietary needs or religious beliefs the detainee may have. The detainee may, at the custody officer's discretion, have meals supplied by their family or friends at their expense. See Note 8A

8.7   Brief outdoor exercise shall be offered daily if practicable.

8.8   A juvenile shall not be placed in a police cell unless no other secure accommodation is available and the custody officer considers it is not practicable to supervise them if they are not placed in a cell or that a cell provides more comfortable accommodation than other secure accommodation in the station. A juvenile may not be placed in a cell with a detained adult.

(b)   Documentation

8.9   A record must be kept of replacement clothing and meals offered.

8.10   If a juvenile is placed in a cell, the reason must be recorded.

8.11   The use of any restraints on a detainee whilst in a cell, the reasons for it and, if appropriate, the arrangements for enhanced supervision of the detainee whilst so restrained, shall be recorded. See paragraph 3.9

Notes for guidance

8A   The provisions in paragraph 8.3 and 8.6 respectively are of particular importance in the case of a person likely to be detained for an extended period. In deciding whether to allow meals to be supplied by family or friends, the custody officer is entitled to take account of the risk of items being concealed in any food or package and the officer's duties and responsibilities under food handling legislation.

8B   Meals should, so far as practicable, be offered at recognised meal times, or at other times that take account of when the detainee last had a meal.

9   Care and treatment of detained persons

(a)   General

9.1   Nothing in this section prevents the police from calling the police surgeon or, if appropriate, some other health care professional, to examine a detainee for the purposes of obtaining evidence relating to any offence in which the detainee is suspected of being involved. See Note 9A

9.2   If a complaint is made by, or on behalf of, a detainee about their treatment since their arrest, or it comes to notice that a detainee may have been treated improperly, a report must be made as soon as practicable to an officer of inspector rank or above not connected with the investigation. If the matter concerns a possible assault or the possibility of the unnecessary or unreasonable use of force, an appropriate health care professional must also be called as soon as practicable.

9.3   Detainees should be visited at least every hour. If no reasonably foreseeable risk was identified in a risk assessment, see paragraphs 3.6 – 3.10, there is no need to wake a sleeping detainee. Those suspected of being intoxicated through drink or drugs or having swallowed drugs, see Note 9CA, or whose level of consciousness causes concern must, subject to any clinical directions given by the appropriate health care professional, see paragraph 9.13:

•   be visited and roused at least every half hour

•   have their condition assessed as in Annex H

•   and clinical treatment arranged if appropriate

See Notes 9B, 9C and 9H

9.4   When arrangements are made to secure clinical attention for a detainee, the custody officer must make sure all relevant information which might assist in the treatment of the detainee's condition is made available to the responsible health care professional. This applies whether or not the health care professional asks for such information. Any officer or police staff with relevant information must inform the custody officer as soon as practicable.

(b)   Clinical treatment and attention

9.5   The custody officer must make sure a detainee receives appropriate clinical attention as soon as reasonably practicable if the person:

(a)   appears to be suffering from physical illness; or

(b)   is injured; or

(c)   appears to be suffering from a mental disorder; or

(d)   appears to need clinical attention

9.5A   This applies even if the detainee makes no request for clinical attention and whether or not they have already received clinical attention elsewhere. If the need for attention appears urgent, e.g. when indicated as in Annex H, the nearest available health care professional or an ambulance must be called immediately.

9.5B   The custody officer must also consider the need for clinical attention as set out in Note for Guidance 9C in relation to those suffering the effects of alcohol or drugs.

9.6   Paragraph 9.5 is not meant to prevent or delay the transfer to a hospital if necessary of a person detained under the Mental Health Act 1983, section 136. See Note 9D. When an assessment under that Act takes place at a police station, see paragraph 3.16, the custody officer must consider whether an appropriate health care professional should be called to conduct an initial clinical check on the detainee. This applies particularly when there is likely to be any significant delay in the arrival of a suitably qualified medical practitioner.

9.7   If it appears to the custody officer, or they are told, that a person brought to a station under arrest may be suffering from an infectious disease or condition, the custody officer must take reasonable steps to safeguard the health of the detainee and others at the station. In deciding what action to take, advice must be sought from an appropriate health care professional. See Note 9E. The custody officer has discretion to isolate the person and their property until clinical directions have been obtained.

9.8   If a detainee requests a clinical examination, an appropriate health care professional must be called as soon as practicable to assess the detainee's clinical needs. If a safe and appropriate care plan cannot be provided, the police surgeon's advice must be sought. The detainee may also be examined by a medical practitioner of their choice at their expense.

9.9   If a detainee is required to take or apply any medication in compliance with clinical directions prescribed before their detention, the custody officer must consult the appropriate health care professional before the use of the medication. Subject to the restrictions in paragraph 9.10, the custody officer is responsible for the safekeeping of any medication and for making sure the detainee is given the opportunity to take or apply prescribed or approved medication. Any such consultation and its outcome shall be noted in the custody record.

9.10   No police officer may administer or supervise the self-administration of medically prescribed controlled drugs of the types and forms listed in the Misuse of Drugs Regulations 2001, Schedule 2 or 3. A detainee may only self-administer such drugs under the personal supervision of the registered medical practitioner authorising their use. Drugs listed in Schedule 4 or 5 may be distributed by the custody officer for self- administration if they have consulted the registered medical practitioner authorising their use, this may be done by telephone, and both parties are satisfied self-administration will not expose the detainee, police officers or anyone else to the risk of harm or injury.

9.11   When appropriate health care professionals administer drugs or other medications, or supervise their self-administration, it must be within current medicines legislation and the scope of practice as determined by their relevant professional body.

9.12   If a detainee has in their possession, or claims to need, medication relating to a heart condition, diabetes, epilepsy or a condition of comparable potential seriousness then, even though paragraph 9.5 may not apply, the advice of the appropriate health care professional must be obtained.

9.13   Whenever the appropriate health care professional is called in accordance with this section to examine or treat a detainee, the custody officer shall ask for their opinion about:

•   any risks or problems which police need to take into account when making

decisions about the detainee's continued detention;

•   when to carry out an interview if applicable; and

- the need for safeguards.

9.14   When clinical directions are given by the appropriate health care professional, whether orally or in writing, and the custody officer has any doubts or is in any way uncertain about any aspect of the directions, the custody officer shall ask for clarification. It is particularly important that directions concerning the frequency of visits are clear, precise and capable of being implemented. See Note 9F.

(c)   Documentation

9.15   A record must be made in the custody record of:

(a)   the arrangements made for an examination by   an   appropriate health care professional under paragraph 9.2 and of any complaint reported under that paragraph together with any relevant remarks by the custody officer;

(b)   any arrangements made in accordance with paragraph 9.5;

(c)   any request for a clinical examination under paragraph 9.8 and any arrangements made in response;

(d)   the injury, ailment, condition or other reason which made it necessary to make the arrangements in (a) to (c), see Note 9G;

(e)   any clinical directions and advice, including any further clarifications, given to police by a health care professional concerning the care and treatment of the detainee in connection with any of the arrangements made in (a) to (c), see Note 9F;

(f)   if applicable, the responses received when attempting to rouse a person using the procedure in Annex H, see Note 9H.

9.16   If a health care professional does not record their clinical findings in the custody record, the record must show where they are recorded. See Note 9G. However, information which is necessary to custody staff to ensure the effective ongoing care and well being of the detainee must be recorded openly in the custody record, see paragraph 3.8 and Annex G, paragraph 7.

9.17   Subject to the requirements of Section 4, the custody record shall include:

- a record of all medication a detainee has in their possession on arrival at the police station;

- a note of any such medication they claim to need but do not have with them.

Notes for guidance

9A   A 'health care professional' means a clinically qualified person working within the scope of practice as determined by their relevant professional body. Whether a health care professional is 'appropriate' depends on the circumstances of the duties they carry out at the time.

9B   Whenever possible juveniles and mentally vulnerable detainees should be visited more frequently.

9C   A detainee who appears drunk or behaves abnormally may be suffering from illness, the effects of drugs or may have sustained injury, particularly a head injury which is not apparent. A detainee needing or dependent on certain drugs, including alcohol, may experience harmful effects within a short time of being deprived of their supply. In these circumstances, when there is any doubt, police should always act urgently to call an appropriate health care professional or an ambulance. Paragraph 9.5 does not apply to minor ailments or injuries which do not need attention. However, all such ailments or injuries must be recorded in the custody record and any doubt must be resolved in favour of calling the appropriate health care professional.

9CA Paragraph 9.3 would apply to a person in police custody by order of a magistrates' court under the Criminal Justice Act 1988, section 152 (as amended by the Drugs Act 2005, section 8) to facilitate the recovery of evidence after being charged with drug possession or drug trafficking and suspected of having swallowed drugs. In the case of the healthcare needs of a person who has swallowed drugs, the custody officer subject to any clinical directions, should consider the necessity for rousing every half hour. This does not negate the need for regular visiting of the suspect in the cell.

9D Whenever practicable, arrangements should be made for persons detained for assessment under the Mental Health Act 1983, section 136 to be taken to a hospital. There is no power under that Act to transfer a person detained under section 136 from one place of safety to another place of safety for assessment.

9E It is important to respect a person's right to privacy and information about their health must be kept confidential and only disclosed with their consent or in accordance with clinical advice when it is necessary to protect the detainee's health or that of others who come into contact with them.

9F The custody officer should always seek to clarify directions that the detainee requires constant observation or supervision and should ask the appropriate health care professional to explain precisely what action needs to be taken to implement such directions.

9G Paragraphs 9.15 and 9.16 do not require any information about the cause of any injury, ailment or condition to be recorded on the custody record if it appears capable of providing evidence of an offence.

9H The purpose of recording a person's responses when attempting to rouse them using the procedure in Annex H is to enable any change in the individual's consciousness level to be noted and clinical treatment arranged if appropriate.

10 Cautions

(a) When a caution must be given

10.1 A person whom there are grounds to suspect of an offence, see Note 10A, must be cautioned before any questions about an offence, or further questions if the answers provide the grounds for suspicion, are put to them if either the suspect's answers or silence, (i.e. failure or refusal to answer or answer satisfactorily) may be given in evidence to a court in a prosecution. A person need not be cautioned if questions are for other necessary purposes, e.g.:

(a) solely to establish their identity or ownership of any vehicle;

(b) to obtain information in accordance with any relevant statutory requirement, see

paragraph 10.9;

(c)   in furtherance of the proper and effective conduct of a search, e.g. to determine the need to search in the exercise of powers of stop and search or to seek co- operation while carrying out a search;

(d)   to seek verification of a written record as in paragraph 11.13;

(e)   Not used

10.2   Whenever a person not under arrest is initially cautioned, or reminded they are under caution, that person must at the same time be told they are not under arrest and are free to leave if they want to. See Note 10C

10.3   A person who is arrested, or further arrested, must be informed at the time, or as soon as practicable thereafter, that they are under arrest and the grounds for their arrest, see paragraph 3.4, Note 10B and Code G, paragraphs 2.2 and 4.3..

10.4   As per Code G, section 3, a person who is arrested, or further arrested, must also be cautioned unless:

(a)   it is impracticable to do so by reason of their condition or behaviour at the time;

(b)   they have already been cautioned immediately prior to arrest as in paragraph 10.1.

(b)   Terms of the cautions

10.5   The caution which must be given on: (a)   arrest;

(b)   all other occasions before a person is charged or informed they may be prosecuted, see section 16, should, unless the restriction on drawing adverse inferences from silence applies, see Annex C, be in the following terms:

"You do not have to say anything. But it may harm your defence if you do not mention when questioned something which you later rely on in Court. Anything you do say may be given in evidence."

Where the use of the Welsh Language is appropriate, a constable may provide the caution directly in Welsh in the following terms:

"Does dim rhaid i chi ddweud dim byd. Ond gall niweidio eich amddiffyniad os na fyddwch chi'n sôn, wrth gael eich holi, am rywbeth y byddwch chi'n dibynnu arno nes ymlaen yn y Llys. Gall unrhyw beth yr ydych yn ei ddweud gael ei roi fel tystiolaeth."

See Note 10G

10.6   Annex C, paragraph 2 sets out the alternative terms of the caution to be used when the restriction on drawing adverse inferences from silence applies.

10.7   Minor deviations from the words of any caution given in accordance with this Code do not constitute a breach of this Code, provided the sense of the relevant caution is preserved. See Note 10D

10.8   After any break in questioning under caution, the person being questioned must be made aware they remain under caution. If there is any doubt the relevant caution should be given again in full when the interview resumes. See Note 10E

10.9   When, despite being cautioned, a person fails to co-operate or to answer particular questions which may affect their immediate treatment, the person should be informed of any relevant consequences and that those consequences are not affected by the caution. Examples are when a person's refusal to provide:

•   their name and address when charged may make them liable to detention;

•   particulars and information in accordance with a statutory requirement, e.g. under the Road Traffic Act 1988, may amount to an offence or may make the person liable to a further arrest.

(c)   Special warnings under the Criminal Justice and Public Order Act 1994, sections 36 and 37

10.10 When a suspect interviewed at a police station or authorised place of detention after arrest fails or refuses to answer certain questions, or to answer satisfactorily, after due warning, see Note 10F, a court or jury may draw such inferences as appear proper under the Criminal Justice and Public Order Act 1994, sections 36 and 37. Such inferences may only be drawn when:

(a)   the restriction on drawing adverse inferences from silence, see Annex C, does not apply; and

(b)   the suspect is arrested by a constable and fails or refuses to account for any objects, marks or substances, or marks on such objects found:

•   on their person;

•   in or on their clothing or footwear;

•   otherwise in their possession; or

•   in the place they were arrested;

(c)   the arrested suspect was found by a constable at a place at or about the time the offence for which that officer has arrested them is alleged to have been committed, and the suspect fails or refuses to account for their presence there.

When the restriction on drawing adverse inferences from silence applies, the suspect may still be asked to account for any of the matters in (b) or (c) but the special warning described in paragraph 10.11 will not apply and must not be given.

10.11 For an inference to be drawn when a suspect fails or refuses to answer a question about one of these matters or to answer it satisfactorily, the suspect must first be told in ordinary language:

(a)   what offence is being investigated;

(b)   what fact they are being asked to account for;

(c)   this fact may be due to them taking part in the commission of the offence;

(d)   a court may draw a proper inference if they fail or refuse to account for this fact; (e) a record is being made of the interview and it may be given in evidence if they are brought to trial.

(d)   Juveniles and persons who are mentally disordered or otherwise mentally vulnerable

10.12 If a juvenile or a person who is mentally disordered or otherwise mentally vulnerable is cautioned in the absence of the appropriate adult, the caution must be repeated in the adult's presence.

(e)   Documentation

10.13 A record shall be made when a caution is given under this section, either in the interviewer's pocket book or in the interview record.

Notes for guidance

10A   There must be some reasonable, objective grounds for the suspicion, based on known facts or information which are relevant to the likelihood the offence has been committed and the person to be questioned committed it.

10B   An arrested person must be given sufficient information to enable them to understand that they have been deprived of their liberty and the reason they have been arrested, e.g. when a person is arrested on suspicion of committing an offence they must be informed of the suspected offence's nature, when and where it was committed. The suspect must also be informed of the reason or reasons why the arrest is considered necessary. Vague or technical language should be avoided.

10C   The restriction on drawing inferences from silence, see Annex C, paragraph 1, does not apply to a person who has not been detained and who therefore cannot be prevented from seeking legal advice if they want, see paragraph 3.21.

10D   If it appears a person does not understand the caution, the person giving it should explain it in their own words.

10E   It may be necessary to show to the court that nothing occurred during an interview break or between interviews which influenced the suspect's recorded evidence. After a break in an interview or at the beginning of a subsequent interview, the interviewing officer should summarise the reason for the break and confirm this with the suspect.

10F   The Criminal Justice and Public Order Act 1994, sections 36 and 37 apply only to suspects who have been arrested by a constable or Customs and Excise officer and are given the relevant warning by the police or customs officer who made the arrest or who is investigating the offence. They do not apply to any interviews with suspects who have not been arrested.

10G   Nothing in this Code requires a caution to be given or repeated when informing a person not under arrest they may be prosecuted for an offence. However, a court will not be able to draw any inferences under the Criminal Justice and Public Order Act 1994, section 34, if the person was not cautioned.

11   Interviews – general

(a)   Action

11.1A An interview is the questioning of a person regarding their involvement or suspected involvement in a criminal offence or offences which, under paragraph 10.1, must be carried out under caution. Whenever a person is interviewed they must be informed of the nature of the offence, or further offence. Procedures under the Road Traffic Act 1988, section 7 or the Transport and Works Act 1992, section 31 do not constitute interviewing for the purpose of this Code.

11.1   Following a decision to arrest a suspect, they must not be interviewed about the relevant offence except at a police station or other authorised place of detention, unless the consequent delay would be likely to:

(a)   lead to:

•   interference with, or harm to, evidence connected with an offence;

•   interference with, or physical harm to, other people; or

•   serious loss of, or damage to, property;

(b)   lead to alerting other people suspected of committing an offence but not yet arrested for it; or

(c)   hinder the recovery of property obtained in consequence of the commission of an offence.

Interviewing in any of these circumstances shall cease once the relevant risk has been averted or the necessary questions have been put in order to attempt to avert that risk.

11.2   Immediately prior to the commencement or re-commencement of any interview at a police station or other authorised place of detention, the interviewer should remind the suspect of their entitlement to free legal advice and that the interview can be delayed for legal advice to be obtained, unless one of the exceptions in paragraph 6.6 applies. It is the interviewer's responsibility to make sure all reminders are recorded in the interview record.

11.3 Not Used

11.4 At the beginning of an interview the interviewer, after cautioning the suspect, see section

10, shall put to them any significant statement or silence which occurred in the presence and hearing of a police officer or other police staff before the start of the interview and which have not been put to the suspect in the course of a previous interview. See Note

11A. The interviewer shall ask the suspect whether they confirm or deny that earlier statement or silence and if they want to add anything.

11.4A A significant statement is one which appears capable of being used in evidence against the suspect, in particular a direct admission of guilt. A significant silence is a failure or refusal to answer a question or answer satisfactorily when under caution, which might, allowing for the restriction on drawing adverse inferences from silence, see Annex C, give rise to an inference under the Criminal Justice and Public Order Act 1994, Part III.

11.5 No interviewer may try to obtain answers or elicit a statement by the use of oppression.

Except as in paragraph 10.9, no interviewer shall indicate, except to answer a direct question, what action will be taken by the police if the person being questioned answers questions, makes a statement or refuses to do either. If the person asks directly what action will be taken if they answer questions, make a statement or refuse to do either, the interviewer may inform them what action the police propose to take provided that action is itself proper and warranted.

11.6 The interview or further interview of a person about an offence with which that person has not been charged or for which they have not been informed they may be prosecuted, must cease when:

(a)   the officer in charge of the investigation is satisfied all the questions they consider relevant to obtaining accurate and reliable information about the offence have been put to the suspect, this includes allowing the suspect an opportunity to give an innocent explanation and asking questions to test if the explanation is accurate and reliable, e.g. to clear up ambiguities or clarify what the suspect said;

(b)   the officer in charge of the investigation has taken account of any other available evidence; and

(c)   the officer in charge of the investigation, or in the case of a detained suspect, the custody officer, see paragraph 16.1, reasonably believes there is sufficient evidence to provide a realistic prospect of conviction for that offence. See Note 11B

This paragraph does not prevent officers in revenue cases or acting under the confiscation provisions of the Criminal Justice Act 1988 or the Drug Trafficking Act 1994 from inviting suspects to complete a formal question and answer record after the interview is concluded.

(b)   Interview records

11.7 (a)   An accurate record must be made of each interview, whether or not the interview takes place at a police station

(b)   The record must state the place of interview, the time it begins and ends, any interview breaks and, subject to paragraph 2.6A, the names of all those present; and must be made on the forms provided for this purpose or in the interviewer's pocket book or in accordance with the Codes of Practice E or F;

(c)   Any written record must be made and completed during the interview, unless this would not be practicable or would interfere with the conduct of the interview, and must constitute either a verbatim record of what has been said or, failing this, an account of the interview which adequately and accurately summarises it.

11.8 If a written record is not made during the interview it must be made as soon as practicable after its completion.

11.9 Written interview records must be timed and signed by the maker.

11.10 If a written record is not completed during the interview the reason must be recorded in the interview record.

11.11 Unless it is impracticable, the person interviewed shall be given the opportunity to read the interview record and to sign it as correct or to indicate how they consider it inaccurate. If the person interviewed cannot read or refuses to read the record or sign it, the senior interviewer present shall read it to them and ask whether they would like to sign it as correct or make their mark or to indicate how they consider it inaccurate. The interviewer shall certify on the interview record itself what has occurred. See Note 11E

11.12 If the appropriate adult or the person's solicitor is present during the interview, they should also be given an opportunity to read and sign the interview record or any written statement taken down during the interview.

11.13 A written record shall be made of any comments made by a suspect, including unsolicited comments, which are outside the context of an interview but which might be relevant to the offence. Any such record must be timed and signed by the maker. When practicable the suspect shall be given the opportunity to read that record and to sign it as correct or to indicate how they consider it inaccurate. See Note 11E

11.14 Any refusal by a person to sign an interview record when asked in accordance with this Code must itself be recorded.

(c)   Juveniles and mentally disordered or otherwise mentally vulnerable people

11.15 A juvenile or person who is mentally disordered or otherwise mentally vulnerable must not be interviewed regarding their involvement or suspected involvement in a criminal offence or offences, or asked to provide or sign a written statement under caution or record of interview, in the absence of the appropriate adult unless paragraphs 11.1, 11.18 to 11.20 apply. See Note 11C

11.16 Juveniles may only be interviewed at their place of education in exceptional circumstances and only when the principal or their nominee agrees. Every effort should be made to notify the parent(s) or other person responsible for the juvenile's welfare and the appropriate adult, if this is a different person, that the police want to interview the juvenile and reasonable time should be allowed to enable the appropriate adult to be present at the interview. If awaiting the appropriate adult would cause unreasonable delay, and unless the juvenile is suspected of an offence against the educational establishment, the principal or their nominee can act as the appropriate adult for the purposes of the interview.

11.17 If an appropriate adult is present at an interview, they shall be informed:

•   they are not expected to act simply as an observer; and

•   the purpose of their presence is to:

–   advise the person being interviewed;

–   observe whether the interview is being conducted properly and fairly;

–   facilitate communication with the person being interviewed.

(d)   Vulnerable suspects – urgent interviews at police stations

11.18 The following persons may not be interviewed unless an officer of superintendent rank or above considers delay will lead to the consequences in paragraph 11.1(a) to (c), and is satisfied the interview would not significantly harm the person's physical or mental state (see Annex G):

(a)   a juvenile or person who is mentally disordered or otherwise mentally vulnerable if at the time of the interview the appropriate adult is not present;

(b)   anyone other than in (a) who at the time of the interview appears unable to:

•   appreciate the significance of questions and their answers; or

•   understand what is happening because of the effects of drink, drugs or any illness, ailment or condition;

(c)   a person who has difficulty understanding English or has a hearing disability, if at the time of the interview an interpreter is not present.

11.19 These interviews may not continue once sufficient information has been obtained to avert the consequences in paragraph 11.1(a) to (c).

11.20 A record shall be made of the grounds for any decision to interview a person under paragraph 11.18.

Notes for guidance

11A   Paragraph 11.4 does not prevent the interviewer from putting significant statements and silences to a suspect again at a later stage or a further interview.

11B   The Criminal Procedure and Investigations Act 1996 Code of Practice, paragraph 3.4 states 'In conducting an investigation, the investigator should pursue all reasonable lines of enquiry, whether these point towards or away from the suspect. What is reasonable will depend on the particular circumstances.' Interviewers should keep this in mind when deciding what questions to ask in an interview.

11C   Although juveniles or people who are mentally disordered or otherwise mentally vulnerable are often capable of providing reliable evidence, they may, without knowing or wishing to do so, be particularly prone in certain circumstances to provide information that may be unreliable, misleading or self-incriminating. Special care should always be taken when questioning such a person, and the appropriate adult should be involved if there is any doubt about a person's age, mental state or capacity. Because of the risk of unreliable evidence it is also important to obtain corroboration of any facts admitted whenever possible.

11D   Juveniles should not be arrested at their place of education unless this is unavoidable.

When a juvenile is arrested at their place of education, the principal or their nominee must be informed.

11E   Significant statements described in paragraph 11.4 will always be relevant to the offence and must be recorded. When a suspect agrees to read records of interviews and other comments and sign them as correct, they should be asked to endorse the record with, e.g. 'I agree that this is a correct record of what was said' and add their signature. If the suspect does not agree with the record, the interviewer should record the details of any disagreement and ask the suspect to read these details and sign them to the effect that they accurately reflect their disagreement. Any refusal to sign should be recorded.

12   Interviews in police stations

(a)   Action

12.1   If a police officer wants to interview or conduct enquiries which require the presence of a detainee, the custody officer is responsible for deciding whether to deliver the detainee into the officer's custody.

12.2   Except as below, in any period of 24 hours a detainee must be allowed a continuous period of at least 8 hours for rest, free from questioning, travel or any interruption in connection with the investigation concerned. This period should normally be at night or other appropriate time which takes account of when the detainee last slept or rested. If a detainee is arrested at a police station after going there voluntarily, the period of 24 hours runs from the time of their arrest and not the time of arrival at the police station. The period may not be interrupted or delayed, except:

(a)   when there are reasonable grounds for believing not delaying or interrupting the period would:

(i)   involve a risk of harm to people or serious loss of, or damage to, property;

(ii)   delay unnecessarily the person's release from custody;

(iii) otherwise prejudice the outcome of the investigation;

(b)   at the request of the detainee, their appropriate adult or legal representative;

(c)   when a delay or interruption is necessary in order to:

(i)   comply with the legal obligations and duties arising under section 15;

(ii)   to take action required under section 9 or in accordance with medical advice.

If the period is interrupted in accordance with (a), a fresh period must be allowed. Interruptions under (b) and (c), do not require a fresh period to be allowed.

12.3   Before a detainee is interviewed the custody officer, in consultation with the officer in charge of the investigation and appropriate health care professionals as necessary, shall assess whether the detainee is fit enough to be interviewed. This means determining and considering the risks to the detainee's physical and mental state if the interview took place and determining what safeguards are needed to allow the interview to take place. See Annex G. The custody officer shall not allow a detainee to be interviewed if the custody officer considers it would cause significant harm to the detainee's physical or mental state. Vulnerable suspects listed at paragraph 11.18 shall be treated as always being at some risk during an interview and these persons may not be interviewed except in accordance with paragraphs 11.18 to 11.20.

12.4   As far as practicable interviews shall take place in interview rooms which are adequately heated, lit and ventilated.

12.5   A suspect whose detention without charge has been authorised under PACE, because the detention is necessary for an interview to obtain evidence of the offence for which they have been arrested, may choose not to answer questions but police do not require the suspect's consent or agreement to interview them for this purpose. If a suspect takes steps to prevent themselves being questioned or further questioned, e.g. by refusing to leave their cell to go to a suitable interview room or by trying to leave the interview room, they shall be advised their consent or agreement to interview is not required. The suspect shall be cautioned as in section 10, and informed if they fail or refuse to co-operate, the interview may take place in the cell and that their failure or refusal to co- operate may be given in evidence. The suspect shall then be invited to co-operate and go into the interview room.

12.6 People being questioned or making statements shall not be required to stand.

12.7 Before the interview commences each interviewer shall, subject to paragraph 2.6A, identify themselves and any other persons present to the interviewee.

12.8 Breaks from interviewing should be made at recognised meal times or at other times that take account of when an interviewee last had a meal. Short refreshment breaks shall be provided at approximately two hour intervals, subject to the interviewer's discretion to delay a break if there are reasonable grounds for believing it would:

(i)   involve a:

•   risk of harm to people;

•   serious loss of, or damage to, property;

(ii)   unnecessarily delay the detainee's release;

(iii)   otherwise prejudice the outcome of the investigation. See Note 12B

12.9 If during the interview a complaint is made by or on behalf of the interviewee concerning the provisions of this Code, the interviewer should:

(i)   record it in the interview record;

(ii)   inform the custody officer, who is then responsible for dealing with it as in section 9.

(b)   Documentation

12.10 A record must be made of the:

•   time a detainee is not in the custody of the custody officer, and why

•   reason for any refusal to deliver the detainee out of that custody

12.11 A record shall be made of:

(a)   the reasons it was not practicable to use an interview room; and

(b)   any action taken as in paragraph 12.5.

The record shall be made on the custody record or in the interview record for action taken whilst an interview record is being kept, with a brief reference to this effect in the custody record.

12.12 Any decision to delay a break in an interview must be recorded, with reasons, in the interview record.

12.13 All written statements made at police stations under caution shall be written on forms provided for the purpose.

12.14 All written statements made under caution shall be taken in accordance with Annex D.

Before a person makes a written statement under caution at a police station they shall be reminded about the right to legal advice. See Note 12A

Notes for guidance

12A   It is not normally necessary to ask for a written statement if the interview was recorded in writing and the record signed in accordance with paragraph 11.11 or audibly or visually recorded in accordance with Code E or F. Statements under caution should normally be taken in these circumstances only at the person's express wish. A person may however be asked if they want to make such a statement.

12B   Meal breaks should normally last at least 45 minutes and shorter breaks after two hours should last at least 15 minutes. If the interviewer delays a break in accordance with paragraph 12.8 and prolongs the interview, a longer break should be provided. If there is a short interview, and another short interview is contemplated, the length of the break may be reduced if there are reasonable grounds to believe this is necessary to avoid any of the consequences in paragraph 12.8(i) to (iii).

13   Interpreters

(a)   General

13.1   Chief officers are responsible for making sure appropriate arrangements are in place for provision of suitably qualified interpreters for people who:

•   are deaf;

•   do not understand English.

Whenever possible, interpreters should be drawn from the National Register of Public Service Interpreters (NRPSI) or the Council for the Advancement of Communication with Deaf People (CACDP) Directory of British Sign Language/English Interpreters.

(b)   Foreign languages

13.2   Unless paragraphs 11.1, 11.18 to 11.20 apply, a person must not be interviewed in the absence of a person capable of interpreting if:

(a)   they have difficulty understanding English;

(b)   the interviewer cannot speak the person's own language; (c)   the person wants an interpreter present.

13.3   The interviewer shall make sure the interpreter makes a note of the interview at the time in the person's language for use in the event of the interpreter being called to give evidence, and certifies its accuracy. The interviewer should allow sufficient time for the interpreter to note each question and answer after each is put, given and interpreted.

The person should be allowed to read the record or have it read to them and sign it as correct or indicate the respects in which they consider it inaccurate. If the interview is audibly recorded or visually recorded, the arrangements in Code E or F apply.

13.4 In the case of a person making a statement to a police officer or other police staff other than in English:

(a)   the interpreter shall record the statement in the language it is made; (b)   the   person shall be invited to sign it;

(c)   an official English translation shall be made in due course.

(c)   Deaf people and people with speech difficulties

13.5 If a person appears to be deaf or there is doubt about their hearing or speaking ability, they must not be interviewed in the absence of an interpreter unless they agree in writing to being interviewed without one or paragraphs 11.1, 11.18 to 11.20 apply.

13.6 An interpreter should also be called if a juvenile is interviewed and the parent or guardian present as the appropriate adult appears to be deaf or there is doubt about their hearing or speaking ability, unless they agree in writing to the interview proceeding without one or paragraphs 11.1, 11.18 to 11.20 apply.

13.7 The interviewer shall make sure the interpreter is allowed to read the interview record and certify its accuracy in the event of the interpreter being called to give evidence. If the interview is audibly recorded or visually recorded, the arrangements in Code E or F apply.

(d)   Additional rules for detained persons

13.8 All reasonable attempts should be made to make the detainee understand that interpreters will be provided at public expense.

13.9 If paragraph 6.1 applies and the detainee cannot communicate with the solicitor because of language, hearing or speech difficulties, an interpreter must be called. The interpreter may not be a police officer or any other police staff when interpretation is needed for the purposes of obtaining legal advice. In all other cases a police officer or other police staff may only interpret if the detainee and the appropriate adult, if applicable, give their agreement in writing or if the interview is audibly recorded or visually recorded as in Code E or F.

13.10 When the custody officer cannot establish effective communication with a person charged with an offence who appears deaf or there is doubt about their ability to hear, speak or to understand English, arrangements must be made as soon as practicable for an interpreter to explain the offence and any other information given by the custody officer.

(e)   Documentation

13.11 Action taken to call an interpreter under this section and any agreement to be interviewed in the absence of an interpreter must be recorded.

14   Questioning – special restrictions

14.1 If a person is arrested by one police force on behalf of another and the lawful period of detention in respect of that offence has not yet commenced in accordance with PACE, section 41 no questions may be put to them about the offence while they are in transit between the forces except to clarify any voluntary statement they make.

14.2   If a person is in police detention at a hospital they may not be questioned without the agreement of a responsible doctor. See Note 14A

Note for guidance

14A   If questioning takes place at a hospital under paragraph 14.2, or on the way to or from a hospital, the period of questioning concerned   counts towards the total period of detention permitted.

15   Reviews and extensions of detention

(a)   Persons detained under PACE

15.1   The review officer is responsible under PACE, section 40 for periodically determining if a person's detention, before or after charge, continues to be necessary. This requirement continues throughout the detention period and except as in paragraph 15.10, the review officer must be present at the police station holding the detainee. See Notes 15A and 15B

15.2   Under PACE, section 42, an officer of superintendent rank or above who is responsible for the station holding the detainee may give authority any time after the second review to extend the maximum period the person may be detained without charge by up to 12 hours. Further detention without charge may be authorised only by a magistrates' court in accordance with PACE, sections 43 and 44. See Notes 15C, 15D and 15E

15.2A Section 42(1) of PACE as amended extends the maximum period of detention for indictable offences from 24 hours to 36 hours. Detaining a juvenile or mentally vulnerable person for longer than 24 hours will be dependent on the circumstances of the case and with regard to the person's:

(a)   special vulnerability;

(b)   the legal obligation to provide an opportunity for representations to be made prior to a decision about extending detention;

(c)   the need to consult and consider the views of any appropriate adult; and

(d)   any alternatives to police custody.

15.3   Before deciding whether to authorise continued detention the officer responsible under paragraphs 15.1 or 15.2 shall give an opportunity to make representations about the detention to:

(a)   the detainee, unless in the case of a review as in paragraph 15.1, the detainee is asleep;

(b)   the detainee's solicitor if available at the time; and

(c)   the appropriate adult if available at the time.

15.3A Other people having an interest in the detainee's welfare may also make representations at the authorising officer's discretion.

15.3B Subject to paragraph 15.10, the representations may be made orally in person or by telephone or in writing. The authorising officer may, however, refuse to hear oral representations from the detainee if the officer considers them unfit to make representations because of their condition or behaviour. See Note 15C

15.3C The decision on whether the review takes place in person or by telephone or by video conferencing (see Note 15G) is a matter for the review officer. In determining the form the review may take, the review officer must always take full account of the needs of the person in custody. The benefits of carrying out a review in person should always be considered, based on the individual circumstances of each case with specific additional consideration if the person is:

(a)   a juvenile (and the age of the juvenile); or

(b)   mentally vulnerable; or

(c)   has been subject to medical attention for other than routine minor ailments; or

(d)   there are presentational or community issues around the person's detention.

15.4   Before conducting a review or determining whether to extend the maximum period of detention without charge, the officer responsible must make sure the detainee is reminded of their entitlement to free legal advice, see paragraph 6.5, unless in the case of a review the person is asleep.

15.5 If, after considering any representations, the officer decides to keep the detainee in detention or extend the maximum period they may be detained without charge, any comment made by the detainee shall be recorded. If applicable, the officer responsible under paragraph 15.1 or 15.2 shall be informed of the comment as soon as practicable. See also paragraphs 11.4 and 11.13

15.6 No officer shall put specific questions to the detainee:

•   regarding their involvement in any offence; or

•   in respect of any comments they may make:

–   when given the opportunity to make representations; or

–   in response to a decision to keep them in detention or extend the maximum period of detention.

Such an exchange could constitute an interview as in paragraph 11.1A and would be subject to the associated safeguards in section 11 and, in respect of a person who has been charged, paragraph 16.5. See also paragraph 11.13

15.7 A detainee who is asleep at a review, see paragraph 15.1, and whose continued detention is authorised must be informed about the decision and reason as soon as practicable after waking.

15.8 Not used

(b)   Telephone review of detention

15.9 PACE, section 40A provides that the officer responsible under section 40 for reviewing the detention of a person who has not been charged, need not attend the police station holding the detainee and may carry out the review by telephone.

15.9A PACE, section 45A(2) provides that the officer responsible under section 40 for reviewing the detention of a person who has not been charged, need not attend the police station holding the detainee and may carry out the review by video conferencing facilities (See Note 15G).

15.9B A telephone review is not permitted where facilities for review by video conferencing exist and it is practicable to use them.

15.9C The review officer can decide at any stage that a telephone review or review by video conferencing should be terminated and that the review will be conducted in person. The reasons for doing so should be noted in the custody record. See Note 15F

15.10 When a telephone review is carried out, an officer at the station holding the detainee shall be required by the review officer to fulfil that officer's obligations under PACE section 40 or this Code by:

(a)   making any record connected with the review in the detainee's custody record; (b)   if applicable, making a record in (a) in the presence of the detainee; and

(c)   giving the detainee information about the review.

15.11 When a telephone review is carried out, the requirement in paragraph 15.3 will be satisfied:

(a)   if facilities exist for the immediate transmission of written representations to the review officer, e.g. fax or email message, by giving the detainee an opportunity to make representations:

(i)   orally by telephone; or

(ii)   in writing using those facilities; and

(b)   in all other cases, by giving the detainee an opportunity to make their representations orally by telephone.

(c)   Documentation

15.12 It is the officer's responsibility to make sure all reminders given under paragraph 15.4 are noted in the custody record.

15.13 The grounds for, and extent of, any delay in conducting a review shall be recorded.

15.14 When a telephone review is carried out, a record shall be made of:

(a)   the reason the review officer did not attend the station holding the detainee; (b)   the place the review officer was;

(c)   the method representations, oral or written, were made to the review officer, see paragraph 15.11.

15.15 Any written representations shall be retained.

15.16 A record shall be made as soon as practicable about the outcome of each review or determination whether to extend the maximum detention period without charge or an application for a warrant of further detention or its extension. If paragraph 15.7 applies, a record shall also be made of when the person was informed and by whom. If an authorisation is given under PACE, section 42, the record shall state the number of hours and minutes by which the detention period is extended or further extended. If a warrant for further detention, or extension, is granted under section 43 or 44, the record shall state the detention period authorised by the warrant and the date and time it was granted.

Notes for guidance

15A   Review officer for the purposes of:

•   PACE, sections 40 and 40A means, in the case of a person arrested but not charged, an officer of at least inspector rank not directly involved in the investigation and, if a person has been arrested and charged, the custody officer;

15B   The detention of persons in police custody not subject to the statutory review requirement in paragraph 15.1 should still be reviewed periodically as a matter of good practice. Such reviews can be carried out by an officer of the rank of sergeant or above. The purpose of such reviews is to check the particular power under which a detainee is held continues to apply, any associated conditions are complied with and to make sure appropriate action is taken to deal with any changes. This includes the detainee's prompt release when the power no longer applies, or their transfer if the power requires the detainee be taken elsewhere as soon as the necessary arrangements are made. Examples include persons:

(a)   arrested on warrant because they failed to answer bail to appear at court;

(b)   arrested under the Bail Act 1976, section 7(3) for breaching a condition of bail granted after charge;

(c)   in police custody for specific purposes and periods under the Crime (Sentences) Act 1997, Schedule 1;

(d)   convicted, or remand prisoners, held in police stations on behalf of the Prison

Service under the Imprisonment (Temporary Provisions) Act 1980, section 6; (e)   being detained to prevent them causing a breach of the peace;

(f)   detained at police stations on behalf of the Immigration Service.

(g)   detained by order of a magistrates' court under the Criminal Justice Act 1988, section 152 (as amended by the Drugs Act 2005, section 8) to facilitate the recovery of evidence after being charged with drug possession or drug trafficking and suspected of having swallowed drugs.

The detention of persons remanded into police detention by order of a court under the Magistrates' Courts Act 1980, section 128 is subject to a statutory requirement to review that detention. This is to make sure the detainee is taken back to court no later than the end of the period authorised by the court or when the need for their detention by police ceases, whichever is the sooner.

15C   In the case of a review of detention, but not an extension, the detainee need not be woken for the review. However, if the detainee is likely to be asleep, e.g. during a period of rest allowed as in paragraph 12.2, at the latest time a review or authorisation to extend detention may take place, the officer should, if the legal obligations and time constraints permit, bring forward the procedure to allow the detainee to make representations. A detainee not asleep during the review must be present when the grounds for their continued detention are recorded and must at the same time be informed of those grounds unless the review officer considers the person is incapable of understanding what is said, violent or likely to become violent or in urgent need of medical attention.

15D   An application to a Magistrates' Court under PACE, sections 43 or 44 for a warrant of further detention or its extension should be made between 10am and 9pm, and if possible during normal court hours. It will not usually be practicable to arrange for a court to sit specially outside the hours of 10am to 9pm. If it appears a special sitting may be needed outside normal court hours but between 10am and 9pm, the clerk to the justices should be given notice and informed of this possibility, while the court is sitting if possible.

15E   In paragraph 15.2, the officer responsible for the station holding the detainee includes a superintendent or above who, in accordance with their force operational policy or police regulations, is given that responsibility on a temporary basis whilst the appointed long- term holder is off duty or otherwise unavailable.

15F   The provisions of PACE, section 40A allowing telephone reviews do not apply to reviews of detention after charge by the custody officer When video conferencing is not required, they allow the use of a telephone to carry out a review of detention before charge. The procedure under PACE, section 42 must be done in person.

15G   The use of video conferencing facilities for decisions about detention under section 45A of PACE is subject to the introduction of regulations by the Secretary of State.

16   Charging detained persons

(a)   Action

16.1   When the officer in charge of the investigation reasonably believes there is sufficient evidence to provide a realistic prospect of conviction for the offence (see paragraph

11.6), they shall without delay, and subject to the following qualification, inform the custody officer who will be responsible for considering whether the detainee should be charged. See Notes 11B and 16A. When a person is detained in respect of more than one offence it is permissible to delay informing the custody officer until the above conditions are satisfied in respect of all the offences, but see paragraph 11.6. If the detainee is a juvenile, mentally disordered or otherwise mentally vulnerable, any resulting action shall be taken in the presence of the appropriate adult if they are present at the time. See Notes 16B and 16C

16.1A Where guidance issued by the Director of Public Prosecutions under section 37A is in force the custody officer must comply with that Guidance in deciding how to act in dealing with the detainee. See Notes 16AA and 16AB.

16.1B Where in compliance with the DPP's Guidance the custody officer decides that the case should be immediately referred to the CPS to make the charging decision, consultation should take place with a Crown Prosecutor as soon as is reasonably practicable. Where the Crown Prosecutor is unable to make the charging decision on the information available at that time, the detainee may be released without charge and on bail (with conditions if necessary) under section 37(7)(a). In such circumstances, the detainee should be informed that they are being released to enable the Director of Public Prosecutions to make a decision under section 37B.

16.2   When a detainee is charged with or informed they may be prosecuted for an offence, see Note 16B, they shall, unless the restriction on drawing adverse inferences from silence applies, see Annex C, be cautioned as follows:

'You do not have to say anything. But it may harm your defence if you do not mention now something which you later rely on in court. Anything you do say may be given in evidence.'

Where the use of the Welsh Language is appropriate, a constable may provide the caution directly in Welsh in the following terms:

'Does dim rhaid i chi ddweud dim byd. Ond gall niweidio eich amddiffyniad os na fyddwch chi'n sôn, yn awr, am rywbeth y byddwch chi'n dibynnu arno nes ymlaen yn y llys. Gall unrhyw beth yr ydych yn ei ddweud gael ei roi fel tystiolaeth.'

Annex C, paragraph 2 sets out the alternative terms of the caution to be used when the restriction on drawing adverse inferences from silence applies.

16.3   When a detainee is charged they shall be given a written notice showing particulars of the offence and, subject to paragraph 2.6A, the officer's name and the case reference number. As far as possible the particulars of the charge shall be stated in simple terms, but they shall also show the precise offence in law with which the detainee is charged. The notice shall begin:

'You are charged with the offence(s) shown below.' Followed by the caution.

If the detainee is a juvenile, mentally disordered or otherwise mentally vulnerable, the notice should be given to the appropriate adult.

16.4   If, after a detainee has been charged with or informed they may be prosecuted for an offence, an officer wants to tell them about any written statement or interview with another person relating to such an offence, the detainee shall either be handed a true copy of the written statement or the content of the interview record brought to their attention. Nothing shall be done to invite any reply or comment except to:

(a)   caution the detainee, 'You do not have to say anything, but anything you do say may be given in evidence.';

Where the use of the Welsh Language is appropriate, caution the detainee in the following terms:

'Does dim rhaid i chi ddweud dim byd, ond gall unrhyw beth yr ydych yn ei ddweud gael ei roi fel tystiolaeth.'

and

(b)   remind the detainee about their right to legal advice.

16.4A If the detainee:

•   cannot read, the document may be read to them

•   is a juvenile, mentally disordered or otherwise mentally vulnerable, the appropriate adult shall also be given a copy, or the interview record shall be brought to their attention

16.5   A detainee may not be interviewed about an offence after they have been charged with, or informed they may be prosecuted for it, unless the interview is necessary:

•   to prevent or minimise harm or loss to some other person, or the public

•   to clear up an ambiguity in a previous answer or statement

- in the interests of justice for the detainee to have put to them, and have an opportunity to comment on, information concerning the offence which has come to light since they were charged or informed they might be prosecuted

Before any such interview, the interviewer shall:

(a)   caution the detainee, 'You do not have to say anything, but anything you do say may be given in evidence.'

Where the use of the Welsh Language is appropriate, the interviewer shall caution the detainee, 'Does dim rhaid i chi ddweud dim byd, ond gall unrhyw beth yr ydych yn ei ddweud gael ei roi fel tystiolaeth.'

(b)   remind the detainee about their right to legal advice. See Note 16B

16.6   The provisions of paragraphs 16.2 to 16.5 must be complied with in the appropriate adult's presence if they are already at the police station. If they are not at the police station then these provisions must be complied with again in their presence when they arrive unless the detainee has been released. See Note 16C

16.7   When a juvenile is charged with an offence and the custody officer authorises their continued detention after charge, the custody officer must try to make arrangements for the juvenile to be taken into the care of a local authority to be detained pending appearance in court unless the custody officer certifies it is impracticable to do so or, in the case of a juvenile of at least 12 years old, no secure accommodation is available and there is a risk to the public of serious harm from that juvenile, in accordance with PACE, section 38(6). See Note 16D

(b)   Documentation

16.8   A record shall be made of anything a detainee says when charged.

16.9   Any questions put in an interview after charge and answers given relating to the offence shall be recorded in full during the interview on forms for that purpose and the record signed by the detainee or, if they refuse, by the interviewer and any third parties present. If the questions are audibly recorded or visually recorded the arrangements in Code E or F apply.

16.10   If it is not practicable to make arrangements for a juvenile's transfer into local authority care as in paragraph 16.7, the custody officer must record the reasons and complete a certificate to be produced before the court with the juvenile. See Note 16D

Notes for guidance

16A   The custody officer must take into account alternatives to prosecution under the Crime and Disorder Act 1998, reprimands and warning applicable to persons under 18, and in national guidance on the cautioning of offenders, for persons aged 18 and over.

16AA When a person is arrested under the provisions of the Criminal Justice Act 2003 which allow a person to be re-tried after being acquitted of a serious offence which is a qualifying offence specified in Schedule 5 to that Act and not precluded from further prosecution by virtue of section 75(3) of that Act the detention provisions of PACE are modified and make an officer of the rank of superintendent or above who has not been directly involved in the investigation responsible for determining whether the evidence is sufficient to charge.

16AB Where Guidance issued by the Director of Public Prosecutions under section 37B is in force, a custody officer who determines in accordance with that Guidance that there is sufficient evidence to charge the detainee, may detain that person for no longer than is reasonably necessary to decide how that person is to be dealt with under PACE, section

37(7)(a) to (d), including, where appropriate, consultation with the Duty Prosecutor. The period is subject to the maximum period of detention before charge determined by PACE, sections 41 to 44. Where in accordance with the Guidance the case is referred to the CPS for decision, the custody officer should ensure that an officer involved in the investigation sends to the CPS such information as is specified in the Guidance.

16B   The giving of a warning or the service of the Notice of Intended Prosecution required by the Road Traffic Offenders Act 1988, section 1 does not amount to informing a detainee they may be prosecuted for an offence and so does not preclude further questioning in relation to that offence.

16C   There is no power under PACE to detain a person and delay action under paragraphs

16.2 to 16.5 solely to await the arrival of the appropriate adult. After charge, bail cannot be refused, or release on bail delayed, simply because an appropriate adult is not available, unless the absence of that adult provides the custody officer with the necessary grounds to authorise detention after charge under PACE, section 38.

16D   Except as in paragraph 16.7, neither a juvenile's behaviour nor the nature of the offence provides grounds for the custody officer to decide it is impracticable to arrange the juvenile's transfer to local authority care. Similarly, the lack of secure local authority accommodation does not make it impracticable to transfer the juvenile. The availability of secure accommodation is only a factor in relation to a juvenile aged 12 or over when the local authority accommodation would not be adequate to protect the public from serious harm from them. The obligation to transfer a juvenile to local authority accommodation applies as much to a juvenile charged during the daytime as to a juvenile to be held overnight, subject to a requirement to bring the juvenile before a court under PACE, section 46.

17   testing persons for the presence of specified Class A drugs

(a)   Action

17.1   This section of Code C applies only in selected police stations in police areas where the provisions for drug testing under section 63B of PACE (as amended by section 5 of the Criminal Justice Act 2003 and section 7 of the Drugs Act 2005) are in force and in respect of which the Secretary of State has given a notification to the relevant chief officer of police that arrangements for the taking of samples have been made. Such a notification will cover either a police area as a whole or particular stations within a police area. The notification indicates whether the testing applies to those arrested or charged or under the age of 18 as the case may be and testing can only take place in respect of the persons so indicated in the notification. Testing cannot be carried out unless the relevant notification has been given and has not been withdrawn. See Note 17F

17.2   A sample of urine or a non-intimate sample may be taken from a person in police detention for the purpose of ascertaining whether he has any specified Class A drug in his body only where they have been brought before the custody officer and:

(a)   either the arrest condition, see paragraph 17.3, or the charge condition, see paragraph 17.4 is met;

(b)   the age condition see paragraph 17.5, is met;

(c)   the notification condition is met in relation to the arrest condition, the charge condition, or the age condition, as the case may be. (Testing on charge and/or arrest must be specifically provided for in the notification for the power to apply. In addition, the fact that testing of under 18s is authorised must be expressly provided for in the notification before the power to test such persons applies.). See paragraph 17.1; and

(d)   a police officer has requested the person concerned to give the sample (the request condition).

17.3 The arrest condition is met where the detainee:

(a)   has been arrested for a trigger offence, see Note 17E, but not charged with that offence; or

(b)   has been arrested for any other offence but not charged with that offence and a police officer of inspector rank or above, who has reasonable grounds for suspecting that their misuse of any specified Class A drug caused or contributed to the offence, has authorised the sample to be taken.

17.4 The charge condition is met where the detainee: (a) has been charged with a trigger offence, or

(b)   has been charged with any other offence and a police officer of inspector rank or above, who has reasonable grounds for suspecting that the detainee's misuse of any specified Class A drug caused or contributed to the offence, has authorised the sample to be taken.

17.5 The age condition is met where:

(a)   in the case of a detainee who has been arrested but not charged as in paragraph

17.3, they are aged 18 or over;

(b)   in the case of a detainee who has been charged as in paragraph 17.4, they are aged 14 or over.

17.6 Before requesting a sample from the person concerned, an officer must:

(a)   inform them that the purpose of taking the sample is for drug testing under PACE.

This is to ascertain whether they have a specified Class A drug present in their body;

(b)   warn them that if, when so requested, they fail without good cause to provide a sample they may be liable to prosecution;

(c)   where the taking of the sample has been authorised by an inspector or above in accordance with paragraph 17.3(b) or 17.4(b) above, inform them that the authorisation has been given and the grounds for giving it;

(d)   remind them of the following rights, which may be exercised at any stage during the period in custody:

(i)   the right to have someone informed of their arrest [see section 5];

(ii)   the right to consult privately with a solicitor and that free independent legal advice is available [see section 6]; and

(iii)   the right to consult these Codes of Practice [see section 3].

17.7   In the case of a person who has not attained the age of 17 —

(a)   the making of the request for a sample under paragraph 17.2(d) above;

(b)   the giving of the warning and the information under paragraph 17.6 above; and

(c)   the taking of the sample,

may not take place except in the presence of an appropriate adult. (see Note 17G)

17.8   Authorisation by an officer of the rank of inspector or above within paragraph 17.3(b) or

17.4(b) may be given orally or in writing but, if it is given orally, it must be confirmed in writing as soon as practicable.

17.9   If a sample is taken from a detainee who has been arrested for an offence but not charged with that offence as in paragraph 17.3, no further sample may be taken during the same continuous period of detention. If during that same period the charge condition is also met in respect of that detainee, the sample which has been taken shall be treated as being taken by virtue of the charge condition, see paragraph 17.4, being met.

17.10 A detainee from whom a sample may be taken may be detained for up to six hours from the time of charge if the custody officer reasonably believes the detention is necessary to enable a sample to be taken. Where the arrest condition is met, a detainee whom the custody officer has decided to release on bail without charge may continue to be detained, but not beyond 24 hours from the relevant time (as defined in section 41(2) of PACE), to enable a sample to be taken.

17.11 A detainee in respect of whom the arrest condition is met, but not the charge condition, see paragraphs 17.3 and 17.4, and whose release would be required before a sample can be taken had they not continued to be detained as a result of being arrested for a further offence which does not satisfy the arrest condition, may have a sample taken at any time within 24 hours after the arrest for the offence that satisfies the arrest condition.

(b)   Documentation

17.12 The following must be recorded in the custody record:

(a)   if a sample is taken following authorisation by an officer of the rank of inspector or above, the authorisation and the grounds for suspicion;

(b)   the giving of a warning of the consequences of failure to provide a sample;

(c)   the time at which the sample was given; and

(d)   the time of charge or, where the arrest condition is being relied upon, the time of arrest and, where applicable, the fact that a sample taken after arrest but before charge is to be treated as being taken by virtue of the charge condition, where that is met in the same period of continuous detention. See paragraph 17.9

(c)   General

17.13 A sample may only be taken by a prescribed person. See Note 17C.

17.14 Force may not be used to take any sample for the purpose of drug testing.

17.15 The terms "Class A drug" and "misuse" have the same meanings as in the Misuse of Drugs Act 1971. "Specified" (in relation to a Class A drug) and "trigger offence" have the same meanings as in Part III of the Criminal Justice and Court Services Act 2000.

17.16 Any sample taken:

(a)   may not be used for any purpose other than to ascertain whether the person concerned has a specified Class A drug present in his body; and

(b)   can be disposed of as clinical waste unless it is to be sent for further analysis in cases where the test result is disputed at the point when the result is known, or where medication has been taken, or for quality assurance purposes.

(d)   Assessment of misuse of drugs

17.17 Under the provisions of Part 3 of the Drugs Act 2005, where a detainee has tested positive for a specified Class A drug under section 63B of PACE a police officer may, at any time before the person's release from the police station, impose a requirement on the detainee to attend an initial assessment of their drug misuse by a suitably qualified person and to remain for its duration. Where such a requirement is imposed, the officer must, at the same time, impose a second requirement on the detainee to attend and remain for a follow-up assessment. The officer must inform the detainee that the second requirement will cease to have effect if, at the initial assessment they are informed that a follow-up assessment is not necessary. These requirements may only be imposed on a person if:

(a)   they have reached the age of 18

(b)   notification has been given by the Secretary of State to the relevant chief officer of police that arrangements for conducting initial and follow-up assessments have been made for those from whom samples for testing have been taken at the police station where the detainee is in custody.

17.18 When imposing a requirement to attend an initial assessment and a follow-up assessment the police officer must:

(a)   inform the person of the time and place at which the initial assessment is to take place;

(b)   explain that this information will be confirmed in writing; and

(c)   warn the person that they may be liable to prosecution if they fail without good cause to attend the initial assessment and remain for its duration and if they fail to attend the follow-up assessment and remain for its duration (if so required).

17.19 Where a police officer has imposed a requirement to attend an initial assessment and a follow-up assessment in accordance with paragraph 17.17, he must, before the person is released from detention, give the person notice in writing which:

(a)   confirms their requirement to attend and remain for the duration of the assessments; and

(b)   confirms the information and repeats the warning referred to in paragraph 17.18.

17.20 The following must be recorded in the custody record:

(a)   that the requirement to attend an initial assessment and a follow-up assessment has been imposed; and

(b)   the information, explanation, warning and notice given in accordance with paragraphs 17.17 and 17.19.

17.21 Where a notice is given in accordance with paragraph 17.19, a police officer can give the person a further notice in writing which informs the person of any change to the time or place at which the initial assessment is to take place and which repeats the warning referred to in paragraph 17.18(c).

17.22 Part 3 of the Drugs Act 2005 also requires police officers to have regard to any guidance issued by the Secretary of State in respect of the assessment provisions.

Notes for guidance

17A   When warning a person who is asked to provide a urine or non-intimate sample in accordance with paragraph 17.6(b), the following form of words may be used:

"You do not have to provide a sample, but I must warn you that if you fail or refuse without good cause to do so, you will commit an offence for which you may be imprisoned, or fined, or both".

Where the Welsh language is appropriate, the following form of words may be used:

'Does dim rhaid i chi roi sampl, ond mae'n rhaid i mi eich rhybuddio y byddwch chi'n cyflawni trosedd os byddwch chi'n methu neu yn gwrthod gwneud hynny heb reswm da, ac y gellir, oherwydd hynny, eich carcharu, eich dirwyo, neu'r ddau.'

17B   A sample has to be sufficient and suitable. A sufficient sample is sufficient in quantity and quality to enable drug-testing analysis to take place. A suitable sample is one which by its nature, is suitable for a particular form of drug analysis.

17C   A prescribed person in paragraph 17.13 is one who is prescribed in regulations made by the Secretary of State under section 63B(6) of the Police and Criminal Evidence Act

1984. [The regulations are currently contained in regulation SI 2001 No. 2645, the Police and Criminal Evidence Act 1984 (Drug Testing Persons in Police Detention) (Prescribed Persons) Regulations 2001.]

17D   Samples, and the information derived from them, may not be subsequently used in the investigation of any offence or in evidence against the persons from whom they were taken.

17E   Trigger offences are:

1.   Offences under the following provisions of the Theft Act 1968:

section 1   (theft) section 8 (robbery)

section 9   (burglary)

section 10   (aggravated burglary)

section 12   (taking a motor vehicle or other conveyance without authority)

section 12A   (aggravated vehicle-taking)

section 22   (handling stolen goods)

section 25   (going equipped for stealing etc.)

2.   Offences under the following provisions of the Misuse of Drugs Act 1971, if committed in respect of a specified Class A drug:–

section 4   (restriction on production and supply of controlled drugs)

section 5(2)   (possession of a controlled drug)

section 5(3)   (possession of a controlled drug with intent to supply)

3.   Offences under the following provisions of the Fraud Act 2006:

section 1   (fraud)

section 6   (possession etc. of articles for use in frauds)

section 7   (making or supplying articles for use in frauds)

3A.   An offence under section 1(1) of the Criminal Attempts Act 1981 if committed in respect of an offence under

(a)   any of the following provisions of the Theft Act 1968:

section 1   (theft)

section 8   (robbery)

section 9   (burglary)

section 22   (handling stolen goods)

(b)   section 1 of the Fraud Act 2006 (fraud)

4.   Offences under the following provisions of the Vagrancy Act 1824:

section 3   (begging)

section 4   (persistent begging)

17F   The power to take samples is subject to notification by the Secretary of State that appropriate arrangements for the taking of samples have been made for the police area as a whole or for the particular police station concerned for whichever of the following is specified in the notification:

(a)   persons in respect of whom the arrest condition is met;

(b)   persons in respect of whom the charge condition is met;

(c)   persons who have not attained the age of 18.

Note: Notification is treated as having been given for the purposes of the charge condition in relation to a police area, if testing (on charge) under section 63B(2) of PACE was in force immediately before section 7 of the Drugs Act 2005 was brought into force; and for the purposes of the age condition, in relation to a police area or police station, if immediately before that day, notification that arrangements had been made for the taking of samples from persons under the age of 18 (those aged 14-17) had been given and had not been withdrawn.

17G   Appropriate adult in paragraph 17.7 means the person's –

(a)   parent or guardian or, if they are in the care of a local authority or voluntary organisation, a person representing that authority or organisation; or

(b)   a social worker of a local authority; or

(c)   if no person falling within (a) or (b) above is available, any responsible person aged 18 or over who is not a police officer or a person employed by the police.

Annex A – Intimate and strip searches

A   Intimate search

1.   An intimate search consists of the physical examination of a person's body orifices other than the mouth. The intrusive nature of such searches means the actual and potential risks associated with intimate searches must never be underestimated.

(a)   Action

2.   Body orifices other than the mouth may be searched only:

(a)   if authorised by an officer of inspector rank or above who has reasonable grounds for believing that the person may have concealed on themselves:

(i)   anything which they could and might use to cause physical injury to themselves or others at the station; or

(ii)   a Class A drug which they intended to supply to another or to export;

and the officer has reasonable grounds for believing that an intimate search is the only means of removing those items; and

(b)   if the search is under paragraph 2(a)(ii) (a drug offence search), the detainee's appropriate consent has been given in writing.

2A.   Before the search begins, a police officer, designated detention officer or staff custody officer, must tell the detainee:-

(a)   that the authority to carry out the search has been given;

(b)   the grounds for giving the authorisation and for believing that the article cannot be removed without an intimate search.

2B   Before a detainee is asked to give appropriate consent to a search under paragraph

2(a)(ii) (a drug offence search) they must be warned that if they refuse without good cause their refusal may harm their case if it comes to trial, see Note A6. This warning may be given by a police officer or member of police staff. A detainee who is not legally represented must be reminded of their entitlement to have free legal advice, see Code C, paragraph 6.5, and the reminder noted in the custody record.

3.   An intimate search may only be carried out by a registered medical practitioner or registered nurse, unless an officer of at least inspector rank considers this is not practicable and the search is to take place under paragraph 2(a)(i), in which case a police officer may carry out the search. See Notes A1 to A5

3A.   Any proposal for a search under paragraph 2(a)(i) to be carried out by someone other than a registered medical practitioner or registered nurse must only be considered as a last resort and when the authorising officer is satisfied the risks associated with allowing the item to remain with the detainee outweigh the risks associated with removing it. See Notes A1 to A5

4.   An intimate search under:

•   paragraph 2(a)(i) may take place only at a hospital, surgery, other medical premises or police station

•   paragraph 2(a)(ii) may take place only at a hospital, surgery or other medical premises and must be carried out by a registered medical practitioner or a registered nurse

5.   An intimate search at a police station of a juvenile or mentally disordered or otherwise mentally vulnerable person may take place only in the presence of an appropriate adult of the same sex, unless the detainee specifically requests a particular adult of the opposite sex who is readily available. In the case of a juvenile the search may take place in the absence of the appropriate adult only if the juvenile signifies in the presence of the appropriate adult they do not want the adult present during the search and the adult agrees. A record shall be made of the juvenile's decision and signed by the appropriate adult.

6.   When an intimate search under paragraph 2(a)(i) is carried out by a police officer, the officer must be of the same sex as the detainee. A minimum of two people, other than the detainee, must be present during the search. Subject to paragraph 5, no person of the opposite sex who is not a medical practitioner or nurse shall be present, nor shall anyone whose presence is unnecessary. The search shall be conducted with proper regard to the sensitivity and vulnerability of the detainee.

(b)   Documentation

7.   In the case of an intimate search, the following shall be recorded as soon as practicable, in the detainee's custody record:

(a)   for searches under paragraphs 2(a)(i) and (ii);

*   the authorisation to carry out the search;

*   the grounds for giving the authorisation;

*   the grounds for believing the article could not be removed without an intimate search

*   which parts of the detainee's body were searched

*   who carried out the search

*   who was present

*   the result.

(b)   for searches under paragraph 2(a)(ii):

*   the giving of the warning required by paragraph 2B;

*   the fact that the appropriate consent was given or (as the case may be)

refused, and if refused, the reason given for the refusal (if any).

8.   If an intimate search is carried out by a police officer, the reason why it was impracticable for a registered medical practitioner or registered nurse to conduct it must be recorded.

B   strip search

9.   A strip search is a search involving the removal of more than outer clothing. In this Code, outer clothing includes shoes and socks.

(a)   Action

10.   A strip search may take place only if it is considered necessary to remove an article which a detainee would not be allowed to keep, and the officer reasonably considers the detainee might have concealed such an article. Strip searches shall not be routinely carried out if there is no reason to consider that articles are concealed.

The conduct of strip searches

11.   When strip searches are conducted:

(a)   a police officer carrying out a strip search must be the same sex as the detainee; (b) the search shall take place in an area where the detainee cannot be seen by anyone who does not need to be present, nor by a member of the opposite sex except an appropriate adult who has been specifically requested by the detainee;

(c)   except in cases of urgency, where there is risk of serious harm to the detainee or to others, whenever a strip search involves exposure of intimate body parts, there must be at least two people present other than the detainee, and if the search is of a juvenile or mentally disordered or otherwise mentally vulnerable person, one of the people must be the appropriate adult. Except in urgent cases as above, a search of a juvenile may take place in the absence of the appropriate adult only if the juvenile signifies in the presence of the appropriate adult that they do not want the adult to be present during the search and the adult agrees. A record shall be made of the juvenile's decision and signed by the appropriate adult. The presence of more than two people, other than an appropriate adult, shall be permitted only in the most exceptional circumstances;

(d)   the search shall be conducted with proper regard to the sensitivity and vulnerability of the detainee in these circumstances and every reasonable effort shall be made to secure the detainee's co-operation and minimise embarrassment. Detainees who are searched shall not normally be required to remove all their clothes at the same time, e.g. a person should be allowed to remove clothing above the waist and redress before removing further clothing;

(e)   if necessary to assist the search, the detainee may be required to hold their arms in the air or to stand with their legs apart and bend forward so a visual examination may be made of the genital and anal areas provided no physical contact is made with any body orifice;

(f)   if articles are found, the detainee shall be asked to hand them over. If articles are found within any body orifice other than the mouth, and the detainee refuses to hand them over, their removal would constitute an intimate search, which must be carried out as in Part A;

(g)   a strip search shall be conducted as quickly as possible, and the detainee allowed to dress as soon as the procedure is complete.

(b)   Documentation

12.   A record shall be made on the custody record of a strip search including the reason it was considered necessary, those present and any result.

Notes for guidance

A1   Before authorising any intimate search, the authorising officer must make every reasonable effort to persuade the detainee to hand the article over without a search. If the detainee agrees, a registered medical practitioner or registered nurse should whenever possible be asked to assess the risks involved and, if necessary, attend to assist the detainee.

A2   If the detainee does not agree to hand the article over without a search, the authorising officer must carefully review all the relevant factors before authorising an intimate search.

In particular, the officer must consider whether the grounds for believing an article may be concealed are reasonable.

A3   If authority is given for a search under paragraph 2(a)(i), a registered medical practitioner or registered nurse shall be consulted whenever possible. The presumption should be that the search will be conducted by the registered medical practitioner or registered nurse and the authorising officer must make every reasonable effort to persuade the detainee to allow the medical practitioner or nurse to conduct the search.

A4   A constable should only be authorised to carry out a search as a last resort and when all other approaches have failed. In these circumstances, the authorising officer must be satisfied the detainee might use the article for one or more of the purposes in paragraph

2(a)(i) and the physical injury likely to be caused is sufficiently severe to justify authorising a constable to carry out the search.

A5   If an officer has any doubts whether to authorise an intimate search by a constable, the officer should seek advice from an officer of superintendent rank or above.

A6   In warning a detainee who is asked to consent to an intimate drug offence search, as in paragraph 2B, the following form of words may be used:

"You do not have to allow yourself to be searched, but I must warn you that if you refuse without good cause, your refusal may harm your case if it comes to trial."

Where the use of the Welsh Language is appropriate, the following form of words may be used:

'Nid oes rhaid i chi roi caniatâd i gael eich archwilio, ond mae'n rhaid i mi eich rhybuddio os gwrthodwch heb reswm da, y gallai eich penderfyniad i wrthod wneud niwed i'ch achos pe bai'n dod gerbron llys.'

Annex B –Delay in notifying arrest or allowing access to legal advice

A   Persons detained under PACE

1.   The exercise of the rights in Section 5 or Section 6, or both, may be delayed if the person is in police detention, as in PACE, section 118(2), in connection with an indictable offence, has not yet been charged with an offence and an officer of superintendent rank or above, or inspector rank or above only for the rights in Section 5, has reasonable grounds for believing their exercise will:

(i)   lead to:

•   interference with, or harm to, evidence connected with an indictable offence; or

•   interference with, or physical harm to, other people; or

(ii)   lead to alerting other people suspected of having committed an indictable offence but not yet arrested for it; or

(iii)   hinder the recovery of property obtained in consequence of the commission of such an offence.

2.   These rights may also be delayed if the officer has reasonable grounds to believe that:

(i)   the person detained for an indictable offence has benefited from their criminal conduct (decided in accordance with Part 2 of the Proceeds of Crime Act 2002); and

(ii)   the recovery of the value of the property constituting that benefit will be hindered by the exercise of either right.

3.   Authority to delay a detainee's right to consult privately with a solicitor may be given only if the authorising officer has reasonable grounds to believe the solicitor the detainee wants to consult

will, inadvertently or otherwise, pass on a message from the detainee or act in some other way which will have any of the consequences specified under paragraphs 1 or 2. In these circumstances the detainee must be allowed to choose another solicitor. See Note B3

4.   If the detainee wishes to see a solicitor, access to that solicitor may not be delayed on the grounds they might advise the detainee not to answer questions or the solicitor was initially asked to attend the police station by someone else. In the latter case the detainee must be told the solicitor has come to the police station at another person's request, and must be asked to sign the custody record to signify whether they want to see the solicitor.

5.   The fact the grounds for delaying notification of arrest may be satisfied does not automatically mean the grounds for delaying access to legal advice will also be satisfied.

6.   These rights may be delayed only for as long as grounds exist and in no case beyond 36 hours after the relevant time as in PACE, section 41. If the grounds cease to apply within this time, the detainee must, as soon as practicable, be asked if they want to exercise either right, the custody record must be noted accordingly, and action taken in accordance with the relevant section of the Code.

7.   A detained person must be permitted to consult a solicitor for a reasonable time before any court hearing.

B   Not used

C   Documentation

13.   The grounds for action under this Annex shall be recorded and the detainee informed of them as soon as practicable.

14.   Any reply given by a detainee under paragraphs 6 or 11 must be recorded and the detainee asked to endorse the record in relation to whether they want to receive legal advice at this point.

D   Cautions and special warnings

15.   When a suspect detained at a police station is interviewed during any period for which access to legal advice has been delayed under this Annex, the court or jury may not draw adverse inferences from their silence.

Notes for guidance

B1   Even if Annex B applies in the case of a juvenile, or a person who is mentally disordered or otherwise mentally vulnerable, action to inform the appropriate adult and the person responsible for a juvenile's welfare if that is a different person, must nevertheless be taken as in paragraph 3.13 and 3.15.

B2   In the case of Commonwealth citizens and foreign nationals, see Note 7A.

B3   A decision to delay access to a specific solicitor is likely to be a rare occurrence and only when it can be shown the suspect is capable of misleading that particular solicitor and there is more than a substantial risk that the suspect will succeed in causing information to be conveyed which will lead to one or more of the specified consequences.

Annex C – Restriction on drawing adverse inferences from silence and terms of the caution when the restriction applies

(a)   The restriction on drawing adverse inferences from silence

1.   The Criminal Justice and Public Order Act 1994, sections 34, 36 and 37 as amended by the Youth Justice and Criminal Evidence Act 1999, section 58 describe the conditions under which adverse inferences may be drawn from a person's failure or refusal to say anything about their involvement in the offence when interviewed, after being charged or informed they may be prosecuted. These provisions are subject to an overriding restriction on the ability of a court or jury to draw adverse inferences from a person's silence. This restriction applies:

(a)   to any detainee at a police station, see Note 10C who, before being interviewed, see section 11 or being charged or informed they may be prosecuted, see section 16, has:

(i)   asked for legal advice, see section 6, paragraph 6.1;

(ii)   not been allowed an opportunity to consult a solicitor, including the duty solicitor, as in this Code; and

(iii)   not changed their mind about wanting legal advice, see section 6, paragraph 6.6(d)

Note the condition in (ii) will

–   apply when a detainee who has asked for legal advice is interviewed before speaking to a solicitor as in section 6, paragraph 6.6(a) or (b).

–   not apply if the detained person declines to ask for the duty solicitor, see section 6, paragraphs 6.6(c) and (d);

(b)   to any person charged with, or informed they may be prosecuted for, an offence who:

(i)   has had brought to their notice a written statement made by another person or the content of an interview with another person which relates to that offence, see section 16, paragraph 16.4;

(ii)   is interviewed about that offence, see section 16, paragraph 16.5; or

(iii)   makes a written statement about that offence, see Annex D paragraphs 4 and 9.

(b)   Terms of the caution when the restriction applies

2.   When a requirement to caution arises at a time when the restriction on drawing adverse inferences from silence applies, the caution shall be:

'You do not have to say anything, but anything you do say may be given in evidence.'

Where the use of the Welsh Language is appropriate, the caution may be used directly in Welsh in the following terms:

'Does dim rhaid i chi ddweud dim byd, ond gall unrhyw beth yr ydych chi'n ei ddweud gael ei roi fel tystiolaeth.'

3.   Whenever the restriction either begins to apply or ceases to apply after a caution has already been given, the person shall be re-cautioned in the appropriate terms. The changed position on drawing inferences and that the previous caution no longer applies shall also be explained to the detainee in ordinary language. See Note C2

Notes for guidance

C1   The restriction on drawing inferences from silence does not apply to a person who has not been detained and who therefore cannot be prevented from seeking legal advice if they want to, see paragraphs 10.2 and 3.15.

C2   The following is suggested as a framework to help explain changes in the position on drawing adverse inferences if the restriction on drawing adverse inferences from silence:

(a)   begins to apply:

'The caution you were previously given no longer applies. This is because after that caution:

(i)   you asked to speak to a solicitor but have not yet been allowed an opportunity to speak to a solicitor. See paragraph 1(a); or

(ii)   you have been charged with/informed you may be prosecuted. See paragraph 1(b).

'This means that from now on, adverse inferences cannot be drawn at court and your defence will not be harmed just because you choose to say nothing. Please listen carefully to the caution I am about to give you because it will apply from now on. You will see that it does not say anything about your defence being harmed.'

(b)   ceases to apply before or at the time the person is charged or informed they may be prosecuted, see paragraph 1(a);

'The caution you were previously given no longer applies. This is because after that caution you have been allowed an opportunity to speak to a solicitor. Please listen carefully to the caution I am about to give you because it will apply from now on. It explains how your defence at court may be affected if you choose to say nothing.'

Annex D –Written statements under caution

(a)   Written by a person under caution

1.   A person shall always be invited to write down what they want to say.

2.   A person who has not been charged with, or informed they may be prosecuted for, any offence to which the statement they want to write relates, shall:

(a)   unless the statement is made at a time when the restriction on drawing adverse inferences from silence applies, see Annex C, be asked to write out and sign the following before writing what they want to say:

'I make this statement of my own free will. I understand that I do not have to say anything but that it may harm my defence if I do not mention when questioned something which I later rely on in court. This statement may be given in evidence.';

(b)   if the statement is made at a time when the restriction on drawing adverse inferences from silence applies, be asked to write out and sign the following before writing what they want to say;

'I make this statement of my own free will. I understand that I do not have to say anything. This statement may be given in evidence.'

3.   When a person, on the occasion of being charged with or informed they may be prosecuted for any offence, asks to make a statement which relates to any such offence and wants to write it they shall:

(a)   unless the restriction on drawing adverse inferences from silence, see Annex C, applied when they were so charged or informed they may be prosecuted, be asked to write out and sign the following before writing what they want to say:

'I make this statement of my own free will. I understand that I do not have to say anything but that it may harm my defence if I do not mention when questioned something which I later rely on in court. This statement may be given in evidence.';

(b)   if the restriction on drawing adverse inferences from silence applied when they were so charged or informed they may be prosecuted, be asked to write out and sign the following before writing what they want to say:

'I make this statement of my own free will. I understand that I do not have to say anything. This statement may be given in evidence.'

4.   When a person, who has already been charged with or informed they may be prosecuted for any offence, asks to make a statement which relates to any such offence and wants to write it they shall be asked to write out and sign the following before writing what they want to say:

'I make this statement of my own free will. I understand that I do not have to say anything. This statement may be given in evidence.';

5.   Any person writing their own statement shall be allowed to do so without any prompting except a police officer or other police staff may indicate to them which matters are material or question any ambiguity in the statement.

(b)   Written by a police officer or other police staff

6.   If a person says they would like someone to write the statement for them, a police officer, or other police staff shall write the statement.

7.   If the person has not been charged with, or informed they may be prosecuted for, any offence to which the statement they want to make relates they shall, before starting, be asked to sign, or make their mark, to the following:

(a)   unless the statement is made at a time when the restriction on drawing adverse inferences from silence applies, see Annex C:

'I, ..., wish to make a statement. I want someone to write down what I say. I understand that I do not have to say anything but that it may harm my defence if I do not mention when questioned something which I later rely on in court. This statement may be given in evidence.';

(b)   if the statement is made at a time when the restriction on drawing adverse inferences from silence applies:

'I, ..., wish to make a statement. I want someone to write down what I say. I understand that I do not have to say anything. This statement may be given in evidence.'

8.   If, on the occasion of being charged with or informed they may be prosecuted for any offence, the person asks to make a statement which relates to any such offence they shall before starting be asked to sign, or make their mark to, the following:

(a)   unless the restriction on drawing adverse inferences from silence applied, see

Annex C, when they were so charged or informed they may be prosecuted:

'I, ..., wish to make a statement. I want someone to write down what I say. I understand that I do not have to say anything but that it may harm my defence if I do not mention when questioned something which I later rely on in court. This statement may be given in evidence.';

(b)   if the restriction on drawing adverse inferences from silence applied when they were so charged or informed they may be prosecuted:

'I, ..., wish to make a statement. I want someone to write down what I say. I understand that I do not have to say anything. This statement may be given in evidence.'

9.   If, having already been charged with or informed they may be prosecuted for any offence, a person asks to make a statement which relates to any such offence they shall before starting, be asked to sign, or make their mark to:

'I, ..., wish to make a statement. I want someone to write down what I say. I understand that I do not have to say anything. This statement may be given in evidence.'

10.   The person writing the statement must take down the exact words spoken by the person making it and must not edit or paraphrase it. Any questions that are necessary, e.g. to make it more intelligible, and the answers given must be recorded at the same time on the statement form.

11.   When the writing of a statement is finished the person making it shall be asked to read it and to make any corrections, alterations or additions they want. When they have finished reading they shall be asked to write and sign or make their mark on the following certificate at the end of the statement:

'I have read the above statement, and I have been able to correct, alter or add anything I wish. This statement is true. I have made it of my own free will.'

12.   If the person making the statement cannot read, or refuses to read it, or to write the above mentioned certificate at the end of it or to sign it, the person taking the statement shall read it to them and ask them if they would like to correct, alter or add anything and to put their signature or make their mark at the end. The person taking the statement shall certify on the statement itself what has occurred.

Annex E – Summary of provisions relating to mentally disordered and otherwise mentally vulnerable people

1.   If an officer has any suspicion, or is told in good faith, that a person of any age may be mentally disordered or otherwise mentally vulnerable, or mentally incapable of understanding the significance of questions or their replies that person shall be treated as mentally disordered or otherwise mentally vulnerable for the purposes of this Code. See paragraph 1.4

2.   In the case of a person who is mentally disordered or otherwise mentally vulnerable, 'the appropriate adult' means:

(a)   a relative, guardian or other person responsible for their care or custody;

(b)   someone experienced in dealing with mentally disordered or mentally vulnerable people but who is not a police officer or employed by the police;

(c)   failing these, some other responsible adult aged 18 or over who is not a police officer or employed by the police. See paragraph 1.7(b) and Note 1D

3.   If the custody officer authorises the detention of a person who is mentally vulnerable or appears to be suffering from a mental disorder, the custody officer must as soon as practicable inform the appropriate adult of the grounds for detention and the person's whereabouts, and ask the adult to come to the police station to see them. If the appropriate adult:

•   is already at the station when information is given as in paragraphs 3.1 to 3.5 the information must be given in their presence

•   is not at the station when the provisions of paragraph 3.1 to 3.5 are complied with these provisions must be complied with again in their presence once they arrive. See paragraphs 3.15 to 3.17

4.   If the appropriate adult, having been informed of the right to legal advice, considers legal advice should be taken, the provisions of section 6 apply as if the mentally disordered or otherwise mentally vulnerable person had requested access to legal advice. See paragraph 3.19 and Note E1.

5.   The custody officer must make sure a person receives appropriate clinical attention as soon as reasonably practicable if the person appears to be suffering from a mental disorder or in urgent cases immediately call the nearest health care professional or an ambulance. It is not intended these provisions delay the transfer of a detainee to a place of safety under the Mental Health Act 1983, section 136 if that is applicable. If an assessment under that Act is to take place at a police station, the custody officer must consider whether an appropriate health care professional should be called to conduct an initial clinical check on the detainee. See paragraph 9.5 and 9.6

6.   It is imperative a mentally disordered or otherwise mentally vulnerable person detained under the Mental Health Act 1983, section 136 be assessed as soon as possible. If that assessment is to take place at the police station, an approved social worker and registered medical practitioner shall be called to the station as soon as possible in order to interview and examine the detainee. Once the detainee has been interviewed, examined and suitable arrangements been made for their treatment or care, they can no longer be detained under section 136. A detainee should be immediately discharged from detention if a registered medical practitioner having examined them, concludes they are not mentally disordered within the meaning of the Act. See paragraph 3.16

7.   If a mentally disordered or otherwise mentally vulnerable person is   cautioned in the absence of the appropriate adult, the caution must be repeated in the appropriate adult's presence. See paragraph 10.12

8.   A mentally disordered or otherwise mentally vulnerable person must not be interviewed or asked to provide or sign a written statement in the absence of the appropriate adult unless the provisions of paragraphs 11.1 or 11.18 to 11.20 apply. Questioning in these circumstances may not continue in the absence of the appropriate adult once sufficient information to avert the risk has been obtained. A record shall be made of the grounds for any decision to begin an interview in these circumstances. See paragraphs 11.1, 11.15 and 11.18 to 11.20

9.   If the appropriate adult is present at an interview, they shall be informed they are not expected to act simply as an observer and the purposes of their presence are to:

•   advise the interviewee

•   observe whether or not the interview is being conducted properly and fairly

•   facilitate communication with the interviewee

See paragraph 11.17

10.   If the detention of a mentally disordered or otherwise mentally vulnerable person is reviewed by a review officer or a superintendent, the appropriate adult must, if available at the time, be given an opportunity to make representations to the officer about the need for continuing detention. See paragraph 15.3

11.   If the custody officer charges a mentally disordered or otherwise mentally vulnerable person with an offence or takes such other action as is appropriate when there is sufficient evidence for a prosecution this must be done in the presence of the appropriate adult. The written notice embodying any charge must be given to the appropriate adult. See paragraphs 16.1 to 16.4A

12.   An intimate or strip search of a mentally disordered or otherwise mentally vulnerable person may take place only in the presence of the appropriate adult of the same sex, unless the detainee specifically requests the presence of a particular adult of the opposite sex. A strip search may take place in the absence of an appropriate adult only in cases of urgency when there is a risk of serious harm to the detainee or others. See Annex A, paragraphs 5 and 11(c)

13.   Particular care must be taken when deciding whether to use any form of approved restraints on a mentally disordered or otherwise mentally vulnerable person in a locked cell. See paragraph 8.2 Notes for guidance.

E1   The purpose of the provision at paragraph 3.19 is to protect the rights of a mentally disordered or otherwise mentally vulnerable detained person who does not understand the significance of what is said to them. If the detained person wants to exercise the right to legal advice, the appropriate action should be taken and not delayed until the appropriate adult arrives. A mentally disordered or otherwise mentally vulnerable detained person should always be given an opportunity, when an appropriate adult is called to the police station, to consult privately with a solicitor in the absence of the appropriate adult if they want.

E2   Although people who are mentally disordered or otherwise mentally vulnerable are often capable of providing reliable evidence, they may, without knowing or wanting to do so, be particularly prone in certain circumstances to provide information that may be unreliable, misleading or self-incriminating. Special care should always be taken when questioning such a person, and the appropriate adult should be involved if there is any doubt about a person's mental state or capacity. Because of the risk of unreliable evidence, it is important to obtain corroboration of any facts admitted whenever possible.

E3   Because of the risks referred to in Note E2, which the presence of the appropriate adult is intended to minimise, officers of superintendent rank or above should exercise their discretion to authorise the commencement of an interview in the appropriate adult's absence only in exceptional cases, if it is necessary to avert an immediate risk of serious harm. See paragraphs 11.1, 11.18 to 11.20

Annex F – Countries with which bilateral consular conventions or agreements requiring notification of the arrest and detention of their nationals are in force as at 1 April 2003

Armenia, Austria, Azerbaijan, Belarus, Belgium, Bosnia-Herzegovina, Bulgaria, China*, Croatia, Cuba, Czech Republic, Denmark, Egypt, France, Georgia, German Federal Republic, Greece, Hungary, Italy, Japan, Kazakhstan, Macedonia, Mexico, Moldova, Mongolia, Norway, Poland, Romania, Russia, Slovak Republic, Slovenia, Spain, Sweden, Tajikistan, Turkmenistan, Ukraine, USA, Uzbekistan, Yugoslavia

* Police are required to inform Chinese officials of arrest/detention in the Manchester consular district only. This comprises Derbyshire, Durham, Greater Manchester, Lancashire, Merseyside, North South and West Yorkshire, and Tyne and Wear.

Annex G – Fitness to be interviewed

1.   This Annex contains general guidance to help police officers and health care professionals assess whether a detainee might be at risk in an interview.

2.   A detainee may be at risk in a interview if it is considered that:

(a)   conducting the interview could significantly harm the detainee's physical or mental state;

(b)   anything the detainee says in the interview about their involvement or suspected involvement in the offence about which they are being interviewed might be considered unreliable in subsequent court proceedings because of their physical or mental state.

3.   In assessing whether the detainee should be interviewed, the following must be considered:

(a)   how the detainee's physical or mental state might affect their ability to understand the nature and purpose of the interview, to comprehend what is being asked and to appreciate the significance of any answers given and make rational decisions about whether they want to say anything;

(b)   the extent to which the detainee's replies may be affected by their physical or mental condition rather than representing a rational and accurate explanation of their involvement in the offence;

(c)   how the nature of the interview, which could include particularly probing questions, might affect the detainee.

4.   It is essential health care professionals who are consulted consider the functional ability of the detainee rather than simply relying on a medical diagnosis, e.g. it is possible for a person with severe mental illness to be fit for interview.

5.   Health care professionals should advise on the need for an appropriate adult to be present, whether reassessment of the person's fitness for interview may be necessary if the interview lasts beyond a specified time, and whether a further specialist opinion may be required.

6.   When health care professionals identify risks they should be asked to quantify the risks.

They should inform the custody officer:

- whether the person's condition:

– is likely to improve

– will require or be amenable to treatment; and

- indicate how long it may take for such improvement to take effect

7.   The role of the health care professional is to consider the risks and advise the custody officer of the outcome of that consideration. The health care professional's determination and any advice or recommendations should be made in writing and form part of the custody record.

8.   Once the health care professional has provided that information, it is a matter for the custody officer to decide whether or not to allow the interview to go ahead and if the interview is to proceed, to determine what safeguards are needed. Nothing prevents safeguards being provided in addition to those required under the Code. An example might be to have an appropriate health care professional present during the interview, in addition to an appropriate adult, in order constantly to monitor the person's condition and how it is being affected by the interview.

Annex H – Detained person: observation list

1.   If any detainee fails to meet any of the following criteria, an appropriate health care professional or an ambulance must be called.

2.   When assessing the level of rousability, consider:

Rousability – can they be woken?

- go into the cell

- call their name

- shake gently

Response to questions – can they give appropriate answers to questions such as:

- What's your name?

- Where do you live?

- Where do you think you are?

Response to commands – can they respond appropriately to commands such as:

- Open your eyes!

- Lift one arm, now the other arm!

3.   Remember to take into account the possibility or presence of other illnesses, injury, or mental condition, a person who is drowsy and smells of alcohol may also have the following:

- Diabetes

- Epilepsy

- Head injury

- Drug intoxication or overdose

- Stroke

Annex I – Not Used

Annex J – Not Used

Annex K – X-RAYs and ultrasound scans

(a)   Action

1.   PACE, section 55A allows a person who has been arrested and is in police detention to have an X-ray taken of them or an ultrasound scan to be carried out on them (or both) if:

(a)   authorised by an officer of inspector rank or above who has reasonable grounds for believing that the detainee:

(i)   may have swallowed a Class A drug; and

(ii)   was in possession of that Class A drug with the intention of supplying it to another or to export; and

(b)   the detainee's appropriate consent has been given in writing.

2.   Before an x-ray is taken or an ultrasound scan carried out, a police officer, designated detention officer or staff custody officer must tell the detainee:-

(a)   that the authority has been given; and

(b)   the grounds for giving the authorisation.

3.   Before a detainee is asked to give appropriate consent to an x-ray or an ultrasound scan, they must be warned that if they refuse without good cause their refusal may harm their case if it comes to trial, see Notes K1 and K2. This warning may be given by a police officer or member of

police staff. A detainee who is not legally represented must be reminded of their entitlement to have free legal advice, see Code C, paragraph 6.5, and the reminder noted in the custody record.

4.   An x-ray may be taken, or an ultrasound scan may be carried out, only by a registered medical practitioner or registered nurse, and only at a hospital, surgery or other medical premises.

(b)   Documentation

5.   The following shall be recorded as soon as practicable in the detainee's custody record:

(a)   the authorisation to take the x-ray or carry out the ultrasound scan (or both);

(b)   the grounds for giving the authorisation;

(c)   the giving of the warning required by paragraph 3; and

(d)   the fact that the appropriate consent was given or (as the case may be) refused, and if refused, the reason given for the refusal (if any); and

(e)   if an x-ray is taken or an ultrasound scan carried out:

•   where it was taken or carried out

•   who took it or carried it out

•   who was present

•   the result

6   Paragraphs 1.4 – 1.7 of this Code apply and an appropriate adult should be present when consent is sought to any procedure under this Annex.

Notes for guidance

K1   If authority is given for an x-ray to be taken or an ultrasound scan to be carried out (or both), consideration should be given to asking a registered medical practitioner or registered nurse to explain to the detainee what is involved and to allay any concerns the detainee might have about the effect which taking an x-ray or carrying out an ultrasound scan might have on them. If appropriate consent is not given, evidence of the explanation may, if the case comes to trial, be relevant to determining whether the detainee had a good cause for refusing.

K2   In warning a detainee who is asked to consent to an X-ray being taken or an ultrasound scan being carried out (or both), as in paragraph 3, the following form of words may be used:

"You do not have to allow an x-ray of you to be taken or an ultrasound scan to be carried out on you, but I must warn you that if you refuse without good cause, your refusal may harm your case if it comes to trial."

Where the use of the Welsh Language is appropriate, the following form of words may be provided in Welsh:

'Does dim rhaid i chi ganiatáu cymryd sgan uwchsain neu belydr-x (neu'r ddau) arnoch, ond mae'n rhaid i mi eich rhybuddio os byddwch chi'n gwrthod gwneud hynny heb reswm da, fe allai hynny niweidio eich achos pe bai'n dod gerbron llys.'

Codes of Practice – Code D Identification of persons by police officers

1   Introduction

1.1   This Code of Practice concerns the principal methods used by police to identify people in connection with the investigation of offences and the keeping of accurate and reliable criminal records. The powers and procedures in this code must be used fairly, responsibly, with respect for the people to whom they apply and without unlawful discrimination. The Equality Act 2010 makes it unlawful for police officers to discriminate against, harass or victimise any person on the

grounds of the 'protected characteristics' of age, disability, gender reassignment, race, religion or belief, sex and sexual orientation, marriage and civil partnership, pregnancy and maternity when using their powers. When police forces are carrying out their functions they also have a duty to have regard to the need to eliminate unlawful discrimination, harassment and victimisation and to take steps to foster good relations.

1.2   In this code, identification by an eye-witness arises when a witness who has seen the offender committing the crime and is given an opportunity to identify a person suspected of involvement in the offence in a video identification, identification parade or similar procedure. These eye- witness identification procedures (see Part A of section 3 below) are designed to:

• test the witness' ability to identify the suspect as the person they saw on a previous occasion

• provide safeguards against mistaken identification.

While this Code concentrates on visual identification procedures, it does not preclude the police making use of aural identification procedures such as a "voice identification parade", where they judge that appropriate.

1.2A   In this code, separate provisions in Part B of section 3 below apply when any person, including a police officer, is asked if they recognise anyone they see in an image as being someone they know and to test their claim that they recognise that person as someone who is known to them. Except where stated, these separate provisions are not subject to the eye-witnesses identification procedures described in paragraph 1.2.

1.3   Identification by fingerprints applies when a person's fingerprints are taken to:

• compare with fingerprints found at the scene of a crime

• check and prove convictions

• help to ascertain a person's identity.

1.3A   Identification using footwear impressions applies when a person's footwear impressions are taken to compare with impressions found at the scene of a crime.

1.4   Identification by body samples and impressions includes taking samples such as blood or hair to generate a DNA profile for comparison with material obtained from the scene of a crime, or a victim.

1.5   Taking photographs of arrested people applies to recording and checking identity and locating and tracing persons who:

• are wanted for offences

• fail to answer their bail.

1.6   Another method of identification involves searching and examining detained suspects to find, e.g., marks such as tattoos or scars which may help establish their identity or whether they have been involved in committing an offence.

1.7   The provisions of the Police and Criminal Evidence Act 1984 (PACE) and this Code are designed to make sure fingerprints, samples, impressions and photographs are taken, used and retained, and identification procedures carried out, only when justified and necessary for preventing, detecting or investigating crime. If these provisions are not observed, the application of the relevant procedures in particular cases may be open to question.

2   General

2.1   This Code must be readily available at all police stations for consultation by:

• police officers and police staff

• detained persons

• members of the public

2.2   The provisions of this Code:

• include the Annexes

• do not include the Notes for guidance.

2.3   Code C, paragraph 1.4, regarding a person who may be mentally disordered or otherwise mentally vulnerable and the Notes for guidance applicable to those provisions apply to this Code.

2.4   Code C, paragraph 1.5, regarding a person who appears to be under the age of 17 applies to this

Code.

2.5   Code C, paragraph 1.6, regarding a person who appears to be blind, seriously visually impaired, deaf, unable to read or speak or has difficulty communicating orally because of a speech impediment applies to this Code.

2.6   In this Code:

• 'appropriate adult' means the same as in Code C, paragraph 1.7

• 'solicitor' means the same as in Code C, paragraph 6.12

and the Notes for guidance applicable to those provisions apply to this Code.

- where a search or other procedure under this code may only be carried out or observed by a person of the same sex as the person to whom the search or procedure applies, the gender of the detainee and other persons present should be established and recorded in line with Annex F of Code A.

2.7   References to custody officers include those performing the functions of custody officer, see

paragraph 1.9 of Code C.

2.8   When a record of any action requiring the authority of an officer of a specified rank is made under this Code, subject to paragraph 2.18, the officer's name and rank must be recorded.

2.9   When this Code requires the prior authority or agreement of an officer of at least inspector or superintendent rank, that authority may be given by a sergeant or chief inspector who has been authorised to perform the functions of the higher rank under PACE, section 107.

2.10   Subject to paragraph 2.18, all records must be timed and signed by the maker.

2.11   Records must be made in the custody record, unless otherwise specified. References to 'pocket book' include any official report book issued to police officers or police staff.

2.12   If any procedure in this Code requires a person's consent, the consent of a:

- mentally disordered or otherwise mentally vulnerable person is only valid if given in the presence of the appropriate adult

- juvenile is only valid if their parent's or guardian's consent is also obtained unless the juvenile is under 14, when their parent's or guardian's consent is sufficient in its own right. If the only obstacle to an identification procedure in section 3 is that a juvenile's parent or guardian refuses consent or reasonable efforts to obtain it have failed, the identification officer may apply the provisions of paragraph 3.21. See Note 2A

2.13   If a person is blind, seriously visually impaired or unable to read, the custody officer or identification officer shall make sure their solicitor, relative, appropriate adult or some other person likely to take an interest in them and not involved in the investigation is available to help check any documentation. When this Code requires written consent or signing, the person

assisting may be asked to sign instead, if the detainee prefers. This paragraph does not require an appropriate adult to be called solely to assist in checking and signing documentation for a person who is not a juvenile, or mentally disordered or otherwise mentally vulnerable (see Note 2B and Code C paragraph 3.15).

2.14   If any procedure in this Code requires information to be given to or sought from a suspect, it must be given or sought in the appropriate adult's presence if the suspect is mentally disordered, otherwise mentally vulnerable or a juvenile. If the appropriate adult is not present when the information is first given or sought, the procedure must be repeated in the presence of the appropriate adult when they arrive. If the suspect appears deaf or there is doubt about their hearing or speaking ability or ability to understand English, and effective communication cannot be established, the information must be given or sought through an interpreter.

2.15   Any procedure in this Code involving the participation of a suspect who is mentally disordered, otherwise mentally vulnerable or a juvenile must take place in the presence of the appropriate adult. See Code C paragraph 1.4.

2.15A   Any procedure in this Code involving the participation of a witness who is or appears to be mentally disordered, otherwise mentally vulnerable or a juvenile should take place in the presence of a pre-trial support person unless the witness states that they do not want a support person to be present. A support person must not be allowed to prompt any identification of a suspect by a witness. See Note 2AB.

2.16   References to:

• 'taking a photograph', include the use of any process to produce a single, still or moving, visual image

• 'photographing a person', should be construed accordingly

• 'photographs', 'films', 'negatives' and 'copies' include relevant visual images recorded, stored, or reproduced through any medium

• 'destruction' includes the deletion of computer data relating to such images or making access to that data impossible

2.17   Except as described, nothing in this Code affects the powers and procedures:

(i)   for requiring and taking samples of breath, blood and urine in relation to driving offences, etc, when under the influence of drink, drugs or excess alcohol under the:

•   Road Traffic Act 1988, sections 4 to 11

•   Road Traffic Offenders Act 1988, sections 15 and 16

•   Transport and Works Act 1992, sections 26 to 38;

(ii)   under the Immigration Act 1971, Schedule 2, paragraph 18, for taking photographs and fingerprints from persons detained under that Act, Schedule 2, paragraph 16 (Administrative Controls as to Control on Entry etc.); for taking fingerprints in accordance with the Immigration and Asylum Act 1999; sections 141 and 142(3), or other methods for collecting information about a person's external physical characteristics provided for by regulations made under that Act, section 144;

(iii)   under the Terrorism Act 2000, Schedule 8, for taking photographs, fingerprints, skin impressions, body samples or impressions from people:

•   arrested under that Act, section 41,

•   detained for the purposes of examination under that Act, Schedule 7, and to whom the Code of Practice issued under that Act, Schedule 14, paragraph 6, applies ('the terrorism provisions') See Note 2C;

(iv) for taking photographs, fingerprints, skin impressions, body samples or impressions from people who have been:

• arrested on warrants issued in Scotland, by officers exercising powers under the Criminal Justice and Public Order Act 1994, section 136(2)

• arrested or detained without warrant by officers from a police force in Scotland exercising their powers of arrest or detention under the Criminal Justice and Public Order Act 1994, section 137(2), (Cross Border powers of arrest etc.).

Note: In these cases, police powers and duties and the person's rights and entitlements whilst at a police station in England and Wales are the same as if the person had been arrested in Scotland by a Scottish police officer.

2.18   Nothing in this Code requires the identity of officers or police staff to be recorded or disclosed: (a) in the case of enquiries linked to the investigation of terrorism;

(b) if the officers or police staff reasonably believe recording or disclosing their names might put

them in danger.

In these cases, they shall use warrant or other identification numbers and the name of their police station. See Note 2D

2.19   In this Code:

(a) 'designated person' means a person other than a police officer, designated under the Police Reform Act 2002, Part 4, who has specified powers and duties of police officers conferred or imposed on them;

(b) any reference to a police officer includes a designated person acting in the exercise or performance of the powers and duties conferred or imposed on them by their designation.

2.20   If a power conferred on a designated person:

(a) allows reasonable force to be used when exercised by a police officer, a designated person exercising that power has the same entitlement to use force;

(b) includes power to use force to enter any premises, that power is not exercisable by that designated person except:

(i) in the company, and under the supervision, of a police officer; or

(ii) for the purpose of:

• saving life or limb; or

• preventing serious damage to property.

2.21   Nothing in this Code prevents the custody officer, or other officer given custody of the detainee, from allowing police staff who are not designated persons to carry out individual procedures or tasks at the police station if the law allows. However, the officer remains responsible for making sure the procedures and tasks are carried out correctly in accordance with the Codes of Practice. Any such person must be:

(a) a person employed by a police authority maintaining a police force and under the control and direction of the Chief Officer of that force;

(b) employed by a person with whom a police authority has a contract for the provision of services relating to persons arrested or otherwise in custody.

2.22   Designated persons and other police staff must have regard to any relevant provisions of the Codes of Practice.

Notes for guidance

2A   For the purposes of paragraph 2.12, the consent required from a parent or guardian may, for a juvenile in the care of a local authority or voluntary organisation, be given by that authority or organisation. In the case of a juvenile, nothing in paragraph 2.12 requires the parent, guardian or representative of a local authority or voluntary organisation to be present to give their consent, unless they are acting as the appropriate adult under paragraphs 2.14 or 2.15. However, it is important that a parent or guardian not present is fully informed before being asked to consent. They must be given the same information about the procedure and the juvenile's suspected involvement in the offence as the juvenile and appropriate adult. The parent or guardian must also be allowed to speak to the juvenile and the appropriate adult if they wish. Provided the consent is fully informed and is not withdrawn, it may be obtained at any time before the procedure takes place.

2AB   The Youth Justice and Criminal Evidence Act 1999 guidance "Achieving Best Evidence in Criminal Proceedings" indicates that a pre-trial support person should accompany a vulnerable witness during any identification procedure unless the witness states that they do not want a support person to be present. It states that this support person should not be (or not be likely to be) a witness in the investigation.

2B   People who are seriously visually impaired or unable to read may be unwilling to sign police documents. The alternative, i.e. their representative signing on their behalf, seeks to protect the interests of both police and suspects.

2C   Photographs, fingerprints, samples and impressions may be taken from a person detained under the terrorism provisions to help determine whether they are, or have been, involved in terrorism, as well as when there are reasonable grounds for suspecting their involvement in a particular offence.

2D   The purpose of paragraph 2.18(b) is to protect those involved in serious organised crime investigations or arrests of particularly violent suspects when there is reliable information that those arrested or their associates may threaten or cause harm to the officers. In cases of doubt, an officer of inspector rank or above should be consulted.

3   Identification and recognition of suspects

(A) Identification of a suspect by an eye-witness

3.0   This part applies when an eye-witness has seen the offender committing the crime or in any other circumstances which tend to prove or disprove the involvement of the person they saw in the crime, for example, close to the scene of the crime, immediately before or immediately after it was committed. It sets out the procedures to be used to test the ability of that eye-witness to identify a person suspected of involvement in the offence as the person they saw on the previous occasion. Except where stated, this part does not apply to the procedures described in Part B and Note 3AA.

3.1   A record shall be made of the suspect's description as first given by a potential witness. This record must:

(a) be made and kept in a form which enables details of that description to be accurately produced from it, in a visible and legible form, which can be given to the suspect or the suspect's solicitor in accordance with this Code; and

(b) unless otherwise specified, be made before the witness takes part in any identification procedures under paragraphs 3.5 to 3.10, 3.21 or 3.23.

A copy of the record shall where practicable, be given to the suspect or their solicitor before any procedures under paragraphs 3.5 to 3.10, 3.21 or 3.23 are carried out. See Note 3E

(a) Cases when the suspect's identity is not known

3.2   In cases when the suspect's identity is not known, a witness may be taken to a particular neighbourhood or place to see whether they can identify the person they saw on a previous occasion. Although the number, age, sex, race, general description and style of clothing of other people present at the location and the way in which any identification is made cannot be controlled, the principles applicable to the formal procedures under paragraphs 3.5 to 3.10 shall be followed as far as practicable. For example:

(a) where it is practicable to do so, a record should be made of the witness' description of the suspect, as in paragraph 3.1 (a), before asking the witness to make an identification;

(b) care must be taken not to direct the witness' attention to any individual unless, taking into account all the circumstances, this cannot be avoided. However, this does not prevent a witness being asked to look carefully at the people around at the time or to look towards a group or in a particular direction, if this appears necessary to make sure that the witness does not overlook a possible suspect simply because the witness is looking in the opposite direction and also to enable the witness to make comparisons between any suspect and others who are in the area; See Note 3F

(c) where there is more than one witness, every effort should be made to keep them separate and witnesses should be taken to see whether they can identify a person independently;

(d) once there is sufficient information to justify the arrest of a particular individual for suspected involvement in the offence, e.g., after a witness makes a positive identification, the provisions set out from paragraph 3.4 onwards shall apply for any other witnesses in relation to that individual.;

(e) the officer or police staff accompanying the witness must record, in their pocket book, the action taken as soon as, and in as much detail, as possible. The record should include: the date, time and place of the relevant occasion the witness claims to have previously seen the suspect; where any identification was made; how it was made and the conditions at the time (e.g., the distance the witness was from the suspect, the weather and light); if the witness's attention was drawn to the suspect; the reason for this; and anything said by the witness or the suspect about the identification or the conduct of the procedure.

3.3   A witness must not be shown photographs, computerised or artist's composite likenesses or similar likenesses or pictures (including 'E-fit' images) if the identity of the suspect is known to the police and the suspect is available to take part in a video identification, an identification parade or a group identification. If the suspect's identity is not known, the showing of such images to a witness to obtain identification evidence must be done in accordance with Annex E.

(b) Cases when the suspect is known and available

3.4 If the suspect's identity is known to the police and they are available, the identification procedures set out in paragraphs 3.5 to 3.10 may be used. References in this section to a suspect being 'known' mean there is sufficient information known to the police to justify the arrest of a particular person for suspected involvement in the offence. A suspect being 'available' means they are immediately available or will be within a reasonably short time and willing to take an effective part in at least one of the following which it is practicable to arrange:

• video identification;

• identification parade; or

• group identification.

Video identification

3.5 A 'video identification' is when the witness is shown moving images of a known suspect, together with similar images of others who resemble the suspect. Moving images must be used unless:

• the suspect is known but not available (see paragraph 3.21 of this Code); or

• in accordance with paragraph 2A of Annex A of this Code, the identification officer does not consider that replication of a physical feature can be achieved or that it is not possible to conceal the location of the feature on the image of the suspect. The identification officer may then decide to make use of video identification but using still images.

3.6 Video identifications must be carried out in accordance with Annex A.

Identification parade

3.7 An 'identification parade' is when the witness sees the suspect in a line of others who resemble the suspect.

3.8 Identification parades must be carried out in accordance with Annex B.

Group identification

3.9 A 'group identification' is when the witness sees the suspect in an informal group of people.

3.10 Group identifications must be carried out in accordance with Annex C.

Arranging eye-witness identification procedures

3.11   Except for the provisions in paragraph 3.19, the arrangements for, and conduct of, the identification procedures in paragraphs 3.5 to 3.10 and circumstances in which an identification procedure must be held shall be the responsibility of an officer not below inspector rank who is not involved with the investigation, 'the identification officer'. Unless otherwise specified, the identification officer may allow another officer or police staff, see paragraph 2.21, to make arrangements for, and conduct, any of these identification procedures. In delegating these procedures, the identification officer must be able to supervise effectively and either intervene or be contacted for advice. No officer or any other person involved with the investigation of the case against the suspect, beyond the extent required by these procedures, may take any part in these procedures or act as the identification officer. This does not prevent the identification officer from consulting the officer in charge of the investigation to determine which procedure to use. When an identification procedure is required, in the interest of fairness to suspects and witnesses, it must be held as soon as practicable.

Circumstances in which an eye-witness identification procedure must be held

3.12   Whenever:

(i)   an eye witness has identified a suspect or purported to have identified them prior to any identification procedure set out in paragraphs 3.5 to 3.10 having been held; or

(ii)   there is a witness available who expresses an ability to identify the suspect, or where there is a reasonable chance of the witness being able to do so, and they have not been given an opportunity to identify the suspect in any of the procedures set out in paragraphs 3.5 to 3.10,

and the suspect disputes being the person the witness claims to have seen, an identification procedure shall be held unless it is not practicable or it would serve no useful purpose in proving or disproving whether the suspect was involved in committing the offence, for example:

•   where the suspect admits being at the scene of the crime and gives an account of what took place and the eye-witness does not see anything which contradicts that.

•   when it is not disputed that the suspect is already known to the witness who claims to have recognised them when seeing them commit the crime.

3.13   An eye-witness identification procedure may also be held if the officer in charge of the investigation considers it would be useful.

Selecting an eye-witness identification procedure

3.14   If, because of paragraph 3.12, an identification procedure is to be held, the suspect shall initially be offered a video identification unless:

(a) a video identification is not practicable; or

(b) an identification parade is both practicable and more suitable than a video identification; or

(c) paragraph 3.16 applies.

The identification officer and the officer in charge of the investigation shall consult each other to determine which option is to be offered. An identification parade may not be practicable because of factors relating to the witnesses, such as their number, state of health, availability and travelling requirements. A video identification would normally be more suitable if it could be arranged and completed sooner than an identification parade. Before an option is offered the suspect must also be reminded of their entitlement to have free legal advice, see Code C, paragraph 6.5.

3.15   A suspect who refuses the identification procedure first offered shall be asked to state their reason for refusing and may get advice from their solicitor and/or if present, their appropriate adult. The suspect, solicitor and/or appropriate adult shall be allowed to make representations about why another procedure should be used. A record should be made of the reasons for refusal and any representations made. After considering any reasons given, and representations made, the identification officer shall, if appropriate, arrange for the suspect to be offered an alternative which the officer considers suitable and practicable. If the officer decides it is not suitable and practicable to offer an alternative identification procedure, the reasons for that decision shall be recorded.

3.16   A group identification may initially be offered if the officer in charge of the investigation considers it is more suitable than a video identification or an identification parade and the identification officer considers it practicable to arrange.

Notice to suspect

3.17   Unless paragraph 3.20 applies, before a video identification, an identification parade or group identification is arranged, the following shall be explained to the suspect:

(i)   the purposes of the video identification, identification parade or group identification; (ii) their entitlement to free legal advice; see Code C, paragraph 6.5;

(iii)   the procedures for holding it, including their right to have a solicitor or friend present;

(iv)   that they do not have to consent to or co-operate in a video identification, identification parade or group identification;

(v)   that if they do not consent to, and co-operate in, a video identification, identification parade or group identification, their refusal may be given in evidence in any subsequent trial and police may proceed covertly without their consent or make other arrangements to test whether a witness can identify them, see paragraph 3.21;

(vi)   whether, for the purposes of the video identification procedure, images of them have previously been obtained, see paragraph 3.20, and if so, that they may co-operate in providing further, suitable images to be used instead;

(vii)   if appropriate, the special arrangements for juveniles;

(viii)   if appropriate, the special arrangements for mentally disordered or otherwise mentally vulnerable people;

(ix)   that if they significantly alter their appearance between being offered an identification procedure and any attempt to hold an identification procedure, this may be given in evidence if the case comes to trial, and the identification officer may then consider other forms of identification, see paragraph 3.21 and Note 3C;

(x)   that a moving image or photograph may be taken of them when they attend for any identification procedure;

(xi)   whether, before their identity became known, the witness was shown photographs, a computerised or artist's composite likeness or similar likeness or image by the police, see Note 3B;

(xii)   that if they change their appearance before an identification parade, it may not be practicable to arrange one on the day or subsequently and, because of the appearance change, the identification officer may consider alternative methods of identification, see Note 3C;

(xiii)   that they or their solicitor will be provided with details of the description of the suspect as first given by any witnesses who are to attend the video identification, identification parade, group identification or confrontation, see paragraph 3.1.

3.18   This information must also be recorded in a written notice handed to the suspect. The suspect must be given a reasonable opportunity to read the notice, after which, they should be asked to sign a second copy to indicate if they are willing to co-operate with the making of a video or take part in the identification parade or group identification. The signed copy shall be retained by the identification officer.

3.19   The duties of the identification officer under paragraphs 3.17 and 3.18 may be performed by the custody officer or other officer not involved in the investigation if:

(a) it is proposed to release the suspect in order that an identification procedure can be arranged and carried out and an inspector is not available to act as the identification officer, see paragraph 3.11, before the suspect leaves the station; or

(b) it is proposed to keep the suspect in police detention whilst the procedure is arranged and carried out and waiting for an inspector to act as the identification officer, see paragraph 3.11, would cause unreasonable delay to the investigation.

The officer concerned shall inform the identification officer of the action taken and give them the signed copy of the notice. See Note 3C

3.20   If the identification officer and officer in charge of the investigation suspect, on reasonable grounds that if the suspect was given the information and notice as in paragraphs 3.17 and 3.18, they would then take steps to avoid being seen by a witness in any identification procedure, the identification officer may arrange for images of the suspect suitable for use in a video identification procedure to be obtained before giving the information and notice. If suspect's images are obtained in these circumstances, the suspect may, for the purposes of a video identification procedure, co-operate in providing new images which if suitable, would be used instead, see paragraph 3.17(vi).

(c) Cases when the suspect is known but not available

3.21   When a known suspect is not available or has ceased to be available, see paragraph 3.4, the identification officer may make arrangements for a video identification (see Annex A). If necessary, the identification officer may follow the video identification procedures but using still images. Any suitable moving or still images may be used and these may be obtained covertly if necessary. Alternatively, the identification officer may make arrangements for a group identification. See Note 3D. These provisions may also be applied to juveniles where the consent of their parent or guardian is either refused or reasonable efforts to obtain that consent have failed. (see paragraph 2.12).

3.22   Any covert activity should be strictly limited to that necessary to test the ability of the witness to identify the suspect.

3.23   The identification officer may arrange for the suspect to be confronted by the witness if none of the options referred to in paragraphs 3.5 to 3.10 or 3.21 are practicable. A "confrontation" is when the suspect is directly confronted by the witness. A confrontation does not require the suspect's consent. Confrontations must be carried out in accordance with Annex D.

3.24   Requirements for information to be given to, or sought from, a suspect or for the suspect to be given an opportunity to view images before they are shown to a witness, do not apply if the suspect's lack of co-operation prevents the necessary action.

(d) Documentation

3.25   A record shall be made of the video identification, identification parade, group identification or confrontation on forms provided for the purpose.

3.26   If the identification officer considers it is not practicable to hold a video identification or identification parade requested by the suspect, the reasons shall be recorded and explained to the suspect.

3.27   A record shall be made of a person's failure or refusal to co-operate in a video identification, identification parade or group identification and, if applicable, of the grounds for obtaining images in accordance with paragraph 3.20.

(e) Showing films and photographs of incidents and information released to the media

3.28   Nothing in this Code inhibits showing films, photographs or other images to the public through the national or local media, or to police officers for the purposes of recognition and tracing suspects. However, when such material is shown to obtain evidence of recognition, the procedures in Part B will apply. See Note 3AA.

3.29   When a broadcast or publication is made, see paragraph 3.28, a copy of the relevant material released to the media for the purposes of recognising or tracing the suspect, shall be kept. The suspect or their solicitor shall be allowed to view such material before any eye-witness identification procedures under paragraphs 3.5 to 3.10, 3.21 or 3.23 of Part A are carried out, provided it is practicable and would not unreasonably delay the investigation. Each eye-witness involved in the procedure shall be asked, after they have taken part, whether they have seen any film, photograph or image relating to the offence or any description of the suspect which has been broadcast or published in any national or local media or on any social networking site and if they have, they should be asked to give details of the circumstances, such as the date and place as relevant. Their replies shall be recorded. This paragraph does not affect any separate requirement under the Criminal Procedure and Investigations Act 1996 to retain material in connection with criminal investigations.

(f)   Destruction and retention of photographs taken or used in eye-witness identification procedures

3.30   PACE, section 64A, see paragraph 5.12, provides powers to take photographs of suspects and allows these photographs to be used or disclosed only for purposes related to the prevention or detection of crime, the investigation of offences or the conduct of prosecutions by, or on behalf of, police or other law enforcement and prosecuting authorities inside and outside the United Kingdom or the enforcement of a sentence. After being so used or disclosed, they may be retained but can only be used or disclosed for the same purposes.

3.31   Subject to paragraph 3.33, the photographs (and all negatives and copies), of suspects not taken in accordance with the provisions in paragraph 5.12 which are taken for the purposes of, or in connection with, the identification procedures in paragraphs 3.5 to 3.10, 3.21 or 3.23 must be destroyed unless the suspect:

(a)   is charged with, or informed they may be prosecuted for, a recordable offence; (b)   is prosecuted for a recordable offence;

(c) is cautioned for a recordable offence or given a warning or reprimand in accordance with the

Crime and Disorder Act 1998 for a recordable offence; or

(d) gives informed consent, in writing, for the photograph or images to be retained for purposes described in paragraph 3.30.

3.32   When paragraph 3.31 requires the destruction of any photograph, the person must be given an opportunity to witness the destruction or to have a certificate confirming the destruction if they request one within five days of being informed that the destruction is required.

3.33   Nothing in paragraph 3.31 affects any separate requirement under the Criminal Procedure and

Investigations Act 1996 to retain material in connection with criminal investigations.

(B) Evidence of recognition by showing films, photographs and other images

3.34   This Part of this section applies when, for the purposes of obtaining evidence of recognition, any person, including a police officer:

(a) views the image of an individual in a film, photograph or any other visual medium; and

(b) is asked whether they recognise that individual as someone who is known to them. See Notes 3AA and 3G

3.35   The films, photographs and other images shall be shown on an individual basis to avoid any possibility of collusion and to provide safeguards against mistaken recognition (see Note 3G), the showing shall as far as possible follow the principles for video identification if the suspect is known, see Annex A, or identification by photographs if the suspect is not known, see Annex E.

3.36   A record of the circumstances and conditions under which the person is given an opportunity to recognise the individual must be made and the record must include:

(a) Whether the person knew or was given information concerning the name or identity of any suspect.

(b) What the person has been told before the viewing about the offence, the person(s) depicted in the images or the offender and by whom.

(c) How and by whom the witness was asked to view the image or look at the individual. (d) Whether the viewing was alone or with others and if with others, the reason for it.

(e) The arrangements under which the person viewed the film or saw the individual and by whom those arrangements were made.

(f) Whether the viewing of any images was arranged as part of a mass circulation to police and the public or for selected persons.

(g) The date time and place images were viewed or further viewed or the individual was seen. (h) The times between which the images were viewed or the individual was seen.

(i) How the viewing of images or sighting of the individual was controlled and by whom.

(j) Whether the person was familiar with the location shown in any images or the place where they saw the individual and if so, why.

(k) Whether or not on this occasion, the person claims to recognise any image shown, or any individual seen, as being someone known to them, and if they do:

(i) the reason

(ii) the words of recognition

(iii) any expressions of doubt

(iv) what features of the image or the individual triggered the recognition.

3.37   The record under paragraph 3.36 may be made by:

•   the person who views the image or sees the individual and makes the recognition.

•   the officer or police staff in charge of showing the images to the person or in charge of the conditions under which the person sees the individual.

Notes for guidance

3AA   The eye-witness identification procedures in Part A should not be used to test whether a witness can recognise a person as someone they know and would be able to give evidence of recognition along the lines that "On (describe date, time location) I saw an image of an individual who I recognised as AB." In these cases, the procedures in Part B shall apply.

3A   Except for the provisions of Annex E, paragraph 1, a police officer who is a witness for the purposes of this part of the Code is subject to the same principles and procedures as a civilian witness.

3B   When a witness attending an identification procedure has previously been shown photographs, or been shown or provided with computerised or artist's composite likenesses, or similar likenesses or pictures, it is the officer in charge of the investigation's responsibility to make the identification officer aware of this.

3C   The purpose of paragraph 3.19 is to avoid or reduce delay in arranging identification procedures by enabling the required information and warnings, see sub-paragraphs 3.17(ix) and 3.17(xii), to be given at the earliest opportunity.

3D   Paragraph 3.21 would apply when a known suspect deliberately makes themselves 'unavailable' in order to delay or frustrate arrangements for obtaining identification evidence. It also applies when a suspect refuses or fails to take part in a video identification, an identification parade or a group identification, or refuses or fails to take part in the only practicable options from that list. It enables any suitable images of the suspect, moving or still, which are available or can be obtained, to be used in an identification procedure. Examples include images from custody and other CCTV systems and from visually recorded interview records, see Code F Note for Guidance 2D.

3E   When it is proposed to show photographs to a witness in accordance with Annex E, it is the responsibility of the officer in charge of the investigation to confirm to the officer responsible for supervising and directing the showing, that the first description of the suspect given by that witness has been recorded. If this description has not been recorded, the procedure under Annex E must be postponed. See Annex E paragraph 2

3F   The admissibility and value of identification evidence obtained when carrying out the procedure under paragraph 3.2 may be compromised if:

(a) before a person is identified, the witness' attention is specifically drawn to that person; or

(b) the suspect's identity becomes known before the procedure.

3G   The admissibility and value of evidence of recognition obtained when carrying out the procedures in Part B may be compromised if before the person is recognised, the witness who has claimed to know them is given or is made, or becomes aware of, information about the person which was not previously known to them personally but which they have purported to rely on to support their claim that the person is in fact known to them.

4   Identification by fingerprints and footwear impressions

(A) Taking fingerprints in connection with a criminal investigation

(a) General

4.1   References to 'fingerprints' means any record, produced by any method, of the skin pattern and other physical characteristics or features of a person's:

(i)   fingers; or

(ii) palms.

(b) Action

4.2   A person's fingerprints may be taken in connection with the investigation of an offence only with their consent or if paragraph 4.3 applies. If the person is at a police station consent must be in writing.

4.3   PACE, section 61, provides powers to take fingerprints without consent from any person over the age of ten years:

(a) under section 61(3), from a person detained at a police station in consequence of being arrested for a recordable offence, see Note 4A, if they have not had their fingerprints taken in the course of the investigation of the offence unless those previously taken fingerprints are not a complete set or some or all of those fingerprints are not of sufficient quality to allow satisfactory analysis, comparison or matching.

(b) under section 61(4), from a person detained at a police station who has been charged with a recordable offence, see Note 4A, or informed they will be reported for such an offence if they have not had their fingerprints taken in the course of the investigation of the offence unless those previously taken fingerprints are not a complete set or some or all of those fingerprints are not of sufficient quality to allow satisfactory analysis, comparison or matching.

(c) under section 61(4A), from a person who has been bailed to appear at a court or police station if the person:

(i)   has answered to bail for a person whose fingerprints were taken previously and there are reasonable grounds for believing they are not the same person; or

(ii) who has answered to bail claims to be a different person from a person whose fingerprints were previously taken;

and in either case, the court or an officer of inspector rank or above, authorises the fingerprints to be taken at the court or police station (an inspector's authority may be given in writing or orally and confirmed in writing, as soon as practicable);

(ca) under section 61(5A) from a person who has been arrested for a recordable offence and released if the person:

(i)   is on bail and has not had their fingerprints taken in the course of the investigation of the offence, or;

(ii) has had their fingerprints taken in the course of the investigation of the offence, but they do not constitute a complete set or some, or all, of the fingerprints are not of sufficient quality to allow satisfactory analysis, comparison or matching.

(cb) under section 61(5B) from a person not detained at a police station who has been charged with a recordable offence or informed they will be reported for such an offence if they have not had their fingerprints taken in the course of the investigation or their fingerprints have been taken in the course of the investigation of the offence, but they do not constitute a complete set or some, or all, of the fingerprints are not of sufficient quality to allow satisfactory analysis, comparison or matching.

(d) under section 61(6), from a person who has been: (i)   convicted of a recordable offence;

(ii) given a caution in respect of a recordable offence which, at the time of the caution, the person admitted; or

(iii) warned or reprimanded under the Crime and Disorder Act 1998, section 65, for a recordable offence,

if, since their conviction, caution, warning or reprimand their fingerprints have not been taken or their fingerprints which have been taken since then do not constitute a complete set or some, or all, of the fingerprints are not of sufficient quality to allow satisfactory analysis, comparison or matching, and in either case, an officer of inspector rank or above, is satisfied that taking the fingerprints is necessary to assist in the prevention or detection of crime and authorises the taking;

(e) under section 61(6A) from a person a constable reasonably suspects is committing or attempting to commit, or has committed or attempted to commit, any offence if either:

•   the person's name is unknown and cannot be readily ascertained by the constable; or

•   the constable has reasonable grounds for doubting whether a name given by the person is their real name.

Note: fingerprints taken under this power are not regarded as having been taken in the course of the investigation of an offence.

(f) under section 61(6D) from a person who has been convicted outside England and Wales of an offence which if committed in England and Wales would be a qualifying offence as defined by PACE, section 65A (see Note 4AB) if:

(i) the person's fingerprints have not been taken previously under this power or their fingerprints have been so taken on a previous occasion but they do not constitute a complete set or some, or all, of the fingerprints are not of sufficient quality to allow satisfactory analysis, comparison or matching; and

(ii) a police officer of inspector rank or above is satisfied that taking fingerprints is necessary to assist in the prevention or detection of crime and authorises them to be taken.

4.4   PACE, section 63A(4) and Schedule 2A provide powers to:

(a) make a requirement (in accordance with Annex G) for a person to attend a police station to have their fingerprints taken in the exercise of certain powers in paragraph 4.3 above when that power applies at the time the fingerprints would be taken in accordance with the requirement. Those powers are:

(i)   section 61(5A) – Persons arrested for a recordable offence and released, see paragraph

4.3(ca): The requirement may not be made more than six months from the day the investigating officer was informed that the fingerprints previously taken were incomplete or below standard.

(ii) section 61(5B) – Persons charged etc. with a recordable offence, see paragraph 4.3(cb): The requirement may not be made more than six months from:

• the day the person was charged or reported if fingerprints have not been taken since then; or

• the day the investigating officer was informed that the fingerprints previously taken were incomplete or below standard.

(iii) section 61(6) – Person convicted, cautioned, warned or reprimanded for a recordable offence in England and Wales, see paragraph 4.3(d): Where the offence for which the person was convicted etc is also a qualifying offence (see Note 4AB), there is no time limit for the exercise of this power. Where the conviction etc. is for a recordable offence which is not a qualifying offence, the requirement may not be made more than two years from:

• the day the person was convicted, cautioned, warned or reprimanded, or the day Schedule 2A comes into force (if later), if fingerprints have not been taken since then; or

• the day an officer from the force investigating the offence was informed that the fingerprints previously taken were incomplete or below standard or the day Schedule

2A comes into force (if later).

(v) section 61(6D) – A person who has been convicted of a qualifying offence (see Note 4AB) outside England and Wales, see paragraph 4.3(g): There is no time limit for making the requirement.

Note: A person who has had their fingerprints taken under any of the powers in section 61 mentioned in paragraph 4.3 on two occasions in relation to any offence may not be required under Schedule 2A to attend a police station for their fingerprints to be taken again under section 61 in relation to that offence, unless authorised by an officer of inspector rank or above. The fact of the authorisation and the reasons for giving it must be recorded as soon as practicable.

(b) arrest, without warrant, a person who fails to comply with the requirement.

4.5   A person's fingerprints may be taken, as above, electronically.

4.6   Reasonable force may be used, if necessary, to take a person's fingerprints without their consent under the powers as in paragraphs 4.3 and 4.4.

4.7   Before any fingerprints are taken:

(a) without consent under any power mentioned in paragraphs 4.3 and 4.4 above, the person must be informed of:

(i)   the reason their fingerprints are to be taken;

(ii) the power under which they are to be taken; and

(iii) the fact that the relevant authority has been given if any power mentioned in paragraph

4.3(c), (d) or (f) applies

(b) with or without consent at a police station or elsewhere, the person must be informed:

(i)   that their fingerprints may be subject of a speculative search against other fingerprints, see Note 4B; and

(ii) that their fingerprints may be retained in accordance with Annex F, Part (a) unless they were taken under the power mentioned in paragraph 4.3(e) when they must be destroyed after they have being checked (See Note 4C).

(c) Documentation

4.8A   A record must be made as soon as practicable after the fingerprints are taken, of:

•   the matters in paragraph 4.7(a)(i) to (iii) and the fact that the person has been informed of those matters; and

•   the fact that the person has been informed of the matters in paragraph 4.7(b)(i) and (ii). The record must be made in the person's custody record if they are detained at a police station when the fingerprints are taken.

4.8   If force is used, a record shall be made of the circumstances and those present.

4.9   Not used

(B) Taking fingerprints in connection with immigration enquiries

Action

4.10   A person's fingerprints may be taken and retained for the purposes of immigration law enforcement and control in accordance with powers and procedures other than under PACE and for which the UK Border Agency (not the police) are responsible. Details of these powers and procedures which are under the Immigration Act 1971, Schedule 2 and Immigration and Asylum Act 1999, section 141, including modifications to the PACE Codes of Practice are contained in Chapter 24 of the Operational Instructions and Guidance manual which is published by the UK Border Agency (See Note 4D).

4.11   Not used

4.12   Not used

4.13   Not used

4.14   Not used

4.15   Not used

(C) Taking footwear impressions in connection with a criminal investigation

(a) Action

4.16   Impressions of a person's footwear may be taken in connection with the investigation of an offence only with their consent or if paragraph 4.17 applies. If the person is at a police station consent must be in writing.

4.17   PACE, section 61A, provides power for a police officer to take footwear impressions without consent from any person over the age of ten years who is detained at a police station:

(a) in consequence of being arrested for a recordable offence, see Note 4A; or if the detainee has been charged with a recordable offence, or informed they will be reported for such an offence; and

(b) the detainee has not had an impression of their footwear taken in the course of the investigation of the offence unless the previously taken impression is not complete or is not of sufficient quality to allow satisfactory analysis, comparison or matching (whether in the case in question or generally).

4.18   Reasonable force may be used, if necessary, to take a footwear impression from a detainee without consent under the power in paragraph 4.17.

4.19   Before any footwear impression is taken with, or without, consent as above, the person must be informed:

(a) of the reason the impression is to be taken;

(b) that the impression may be retained and may be subject of a speculative search against other impressions, see Note 4B, unless destruction of the impression is required in accordance with Annex F, Part (a); and

(c) that if their footwear impressions are required to be destroyed, they may witness their destruction as provided for in Annex F, Part (a).

(b) Documentation

4.20 A record must be made as soon as possible, of the reason for taking a person's footwear impressions without consent. If force is used, a record shall be made of the circumstances and those present.

4.21 A record shall be made when a person has been informed under the terms of paragraph 4.19(b), of the possibility that their footwear impressions may be subject of a speculative search.

Notes for guidance

4A References to 'recordable offences' in this Code relate to those offences for which convictions, cautions, reprimands and warnings may be recorded in national police records. See PACE, section

27(4). The recordable offences current at the time when this Code was prepared, are any offences which carry a sentence of imprisonment on conviction (irrespective of the period, or the age of the offender or actual sentence passed) as well as the non-imprisonable offences under the Vagrancy Act 1824 sections 3 and 4 (begging and persistent begging), the Street Offences Act 1959, section 1 (loitering or soliciting for purposes of prostitution), the Road Traffic Act 1988, section 25 (tampering with motor vehicles), the Criminal Justice and Public Order Act 1994, section 167 (touting for hire car services) and others listed in the National Police Records (Recordable Offences) Regulations 2000 as amended.

4AB A qualifying offence is one of the offences specified in PACE, section 65A. These indictable offences which concern the use or threat of violence or unlawful force against persons, sexual offences and offences against children include, for example, murder, manslaughter, false imprisonment, kidnapping and other offences such as:

•	sections 4, 16, 18, 20 to 24 or 47 of the Offences Against the Person Act 1861;

•	sections 16 to 18 of the Firearms Act 1968;

•	sections 9 or 10 of the Theft Act 1968 or under section 12A of that Act involving an accident which caused a person's death;

•	section 1 of the Criminal Damage Act 1971 required to be charged as arson;

•	section 1 of the Protection of Children Act 1978 and;

•	sections 1 to 19, 25, 26, 30 to 41, 47 to 50, 52, 53, 57 to 59, 61 to 67, 69 and 70 of the Sexual

Offences Act 2003.

4B Fingerprints, footwear impressions or a DNA sample (and the information derived from it) taken from a person arrested on suspicion of being involved in a recordable offence, or charged with such an offence, or informed they will be reported for such an offence, may be subject of a speculative search. This means the fingerprints, footwear impressions or DNA sample may be checked against other fingerprints, footwear impressions and DNA records held by, or on behalf of, the police and other law enforcement authorities in, or outside, the UK, or held in connection with, or as a result of, an investigation of an offence inside or outside the UK. Fingerprints, footwear impressions and samples taken from a person suspected of committing a recordable offence but not arrested, charged or informed they will be reported for it, may be subject to a speculative search only if the person consents in writing. The following is an example of a basic form of words:

"I consent to my fingerprints, footwear impressions and DNA sample and information derived from it being retained and used only for purposes related to the prevention and detection of a crime, the investigation of an offence or the conduct of a prosecution either nationally or internationally.

I understand that my fingerprints, footwear impressions or DNA sample may be checked against other fingerprint, footwear impressions and DNA records held by or on behalf of relevant law enforcement authorities, either nationally or internationally.

I understand that once I have given my consent for my fingerprints, footwear impressions or

DNA sample to be retained and used I cannot withdraw this consent."

See Annex F regarding the retention and use of fingerprints and footwear impressions taken with consent for elimination purposes.

4C   The power under section 61(6A) of PACE described in paragraph 4.3(e) allows fingerprints of a suspect who has not been arrested to be taken in connection with any offence (whether recordable or not) using a mobile device and then checked on the street against the database containing the national fingerprint collection. Fingerprints taken under this power cannot be retained after they have been checked. The results may make an arrest for the suspected offence based on the name condition unnecessary (See Code G paragraph 2.9(a)) and enable the offence to be disposed of without arrest, for example, by summons/charging by post, penalty notice or words of advice. If arrest for a non-recordable offence is necessary for any other reasons, this power may also be exercised at the station. Before the power is exercised, the officer should:

•   inform the person of the nature of the suspected offence and why they are suspected of committing it.

•   give them a reasonable opportunity to establish their real name before deciding that their name is unknown and cannot be readily ascertained or that there are reasonable grounds to doubt that a name they have given is their real name.

•   as applicable, inform the person of the reason why their name is not know and cannot be readily ascertained or of the grounds for doubting that a name they have given is their real name, including, for example, the reason why a particular document the person has produced to verify their real name, is not sufficient.

4D   Powers to take fingerprints without consent for immigration purposes are given to police and immigration officers under the:

(a) Immigration Act 1971, Schedule 2, paragraph 18(2), when it is reasonably necessary for the purposes of identifying a person detained under the Immigration Act 1971, Schedule 2, paragraph 16 (Detention of person liable to examination or removal), and

(b) Immigration and Asylum Act 1999, section 141(7) when a person:

•   fails without reasonable excuse to produce, on arrival, a valid passport with a photograph or some other document satisfactorily establishing their identity and nationality;

- is refused entry to the UK but is temporarily admitted if an immigration officer reasonably suspects the person might break a residence or reporting condition;

- is subject to directions for removal from the UK;

- has been arrested under the Immigration Act 1971, Schedule 2, paragraph 17;

- has made a claim for asylum

- is a dependant of any of the above.

The Immigration and Asylum Act 1999, section 142(3), also gives police and immigration officers power to arrest without warrant, a person who fails to comply with a requirement imposed by the Secretary of State to attend a specified place for fingerprinting.

5   Examinations to establish identity and the taking of photographs

(A) Detainees at police stations

(a) Searching or examination of detainees at police stations

5.1   PACE, section 54A(1), allows a detainee at a police station to be searched or examined or both, to establish:

(a) whether they have any marks, features or injuries that would tend to identify them as a person involved in the commission of an offence and to photograph any identifying marks, see paragraph 5.5; or

(b) their identity, see Note 5A.

A person detained at a police station to be searched under a stop and search power, see Code A, is not a detainee for the purposes of these powers.

5.2   A search and/or examination to find marks under section 54A (1) (a) may be carried out without the detainee's consent, see paragraph 2.12, only if authorised by an officer of at least inspector rank when consent has been withheld or it is not practicable to obtain consent, see Note 5D.

5.3   A search or examination to establish a suspect's identity under section 54A (1) (b) may be carried out without the detainee's consent, see paragraph 2.12, only if authorised by an officer of at least inspector rank when the detainee has refused to identify themselves or the authorising officer has reasonable grounds for suspecting the person is not who they claim to be.

5.4   Any marks that assist in establishing the detainee's identity, or their identification as a person involved in the commission of an offence, are identifying marks. Such marks may be photographed with the detainee's consent, see paragraph 2.12; or without their consent if it is withheld or it is not practicable to obtain it, see Note 5D.

5.5   A detainee may only be searched, examined and photographed under section 54A, by a police officer of the same sex.

5.6   Any photographs of identifying marks, taken under section 54A, may be used or disclosed only for purposes related to the prevention or detection of crime, the investigation of offences or the conduct of prosecutions by, or on behalf of, police or other law enforcement and prosecuting authorities inside, and outside, the UK. After being so used or disclosed, the photograph may be retained but must not be used or disclosed except for these purposes, see Note 5B.

5.7   The powers, as in paragraph 5.1, do not affect any separate requirement under the Criminal Procedure and Investigations Act 1996 to retain material in connection with criminal investigations.

5.8   Authority for the search and/or examination for the purposes of paragraphs 5.2 and 5.3 may be given orally or in writing. If given orally, the authorising officer must confirm it in writing as soon as practicable. A separate authority is required for each purpose which applies.

5.9   If it is established a person is unwilling to co-operate sufficiently to enable a search and/or examination to take place or a suitable photograph to be taken, an officer may use reasonable force to:

(a) search and/or examine a detainee without their consent; and

(b) photograph any identifying marks without their consent.

5.10   The thoroughness and extent of any search or examination carried out in accordance with the powers in section 54A must be no more than the officer considers necessary to achieve the required purpose. Any search or examination which involves the removal of more than the person's outer clothing shall be conducted in accordance with Code C, Annex A, paragraph 11.

5.11   An intimate search may not be carried out under the powers in section 54A.

 (b) Photographing detainees at police stations and other persons elsewhere than at a police station

5.12   Under PACE, section 64A, an officer may photograph:

(a) any person whilst they are detained at a police station; and

(b) any person who is elsewhere than at a police station and who has been:

(i)   arrested by a constable for an offence;

(ii)   taken into custody by a constable after being arrested for an offence by a person other than a constable;

(iii) made subject to a requirement to wait with a community support officer under paragraph 2(3) or (3B) of Schedule 4 to the Police Reform Act 2002;

(iiia) given a direction by a constable under section 27 of the Violent Crime Reduction Act

2006.

(iv) given a penalty notice by a constable in uniform under Chapter 1 of Part 1 of the Criminal Justice and Police Act 2001, a penalty notice by a constable under section 444A of the Education Act 1996, or a fixed penalty notice by a constable in uniform under section 54 of the Road Traffic Offenders Act 1988;

(v) given a notice in relation to a relevant fixed penalty offence (within the meaning of paragraph 1 of Schedule 4 to the Police Reform Act 2002) by a community support officer by virtue of a designation applying that paragraph to him;

(vi) given a notice in relation to a relevant fixed penalty offence (within the meaning of paragraph 1 of Schedule 5 to the Police Reform Act 2002) by an accredited person by virtue of accreditation specifying that that paragraph applies to him; or

(vii) given a direction to leave and not return to a specified location for up to 48 hours by a police constable (under section 27 of the Violent Crime Reduction Act 2006).

5.12A   Photographs taken under PACE, section 64A:

(a) may be taken with the person's consent, or without their consent if consent is withheld or it is not practicable to obtain their consent, see Note 5E; and

(b) may be used or disclosed only for purposes related to the prevention or detection of crime, the investigation of offences or the conduct of prosecutions by, or on behalf of, police or other law enforcement and prosecuting authorities inside and outside the United Kingdom or the enforcement of any sentence or order made by a court when dealing with an offence. After being so used or disclosed, they may be retained but can only be used or disclosed for the same purposes. See Note 5B.

5.13   The officer proposing to take a detainee's photograph may, for this purpose, require the person to remove any item or substance worn on, or over, all, or any part of, their head or face. If they do not comply with such a requirement, the officer may remove the item or substance.

5.14   If it is established the detainee is unwilling to co-operate sufficiently to enable a suitable photograph to be taken and it is not reasonably practicable to take the photograph covertly, an officer may use reasonable force, see Note 5F.

(a) to take their photograph without their consent; and

(b) for the purpose of taking the photograph, remove any item or substance worn on, or over, all, or any part of, the person's head or face which they have failed to remove when asked.

5.15   For the purposes of this Code, a photograph may be obtained without the person's consent by making a copy of an image of them taken at any time on a camera system installed anywhere in the police station.

(c) Information to be given

5.16   When a person is searched, examined or photographed under the provisions as in paragraph 5.1

and 5.12, or their photograph obtained as in paragraph 5.15, they must be informed of the:

(a) purpose of the search, examination or photograph;

(b) grounds on which the relevant authority, if applicable, has been given; and

(c) purposes for which the photograph may be used, disclosed or retained.

This information must be given before the search or examination commences or the photograph is taken, except if the photograph is:

(i)   to be taken covertly;

(ii) obtained as in paragraph 5.15, in which case the person must be informed as soon as practicable after the photograph is taken or obtained.

(d) Documentation

5.17   A record must be made when a detainee is searched, examined, or a photograph of the person, or any identifying marks found on them, are taken. The record must include the:

(a) identity, subject to paragraph 2.18, of the officer carrying out the search, examination or taking the photograph;

(b) purpose of the search, examination or photograph and the outcome;

(c) detainee's consent to the search, examination or photograph, or the reason the person was searched, examined or photographed without consent;

(d) giving of any authority as in paragraphs 5.2 and 5.3, the grounds for giving it and the authorising officer.

5.18   If force is used when searching, examining or taking a photograph in accordance with this section, a record shall be made of the circumstances and those present.

(B) Persons at police stations not detained

5.19   When there are reasonable grounds for suspecting the involvement of a person in a criminal offence, but that person is at a police station voluntarily and not detained, the provisions of paragraphs 5.1 to 5.18 should apply, subject to the modifications in the following paragraphs.

5.20   References to the 'person being detained' and to the powers mentioned in paragraph 5.1 which apply only to detainees at police stations shall be omitted.

5.21   Force may not be used to:

(a) search and/or examine the person to:

(i) discover whether they have any marks that would tend to identify them as a person involved in the commission of an offence; or

(ii) establish their identity, see Note 5A;

(b) take photographs of any identifying marks, see paragraph 5.4; or

(c) take a photograph of the person.

5.22   Subject to paragraph 5.24, the photographs of persons or of their identifying marks which are not taken in accordance with the provisions mentioned in paragraphs 5.1 or 5.12, must be destroyed (together with any negatives and copies) unless the person:

(a) is charged with, or informed they may be prosecuted for, a recordable offence; (b) is prosecuted for a recordable offence;

(c) is cautioned for a recordable offence or given a warning or reprimand in accordance with the

Crime and Disorder Act 1998 for a recordable offence; or

(d) gives informed consent, in writing, for the photograph or image to be retained as in paragraph 5.6.

5.23   When paragraph 5.22 requires the destruction of any photograph, the person must be given an opportunity to witness the destruction or to have a certificate confirming the destruction provided they so request the certificate within five days of being informed the destruction is required.

5.24   Nothing in paragraph 5.22 affects any separate requirement under the Criminal Procedure and

Investigations Act 1996 to retain material in connection with criminal investigations.

Notes for guidance

5A   The conditions under which fingerprints may be taken to assist in establishing a person's identity, are described in Section 4.

5B   Examples of purposes related to the prevention or detection of crime, the investigation of offences or the conduct of prosecutions include:

(a) checking the photograph against other photographs held in records or in connection with, or as a result of, an investigation of an offence to establish whether the person is liable to arrest for other offences;

(b) when the person is arrested at the same time as other people, or at a time when it is likely that other people will be arrested, using the photograph to help establish who was arrested, at what time and where;

(c) when the real identity of the person is not known and cannot be readily ascertained or there are reasonable grounds for doubting a name and other personal details given by the person, are their real name and personal details. In these circumstances, using or disclosing the photograph to help to establish or verify their real identity or determine whether they are liable to arrest for some other offence, e.g. by checking it against other photographs held in records or in connection with, or as a result of, an investigation of an offence;

(d) when it appears any identification procedure in section 3 may need to be arranged for which the person's photograph would assist;

(e) when the person's release without charge may be required, and if the release is:

(i)   on bail to appear at a police station, using the photograph to help verify the person's identity when they answer their bail and if the person does not answer their bail, to assist in arresting them; or

(ii) without bail, using the photograph to help verify their identity or assist in locating them for the purposes of serving them with a summons to appear at court in criminal proceedings;

(f) when the person has answered to bail at a police station and there are reasonable grounds for doubting they are the person who was previously granted bail, using the photograph to help establish or verify their identity;

(g) when the person arrested on a warrant claims to be a different person from the person named on the warrant and a photograph would help to confirm or disprove their claim;

(h) when the person has been charged with, reported for, or convicted of, a recordable offence and their photograph is not already on record as a result of (a) to (f) or their photograph is on record but their appearance has changed since it was taken and the person has not yet been released or brought before a court.

5C   There is no power to arrest a person convicted of a recordable offence solely to take their photograph. The power to take photographs in this section applies only where the person is in custody as a result of the exercise of another power, e.g. arrest for fingerprinting under PACE, section 27.

5D   Examples of when it would not be practicable to obtain a detainee's consent, see paragraph 2.12, to a search, examination or the taking of a photograph of an identifying mark include:

(a) when the person is drunk or otherwise unfit to give consent;

(b) when there are reasonable grounds to suspect that if the person became aware a search or examination was to take place or an identifying mark was to be photographed, they would take steps to prevent this happening, e.g. by violently resisting, covering or concealing the mark etc and it would not otherwise be possible to carry out the search or examination or to photograph any identifying mark;

(c) in the case of a juvenile, if the parent or guardian cannot be contacted in sufficient time to allow the search or examination to be carried out or the photograph to be taken.

5E   Examples of when it would not be practicable to obtain the person's consent, see paragraph 2.12, to a photograph being taken include:

(a) when the person is drunk or otherwise unfit to give consent;

(b) when there are reasonable grounds to suspect that if the person became aware a photograph, suitable to be used or disclosed for the use and disclosure described in paragraph 5.6, was to be taken, they would take steps to prevent it being taken, e.g. by violently resisting, covering or distorting their face etc, and it would not otherwise be possible to take a suitable photograph;

(c) when, in order to obtain a suitable photograph, it is necessary to take it covertly; and

(d) in the case of a juvenile, if the parent or guardian cannot be contacted in sufficient time to allow the photograph to be taken.

5F   The use of reasonable force to take the photograph of a suspect elsewhere than at a police station must be carefully considered. In order to obtain a suspect's consent and co-operation to remove an item of religious headwear to take their photograph, a constable should consider whether in the circumstances of the situation the removal of the headwear and the taking of the photograph should be by an officer of the same sex as the person. It would be appropriate for these actions to be conducted out of public view.

6   Identification by body samples and impressions

(A) General

6.1   References to:

(a) an 'intimate sample' mean a dental impression or sample of blood, semen or any other tissue fluid, urine, or pubic hair, or a swab taken from any part of a person's genitals or from a person's body orifice other than the mouth;

(b) a 'non-intimate sample' means:

(i)   a sample of hair, other than pubic hair, which includes hair plucked with the root, see Note 6A;

(ii) a sample taken from a nail or from under a nail;

(iii) a swab taken from any part of a person's body other than a part from which a swab taken would be an intimate sample;

(iv) saliva;

(v) a skin impression which means any record, other than a fingerprint, which is a record, in any form and produced by any method, of the skin pattern and other physical characteristics or features of the whole, or any part of, a person's foot or of any other part of their body.

(B) Action

(a) Intimate samples

6.2   PACE, section 62, provides that intimate samples may be taken under: (a) section 62(1), from a person in police detention only:

(i) if a police officer of inspector rank or above has reasonable grounds to believe such an

impression or sample will tend to confirm or disprove the suspect's involvement in a recordable offence, see Note 4A, and gives authorisation for a sample to be taken; and

(ii) with the suspect's written consent;

(b) section 62(1A), from a person not in police detention but from whom two or more non-intimate samples have been taken in the course of an investigation of an offence and the samples, though suitable, have proved insufficient if:

(i) a police officer of inspector rank or above authorises it to be taken; and

(ii) the person concerned gives their written consent. See Notes 6B and 6C

(c) section 62(2A), from a person convicted outside England and Wales of an offence which if committed in England and Wales would be qualifying offence as defined by PACE, section 65A (see Note 4AB) from whom two or more non-intimate samples taken under section 63(3E) (see paragraph 6.6(h) have proved insufficient if:

(i)   a police officer of inspector rank or above is satisfied that taking the sample is necessary to assist in the prevention or detection of crime and authorises it to be taken; and

(ii) the person concerned gives their written consent.

6.2A   PACE, section 63A(4) and Schedule 2A provide powers to:

(a) make a requirement (in accordance with Annex G) for a person to attend a police station to have an intimate sample taken in the exercise of one of the following powers in paragraph 6.2 when that power applies at the time the sample is to be taken in accordance with the requirement or after the person's arrest if they fail to comply with the requirement:

(i)   section 62(1A) – Persons from whom two or more non-intimate samples have been taken and proved to be insufficient, see paragraph 6.2(b): There is no time limit for making the requirement.

(ii) section 62(2A) – Persons convicted outside England and Wales from whom two or more non-intimate samples taken under section 63(3E) (see paragraph 6.6(h) have proved insufficient, see paragraph 6.2(c): There is no time limit for making the requirement.

6.3   Before a suspect is asked to provide an intimate sample, they must be: (a) informed:

(i)   of the reason, including the nature of the suspected offence (except if taken under

paragraph 6.2(c) from a person convicted outside England and Wales.

(ii) that authorisation has been given and the provisions under which given;

(iii) that a sample taken at a police station may be subject of a speculative search;

(b) warned that if they refuse without good cause their refusal may harm their case if it comes to trial, see Note 6D. If the suspect is in police detention and not legally represented, they

must also be reminded of their entitlement to have free legal advice, see Code C, paragraph

6.5, and the reminder noted in the custody record. If paragraph 6.2(b) applies and the person is attending a station voluntarily, their entitlement to free legal advice as in Code C, paragraph 3.21 shall be explained to them.

6.4   Dental impressions may only be taken by a registered dentist. Other intimate samples, except for samples of urine, may only be taken by a registered medical practitioner or registered nurse or registered paramedic.

(b)   Non-intimate samples

6.5   A non-intimate sample may be taken from a detainee only with their written consent or if paragraph 6.6 applies.

6.6   a non-intimate sample may be taken from a person without the appropriate consent in the following circumstances:

(a) under section 63(2A) from a person who is in police detention as a consequence of being arrested for a recordable offence and who has not had a non-intimate sample of the same type and from the same part of the body taken in the course of the investigation of the offence by the police or they have had such a sample taken but it proved insufficient.

(b) Under section 63(3) from a person who is being held in custody by the police on the authority of a court if an officer of at least the rank of inspector authorises it to be taken. An authorisation may be given:

(i)   if the authorising officer has reasonable grounds for suspecting the person of involvement in a recordable offence and for believing that the sample will tend to confirm or disprove that involvement, and

(ii) in writing or orally and confirmed in writing, as soon as practicable;

but an authorisation may not be given to take from the same part of the body a further non-intimate sample consisting of a skin impression unless the previously taken impression proved insufficient

(c) under section 63(3ZA) from a person who has been arrested for a recordable offence and released if the person:

(i)   is on bail and has not had a sample of the same type and from the same part of the body taken in the course of the investigation of the offence, or;

(ii) has had such a sample taken in the course of the investigation of the offence, but it proved unsuitable or insufficient.

(d) under section 63(3A), from a person (whether or not in police detention or held in custody by the police on the authority of a court) who has been charged with a recordable offence or informed they will be reported for such an offence if the person:

(i)   has not had a non-intimate sample taken from them in the course of the investigation of the offence;

(ii) has had a sample so taken, but it proved unsuitable or insufficient, see Note 6B; or

(iii) has had a sample taken in the course of the investigation of the offence and the sample has been destroyed and in proceedings relating to that offence there is a dispute as to whether a DNA profile relevant to the proceedings was derived from the destroyed sample.

(e) under section 63(3B), from a person who has been: (i) convicted of a recordable offence;

(ii) given a caution in respect of a recordable offence which, at the time of the caution, the person admitted; or

(iii) warned or reprimanded under the Crime and Disorder Act 1998, section 65, for a recordable offence, if, since their conviction, caution, warning or reprimand a non-intimate sample has not been taken from them or a sample which has been taken since then has proved to be unsuitable or insufficient and in either case, an officer of inspector rank or above, is satisfied that taking the fingerprints is necessary to assist in the prevention or detection of crime and authorises the taking;

(f) under section 63(3C) from a person to whom section 2 of the Criminal Evidence (Amendment) Act 1997 applies (persons detained following acquittal on grounds of insanity or finding of unfitness to plead).

(g) under section 63(3E) from a person who has been convicted outside England and Wales of an offence which if committed in England and Wales would be a qualifying offence as defined by PACE, section 65A (see Note 4AB) if:

(i) a non-intimate sample has not been taken previously under this power or unless a sample was so taken but was unsuitable or insufficient; and

(ii) a police officer of inspector rank or above is satisfied that taking a sample is necessary to assist in the prevention or detection of crime and authorises it to be taken.

6.6A   PACE, section 63A(4) and Schedule 2A provide powers to:

(a) make a requirement (in accordance with Annex G) for a person to attend a police station to have a non-intimate sample taken in the exercise of one of the following powers in paragraph

6.6 when that power applies at the time the sample would be taken in accordance with the requirement:

(i)   section 63(3ZA) – Persons arrested for a recordable offence and released, see paragraph

6.6(c): The requirement may not be made more than six months from the day the investigating officer was informed that the sample previously taken was unsuitable or insufficient.

(ii) section 63(3A) – Persons charged etc. with a recordable offence, see paragraph 6.6(d): The requirement may not be made more than six months from:

- · the day the person was charged or reported if a sample has not been taken since then; or

- the day the investigating officer was informed that the sample previously taken was unsuitable or insufficient.

(iii) section 63(3B) – Person convicted, cautioned, warned or reprimanded for a recordable offence in England and Wales, see paragraph 6.6(e): Where the offence for which the person was convicted etc is also a qualifying offence (see Note 4AB), there is no time limit for the exercise of this power. Where the conviction etc was for a recordable offence that is not a qualifying offence, the requirement may not be made more than two years from:

- the day the person was convicted, cautioned, warned or reprimanded, or the day Schedule 2A comes into force (if later), if a samples has not been taken since then; or

- the day an officer from the force investigating the offence was informed that the sample previously taken was unsuitable or insufficient or the day Schedule 2A comes into force (if later).

(iv) section 63(3E) – A person who has been convicted of qualifying offence (see Note 4AB) outside England and Wales, see paragraph 6.6(h): There is no time limit for making the requirement. Note: A person who has had a non-intimate sample taken under any of the powers in section

63 mentioned in paragraph 6.6 on two occasions in relation to any offence may not be required under Schedule 2A to attend a police station for a sample to be taken again under section 63 in relation to that offence, unless authorised by an officer of inspector rank or above. The fact of the authorisation and the reasons for giving it must be recorded as soon as practicable.

(b) arrest, without warrant, a person who fails to comply with the requirement.

6.7   Reasonable force may be used, if necessary, to take a non-intimate sample from a person without their consent under the powers mentioned in paragraph 6.6.

6.8   Before any non-intimate sample is taken:

(a) without consent under any power mentioned in paragraphs 6.6 and 6.6A, the person must be informed of:

(i)   the reason for taking the sample;

(ii) the power under which the sample is to be taken;

(iii) the fact that the relevant authority has been given if any power mentioned in paragraph 6.6(b), (e) or (h) applies;

(b) with or without consent at a police station or elsewhere, the person must be informed:

(i)   that their sample or information derived from it may be subject of a speculative search against other samples and information derived from them, see Note 6E and

(ii) that their sample and the information derived from it may be retained in accordance with Annex F, Part (a).

(c)   Removal of clothing

6.9   When clothing needs to be removed in circumstances likely to cause embarrassment to the person, no person of the opposite sex who is not a registered medical practitioner or registered health care professional shall be present, (unless in the case of a juvenile, mentally disordered or mentally vulnerable person, that person specifically requests the presence of an appropriate adult of the opposite sex who is readily available) nor shall anyone whose presence is unnecessary. However, in the case of a juvenile, this is subject to the overriding proviso that such a removal of clothing may take place in the absence of the appropriate adult only if the juvenile signifies in their presence, that they prefer the adult's absence and they agree.

(c)   Documentation

6.10   A record must be made as soon as practicable after the sample is taken of:

•   The matters in paragraph 6.8(a)(i) to (iii) and the fact that the person has been informed of those matters; and

- The fact that the person has been informed of the matters in paragraph 6.8(b)(i) and (ii).

6.10A   If force is used, a record shall be made of the circumstances and those present.

6.11   A record must be made of a warning given as required by paragraph 6.3.

6.12   Not used

Notes for guidance

6A   When hair samples are taken for the purpose of DNA analysis (rather than for other purposes such as making a visual match), the suspect should be permitted a reasonable choice as to what part

of the body the hairs are taken from. When hairs are plucked, they should be plucked individually, unless the suspect prefers otherwise and no more should be plucked than the person taking them reasonably considers necessary for a sufficient sample.

6B   (a)   An insufficient sample is one which is not sufficient either in quantity or quality to provide information for a particular form of analysis, such as DNA analysis. A sample may also be insufficient if enough information cannot be obtained from it by analysis because of loss, destruction, damage or contamination of the sample or as a result of an earlier, unsuccessful attempt at analysis.

(b)   An unsuitable sample is one which, by its nature, is not suitable for a particular form of analysis.

6C   Nothing in paragraph 6.2 prevents intimate samples being taken for elimination purposes with the consent of the person concerned but the provisions of paragraph 2.12 relating to the role of the appropriate adult, should be applied. Paragraph 6.2(b) does not, however, apply where the non-intimate samples were previously taken under the Terrorism Act 2000, Schedule 8, paragraph 10.

6D   In warning a person who is asked to provide an intimate sample as in paragraph 6.3, the following form of words may be used:

'You do not have to provide this sample/allow this swab or impression to be taken, but I must warn you that if you refuse without good cause, your refusal may harm your case if it comes to trial.'

6E   Fingerprints or a DNA sample and the information derived from it taken from a person arrested on suspicion of being involved in a recordable offence, or charged with such an offence, or informed they will be reported for such an offence, may be subject of a speculative search. This means they may be checked against other fingerprints and DNA records held by, or on behalf of, the police and other law enforcement authorities in or outside the UK or held in connection with, or as a result of, an investigation of an offence inside or outside the UK. Fingerprints and samples taken from any other person, e.g. a person suspected of committing a recordable offence but who has not been arrested, charged or informed they will be reported for it, may be subject to a speculative search only if the person consents in writing to their fingerprints being subject of such a search. The following is an example of a basic form of words:

"I consent to my fingerprints/DNA sample and information derived from it being retained and used only for purposes related to the prevention and detection of a crime, the investigation of an offence or the conduct of a prosecution either nationally or internationally.

I understand that this sample may be checked against other fingerprint/DNA records held by or on behalf of relevant law enforcement authorities, either nationally or internationally.

I understand that once I have given my consent for the sample to be retained and used I cannot withdraw this consent."

See Annex F regarding the retention and use of fingerprints and samples taken with consent for elimination purposes.

6F   Samples of urine and non-intimate samples taken in accordance with sections 63B and 63C of PACE may not be used for identification purposes in accordance with this Code. See Code C note for guidance 17D.

Annex A - Video identification

(a) General

1.   The arrangements for obtaining and ensuring the availability of a suitable set of images to be used in a video identification must be the responsibility of an identification officer, who has no direct involvement with the case.

2.   The set of images must include the suspect and at least eight other people who, so far as possible, resemble the suspect in age, general appearance and position in life. Only one suspect shall appear in any set unless there are two suspects of roughly similar appearance, in which case they may be shown together with at least twelve other people.

2A   If the suspect has an unusual physical feature, e.g., a facial scar, tattoo or distinctive hairstyle or hair colour which does not appear on the images of the other people that are available to be used, steps may be taken to:

(a) conceal the location of the feature on the images of the suspect and the other people; or

(b) replicate that feature on the images of the other people.

For these purposes, the feature may be concealed or replicated electronically or by any other method which it is practicable to use to ensure that the images of the suspect and other people resemble each other. The identification officer has discretion to choose whether to conceal or replicate the feature and the method to be used. If an unusual physical feature has been described by the witness, the identification officer should, if practicable, have that feature replicated. If it has not been described, concealment may be more appropriate.

2B   If the identification officer decides that a feature should be concealed or replicated, the reason for the decision and whether the feature was concealed or replicated in the images shown to any witness shall be recorded.

2C   If the witness requests to view an image where an unusual physical feature has been concealed or replicated without the feature being concealed or replicated, the witness may be allowed to do so.

3.   The images used to conduct a video identification shall, as far as possible, show the suspect and other people in the same positions or carrying out the same sequence of movements. They shall also show the suspect and other people under identical conditions unless the identification officer reasonably believes:

(a) because of the suspect's failure or refusal to co-operate or other reasons, it is not practicable for the conditions to be identical; and

(b) any difference in the conditions would not direct a witness' attention to any individual image.

4.   The reasons identical conditions are not practicable shall be recorded on forms provided for the purpose.

5.   Provision must be made for each person shown to be identified by number.

6.   If police officers are shown, any numerals or other identifying badges must be concealed. If a prison inmate is shown, either as a suspect or not, then either all, or none of, the people shown should be in prison clothing.

7.   The suspect or their solicitor, friend, or appropriate adult must be given a reasonable opportunity to see the complete set of images before it is shown to any witness. If the suspect has a reasonable objection to the set of images or any of the participants, the suspect shall be asked to state the reasons for the objection. Steps shall, if practicable, be taken to remove the grounds for objection. If this is not practicable, the suspect and/or their representative shall be told why their objections cannot be met and the objection, the reason given for it and why it cannot be met shall be recorded on forms provided for the purpose.

8.   Before the images are shown in accordance with paragraph 7, the suspect or their solicitor shall be provided with details of the first description of the suspect by any witnesses who are to attend the video identification. When a broadcast or publication is made, as in paragraph 3.28, the suspect or their solicitor must also be allowed to view any material released to the media by the police for the purpose of recognising or tracing the suspect, provided it is practicable and would not unreasonably delay the investigation.

9.   The suspect's solicitor, if practicable, shall be given reasonable notification of the time and place the video identification is to be conducted so a representative may attend on behalf of the suspect. The suspect may not be present when the images are shown to the witness(es). In the absence of the suspect's solicitor, the viewing itself shall be recorded on video. No unauthorised people may be present.

(b)   Conducting the video identification

10.   The identification officer is responsible for making the appropriate arrangements to make sure, before they see the set of images, witnesses are not able to communicate with each other about the case, see any of the images which are to be shown, see, or be reminded of, any photograph or description of the suspect or be given any other indication as to the suspect's identity, or overhear a witness who has already seen the material. There must be no discussion with the witness about the composition of the set of images and they must not be told whether a previous witness has made any identification.

11.   Only one witness may see the set of images at a time. Immediately before the images are shown, the witness shall be told that the person they saw on a specified earlier occasion may, or may not, appear in the images they are shown and that if they cannot make a positive identification, they should say so. The witness shall be advised that at any point, they may ask to see a particular

part of the set of images or to have a particular image frozen for them to study. Furthermore, it should be pointed out to the witness that there is no limit on how many times they can view the whole set of images or any part of them. However, they should be asked not to make any decision as to whether the person they saw is on the set of images until they have seen the whole set at least twice.

12.   Once the witness has seen the whole set of images at least twice and has indicated that they do not want to view the images, or any part of them, again, the witness shall be asked to say whether the individual they saw in person on a specified earlier occasion has been shown and, if so, to identify them by number of the image. The witness will then be shown that image to confirm the identification, see paragraph 17.

13.   Care must be taken not to direct the witness' attention to any one individual image or give any indication of the suspect's identity. Where a witness has previously made an identification by photographs, or a computerised or artist's composite or similar likeness, the witness must not be reminded of such a photograph or composite likeness once a suspect is available for identification by other means in accordance with this Code. Nor must the witness be reminded of any description of the suspect.

14.   After the procedure, each witness shall be asked whether they have seen any broadcast or published films or photographs, or any descriptions of suspects relating to the offence and their reply shall be recorded.

(c) Image security and destruction

15.   Arrangements shall be made for all relevant material containing sets of images used for specific identification procedures to be kept securely and their movements accounted for. In particular, no-one involved in the investigation shall be permitted to view the material prior to it being shown to any witness.

16.   As appropriate, paragraph 3.30 or 3.31 applies to the destruction or retention of relevant sets of images.

(d) Documentation

17.   A record must be made of all those participating in, or seeing, the set of images whose names are known to the police.

18.   A record of the conduct of the video identification must be made on forms provided for the purpose. This shall include anything said by the witness about any identifications or the conduct of the procedure and any reasons it was not practicable to comply with any of the provisions of this Code governing the conduct of video identifications.

Annex B - Identification parades

(a) General

1.   A suspect must be given a reasonable opportunity to have a solicitor or friend present, and the suspect shall be asked to indicate on a second copy of the notice whether or not they wish to do so.

2.   An identification parade may take place either in a normal room or one equipped with a screen permitting witnesses to see members of the identification parade without being seen. The procedures for the composition and conduct of the identification parade are the same in both cases, subject to paragraph 8 (except that an identification parade involving a screen may take place only

when the suspect's solicitor, friend or appropriate adult is present or the identification parade is recorded on video).

3.   Before the identification parade takes place, the suspect or their solicitor shall be provided with details of the first description of the suspect by any witnesses who are attending the identification parade. When a broadcast or publication is made as in paragraph 3.28, the suspect or their solicitor should also be allowed to view any material released to the media by the police for the purpose of recognising or tracing the suspect, provided it is practicable to do so and would not unreasonably delay the investigation.

(b) Identification parades involving prison inmates

4.   If a prison inmate is required for identification, and there are no security problems about the person leaving the establishment, they may be asked to participate in an identification parade or video identification.

5.   An identification parade may be held in a Prison Department establishment but shall be conducted, as far as practicable under normal identification parade rules. Members of the public shall make up the identification parade unless there are serious security, or control, objections to their admission to the establishment. In such cases, or if a group or video identification is arranged within the establishment, other inmates may participate. If an inmate is the suspect, they are not required to wear prison clothing for the identification parade unless the other people taking part are other inmates in similar clothing, or are members of the public who are prepared to wear prison clothing for the occasion.

(c) Conduct of the identification parade

6.   Immediately before the identification parade, the suspect must be reminded of the procedures governing its conduct and cautioned in the terms of Code C, paragraphs 10.5 or 10.6, as appropriate.

7.   All unauthorised people must be excluded from the place where the identification parade is held.

8.   Once the identification parade has been formed, everything afterwards, in respect of it, shall take place in the presence and hearing of the suspect and any interpreter, solicitor, friend or appropriate adult who is present (unless the identification parade involves a screen, in which case everything said to, or by, any witness at the place where the identification parade is held, must be said in the hearing and presence of the suspect's solicitor, friend or appropriate adult or be recorded on video).

9.   The identification parade shall consist of at least eight people (in addition to the suspect) who, so far as possible, resemble the suspect in age, height, general appearance and position in life. Only one suspect shall be included in an identification parade unless there are two suspects of roughly similar appearance, in which case they may be paraded together with at least twelve other people. In no circumstances shall more than two suspects be included in one identification parade and where there are separate identification parades, they shall be made up of different people.

10.   If the suspect has an unusual physical feature, e.g., a facial scar, tattoo or distinctive hairstyle or hair colour which cannot be replicated on other members of the identification parade, steps may be taken to conceal the location of that feature on the suspect and the other members of the identification parade if the suspect and their solicitor, or appropriate adult, agree. For example, by use of a plaster or a hat, so that all members of the identification parade resemble each other in general appearance.

11.   When all members of a similar group are possible suspects, separate identification parades shall be held for each unless there are two suspects of similar appearance when they may appear on the same identification parade with at least twelve other members of the group who are not suspects. When police officers in uniform form an identification parade any numerals or other identifying badges shall be concealed.

12.   When the suspect is brought to the place where the identification parade is to be held, they shall be asked if they have any objection to the arrangements for the identification parade or to any of the other participants in it and to state the reasons for the objection. The suspect may obtain advice from their solicitor or friend, if present, before the identification parade proceeds. If the suspect has a reasonable objection to the arrangements or any of the participants, steps shall, if practicable, be taken to remove the grounds for objection. When it is not practicable to do so, the suspect shall be told why their objections cannot be met and the objection, the reason given for it and why it cannot be met, shall be recorded on forms provided for the purpose.

13.   The suspect may select their own position in the line, but may not otherwise interfere with the order of the people forming the line. When there is more than one witness, the suspect must be told, after each witness has left the room, that they can, if they wish, change position in the line. Each position in the line must be clearly numbered, whether by means of a number laid on the floor in front of each identification parade member or by other means.

14.   Appropriate arrangements must be made to make sure, before witnesses attend the identification parade, they are not able to:

(i)   communicate with each other about the case or overhear a witness who has already seen the identification parade;

(ii) see any member of the identification parade;

(iii) see, or be reminded of, any photograph or description of the suspect or be given any other indication as to the suspect's identity; or

(iv) see the suspect before or after the identification parade.

15.   The person conducting a witness to an identification parade must not discuss with them the composition of the identification parade and, in particular, must not disclose whether a previous witness has made any identification.

16.   Witnesses shall be brought in one at a time. Immediately before the witness inspects the identification parade, they shall be told the person they saw on a specified earlier occasion may, or may not, be present and if they cannot make a positive identification, they should say so. The witness must also be told they should not make any decision about whether the person they saw is on the identification parade until they have looked at each member at least twice.

17.   When the officer or police staff (see paragraph 3.11) conducting the identification procedure is satisfied the witness has properly looked at each member of the identification parade, they shall ask the witness whether the person they saw on a specified earlier occasion is on the identification parade and, if so, to indicate the number of the person concerned, see paragraph 28.

18.   If the witness wishes to hear any identification parade member speak, adopt any specified posture or move, they shall first be asked whether they can identify any person(s) on the identification parade on the basis of appearance only. When the request is to hear members of the identification parade speak, the witness shall be reminded that the participants in the identification parade have been chosen on the basis of physical appearance only. Members of the identification

parade may then be asked to comply with the witness' request to hear them speak, see them move or adopt any specified posture.

19.   If the witness requests that the person they have indicated remove anything used for the purposes of paragraph 10 to conceal the location of an unusual physical feature, that person may be asked to remove it.

20.   If the witness makes an identification after the identification parade has ended, the suspect and, if present, their solicitor, interpreter or friend shall be informed. When this occurs, consideration should be given to allowing the witness a second opportunity to identify the suspect.

21   After the procedure, each witness shall be asked whether they have seen any broadcast or published films or photographs or any descriptions of suspects relating to the offence and their reply shall be recorded.

22.   When the last witness has left, the suspect shall be asked whether they wish to make any comments on the conduct of the identification parade.

(d) Documentation

23.   A video recording must normally be taken of the identification parade. If that is impracticable, a colour photograph must be taken. A copy of the video recording or photograph shall be supplied, on request, to the suspect or their solicitor within a reasonable time.

24.   As appropriate, paragraph 3.30 or 3.31, should apply to any photograph or video taken as in

paragraph 23.

25.   If any person is asked to leave an identification parade because they are interfering with its conduct, the circumstances shall be recorded.

26.   A record must be made of all those present at an identification parade whose names are known to the police.

27.   If prison inmates make up an identification parade, the circumstances must be recorded.

28.   A record of the conduct of any identification parade must be made on forms provided for the purpose. This shall include anything said by the witness or the suspect about any identifications or the conduct of the procedure, and any reasons it was not practicable to comply with any of this Code's provisions.

Annex C - Group identification

(a) General

1.   The purpose of this Annex is to make sure, as far as possible, group identifications follow the principles and procedures for identification parades so the conditions are fair to the suspect in the way they test the witness' ability to make an identification.

2.   Group identifications may take place either with the suspect's consent and co-operation or covertly without their consent.

3.   The location of the group identification is a matter for the identification officer, although the officer may take into account any representations made by the suspect, appropriate adult, their solicitor or friend.

4.   The place where the group identification is held should be one where other people are either passing by or waiting around informally, in groups such that the suspect is able to join them and be capable of being seen by the witness at the same time as others in the group. For example people leaving an escalator, pedestrians walking through a shopping centre, passengers on railway and bus stations, waiting in queues or groups or where people are standing or sitting in groups in other public places.

5.   If the group identification is to be held covertly, the choice of locations will be limited by the places where the suspect can be found and the number of other people present at that time. In these cases, suitable locations might be along regular routes travelled by the suspect, including buses or trains or public places frequented by the suspect.

6.   Although the number, age, sex, race and general description and style of clothing of other people present at the location cannot be controlled by the identification officer, in selecting the location the officer must consider the general appearance and numbers of people likely to be present. In particular, the officer must reasonably expect that over the period the witness observes the group, they will be able to see, from time to time, a number of others whose appearance is broadly similar to that of the suspect.

7.   A group identification need not be held if the identification officer believes, because of the unusual appearance of the suspect, none of the locations it would be practicable to use, satisfy the requirements of paragraph 6 necessary to make the identification fair.

8.   Immediately after a group identification procedure has taken place (with or without the suspect's consent), a colour photograph or video should be taken of the general scene, if practicable, to give a general impression of the scene and the number of people present. Alternatively, if it is practicable, the group identification may be video recorded.

9.   If it is not practicable to take the photograph or video in accordance with paragraph 8, a photograph or film of the scene should be taken later at a time determined by the identification officer if the officer considers it practicable to do so.

10.   An identification carried out in accordance with this Code remains a group identification even though, at the time of being seen by the witness, the suspect was on their own rather than in a group.

11.   Before the group identification takes place, the suspect or their solicitor shall be provided with details of the first description of the suspect by any witnesses who are to attend the identification. When a broadcast or publication is made, as in paragraph 3.28, the suspect or their solicitor should also be allowed to view any material released by the police to the media for the purposes of recognising or tracing the suspect, provided that it is practicable and would not unreasonably delay the investigation.

12.   After the procedure, each witness shall be asked whether they have seen any broadcast or published films or photographs or any descriptions of suspects relating to the offence and their reply recorded.

(b) Identification with the consent of the suspect

13.   A suspect must be given a reasonable opportunity to have a solicitor or friend present. They shall be asked to indicate on a second copy of the notice whether or not they wish to do so.

14.   The witness, the person carrying out the procedure and the suspect's solicitor, appropriate adult, friend or any interpreter for the witness, may be concealed from the sight of the individuals in the group they are observing, if the person carrying out the procedure considers this assists the conduct of the identification.

15.   The person conducting a witness to a group identification must not discuss with them the forthcoming group identification and, in particular, must not disclose whether a previous witness has made any identification.

16.   Anything said to, or by, the witness during the procedure about the identification should be said in the presence and hearing of those present at the procedure.

17.   Appropriate arrangements must be made to make sure, before witnesses attend the group identification, they are not able to:

(i)   communicate with each other about the case or overhear a witness who has already been given an opportunity to see the suspect in the group;

(ii) see the suspect; or

(iii) see, or be reminded of, any photographs or description of the suspect or be given any other indication of the suspect's identity.

18.   Witnesses shall be brought one at a time to the place where they are to observe the group. Immediately before the witness is asked to look at the group, the person conducting the procedure shall tell them that the person they saw may, or may not, be in the group and that if they cannot make a positive identification, they should say so. The witness shall be asked to observe the group in which the suspect is to appear. The way in which the witness should do this will depend on whether the group is moving or stationary.

Moving group

19.   When the group in which the suspect is to appear is moving, e.g. leaving an escalator, the provisions of paragraphs 20 to 24 should be followed.

20.   If two or more suspects consent to a group identification, each should be the subject of separate identification procedures. These may be conducted consecutively on the same occasion.

21.   The person conducting the procedure shall tell the witness to observe the group and ask them to point out any person they think they saw on the specified earlier occasion.

22.   Once the witness has been informed as in paragraph 21 the suspect should be allowed to take whatever position in the group they wish.

23.   When the witness points out a person as in paragraph 21 they shall, if practicable, be asked to take a closer look at the person to confirm the identification. If this is not practicable, or they cannot confirm the identification, they shall be asked how sure they are that the person they have indicated is the relevant person.

24.   The witness should continue to observe the group for the period which the person conducting the procedure reasonably believes is necessary in the circumstances for them to be able to make comparisons between the suspect and other individuals of broadly similar appearance to the suspect as in paragraph 6.

Stationary groups

25.   When the group in which the suspect is to appear is stationary, e.g. people waiting in a queue, the provisions of paragraphs 26 to 29 should be followed.

26.   If two or more suspects consent to a group identification, each should be subject to separate identification procedures unless they are of broadly similar appearance when they may appear in the same group. When separate group identifications are held, the groups must be made up of different people.

27.   The suspect may take whatever position in the group they wish. If there is more than one witness, the suspect must be told, out of the sight and hearing of any witness, that they can, if they wish, change their position in the group.

28.   The witness shall be asked to pass along, or amongst, the group and to look at each person in the group at least twice, taking as much care and time as possible according to the circumstances, before making an identification. Once the witness has done this, they shall be asked whether the person they saw on the specified earlier occasion is in the group and to indicate any such person by whatever means the person conducting the procedure considers appropriate in the circumstances. If this is not practicable, the witness shall be asked to point out any person they think they saw on the earlier occasion.

29.   When the witness makes an indication as in paragraph 28, arrangements shall be made, if practicable, for the witness to take a closer look at the person to confirm the identification. If this is not practicable, or the witness is unable to confirm the identification, they shall be asked how sure they are that the person they have indicated is the relevant person.

All cases

30.   If the suspect unreasonably delays joining the group, or having joined the group, deliberately conceals themselves from the sight of the witness, this may be treated as a refusal to co-operate in a group identification.

31.   If the witness identifies a person other than the suspect, that person should be informed what has happened and asked if they are prepared to give their name and address. There is no obligation upon any member of the public to give these details. There shall be no duty to record any details of any other member of the public present in the group or at the place where the procedure is conducted.

32.   When the group identification has been completed, the suspect shall be asked whether they wish to make any comments on the conduct of the procedure.

33.   If the suspect has not been previously informed, they shall be told of any identifications made by the witnesses.

(c) Identification without the suspect's consent

34.   Group identifications held covertly without the suspect's consent should, as far as practicable, follow the rules for conduct of group identification by consent.

35.   A suspect has no right to have a solicitor, appropriate adult or friend present as the identification will take place without the knowledge of the suspect.

36.   Any number of suspects may be identified at the same time.

(d) Identifications in police stations

37.   Group identifications should only take place in police stations for reasons of safety, security or because it is not practicable to hold them elsewhere.

38.   The group identification may take place either in a room equipped with a screen permitting witnesses to see members of the group without being seen, or anywhere else in the police station that the identification officer considers appropriate.

39.   Any of the additional safeguards applicable to identification parades should be followed if the identification officer considers it is practicable to do so in the circumstances.

(e) Identifications involving prison inmates

40.   A group identification involving a prison inmate may only be arranged in the prison or at a police station.

41.   When a group identification takes place involving a prison inmate, whether in a prison or in a police station, the arrangements should follow those in paragraphs 37 to 39. If a group identification takes place within a prison, other inmates may participate. If an inmate is the suspect, they do not have to wear prison clothing for the group identification unless the other participants are wearing the same clothing.

(f) Documentation

42.   When a photograph or video is taken as in paragraph 8 or 9, a copy of the photograph or video shall be supplied on request to the suspect or their solicitor within a reasonable time.

43.   Paragraph 3.30 or 3.31, as appropriate, shall apply when the photograph or film taken in accordance with paragraph 8 or 9 includes the suspect.

44.   A record of the conduct of any group identification must be made on forms provided for the purpose. This shall include anything said by the witness or suspect about any identifications or the conduct of the procedure and any reasons why it was not practicable to comply with any of the provisions of this Code governing the conduct of group identifications.

Annex D - Confrontation by a witness

1.   Before the confrontation takes place, the witness must be told that the person they saw may, or may not, be the person they are to confront and that if they are not that person, then the witness should say so.

2.   Before the confrontation takes place the suspect or their solicitor shall be provided with details of the first description of the suspect given by any witness who is to attend. When a broadcast or publication is made, as in paragraph 3.28, the suspect or their solicitor should also be

allowed to view any material released to the media for the purposes of recognising or tracing the suspect, provided it is practicable to do so and would not unreasonably delay the investigation.

3.   Force may not be used to make the suspect's face visible to the witness.

4.   Confrontation must take place in the presence of the suspect's solicitor, interpreter or friend unless this would cause unreasonable delay.

5.   The suspect shall be confronted independently by each witness, who shall be asked "Is this the person?". If the witness identifies the person but is unable to confirm the identification, they shall be asked how sure they are that the person is the one they saw on the earlier occasion.

6.   The confrontation should normally take place in the police station, either in a normal room or one equipped with a screen permitting a witness to see the suspect without being seen. In both cases, the procedures are the same except that a room equipped with a screen may be used only when the suspect's solicitor, friend or appropriate adult is present or the confrontation is recorded on video.

7.   After the procedure, each witness shall be asked whether they have seen any broadcast or published films or photographs or any descriptions of suspects relating to the offence and their reply shall be recorded.

Annex E - Showing photographs

(a) Action

1.   An officer of sergeant rank or above shall be responsible for supervising and directing the showing of photographs. The actual showing may be done by another officer or police staff, see paragraph 3.11.

2.   The supervising officer must confirm the first description of the suspect given by the witness has been recorded before they are shown the photographs. If the supervising officer is unable to confirm the description has been recorded they shall postpone showing the photographs.

3.   Only one witness shall be shown photographs at any one time. Each witness shall be given as much privacy as practicable and shall not be allowed to communicate with any other witness in the case.

4.   The witness shall be shown not less than twelve photographs at a time, which shall, as far as possible, all be of a similar type.

5.   When the witness is shown the photographs, they shall be told the photograph of the person they saw may, or may not, be amongst them and if they cannot make a positive identification, they should say so. The witness shall also be told they should not make a decision until they have viewed at least twelve photographs. The witness shall not be prompted or guided in any way but shall be left to make any selection without help.

6.   If a witness makes a positive identification from photographs, unless the person identified is otherwise eliminated from enquiries or is not available, other witnesses shall not be shown photographs. But both they, and the witness who has made the identification, shall be asked to attend a video identification, an identification parade or group identification unless there is no dispute about the suspect's identification.

7.   If the witness makes a selection but is unable to confirm the identification, the person showing the photographs shall ask them how sure they are that the photograph they have indicated is the person they saw on the specified earlier occasion.

8.   When the use of a computerised or artist's composite or similar likeness has led to there being a known suspect who can be asked to participate in a video identification, appear on an identification parade or participate in a group identification, that likeness shall not be shown to other potential witnesses.

9.   When a witness attending a video identification, an identification parade or group identification has previously been shown photographs or computerised or artist's composite or similar likeness (and it is the responsibility of the officer in charge of the investigation to make the identification officer aware that this is the case), the suspect and their solicitor must be informed of this fact before the identification procedure takes place.

10.   None of the photographs shown shall be destroyed, whether or not an identification is made, since they may be required for production in court. The photographs shall be numbered and a separate photograph taken of the frame or part of the album from which the witness made an identification as an aid to reconstituting it.

(b) Documentation

11.   Whether or not an identification is made, a record shall be kept of the showing of photographs on forms provided for the purpose. This shall include anything said by the witness about any identification or the conduct of the procedure, any reasons it was not practicable to comply with any of the provisions of this Code governing the showing of photographs and the name and rank of the supervising officer.

12.   The supervising officer shall inspect and sign the record as soon as practicable.

Annex F - Fingerprints, footwear impressions and samples - destruction and speculative searches

(a)   Fingerprints, footwear impressions and samples taken in connection with a criminal investigation from a person suspected of committing the offence under investigation.

1.   The retention and destruction of fingerprints, footwear impressions and samples taken in connection with a criminal investigation from a person suspected of committing the offence under investigation is subject to PACE, section 64.

(b)   Fingerprints, footwear impressions and samples taken in connection with a criminal investigation from a person not suspected of committing the offence under investigation.

2.   When fingerprints, footwear impressions or DNA samples are taken from a person in connection with an investigation and the person is not suspected of having committed the offence, see Note F1, they must be destroyed as soon as they have fulfilled the purpose for which they were taken unless:

(a) they were taken for the purposes of an investigation of an offence for which a person has been convicted; and

(b) fingerprints, footwear impressions or samples were also taken from the convicted person for the purposes of that investigation.

However, subject to paragraph 2, the fingerprints, footwear impressions and samples, and the information derived from samples, may not be used in the investigation of any offence or in evidence against the person who is, or would be, entitled to the destruction of the fingerprints, footwear impressions and samples, see Note F2.

3.   The requirement to destroy fingerprints, footwear impressions and DNA samples, and information derived from samples, and restrictions on their retention and use in paragraph 1 do not apply if the person gives their written consent for their fingerprints, footwear impressions or sample to be retained and used after they have fulfilled the purpose for which they were taken, see Note F1.

4.   When a person's fingerprints, footwear impressions or sample are to be destroyed: (a) any copies of the fingerprints and footwear impressions must also be destroyed;

(b) the person may witness the destruction of their fingerprints, footwear impressions or copies if

they ask to do so within five days of being informed destruction is required;

(c) access to relevant computer fingerprint data shall be made impossible as soon as it is practicable to do so and the person shall be given a certificate to this effect within three months of asking; and

(d) neither the fingerprints, footwear impressions, the sample, or any information derived from the sample, may be used in the investigation of any offence or in evidence against the person who is, or would be, entitled to its destruction.

5.   Fingerprints, footwear impressions or samples, and the information derived from samples, taken in connection with the investigation of an offence which are not required to be destroyed, may be retained after they have fulfilled the purposes for which they were taken but may be used only for purposes related to the prevention or detection of crime, the investigation of an offence or the conduct of a prosecution in, as well as outside, the UK and may also be subject to a speculative search. This includes checking them against other fingerprints, footwear impressions and DNA records held by, or on behalf of, the police and other law enforcement authorities in, as well as outside, the UK.

(b) Fingerprints taken in connection with Immigration Service enquiries

6.   See paragraph 4.10.

Notes for guidance

F1   Fingerprints, footwear impressions and samples given voluntarily for the purposes of elimination play an important part in many police investigations. It is, therefore, important to make sure innocent volunteers are not deterred from participating and their consent to their fingerprints, footwear impressions and DNA being used for the purposes of a specific investigation is fully informed and voluntary. If the police or volunteer seek to have the fingerprints, footwear impressions or samples retained for use after the specific investigation ends, it is important the volunteer's consent to this is also fully informed and voluntary.

Examples of consent for:

•   DNA/fingerprints/footwear impressions - to be used only for the purposes of a specific investigation;

- DNA/fingerprints/footwear impressions - to be used in the specific investigation and

retained by the police for future use.

To minimise the risk of confusion, each consent should be physically separate and the volunteer should be asked to sign each consent.

(a) DNA:

(i)   DNA sample taken for the purposes of elimination or as part of an intelligence-led screening and to be used only for the purposes of that investigation and destroyed afterwards:

"I consent to my DNA/mouth swab being taken for forensic analysis. I understand that the sample will be destroyed at the end of the case and that my profile will only be compared to the crime stain profile from this enquiry. I have been advised that the person taking the sample may be required to give evidence and/or provide a written statement to the police in relation to the taking of it".

(ii) DNA sample to be retained on the National DNA database and used in the future:

"I consent to my DNA sample and information derived from it being retained and used only for purposes related to the prevention and detection of a crime, the investigation of an offence or the conduct of a prosecution either nationally or internationally."

"I understand that this sample may be checked against other DNA records held by, or on behalf of, relevant law enforcement authorities, either nationally or internationally".

"I understand that once I have given my consent for the sample to be retained and used

I cannot withdraw this consent." (b) Fingerprints:

(i)   Fingerprints taken for the purposes of elimination or as part of an intelligence-led

screening and to be used only for the purposes of that investigation and destroyed afterwards:

"I consent to my fingerprints being taken for elimination purposes. I understand that the fingerprints will be destroyed at the end of the case and that my fingerprints will only be compared to the fingerprints from this enquiry. I have been advised that the person taking the fingerprints may be required to give evidence and/or provide a written statement to the police in relation to the taking of it."

(ii) Fingerprints to be retained for future use:

"I consent to my fingerprints being retained and used only for purposes related to the prevention and detection of a crime, the investigation of an offence or the conduct of a prosecution either nationally or internationally".

"I understand that my fingerprints may be checked against other records held by, or on behalf of, relevant law enforcement authorities, either nationally or internationally." "I understand that once I have given my consent for my fingerprints to be retained and used I cannot withdraw this consent."

(c) Footwear impressions:

(i)   Footwear impressions taken for the purposes of elimination or as part of an intelligence-led screening and to be used only for the purposes of that investigation and destroyed afterwards:

"I consent to my footwear impressions being taken for elimination purposes. I understand that the footwear impressions will be destroyed at the end of the case and that my footwear impressions will only be compared to the footwear impressions from this enquiry. I have been advised that the person taking the footwear impressions may be required to give evidence and/or provide a written statement to the police in relation to the taking of it."

(ii) Footwear impressions to be retained for future use:

"I consent to my footwear impressions being retained and used only for purposes related to the prevention and detection of a crime, the investigation of an offence or the conduct of a prosecution, either nationally or internationally".

"I understand that my footwear impressions may be checked against other records held by, or on behalf of, relevant law enforcement authorities, either nationally or internationally."

"I understand that once I have given my consent for my footwear impressions to be retained and used I cannot withdraw this consent."

F2   The provisions for the retention of fingerprints, footwear impressions and samples in paragraph 1 allow for all fingerprints, footwear impressions and samples in a case to be available for any subsequent miscarriage of justice investigation.

Annex G –Requirement for a person to attend a police station for fingerprints and samples.

1.   A requirement under Schedule 2A for a person to attend a police station to have fingerprints or samples taken:

(a) must give the person a period of at least seven days within which to attend the police station;

and

(b) may direct them to attend at a specified time of day or between specified times of day.

2.   When specifying the period and times of attendance, the officer making the requirements must consider whether the fingerprints or samples could reasonably be taken at a time when the person is required to attend the police station for any other reason. See Note G1.

3.   An officer of the rank of inspector or above may authorise a period shorter than 7 days if there is an urgent need for person's fingerprints or sample for the purposes of the investigation of an offence. The fact of the authorisation and the reasons for giving it must be recorded as soon as practicable.

4.   The constable making a requirement and the person to whom it applies may agree to vary it so as to specify any period within which, or date or time at which, the person is to attend. However, variation shall not have effect for the purposes of enforcement, unless it is confirmed by the constable in writing.

Notes for Guidance

G1   The specified period within which the person is to attend need not fall within the period allowed

(if applicable) for making the requirement.

G2   To justify the arrest without warrant of a person who fails to comply with a requirement, (see paragraph 4.4(b) above), the officer making the requirement, or confirming a variation, should be prepared to explain how, when and where the requirement was made or the variation was confirmed and what steps were taken to ensure the person understood what to do and the consequences of not complying with the requirement.

Codes of Practice – Code E Audio recording interviews with suspects

1   **General**

1.1   This Code of Practice must be readily available for consultation by:

.   police officers

.   police staff

.   detained persons

.   members of the public.

1.2   The Notes for Guidance included are not provisions of this Code.

1.3   Nothing in this Code shall detract from the requirements of Code C, the Code of

Practice for the detention, treatment and questioning of persons by police officers.

1.4   This Code does not apply to those people listed in Code C, paragraph 1.12.

E   1.5   The term:

.   'appropriate adult' has the same meaning as in Code C, paragraph 1.7

.   'solicitor' has the same meaning as in Code C, paragraph 6.12.

1.5A   Recording of interviews shall be carried out openly to instil confidence in its reliability as an impartial and accurate record of the interview.

1.6   In this Code:

(aa)   'recording media' means any removable, physical audio recording medium (such as magnetic tape, optical disc or solid state memory) which can be played and copied.

(a)   'designated person' means a person other than a police officer, designated under the Police Reform Act 2002, Part 4 who has specified powers and duties of police officers conferred or imposed on them;

(b)   any reference to a police officer includes a designated person acting in the exercise or performance of the powers and duties conferred or imposed on them by their designation.

(c)   'secure digital network' is a computer network system which enables an original interview recording to be stored as a digital multi media file or a series of such files, on a secure file server which is accredited by the National Accreditor for Police Information Systems in the National Police Improvement Agency (NPIA) in accordance with the UK Government Protective Marking Scheme. (see section 7 of this Code).

1.7   Sections 2 to 6 of this code set out the procedures and requirements which apply to all interviews together with the provisions which apply only to interviews recorded using removable media. Section 7 sets out the provisions which apply to interviews recorded using a secure digital network and specifies the provisions in sections 2 to 6 which do not apply to secure digital network recording.

1.8   Nothing in this Code prevents the custody officer, or other officer given custody of the detainee, from allowing police staff who are not designated persons to carry out individual procedures or tasks at the police station if the law allows. However, the officer remains responsible for making sure the procedures and tasks are carried out correctly in accordance with this Code. Any such police staff must be:

(a)   a person employed by a police authority maintaining a police force and under the control and direction of the Chief Officer of that force; or

(b)   employed by a person with whom a police authority has a contract for the provision of services relating to persons arrested or otherwise in custody.

1.9   Designated persons and other police staff must have regard to any relevant provisions of the Codes of Practice.

1.10   References to pocket book include any official report book issued to police officers or police staff.

1.11   References to a custody officer include those performing the functions of a custody officer as in paragraph 1.9 of Code C.

2   **Recording and sealing master recordings**

2.1   Not used.

2.2   One recording, the master recording, will be sealed in the suspect's presence. A second recording will be used as a working copy. The master recording is either of the two recordings used in a twin deck/drive machine or the only recording in a single deck/drive machine. The working copy is either the second/third recording used in a twin/triple deck/drive machine or a copy of the master recording made by a single deck/drive machine. See Notes 2A and 2B [This paragraph does not apply to interviews recorded using a secure digital network, see paragraphs 7.4 to 7.6]

2.3   Nothing in this Code requires the identity of officers or police staff conducting interviews to be recorded or disclosed:

(a)   in the case of enquiries linked to the investigation of terrorism (see paragraph 3.2); or

(b)   if the interviewer reasonably believes recording or disclosing their name might put them in danger.

In these cases interviewers should use warrant or other identification numbers and the name of their police station. See Note 2C

Notes for guidance

2A   The purpose of sealing the master recording in the suspect's presence is to show the recording's integrity is preserved. If a single deck/drive machine is used the working copy of the master recording must be made in the suspect's presence and without the master recording leaving their sight. The working copy shall be used for making further copies if needed.

2B   Not used.

2C   The purpose of paragraph 2.3(b) is to protect those involved in serious organised crime investigations or arrests of particularly violent suspects when there is reliable information that those arrested or their associates may threaten or cause harm to those involved. In cases of doubt, an officer of inspector rank or above should be consulted.

3   Interviews to be audio recorded

3.1   Subject to paragraphs 3.3 and 3.4, audio recording shall be used at police stations for any interview:

(a)   with a person cautioned under Code C, section 10 in respect of any indictable offence, including an offence triable either way, see Note 3A

(b)   which takes place as a result of an interviewer exceptionally putting further questions to a suspect about an offence described in paragraph 3.1(a) after they have been charged with, or told they may be prosecuted for, that offence, see Code C, paragraph 16.5

(c)   when an interviewer wants to tell a person, after they have been charged with, or informed they may be prosecuted for, an offence described in paragraph 3.1(a), about any written statement or interview with another person, see Code C, paragraph 16.4.

3.2   The Terrorism Act 2000 makes separate provision for a Code of Practice for the audio recording of interviews of those arrested under Section 41 of, or Schedule 7 to, the 2000 Act. The provisions of this Code do not apply to such interviews. [See Note 3C].

3.3   The custody officer may authorise the interviewer not to audio record the interview when it is:

(a)   not reasonably practicable because of equipment failure or the unavailability of a suitable interview room or recording equipment and the authorising officer considers, on reasonable grounds, that the interview should not be delayed; or

(b)   clear from the outset there will not be a prosecution.

Note: In these cases the interview should be recorded in writing in accordance with Code C, section 11. In all cases the custody officer shall record the specific reasons for not audio recording. See Note 3B

3.4   If a person refuses to go into or remain in a suitable interview room, see Code C paragraph 12.5, and the custody officer considers, on reasonable grounds, that the interview should not be delayed the interview may, at the custody officer's discretion, be conducted in a cell using portable recording equipment or, if none is available, recorded in writing as in Code C, section 11. The reasons for this shall be recorded.

3.5   The whole of each interview shall be audio recorded, including the taking and reading back of any statement.

3.6   A sign or indicator which is visible to the suspect must show when the recording equipment is recording.

Notes for guidance

3A   Nothing in this Code is intended to preclude audio recording at police discretion of interviews at police stations with people cautioned in respect of offences not covered by paragraph 3.1, or responses made by persons after they have been charged with, or told they may be prosecuted for, an offence, provided this Code is complied with.

3B   A decision not to audio record an interview for any reason may be the subject of comment in court. The authorising officer should be prepared to justify that decision.

3C   If, during the course of an interview under this Code, it becomes apparent that the interview should be conducted under one of the terrorism codes for recording of interviews the interview should only continue in accordance with the relevant code.

4   The interview

(a)   General

4.1   The provisions of Code C:

.   sections 10 and 11, and the applicable Notes for Guidance apply to the conduct of interviews to which this Code applies

.   paragraphs 11.7 to 11.14 apply only when a written record is needed.

4.2   Code C, paragraphs 10.10, 10.11 and Annex C describe the restriction on drawing adverse inferences from a suspect's failure or refusal to say anything about their involvement in the offence when interviewed or after being charged or informed they may be prosecuted, and how it affects the terms of the caution and determines if and by whom a special warning under sections 36 and 37 of the Criminal Justice and Public Order Act 1994 can be given.

(b)   Commencement of interviews

4.3   When the suspect is brought into the interview room the interviewer shall, without delay but in the suspect's sight, load the recorder with new recording media and set it to record. The recording media must be unwrapped or opened in the suspect's presence. [This paragraph does not apply to interviews recorded using a secure digital network, see paragraphs 7.4 and 7.5].

4.4   The interviewer should tell the suspect about the recording process and point out the sign or indicator which shows that the recording equipment is activated and recording. See paragraph 3.6. The interviewer shall:

(a)   say the interview is being audibly recorded

(b)   subject to paragraph 2.3, give their name and rank and that of any other interviewer present

(c)   ask the suspect and any other party present, e.g. a solicitor, to identify themselves

(d)   state the date, time of commencement and place of the interview

(e)   state the suspect will be given a notice about what will happen to the copies of the recording. [This sub-paragraph does not apply to interviews recorded using a secure digital network, see paragraphs 7.4 and 7.6 to 7.7] See Note 4A

4.5   The interviewer shall:

.   caution the suspect, see Code C, section 10

.   remind the suspect of their entitlement to free legal advice, see Code C, paragraph 11.2.

4.6   The interviewer shall put to the suspect any significant statement or silence, see Code C, paragraph 11.4.

(c)   Interviews with deaf persons

4.7   If the suspect is deaf or is suspected of having impaired hearing, the interviewer shall make a written note of the interview in accordance with Code C, at the same time as audio recording it in accordance with this Code. See Notes 4B and 4C

(d)   Objections and complaints by the suspect

4.8   If the suspect objects to the interview being audibly recorded at the outset, during the interview or during a break, the interviewer shall explain that the interview is being audibly recorded and that this Code requires the suspect's objections to be recorded on the audio recording. When any objections have been audibly recorded or the suspect has refused to have their objections recorded, the interviewer shall say they are turning off the recorder, give their reasons and turn it off. The interviewer shall then make a written record of the interview as in Code C, section 11. If, however, the interviewer reasonably considers they may proceed to question the suspect with the audio recording still on, the interviewer may do so. This procedure also applies in cases where the suspect has previously objected to the interview being visually recorded, see Code F 4.8, and the investigating officer has decided to audibly record the interview. See Note 4D

4.9   If in the course of an interview a complaint is made by or on behalf of the person being questioned concerning the provisions of this Code or Code C, the interviewer shall act as in Code C, paragraph 12.9. See Notes 4E and 4F

4.10   If the suspect indicates they want to tell the interviewer about matters not directly connected with the offence and they are unwilling for these matters to be audio recorded, the suspect should be given the opportunity to tell the interviewer at the end of the formal interview.

(e)   Changing recording media

4.11   When the recorder shows the recording media only has a short time left, the interviewer shall tell the suspect the recording media are coming to an end and round off that part of the interview. If the interviewer leaves the room for a second set of recording media, the suspect shall not be left unattended. The interviewer will remove the recording media from the recorder and insert the new recording media which shall be unwrapped or opened in the suspect's presence. The recorder should be set to record on the new media. To avoid confusion between the recording media, the interviewer shall mark the media with an identification number immediately after they are removed from the recorder. [This paragraph does not apply to interviews recorded using a secure digital network as this does not use removable media, see paragraphs 1.6(c), 7.4 and 7.14 to 7.15.]

(f)   Taking a break during interview

4.12   When a break is taken, the fact that a break is to be taken, the reason for it and the time shall be recorded on the audio recording.

4.12A When the break is taken and the interview room vacated by the suspect, the recording media shall be removed from the recorder and the procedures for the conclusion of an interview followed, see paragraph 4.18.

4.13   When a break is a short one and both the suspect and an interviewer remain in the interview room, the recording may be stopped.   There is no need to remove the recording media and when the interview recommences the recording should continue on the same recording media. The time the interview recommences shall be recorded on the audio recording.

4.14   After any break in the interview the interviewer must, before resuming the interview, remind the person being questioned that they remain under caution or, if there is any doubt, give the caution in full again. See Note 4G.

[Paragraphs 4.12 to 4.14 do not apply to interviews recorded using a secure digital network, see paragraphs 7.4 and 7.8 to 7.10]

(g)   Failure of recording equipment

4.15   If there is an equipment failure which can be rectified quickly, e.g. by inserting new recording media, the interviewer shall follow the appropriate procedures as in paragraph 4.11. When the recording is resumed the interviewer shall explain what happened and record the time the interview recommences. If, however, it will not be possible to continue recording on that recorder and no replacement recorder is readily available, the interview may continue without being audibly recorded. If this happens, the interviewer shall seek the custody officer's authority as in paragraph 3.3.   See Note 4H [This paragraph does not apply to interviews recorded using a secure digital network, see paragraphs 7.4 and 7.11]

(h)   Removing recording media from the recorder

4.16   When recording media is removed from the recorder during the interview, they shall be retained and the procedures in paragraph 4.18 followed.   [This paragraph does not apply to interviews recorded using a secure digital network as this does not use removable media, see 1.6(c), 7.4 and 7.14 to 7.15.]

(i)   Conclusion of interview

4.17   At the conclusion of the interview, the suspect shall be offered the opportunity to clarify anything he or she has said and asked if there is anything they want to add.

4.18   At the conclusion of the interview, including the taking and reading back of any written statement, the time shall be recorded and the recording shall be stopped. The interviewer shall seal the master recording with a master recording label and treat it as an exhibit in accordance with force standing orders. The interviewer shall sign the label and ask the suspect and any third party present during the interview to sign it. If the suspect or third party refuse to sign the label an officer of at least inspector rank, or if not available the custody officer, shall be called into the interview room and asked, subject to paragraph 2.3, to sign it.

4.19   The suspect shall be handed a notice which explains:

.   how the audio recording will be used

.   the arrangements for access to it

.   that if the person is charged or informed they will be prosecuted, a copy of the audio recording will be supplied as soon as practicable or as otherwise agreed between the suspect and the police or on the order of a court.

[Paragraphs 4.17 to 4.19 do not apply to interviews recorded using a secure digital network, see paragraphs 7.4 and 7.12 to 7.13]

Notes for guidance

4A   For the purpose of voice identification the interviewer should ask the suspect and any other people present to identify themselves.

4B   This provision is to give a person who is deaf or has impaired hearing equivalent rights of access to the full interview record as far as this is possible using audio recording.

4C   The provisions of Code C, section 13 on interpreters for deaf persons or for interviews with suspects who have difficulty understanding English continue to apply.

4D   The interviewer should remember that a decision to continue recording against the wishes of the suspect may be the subject of comment in court.

4E   If the custody officer is called to deal with the complaint, the recorder should, if possible, be left on until the custody officer has entered the room and spoken to the person being interviewed. Continuation or termination of the interview should be at the interviewer's discretion pending action by an inspector under Code C, paragraph 9.2.

4F   If the complaint is about a matter not connected with this Code or Code C, the decision to continue is at the interviewer's discretion. When the interviewer decides to continue the interview, they shall tell the suspect the complaint will be brought to the custody officer's attention at the conclusion of the interview. When the interview is concluded the interviewer must, as soon as practicable, inform the custody officer about the existence and nature of the complaint made.

4G   The interviewer should remember that it may be necessary to show to the court that nothing occurred during a break or between interviews which influenced the suspect's recorded evidence. After a break or at the beginning of a subsequent interview, the interviewer should consider summarising on the record the reason for the break and confirming this with the suspect.

4H   Where the interview is being recorded and the media or the recording equipment fails the officer conducting the interview should stop the interview immediately. Where part of the interview is unaffected by the error and is still accessible on the media, that media shall be copied and sealed in the suspect's presence and the interview recommenced using new equipment/media as required. Where the content of the interview has been lost in its entirety the media should be sealed in the suspect's presence and the interview begun again. If the recording equipment cannot be fixed or no replacement is immediately available the interview should be recorded in accordance with Code C, section 11.

5   After the interview

5.1   The interviewer shall make a note in their pocket book that the interview has taken place, was audibly recorded, its time, duration and date and the master recording's identification number.

5.2   If no proceedings follow in respect of the person whose interview was recorded, the recording media must be kept securely as in paragraph 6.1 and Note 6A.

[This section (paragraphs 5.1, 5.2 and Note 5A) does not apply to interviews recorded using a secure digital network, see paragraphs 7.4 and 7.14 to 7.15]

Note for guidance

5A   Any written record of an audibly recorded interview should be made in accordance with national guidelines approved by the Secretary of State, and with regard to the advice contained in the Manual of Guidance for the preparation, processing and submission of prosecution files.

6   Media security

6.1   The officer in charge of each police station at which interviews with suspects are recorded shall make arrangements for master recordings to be kept securely and their movements accounted for on the same basis as material which may be used for evidential purposes, in accordance with force standing orders. See Note 6A

6.2   A police officer has no authority to break the seal on a master recording required for criminal trial or appeal proceedings. If it is necessary to gain access to the master recording, the police officer shall arrange for its seal to be broken in the presence of a representative of the Crown Prosecution Service. The defendant or their legal adviser should be informed and given a reasonable opportunity to be present. If the defendant or their legal representative is present they shall be invited to reseal and sign the master recording. If either refuses or neither is present this should be done by the representative of the Crown Prosecution Service. See Notes 6B and 6C

6.3   If no criminal proceedings result or the criminal trial and, if applicable, appeal proceedings to which the interview relates have been concluded, the chief officer of police is responsible for establishing arrangements for breaking the seal on the master recording, if necessary.

6.4   When the master recording seal is broken, a record must be made of the procedure followed, including the date, time, place and persons present.

[This section (paragraphs 6.1 to 6.4 and Notes 6A to 6C) does not apply to interviews recorded using a secure digital network, see paragraphs 7.4 and 7.14 to 7.15]

Notes for guidance

6A   This section is concerned with the security of the master recording sealed at the conclusion of the interview. Care must be taken of working copies of recordings because their loss or destruction may lead to the need to access master recordings.

6B   If the recording has been delivered to the crown court for their keeping after committal for trial the crown prosecutor will apply to the chief clerk of the crown court centre for the release of the recording for unsealing by the crown prosecutor.

6C   Reference to the Crown Prosecution Service or to the crown prosecutor in this part of the Code should be taken to include any other body or person with a statutory responsibility for prosecution for whom the police conduct any audibly recorded interviews.

7   Recording of Interviews by Secure Digital Network

7.1   A secure digital network does not use removable media and this section specifies the provisions which will apply when a secure digital network is used.

7.2   Not used.

7.3   The following requirements are solely applicable to the use of a secure digital network for the recording of interviews.

(a)   Application of sections 1 to 6 of Code E

7.4   Sections 1 to 6 of Code E above apply except for the following paragraphs:

.   Paragraph 2.2 under "Recording and sealing of master recordings"

.   Paragraph 4.3 under "(b) Commencement of interviews"

.   Paragraph 4.4 (e) under "(b) Commencement of interviews"

.   Paragraphs 4.11 – 4.19 under "(e) Changing recording media", "(f) Taking a break during interview", "(g) Failure of recording equipment", "(h) Removing recording media from the recorder" and "(i) Conclusion of interview"

.   Paragraphs 6.1 – 6.4 and Notes 6A to 6C under "Media security"

(b)   Commencement of Interview

7.5   When the suspect is brought into the interview room, the interviewer shall without delay and in the sight of the suspect, switch on the recording equipment and enter the information necessary to log on to the secure network and start recording.

7.6   The interviewer must then inform the suspect that the interview is being recorded using a secure digital network and that recording has commenced.

7.7   In addition to the requirements of paragraph 4.4 (a – d) above, the interviewer must inform the person that:

.   they will be given access to the recording of the interview in the event that they are charged or informed that they will be prosecuted but if they are not charged or informed that they will be prosecuted they will only be given access as agreed with the police or on the order of a court; and

.   they will be given a written notice at the end of the interview setting out their rights to access the recording and what will happen to the recording.

(c)   Taking a break during interview

7.8   When a break is taken, the fact that a break is to be taken, the reason for it and the time shall be recorded on the audio recording. The recording shall be stopped and the procedures in paragraphs 7.12 and 7.13 for the conclusion of an interview followed.

7.9   When the interview recommences the procedures in paragraphs 7.5 to 7.7 for commencing an interview shall be followed to create a new file to record the continuation of the interview. The time the interview recommences shall be recorded on the audio recording.

7.10   After any break in the interview the interviewer must, before resuming the interview, remind the person being questioned that they remain under caution or, if there is any doubt, give the caution in full again. See Note 4G

(d)   Failure of recording equipment

7.11   If there is an equipment failure which can be rectified quickly, e.g. by commencing a new secure digital network recording, the interviewer shall follow the appropriate procedures as in paragraphs 7.8 to 7.10. When the recording is resumed the interviewer shall explain what happened and record the time the interview recommences.   If, however, it is not possible to continue recording on the secure digital network the interview should be recorded on removable media as in paragraph 4.3 unless the necessary equipment is not available. If this happens the interview may continue without being audibly recorded and the interviewer shall seek the custody officer's authority as in paragraph 3.3. See Note 4H.

(e)   Conclusion of interview

7.12   At the conclusion of the interview, the suspect shall be offered the opportunity to clarify anything he or she has said and asked if there is anything they want to add.

7.13   At the conclusion of the interview, including the taking and reading back of any written statement:

(a)   the time shall be orally recorded

(b)   the suspect shall be handed a notice which explains:

.   how the audio recording will be used

.   the arrangements for access to it

.   that if they are charged or informed that they will be prosecuted, they will be given access to the recording of the interview either electronically or by being given a copy on removable recording media, but if they are not charged or informed that they will prosecuted, they will only be given access as agreed with the police or on the order of a court. See Note 7A.

(c)   the suspect must be asked to confirm that he or she has received a copy of the notice at paragraph 7.13(b) above. If the suspect fails to accept or to acknowledge receipt of the notice, the interviewer will state for the recording that a copy of the notice has been provided to the suspect and that he or she has refused to take a copy of the notice or has refused to acknowledge receipt.

(d)   the time shall be recorded and the interviewer shall notify the suspect that the recording is being saved to the secure network. The interviewer must save the recording in the presence of the suspect. The suspect should then be informed that the interview is terminated.

(f)   After the interview

7.14   The interviewer shall make a note in their pocket book that the interview has taken place, was audibly recorded, its time, duration and date and the original recording's identification number.

7.15   If no proceedings follow in respect of the person whose interview was recorded, the recordings must be kept securely as in paragraphs 7.16 and 7.17. See Note 5A

(g)   Security of secure digital network interview records

7.16   Interview record files are stored in read only format on non-removable storage devices, for example, hard disk drives, to ensure their integrity. The recordings are first saved locally to a secure non-removable device before being transferred to the remote network device. If for any reason the network connection fails, the recording remains on the local device and will be transferred when the network connections are restored.

7.17   Access to interview recordings, including copying to removable media, must be strictly controlled and monitored to ensure that access is restricted to those who have been given specific permission to access for specified purposes when this is necessary. For example, police officers and CPS lawyers involved in the preparation of any prosecution case, persons interviewed if they have been charged or informed they may be prosecuted and their legal representatives.

Note for Guidance

7A   The notice at paragraph 7.13 above should provide a brief explanation of the secure digital network and how access to the recording is strictly limited. The notice should also explain the access rights of the suspect, his or her legal representative, the police and the prosecutor to the recording of the interview. Space should be provided on the form to insert the date and the file reference number for the interview.

Codes of Practice – Code F Visual recording with sound of interviews with suspects

1   General

1.1   This code of practice must be readily available for consultation by police officers and other police staff, detained persons and members of the public.

1.2   The notes for guidance included are not provisions of this code. They form guidance to police officers and others about its application and interpretation.

1.3   Nothing in this code shall be taken as detracting in any way from the requirements of the Code of Practice for the Detention, Treatment and Questioning of Persons by Police Officers (Code C). [See Note 1A].

1.4   The interviews to which this Code applies are set out in paragraphs 3.1 - 3.3.

1.5   In this code, the term "appropriate adult", "solicitor" and "interview" have the same meaning as those set out in Code C. The corresponding provisions and Notes for Guidance in Code C applicable to those terms shall also apply where appropriate.

1.5A   The visual recording of interviews shall be carried out openly to instil confidence in its reliability as an impartial and accurate record of the interview.

1.6   Any reference in this code to visual recording shall be taken to mean visual recording with sound and in this code:

(aa)   'recording media' means any removable, physical audio recording medium (such as magnetic tape, optical disc or solid state memory) which can be played and copied.

(a)   'designated person' means a person other than a police officer, designated under the Police Reform Act 2002, Part 4 who has specified powers and duties of police officers conferred or imposed on them;

(b)   any reference to a police officer includes a designated person acting in the exercise or performance of the powers and duties conferred or imposed on them by their designation.

(c)   'secure digital network' is a computer network system which enables an original interview recording to be stored as a digital multi media file or a series of such files, on a secure file server which is accredited by the National Accreditor for Police Information Systems in the National Police Improvement Agency (NPIA) in accordance with the UK Government Protective Marking Scheme. (see section 7 of this Code).

1.7   References to "pocket book" in this Code include any official report book issued to police officers.

Note for Guidance

1A   As in paragraph 1.9 of Code C, references to custody officers include those carrying out the functions of a custody officer.

2   Recording and sealing of master recordings

2.1   Not used

2.2   The camera(s) shall be placed in the interview room so as to ensure coverage of as much of the room as is practicably possible whilst the interviews are taking place. [See Note 2A].

2.3   The certified recording medium will be of a high quality, new and previously unused.

When the certified recording medium is placed in the recorder and switched on to record, the correct date and time, in hours, minutes and seconds, will be superimposed automatically, second by second, during the whole recording. [See Note 2B]. See section 7 regarding the use of a secure digital network to record the interview.

2.4   One copy of the certified recording medium, referred to in this code as the master copy, will be sealed before it leaves the presence of the suspect. A second copy will be used as a working copy. [See Note 2C and 2D].

2.5   Nothing in this code requires the identity of an officer to be recorded or disclosed if:

(a)   the interview or record relates to a person detained under the Terrorism Act

2000 (see paragraph 3.2); or

(b)   otherwise where the officer reasonably believes that recording or disclosing their name might put them in danger.

2.6   In these cases, the officer will have their back to the camera and shall use their warrant or other identification number and the name of the police station to which they are attached. Such instances and the reasons for them shall be recorded in the custody record. [See Note 2E]

Notes for Guidance

2A   Interviewing officers will wish to arrange that, as far as possible, visual recording arrangements are unobtrusive. It must be clear to the suspect, however, that there is no opportunity to interfere with the recording equipment or the recording media.

2B   In this context, the certified recording media should be capable of having an image of the date and time superimposed upon them as they record the interview.

2C   The purpose of sealing the master copy before it leaves the presence of the suspect is to establish their confidence that the integrity of the copy is preserved.

2D   The recording of the interview may be used for identification procedures in accordance with paragraph 3.21 or Annex E of Code D.

2E   The purpose of the paragraph 2.5(b) is to protect police officers and others involved in the investigation of serious organised crime or the arrest of particularly violent suspects when there is reliable information that those arrested or their associates may threaten or cause harm to the officers, their families or their personal property.

3   Interviews to be visually recorded

3.1   Subject to paragraph 3.2 below, if an interviewing officer decides to make a visual recording these are the areas where it might be appropriate:

(a)   with a suspect in respect of an indictable offence (including an offence triable either way) [see Notes 3A and 3B];

(b)   which takes place as a result of an interviewer exceptionally putting further questions to a suspect about an offence described in sub-paragraph (a) above after they have been charged with, or informed they may be prosecuted for, that offence [see Note 3C];

(c)   in which an interviewer wishes to bring to the notice of a person, after that person has been charged with, or informed they may be prosecuted for an offence described in sub-paragraph (a) above, any written statement made by another person, or the content of an interview with another person [see Note 3D]

(d)   with, or in the presence of, a deaf or deaf/blind or speech impaired person who uses sign language to communicate;

(e)   with, or in the presence of anyone who requires an "appropriate adult"; or

(f)   in any case where the suspect or their representative requests that the interview be recorded visually.

3.2   The Terrorism Act 2000 makes separate provision for a code of practice for the video recording of interviews in a police station of those detained under Schedule 7 or section 41 of the Act. The provisions of this code do not therefore apply to such interviews [see Note 3E].

3.3   The custody officer may authorise the interviewing officer not to record the interview visually:

(a)   where it is not reasonably practicable to do so because of failure of the equipment, or the non-availability of a suitable interview room, or recorder, and the authorising officer considers on reasonable grounds that the interview should not be delayed until the failure has been rectified or a suitable room or recorder becomes available. In such cases the custody officer may authorise the interviewing officer to audio record the interview in accordance with the guidance set out in Code E;

(b)   where it is clear from the outset that no prosecution will ensue; or

(c)   where it is not practicable to do so because at the time the person resists being taken to a suitable interview room or other location which would enable the interview to be recorded, or otherwise fails or refuses to go into such a room or location, and the authorising officer considers on reasonable grounds that the interview should not be delayed until these conditions cease to apply.

In all cases the custody officer shall make a note in the custody records of the reasons for not taking a visual record. [See Note 3F].

3.4   When a person who is voluntarily attending the police station is required to be cautioned in accordance with Code C prior to being interviewed, the subsequent interview shall be recorded, unless the custody officer gives authority in accordance with the provisions of paragraph 3.3 above for the interview not to be so recorded.

3.5   The whole of each interview shall be recorded visually, including the taking and reading back of any statement.

3.6   A sign or indicator which is visible to the suspect must show when the visual recording equipment is recording.

Notes for Guidance

3A   Nothing in the code is intended to preclude visual recording at police discretion of interviews at police stations with people cautioned in respect of offences not covered by paragraph 3.1, or responses made by interviewees after they have been charged with, or informed they may be prosecuted for, an offence, provided that this code is complied with.

3B   Attention is drawn to the provisions set out in Code C about the matters to be considered when deciding whether a detained person is fit to be interviewed.

3C   Code C sets out the circumstances in which a suspect may be questioned about an offence after being charged with it.

3D   Code C sets out the procedures to be followed when a person's attention is drawn after charge, to a statement made by another person. One method of bringing the content of an interview with another person to the notice of a suspect may be to play him a recording of that interview.

3E   If, during the course of an interview under this Code, it becomes apparent that the interview should be conducted under one of the terrorism codes for video recording of interviews the interview should only continue in accordance with the relevant code.

3F   A decision not to record an interview visually for any reason may be the subject of comment in court. The authorising officer should therefore be prepared to justify their decision in each case.

4   The Interview

(a)   General

4.1   The provisions of Code C in relation to cautions and interviews and the Notes for Guidance applicable to those provisions shall apply to the conduct of interviews to which this Code applies.

4.2   Particular attention is drawn to those parts of Code C that describe the restrictions on drawing adverse inferences from a suspect's failure or refusal to say anything about their involvement in the offence when interviewed, or after being charged or informed they may be prosecuted and how those restrictions affect the terms of the caution and determine whether a special warning under Sections 36 and 37 of the Criminal Justice and Public Order Act 1994 can be given.

(b)   Commencement of interviews

4.3   When the suspect is brought into the interview room the interviewer shall without delay, but in sight of the suspect, load the recording equipment and set it to record. The recording media must be unwrapped or otherwise opened in the presence of the suspect. [See Note 4A]

4.4   The interviewer shall then tell the suspect formally about the visual recording and point out the sign or indicator which shows that the recording equipment is activated and recording. See paragraph 3.6. The interviewer shall:

(a)   explain the interview is being visually recorded;

(b)   subject to paragraph 2.5, give his or her name and rank, and that of any other interviewer present;

(c)   ask the suspect and any other party present (e.g. his solicitor) to identify themselves. (d) state the date, time of commencement and place of the interview; and

(e)   state that the suspect will be given a notice about what will happen to the recording.

4.5   The interviewer shall then caution the suspect, which should follow that set out in Code C, and remind the suspect of their entitlement to free and independent legal advice and that they can speak to a solicitor on the telephone.

4.6   The interviewer shall then put to the suspect any significant statement or silence (i.e. failure or refusal to answer a question or to answer it satisfactorily) which occurred before the start of the interview, and shall ask the suspect whether they wish to confirm or deny that earlier statement or silence or whether they wish to add anything. The definition of a "significant" statement or silence is the same as that set out in Code C.

(c)   Interviews with the deaf

4.7   If the suspect is deaf or there is doubt about their hearing ability, the provisions of Code C on interpreters for the deaf or for interviews with suspects who have difficulty in understanding English continue to apply.

(d)   Objections and complaints by the suspect

4.8   If the suspect raises objections to the interview being visually recorded either at the outset or during the interview or during a break in the interview, the interviewer shall explain the fact that the interview is being visually recorded and that the provisions of this code require that the suspect's objections shall be recorded on the visual recording.   When any objections have been visually recorded or the suspect has refused to have their objections recorded, the interviewer shall say that they are turning off the recording equipment, give their reasons and turn it off. If a separate audio recording is being maintained, the officer shall ask the person to record the reasons for refusing to agree to visual recording of the interview. Paragraph 4.8 of Code E will apply if the person objects to audio recording of the interview. The officer shall then make a written record of the interview. If the interviewer reasonably considers they may proceed to question the suspect with the visual recording still on, the interviewer may do so. See Note 4G.

4.9   If in the course of an interview a complaint is made by the person being questioned, or on their behalf, concerning the provisions of this code or of Code C, then the interviewer shall act in accordance with Code C, record it in the interview record and inform the custody officer. [See Notes 4B and 4C].

4.10   If the suspect indicates that they wish to tell the interviewer about matters not directly connected with the offence of which they are suspected and that they are unwilling for these matters to be recorded, the suspect shall be given the opportunity to tell the interviewer about these matters after the conclusion of the formal interview.

(e) Changing the recording media

4.11   In instances where the recording medium is not of sufficient length to record all of the interview with the suspect, further certified recording medium will be used. When the recording equipment indicates that the recording medium has only a short time left to run, the interviewer shall advise the suspect and round off that part of the interview. If the interviewer wishes to continue the interview but does not already have further certified recording media with him, they shall obtain a set. The suspect should not be left unattended in the interview room. The interviewer will remove the recording media from the recording equipment and insert the new ones which have been unwrapped or otherwise opened in the suspect's presence. The recording equipment shall then be set to record. Care must be taken, particularly when a number of sets of recording media have been used, to ensure that there is no confusion between them. This could be achieved by marking the sets of recording media with consecutive identification numbers.

(f)   Taking a break during the interview

4.12   When a break is to be taken during the course of an interview and the interview room is to be vacated by the suspect, the fact that a break is to be taken, the reason for it and the time shall be recorded. The recording equipment must be turned off and the recording media removed. The procedures for the conclusion of an interview set out in paragraph 4.19, below, should be followed.

4.13   When a break is to be a short one, and both the suspect and a police officer are to remain in the interview room, the fact that a break is to be taken, the reasons for it and the time shall be recorded on the recording media. The recording equipment may be turned off, but there is no need to remove the recording media. When the interview is recommenced the recording shall continue on the same recording media and the time at which the interview recommences shall be recorded.

4.14   When there is a break in questioning under caution, the interviewing officer must ensure that the person being questioned is aware that they remain under caution. If there is any doubt, the caution must be given again in full when the interview resumes. [See Note 4D and 4E].

(g)   Failure of recording equipment

4.15   If there is a failure of equipment which can be rectified quickly, the appropriate procedures set out in paragraph 4.12 shall be followed. When the recording is resumed the interviewer shall explain what has happened and record the time the interview recommences. If, however, it is not possible to continue recording on that particular recorder and no alternative equipment is readily available, the interview may continue without being recorded visually. In such circumstances, the procedures set out in paragraph 3.3 of this code for seeking the authority of the custody officer will be followed. [See Note 4F].

(h)   Removing used recording media from recording equipment

4.16   Where used recording media are removed from the recording equipment during the course of an interview, they shall be retained and the procedures set out in paragraph 4.18 below followed.

(i)   Conclusion of interview

4.17   Before the conclusion of the interview, the suspect shall be offered the opportunity to clarify anything he or she has said and asked if there is anything that they wish to add.

4.18   At the conclusion of the interview, including the taking and reading back of any written statement, the time shall be recorded and the recording equipment switched off. The master recording shall be removed from the recording equipment, sealed with a master recording label and treated as an exhibit in accordance with the force standing orders. The interviewer shall sign the label and also ask the suspect and any third party present during the interview to sign it. If the suspect or third party refuses to sign the label, an officer of at least the rank of inspector, or if one is not available, the custody officer, shall be called into the interview room and asked, subject to paragraph 2.5, to sign it.

4.19   The suspect shall be handed a notice which explains the use which will be made of the recording and the arrangements for access to it. The notice will also advise the suspect that a copy of the tape shall be supplied as soon as practicable if the person is charged or informed that he will be prosecuted.

Notes for Guidance

4A   The interviewer should attempt to estimate the likely length of the interview and ensure that an appropriate quantity of certified recording media and labels with which to seal the master copies are available in the interview room.

4B   Where the custody officer is called immediately to deal with the complaint, wherever possible the recording equipment should be left to run until the custody officer has entered the interview room and spoken to the person being interviewed. Continuation or termination of the interview should be at the discretion of the interviewing officer pending action by an inspector as set out in Code C.

4C   Where the complaint is about a matter not connected with this code of practice or Code C, the decision to continue with the interview is at the discretion of the interviewing officer. Where the interviewing officer decides to continue with the interview, the person being interviewed shall be told that the complaint will be brought to the attention of the custody officer at the conclusion of the interview. When the interview is concluded, the interviewing officer must, as soon as practicable, inform the custody officer of the existence and nature of the complaint made.

4D   In considering whether to caution again after a break, the officer should bear in mind that he may have to satisfy a court that the person understood that he was still under caution when the interview resumed.

4E   The officer should bear in mind that it may be necessary to satisfy the court that nothing occurred during a break in an interview or between interviews which influenced the suspect's recorded evidence. On the re-commencement of an interview, the officer should consider summarising on the record the reason for the break and confirming this with the suspect.

4F   If any part of the recording media breaks or is otherwise damaged during the interview, it should be sealed as a master copy in the presence of the suspect and the interview resumed where it left off. The undamaged part should be copied and the original sealed as a master tape in the suspect's presence, if necessary after the interview. If equipment for copying is not readily available, both parts should be sealed in the suspect's presence and the interview begun again.

4G   The interviewer should be aware that a decision to continue recording against the wishes of the suspect may be the subject of comment in court.

5   After the Interview

5.1   The interviewer shall make a note in his or her pocket book of the fact that the interview has taken place and has been recorded, its time, duration and date and the identification number of the master copy of the recording media.

5.2   Where no proceedings follow in respect of the person whose interview was recorded, the recording media must nevertheless be kept securely in accordance with paragraph 6.1 and Note 6A.

Note for Guidance

5A   Any written record of a recorded interview shall be made in accordance with national guidelines approved by the Secretary of State, and with regard to the advice contained in the Manual of Guidance for the preparation, processing and submission of files.

6   Master Copy Security

(a)   General

6.1   The officer in charge of the police station at which interviews with suspects are recorded shall make arrangements for the master copies to be kept securely and their movements accounted for on the same basis as other material which may be used for evidential purposes, in accordance with force standing orders [See Note 6A].

(b)   Breaking master copy seal for criminal proceedings

6.2   A police officer has no authority to break the seal on a master copy which is required for criminal trial or appeal proceedings. If it is necessary to gain access to the master copy, the police officer shall arrange for its seal to be broken in the presence of a representative of the Crown Prosecution Service. The defendant or their legal adviser shall be informed and given a reasonable opportunity to be present. If the defendant or their legal representative is present they shall be invited to reseal and sign the master copy. If either refuses or neither is present, this shall be done by the representative of the Crown Prosecution Service. [See Notes 6B and 6C].

(c)   Breaking master copy seal: other cases

6.3   The chief officer of police is responsible for establishing arrangements for breaking the seal of the master copy where no criminal proceedings result, or the criminal proceedings, to which the interview relates, have been concluded and it becomes necessary to break the seal. These arrangements should be those which the chief officer considers are reasonably necessary to demonstrate to the person interviewed and any other party who may wish to use or refer to the interview record that the master   copy has not been tampered with and that the interview record remains accurate. [See Note 6D]

6.4   Subject to paragraph 6.6, a representative of each party must be given a reasonable opportunity to be present when the seal is broken, the master copy copied and re- sealed.

6.5   If one or more of the parties is not present when the master copy seal is broken because they cannot be contacted or refuse to attend or paragraph 6.6 applies, arrangements should be made for an independent person such as a custody visitor, to be present. Alternatively, or as an additional safeguard, arrangement should be made for a film or photographs to be taken of the procedure.

6.6   Paragraph 6.5 does not require a person to be given an opportunity to be present when;

(a)   it is necessary to break the master copy seal for the proper and effective further investigation of the original offence or the investigation of some other offence; and

(b) the officer in charge of the investigation has reasonable grounds to suspect that allowing an opportunity might prejudice any such an investigation or criminal proceedings which may be brought as a result or endanger any person. [See Note 6E]

(d) Documentation

6.7 When the master copy seal is broken, copied and re-sealed, a record must be made of the procedure followed, including the date time and place and persons present.

Notes for Guidance

6A This section is concerned with the security of the master copy which will have been sealed at the conclusion of the interview. Care should, however, be taken of working copies since their loss or destruction may lead unnecessarily to the need to have access to master copies.

6B If the master copy has been delivered to the Crown Court for their keeping after committal for trial the Crown Prosecutor will apply to the Chief Clerk of the Crown Court Centre for its release for unsealing by the Crown Prosecutor.

6C Reference to the Crown Prosecution Service or to the Crown Prosecutor in this part of the code shall be taken to include any other body or person with a statutory responsibility for prosecution for whom the police conduct any recorded interviews.

6D The most common reasons for needing access to master copies that are not required for criminal proceedings arise from civil actions and complaints against police and civil actions between individuals arising out of allegations of crime investigated by police.

6E Paragraph 6.6 could apply, for example, when one or more of the outcomes or likely outcomes of the investigation might be; (i) the prosecution of one or more of the original suspects, (ii) the prosecution of someone previously not suspected, including someone who was originally a witness; and (iii) any original suspect being treated as a prosecution witness and when premature disclosure of any police action, particularly through contact with any parties involved, could lead to a real risk of compromising the investigation and endangering witnesses.

7 Visual Recording of Interviews by Secure Digital Network

7.1 This section applies if an officer wishes to make a visual recording with sound of an interview mentioned in section 3 of this Code using a secure digital network which does not use removable media (see paragraph 1.6(c) above).

7.3 The provisions of sections 1 to 6 of this Code which relate or apply only to removable media will not apply to a secure digital network recording.

7.4 The statutory requirement and provisions for the audio recording of interviews using a secure digital network set out in section 7 of Code E should be applied to the visual recording with sound of interviews mentioned in section 3 of this code as if references to audio recordings of interviews include visual recordings with sound.

Codes of Practice – Code G Statutory power of arrest by police officers

1.   Introduction

1.1   This Code of Practice deals with statutory power of police to arrest persons suspected of involvement in a criminal offence.

1.2   The right to liberty is a key principle of the Human Rights Act 1998. The exercise of the power of arrest represents an obvious and significant interference with that right.

1.3   The use of the power must be fully justified and officers exercising the power should consider if the necessary objectives can be met by other, less intrusive means. Arrest must never be used simply because it can be used. Absence of justification for exercising the powers of arrest may lead to challenges should the case proceed to court. When the power of arrest is exercised it is essential that it is exercised in a non- discriminatory and proportionate manner.

1.4   Section 24 of the Police and Criminal Evidence Act 1984 (as substituted by section

110 of the Serious Organised Crime and Police Act 2005) provides the statutory power of arrest. If the provisions of the Act and this Code are not observed, both the arrest and the conduct of any subsequent investigation may be open to question.

1.5   This code of practice must be readily available at all police stations for consultation by police officers and police staff, detained persons and members of the public.

1.6   The notes for guidance are not provisions of this code.

2   Elements of Arrest under section 24 PACE

2.1   A lawful arrest requires two elements:

A person's involvement or suspected involvement or attempted involvement in the commission of a criminal offence;

AND

Reasonable grounds for believing that the person's arrest is necessary.

2.2   Arresting officers are required to inform the person arrested that they have been arrested, even if this fact is obvious, and of the relevant circumstances of the arrest in relation to both elements and to inform the custody officer of these on arrival at the police station. See Code C paragraph 3.4.

Involvement in the commission of an offence'

2.3   A constable may arrest without warrant in relation to any offence, except for the single exception listed in Note for Guidance 1. A constable may arrest anyone:

•   who is about to commit an offence or is in the act of committing an offence

- whom the officer has reasonable grounds for suspecting is about to commit an offence or to be committing an offence

- whom the officer has reasonable grounds to suspect of being guilty of an offence which he or she has reasonable grounds for suspecting has been committed

- anyone who is guilty of an offence which has been committed or anyone whom the officer has reasonable grounds for suspecting to be guilty of that offence.

Necessity criteria

2.4   The power of arrest is only exercisable if the constable has reasonable grounds for believing that it is necessary to arrest the person. The criteria for what may constitute necessity are set out in paragraph 2.9. It remains an operational decision at the discretion of the arresting officer as to:

- what action he or she may take at the point of contact with the individual;

- the necessity criterion or criteria (if any) which applies to the individual; and

- whether to arrest, report for summons, grant street bail, issue a fixed penalty notice or take any other action that is open to the officer.

2.5   In applying the criteria, the arresting officer has to be satisfied that at least one of the reasons supporting the need for arrest is satisfied.

2.6   Extending the power of arrest to all offences provides a constable with the ability to use that power to deal with any situation.   However applying the necessity criteria requires the constable to examine and justify the reason or reasons why a person needs to be taken to a police station for the custody officer to decide whether the person should be placed in police detention.

2.7   The criteria below are set out in section 24 of PACE as substituted by section 110 of the Serious Organised Crime and Police Act   2005.   The criteria are exhaustive. However, the circumstances that may satisfy those criteria remain a matter for the operational discretion of individual officers. Some examples are given below of what those circumstances may be.

2.8   In considering the individual circumstances, the constable must take into account the situation of the victim, the nature of the offence, the circumstances of the suspect and the needs of the investigative process.

2.9   The criteria are that the arrest is necessary:

(a)   to enable the name of the person in question to be ascertained (in the case where the constable does not know, and cannot readily ascertain, the person's name, or has reasonable grounds for doubting whether a name given by the person as his name is his real name)

(b)   correspondingly as regards the person's address

an address is a satisfactory address for service of summons if the person will be at it for a sufficiently long period for it to be possible to serve him or her with a summons; or, that some other person at that address specified by the person will accept service of the summons on their behalf.

(c)   to prevent the person in question –

(i)   causing physical injury to himself or any other person; (ii)   suffering physical injury ;

(iii)   causing loss or damage to property;

(iv)   committing an offence against public decency (only applies where members of the public going about their normal business cannot reasonably be expected to avoid the person in question); or

(v)   causing an unlawful obstruction of the highway;

(d)   to protect a child or other vulnerable person from the person in question

(e)   to allow the prompt and effective investigation of the offence or of the conduct of the person in question.

This may include cases such as:

(i)   Where there are reasonable grounds to believe that the person:

- has made false statements;

- has made statements which cannot be readily verified;

- has presented false evidence;

- may steal or destroy evidence;

- may make contact with co-suspects or conspirators;

- may intimidate or threaten or make contact with witnesses;

- where it is necessary to obtain evidence by questioning; or

(ii)   when considering arrest in connection with an indictable offence, there is a need to:

- enter and search any premises occupied or controlled by a person

- search the person

- prevent contact with others

- take fingerprints, footwear impressions, samples or photographs of the suspect

(iii)   ensuring compliance with statutory drug testing requirements.

(f)   to prevent any prosecution for the offence from being hindered by the disappearance of the person in question.

This may arise if there are reasonable grounds for believing that

• if the person is not arrested he or she will fail to attend court

• street bail after arrest would be insufficient to deter the suspect from trying to evade prosecution

3   Information to be given on Arrest

(a)   Cautions - when a caution must be given (taken from Code C section 10)

3.1   A person whom there are grounds to suspect of an offence (see Note 2) must be cautioned before any questions about an offence, or further questions if the answers provide the grounds for suspicion, are put to them if either the suspect's answers or silence, (i.e. failure or refusal to answer or answer satisfactorily) may be given in evidence to a court in a prosecution. A person need not be cautioned if questions are for other necessary purposes e.g.:

(a)   solely to establish their identity or ownership of any vehicle;

(b)   to obtain information in accordance with any relevant statutory requirement;

(c)   in furtherance of the proper and effective conduct of a search, e.g. to determine the need to search in the exercise of powers of stop and search or to seek co- operation while carrying out a search;

(d)   to seek verification of a written record as in Code C paragraph 11.13;

(e)   when examining a person in accordance with the Terrorism Act 2000, Schedule

7 and the Code of Practice for Examining Officers issued under that Act, Schedule 14, paragraph 6.

3.2   Whenever a person not under arrest is initially cautioned, or reminded they are under caution, that person must at the same time be told they are not under arrest and are free to leave if they want to.

3.3   A person who is arrested, or further arrested, must be informed at the time, or as soon as practicable thereafter, that they are under arrest and the grounds for their arrest, see Note 3.

3.4   A person who is arrested, or further arrested, must also be cautioned unless:

(a)   it is impracticable to do so by reason of their condition or behaviour at the time; (b) they have already been cautioned immediately prior to arrest as in paragraph 3.1.

(c)   Terms of the caution (Taken from Code C section 10)

3.5   The caution, which must be given on arrest, should be in the following terms:

"You do not have to say anything. But it may harm your defence if you do not mention when questioned something which you later rely on in Court. Anything you do say may be given in evidence." See Note 5

3.6   Minor deviations from the words of any caution given in accordance with this Code do not constitute a breach of this Code, provided the sense of the relevant caution is preserved. See Note 6

3.7   When, despite being cautioned, a person fails to co-operate or to answer particular questions which may affect their immediate treatment, the person should be informed of any relevant consequences and that those consequences are not affected by the caution. Examples are when a person's refusal to provide:

•   their name and address when charged may make them liable to detention;

•   particulars and information in accordance with a statutory requirement, e.g. under the Road Traffic Act 1988, may amount to an offence or may make the person liable to a further arrest.

4   Records of Arrest

(a) General

4.1   The arresting officer is required to record in his pocket book or by other methods used for recording information:

•   the nature and circumstances of the offence leading to the arrest

•   the reason or reasons why arrest was necessary

•   the giving of the caution

•   anything said by the person at the time of arrest

4.2   Such a record should be made at the time of the arrest unless impracticable to do. If not made at that time, the record should then be completed as soon as possible thereafter.

4.3   On arrival at the police station, the custody officer shall open the custody record (see paragraph 1.1A and section 2 of Code C). The information given by the arresting officer on the circumstances and reason or reasons for arrest shall be recorded as part of the custody record. Alternatively, a copy of the record made by the officer in accordance with paragraph 4.1 above shall be attached as part of the custody record. See paragraph 2.2 and Code C paragraphs 3.4 and 10.3.

4.4   The custody record will serve as a record of the arrest. Copies of the custody record will be provided in accordance with paragraphs 2.4 and 2.4A of Code C and access for inspection of the original record in accordance with paragraph 2.5 of Code C.

(b) Interviews and arrests

4.5   Records of interview, significant statements or silences will be treated in the same way as set out in sections 10 and 11 of Code C and in Code E (tape recording of interviews).

Notes for guidance

1   The powers of arrest for offences under sections 4(1) and 5(1) of the Criminal Law Act 1967 require that the offences to which they relate must carry a sentence fixed by law or one in which a first time offender aged 18 or over could be sentenced to 5 years or more imprisonment

2   There must be some reasonable, objective grounds for the suspicion, based on known facts or information which are relevant to the likelihood the offence has been committed and the person to be questioned committed it.

3   An arrested person must be given sufficient information to enable them to understand they have been deprived of their liberty and the reason they have been arrested, e.g. when a person is arrested on suspicion of committing an offence they must be informed of the suspected offence's nature, when and where it was committed. The suspect must also be informed of the reason or reasons why arrest is considered necessary. Vague or technical language should be avoided.

4   Nothing in this Code requires a caution to be given or repeated when informing a person not under arrest they may be prosecuted for an offence. However, a court will not be able to draw any inferences under the Criminal Justice and Public Order Act 1994, section 34, if the person was not cautioned.

5   If it appears a person does not understand the caution, the people giving it should explain it in their own words.

6   The powers available to an officer as the result of an arrest – for example, entry and search of premises, holding a person incommunicado, setting up road blocks – are only available in respect of indictable offences and are subject to the specific requirements on authorisation as set out in the 1984 Act and relevant PACE Code of Practice.

Codes of Practice - Code H in connection with the detention, treatment and questioning by police officers and of persons under section 41 of, and Schedule 8 to, the Terrorism Act 2000

1   General

1.1   This Code of Practice applies to, and only to, persons arrested under section 41 of the Terrorism Act 2000 (TACT) and detained in police custody under those provisions and Schedule 8 of the Act. References to detention under this provision that were previously included in PACE Code C – Code for the Detention, Treatment, and Questioning of Persons by Police Officers, no longer apply.

1.2   The Code ceases to apply at any point that a detainee is: (a) charged with an offence

(b)   released without charge, or

(c)   transferred to a prison see section 14.5

1.3   References to an offence in this Code include being concerned in the commission, preparation or instigation of acts of terrorism.

1.4   This Code's provisions do not apply to detention of individuals under any other terrorism legislation. This Code does not apply to people:

(i)   detained under section 5(1) of the Prevention of Terrorism Act 2005.

(ii)   detained for examination under TACT Schedule 7 and to whom the Code of

Practice issued under that Act, Schedule 14, paragraph 6 applies;

(iii)   detained for searches under stop and search powers.

The provisions for the detention, treatment and questioning by police officers of persons other than those in police detention following arrest under section 41 of TACT, are set out in Code C issued under section 66(1) of the Police & Criminal Evidence Act (PACE)1984 (PACE Code C).

1.5   All persons in custody must be dealt with expeditiously, and released as soon as the need for detention no longer applies.

1.6   There is no provision for bail under TACT prior to charge.

1.7   An officer must perform the assigned duties in this Code as soon as practicable. An officer will not be in breach of this Code if delay is justifiable and reasonable steps are taken to prevent unnecessary delay. The custody record shall show when a delay has occurred and the reason. See Note 1H

1.8   This Code of Practice must be readily available at all police stations for consultation by:

•   police officers

- police staff

- detained persons

- members of the public.

1.9   The provisions of this Code:

- include the Annexes

- do not include the Notes for Guidance.

1.10   If an officer has any suspicion, or is told in good faith, that a person of any age may be mentally disordered or otherwise mentally vulnerable, in the absence of clear evidence to dispel that suspicion, the person shall be treated as such for the purposes of this Code. See Note 1G

1.11   For the purposes of this Code, a juvenile is any person under the age of 17. If anyone appears to be under 17, and there is no clear evidence that they are 17 or over, they shall be treated as a juvenile for the purposes of this Code.

1.12   If a person appears to be blind, seriously visually impaired, deaf, unable to read or speak or has difficulty orally because of a speech impediment, they shall be treated as such for the purposes of this Code in the absence of clear evidence to the contrary.

1.13   'The appropriate adult' means, in the case of a:

(a)   juvenile:

(i)   the parent, guardian or, if the juvenile is in local authority or voluntary organisation care, or is otherwise being looked after under the Children Act 1989, a person representing that authority or organisation;

(ii)   a social worker of a local authority social services department;

(iii)   failing these, some other responsible adult aged 18 or over who is not a police officer or employed by the police.

(b)   person who is mentally disordered or mentally vulnerable: See Note 1D

(i)   a relative, guardian or other person responsible for their care or custody; (ii) someone experienced in dealing with mentally disordered or mentally vulnerable people but who is not a police officer or employed by the police;

(iii)   failing these, some other responsible adult aged 18 or over who is not a police officer or employed by the police.

1.14   If this Code requires a person be given certain information, they do not have to be given it if at the time they are incapable of understanding what is said, are violent or may become violent or in urgent need of medical attention, but they must be given it as soon as practicable.

1.15   References to a custody officer include any:-

- police officer; or

• designated staff custody officer acting in the exercise or performance of the powers and duties conferred or imposed on them by their designation, performing the functions of a custody officer. See Note 1J.

1.16 When this Code requires the prior authority or agreement of an officer of at least inspector or superintendent rank, that authority may be given by a sergeant or chief inspector authorised by section 107 of PACE to perform the functions of the higher rank under TACT.

1.17 In this Code:

(a) 'designated person' means a person other than a police officer, designated under the Police Reform Act 2002, Part 4 who has specified powers and duties of police officers conferred or imposed on them;

(b) reference to a police officer includes a designated person acting in the exercise or performance of the powers and duties conferred or imposed on them by their designation.

1.18 Designated persons are entitled to use reasonable force as follows:-

(a) when exercising a power conferred on them which allows a police officer exercising that power to use reasonable force, a designated person has the same entitlement to use force; and

(b) at other times when carrying out duties conferred or imposed on them that also entitle them to use reasonable force, for example:

• when at a police station carrying out the duty to keep detainees for whom they are responsible under control and to assist any other police officer or designated person to keep any detainee under control and to prevent their escape.

• when securing, or assisting any other police officer or designated person

in securing, the detention of a person at a police station.

• when escorting, or assisting any other police officer or designated person in

escorting, a detainee within a police station.

• for the purpose of saving life or limb; or

• preventing serious damage to property.

1.19 Nothing in this Code prevents the custody officer, or other officer given custody of the detainee, from allowing police staff who are not designated persons to carry out individual procedures or tasks at the police station if the law allows. However, the officer remains responsible for making sure the procedures and tasks are carried out correctly in accordance with the Codes of Practice. Any such person must be:

(a) a person employed by a police authority maintaining a police force and under the control and direction of the Chief Officer of that force;

(b) employed by a person with whom a police authority has a contract for the provision of services relating to persons arrested or otherwise in custody.

1.20   Designated persons and other police staff must have regard to any relevant provisions of this Code.

1.21   References to pocket books include any official report book issued to police officers or other police staff.

Notes for guidance

1A   Although certain sections of this Code apply specifically to people in custody at police stations, those there voluntarily to assist with an investigation should be treated with no less consideration, e.g. offered refreshments at appropriate times, and enjoy an absolute right to obtain legal advice or communicate with anyone outside the police station.

1B   A person, including a parent or guardian, should not be an appropriate adult if they:

•   are

–   suspected of involvement in the offence or involvement in the commission, preparation or instigation of acts of terrorism

–   the victim

–   a witness

–   involved in the investigation

•   received admissions prior to attending to act as the appropriate adult.

Note: If a juvenile's parent is estranged from the juvenile, they should not be asked to act as the appropriate adult if the juvenile expressly and specifically objects to their presence.

1C   If a juvenile admits an offence to, or in the presence of, a social worker or member of a youth offending team other than during the time that person is acting as the juvenile's appropriate adult, another appropriate adult should be appointed in the interest of fairness.

1D   In the case of people who are mentally disordered or otherwise mentally vulnerable, it may be more satisfactory if the appropriate adult is someone experienced or trained in their care rather than a relative lacking such qualifications. But if the detainee prefers a relative to a better qualified stranger or objects to a particular person their wishes should, if practicable, be respected.

1E   A detainee should always be given an opportunity, when an appropriate adult is called to the police station, to consult privately with a solicitor in the appropriate adult's absence if they want. An appropriate adult is not subject to legal privilege.

1F   A solicitor or independent custody visitor (formerly a lay visitor) present at the police station in that capacity may not be the appropriate adult.

1G   'Mentally vulnerable' applies to any detainee who, because of their mental state or capacity, may not understand the significance of what is said, of questions or of their replies. 'Mental disorder' is defined in the Mental Health Act 1983, section 1(2) as

'mental illness, arrested or incomplete development of mind, psychopathic disorder and any other disorder or disability of mind'. When the custody officer has any doubt about the mental state or capacity of a detainee, that detainee should be treated as mentally vulnerable and an appropriate adult called.

1H   Paragraph 1.7 is intended to cover delays which may occur in processing detainees e.g if:

•   a large number of suspects are brought into the station simultaneously to be placed in custody;

•   interview rooms are all being used;

•   there are difficulties contacting an appropriate adult, solicitor or interpreter.

1I   The custody officer must remind the appropriate adult and detainee about the right to legal advice and record any reasons for waiving it in accordance with section 6.

1J   The designation of police staff custody officers applies only in police areas where an order commencing the provisions of the Police Reform Act 2002, section 38 and Schedule 4A, for designating police staff custody officers is in effect.

1K   This Code does not affect the principle that all citizens have a duty to help police officers to prevent crime and discover offenders. This is a civic rather than a legal duty; but when a police officer is trying to discover whether, or by whom, an offence has been committed he is entitled to question any person from whom he thinks useful information can be obtained, subject to the restrictions imposed by this Code. A person's declaration that he is unwilling to reply does not alter this entitlement.

1L   If a person is moved from a police station to receive medical treatment, or for any other reason, the period of detention is still calculated from the time of arrest under section 41 of TACT (or, if a person was being detained under TACT Schedule 7 when arrested, from the time at which the examination under Schedule 7 began).

1M   Under Paragraph 1 of Schedule 8 to TACT, all police stations are designated for detention of persons arrested under section 41 of TACT. Paragraph 4 of Schedule 8 requires that the constable who arrests a person under section 41 takes him as soon as practicable to the police station which he considers is "most appropriate".

2   Custody records

2.1   When a person is brought to a police station:

•   under TACT section 41 arrest, or

•   is arrested under TACT section 41 at the police station having attended there voluntarily,

they should be brought before the custody officer as soon as practicable after their arrival at the station or, if appropriate, following arrest after attending the police station voluntarily see Note 3H. A person is deemed to be "at a police station" for these purposes if they are within the boundary of any building or enclosed yard which forms part of that police station.

2.2   A separate custody record must be opened as soon as practicable for each person brought to a police station under arrest or arrested at the station having gone there voluntarily. All information recorded under this Code must be recorded as soon as practicable in the custody record unless otherwise specified. Any audio or video recording made in the custody area is not part of the custody record.

2.3   If any action requires the authority of an officer of a specified rank, this must be noted in the custody record, subject to paragraph 2.8.

2.4   The custody officer is responsible for the custody record's accuracy and completeness and for making sure the record or copy of the record accompanies a detainee if they are transferred to another police station. The record shall show the:

*   time and reason for transfer;

*   time a person is released from detention.

2.5   A solicitor or appropriate adult must be permitted to consult a detainee's custody record as soon as practicable after their arrival at the station and at any other time whilst the person is detained. Arrangements for this access must be agreed with the custody officer and may not unreasonably interfere with the custody officer's duties or the justifiable needs of the investigation.

2.6   When a detainee leaves police detention or is taken before a court they, their legal representative or appropriate adult shall be given, on request, a copy of the custody record as soon as practicable. This entitlement lasts for 12 months after release.

2.7   The detainee, appropriate adult or legal representative shall be permitted to inspect the original custody record once the detained person is no longer held under the provisions of TACT section 41 and Schedule 8, provided they give reasonable notice of their request. Any such inspection shall be noted in the custody record.

2.8   All entries in custody records must be timed and identified by the maker. Nothing in this Code requires the identity of officers or other police staff to be recorded or disclosed in the case of enquiries linked to the investigation of terrorism. In these cases, they shall use their warrant or other identification numbers and the name of their police station see Note 2A. If records are entered on computer these shall also be timed and contain the operator's identification.

2.9   The fact and time of any detainee's refusal to sign a custody record, when asked in accordance with this Code, must be recorded.

Note for guidance

2A   The purpose of paragraph 2.8 is to protect those involved in terrorist investigations or arrests of terrorist suspects from the possibility that those arrested, their associates or other individuals or groups may threaten or cause harm to those involved.

3   Initial action

(a)   Detained persons – normal procedure

3.1   When a person is brought to a police station under arrest or arrested at the station having gone there voluntarily, the custody officer must make sure the person is told clearly about the following continuing rights which may be exercised at any stage during the period in custody:

(i)   the right to have someone informed of their arrest as in section 5;

(ii)   the right to consult privately with a solicitor and that free independent legal advice is available;

(iii)   the right to consult this Code of Practice. See Note 3D

3.2   The detainee must also be given:

•   a written notice setting out:

–   the above three rights;

–   the arrangements for obtaining legal advice;

–   the right to a copy of the custody record as in paragraph 2.6;

–   the caution in the terms prescribed in section 10.

•   an additional written notice briefly setting out their entitlements while in custody, see Notes 3A and 3B.

Note: The detainee shall be asked to sign the custody record to acknowledge receipt of these notices. Any refusal must be recorded on the custody record.

3.3   A citizen of an independent Commonwealth country or a national of a foreign country, including the Republic of Ireland, must be informed as soon as practicable about their rights of communication with their High Commission, Embassy or Consulate. See section 7

3.4   The custody officer shall:

•   record that the person was arrested under section 41 of TACT and the reason(s)

for the arrest on the custody record. See paragraph 10.2 and Note for Guidance 3G.

•   note on the custody record any comment the detainee makes in relation to the arresting officer's account but shall not invite comment. If the arresting officer is not physically present when the detainee is brought to a police station, the arresting officer's account must be made available to the custody officer remotely or by a third party on the arresting officer's behalf;

•   note any comment the detainee makes in respect of the decision to detain them but shall not invite comment;

•   not put specific questions to the detainee regarding their involvement in any offence, nor in respect of any comments they may make in response to the arresting officer's account or the decision to place them in detention See paragraphs 14.1 and 14.2 and Notes for Guidance 3H, 14A and 14B. Such an exchange is likely to constitute an interview as in paragraph 11.1 and require the associated safeguards in section 11.

See paragraph 5.9 of the Code of Practice issued under TACT Schedule 8 Paragraph 3 in respect of unsolicited comments.

If the first review of detention is carried out at this time, see paragraphs 14.1 and 14.2, and Part II of Schedule 8 to the Terrorism Act 2000 in respect of action by the review officer.

3.5   The custody officer shall:

(a)   ask the detainee, whether at this time, they: (vii)   would like legal advice, see section 6;

(viii)   want someone informed of their detention, see section 5;

(b)   ask the detainee to sign the custody record to confirm their decisions in respect of (a);

(c)   determine whether the detainee:

(i)   is, or might be, in need of medical treatment or attention, see section 9; (ii)   requires:

•   an appropriate adult;

•   help to check documentation;

•   an interpreter;

(d)   record the decision in respect of (c).

3.6   When determining these needs the custody officer is responsible for initiating an assessment to consider whether the detainee is likely to present specific risks to custody staff, any individual who may have contact with detainee (e.g. legal advisers, medical staff), or themselves. Such assessments should always include a check on the Police National Computer, to be carried out as soon as practicable, to identify any risks highlighted in relation to the detainee. Although such assessments are primarily the custody officer's responsibility, it will be necessary to obtain information from other sources, especially the investigation team See Note 3E, the arresting officer or an appropriate health care professional, see paragraph 9.15. Reasons for delaying the initiation or completion of the assessment must be recorded.

3.7   Chief Officers should ensure that arrangements for proper and effective risk assessments required by paragraph 3.6 are implemented in respect of all detainees at police stations in their area.

3.8   Risk assessments must follow a structured process which clearly defines the categories of risk to be considered and the results must be incorporated in the detainee's custody record. The custody officer is responsible for making sure those responsible for the detainee's custody are appropriately briefed about the risks. The content of any risk assessment and any analysis of the level of risk relating to the person's detention is not required to be shown or provided to the detainee or any person acting on behalf of the detainee. If no specific risks are identified by the assessment, that should be noted in the custody record. See Note 3F and paragraph 9.15

3.9   Custody officers are responsible for implementing the response to any specific risk assessment, which should include for example:

•   reducing opportunities for self harm;

•   calling a health care professional;

•   increasing levels of monitoring or observation;

- reducing the risk to those who come into contact with the detainee .

See Note for Guidance 3F

3.10   Risk assessment is an ongoing process and assessments must always be subject to review if circumstances change.

3.11   If video cameras are installed in the custody area, notices shall be prominently displayed showing cameras are in use. Any request to have video cameras switched off shall be refused.

3.12   A constable, prison officer or other person authorised by the Secretary of State may take any steps which are reasonably necessary for

(a)   photographing the detained person

(b)   measuring him, or

(c)   identifying him.

3.13   Paragraph 3.12 concerns the power in TACT Schedule 8 Paragraph 2. The power in TACT Schedule 8 Paragraph 2 does not cover the taking of fingerprints, intimate samples or non-intimate samples, which is covered in TACT Schedule 8 paragraphs 10-15.

(b)   Detained persons – special groups

3.14   If the detainee appears deaf or there is doubt about their hearing or speaking ability or ability to understand English, and the custody officer cannot establish effective communication, the custody officer must, as soon as practicable, call an interpreter for assistance in the action under paragraphs 3.1–3.5. See section 13

3.15   If the detainee is a juvenile, the custody officer must, if it is practicable, ascertain the identity of a person responsible for their welfare. That person:

- may be:

– the parent or guardian;

– if the juvenile is in local authority or voluntary organisation care, or is otherwise being looked after under the Children Act 1989, a person appointed by that authority or organisation to have responsibility for the juvenile's welfare;

– any other person who has, for the time being, assumed responsibility for the juvenile's welfare.

- must be informed as soon as practicable that the juvenile has been arrested, why they have been arrested and where they are detained. This right is in addition to the juvenile's right in section 5 not to be held incommunicado. See Note 3C

3.16   If a juvenile is known to be subject to a court order under which a person or organisation is given any degree of statutory responsibility to supervise or otherwise monitor them, reasonable steps must also be taken to notify that person or organisation (the 'responsible officer'). The responsible officer will normally be a member of a Youth Offending Team, except for a curfew order which involves electronic monitoring when the contractor providing the monitoring will normally be the responsible officer.

3.17 If the detainee is a juvenile, mentally disordered or otherwise mentally vulnerable, the custody officer must, as soon as practicable:

• inform the appropriate adult, who in the case of a juvenile may or may not be a

person responsible for their welfare, as in paragraph 3.15, of:

– the grounds for their detention;

– their whereabouts.

• ask the adult to come to the police station to see the detainee.

3.18 If the appropriate adult is:

• already at the police station, the provisions of paragraphs 3.1 to 3.5 must be complied with in the appropriate adult's presence;

• not at the station when these provisions are complied with, they must be complied

with again in the presence of the appropriate adult when they arrive.

3.19 The detainee shall be advised that:

• the duties of the appropriate adult include giving advice and assistance;

• they can consult privately with the appropriate adult at any time.

3.20 If the detainee, or appropriate adult on the detainee's behalf, asks for a solicitor to be called to give legal advice, the provisions of section 6 apply.

3.21 If the detainee is blind, seriously visually impaired or unable to read, the custody officer shall make sure their solicitor, relative, appropriate adult or some other person likely to take an interest in them and not involved in the investigation is available to help check any documentation. When this Code requires written consent or signing the person assisting may be asked to sign instead, if the detainee prefers. This paragraph does not require an appropriate adult to be called solely to assist in checking and signing documentation for a person who is not a juvenile, or mentally disordered or otherwise mentally vulnerable (see paragraph 3.17).

(c) Documentation

3.22 The grounds for a person's detention shall be recorded, in the person's presence if practicable.

3.23 Action taken under paragraphs 3.14 to 3.22 shall be recorded.

Notes for guidance

3A The notice of entitlements should:

- list the entitlements in this Code, including:

– visits and contact with outside parties where practicable, including special provisions for Commonwealth citizens and foreign nationals;

– reasonable standards of physical comfort;

– adequate food and drink;

– access to toilets and washing facilities, clothing, medical attention, and exercise when practicable.

- mention the:

– provisions relating to the conduct of interviews;

– circumstances in which an appropriate adult should be available to assist the detainee and their statutory rights to make representation whenever the period of their detention is reviewed.

3B   In addition to notices in English, translations should be available in Welsh, the main minority ethnic languages and the principal European languages whenever they are likely to be helpful. Audio versions of the notice should also be made available.

3C   If the juvenile is in local authority or voluntary organisation care but living with their parents or other adults responsible for their welfare, although there is no legal obligation to inform them, they should normally be contacted, as well as the authority or organisation unless suspected of involvement in the offence concerned. Even if the juvenile is not living with their parents, consideration should be given to informing them.

3D   The right to consult this or other relevant Codes of Practice does not entitle the person concerned to delay unreasonably any necessary investigative or administrative action whilst they do so. Examples of action which need not be delayed unreasonably include:

- searching detainees at the police station;

- taking fingerprints or non-intimate samples without consent for evidential purposes.

3E   The investigation team will include any officer involved in questioning a suspect, gathering or analysing evidence in relation to the offences of which the detainee is suspected of having committed. Should a custody officer require information from the investigation team, the first point of contact should be the officer in charge of the investigation.

3F   Home Office Circular 32/2000 provides more detailed guidance on risk assessments and identifies key risk areas which should always be considered. This should be read with the Guidance on Safer Detention & Handling of Persons in Police Custody issued by the National Centre for Policing Excellence in conjunction with the Home Office and Association of Chief Police Officers.

3G   Arrests under TACT section 41 can only be made where an officer has reasonable grounds to suspect that the individual concerned is a "terrorist". This differs from the PACE power of arrest in that it need not be linked to a specific offence. There may also be circumstances where an arrest under TACT is made on the grounds of sensitive information which can not be disclosed. In such circumstances, the grounds for arrest may be given in terms of the interpretation of a "terrorist" set out in TACT sections 40(1)(a) or 40(1)(b).

3H   For the purpose of arrests under TACT section 41, the review officer is responsible for authorising detention (see Paragraphs 14.1 and 14.2, and Notes for Guidance 14A and 14B). The review officer's role is explained in TACT Schedule 8 Part II. A person may be detained after arrest pending the first review, which must take place as soon as practicable after the person's arrest.

4   Detainee's property

(a)   Action

4.1   The custody officer is responsible for:

(a)   ascertaining what property a detainee:

(i)   has with them when they come to the police station, either on first arrival at the police station or any subsequent arrivals at a police station in connection with that detention.

(ii)   might have acquired for an unlawful or harmful purpose while in custody;

(b)   the safekeeping of any property taken from a detainee which remains at the police station.

The custody officer may search the detainee or authorise their being searched to the extent they consider necessary, provided a search of intimate parts of the body or involving the removal of more than outer clothing is only made as in Annex A. A search may only be carried out by an officer of the same sex as the detainee. See Note 4A

4.2   Detainees may retain clothing and personal effects at their own risk unless the custody officer considers they may use them to cause harm to themselves or others, interfere with evidence, damage property, effect an escape or they are needed as evidence. In this event the custody officer may withhold such articles as they consider necessary and must tell the detainee why.

4.3   Personal effects are those items a detainee may lawfully need, use or refer to while in detention but do not include cash and other items of value.

(b)   Documentation

4.4   It is a matter for the custody officer to determine whether a record should be made of the property a detained person has with him or had taken from him on arrest (see Note for Guidance 4D). Any record made is not required to be kept as part of the custody record but the custody record should be noted as to where such a record exists. Whenever a record is made the detainee shall be allowed to check and sign the record of property as correct. Any refusal to sign shall be recorded.

4.5   If a detainee is not allowed to keep any article of clothing or personal effects, the reason must be recorded.

Notes for guidance

4A   PACE, Section 54(1) and paragraph 4.1 require a detainee to be searched when it is clear the custody officer will have continuing duties in relation to that detainee or when that detainee's behaviour or offence makes an inventory appropriate. They do not require every detainee to be searched, e.g. if it is clear a person will only be detained for a short period and is not to be placed in a cell, the custody officer may decide not to search them. In such a case the custody record will be endorsed 'not searched', paragraph 4.4 will not apply, and the detainee will be invited to sign the entry. If the detainee refuses, the custody officer will be obliged to ascertain what property they have in accordance with paragraph 4.1.

4B   Paragraph 4.4 does not require the custody officer to record on the custody record property in the detainee's possession on arrest if, by virtue of its nature, quantity or size, it is not practicable to remove it to the police station.

4C   Paragraph 4.4 does not require items of clothing worn by the person be recorded unless withheld by the custody officer as in paragraph 4.2.

4D   Section 43(2) of TACT allows a constable to search a person who has been arrested under section 41 to discover whether he has anything in his possession that may constitute evidence that he is a terrorist.

5   Right not to be held incommunicado

(a)   Action

5.1   Any person arrested and held in custody at a police station or other premises may, on request, have one named person who is a friend, relative or a person known to them who is likely to take an interest in their welfare informed at public expense of their whereabouts as soon as practicable. If the person cannot be contacted the detainee may choose up to two alternatives. If they cannot be contacted, the person in charge of detention or the investigation has discretion to allow further attempts until the information has been conveyed. See Notes 5D and 5E

5.2   The exercise of the above right in respect of each person nominated may be delayed only in accordance with Annex B.

5.3   The above right may be exercised each time a detainee is taken to another police station or returned to a police station having been previously transferred to prison. This Code does not afford such a right to a person on transfer to a prison, where a detainee's rights will be governed by Prison Rules see paragraph 14.8.

5.4   If the detainee agrees, they may receive visits from friends, family or others likely to take an interest in their welfare, at the custody officer's discretion. Custody Officers should liaise closely with the investigation team (see Note 3E) to allow risk assessments to be made where particular visitors have been requested by the detainee or identified themselves to police. In circumstances where the nature of the investigation means that such requests can not be met, consideration should be given, in conjunction with a representative of the relevant scheme, to increasing the frequency of visits from independent visitor schemes. See Notes 5B and 5C.

5.5   If a friend, relative or person with an interest in the detainee's welfare enquires about their whereabouts, this information shall be given if the suspect agrees and Annex B does not apply. See Note 5E

5.6   The detainee shall be given writing materials, on request, and allowed to telephone one person for a reasonable time, see Notes 5A and 5F. Either or both these privileges may be denied or delayed if an officer of inspector rank or above considers sending a letter or making a telephone call may result in any of the consequences in Annex B paragraphs

1 and 2, particularly in relation to the making of a telephone call in a language which an officer listening to the call (see paragraph 5.7) does not understand. See note 5G. Nothing in this paragraph permits the restriction or denial of the rights in paragraphs 5.1 and 6.1.

5.7   Before any letter or message is sent, or telephone call made, the detainee shall be informed that what they say in any letter, call or message (other than in a communication to a solicitor) may be read or listened to and may be given in evidence. A telephone call may be terminated if it is being abused see Note 5G. The costs can be at public expense at the custody officer's discretion.

5.8   Any delay or denial of the rights in this section should be proportionate and should last no longer than necessary.

(b)   Documentation

5.9   A record must be kept of any:

(a)   request made under this section and the action taken;

(b)   letters, messages or telephone calls made or received or visit received;

(c)   refusal by the detainee to have information about them given to an outside enquirer, or any refusal to see a visitor. The detainee must be asked to countersign the record accordingly and any refusal recorded.

Notes for guidance

5A   A person may request an interpreter to interpret a telephone call or translate a letter.

5B   At the custody officer's discretion (and subject to the detainee's consent), visits from friends, family or others likely to take an interest in the detainee's welfare, should be allowed when possible, subject to sufficient personnel being available to supervise a visit and any possible hindrance to the investigation. Custody Officers should bear in mind the exceptional nature of prolonged TACT detention and consider the potential benefits that visits may bring to the health and welfare of detainees who are held for extended periods.

5C   Official visitors should be given access following consultation with the officer who has overall responsibility for the investigation provided the detainee consents, and they do not compromise safety or security or unduly delay or interfere with the progress of an investigation. Official visitors should still be required to provide appropriate identification and subject to any screening process in place at the place of detention. Official visitors may include:

•   An accredited faith representative

•   Members of either House of Parliament

•   Public officials needing to interview the prisoner in the course of their duties

•   Other persons visiting with the approval of the officer who has overall responsibility for the investigation

•   Consular officials visiting a detainee who is a national of the country they represent subject to Annex F.

Visits from appropriate members of the Independent Custody Visitors Scheme should be dealt with in accordance with the separate Code of Practice on Independent Custody Visiting.

5D   If the detainee does not know anyone to contact for advice or support or cannot contact a friend or relative, the custody officer should bear in mind any local voluntary bodies or other organisations that might be able to help. Paragraph 6.1 applies if legal advice is required.

5E   In some circumstances it may not be appropriate to use the telephone to disclose information under paragraphs 5.1 and 5.5.

5F   The telephone call at paragraph 5.6 is in addition to any communication under paragraphs 5.1 and 6.1. Further calls may be made at the custody officer's discretion.

5G   The nature of terrorism investigations means that officers should have particular regard to the possibility of suspects attempting to pass information which may be detrimental to public safety, or to an investigation.

6   Right to legal advice

(a)   Action

6.1   Unless Annex B applies, all detainees must be informed that they may at any time consult and communicate privately with a solicitor, whether in person, in writing or by telephone, and that free independent legal advice is available from the duty solicitor. Where an appropriate adult is in attendance, they must also be informed of this right. See paragraph 3.1, Note 1I, Note 6B and Note 6I

6.2   A poster advertising the right to legal advice must be prominently displayed in the charging area of every police station. See Note 6G

6.3   No police officer should, at any time, do or say anything with the intention of dissuading a detainee from obtaining legal advice.

6.4   The exercise of the right of access to legal advice may be delayed exceptionally only as in Annex B. Whenever legal advice is requested, and unless Annex B applies, the custody officer must act without delay to secure the provision of such advice. If, on being informed or reminded of this right, the detainee the officer should point out that the right includes the right to speak with a solicitor on the telephone (see paragraph 5.6). If the detainee continues to waive this right the officer should ask them why and any reasons should be recorded on the custody record or the interview record as appropriate. Reminders of the right to legal advice must be given as in paragraphs 3.5, 11.3, and the PACE Code D on the Identification of Persons by Police Officers (PACE Code D), paragraphs 3.19(ii) and 6.2. Once it is clear a detainee does not want to speak to a solicitor in person or by telephone they should cease to be asked their reasons. See Note 6J.

6.5   An officer of the rank of Commander or Assistant Chief Constable may give a direction under TACT Schedule 8 paragraph 9 that a detainee may only consult a solicitor within the sight and hearing of a qualified officer. Such a direction may only be given if the officer has reasonable grounds to believe that if it were not, it may result in one of the consequences set out in TACT Schedule 8 paragraphs 8(4) or 8(5)(c). See Annex B paragraph 3 and Note 6I. A "qualified officer" means a police officer who:

(a)   is at least the rank of inspector;

(b)   is of the uniformed branch of the force of which the officer giving the direction is a member, and

(c)   in the opinion of the officer giving the direction, has no connection with the detained person's case

Officers considering the use of this power should first refer to Home Office Circular 40/2003.

6.6   In the case of a juvenile, an appropriate adult should consider whether legal advice from a solicitor is required. If the juvenile indicates that they do not want legal advice, the appropriate adult has the right to ask for a solicitor to attend if this would be in the best interests of the person. However, the detained person cannot be forced to see the solicitor if he is adamant that he does not wish to do so.

6.7   A detainee who wants legal advice may not be interviewed or continue to be interviewed until they have received such advice unless:

(a)   Annex B applies, when the restriction on drawing adverse inferences from silence in Annex C will apply because the detainee is not allowed an opportunity to consult a solicitor; or

(b)   an officer of superintendent rank or above has reasonable grounds for believing that:

(i)   the consequent delay might:

•   lead to interference with, or harm to, evidence connected with an offence;

•   lead to interference with, or physical harm to, other people;

•   lead to serious loss of, or damage to, property;

•   lead to alerting other people suspected of having committed an offence but not yet arrested for it;

•   hinder the recovery of property obtained in consequence of the commission of an offence.

(ii)   when a solicitor, including a duty solicitor, has been contacted and has agreed to attend, awaiting their arrival would cause unreasonable delay to the process of investigation.

Note: In these cases the restriction on drawing adverse inferences from silence in Annex C will apply because the detainee is not allowed an opportunity to consult a solicitor.

(c)   the solicitor the detainee has nominated or selected from a list:

(i)   cannot be contacted;

(ii)   has previously indicated they do not wish to be contacted; or

(iii)   having been contacted, has declined to attend; and

the detainee has been advised of the Duty Solicitor Scheme but has declined to ask for the duty solicitor.

In these circumstances the interview may be started or continued without further delay provided an officer of inspector rank or above has agreed to the interview proceeding.

Note: The restriction on drawing adverse inferences from silence in Annex C will not apply because the detainee is allowed an opportunity to consult the duty solicitor;

(d)   the detainee changes their mind, about wanting legal advice.

In these circumstances the interview may be started or continued without delay provided that:

(i)   the detainee agrees to do so , in writing or on the interview record made in accordance with the Code of Practice issued under TACT Schedule 8 Paragraph 3; and

(ii)   an officer of inspector rank or above has inquired about the detainee's reasons for their change of mind and gives authority for the interview to proceed.

Confirmation of the detainee's agreement, their change of mind, the reasons for it if given and, subject to paragraph 2.8, the name of the authorising officer shall be recorded in the written interview record or the interview record made in accordance with the Code of Practice issued under Paragraph 3 of Schedule 8 to the Terrorism Act. See Note 6H. Note: In these circumstances the restriction on drawing adverse inferences from silence in Annex C will not apply because the detainee is allowed an opportunity to consult a solicitor if they wish.

6.8   If paragraph 6.7(a) applies, where the reason for authorising the delay ceases to apply, there may be no further delay in permitting the exercise of the right in the absence of a further authorisation unless paragraph 6.7 (b), (c) or (d) applies.

6.9   A detainee who has been permitted to consult a solicitor shall be entitled on request to have the solicitor present when they are interviewed unless one of the exceptions in paragraph 6.7 applies.

6.10   The solicitor may only be required to leave the interview if their conduct is such that the interviewer is unable properly to put questions to the suspect. See Notes 6C and 6D

6.11   If the interviewer considers a solicitor is acting in such a way, they will stop the interview and consult an officer not below superintendent rank, if one is readily available, and otherwise an officer not below inspector rank not connected with the investigation. After speaking to the solicitor, the officer consulted will decide if the interview should continue in the presence of that solicitor. If they decide it should not, the suspect will be given the opportunity to consult another solicitor before the interview continues and that solicitor given an opportunity to be present at the interview. See Note 6D

6.12   The removal of a solicitor from an interview is a serious step and, if it occurs, the officer of superintendent rank or above who took the decision will consider if the incident should be reported to the Law Society. If the decision to remove the solicitor has been taken by an officer below superintendent rank, the facts must be reported to an officer of superintendent rank or above who will similarly consider whether a report to the Law Society would be appropriate. When the solicitor concerned is a duty solicitor, the report should be both to the Law Society and to the Legal Services Commission.

6.13   'Solicitor' in this Code means:

•   a solicitor who holds a current practising certificate

•   an accredited or probationary representative included on the register of representatives maintained by the Legal Services Commission.

6.14   An accredited or probationary representative sent to provide advice by, and on behalf of, a solicitor shall be admitted to the police station for this purpose unless an officer of inspector rank or above considers such a visit will hinder the investigation and directs otherwise. Hindering the investigation does not include giving proper legal advice to a detainee as in Note 6C. Once admitted to the police station, paragraphs 6.7 to 6.11 apply.

6.15   In exercising their discretion under paragraph 6.14, the officer should take into account in particular:

• whether:

–   the identity and status of an accredited or probationary   representative have been satisfactorily established;

–   they are of suitable character to provide legal advice,

–   any other matters in any written letter of authorisation provided by the solicitor on whose behalf the person is attending the police station. See Note 6E

6.16   If the inspector refuses access to an accredited or probationary representative or a decision is taken that such a person should not be permitted to remain at an interview, the inspector must notify the solicitor on whose behalf the representative was acting and give them an opportunity to make alternative arrangements. The detainee must be informed and the custody record noted.

6.17   If a solicitor arrives at the station to see a particular person, that person must, unless Annex B applies, be so informed whether or not they are being interviewed and asked if they would like to see the solicitor. This applies even if the detainee has declined legal advice or, having requested it, subsequently agreed to be interviewed without receiving advice. The solicitor's attendance and the detainee's decision must be noted in the custody record.

(b)   Documentation

6.18   Any request for legal advice and the action taken shall be recorded.

6.19   A record shall be made in the interview record if a detainee asks for legal advice and an interview is begun either in the absence of a solicitor or their representative, or they have been required to leave an interview.

Notes for guidance

6A   If paragraph 6.7(b) applies, the officer should, if practicable, ask the solicitor for

an estimate of how long it will take to come to the station and relate this to the time detention is permitted, the time of day (i.e. whether the rest period under paragraph 12.2 is imminent) and the requirements of other investigations. If the solicitor is on their way or is to set off immediately, it will not normally be appropriate to begin an interview before they arrive. If it appears necessary to begin an interview before the solicitor's arrival, they should be given an indication of how long the police would be able to wait so there is an opportunity to make arrangements for someone else to provide legal advice. Nothing within this section is intended to prevent police from ascertaining immediately after the arrest of an individual whether a threat to public safety exists (see paragraph 11.2).

6B   A detainee who asks for legal advice should be given an opportunity to consult a specific solicitor or another solicitor from that solicitor's firm or the duty solicitor. If advice is not available by these means, or they do not want to consult the duty solicitor, the detainee should be given an opportunity to choose a solicitor from a list of those willing to provide legal advice. If this solicitor is unavailable, they may   choose up to two alternatives. If these attempts are unsuccessful, the custody officer has discretion to allow further attempts until a solicitor has been contacted and agrees to provide legal advice. Apart from carrying out these duties, an officer must not advise the suspect about any particular firm of solicitors.

6C   A detainee has a right to free legal advice and to be represented by a solicitor. The solicitor's only role in the police station is to protect and advance the legal rights of their client. On occasions this may require the solicitor to give advice which has the effect of the client avoiding giving evidence which strengthens a prosecution case. The solicitor may intervene in order to seek clarification, challenge an improper question to their client or the manner in which it is put, advise their client not to reply to particular questions, or if they wish to give their client further legal advice. Paragraph 6.9 only applies if the solicitor's approach or conduct prevents or unreasonably obstructs proper questions being put to the suspect or the suspect's response being recorded. Examples of unacceptable conduct include answering questions on a suspect's behalf or providing written replies for the suspect to quote.

6D   An officer who takes the decision to exclude a solicitor must be in a position to satisfy the court the decision was properly made. In order to do this they may need to witness what is happening.

6E   If an officer of at least inspector rank considers a particular solicitor or firm of solicitors is persistently sending probationary representatives who are unsuited to provide legal advice, they should inform an officer of at least superintendent rank, who may wish to take the matter up with the Law Society.

6F   Subject to the constraints of Annex B, a solicitor may advise more than one client in an investigation if they wish. Any question of a conflict of interest is for the solicitor under their professional code of conduct. If, however, waiting for a solicitor to give advice to one client may lead to unreasonable delay to the interview with another, the provisions of paragraph 6.7(b) may apply.

6G   In addition to a poster in English, a poster or posters containing translations into Welsh, the main minority ethnic languages and the principal European languages should be displayed wherever they are likely to be helpful and it is practicable to do so.

6H   Paragraph 6.7(d) requires the authorisation of an officer of inspector rank or above to the continuation of an interview when a detainee who wanted legal advice changes their mind. It is permissible for such authorisation to be given over the telephone, if the authorising officer is able to satisfy themselves about the reason for the detainee's change of mind and is satisfied it is proper to continue the interview in those circumstances.

6I   Whenever a detainee exercises their right to legal advice by consulting or communicating with a solicitor, they must be allowed to do so in private. This right to consult or communicate in private is fundamental. Except as allowed by the Terrorism Act 2000, Schedule 8, paragraph 9, if the requirement for privacy is compromised because what is said or written by the detainee or solicitor for the purpose of giving and receiving legal advice is overheard, listened to, or read by others without the informed consent of the detainee, the right will effectively have been denied. When a detainee chooses to speak to a solicitor on the telephone, they should be allowed to do so in private unless a direction under Schedule 8, paragraph 9 of the Terrorism Act 2000 has been given or this is impractical because of the design and layout of the custody area, or the location of telephones. However, the normal expectation should be that facilities will be available, unless they are being used, at all police stations to enable detainees to speak in private to a solicitor either face to face or over the telephone.

6J   A detainee is not obliged to give reasons for declining legal advice and should not be pressed to do so.

7   Citizens of independent Commonwealth countries or foreign nationals

(a)   Action

7.1   Any citizen of an independent Commonwealth country or a national of a foreign country, including the Republic of Ireland, may communicate at any time with the appropriate High Commission, Embassy or Consulate. The detainee must be informed as soon as practicable of:

• this right;

• their right, upon request, to have their High Commission, Embassy or Consulate told of their whereabouts and the grounds for their detention. Such a request should be acted upon as soon as practicable.

7.2   If a detainee is a citizen of a country with which a bilateral consular convention or agreement is in force requiring notification of arrest, the appropriate High Commission, Embassy or Consulate shall be informed as soon as practicable, subject to paragraph

7.4. The countries to which this applies as at 1 April 2003 are listed in Annex F.

7.3   Consular officers may visit one of their nationals in police detention to talk to them and, if required, to arrange for legal advice. Such visits shall take place out of the hearing of a police officer.

7.4   Notwithstanding the provisions of consular conventions, if the detainee is a political refugee whether for reasons of race, nationality, political opinion or religion, or is seeking political asylum, consular officers shall not be informed of the arrest of one of their nationals or given access or information about them except at the detainee's express request.

(b)   Documentation

7.5   A record shall be made when a detainee is informed of their rights under this section and of any communications with a High Commission, Embassy or Consulate.

Note for guidance

7A   The exercise of the rights in this section may not be interfered with even though Annex B applies.

8   Conditions of detention

(a)   Action

8.1   So far as it is practicable, not more than one detainee should be detained in each cell.

8.2   Cells in use must be adequately heated, cleaned and ventilated. They must be adequately lit, subject to such dimming as is compatible with safety and security to allow people detained overnight to sleep. No additional restraints shall be used within a locked cell unless absolutely necessary and then only restraint equipment, approved for use in that force by the Chief Officer, which is reasonable and necessary in the circumstances having regard to the detainee's demeanour and with a view to ensuring their safety and the safety of others. If a detainee is deaf, mentally disordered or otherwise mentally vulnerable, particular care must be taken when deciding whether to use any form of approved restraints.

8.3   Blankets, mattresses, pillows and other bedding supplied shall be of a reasonable standard and in a clean and sanitary condition.

8.4   Access to toilet and washing facilities must be provided.

8.5   If it is necessary to remove a detainee's clothes for the purposes of investigation, for hygiene, health reasons or cleaning, replacement clothing of a reasonable standard of comfort and cleanliness shall be provided. A detainee may not be interviewed unless adequate clothing has been offered.

8.6   At least two light meals and one main meal should be offered in any 24 hour period.

See Note 8B. Drinks should be provided at meal times and upon reasonable request between meals. Whenever necessary, advice shall be sought from the appropriate health care professional, see Note 9A, on medical and dietary matters. As far as practicable, meals provided shall offer a varied diet and meet any specific dietary needs or religious beliefs the detainee may have. Detainees should also be made aware that the meals offered meet such needs. The detainee may, at the custody officer's discretion, have meals supplied by their family or friends at their expense. See Note 8A

8.7   Brief outdoor exercise shall be offered daily if practicable. Where facilities exist, indoor exercise shall be offered as an alternative if outside conditions are such that a detainee can not be reasonably expected to take outdoor exercise (e.g., in cold or wet weather) or if requested by the detainee or for reasons of security, see Note 8C.

8.8   Where practicable, provision should be made for detainees to practice religious observance. Consideration should be given to providing a separate room which can be used as a prayer room. The supply of appropriate food and clothing, and suitable provision for prayer facilities, such as uncontaminated copies of religious books, should also be considered. See Note 8D.

8.9   A juvenile shall not be placed in a cell unless no other secure accommodation is available and the custody officer considers it is not practicable to supervise them if they are not placed in a cell or that cell provides more comfortable accommodation than other secure accommodation in the station. A juvenile may not be placed in a cell with a detained adult.

8.10   Police stations should keep a reasonable supply of reading material available for detainees, including but not limited to, the main religious texts. See Note 8D. Detainees should be made aware that such material is available and reasonable requests for such material should be met as soon as practicable unless to do so would:

(i)   interfere with the investigation; or

(ii)   prevent or delay an officer from discharging his statutory duties, or those in this Code.

If such a request is refused on the grounds of (i) or (ii) above, this should be noted in the custody record and met as soon as possible after those grounds cease to apply.

(b)   Documentation

8.11   A record must be kept of replacement clothing and meals offered.

8.12   The use of any restraints on a detainee whilst in a cell, the reasons for it and, if appropriate, the arrangements for enhanced supervision of the detainee whilst so restrained, shall be recorded. See paragraph 3.9

Notes for guidance

8A   In deciding whether to allow meals to be supplied by family or friends, the custody officer is entitled to take account of the risk of items being concealed in any food or package and the officer's duties and responsibilities under food handling legislation. If an officer needs to examine food or other items supplied by family and friends before deciding whether they can be given to the detainee, he should inform the person who has brought the item to the police station of this and the reasons for doing so.

8B   Meals should, so far as practicable, be offered at recognised meal times, or at other times that take account of when the detainee last had a meal.

8C   In light of the potential for detaining individuals for extended periods of time, the overriding principle should be to accommodate a period of exercise, except where to do so would hinder the investigation, delay the detainee's release or charge, or it is declined by the detainee.

8D   Police forces should consult with representatives of the main religious communities to ensure the provision for religious observance is adequate, and to seek advice on the appropriate storage and handling of religious texts or other religious items.

9   Care and treatment of detained persons

(a)   General

9.1   Notwithstanding other requirements for medical attention as set out in this section, detainees who are held for more than 96 hours must be visited by a healthcare professional at least once every 24 hours.

9.2   Nothing in this section prevents the police from calling the police surgeon or, if appropriate, some other health care professional, to examine a detainee for the purposes of obtaining evidence relating to any offence in which the detainee is suspected of being involved. See Note 9A

9.3   If a complaint is made by, or on behalf of, a detainee about their treatment since their arrest, or it comes to notice that a detainee may have been treated improperly, a report must be made as soon as practicable to an officer of inspector rank or above not connected with the investigation. If the matter concerns a possible assault or the possibility of the unnecessary or unreasonable use of force, an appropriate health care professional must also be called as soon as practicable.

9.4   Detainees should be visited at least every hour. If no reasonably foreseeable risk was identified in a risk assessment, see paragraphs 3.6 – 3.10, there is no need to wake a sleeping detainee. Those suspected of being intoxicated through drink or drugs or having swallowed drugs, see Note 9C, or whose level of consciousness causes concern must, subject to any clinical directions given by the appropriate health care professional, see paragraph 9.15:

•   be visited and roused at least every half hour

•   have their condition assessed as in Annex H

•   and clinical treatment arranged if appropriate

See Notes 9B, 9C and 9G

9.5   When arrangements are made to secure clinical attention for a detainee, the custody officer must make sure all relevant information which might assist in the treatment of the detainee's condition is made available to the responsible health care professional. This applies whether or not the health care professional asks for such information. Any officer or police staff with relevant information must inform the custody officer as soon as practicable.

(b)   Clinical treatment and attention

9.6   The custody officer must make sure a detainee receives appropriate clinical attention as soon as reasonably practicable if the person:

(a)   appears to be suffering from physical illness; or

(b)   is injured; or

(c)   appears to be suffering from a mental disorder; or

(d)   appears to need clinical attention

9.7   This applies even if the detainee makes no request for clinical attention and whether or not they have already received clinical attention elsewhere. If the need for attention appears urgent, e.g. when indicated as in Annex H, the nearest available health care professional or an ambulance must be called immediately.

9.8   The custody officer must also consider the need for clinical attention as set out in Note 9C in relation to those suffering the effects of alcohol or drugs.

9.9   If it appears to the custody officer, or they are told, that a person brought to a station under arrest may be suffering from an infectious disease or condition, the custody officer must take reasonable steps to safeguard the health of the detainee and others at the station. In deciding what action to take, advice must be sought from an appropriate health care professional. See Note 9D. The custody officer has discretion to isolate the person and their property until clinical directions have been obtained.

9.10   If a detainee requests a clinical examination, an appropriate health care professional must be called as soon as practicable to assess the detainee's clinical needs. If a safe and appropriate care plan cannot be provided, the police surgeon's advice must be sought. The detainee may also be examined by a medical practitioner of their choice at their expense.

9.11 If a detainee is required to take or apply any medication in compliance with clinical directions prescribed before their detention, the custody officer must consult the appropriate health care professional before the use of the medication. Subject to the restrictions in paragraph 9.12, the custody officer is responsible for the safekeeping of any medication and for making sure the detainee is given the opportunity to take or apply prescribed or approved medication. Any such consultation and its outcome shall be noted in the custody record.

9.12 No police officer may administer or supervise the self-administration of medically prescribed controlled drugs of the types and forms listed in the Misuse of Drugs Regulations 2001, Schedule 2 or 3. A detainee may only self-administer such drugs under the personal supervision of the registered medical practitioner authorising their use. Drugs listed in Schedule 4 or 5 may be distributed by the custody officer for self- administration if they have consulted the registered medical practitioner authorising their use, this may be done by telephone, and both parties are satisfied self-administration will not expose the detainee, police officers or anyone else to the risk of harm or injury.

9.13 When appropriate health care professionals administer drugs or other medications, or supervise their self-administration, it must be within current medicines legislation and the scope of practice as determined by their relevant professional body.

9.14 If a detainee has in their possession, or claims to need, medication relating to a heart condition, diabetes, epilepsy or a condition of comparable potential seriousness then, even though paragraph 9.6 may not apply, the advice of the appropriate health care professional must be obtained.

9.15 Whenever the appropriate health care professional is called in accordance with this section to examine or treat a detainee, the custody officer shall ask for their opinion about:

•   any risks or problems which police need to take into account when making decisions about the detainee's continued detention;

•   when to carry out an interview if applicable; and

•   the need for safeguards.

9.16 When clinical directions are given by the appropriate health care professional, whether orally or in writing, and the custody officer has any doubts or is in any way uncertain about any aspect of the directions, the custody officer shall ask for clarification. It is particularly important that directions concerning the frequency of visits are clear, precise and capable of being implemented. See Note 9E.

(c)   Documentation

9.17 A record must be made in the custody record of:

(a)   the arrangements made for an examination by an appropriate health care professional under paragraph 9.3 and of any complaint reported under that paragraph together with any relevant remarks by the custody officer;

(b)   any arrangements made in accordance with paragraph 9.6;

(c)   any request for a clinical examination under paragraph 9.10 and any arrangements made in response;

(d)   the injury, ailment, condition or other reason which made it necessary to make the arrangements in (a) to (c), see Note 9F;

(e)   any clinical directions and advice, including any further clarifications, given to police by a health care professional concerning the care and treatment of the detainee in connection with any of the arrangements made in (a) to (c), see Note 9E;

(f)   if applicable, the responses received when attempting to rouse a person using the procedure in Annex H, see Note 9G.

9.18 If a health care professional does not record their clinical findings in the custody record, the record must show where they are recorded. See Note 9F. However, information which is necessary to custody staff to ensure the effective ongoing care and well being of the detainee must be recorded openly in the custody record, see paragraph 3.8 and Annex G, paragraph 7.

9.19 Subject to the requirements of Section 4, the custody record shall include:

•   a record of all medication a detainee has in their possession on arrival at the police station;

•   a note of any such medication they claim to need but do not have with them.

Notes for guidance

9A   A 'health care professional' means a clinically qualified person working within the scope of practice as determined by their relevant professional body. Whether a health care professional is 'appropriate' depends on the circumstances of the duties they carry out at the time.

9B   Whenever possible juveniles and mentally vulnerable detainees should be visited more frequently.

9C   A detainee who appears drunk or behaves abnormally may be suffering from illness, the effects of drugs or may have sustained injury, particularly a head injury which is not apparent. A detainee needing or dependent on certain drugs, including alcohol, may experience harmful effects within a short time of being deprived of their supply. In these circumstances, when there is any doubt, police should always act urgently to call an appropriate health care professional or an ambulance. Paragraph 9.6 does not apply to minor ailments or injuries which do not need attention. However, all such ailments or injuries must be recorded in the custody record and any doubt must be resolved in favour of calling the appropriate health care professional.

9D   It is important to respect a person's right to privacy and information about their health must be kept confidential and only disclosed with their consent or in accordance with clinical advice when it is necessary to protect the detainee's health or that of others who come into contact with them.

9E   The custody officer should always seek to clarify directions that the detainee requires constant observation or supervision and should ask the appropriate health care professional to explain precisely what action needs to be taken to implement such directions.

9F   Paragraphs 9.17 and 9.18 do not require any information about the cause of any injury, ailment or condition to be recorded on the custody record if it appears capable of providing evidence of an offence.

9G   The purpose of recording a person's responses when attempting to rouse them using the procedure in Annex H is to enable any change in the individual's consciousness level to be noted and clinical treatment arranged if appropriate.

10   Cautions

(a)   When a caution must be given

10.1 A person whom there are grounds to suspect of an offence, see Note 10A, must be cautioned before any questions about an offence, or further questions if the answers provide the grounds for suspicion, are put to them if either the suspect's answers or silence, (i.e. failure or refusal to answer or answer satisfactorily) may be given in evidence to a court in a prosecution.

10.2 A person who is arrested, or further arrested, must be informed at the time, or as soon as practicable thereafter, that they are under arrest and the grounds for their arrest, see paragraph 3.4, Note 3G and Note 10B.

10.3 As per section 3 of PACE Code G, a person who is arrested, or further arrested, must also be cautioned unless:

(a)   it is impracticable to do so by reason of their condition or behaviour at the time;

(b)   they have already been cautioned immediately prior to arrest as in paragraph 10.1.

(b)   Terms of the cautions

10.4 The caution which must be given on:

(a)   arrest;

(b)   all other occasions before a person is charged or informed they may be prosecuted, see PACE Code C, section 16. should, unless the restriction on drawing adverse inferences from silence applies, see Annex C, be in the following terms:

"You do not have to say anything. But it may harm your defence if you do not mention when questioned something which you later rely on in Court. Anything you do say may be given in evidence." See Note 10F

10.5 Annex C, paragraph 2 sets out the alternative terms of the caution to be used when the restriction on drawing adverse inferences from silence applies.

10.6 Minor deviations from the words of any caution given in accordance with this Code do not constitute a breach of this Code, provided the sense of the relevant caution is preserved. See Note 10C

10.7 After any break in questioning under caution, the person being questioned must be made aware they remain under caution. If there is any doubt the relevant caution should be given again in full when the interview resumes. See Note 10D

10.8   When, despite being cautioned, a person fails to co-operate or to answer particular questions which may affect their immediate treatment, the person should be informed of any relevant consequences and that those consequences are not affected by the caution. Examples are when a person's refusal to provide:

- their name and address when charged may make them liable to detention;

- particulars and information in accordance with a statutory requirement

(c)   Special warnings under the Criminal Justice and Public Order Act 1994, sections 36 and 37

10.9   When a suspect interviewed at a police station or authorised place of detention after arrest fails or refuses to answer certain questions, or to answer satisfactorily, after due warning, see Note 10E, a court or jury may draw such inferences as appear proper under the Criminal Justice and Public Order Act 1994, sections 36 and 37. Such inferences may only be drawn when:

(a)   the restriction on drawing adverse inferences from silence, see Annex C, does not apply; and

(b)   the suspect is arrested by a constable and fails or refuses to account for any objects, marks or substances, or marks on such objects found:

- on their person;

- in or on their clothing or footwear;

- otherwise in their possession; or

- in the place they were arrested;

(c)   the arrested suspect was found by a constable at a place at or about the time the offence for which that officer has arrested them is alleged to have been committed, and the suspect fails or refuses to account for their presence there.

When the restriction on drawing adverse inferences from silence applies, the suspect may still be asked to account for any of the matters in (b) or (c) but the special warning described in paragraph 10.10 will not apply and must not be given.

10.10 For an inference to be drawn when a suspect fails or refuses to answer a question about one of these matters or to answer it satisfactorily, the suspect must first be told in ordinary language:

(a)   what offence is being investigated;

(b)   what fact they are being asked to account for;

(c)   this fact may be due to them taking part in the commission of the offence;

(d)   a court may draw a proper inference if they fail or refuse to account for this fact; (e) a record is being made of the interview and it may be given in evidence if they are brought to trial.

(d)   Juveniles and persons who are mentally disordered or otherwise mentally vulnerable

10.11 If a juvenile or a person who is mentally disordered or otherwise mentally vulnerable is cautioned in the absence of the appropriate adult, the caution must be repeated in the adult's presence.

(e)   Documentation

10.12 A record shall be made when a caution is given under this section, either in the interviewer's pocket book or in the interview record.

Notes for guidance

10A   There must be some reasonable, objective grounds for the suspicion, based on known facts or information which are relevant to the likelihood the offence has been committed and the person to be questioned committed it.

10B   An arrested person must be given sufficient information to enable them to understand that they have been deprived of their liberty and the reason they have been arrested, e.g. when a person is arrested on suspicion of committing an offence they must be informed of the suspected offence's nature, when and where it was committed see Note 3G. The suspect must also be informed of the reason or reasons why the arrest is considered necessary. Vague or technical language should be avoided.

10C   If it appears a person does not understand the caution, the person giving it should explain it in their own words.

10D   It may be necessary to show to the court that nothing occurred during an interview break or between interviews which influenced the suspect's recorded evidence. After a break in an interview or at the beginning of a subsequent interview, the interviewing officer should summarise the reason for the break and confirm this with the suspect.

10E   The Criminal Justice and Public Order Act 1994, sections 36 and 37 apply only to suspects who have been arrested by a constable or Customs and Excise officer and are given the relevant warning by the police or customs officer who made the arrest or who is investigating the offence. They do not apply to any interviews with suspects who have not been arrested.

10F   Nothing in this Code requires a caution to be given or repeated when informing a person not under arrest they may be prosecuted for an offence. However, a court will not be able to draw any inferences under the Criminal Justice and Public Order Act 1994, section 34, if the person was not cautioned.

11   Interviews – general

(a)   Action

11.1   An interview in this Code is the questioning of a person arrested on suspicion of being a terrorist which, under paragraph 10.1, must be carried out under caution. Whenever a person is interviewed they must be informed of the grounds for arrest see Note 3G.

11.2   Following a decision to arrest a suspect, they must not be interviewed about the relevant offence except at a place designated for detention under Schedule 8 paragraph 1 of the Terrorism Act 2000, unless the consequent delay would be likely to:

(a)   lead to:

- interference with, or harm to, evidence connected with an offence;

- interference with, or physical harm to, other people; or

- serious loss of, or damage to, property;

(b)   lead to alerting other people suspected of committing an offence but not yet arrested for it; or

(c)   hinder the recovery of property obtained in consequence of the commission of an offence.

Interviewing in any of these circumstances shall cease once the relevant risk has been averted or the necessary questions have been put in order to attempt to avert that risk.

11.3   Immediately prior to the commencement or re-commencement of any interview at a designated place of detention, the interviewer should remind the suspect of their entitlement to free legal advice and that the interview can be delayed for legal advice to be obtained, unless one of the exceptions in paragraph 6.7 applies. It is the interviewer's responsibility to make sure all reminders are recorded in the interview record.

11.4   At the beginning of an interview the interviewer, after cautioning the suspect, see section

10, shall put to them any significant statement or silence which occurred in the presence and hearing of a police officer or other police staff before the start of the interview and which have not been put to the suspect in the course of a previous interview. See Note

11A. The interviewer shall ask the suspect whether they confirm or deny that earlier statement or silence and if they want to add anything.

11.5   A significant statement is one which appears capable of being used in evidence against the suspect, in particular a direct admission of guilt. A significant silence is a failure or refusal to answer a question or answer satisfactorily when under caution, which might, allowing for the restriction on drawing adverse inferences from silence, see Annex C, give rise to an inference under the Criminal Justice and Public Order Act 1994, Part III.

11.6   No interviewer may try to obtain answers or elicit a statement by the use of oppression.

Except as in paragraph 10.8, no interviewer shall indicate, except to answer a direct question, what action will be taken by the police if the person being questioned answers questions, makes a statement or refuses to do either. If the person asks directly what action will be taken if they answer questions, make a statement or refuse to do either, the interviewer may inform them what action the police propose to take provided that action is itself proper and warranted.

11.7   The interview or further interview of a person about an offence with which that person has not been charged or for which they have not been informed they may be prosecuted, must cease when:

(a)   the officer in charge of the investigation is satisfied all the questions they consider relevant to obtaining accurate and reliable information about the offence have been put to the suspect, this includes allowing the suspect an opportunity to give an innocent explanation and asking questions to test if the explanation is accurate and reliable, e.g. to clear up ambiguities or clarify what the suspect said;

(b)   the officer in charge of the investigation has taken account of any other available evidence; and

(c)   the officer in charge of the investigation, or in the case of a detained suspect, the custody officer, see PACE Code C paragraph 16.1, reasonably believes there is sufficient evidence to provide a realistic prospect of conviction for that offence. See Note 11B

(b)   Interview records

11.8   Interview records should be made in accordance with the Code of Practice issued under Schedule 8 Paragraph 3 to the Terrorism Act where the interview takes place at a designated place of detention.

(c)   Juveniles and mentally disordered or otherwise mentally vulnerable people

11.9   A juvenile or person who is mentally disordered or otherwise mentally vulnerable must not be interviewed regarding their involvement or suspected involvement in a criminal offence or offences, or asked to provide or sign a written statement under caution or record of interview, in the absence of the appropriate adult unless paragraphs 11.2, 11.11 to 11.13 apply. See Note 11C

11.10 If an appropriate adult is present at an interview, they shall be informed:

•   they are not expected to act simply as an observer; and

•   the purpose of their presence is to:

–   advise the person being interviewed;

–   observe whether the interview is being conducted properly and fairly;

–   facilitate communication with the person being interviewed.

The appropriate adult may be required to leave the interview if their conduct is such that the interviewer is unable properly to put questions to the suspect. This will include situations where the appropriate adult's approach or conduct prevents or unreasonably obstructs proper questions being put to the suspect or the suspect's responses being recorded. If the interviewer considers an appropriate adult is acting in such a way, they will stop the interview and consult an officer not below superintendent rank, if one is readily available, and otherwise an officer not below inspector rank not connected with the investigation. After speaking to the appropriate adult, the officer consulted will decide if the interview should continue without the attendance of that appropriate adult. If they decide it should not, another appropriate adult should be obtained before the interview continues, unless the provisions of paragraph 11.11 below apply.

(d)   Vulnerable suspects – urgent interviews at police stations

11.11 The following persons may not be interviewed unless an officer of superintendent rank or above considers delay will lead to the consequences in paragraph 11.2(a) to (c), and is satisfied the interview would not significantly harm the person's physical or mental state (see Annex G):

(a)   a juvenile or person who is mentally disordered or otherwise mentally vulnerable if at the time of the interview the appropriate adult is not present;

(b)   anyone other than in (a) who at the time of the interview appears unable to:

•   appreciate the significance of questions and their answers; or

•   understand what is happening because of the effects of drink, drugs or any illness, ailment or condition;

(c)   a person who has difficulty understanding English or has a hearing disability, if at the time of the interview an interpreter is not present.

11.12 These interviews may not continue once sufficient information has been obtained to avert the consequences in paragraph 11.2(a) to (c).

11.13 A record shall be made of the grounds for any decision to interview a person under paragraph 11.11.

Notes for guidance

11A   Paragraph 11.4 does not prevent the interviewer from putting significant statements and silences to a suspect again at a later stage or a further interview.

11B   The Criminal Procedure and Investigations Act 1996 Code of Practice, paragraph 3.4 states 'In conducting an investigation, the investigator should pursue all reasonable lines of enquiry, whether these point towards or away from the suspect. What is reasonable will depend on the particular circumstances.' Interviewers should keep this in mind when deciding what questions to ask in an interview.

11C   Although juveniles or people who are mentally disordered or otherwise mentally vulnerable are often capable of providing reliable evidence, they may, without knowing or wishing to do so, be particularly prone in certain circumstances to provide information that may be unreliable, misleading or self-incriminating. Special care should always be taken when questioning such a person, and the appropriate adult should be involved if there is any doubt about a person's age, mental state or capacity. Because of the risk of unreliable evidence it is also important to obtain corroboration of any facts admitted whenever possible.

11D   Consideration should be given to the effect of extended detention on a detainee and any subsequent information they provide, especially if it relates to information on matters that they have failed to provide previously in response to similar questioning see Annex G.

11E   Significant statements described in paragraph 11.4 will always be relevant to the offence and must be recorded. When a suspect agrees to read records of interviews and other comments and sign them as correct, they should be asked to endorse the record with, e.g. 'I agree that this is a correct record of what was said' and add their signature. If the suspect does not agree with the record, the interviewer should record the details of any disagreement and ask the suspect to read these details and sign them to the effect that they accurately reflect their disagreement. Any refusal to sign should be recorded.

12   Interviews in police stations

(a)   Action

12.1   If a police officer wants to interview or conduct enquiries which require the presence of a detainee, the custody officer is responsible for deciding whether to deliver the detainee into the officer's custody.

12.2   Except as below, in any period of 24 hours a detainee must be allowed a continuous period of at least 8 hours for rest, free from questioning, travel or any interruption in connection with the investigation concerned. This period should normally be at night or other appropriate time which takes account of when the detainee last slept or rested. If a detainee is arrested at a police station after going there voluntarily, the period of 24 hours runs from the time of their arrest (or, if a person was being detained under TACT Schedule 7 when arrested, from the time at which the examination under Schedule 7 began) and not the time of arrival at the police station. The period may not be interrupted or delayed, except:

(a)   when there are reasonable grounds for believing not delaying or interrupting the period would:

(i)   involve a risk of harm to people or serious loss of, or damage to, property;

(ii)   delay unnecessarily the person's release from custody; (iii) otherwise   prejudice   the outcome of the investigation;

(b)   at the request of the detainee, their appropriate adult or legal representative; (c)   when a delay or interruption is necessary in order to:

(i)   comply with the legal obligations and duties arising under section 14;

(ii)   to take action required under section 9 or in accordance with medical advice.

If the period is interrupted in accordance with (a), a fresh period must be allowed. Interruptions under (b) and (c), do not require a fresh period to be allowed.

12.3   Before a detainee is interviewed the custody officer, in consultation with the officer in charge of the investigation and appropriate health care professionals as necessary, shall assess whether the detainee is fit enough to be interviewed. This means determining and considering the risks to the detainee's physical and mental state if the interview took place and determining what safeguards are needed to allow the interview to take place. The custody officer shall not allow a detainee to be interviewed if the custody officer considers it would cause significant harm to the detainee's physical or mental state. Vulnerable suspects listed at paragraph 11.11 shall be treated as always being at some risk during an interview and these persons may not be interviewed except in accordance with paragraphs 11.11 to 11.13.

12.4   As far as practicable interviews shall take place in interview rooms which are adequately heated, lit and ventilated.

12.5   A suspect whose detention without charge has been authorised under TACT Schedule

8, because the detention is necessary for an interview to obtain evidence of the offence for which they have been arrested, may choose not to answer questions but police do not require the suspect's consent or agreement to interview them for this purpose. If a suspect takes steps to prevent themselves being questioned or further questioned, e.g. by refusing to leave their cell to go to a suitable interview room or by trying to leave the interview room, they shall be advised their consent or agreement to interview is not required. The suspect shall be cautioned as in section 10, and informed if they fail or refuse to co-operate, the interview may take place in the cell and that their failure or refusal to co-operate may be given in evidence. The suspect shall then be invited to co-operate and go into the interview room.

12.6   People being questioned or making statements shall not be required to stand.

12.7   Before the interview commences each interviewer shall, subject to the qualification at

paragraph 2.8, identify themselves and any other persons present to the interviewee.

12.8   Breaks from interviewing should be made at recognised meal times or at other times that take account of when an interviewee last had a meal. Short refreshment breaks shall be provided at approximately two hour intervals, subject to the interviewer's discretion to delay a break if there are reasonable grounds for believing it would:

(i)   involve a:

•   risk of harm to people;

•   serious loss of, or damage to, property;

(ii)   unnecessarily delay the detainee's release;

(iii)   otherwise prejudice the outcome of the investigation. See Note 12B

12.9   During extended periods where no interviews take place, because of the need to gather further evidence or analyse existing evidence, detainees and their legal representative shall be informed that the investigation into the relevant offence remains ongoing. If practicable, the detainee and legal representative should also be made aware in general terms of any reasons for long gaps between interviews. Consideration should be given to allowing visits, more frequent exercise, or for reading or writing materials to be offered see paragraph 5.4, section 8 and Note 12C.

12.10 If during the interview a complaint is made by or on behalf of the interviewee concerning the provisions of this Code, the interviewer should:

(i)   record it in the interview record;

(ii)   inform the custody officer, who is then responsible for dealing with it as in section 9.

(b)   Documentation

12.11 A record must be made of the:

•   time a detainee is not in the custody of the custody officer, and why

•   reason for any refusal to deliver the detainee out of that custody

12.12 A record shall be made of:

(a)   the reasons it was not practicable to use an interview room; and

(b)   any action taken as in paragraph 12.5.

The record shall be made on the custody record or in the interview record for action taken whilst an interview record is being kept, with a brief reference to this effect in the custody record.

12.13 Any decision to delay a break in an interview must be recorded, with reasons, in the interview record.

12.14 All written statements made at police stations under caution shall be written on forms provided for the purpose.

12.15 All written statements made under caution shall be taken in accordance with Annex D.

Before a person makes a written statement under caution at a police station they shall be reminded about the right to legal advice. See Note 12A

Notes for guidance

12A   It is not normally necessary to ask for a written statement if the interview was recorded in writing and the record signed in accordance with the Code of Practice issued under TACT Schedule 8 Paragraph 3. Statements under caution should normally be taken in these circumstances only at the person's express wish. A person may however be asked if they want to make such a statement.

12B   Meal breaks should normally last at least 45 minutes and shorter breaks after two hours should last at least 15 minutes. If the interviewer delays a break in accordance with paragraph 12.8 and prolongs the interview, a longer break should be provided. If there is a short interview, and another short interview is contemplated, the length of the break may be reduced if there are reasonable grounds to believe this is necessary to avoid any of the consequences in paragraph 12.8(i) to (iii).

12C   Consideration should be given to the matters referred to in paragraph 12.9 after a period of over 24 hours without questioning. This is to ensure that extended periods of detention without an indication that the investigation remains ongoing do not contribute to a deterioration of the detainee's well-being.

13   Interpreters

(a)   General

13.1   Chief officers are responsible for making sure appropriate arrangements are in place for provision of suitably qualified interpreters for people who:

- are deaf;

- do not understand English.

Whenever possible, interpreters should be drawn from the National Register of Public Service Interpreters (NRPSI) or the Council for the Advancement of Communication with Deaf People (CACDP) Directory of British Sign Language/English Interpreters.

(b)   Foreign languages

13.2   Unless paragraphs 11.2, 11.11 to 11.13 apply, a person must not be interviewed in the absence of a person capable of interpreting if:

(a)   they have difficulty understanding English;

(b)   the interviewer cannot speak the person's own language; (c)   the person wants an interpreter present.

13.3   The interviewer shall make sure the interpreter makes a note of the interview at the time in the person's language for use in the event of the interpreter being called to give evidence, and certifies its accuracy. The interviewer should allow sufficient time for the interpreter to note each question and answer after each is put, given and interpreted. The person should be allowed to read the record or have it read to them and sign it as correct or indicate the respects in which they consider it inaccurate. If the interview is audibly recorded or visually recorded with sound, the Code of Practice issued under paragraph 3 of Schedule 8 to the Terrorism Act 2000 will apply.

13.4   In the case of a person making a statement to a police officer or other police staff other than in English:

(a)   the interpreter shall record the statement in the language it is made;

(b)   the person shall be invited to sign it;

(c)   an official English translation shall be made in due course.

(c)   Deaf people and people with speech difficulties

13.5   If a person appears to be deaf or there is doubt about their hearing or speaking ability, they must not be interviewed in the absence of an interpreter unless they agree in writing to being interviewed without one or paragraphs 11.2, 11.11 to 11.13 apply.

13.6   An interpreter should also be called if a juvenile is interviewed and the parent or guardian present as the appropriate adult appears to be deaf or there is doubt about their hearing or speaking ability, unless they agree in writing to the interview proceeding without one or paragraphs 11.2, 11.11 to 11.13 apply.

13.7   The interviewer shall make sure the interpreter is allowed to read the interview record and certify its accuracy in the event of the interpreter being called to give evidence. If the interview is audibly recorded or visually recorded, the Code of Practice issued under TACT Schedule 8 Paragraph 3 will apply.

(d)   Additional rules for detained persons

13.8   All reasonable attempts should be made to make the detainee understand that interpreters will be provided at public expense.

13.9   If paragraph 6.1 applies and the detainee cannot communicate with the solicitor because of language, hearing or speech difficulties, an interpreter must be called. The interpreter may not be a police officer or any other police staff when interpretation is needed for the purposes of obtaining legal advice. In all other cases a police officer or other police staff may only interpret if the detainee and the appropriate adult, if applicable, give their agreement in writing or if the interview is audibly recorded or visually recorded as in the Code of Practice issued under TACT Schedule 8 Paragraph 3.

13.10 When the custody officer cannot establish effective communication with a person charged with an offence who appears deaf or there is doubt about their ability to hear, speak or to understand English, arrangements must be made as soon as practicable for an interpreter to explain the offence and any other information given by the custody officer.

(e)   Documentation

13.11 Action taken to call an interpreter under this section and any agreement to be interviewed in the absence of an interpreter must be recorded.

14   Reviews and extensions of Detention

(a)   Reviews and Extensions of Detention

14.1   The powers and duties of the review officer are in the Terrorism Act 2000, Schedule 8, Part II. See Notes 14A and 14B. A review officer should carry out his duties at the police station where the detainee is held, and be allowed such access to the detainee as is necessary for him to exercise those duties.

14.2   For the purposes of reviewing a person's detention, no officer shall put specific questions to the detainee:

•   regarding their involvement in any offence; or

•   in respect of any comments they may make:

–   when given the opportunity to make representations; or

–   in response to a decision to keep them in detention or extend the maximum period of detention.

Such an exchange could constitute an interview as in paragraph 11.1 and would be subject to the associated safeguards in section 11 and, in respect of a person who has been charged see PACE Code C Section 16.8.

14.3   If detention is necessary for longer than 48 hours, a police officer of at least superintendent rank, or a Crown Prosecutor may apply for warrants of further detention under the Terrorism Act 2000, Schedule 8, Part III.

14.4   When an application for a warrant of further or extended detention is sought under Paragraph 29 or 36 of Schedule 8, the detained person and their representative must be informed of their rights in respect of the application. These include:

a)   the right to a written or oral notice of the warrant See Note 14G.

b)   the right to make oral or written representations to the judicial authority about the application.

c)   the right to be present and legally represented at the hearing of the application, unless specifically excluded by the judicial authority.

d)   their right to free legal advice (see section 6 of this Code).

(b)   Transfer of detained persons to Prison

14.5   Where a warrant is issued which authorises detention beyond a period of 14 days from the time of arrest (or if a person was being detained under TACT Schedule 7, from the time at which the examination under Schedule 7 began), the detainee must be transferred from detention in a police station to detention in a designated prison as soon as is practicable, unless:

a)   the detainee specifically requests to remain in detention at a police station and that request can be accommodated, or

b)   there are reasonable grounds to believe that transferring a person to a prison would:

i)   significantly hinder a terrorism investigation;

ii)   delay charging of the detainee or his release from custody, or

iii)   otherwise prevent the investigation from being conducted diligently and expeditiously.

If any of the grounds in (b)(i) to (iii) above are relied upon, these must be presented to the judicial authority as part of the application for the warrant that would extend detention beyond a period of 14 days from the time of arrest (or if a person was being detained under TACT Schedule 7, from the time at which the examination under Schedule 7 began) See Note 14J.

14.6   If a person remains in detention at a police station under a warrant of further detention as described at section 14.5, they must be transferred to a prison as soon as practicable after the grounds at (b)(i) to (iii) of that section cease to apply.

14.7   Police should maintain an agreement with the National Offender Management Service (NOMS) that stipulates named prisons to which individuals may be transferred under this section. This should be made with regard to ensuring detainees are moved to the most suitable prison for the purposes of the investigation and their welfare, and should include provision for the transfer of male, female and juvenile detainees. Police should ensure that the Governor of a prison to which they intend to transfer a detainee is given reasonable notice of this. Where practicable, this should be no later than the point at which a warrant is applied for that would take the period of detention beyond 14 days.

14.8   Following a detained person's transfer to a designated prison, their detention will be governed by the terms of Schedule 8 and Prison Rules, and this Code of Practice will not apply during any period that the person remains in prison detention. The Code will once more apply if a detained person is transferred back from prison detention to police detention. In order to enable the Governor to arrange for the production of the detainee back into police custody, police should give notice to the Governor of the relevant prison as soon as possible of any decision to transfer a detainee from prison back to a police station. Any transfer between a prison and a police station should be conducted by police, and this Code will be applicable during the period of transit See Note 14K. A detainee should only remain in police custody having been transferred back from a prison, for as long as is necessary for the purpose of the investigation.

14.9   The investigating team and custody officer should provide as much information as necessary to enable the relevant prison authorities to provide appropriate facilities to detain an individual. This should include, but not be limited to:

i)   medical assessments

ii)   security and risk assessments

iii)   details of the detained person's legal representatives

iv)   details of any individuals from whom the detained person has requested visits, or who have requested to visit the detained person.

14.10 Where a detainee is to be transferred to prison, the custody officer should inform the detainee's legal adviser beforehand that the transfer is to take place (including the name of the prison). The custody officer should also make all reasonable attempts to inform:

•   family or friends who have been informed previously of the detainee's detention;

and

•   the person who was initially informed of the detainee's detention as at paragraph 5.1.

(c)   Documentation

14.11 It is the responsibility of the officer who gives any reminders as at paragraph 14.4, to ensure that these are noted in the custody record, as well any comments made by the detained person upon being told of those rights.

14.12 The grounds for, and extent of, any delay in conducting a review shall be recorded.

14.13 Any written representations shall be retained.

14.14 A record shall be made as soon as practicable about the outcome of each review or determination whether to extend the maximum detention period without charge or an application for a warrant of further detention or its extension.

14.15 Any decision not to transfer a detained person to a designated prison under paragraph

14.5, must be recorded, along with the reasons for this decision. If a request under paragraph 14.5(a) is not accommodated, the reasons for this should also be recorded.

Notes for guidance

14A   TACT Schedule 8 Part II sets out the procedures for review of detention up to 48 hours from the time of arrest under TACT section 41 (or if a person was being detained under TACT Schedule 7, from the time at which the examination under Schedule 7 began). These include provisions for the requirement to review detention, postponing a review, grounds for continued detention, designating a review officer, representations, rights of the detained person and keeping a record. The review officer's role ends after a warrant has been issued for extension of detention under Part III of Schedule 8.

14B   Section 24(1) of the Terrorism Act 2006, amended the grounds contained within the 2000 Act on which a review officer may authorise continued detention. Continued detention may be authorised if it is necessary-

a)   to obtain relevant evidence whether by questioning him or otherwise b)   to   preserve relevant evidence

c)   while awaiting the result of an examination or analysis of relevant evidence

d)   for the examination or analysis of anything with a view to obtaining relevant evidence

e)   pending a decision to apply to the Secretary of State for a deportation notice to be served on the detainee, the making of any such application, or the consideration of any such application by the Secretary of State

f)   pending a decision to charge the detainee with an offence.

14C   Applications for warrants to extend detention beyond 48 hours, may be made for periods of 7 days at a time (initially under TACT Schedule 8 paragraph 29, and extensions thereafter under TACT Schedule 8, Paragraph 36), up to a maximum period of 28 days from the time of arrest (or if a person was being detained under TACT Schedule 7, from the time at which the examination under Schedule 7 began). Applications may be made for shorter periods than 7 days, which must be specified. The judicial authority may also substitute a shorter period if he feels a period of 7 days is inappropriate.

14D   Unless Note 14F applies, applications for warrants that would take the total period of detention up to 14 days or less should be made to a judicial authority, meaning a District Judge (Magistrates' Court) designated by the Lord Chancellor to hear such applications.

14E   Any application for a warrant which would take the period of detention beyond 14 days from the time of arrest (or if a person was being detained under TACT Schedule 7, from the time at which the examination under Schedule 7 began), must be made to a High Court Judge.

14F   If an application has been made to a High Court judge for a warrant which would take detention beyond 14 days, and the High Court judge instead issues a warrant for a period of time which would not take detention beyond 14 days, further applications for extension of detention must also be made to a High Court judge, regardless of the period of time to which they refer.

14G   TACT Schedule 8 Paragraph 31 requires a notice to be given to the detained person if a warrant is sought for further detention. This must be provided before the judicial hearing of the application for that warrant and must include:

a)   notification that the application for a warrant has been made b)   the time at which the application was made

c)   the time at which the application is to be heard

d)   the grounds on which further detention is sought.

A notice must also be provided each time an application is made to extend an existing warrant

14H   An officer applying for an order under TACT Schedule 8 Paragraph 34 to withhold specified information on which he intends to rely when applying for a warrant of further detention, may make the application for the order orally or in writing. The most appropriate method of application will depend on the circumstances of the case and the need to ensure fairness to the detainee.

14I   Where facilities exist, hearings relating to extension of detention under Part III of Schedule

8 may take place using video conferencing facilities provided that the requirements set out in Schedule 8 are still met. However, if the judicial authority requires the detained person to be physically present at any hearing, this should be complied with as soon as practicable. Paragraphs 33(4) to 33(9) of TACT Schedule 8 govern the relevant conduct of hearings.

14J   Transfer to prison is intended to ensure that individuals who are detained for extended periods of time are held in a place designed for longer periods of detention than police stations. Prison will provide detainees with a greater range of facilities more appropriate to longer detention periods.

14K   The Code will only apply as is appropriate to the conditions of detention during the period of transit. There is obviously no requirement to provide such things as bed linen or reading materials for the journey between prison and police station.

15   Charging

15.1   Charging of detained persons is covered by PACE and guidance issued under PACE by the Director of Public Prosecutions. General guidance on charging can be found in section 16 of PACE Code C.

16   testing persons for the presence of specified Class A drugs

16.1   The provisions for drug testing under section 63B of PACE (as amended by section 5 of the Criminal Justice Act 2003 and section 7 of the Drugs Act 2005), do not apply to detention under TACT section 41 and Schedule 8. Guidance on these provisions can be found in section 17 of PACE Code C.

Annex A – Intimate and strip searches

A   Intimate search

1.   An intimate search consists of the physical examination of a person's body orifices other than the mouth. The intrusive nature of such searches means the actual and potential risks associated with intimate searches must never be underestimated.

(a)   Action H

2.   Body orifices other than the mouth may be searched only if authorised by an officer

of inspector rank or above who has reasonable grounds for believing that the person may have concealed on themselves anything which they could and might use to cause physical injury to themselves or others at the station and the officer has reasonable grounds for believing that an intimate search is the only means of removing those items.

3.   Before the search begins, a police officer, designated detention officer or staff custody officer, must tell the detainee:-

(a)   that the authority to carry out the search has been given;

(b)   the grounds for giving the authorisation and for believing that the article cannot be removed without an intimate search.

4.   An intimate search may only be carried out by a registered medical practitioner or registered nurse, unless an officer of at least inspector rank considers this is not practicable, in which case a police officer may carry out the search. See Notes A1 to A5

5.   Any proposal for a search under paragraph 2 to be carried out by someone other than a registered medical practitioner or registered nurse must only be considered as a last resort and when the authorising officer is satisfied the risks associated with allowing the item to remain with the detainee outweigh the risks associated with removing it. See Notes A1 to A5

6.   An intimate search at a police station of a juvenile or mentally disordered or otherwise mentally vulnerable person may take place only in the presence of an appropriate adult of the same sex, unless the detainee specifically requests a particular adult of the opposite sex who is readily available. In the case of a juvenile the search may take place in the absence of the appropriate adult only if the juvenile signifies in the presence of the appropriate adult they do not want the adult present during the search and the adult agrees. A record shall be made of the juvenile's decision and signed by the appropriate adult.

7.   When an intimate search under paragraph 2 is carried out by a police officer, the officer must be of the same sex as the detainee. A minimum of two people, other than the detainee, must be present during the search. Subject to paragraph 6, no person of the opposite sex who is not a medical practitioner or nurse shall be present, nor shall anyone whose presence is unnecessary. The search shall be conducted with proper regard to the sensitivity and vulnerability of the detainee.

(b)   Documentation

8.   In the case of an intimate search under paragraph 2, the following shall be recorded as soon as practicable, in the detainee's custody record:

•   the authorisation to carry out the search;

•   the grounds for giving the authorisation;

•   the grounds for believing the article could not be removed without an intimate search

•   which parts of the detainee's body were searched

•   who carried out the search

•   who was present

•   the result.

9.   If an intimate search is carried out by a police officer, the reason why it was impracticable for a registered medical practitioner or registered nurse to conduct it must be recorded.

B   Strip search

10.   A strip search is a search involving the removal of more than outer clothing. In this Code, outer clothing includes shoes and socks.

(a)   Action

11. A strip search may take place only if it is considered necessary to remove an article which a detainee would not be allowed to keep, and the officer reasonably considers the detainee might have concealed such an article. Strip searches shall not be routinely carried out if there is no reason to consider that articles are concealed.

The conduct of strip searches

12. **When strip searches are conducted:**

(a) a police officer carrying out a strip search must be the same sex as the detainee;

(b) the search shall take place in an area where the detainee cannot be seen by anyone who does not need to be present, nor by a member of the opposite sex except an appropriate adult who has been specifically requested by the detainee;

(c) except in cases of urgency, where there is risk of serious harm to the detainee or to others, whenever a strip search involves exposure of intimate body parts, there must be at least two people present other than the detainee, and if the search is of a juvenile or mentally disordered or otherwise mentally vulnerable person, one of the people must be the appropriate adult. Except in urgent cases as above, a search of a juvenile may take place in the absence of the appropriate adult only if the juvenile signifies in the presence of the appropriate adult that they do not want the adult to be present during the search and the adult agrees. A record shall be made of the juvenile's decision and signed by the appropriate adult. The presence of more than two people, other than an appropriate adult, shall be permitted only in the most exceptional circumstances;

(d) the search shall be conducted with proper regard to the sensitivity and vulnerability of the detainee in these circumstances and every reasonable effort shall be made to secure the detainee's co-operation and minimise embarrassment. Detainees who are searched shall not normally be required to remove all their clothes at the same time, e.g. a person should be allowed to remove clothing above the waist and redress before removing further clothing;

(e) if necessary to assist the search, the detainee may be required to hold their arms in the air or to stand with their legs apart and bend forward so a visual examination may be made of the genital and anal areas provided no physical contact is made with any body orifice;

(f) if articles are found, the detainee shall be asked to hand them over. If articles are found within any body orifice other than the mouth, and the detainee refuses to hand them over, their removal would constitute an intimate search, which must be carried out as in Part A;

(g) a strip search shall be conducted as quickly as possible, and the detainee allowed to dress as soon as the procedure is complete.

(b) Documentation

13. A record shall be made on the custody record of a strip search including the reason it was considered necessary, those present and any result.

Notes for guidance

A1 Before authorising any intimate search, the authorising officer must make every reasonable effort to persuade the detainee to hand the article over without a search. If the detainee agrees, a registered medical practitioner or registered nurse should whenever possible be asked to assess the risks involved and, if necessary, attend to assist the detainee.

A2   If the detainee does not agree to hand the article over without a search, the authorising officer must carefully review all the relevant factors before authorising an intimate search. In particular, the officer must consider whether the grounds for believing an article may be concealed are reasonable.

A3   If authority is given for a search under paragraph 2, a registered medical practitioner or registered nurse shall be consulted whenever possible. The presumption should be that the search will be conducted by the registered medical practitioner or registered nurse and the authorising officer must make every reasonable effort to persuade the detainee to allow the medical practitioner or nurse to conduct the search.

A4   A constable should only be authorised to carry out a search as a last resort and when all other approaches have failed. In these circumstances, the authorising officer must be satisfied the detainee might use the article for one or more of the purposes in paragraph 2 and the physical injury likely to be caused is sufficiently severe to justify authorising a constable to carry out the search.

A5   If an officer has any doubts whether to authorise an intimate search by a constable, the officer should seek advice from an officer of superintendent rank or above.

Annex B – Delay in notifying arrest of allowing access to legal advice for persons detained under The Terrorism Act 2000.

A   Delays under TACT Schedule 8

1.   The rights as in sections 5 or 6, may be delayed if the person is detained under the Terrorism Act 2000, section 41, has not yet been charged with an offence and an officer of superintendent rank or above has reasonable grounds for believing the exercise of either right will have one of the following consequences:

(a)   interference with or harm to evidence of a serious offence, (b)   interference with or physical injury to any person,

(c)   the alerting of persons who are suspected of having committed a serious offence but who have not been arrested for it,

(d)   the hindering of the recovery of property obtained as a result of a serious offence or in respect of which a forfeiture order could be made under section 23,

(e)   interference with the gathering of information about the commission, preparation or instigation of acts of terrorism,

(f)   the alerting of a person and thereby making it more difficult to prevent an act of terrorism, or

(g)   the alerting of a person and thereby making it more difficult to secure a person's apprehension, prosecution or conviction in connection with the commission, preparation or instigation of an act of terrorism.

2.   These rights may also be delayed if the officer has reasonable grounds for believing that:

(a)   the detained person has benefited from his criminal conduct (to be decided in accordance with Part 2 of the Proceeds of Crime Act 2002), and

(b)   the recovery of the value of the property constituting the benefit will be hindered by—

(i)   informing the named person of the detained person's detention (in the case of an authorisation under Paragraph 8(1)(a) of Schedule 8 to TACT, or

(ii)   the exercise of the right under paragraph 7 (in the case of an authorisation under Paragraph 8(1)(b) of Schedule 8 to TACT.

3.   Authority to delay a detainee's right to consult privately with a solicitor may be given only if the authorising officer has reasonable grounds to believe the solicitor the detainee wants to consult will, inadvertently or otherwise, pass on a message from the detainee or act in some other way which will have any of the consequences specified under paragraph 8 of Schedule 8 to the Terrorism Act 2000. In these circumstances the detainee must be allowed to choose another solicitor. See Note B3

4.   If the detainee wishes to see a solicitor, access to that solicitor may not be delayed on the grounds they might advise the detainee not to answer questions or the solicitor was initially asked to attend the police station by someone else. In the latter case the detainee must be told the solicitor has come to the police station at another person's request, and must be asked to sign the custody record to signify whether they want to see the solicitor.

5.   The fact the grounds for delaying notification of arrest may be satisfied does not automatically mean the grounds for delaying access to legal advice will also be satisfied.

6.   These rights may be delayed only for as long as is necessary but not beyond 48 hours from the time of arrest (or if a person was being detained under TACT Schedule 7, from the time at which the examination under Schedule 7 began). If the above grounds cease to apply within this time the detainee must as soon as practicable be asked if they wish to exercise either right, the custody record noted accordingly, and action taken in accordance with the relevant section of this Code.

7.   A person must be allowed to consult a solicitor for a reasonable time before any court hearing.

B   Documentation

8.   The grounds for action under this Annex shall be recorded and the detainee informed of them as soon as practicable.

9.   Any reply given by a detainee under paragraph 6 must be recorded and the detainee asked to endorse the record in relation to whether they want to receive legal advice at this point.

C   Cautions and special warnings

10.   When a suspect detained at a police station is interviewed during any period for which access to legal advice has been delayed under this Annex, the court or jury may not draw adverse inferences from their silence.

Notes for guidance

B1   Even if Annex B applies in the case of a juvenile, or a person who is mentally disordered or otherwise mentally vulnerable, action to inform the appropriate adult and the person responsible for a juvenile's welfare if that is a different person, must nevertheless be taken as in paragraph 3.15 and 3.17.

B2   In the case of Commonwealth citizens and foreign nationals, see Note 7A.

B3   A decision to delay access to a specific solicitor is likely to be a rare occurrence and only when it can be shown the suspect is capable of misleading that particular solicitor and there is more than a substantial risk that the suspect will succeed in causing information to be conveyed which will lead to one or more of the specified consequences.

Annex C – Restriction on drawing adverse inferences from silence and terms of the caution when the restriction applies

(a)   The restriction on drawing adverse inferences from silence

1.   The Criminal Justice and Public Order Act 1994, sections 34, 36 and 37 as amended by the Youth Justice and Criminal Evidence Act 1999, section 58 describe the conditions under which adverse inferences may be drawn from a person's failure or refusal to say anything about their involvement in the offence when interviewed, after being charged or informed they may be prosecuted. These provisions are subject to an overriding restriction on the ability of a court or jury to draw adverse inferences from a person's silence. This restriction applies:

(a)   to any detainee at a police station who, before being interviewed, see section 11

or being charged or informed they may be prosecuted, see section 15, has: (i)   asked for legal advice, see section 6, paragraph 6.1;

(ii)   not been allowed an opportunity to consult a solicitor, including the duty solicitor, as in this Code; and

(iii)   not changed their mind about wanting legal advice, see section 6, paragraph 6.7(c)

Note the condition in (ii) will

–   apply when a detainee who has asked for legal advice is interviewed before speaking to a solicitor as in section 6, paragraph 6.6(a) or (b).

–   not apply if the detained person declines to ask for the duty solicitor, see section 6, paragraphs 6.7(b) and (c);

(b)   to any person charged with, or informed they may be prosecuted for, an offence who:

(i)   has had brought to their notice a written statement made by another person or the content of an interview with another person which relates to that offence, see PACE Code C section 16, paragraph 16.6;

(ii)   is interviewed about that offence, see PACE Code C section 16, paragraph 16.8; or

(iii)   makes a written statement about that offence, see Annex D paragraphs 4 and 9.

(b)   Terms of the caution when the restriction applies

2.   When a requirement to caution arises at a time when the restriction on drawing adverse inferences from silence applies, the caution shall be:

'You do not have to say anything, but anything you do say may be given in evidence.'

3.   Whenever the restriction either begins to apply or ceases to apply after a caution has already been given, the person shall be re-cautioned in the appropriate terms. The changed position on drawing inferences and that the previous caution no longer applies shall also be explained to the detainee in ordinary language. See Note C1

Notes for guidance

C1   The following is suggested as a framework to help explain changes in the position on drawing adverse inferences if the restriction on drawing adverse inferences from silence:

(a)   begins to apply:

'The caution you were previously given no longer applies. This is because after that caution:

(i)   you asked to speak to a solicitor but have not yet been allowed an opportunity to speak to a solicitor. See paragraph 1(a); or

(ii)   you have been charged with/informed you may be prosecuted. See paragraph 1(b).

'This means that from now on, adverse inferences cannot be drawn at court and your defence will not be harmed just because you choose to say nothing. Please listen carefully to the caution I am about to give you because it will apply from now on. You will see that it does not say anything about your defence being harmed.'

(b)   ceases to apply before or at the time the person is charged or informed they may be prosecuted, see paragraph 1(a);

'The caution you were previously given no longer applies. This is because after that caution you have been allowed an opportunity to speak to a solicitor. Please listen carefully to the caution I am about to give you because it will apply from now on. It explains how your defence at court may be affected if you choose to say nothing.'

Annex D – Written statements under caution

(a)   Written by a person under caution

1.   A person shall always be invited to write down what they want to say.

2.   A person who has not been charged with, or informed they may be prosecuted for, any offence to which the statement they want to write relates, shall:

(a)   unless the statement is made at a time when the restriction on drawing adverse inferences from silence applies, see Annex C, be asked to write out and sign the following before writing what they want to say:

'I make this statement of my own free will. I understand that I do not have to say anything but that it may harm my defence if I do not mention when questioned something which I later rely on in court. This statement may be given in evidence.';

(b)   if the statement is made at a time when the restriction on drawing adverse inferences from silence applies, be asked to write out and sign the following before writing what they want to say;

'I make this statement of my own free will. I understand that I do not have to say anything. This statement may be given in evidence.'

3.   When a person, on the occasion of being charged with or informed they may be prosecuted for any offence, asks to make a statement which relates to any such offence and wants to write it they shall:

(a)   unless the restriction on drawing adverse inferences from silence, see Annex C, applied when they were so charged or informed they may be prosecuted, be asked to write out and sign the following before writing what they want to say:

'I make this statement of my own free will. I understand that I do not have to say anything but that it may harm my defence if I do not mention when questioned something which I later rely on in court. This statement may be given in evidence.';

(b)   if the restriction on drawing adverse inferences from silence applied when they were so charged or informed they may be prosecuted, be asked to write out and sign the following before writing what they want to say:

'I make this statement of my own free will. I understand that I do not have to say anything. This statement may be given in evidence.'

4.   When a person, who has already been charged with or informed they may be prosecuted for any offence, asks to make a statement which relates to any such offence and wants to write it they shall be asked to write out and sign the following before writing what they want to say:

'I make this statement of my own free will. I understand that I do not have to say anything. This statement may be given in evidence.';

5.   Any person writing their own statement shall be allowed to do so without any prompting except a police officer or other police staff may indicate to them which matters are material or question any ambiguity in the statement.

(b)   Written by a police officer or other police staff

6.   If a person says they would like someone to write the statement for them, a police officer, or other police staff shall write the statement.

7.   If the person has not been charged with, or informed they may be prosecuted for, any offence to which the statement they want to make relates they shall, before starting, be asked to sign, or make their mark, to the following:

(a)   unless the statement is made at a time when the restriction on drawing adverse inferences from silence applies, see Annex C:

'I, ..., wish to make a statement. I want someone to write down what I say. I understand that I do not have to say anything but that it may harm my defence if I do not mention when questioned something which I later rely on in court. This statement may be given in evidence.';

(b)   if the statement is made at a time when the restriction on drawing adverse inferences from silence applies:

'I, ..., wish to make a statement. I want someone to write down what I say. I understand that I do not have to say anything. This statement may be given in evidence.'

8.   If, on the occasion of being charged with or informed they may be prosecuted for any offence, the person asks to make a statement which relates to any such offence they shall before starting be asked to sign, or make their mark to, the following:

(a)   unless the restriction on drawing adverse inferences from silence applied, see Annex C, when they were so charged or informed they may be prosecuted:

'I, ..., wish to make a statement. I want someone to write down what I say. I understand that I do not have to say anything but that it may harm my defence if I do not mention when questioned something which I later rely on in court. This statement may be given in evidence.';

(b)   if the restriction on drawing adverse inferences from silence applied when they were so charged or informed they may be prosecuted:

'I, ..., wish to make a statement. I want someone to write down what I say. I understand that I do not have to say anything. This statement may be given in evidence.'

9.   If, having already been charged with or informed they may be prosecuted for any offence, a person asks to make a statement which relates to any such offence they shall before starting, be asked to sign, or make their mark to:

'I, ..., wish to make a statement. I want someone to write down what I say. I understand that I do not have to say anything. This statement may be given in evidence.'

10.   The person writing the statement must take down the exact words spoken by the person making it and must not edit or paraphrase it. Any questions that are necessary, e.g. to make it more intelligible, and the answers given must be recorded at the same time on the statement form.

11.   When the writing of a statement is finished the person making it shall be asked to read it and to make any corrections, alterations or additions they want. When they have finished reading they shall be asked to write and sign or make their mark on the following certificate at the end of the statement:

'I have read the above statement, and I have been able to correct, alter or add anything I wish. This statement is true. I have made it of my own free will.'

12.   If the person making the statement cannot read, or refuses to read it, or to write the above mentioned certificate at the end of it or to sign it, the person taking the statement shall read it to them and ask them if they would like to correct, alter or add anything and to put their signature or make their mark at the end. The person taking the statement shall certify on the statement itself what has occurred.

Annex E – Summary of provisions relating to mentally disordered and otherwise mentally vulnerable people

1.   If an officer has any suspicion, or is told in good faith, that a person of any age may be mentally disordered or otherwise mentally vulnerable, or mentally incapable of understanding the significance of questions or their replies that person shall be treated as mentally disordered or otherwise mentally vulnerable for the purposes of this Code. See paragraph 1.10

2.   In the case of a person who is mentally disordered or otherwise mentally vulnerable, 'the appropriate adult' means:

(a)   a relative, guardian or other person responsible for their care or custody;

(b)   someone experienced in dealing with mentally disordered or mentally vulnerable people but who is not a police officer or employed by the police;

(c)   failing these, some other responsible adult aged 18 or over who is not a police officer or employed by the police.

See paragraph 1.13(b) and Note 1D

3.   If the detention of a person who is mentally vulnerable or appears to be suffering from a mental disorder is authorised by the review officer (see paragraphs 14.1 and 14.2 and Notes for Guidance 14A and 14B) , the custody officer must as soon as practicable inform the appropriate adult of the grounds for detention and the person's whereabouts, and ask the adult to come to the police station to see them. If the appropriate adult:

•   is already at the station when information is given as in paragraphs 3.1 to 3.5 the information must be given in their presence

•   is not at the station when the provisions of paragraph 3.1 to 3.5 are complied with these provisions must be complied with again in their presence once they arrive.

See paragraphs 3.15 to 3.16

4.   If the appropriate adult, having been informed of the right to legal advice, considers legal advice should be taken, the provisions of section 6 apply as if the mentally disordered or otherwise mentally vulnerable person had requested access to legal advice. See paragraph 3.20 and Note E1.

5.   The custody officer must make sure a person receives appropriate clinical attention as soon as reasonably practicable if the person appears to be suffering from a mental disorder or in urgent cases immediately call the nearest health care professional or an ambulance. It is not intended these provisions delay the transfer of a detainee to a place of safety under the Mental Health Act 1983, section 136 if that is applicable. If an assessment under that Act is to take place at a police station, the custody officer must consider whether an appropriate health care professional should be called to conduct an initial clinical check on the detainee. See paragraph 9.6 and 9.8

6.   If a mentally disordered or otherwise mentally vulnerable person is cautioned in the absence of the appropriate adult, the caution must be repeated in the appropriate adult's presence. See paragraph 10.11

7.   A mentally disordered or otherwise mentally vulnerable person must not be interviewed or asked to provide or sign a written statement in the absence of the appropriate adult unless the

provisions of paragraphs 11.2 or 11.11 to 11.13 apply. Questioning in these circumstances may not continue in the absence of the appropriate adult once sufficient information to avert the risk has been obtained. A record shall be made of the grounds for any decision to begin an interview in these circumstances. See paragraphs 11.2, 11.9 and 11.11 to 11.13

8.   If the appropriate adult is present at an interview, they shall be informed they are not expected to act simply as an observer and the purposes of their presence are to:

•   advise the interviewee

•   observe whether or not the interview is being conducted properly and fairly

•   facilitate communication with the interviewee

See paragraph 11.10

9.   If the custody officer charges a mentally disordered or otherwise mentally vulnerable person with an offence or takes such other action as is appropriate when there is sufficient evidence for a prosecution this must be done in the presence of the appropriate adult. The written notice embodying any charge must be given to the appropriate adult. See paragraphs PACE Code C Section 16.

10.   An intimate or strip search of a mentally disordered or otherwise mentally vulnerable person may take place only in the presence of the appropriate adult of the same sex, unless the detainee specifically requests the presence of a particular adult of the opposite sex. A strip search may take place in the absence of an appropriate adult only in cases of urgency when there is a risk of serious harm to the detainee or others. See Annex A, paragraphs 6 and 12(c)

11.   Particular care must be taken when deciding whether to use any form of approved restraints on a mentally disordered or otherwise mentally vulnerable person in a locked cell. See paragraph 8.2

Notes for guidance

E1   The purpose of the provision at paragraph 3.20 is to protect the rights of a mentally disordered or otherwise mentally vulnerable detained person who does not understand the significance of what is said to them. If the detained person wants to exercise the right to legal advice, the appropriate action should be taken and not delayed until the appropriate adult arrives. A mentally disordered or otherwise mentally vulnerable detained person should always be given an opportunity, when an appropriate adult is called to the police station, to consult privately with a solicitor in the absence of the appropriate adult if they want.

E2   Although people who are mentally disordered or otherwise mentally vulnerable are often capable of providing reliable evidence, they may, without knowing or wanting to do so, be particularly prone in certain circumstances to provide information that may be unreliable, misleading or self-incriminating. Special care should always be taken when questioning such a person, and the appropriate adult should be involved if there is any doubt about a person's mental state or capacity. Because of the risk of unreliable evidence, it is important to obtain corroboration of any facts admitted whenever possible.

E3   Because of the risks referred to in Note E2, which the presence of the appropriate adult is intended to minimise, officers of superintendent rank or above should exercise their discretion to authorise the commencement of an interview in the appropriate adult's absence only in exceptional cases, if it is necessary to avert an immediate risk of serious harm. See paragraphs 11.2, 11.11 to 11.13

Annex F – Countries with which bilateral consular conventions or agreements requiring notification of the arrest and detention of their nationals are in force.

Armenia, Austria, Azerbaijan, Belarus, Belgium, Bosnia-Herzegovina, Bulgaria, China*, Croatia, Cuba, Czech Republic, Denmark, Egypt, France, Georgia, German Federal Republic, Greece, Hungary, Italy, Japan, Kazakhstan, Macedonia, Mexico, Moldova, Mongolia, Norway, Poland, Romania, Russia, Slovak, Republic, Slovenia, Spain, Sweden, Tajikistan, Turkmenistan, Ukraine, USA, Uzbekistan, Yugoslavia

* Police are required to inform Chinese officials of arrest/detention in the Manchester consular district only. This comprises Derbyshire, Durham, Greater Manchester, Lancashire, Merseyside, North South and West Yorkshire, and Tyne and Wear.

Annex G – Fitness to be interviewed

1.   This Annex contains general guidance to help police officers and health care professionals assess whether a detainee might be at risk in an interview.

2.   A detainee may be at risk in a interview if it is considered that:

(a)   conducting the interview could significantly harm the detainee's physical or mental state;

(b)   anything the detainee says in the interview about their involvement or suspected involvement in the offence about which they are being interviewed might be considered unreliable in subsequent court proceedings because of their physical or mental state.

3.   In assessing whether the detainee should be interviewed, the   following must be considered:

(a)   how the detainee's physical or mental state might affect their ability to understand the nature and purpose of the interview, to comprehend what is being asked and to appreciate the significance of any answers given and make rational decisions about whether they want to say anything;

(b)   the extent to which the detainee's replies may be affected by their physical or mental condition rather than representing a rational and accurate explanation of their involvement in the offence;

(c)   how the nature of the interview, which could include particularly probing questions, might affect the detainee.

4.   It is essential health care professionals who are consulted consider the functional ability of the detainee rather than simply relying on a medical diagnosis, e.g. it is possible for a person with severe mental illness to be fit for interview.

5.   Health care professionals should advise on the need for an appropriate adult to be present, whether reassessment of the person's fitness for interview may be necessary if the interview lasts beyond a specified time, and whether a further specialist opinion may be required.

6.   When health care professionals identify risks they should be asked to quantify the risks.

They should inform the custody officer:

- whether the person's condition:

– is likely to improve

– will require or be amenable to treatment; and

- indicate how long it may take for such improvement to take effect

7.   The role of the health care professional is to consider the risks and advise the custody officer of the outcome of that consideration. The health care professional's determination and any advice or recommendations should be made in writing and form part of the custody record.

8.   Once the health care professional has provided that information, it is a matter for the custody officer to decide whether or not to allow the interview to go ahead and if the interview is to proceed, to determine what safeguards are needed. Nothing prevents safeguards being provided in addition to those required under the Code. An example might be to have an appropriate health care professional present during the interview, in addition to an appropriate adult, in order constantly to monitor the person's condition and how it is being affected by the interview.

Annex H – Detained person: observation list

1.   If any detainee fails to meet any of the following criteria, an appropriate health care professional or an ambulance must be called.

2.   When assessing the level of rousability, consider:

Rousability – can they be woken?

- go into the cell

- call their name

- shake gently

Response to questions – can they give appropriate answers to questions such as:

- What's your name?

- Where do you live?

- Where do you think you are?

Response to commands – can they respond appropriately to commands such as:

- Open your eyes!

- Lift one arm, now the other arm!

3.   Remember to take into account the possibility or presence of other illnesses, injury, or mental condition, a person who is drowsy and smells of alcohol may also have the following:

- Diabetes

- Epilepsy

- Head injury

- Drug intoxication or overdose

- Stroke

Appendix 3 – ACPO Gravity Matrix

The following pages show various tables that can be applied to the gravity factor system; the first page deals with offences that would usually be excluded from the options of reprimand or warning, though in exceptional circumstances the general factors may be so significant that they could influence a reduction in gravity; the second and third pages list a number of general factors that might aggravate or mitigate the commission of any type of offence, including excluded offences in exceptional circumstances; and the remaining pages show lists of offences together with their standard gravity scores and those offence specific gravity factors that are considered appropriate to aggravate or mitigate each type of offence, according to the particular circumstances surrounding it. However, it should be remembered throughout the process that each case must be considered on its own merits.

The Criminal Justice Act 2003 passed the responsibility for making charging decisions from the police to the CPS in all indictable only, either way or summary offences, except those cases specified in the Director's Guidance, which the police may continue to charge. The police may still take the decision to issue a reprimand or final warning in all summary and either way offences without reference to the CPS where the police consider that the youth is eligible for diversion.

NB All indictable only offences must be referred to the CPS to decide whether to charge or divert, as only the CPS can make this decision.

The Final Gravity Score

The presumptions applicable to the final gravity score reached, when all the relevant factors have been applied to the circumstances of a particular offence, are listed in the table below. This must be used in conjunction with the legislation in relation to the offender's qualification for reprimand, warning or charge. Where this assessment leads the police officer to consider a warning or charge there is also the option to ask the Youth offending team to undertake a prior assessment of the young offender to inform their decision-making process.

FINAL SCORE	ACTION
4	**Normally result in charge.**
3	**Normally warn for a first offence. If offender does not qualify for a warning then charge. Only in exceptional circumstances should a reprimand be given. Decision maker needs to justify reprimand.**
2	**Normally reprimand for a first offence. If offender does not qualify for a reprimand but qualifies for a warning then give warning. If offender does not qualify for a warning then charge.**
1	**Always the minimum response applicable to the individual offender, i.e. reprimand, warning or charge.**

Discretion does exist to deviate from the normal response, as indicated above, but only in exceptional circumstances, and such action would need to be justified by the decision maker. It would be impossible to articulate those circumstances which could be deemed to be exceptional, but decision makers will be aware that even the most serious of offences could amount to technical offences, the circumstances of which might appropriately attract a reprimand or warning. It would often be inappropriate to charge in such cases.

An 'informal warning', which falls outside the parameters of the table above, should only be given in exceptional circumstances where a minimal response is appropriate and usually when anti-social behaviour falls short of a substantive criminal offence. It may be administered instantly by the officer in the case, or by letter if the decision is made by a police decision-maker, when the case against the young person is unlikely to be proceeded with in the Youth Court.

'No Further Action' also has not been included in the above table as it is not so much a method of disposal for an admitted case of a young offender, as an acknowledgement that no action is appropriate or warranted in a particular case. No substantive offence can be mitigated down to warrant no further action, using the gravity factor decision process alone.

LIST OF EXCLUDED OFFENCES

Abduction - girl under 16 years	Paying for sexual services of child under 13 with penetration
Arson - with intent to endanger life / reckless whether life endangered	Perjury
Assault - GBH/wounding with intent	Pervert course of justice, inc. conspiracy/attempt
Assault by penetration	Poison - administer/cause to be administered noxious substances with intent to injure etc.
Bail personation	
	Prison - escape/aid/assist
Blackmail	
	Rape
Burglary - aggravated	
	Riot
Burglary with intent to commit indictable only offence	
	Robbery & assault with intent to rob
Causing/inciting person to engage in sexual activity without consent but with penetration	Sexual activity with person with mental disorder with penetration
Child destruction	Suicide/attempted - aid/abet/counsel
Corrosive fluid etc. throw with intent to maim etc.	Trespass with Intent to Commit Sexual Offence
Criminal damage - with intent to endanger life/ reckless as to whether life endangered	Traffic:
	• death by dangerous driving

Escape - from lawful custody	
	• death by careless driving aggravated by drugs or drink
Explosive substances offences (most)	
	• Refusing to provide specimen of breath/blood/urine at police station.
False imprisonment	
	• Excess alcohol/driving when unfit through drink/drugs
Firearm - possession with intent to endanger life/injure property	
Firearm - possession while committing offence or with intent to commit offence or use to resist arrest	• drunk in charge
	• driving whilst disqualified
Infanticide	
	• Speeding (above fixed penalty speed)
Kidnap	
	• wanton and furious driving
Murder / Manslaughter	

General factors for consideration

The circumstances surrounding the offence should always be taken into account in determining the most appropriate response. There are a number of general factors that can affect the decision about how to proceed. These are set out in the next two tables below.

Important: only one reprimand may be given. Where an offender has already received a reprimand, the minimum response will be a warning. Only one warning may normally be given. A second warning is only available where the previous offence was committed more that 2 years ago, and the offence is minor. Where an offender has already been warned, a further offence should normally result in a charge.

GENERAL FACTORS FOR ALL OFFENCES

(+)	(-)
Conviction is likely to result in significant sentence.	Conviction is likely to result in unusually small or nominal penalty.
Weapon used or violence threatened during commission of offence.	Prosecution is likely to have bad effect on victim's physical or mental health.
Offence against public servant (e.g. police, nurse, council employee, etc.)	Offender supplied information which reduced risk, loss or harm to others.
Offender abused a position of trust - e.g. banker, baby-sitter, shop assistant.	Offender was influenced by others more criminally sophisticated.
Offender was ringleader / organiser.	Genuine mistake or misunderstanding.
Evidence of premeditation.	Vulnerability of the offender.
Offender was part of an organised team or offence was committed by a group.	Provocation from victim or victim's group and offender reacted impulsively.
Victim was vulnerable, deliberately put in considerable fear or suffered personal attack, damage, disturbance, or domestic violence.	The offence is minor and offender has put right harm or loss caused; has expressed regret; offered reparation or compensation.
Offence motivated by discrimination against victim's racial or ethnic origin religious beliefs, gender, political views or sexual preference.	Offender is or was at time of offence suffering from significant mental or physical ill-health and offence is not likely to be repeated.
There are grounds for believing the offence is likely to be repeated or continued - e.g. by a history of recurring conduct.	The offence is so old that the relevance of any response is minimised, i.e. there has been a long delay between the offence occurring and the point of decision making - Unless the offence is
Evidence of exploitation.	
The offence, though minor, is prevalent in the local area - as identified in the local crime audit, specified in the youth justice plan or specifically agreed with CPS to warrant more serious response.	serious; the offender contributed to the delay; the offence only recently came to light; or the complexity of the offence has contributed to long investigation.
Offence committed with intent to commit a sexual offence	

GENERAL FACTORS FOR TRAFFIC OFFENCES

(+)	(-)
serious injury caused to public or significant damage caused	genuine oversight, technicality of the offence or emergency circumstances
multiple offenders involved in similar offences at same time/location	no danger caused to public

(+)	(-)
potential risk to public or resultant danger	lack of knowledge

OFFENCE SPECIFIC GRAVITY FACTORS

OFFENCE	GRAVITY SCORE	AGGRAVATING/MITIGATING FACTORS	
		+	-
ABDUCTION			
Abduction of Girl Under 16 Yrs	4	**Defer Decision to CPS**	
Kidnap	4	**Defer Decision to CPS**	
False Imprisonment	4	**Defer Decision to CPS**	
ANIMALS			
Causing unnecessary suffering by doing any act (Protection of Animals Act 1911)	3	* serious injury	*minor injury
Causing unnecessary suffering by omitting to do any act (1911 Act)	2	*Not following instructions	*Instructions not given
Cruelly ill-treat etc (1911 Act)	3	*Premeditated instigator	*Reckless participant
Permitting ill-treatment (1911 Act)	2		
Abandonment (Abandonment of Animals Act 1961)	3	*Animal dies	*Animal survives
Dog Worrying Livestock	2		* No apparent injury
Poaching Offences	2	* Organised/Sophistication * Commercial purpose	
Dangerous Dog (Order to be kept under control or destroyed)	4		* Dog destroyed
Abandoning, or allowing to stray, a fighting dog (Sec. 1.2e Dangerous Dogs Act 1991)	4		* Dog destroyed
Possession without exemption of a Pit Bull Terrier, Japanese Tosa or other Designated Fighting Dog (Sec. 1.3 Dangerous Dogs Act 1991)	4		* Dog destroyed
Owner or Person in Charge allowing dog to be dangerously out of control in a Public Place injuring any person (Sec. 3.1 Dangerous Dogs Act 1991)	3	* Serious injury * No effort to control	* Minor Injury * Dog destroyed * Beyond physical limitation of owner/ person in charge * First time in charge
Owner or Person in Charge allowing dog to be dangerously out of control in a Public Place, no injury being caused (Sec. 3.1 Dangerous Dogs Act 1991)	3	* Person placed in fear * Intent/disregard	* No injury/fear * Dog destroyed * Circumstances beyond the control of the offender

OFFENCE	GRAVITY SCORE	AGGRAVATING/MITIGATING FACTORS	
		+	-
Owner or Person in Charge allowing dog to enter a Non-Public Place, and injure any person (Sec. 3.3 Dangerous Dogs Act 1991)	3	* Serious injury	* Minor Injury * Dog destroyed
Owner or Person in Charge allowing dog enter a Non-Public Place, causing Reasonable Apprehension that it would injure a person (Sec. 3.3 Dangerous Dogs Act 1991)	3	* Intent/disregard	* Dog destroyed * Circumstances beyond the control of the offender
Allowing a Fighting Dog to be in a Public Place without a Muzzle or a Lead (Sec. 1.2d Dangerous Dogs Act 1991)	4	* Fear/injury caused	* Escaped despite precautions * Dog destroyed
ANTI-SOCIAL BEHAVIOUR			
Breach of ASBO	3	* Flagrant breach	* Unaware of consequence of breach
Breach of ISO	3	* Flagrant breach	* Unaware of consequence of breach
Failing to disperse	2	* Flagrant breach	
ASSAULTS			
Threats to Kill (Section 16 OAP Act 1861)	3	* Calculated	* Threat made in heat of the moment - no likelihood of violence now existing
Poison - Administer/Cause to be Administered noxious substance with Intent to Injure, etc.	4	**Defer Decision to CPS**	
Corrosive Fluid etc. - Throw with Intent to Maim etc.	4	**Defer Decision to CPS**	
GBH/Wounding with Intent (Section 18 OAP Act 1861)	4	**Defer Decision to CPS**	
GBH/Wounding (Section 20 OAP Act 1861)	4	* Weapon used * More than one blow * Unprovoked attack * Premeditation * Group action * Domestic violence	* Impulsive action * Provocation * Nature of the injury (especially where superficial wound)
ABH (Section 47 OAP Act 1861)	3	* Weapon used * More than one blow	* Impulsive action * Provocation

OFFENCE	GRAVITY SCORE	AGGRAVATING/MITIGATING FACTORS	
		+	-
		* Attacked while victim 'vulnerable/ defenceless' e.g., 'on floor' * Unprovoked attack * Nature of the injury (especially where serious /disfiguring injury) * Premeditation * Domestic violence * Group action	* Minor injury
Assault on Police (Section 51 Police Act 1996)	3	* Sustained assault * Attempt to prevent arrest of another * Weapon used * Premeditation * Any injuries caused * Group action	
Common Assault (Section 39 Criminal Justice Act 1988)	2	* Significant injury caused * Deliberate aggression without provocation * Vulnerable victim * Weapon used * Premeditation * Domestic violence * Group action	* Trivial nature of action * Impulsive action * Injury very minor
BURGLARY			
Aggravated Burglary	4	**Defer Decision to CPS**	
Burglary with Intent to inflict GBH	4		
Burglary with Intent to Steal/Criminal Damage	3	* Night-time * Occupier present * Deliberately frightening	* Vacant premises * Low value * Coercion from others

OFFENCE	GRAVITY SCORE	AGGRAVATING/MITIGATING FACTORS	
		+	-
Burglary Dwelling	4	occupants * Soiling / ransacking / damage	in group on reluctant offender
Burglary Non-Dwelling	3	* Professional operation * Group offence * 'Ram-raiding' * Unrecovered property of considerable value	
CRIMINAL DAMAGE			
Criminal Damage	2	* Damage deliberate rather than reckless * Potential of greater danger * Group offence * Damage £500+ approx.	* Damage £100 or less
Arson (where life not endangered)	3	* Damage deliberate * Potential of greater danger * Group offence * Damage £500+ approx.	* Damage £100 or less
Criminal Damage (including Arson) with Intent to Endanger Life or Reckless as to whether Life is Endangered	4	**Defer Decision to CPS**	
Threat to Destroy Property of Another	2	* Intent to cause fear * Potential value of damage £500+ (approx.)	* Potential value of damage £100 or less
Possession of Articles with Intent to Commit Criminal Damage	2	* Evidence of intent to commit serious criminal damage * Potential value of damage £500+ (approx.)	* Potential value of damage £100 or less
CROSSBOWS			
Purchase/Hire of Crossbow or Part by Person Under 17 (Sec. 2 Crossbows Act 1987)	2	* Supply by Dealer * Aware it was an offence	

OFFENCE	GRAVITY SCORE	AGGRAVATING/MITIGATING FACTORS	
		+	-
		* Evidence of discharge in public place	
Possession of Crossbow or Part by Person Under 17 (Sec. 3 Crossbows Act 1987)	2	* Aware it was an offence * Evidence of discharge in public place	
CRUELTY			
Cruelty/Ill Treatment to a child in a manner likely to cause unnecessary suffering or injury	3	* Persistent neglect * Sadistic violence * Repeated violence * Substantial injury * Premeditation	
DEATHS			
Suicide/Attempted Suicide – aid/abet/counsel	4	**Defer Decision to CPS**	
Child Destruction	4	**Defer Decision to CPS**	
Infanticide	4	**Defer Decision to CPS**	
Familial Homicide	4	**Defer Decision to CPS**	
Murder/Manslaughter	4	**Defer Decision to CPS**	
DRUGS			
CLASS 'A' DRUG – Supply or Possession with intent to supply	4		
CLASS 'B' or 'C' DRUG Supply or Possession with intent to supply	4		* Group of people pooling resources to buy a supply to share between them. * No profit made
CLASS 'A' DRUG Possession	3	* In prison establishment * Large quantity	* Small quantity consistent with personal use
CLASS 'B' or 'C' DRUG Possession	2	* In prison establishment * Large quantity	* Small quantity consistent with personal use
CLASS 'A' DRUG Production	4	* Commercial cultivation * Large quantity	* Small quantity consistent with personal use
CLASS 'B' or 'C' DRUG Production or Cultivation	4		* Small quantity consistent with personal use
Permit use of premises for smoking Cannabis or Cannabis Resin	2	* On commercial basis * Evidence of widespread	* Vulnerable offender

OFFENCE	GRAVITY SCORE	AGGRAVATING/MITIGATING FACTORS	
		+	-
		use	
DRUNKENNESS			
Drunk and Disorderly	1	* Risk of escalation * Busy public place * Offensive language or behaviour * Threatening	* Only witnessed by a police officer and little inconvenience to public * Non-threatening
Drunk and Incapable	1	* Serious alcohol problem	
FALSE MESSAGES			
Bomb Hoax (Section 51 Criminal Law Act 1977)	3	* 'Copy-cat' scenario * Existing climate of fear * Caused dangerous or large scale evacuation i.e. hospital, sporting event * Serious financial loss	* Obvious to recipient that a hoax
Sending Malicious Communication (Section 1 Malicious Communication Act 1988)	3	* Persistency	* Obvious to recipient that a hoax
False Alarms to Emergency Services (Section 43 Telecomms Act 1984)	2	*Persistency	*Obvious to recipient that a hoax
(Also specific offence of False Fire Alarm under Section 31 Fire Services Act 1947)	2	*Persistency	*Obvious to recipient that a hoax
Other False Emergency Calls (Section 43 Telecomms Act 1984)	2	* Persistency	* Obvious to recipient that a hoax
Improper use of Telecom Systems (Section 43 Telecomms Act 1984)	3	* Persistency * Sexual and/or sadistic in nature	* Obvious to recipient that a hoax
FIREARMS			
Possession of firearm with intent to endanger life/injure property (Section 16 Firearms Act 1968)	4	**Defer Decision to CPS**	

OFFENCE	GRAVITY SCORE	AGGRAVATING/MITIGATING FACTORS	
		+	-
Possession of firearm while committing offence or with intent to commit offence (Section 17 & 18 of 1968 Act)	4	**Defer Decision to CPS**	
Carrying in public place (Section 19 of 1968 Act) Loaded firearm Unloaded air weapon/imitation firearm	 3 2	* Type of weapon * Discharge of weapon	
Trespass in building with loaded firearm (Section 20 of 1968 Act)	3	* Type of weapon * Discharge of weapon	
Person under 17 purchasing firearm or ammunition (Section 22 of 1968 Act)	2	* Type of weapon	
Person under 17 having air weapon in public place (Section 22 of 1968 Act)	2	* Impact on the public * Aware it was an offence * Evidence of firing	
Supply (including sale) firearm or ammunition to person under 17 (Section 24 of 1968 Act)	2	* Supply by firearms dealer	
Possession of firearm/shotgun without certificate (Section 1.1 and Section 2.1) a) No certificate ever held b) Following non-renewal	 3	* Any form of usage or possession in public * Type/construction of weapons e.g. sawn-off, prohibited etc.	
	2	* History of slow renewal * Deliberate avoidance of renewal procedure	
Making false statement to procure grant/ renewal/ variation of firearm/ shotgun certificate (Sec. 26.5 & 29.3 of 1968 Act)	3	* Previous conviction(s) omitted which would affect decision to grant/ renew/vary certificate * Deliberate supply of false information	
Failure to comply with condition of certificate relating to security of weapons (Sec. 1.2 & 2.2 of	2	* Degree of carelessness * Previous history of	

OFFENCE	GRAVITY SCORE	AGGRAVATING/MITIGATING FACTORS	
		+	-
1968 Act)		insecurity * Certificate held for period of time - therefore knew of the requirement	
FOOTBALL GROUNDS			
Throwing a missile in ground (Section 2 Football (Offences) Act 1991)	2	* Likelihood of injury * Incitement factors	* No injury or minor injuries
Taking part in racial or indecent chanting (Section 3 Football (Offences) Act 1991)	3	* Intent to incite others to stir up racial hatred * Risk of escalation	* Isolated incident
Going into the playing area or adjacent area without lawful authority or excuse (Section 4 Football (Offences) Act 1991)	2	* Risk of escalation	* No threatening circumstances
Breach of Football Banning Order (14A or 14B) Footbal Spectators Act 1989)	3		* Unaware that Order was in force
FORGERY			
Making a false document (Section 1 Forgery & Counterfeiting Act 1981)	2	* Nature of document & potential consequences * Organised team * Sophistication	* Poverty/personal need * Coercion from others
Using a false document (Section 3 Forgery & Counterfeiting Act 1981)	2	* Nature of document & potential consequences * Organised team * Sophistication	* Poverty/personal need * Coercion from others
Possessing a false document with intent (Section 5 Forgery & Counterfeiting Act 1981)	2	* Nature of document & potential consequences * Organised team * Sophistication	* Poverty/personal need * Coercion from others
Forgery of documents etc. (Road Traffic Act 1988)	2	* Nature of document & potential consequences * Organised team * Sophistication	* Poverty/personal need * Coercion from others
INTERFERENCE WITH THE COURSE OF JUSTICE			
Conspiracy/Attempt to pervert the course of justice	4	**Defer Decision to CPS**	
Perjury	4	**Defer Decision to CPS**	
Bail personation	4	**Defer Decision to CPS**	

OFFENCE	GRAVITY SCORE	AGGRAVATING/MITIGATING FACTORS	
		+	-
Escape from lawful custody	4	Defer Decision to CPS	
Prison - escape/aid/assist	4	Defer Decision to CPS	
MISCELLANEOUS			
Most non-recordable offences	1		
Breach of by-laws	1		*Not a local resident
OBSTRUCTION			
Obstruct Police (Section 51 Police Act 1964)	1	* Attempt to prevent arrest of another * Premeditation * Group action * Violence used or threatened	
Wilful obstruction of highway	2	* Close to traffic hazard e.g. school	* Brief period only * No considerable problems caused to other road users and/or pedestrians
OFFENSIVE WEAPONS			
Possession of Offensive Weapon	3	* Method of use * Concern caused to member(s) of public * Degree of danger	
Possession of Sharp Pointed Blade	3	* Method of use * Concern caused to member(s) of public	* Genuine oversight in retaining blade after a lawful possession
PUBLIC ORDER			
Riot (Section 1)	4	Defer Decision to CPS	
Violent Disorder (Section 2)	3	* Planned/premeditated * Use of weapons * Busy public place * Large group * People put in fear * Damage caused	
Affray (Section 3)	3	* Use of weapons * Busy public place	

OFFENCE	GRAVITY SCORE	AGGRAVATING/MITIGATING FACTORS	
		+	-
		* Group action * People put in fear * Damage caused	
Threatening abusive or insulting words or behaviour intended to cause fear of violence or to provoke violence (Section 4)	2	* Risk of escalation * Use of weapons * Busy public place * Group action * People put in fear	* No risk of escalation
Intentional causing harassment, alarm or distress through threatening abusive or insulting words, behaviour or display (Section 4A)	3	* Racial overtones * Risk of escalation * Group action	* No risk of escalation
Threatening abusive or insulting words or behaviour likely to cause harassment, alarm or distress (Section 5)	2	* Risk of escalation * Group action	* No risk of escalation * Isolated incident
ROAD TRAFFIC			
Causing Death by Dangerous Driving (Section 1 Road Traffic Act 1988)	4	**Defer Decision to CPS**	
Causing Death by Careless Driving under the influence of drink or drugs (Section 3 Road Traffic Act 1988)	4	**Defer Decision to CPS**	
Driving whilst Disqualified	4		
Excess Alcohol/Driving when unfit through Drink/Drugs	4		
Refuse to provide specimen of breath/blood/urine at police stn.	4		
Drunk in Charge	4		
Driving after false declaration as to physical fitness/failing to notify disability and refusal or revocation of licence (Sections 92-94 Road Traffic Act 1988)	2		* Voluntary surrender of licence
Dangerous Driving (Section 2 Road Traffic Act 1988)	4	* Avoiding detection or apprehension * Competitive driving, racing, showing off * Disregard of warnings e.g., from passengers or	* Continuing for only a short period * Contributed to by action of another

OFFENCE	GRAVITY SCORE	AGGRAVATING/MITIGATING FACTORS	
		+	-
		others in vicinity * Evidence alcohol/drugs * Excessive speed * Prolonged, persistent, deliberate bad driving * Serious risk	
Failing to Stop after Accident/Failure to Report Accident	3	* Blatant disregard of need * Serious injury & failure to remain at scene * Serious injury and/or serious damage * Evidence of impairment	* No intent to evade liability for the offence * Genuine belief that relevant person aware * Negligible damage
Careless Driving (Section 3 Road Traffic Act 1988) Inconsiderate Driving (Section 3 Road Traffic Act 1988)	3 2	* Major error of judgement * Excessive speed * Driving with disregard for road safety taking account of road, weather and/or traffic conditions * Re-Test may be appropriate– Sec.36 Road Traffic Off. Act 1988 * Disability - Section 22 RTOA 1988 * Deliberate act of selfishness, impatience or aggressiveness causing inconvenience	* Minor error of judgement * Defect in road surface/signing, etc. * Momentary lapse * Adverse weather conditions * Both (or more) drivers may have been at fault
a)Vehicle left in dangerous position b)Tampering with vehicle (Sec. 25 RTA 1988) c)Causing danger to other road users (Sec. 22a RTA 1988)	2 3 3	*Potential or actual danger intended Danger of serious injury to other road users	
Failure to provide roadside test	2		
Speeding (above fixed penalty	4		

OFFENCE	GRAVITY SCORE	AGGRAVATING/MITIGATING FACTORS	
		+	-
speed)			
Wanton and Furious Driving/Riding	4	**Defer Decision to CPS**	
ROAD TRAFFIC DOCUMENTS			
Driving other than in accordance with driving licence ie		* Blatant disregard of need	
No 'L' plates			
'L' driver unaccompanied	2		
'L' driver carrying passengers	2		
No driving licence	2		
	3		
Drive vehicle subject to Prohibition Notice (Sec 71(1) Road Traffic Act 1988)	4		*Not aware of Notice
No Insurance	3	* Deliberate offence * Offence involving TWOC or other offence giving rise to danger	* Genuine mistake/ technicality * Duty to provide insurance resting with another e.g. parent, company, hirer, etc
No Test Certificate	2	* Blatant disregard of need	* Genuine oversight
Fraudulent Use of Excise Licence	2		* Both vehicles owned by offender
Failure to notify change of ownership	2	* Blatant disregard of need	* Genuine oversight
Construction and use offences	3	* Blatant disregard of need * Seriousness of defect(s)	* Genuine oversight * Minor defect(s)
Motorway Offences	3	* Blatant disregard of Regulations. * Serious risk to offender or other road user	* Genuine mistake
SEXUAL OFFENCES			
Rape (Sec. 1)	4	**Defer Decision to CPS**	
Assault by Penetration (Sec. 2)	4	**Defer Decision to CPS**	
Sexual Assault (Sec. 3)	3	* Force used * Elderly / younger victim * Group action	

OFFENCE	GRAVITY SCORE	AGGRAVATING/MITIGATING FACTORS	
		+	-
Causing Person to Engage in Sexual Activity without Consent (Sec. 4) With Penetration	4	**Defer Decision to CPS**	
Without Penetration	3	* Force used * Elderly / younger victim * Group action	
Rape of Child Under 13 (Sec. 5)	4	**Defer Decision to CPS**	
Assault of Child Under 13 by Penetration (Sec. 6)	4	**Defer Decision to CPS**	
Sexual Assault of Child Under 13 (Sec. 7)	3	* Facilitated by drugs/ alcohol * Force used * Group action	* Offender and victim of similar age and no element of coercion or corruption present
Causing/Inciting Child Under 13 to Engage in Sexual Activity without Consent (Sec. 8) With Penetration	4	**Defer Decision to CPS**	
Without Penetration	3	* Facilitated by drugs/ alcohol * Force used * Group action	
Sexual Activity with Child (Sec. 13) Victim under 13 Victim under 16	3 2	* Facilitated by drugs/ alcohol * Force used * Group action	* Offender and victim of similar age and no element of coercion or corruption present
Causing/Inciting Child to Engage in Sexual Activity (Sec. 13) Victim under 13 Victim under 16	3 2	* Facilitated by drugs/ alcohol * Force used * Group action	

OFFENCE	GRAVITY SCORE	AGGRAVATING/MITIGATING FACTORS	
		+	-
Engaging in Sexual Activity in Presence of Child (Sec. 13) Victim under 13 Victim under 16	 3 2	* Facilitated by drugs/ alcohol * Force used * Group action	* Offender and victim of similar age and no element of coercion or corruption present
Causing Child to Watch Sexual Act (Sec. 13) Victim under 13 Victim under 16	 3 2	* Facilitated by drugs/ alcohol * Force used * Group action	* Offender and victim of similar age and no element of coercion or corruption present
Sexual Activity with Child Family Member (Sec. 25)	3	* Victim did not wholly consent * Element of coercion * Victim Under 13	* Offender & victim are similar in age * Both parties over age of consent and no element of coercion/seduction
Inciting Child Family Member to Engage in Sexual Activity (Sec. 26)	3	* Victim did not wholly consent * Element of coercion * Victim Under 13	* Offender & victim are similar in age * Both parties over age of consent and no element of coercion/seduction
Sex with Adult Relative with Penetration and with or without Consent (Sec. 64 & 65)	2	* Facilitated by drugs/ alcohol * Force used * Element of coercion * Group action	
Sexual Activity with Person with Mental Disorder (Sec. 30) With Penetration	 4	 **Defer Decision to CPS**	
Without Penetration	3	* Facilitated by drugs/ alcohol * Force used * Group action	* Offender & victim are similar in age * Both parties over age of consent and no element of coercion/seduction * Offender has mental disorder

OFFENCE	GRAVITY SCORE	AGGRAVATING/MITIGATING FACTORS	
		+	-
Causing/Inciting Person with Mental Disorder to Engage in Sexual Activity without Consent (Sec. 31) With Penetration Without Penetration	4	**Defer Decision to CPS**	
	3	* Facilitated by drugs/ alcohol * Force used * Group action	* Offender & victim are similar in age * Both parties over age of consent and no element of coercion/seduction * Offender has mental disorder
Engaging in Sexual Activity in Presence of Person with Mental Disorder (Sec. 32)	3	* Facilitated by drugs/ alcohol * Force used * Group action	* Offender and victim of similar age and no element of coercion or corruption present * Offender has mental disorder
Causing Person with Mental Disorder to Watch Sexual Act (Sec. 33)	3	* Facilitated by drugs/ alcohol * Force used * Group action	* Offender and victim of similar age and no element of coercion or corruption present * Offender has mental disorder
Paying for Sexual Services of Child (sec. 47) with Penetration Victim under 13 Victim under 16 Victim under 18	4 3 2		
Causing/Inciting Child Prostitution/Pornography (Sec. 48)	3	* Victim under 13	
Controlling Child Involved in Prostitution/Pornography (Sec. 49)	3	* Victim under 13	
Arranging/Facilitation Child Prostitution/Pornography (Sec. 50)	3	* Victim under 13	
Administering Substance with	3		

OFFENCE	GRAVITY SCORE	AGGRAVATING/MITIGATING FACTORS	
		+	-
Intent to Commit Sexual Offence (Sec. 61)			
Commit Offence with Intent to Commit Sexual Offence (Sec. 62)	**Refer to offence committed and see General Factors for All Offences**		
For Kidnapping/False Imprisonment offences only	4		
Trespass with Intent to Commit Sexual Offence (Sec. 63)	4		
Exposure (Sec. 66)	2	* Victim put in fear * Repeat performances	
Voyeurism (Sec. 67)	2	* Victim distressed * Victim observed in person * Repeat performances	
Sexual Activity in Public Lavatory (Sec. 71)	2	* Genuine chance of public witnessing the offence * Youth victim	* Consenting victim but age of legal consent
Common prostitute loitering for prostitution *Before any formal action is considered, the assumption that a child prostitute is a victim must first be acted on by referral to the multi-agency group. Only when advised by them can formal action be considered.*	2		
'Kerb Crawling'	2	* Affects residential areas	
SPORTING EVENTS			
Intoxicating liquor in possession on specified vehicle (Section 1.3 & 1A.3)	2	* Group involvement * Large quantity	* Small quantity
Drunk in a specified vehicle (Section 1.4 & 1A.4)	2	* Group involvement * Risk of escalation * Threatening	* Non-threatening
Intoxicating liquor/article in possession whilst entering or inside (viewing area) sports ground (Section 2.1)	2	* Group involvement * Risk of escalation	
Entering or being in a sports ground whilst drunk (Section	2	* Group involvement	

OFFENCE	GRAVITY SCORE	AGGRAVATING/MITIGATING FACTORS	
		+	-
2.2)		* Risk of escalation * Threatening	* Non-threatening
THEFT			
Robbery/Assault with Intent to Rob	4	**Defer Decision to CPS**	
Theft - up to £100 in value - over £100	 2 3	* Planned * Sophistication * Organised team * Adult involving children * Significant related damage * Unrecovered property of considerable value * Value £200+ (approx.)	* Theft for reasons of poverty/personal need * Coercion from others in group on reluctant offender
Going Equipped to Steal	2		
Handling Stolen Property	3	* Property stolen to order * Professional receiver * Youth coercing children * Property of high value	* Very low value * Receiving under pressure from another
Abstracting Electricity	2	* Special equipment * High usage * Prolonged period	* Poverty/personal need * Coercion by others
Obtaining Property by Deception (Section 15 Theft Act 1968)	2	* Sophistication * Two or more involved * Committed over lengthy period * Unrecovered property of considerable value * Value £200+ (approx.)	* Poverty/personal need * Coercion by others in group on reluctant offender * Value £50 or less
Obtaining Services by Deception (Section 1 Theft Act 1978)	2	* Sophistication * Organised team * Unrecovered property of	* Poverty/personal need * Coercion by others in group on reluctant

OFFENCE	GRAVITY SCORE	AGGRAVATING/MITIGATING FACTORS	
		+	-
		considerable value	offender
		* Value £200+ (approx.)	* Value £50 or less
Evasion of Liability by Deception (Section 2 Theft Act 1978)	2	* Sophistication * Organised team * Unrecovered property of considerable value * Value £200+ (approx.)	* Poverty/personal need * Coercion by others of reluctant offender * Value £50 or less
False Accounting	2	* Sophistication * Value £200+ (approx.)	* Value £50 or less
Blackmail	4	**Defer Decision to CPS**	
Taking Vehicle without Consent	2	* Premeditated * Group Action * Related damage	* Taken from family member * The taking is a technical offence
Aggravated Vehicle Taking where owing to the Driving of the Vehicle, an Accident occurred causing injury to any person	4		* The taking is a technical offence * Injured is member of driver's family
Aggravated Vehicle Taking where: a) Damage to any Property other than the Vehicle b) Damage was caused to the Vehicle c) the Vehicle was Driven Dangerously on a Road or other Public Place (S1 Aggravated Vehicle - Taking Act 1992)	3	* Avoiding detection or apprehension * Competitive driving: racing, showing off * Disregard for warnings e.g. from passengers or other in vicinity * Excessive speed * Evidence of alcohol or drugs * Group action * Premeditated * Serious risk	* The taking is a technical offence * Damage to own family property * Minor damage

OFFENCE	GRAVITY SCORE	AGGRAVATING/MITIGATING FACTORS	
		+	-
Tampering with Motor Vehicle (S25 RTA 1988)	2	* Potential or actual danger intended	
Interference with Vehicle (S9 Criminal Attempts Act 1981)	2	* Damage to vehicle	
Making Off Without Payment (Section 3 Theft Act 1978)	2	* Deliberate plan * Two or more involved * Large amount involved	* Small amount involved
WASTING POLICE TIME			
Wasting Police Time	2	* Detention of innocent person * Substantial time wasted	* Early retraction and remorse * Innocent prank

Appendix 4 Police Station Fixed Fees, and other payments

All fees in this Payment Annex are exclusive of VAT.

Criminal Investigations

Work conducted at the Police Station: Police Station Advice and Assistance

(Paragraphs 9.1 to 9.116 of the Specification)

Police Station Telephone Advice Fixed Fee

London £31.45 per claim

National £30.25 per claim

The CDS Direct Fixed Acceptance Fee is **£8.00** per Matter.

Payment for Police Station Attendance – (hourly rates for recording time and to determine whether the Exceptional Threshold has been reached)

	London	National
Police Station Attendance hourly rates		
Own or Duty Solicitor	£56.20	£52.00
Duty Solicitor (Unsocial Hours)	£69.05	£69.05
Duty solicitor – serious offences	£65.00	£60.00
Duty Solicitor – serious offences (Unsocial Hours)	£80.00	£80.00
Travelling and waiting hourly rates		
Own Solicitor	£28.80	£28.80
Duty Solicitor	£56.20	£52.00
Duty Solicitor (Unsocial Hours)	£69.05	£69.05

Police Station Attendance Fixed Fees

The fees set out in this Annex are exclusive of VAT.

Table 1

Regional Office 1: Newcastle

Criminal Justice System Area	Scheme	Fixed Fee (£)	Exceptional Case Threshold (£)	Code
Cleveland	Hartlepool	144	444.27	1001
	Teeside	149	457.02	1002
Durham	Darlington	169.36	508.08	1003
	South Durham	167	513.18	1004
	Durham	195	607.65	1005
	Derwentside	188.09	564.27	1006
	Easington	183	561.69	1007
Northumbria	South East Northumberland	162.55	487.65	1008
	Newcastle upon Tyne	151	464.67	1009
	Gateshead	156.60	469.80	1010
	North Tyneside	154	472.35	1011
	South Tyneside	146	449.37	1012
	Sunderland; Houghton Le Spring	163	502.98	1013
	Berwick & Alnwick	194	597.45	1014
	Tynedale & Hexham	169	520.86	1015

Table 2

Regional Office 2: Bristol

Criminal Justice System Area	Scheme	Fixed Fee (£)	Exceptional Case Threshold (£)	Code
Avon & Somerset	Avon North & Thornbury	195	615.33	2001
	Bath & Wansdyke	211.91	635.73	2002

	Mendip; Yeovil & South Somerset	237.45	712.35	2003
	Bristol	175.32	525.96	2004
	Sedgemoor; Taunton Deane	199	674.04	2005
	Weston-Super-Mare	198.30	594.90	2006
Dorset	Central Dorset	200	600	2007
	Bournemouth & Christchurch	159.15	477.45	2008
	Poole East Dorset	168	515.73	2009
	Bridport West Dorset; Weymouth & Dorchester	160	480	2010
Wiltshire	Salisbury	191	587.22	2011
	Chippenham; Trowbridge	205.96	617.88	2012
	Swindon	188	579.57	2013
Gloucestershire	Cheltenham	173	533.61	2014
	Gloucester	170	523.41	2015
	Stroud	195	600	2016
Devon & Cornwall	Barnstaple	190.64	571.92	2017
	Exeter	169.36	508.08	2018
	Plymouth	196.60	589.80	2019
	East Cornwall	218	740.43	2020
	Carrick; Kerrier (Camborne); Penwith	195	617.88	2021
	Teignbridge; Torbay	178.72	536.16	2022

Table 3

Regional Office 3: Birmingham

Criminal Justice System Area	Scheme	Fixed Fee (£)	Exceptional Case Threshold (£)	Code
Staffordshire	Stoke on Trent; Leek	195	617.88	3001

Criminal Justice System Area	Scheme	Fixed Fee (£)	Exceptional Case Threshold (£)	Code
	Stafford; Cannock & Rugeley	195	600	3002
	Lichfield & Tamworth; Burton Upon Trent; Uttoxeter	189	582.12	3003
Warwickshire	Leamington; Nuneaton; Rugby	195.74	587.22	3004
West Mercia	Hereford; Leominster	170.21	510.63	3005
	Kidderminster; Redditch	217.87	653.61	3006
	Shrewsbury	182	559.14	3007
	Telford	189	582.12	3008
	Worcester	198.30	594.90	3009
West Midlands	Sandwell	193	592.35	3010
	Wolverhampton & Seisdon	193	592.35	3011
	Dudley & Halesowen	189.79	569.37	3012
	Walsall	195	602.55	3013
	Birmingham	195	620.43	3014
	Solihull	205.11	615.33	3015
	Coventry	168.51	505.53	3016

Table 4

Regional Office 4: Cardiff

Criminal Justice System Area	Scheme	Fixed Fee (£)	Exceptional Case Threshold (£)	Code
Dyfed Powys	Amman Valley	195	625.53	4001
	Camarthen East Dyfed	221.28	663.84	4002
	Llanelli	152	467.22	4003
	Brecon & Radnor	222.98	668.94	4004
	Mid Wales	170.21	510.63	4005
	North Ceredigion; South Ceredigion	223.83	671.49	4006
	Pembrokeshire	183	564.27	4007

Gwent	East Gwent	186	571.92	4008
	Newport	183	561.69	4009
	Lower Rhymney Valley; North Bedwellty; South Bedwellty	195	610.20	4010
North Wales	Bangor & Caernarfon	207.66	622.98	4011
	Colwyn Bay	190	584.67	4012
	Denbighshire	206.81	620.43	4013
	Dolgellau	206.81	620.43	4014
	Mold & Hawarden	195	607.65	4015
	North Anglesey	216.17	648.51	4016
	Pwlheli	146.38	439.14	4017
	Wrexham	177.02	531.06	4018
South Wales	Cardiff	195	643.41	4019
	Vale of Glamorgan	228.09	684.27	4020
	Cynon Valley	195	617.88	4021
	Mid Glamorgan & Miskin	195	643.41	4022
	Merthyr Tydfil	195	638.31	4023
	Port Talbot	240	811.92	4024
	Newcastle & Ogmore	195	653.61	4025
	Neath	198	671.49	4026
	Swansea	188	579.57	4027

Table 5

Regional Office 5: Liverpool

Criminal Justice System Area	Scheme	Fixed Fee (£)	Exceptional Case Threshold (£)	Code
Merseyside	Bootle & Crosby	178	546.39	5001
	Southport	148.94	446.82	5002
	Liverpool	196.60	589.80	5003
	St Helens	168	518.31	5004

Knowsley	181	556.59	5005
Wirral	173	531.06	5006

Table 6

Regional Office 6: Manchester

Criminal Justice System Area	Scheme	Fixed Fee (£)	Exceptional Case Threshold (£)	Code
Cheshire	Crewe & Nantwich; Sandbach & Congleton; Macclesfield	193	592.35	6001
	Warrington; Halton	169.36	508.08	6002
	Chester; Vale Royal (Northwich)	176.17	528.51	6003
Cumbria	Barrow in Furness	168.51	505.53	6004
	Kendal & Windermere	200.85	602.55	6005
	Penrith; Carlisle	189.79	569.37	6006
	Whitehaven; Workington	157.45	472.35	6007
Greater Manchester	Manchester	195	643.41	6008
	Stockport	183.83	551.49	6009
	Trafford	195	612.78	6010
	Salford	195	625.53	6011
	Bolton	180.43	541.29	6012
	Bury	175.32	525.96	6013
	Wigan	186.38	559.14	6014
	Rochdale; Middleton	185.53	556.59	6015
	Tameside	171	525.96	6016
	Oldham	150.64	451.92	6017
Lancashire	Burnley; Rossendale	177.87	533.61	6018
	Blackburn; Accrington; Ribble Valley	195	635.73	6019
	Blackpool	138.72	416.16	6020
	Fleetwood	142.13	426.39	6021

Lancaster	174.47	523.41		6022
Chorley; Ormskirk; South Ribble & Leyland	191.49	574.47		6023
Preston	156.60	469.80		6024

Table 7

Regional Office 7: Brighton

Criminal Justice System Area	Scheme	Fixed Fee (£)	Exceptional Case Threshold (£)	Code
Kent	Dartford & Gravesend	255.32	765.96	7001
	Ashford & Tenterden; Dover; Folkestone	225	763.41	7002
	Medway	224.68	674.04	7003
	Swale	266.38	799.14	7004
	Maidstone & West Malling	237.45	712.35	7005
	Canterbury; Thanet	195	661.29	7006
	West Kent (Tonbridge)	228.09	684.27	7007
Surrey	Guildford & Farnham	197	668.94	7008
	North West Surrey (Woking)	215	730.20	7009
	South East Surrey	227	771.06	7010
	Epsom	230	781.29	7011
	Staines	264	893.61	7012
Sussex	Brighton & Hove & Lewes	201	681.69	7013
	Chichester & District	178	546.39	7014
	Crawley; Horsham	250.21	750.63	7015
	Hastings	156	480.00	7016
	Worthing	180	554.04	7017
	Eastbourne	189.79	569.37	7018

Table 8

Regional Office 8: Nottingham

Criminal Justice System Area	Scheme	Fixed Fee (£)	Exceptional Case Threshold (£)	Code
Derbyshire	East Derbyshire (Ripley); Ilkeston	226.38	679.14	8001
	Ashbourne; Matlock; High Peak (Buxton)	208.51	625.53	8002
	Chesterfield	194.89	584.67	8003
	Derby; Swadlincote	195	625.53	8004
Leicestershire	Ashby & Coalville; Loughborough; Melton Mowbray	199.15	597.45	8005
	Leicester	195	605.10	8006
	Hinkley; Market Harborough	221.28	663.84	8007
Lincolnshire	Boston; Bourne; Stamford	190	584.67	8008
	Skegness	171.06	513.18	8009
	Lincoln; Gainsborough	177.02	531.06	8010
	Grantham & Sleaford	175	538.71	8011
Nottinghamshire	Mansfield	176	541.29	8012
	Newark	197.45	592.35	8013
	Nottingham	196.60	589.80	8014
	Worksop & East Retford	187	574.47	8015
Northampton-shire	Corby (Kettering); Wellingborough;	172.77	518.31	8016
	Northampton	187.23	561.69	8017

Table 9

Regional Office 9: Cambridge

Criminal Justice System Area	Scheme	Fixed Fee (£)	Exceptional Case Threshold (£)	Code
Bedfordshire	Bedford	184	566.82	9001
	Luton	195	658.71	9002
Cambridgeshire	Cambridge	178	548.94	9003
	Ely	195	630.63	9004
	Huntingdon	189.79	569.37	9005
	March & Wisbech	188.09	564.27	9006
	Peterborough	156.60	469.80	9007
Essex	Basildon	195	602.55	9008
	Brentwood	273	926.82	9009
	Braintree	218	737.88	9010
	Clacton & Harwich; Colchester	195	617.88	9011
	Grays	255	865.53	9012
	Harlow & Loughton	255	865.53	9013
	Stanstead	282	957.45	9014
	Rayleigh; Southend on Sea	182.98	548.94	9015
	Chelmsford; Witham	193	594.90	9016
Hertfordshire	Dacorum (Hemel Hempstead)	230	778.71	9017
	Bishop's Stortford; East Hertfordshire	279	947.22	9018
	Stevenage & North Hertfordshire	259	878.31	9019
	St Albans	235	796.59	9020
	Watford	231	783.84	9021
Norfolk	Cromer & North Walsham	202	684.27	9022

	Great Yarmouth	184.68	554.04	9023
	Kings Lynn & West Norfolk	180.43	541.29	9024
	Norwich & District	185.53	556.59	9025
	Diss; Thetford	192	589.80	9026
	Dereham	217	735.33	9027
Suffolk	Lowestoft; Beccles & Halesworth; Aldeburgh	185.53	556.59	9028
	Felixstowe; Ipswich & District; Woodbridge	188.94	566.82	9029
	Sudbury & Hadleigh; Bury St Edmunds; Haverhill; Newmarket	195	605.10	9030

Table 10

Regional Office 10: Reading

Criminal Justice System Area	Scheme	Fixed Fee (£)	Exceptional Case Threshold (£)	Code
Thames Valley	Abingdon, Didcot & Witney (South Oxfordshire)	229	776.16	1131
	Aylesbury	217.87	653.61	1132
	High Wycombe & Amersham	209	709.80	1133
	Milton Keynes	181	556.59	1134
	Bicester; North Oxon (Banbury)	213	722.55	1135
	Oxford	213	722.55	1136
	Reading	206.81	620.43	1137
	Slough (East Berkshire)	229	776.16	1138
	West Berkshire (Newbury etc)	191.49	574.47	1139
Hampshire	Aldershot; Petersfield (North East Hampshire)	219	742.98	1140
	Andover; Basingstoke; Winchester (North West Hampshire)	230.64	691.92	1141

Isle of Wight	188.09	564.27	1142
Portsmouth; Waterlooville (South East Hampshire)	193.19	579.57	1143
Gosport & Fareham	235.74	707.22	1144
South West Hampshire (Southampton)	217.87	653.61	1145

Table 11

Regional Office 11: Leeds

Criminal Justice System Area	Scheme	Fixed Fee (£)	Exceptional Case Threshold (£)	Code
Humberside	Grimsby & Cleethorpes	147.23	441.69	1201
	Scunthorpe	158	487.65	1202
	Hull	168	515.73	1203
	Beverley; Bridlington	195	643.41	1204
	Goole	200	676.59	1205
North Yorkshire	Northallerton & Richmond	210.21	630.63	1206
	Harrogate & Ripon	201.70	605.10	1207
	Skipton, Settle & Ingleton	195	600	1208
	Scarborough; Whitby	167	513.18	1209
	Malton & Ryedale	160.85	482.55	1210
	York; Selby	175	538.71	1211
South Yorkshire	Barnsley	174	536.16	1212
	Doncaster	168	515.73	1213
	Rotherham	178	548.94	1214
	Sheffield	183	564.27	1215

West Yorkshire	Halifax	190.64	571.92	1216
	Huddersfield	160.85	482.55	1217
	Dewsbury	174.47	523.41	1218
	Bradford	149	459.57	1219
	Keighley &Bingley	168	515.73	1220
	Leeds	158	485.10	1221
	Pontefract & Castleford	154.89	464.67	1222
	Wakefield	153	469.80	1223

Table 12

Regional Office 12: London

Criminal Justice System Area	Scheme	Fixed Fee (£)	Exceptional Case Threshold (£)	Code
London	Barking	246	834.90	1301
	Bexley	220	745.53	1302
	Bishopsgate	257	870.63	1303
	Brent	240	811.92	1304
	Brentford	244	827.22	1305
	Bromley	232	786.39	1306
	Camberwell Green	240	814.47	1307
	Central London	260	880.86	1308
	Clerkenwell; Hampstead	243	822.12	1309
	Croydon	237	801.69	1310
	Ealing	252	855.33	1311
	Enfield	239	809.37	1312
	Greenwich; Woolwich	229	776.16	1313
	Haringey	247	837.45	1314
	Harrow	240	814.47	1315
	Havering	224	758.31	1316

Heathrow	301	1021.29	1317
Hendon; Barnet	242	819.57	1318
Highbury Corner	252	852.78	1319
Kingston-Upon-Thames	250	847.65	1320
Newham	241	817.02	1321
Old Street	240	814.47	1322
Redbridge	247	837.45	1323
Richmond-Upon-Thames	264	893.61	1324
South London	252	852.78	1325
Sutton	239	809.37	1326
Thames	239	809.37	1327
Tower Bridge	255	865.53	1328
Uxbridge	231	783.84	1329
Waltham Forest	224	760.86	1330
West London	258	875.73	1331
Wimbledon	245	829.80	1332

Work conducted outside the Police Station: Free standing Advice and Assistance

(Paragraphs 9.117 to 9.144 of the Specification)

The Upper Limit for this Unit of Work is **£300.**

	London	National
Routine letters written and routine telephone calls per item	**£3.85**	**£3.70**

	London	National
Preparation hourly rate	**£49.70**	**£46.90**
Travel and waiting hourly rate	**£26.30**	**£26.30**

Work conducted outside the Police Station:

Advocacy Assistance on a warrant of further detention

(Paragraphs 9.145 to 9.157 of the Specification)

The Upper Limit for this Unit of Work is **£1,500.**

Magistrates' court or judicial authority

	London	National
Routine letters written and		
Own Solicitor and Duty Solicitor	**£3.85**	**£3.70**
Duty Solicitor (Unsocial Hours)	**£5.10**	**£4.90**
Preparation hourly rate		
Own Solicitor and Duty Solicitor	**£49.70**	**£46.90**
Duty Solicitor (Unsocial Hours)	**£66.30**	**£62.50**
Advocacy hourly rate		
Own Solicitor and Duty Solicitor	**£59.00**	**£59.00**
Duty Solicitor (Unsocial Hours)	**£78.65**	**£78.65**
Travelling and waiting hourly rate		
Own Solicitor and Duty Solicitor	**£26.30**	**£26.30**
Duty Solicitor (Unsocial Hours)	**£35.05**	**£35.05**

High Court or a senior judge

	London	National
Routine letter out per item	**£7.50**	**£7.50**
Routine telephone calls per item	**£4.15**	**£4.15**
All other preparation work, hourly rate	**£79.50**	**£75.00**
Attending counsel in conference or at the trial or hearing of any summons or application at court, or	**£37.00**	**£37.00**
Attending without counsel at the trial or hearing of any cause or the hearing of any summons or application at court, or other	**£75.00**	**£75.00**
Travelling and waiting hourly rate	**£33.25**	**£33.25**

Work conducted outside the Police Station:

Advocacy Assistance for armed forces custody hearings

(Paragraphs 9.158 to 9.170 of the Specification)

The Upper Limit for this Unit of Work is **£1,500.**

	London	National
Routine letters written and		
Own Solicitor and Duty Solicitor	£3.85	£3.70
Duty Solicitor (Unsocial Hours)	£5.10	£4.90
Preparation hourly rate		
Own Solicitor and Duty Solicitor	£49.70	£46.90
Duty Solicitor (Unsocial Hours)	£66.30	£62.50
Advocacy hourly rate		
Own Solicitor and Duty Solicitor	£59.00	£59.00
Duty Solicitor (Unsocial Hours)	£78.65	£78.65
Travelling and waiting hourly rate		
Own Solicitor and Duty Solicitor	£26.30	£26.30
Duty Solicitor (Unsocial Hours)	£35.05	£35.05

Work conducted outside the Police Station:

Advocacy Assistance in the magistrates' court in connection with an application to vary police bail conditions.

(Paragraphs 9.71 to 9.182 of the Specification)

The Upper Limit for this Unit of Work is **£1,500.**

	London	National
Routine letters written and telephone calls per item	£4.05	£3.90
Preparation hourly rate	£52.55	£49.70
Advocacy hourly rate	£62.35	£62.35
Travelling and waiting hourly rate	£26.30	£26.30

Work conducted outside the Police Station:

Advocacy Assistance for armed forces custody hearings

(Paragraphs 9.158 to 9.170 of the Specification)

The Upper Limit for this Unit of Work is £1,500.

	London	National
Routine letters written and		
Own Solicitor and Duty Solicitor	£3.85	£3.70
Duty Solicitor (Unsocial Hours)	£5.10	£4.90
Preparation hourly rate		
Own Solicitor and Duty Solicitor	£49.70	£46.90
Duty Solicitor (Unsocial Hours)	£66.30	£62.50
Advocacy hourly rate		
Own Solicitor and Duty Solicitor	£59.00	£59.00
Duty Solicitor (Unsocial Hours)	£78.65	£78.65
Travelling and waiting hourly rate		
Own Solicitor and Duty Solicitor	£26.30	£26.30
Duty Solicitor (Unsocial Hours)	£35.05	£35.05

Work conducted outside the Police Station:

Advocacy Assistance in the magistrates' court in connection with an application to vary police bail conditions.

(Paragraphs 9.71 to 9.182 of the Specification)

The Upper Limit for this Unit of Work is £1,500.

	London	National
Routine letters written and telephone calls per item	£4.05	£3.90
Preparation hourly rate	£52.55	£49.70
Advocacy hourly rate	£62.35	£62.35
Travelling and waiting hourly rate	£26.30	£26.30

Appendix 5 – Code of Practice on Conditional Cautions

1. Introduction

    1. This Code of Practice has been approved by Parliament and brought into force by statutory instrument (SI2004- 1683). It extends to England and Wales. The Code governs the use of Conditional Cautions under Part 3 of the Criminal Justice Act 2003 ("the Act"). The text of the relevant provisions of the Act is attached at Annex A.

    2. Conditional Cautioning enables offenders to be given a suitable disposal without the involvement of the usual court processes. Where rehabilitative or reparative conditions (or both) are considered preferable to prosecution, Conditional Cautioning provides a statutory means of enforcing them through prosecution for the original offence in the event of non-compliance. The key to determining whether a Conditional Caution should be given - instead of prosecution or a simple caution - is that the imposition of specified conditions will be an appropriate and effective means of addressing an offender's behaviour or making reparation for the effects of the offence on the victim or the community.

    3. The Act defines a Conditional Caution as 'a caution which is given in respect of an offence committed by the offender and which has conditions attached to it'. If an offender fails without reasonable excuse to comply with the conditions attached to a Conditional Caution the Act provides for criminal proceedings to be instituted and the caution cancelled.

    4. Such a caution may only be given by an authorised person, defined as a constable; a person designated as an investigating officer under section 38 of the Police Reform Act 2002; or a person authorised for the purpose by a relevant prosecutor. The authorised person should be suitably trained.

    5. *A relevant prosecutor* is defined as -

        a. the Attorney General,

        b. the Director of the Serious Fraud Office,

        c. the Director of Public Prosecutions,

        d. a Secretary of State,

        e. the Commissioners of Inland Revenue,

f.   the Commissioners of Customs and Excise, or

g.   a person specified as a relevant prosecutor in an order made by the Secretary of State for the purposes of this Part of the Act.

6.   Although this Code is expressed largely in terms of the police and CPS, it applies equally to Conditional Cautions given on the authority of other relevant prosecutors, who should ensure that their procedures (with any necessary adaptations) comply with the relevant provisions of the Code. Where appropriate, references to the police should be read as including other authorised persons, and references to the CPS as including other relevant prosecutors.

2. Conditional Cautioning As A Disposal

1.   A Conditional Caution is a statutory development of the non-statutory police caution ('simple caution') which has long been available, at the discretion of the police and CPS, as an alternative to prosecution in suitable cases. The basic criteria for a Conditional Caution - ie those which must be satisfied before this disposal can be considered - are:

- that the offender is 18 or over;

- that the offender admits the offence to the authorised person; and

- that there is, in the opinion of the relevant prosecutor, evidence sufficient to charge the offender with the offence.

In cases where these criteria are satisfied, a Conditional Caution may be considered as an alternative to charge, taking into account the factors outlined in section 3 of this Code. The simple caution will remain available as a disposal, and may be appropriate in cases where no suitable conditions readily suggest themselves, or where prosecution would not be in the public interest, or where the suspect has forestalled what would otherwise have been a suitable condition by (for example) paying compensation to the victim (and can establish that he has done so). For those offences for which there is the option of issuing a fixed penalty notice, that will generally be the appropriate disposal unless such a notice has previously been issued to the offender, in which case a Conditional Caution might be more suitable.

The issue of simple cautions and penalty notices will continue to be a matter for the police. The discretion of the police in respect of decisions whether to charge has been reduced with the introduction of the arrangements in Schedule 2 to the Criminal Justice Act 2003, whereby the Director of Public Prosecutions is empowered to issue guidance about how custody officers should proceed in cases where they consider that there would be sufficient evidence to prosecute. The effect of the guidance which the DPP has issued pursuant to section 37A of the Police and Criminal Evidence Act 1984 is that it is for the CPS to decide whether or not a suspect should be charged and to determine which charge should be brought, although the police retain the discretion to charge in minor, routine cases.

But the police have no such discretion in respect of Conditional Cautions, which may be given only where the prosecutor considers that it is appropriate to do so, even in cases where it would have been open to the police to charge without reference. It follows that, where it appears to the police that the statutory requirements are met and that a Conditional Caution might be appropriate, it is for the prosecutor to decide that a Conditional Caution is the right disposal and what condition(s) would be suitable. It is also open to the prosecutor to take the view that a Conditional Caution is an appropriate disposal without this having been suggested by the police.

The necessary consultation should be carried out as quickly as possible, either face-to-face with a Crown Prosecutor located in the police station, by telephone, or using any arrangements whereby advice may be sought out of hours. It is acknowledged that Restorative Justice (RJ) processes will involve consultation with the parties at the outset. This process should be carefully managed to balance the benefits of using restorative methods against the desirability of early disposal. Where, exceptionally, the necessary reference to the CPS cannot be done on the spot, the suspect should be bailed under s37(7)(a) of the Police and Criminal Evidence Act 1984 for a sufficient period to enable the CPS to decide whether prosecution or a Conditional Caution would be appropriate.

Where, in RJ cases, the decision of the CPS is that a caution would be appropriate if acceptable conditions can be agreed upon through RJ processes, the suspect should be bailed under s37(7)(a) for a period that will allow those processes to take place before the resulting conditions are approved by the prosecutor and the offer of a caution made to the offender.

Where several related or similar offences are admitted they may be grouped and dealt with by a single Conditional Caution; breach of any of the conditions would make the offender liable for prosecution for all of the offences.

A Conditional Caution is a statutory disposal and may be cited in any subsequent court proceedings.

Deciding When A Conditional Caution May Be Appropriate

Guidance about existing cautions advises the police that, in considering whether an offender should be charged or cautioned, they should have regard to the seriousness of the offence and to the offender's criminal record. The same considerations will apply to Conditional Cautions, and authorised persons as well as relevant prosecutors should apply the principles of the Code for Crown Prosecutors and take into consideration the latest Home Office Circular in relation to cautions, when deciding whether an offence may be suitable for a Conditional Caution. Careful account should be taken of any current guidance in relation to domestic violence and hate crime including homophobic crime and crime involving a racist element.

Conditions attached to cautions must either facilitate the rehabilitation of the offender or ensure that the offender makes reparation for the offence, or both. Where the circumstances of a particular case or offender readily suggest conditions of this type, and where such conditions will provide a proportionate response to the offence bearing in mind the public interest, a Conditional Caution will usually be appropriate. It must be remembered that the offender must consent to the conditions as a pre-requisite to imposing them.

It is not intended to establish a progression so that a Conditional Caution is regarded as the logical next step for an offender who has received a simple caution. Indeed a person who has recently been cautioned for a similar offence should not be given a Conditional Caution, unless exceptionally it is believed that the condition might be effective in breaking the pattern of offending. Previous cautions (or indeed convictions) for quite dissimilar offences may be disregarded, however, as may cautions or convictions more than 5 years old, although failure to complete a previous Conditional Caution would normally rule out the issue of another.

The Requirements Set Out In The Act

The following requirements must be complied with:

The authorised person has evidence that the offender has committed an offence.

This will be the evidence on the basis of which the suspect would otherwise fall to be charged, which must include an admission made under caution in interview and any witness statements. In order to avoid any suggestion that an admission has been obtained by offering an inducement, the prospect of a Conditional Caution should on no account be mentioned until the suspect has made a clear and reliable admission under a cautioned interview to all the elements of the offence.

The relevant prosecutor decides -

a.   that there is sufficient evidence to charge the offender with the offence, and

b.   that a Conditional Caution should be given to the offender in respect of that offence.

The relevant prosecutor will apply the evidential test in the usual way according to the Code for Crown Prosecutors - ie that there would be a realistic prospect of conviction if the offender were to be prosecuted. The prosecutor must also conclude that the public interest would be served by the offender receiving a Conditional Caution, if he accepts it and subject to his performing the agreed conditions. In addition, since the fall-back is that the offender will be prosecuted if he either does not accept or fails to perform the conditions, the prosecutor must be satisfied that prosecution would be in the public interest in those contingencies.

i.   **The offender admits to the authorised person that he committed the offence.**

In addition to the admission made in interview (see (i) above), it is necessary that at the time the Conditional Caution is administered the offender admits to the authorised person that he committed the offence. Offenders should be advised at that point of their right to seek legal advice to ensure they give informed consent to accepting both the caution and the conditions, whether or not they have availed themselves of that right at an earlier stage.

ii.   **The authorised person explains the effect of the Conditional Caution to the offender and warns him that failure to comply with any of the conditions attached to the caution is likely to result in the offender being prosecuted for the original offence.**

The implications of the caution should be explained, including that there are circumstances in which it may be disclosed (such as to certain potential employers, and to a court in any future criminal proceedings) and, where the offence is listed in Schedule 1 to the Sex Offenders Act 1997, that accepting a caution will result in the offender being required to notify the police of their name and address and certain other details.

There should not be any bargaining with the offender over the conditions: if he does not accept them in full, he should be prosecuted.

It should be made clear in explaining the consequences of non-compliance that the conditions are to be performed within the agreed time. It must be explained clearly that failure to comply will prompt a reconsideration of the case and usually result in the offender being prosecuted for the original offence.

iii.   **The offender signs a document which contains -**

a.   details of the offence,

b.   an admission by him that he committed the offence,

c.   his consent to being given the Conditional Caution,

d.   an agreement to comply with the conditions attached to the caution, which must be set out on the face of the document, and

e.   an explanation of the implications referred to in (iv) above.

After the offender has admitted to the offence and, having heard the explanation referred to above, has agreed to the conditions, he must sign a pro-forma to this effect. A standard form is available and must be used by all forces. This document will contain details of the offence, the offender's admission, and the conditions and timescale for completing them to which he has agreed. It must be explained to the offender before the form is signed that it will be admissible as evidence in court if the offender is subsequently prosecuted for the original offence in the event of non-compliance.

Types Of Condition

Conditions attached to a caution must be -

- *Proportionate* to the offence. The offender is unlikely to agree to a condition that is more onerous than the sentence that would probably be imposed if the case were taken to court. On the other hand, conditions that amount to far less than the punishment that would be probably be given by a court are unlikely to satisfy the public interest or engender confidence in the criminal justice system.
- *Achievable*: the conditions must be clearly defined in terms of what must be done and within what period of time. Conditions must be realistic and should take

account of the particular offender's circumstances, including physical and mental capacity, so that he could reasonably be expected to achieve them within the time set; otherwise the only result will be a delayed prosecution.

- Appropriate: the conditions should be relevant to the offence or the offender or both.

The Act requires that conditions should fall into one or both of two categories: rehabilitation and reparation.

- **Rehabilitation**: this might include taking part in treatment for drug or alcohol dependency (e.g. attendance at self-help groups provided it can be verified, or on a drug awareness and education programme including assessment of personal needs and appropriate onward referral), anger management courses, or driving rectification classes and the like, or involvement in a restorative justice process (which may lead to reparation). The offender would be expected to pay reasonable costs, if there are any, and a requirement to do so should be one of the conditions. Where the offender cannot afford to pay and this rules out a particular condition, every effort should be made to identify an alternative. The fact that provision of some sorts of course may be subject to resource implications (and possibly a waiting list) will need to be taken into account, bearing in mind that completion of any conditions should be swift and achievable within a reasonable time (see section 6 below).

- **Reparation**: this might include repairing or otherwise making good any damage caused to property (e.g. by cleaning graffiti), restoring stolen goods, paying modest financial compensation, or in some cases a simple apology to the victim. Compensation may be paid to an individual or to the community in the form of an appropriate charity.

Offenders should be required as standard to comply with a condition not to commit further offences until the conditions have been performed.

Specific conditions such as that the offender should avoid a particular street or public house may be included, but consideration should also be given as to whether alternatives such as Anti-Social Behaviour Orders or Restriction Orders etc would be more appropriate or timely.

The police, CPS and National Probation Service (NPS) should take steps at local level (e.g. through the Local Criminal Justice Board or Crime & Disorder Reduction Partnership) to identify agencies, groups or organizations, voluntary or statutory, which provide courses or other activities that might form part of a Conditional Caution, and which it may be appropriate to consult when deciding whether a case is suitable for a

Conditional Caution. The NPS could be approached in appropriate cases to assist in determining whether certain offenders are suitable for a Conditional Caution, for example where there are concerns about the health, behaviour or background of the offender.

When conditions are imposed that require the performance of some task other than the simple payment of compensation or the attendance on a course supervised by an organization responsible for monitoring attendance, careful thought should be given to how performance will be measured and who will be the appropriate person to give assurances that the condition has been completed. This should be documented as part of the description of the condition, in order that the relevant prosecutor and the offender are in no doubt as to the conditions and the measurement of performance. (See also section 10.1.)

Time Limits

The deadline for the completion of conditions should not be too long. This is particularly important in relation to summary offences, for most of which there is a time limit of six months within which a prosecution must commence; for these offences the deadline set should leave enough time for a prosecution to proceed in the event of non-compliance.

Where the condition is for an offender to go on a course of treatment for behaviour/ substance abuse, which may take longer than six months to deliver, the relevant prosecutor will need to consider whether this is appropriate, depending on the attitude of the offender and the likelihood of compliance. There is no reason why undertaking a course of longer duration should not be a condition, provided that (to satisfy the reasonableness test) the offender is only required under the terms of the Conditional Caution to attend for part of it. For example, a course may last 12 months to achieve best results. In such a case, the offender might agree, under the conditions of his caution, to attend for 4 months, and thereafter it will be up to him to continue the treatment for his own benefit, rather than under any legal compulsion.

Involvement Of Victims

In the course of interviewing the victim about the offence, it would be important to ascertain whether any resulting loss, damage or injury is such that it could readily be made good; what the victim's attitude would be towards an offer of reparation from the offender, should one be made; and whether they would be content for such reparation to be made the condition of a caution. Where a caution (simple or conditional) is at that stage regarded as a possibility, the fact may be mentioned to the victim in order to ascertain their views, but it is vital not to give the impression that the victim's views (if any) will be conclusive as to the outcome, which (it should be explained) is at the discretion of the CPS. In some circumstances the relevant prosecutor may consider that in order to be proportionate to the level of the offence, conditions should be more or less onerous than those the victim would accept, in which case the prosecutor should consider whether some explanation to this effect will be helpful to the victim or to the offender.

The Victim Personal Statement (VPS) scheme provides victims with the opportunity to describe the effects of the crime and to have these effects taken into account as the case progresses through the criminal justice system. If it is subsequently proposed to approach the victim for an interview specifically about Conditional Cautioning, the contents of the VPS (if he or she has made one) should be considered beforehand, but it should not be considered sufficient, on its own, to inform a decision to pursue a restorative justice route.

Further information and guidance on the victim personal statement scheme can be found on the Home Office website at:

www.homeoffice.gov.uk/justice/victims/personal/index.html

Restorative Justice

Restorative justice processes bring victims and offenders, and sometimes community members, into contact, either face to face or indirectly, to focus on the impact of a particular crime, and together to agree what can be done to repair the harm caused by that crime. Such processes must always be voluntary for both the victim and the offender. Any person delivering a restorative process, including preparatory work with victims and offenders, must be trained in restorative justice and must meet the required standards. See guidance on this at

www.homeoffice.gov.uk/justice/victims/restorative/index.html

Restorative justice processes can be used as a condition of the caution (where the contact with the victim, direct or indirect, is itself the condition) if both victim and offender consent to this. Alternatively, they can be used as the decision-making process whereby conditions, such as compensation, rehabilitative activities, or other kinds of reparation, are agreed. It should be noted that in this second case, the 'outcome agreement' arising from the process forms a basis for conditions to be approved or formulated by the prosecutor. Notwithstanding the outcome agreement, the prosecutor retains a duty to ensure that the conditions are proportionate to the offending and meet the public interest requirements of the case. Taking account of the views of the victim, and any other conditions attached to the caution, the CPS/police will need to take a view as to which use of restorative justice is appropriate in a particular case.

It is desirable that, where RJ-trained personnel are available and a case with a personal victim is being considered for a Conditional Caution, the victim should be contacted (unless there are exceptional reasons not to do so) to ask for their views on reparation as a condition of the caution, or (if the offender has already indicated they are willing) whether they would like to be involved in a direct or indirect restorative justice process. Restorative justice processes may also be appropriate for crimes with a corporate victim, or crimes where the community as a whole has suffered. In these cases, or in cases where a personal victim has chosen to have no involvement, it may still be desirable to deliver the caution (and decide any conditions) in a restorative manner.

Places Where Cautions May Be Given

Conditional Cautions will usually be given at the local police station, but there is the option of selecting a location appropriate to the offence; e.g. there may be value in giving it at the place where vandalism has occurred. It will be for the authorised person to determine the venue for administering the caution. However, it is not suitable for Conditional Cautions to be delivered on the street, or in the offender's home.

Monitoring And Compliance

It is essential that there should be robust monitoring of compliance with the conditions of a caution. The onus is on the offender to show that the conditions have been met, and the conditions should be expressed in a way that makes clear to the offender what is to be done, by when, and what will be acceptable as evidence that it has been done. For example, an offender who agrees to attend a course might be required to produce a letter from the organiser confirming that he has done so. Depending on the nature of the condition, it may be appropriate for other agencies managing the Conditional Caution to monitor performance and report to the relevant prosecutor any failure fully to comply. At the end of the process the offender will sign a form that will include a declaration that the conditions have been met.

Failure to comply with any one of the conditions means that the offender may be prosecuted for the original offence. The offender will be required as a standard condition to report any failure to comply and explain whether there are circumstances that might amount to a reasonable excuse. Where the offender fails to report and give reasons, a prosecution may (following a prompt CPS review) be commenced, usually by the issue of a summons.

Whether any excuse given is reasonable or not is a matter for the relevant prosecutor to determine on all the available evidence. Such a decision may be reviewable by a court. The decision and reasons for it should be carefully recorded. Where the CPS are satisfied that there is a reasonable excuse for the offender's failure to meet the conditions, they will have to decide whether the case should be regarded as closed, or whether it would be appropriate to set a new time limit for completing conditions or (exceptionally) to revise the conditions, although they should not be made more onerous. Where this is done, the revisions should be recorded and the offender must sign the revised Conditional Caution form acquiescing in the changes. A refusal by the offender to agree to revised conditions will usually result in prosecution for the original offence. It will not usually be appropriate to revise conditions more than once.

Where conditions have been partially completed, it is for the prosecutor to decide whether the offender should be prosecuted, or whether the extent of the part-compliance is sufficient to regard the Conditional Caution as having been fulfilled (in which case it would remain on the record).

In general, however, failure to complete the conditions without reasonable excuse will lead to the offender being prosecuted for the original offence. The CPS will inform the police of the decision. The charge may be brought at the police station (if the offender attends voluntarily - there is no power of arrest), or more usually by way of summons (or, when the relevant provision of the Criminal Justice Act 2003 has been implemented, in accordance with the 'charge by post' procedure, which may be used by the CPS as well as by the police). Where it is believed that the service of a summons or charge by post will be ineffective, eg because the offender's whereabouts are no longer known, an application for a warrant at first instance should be made to the magistrates' court. At the same time the Conditional Caution should be formally terminated, the offender so informed, and relevant police records (PNC and any locally stored) amended accordingly. Court proceedings will then go ahead in the usual way.

Whenever proceedings are instituted, the Conditional Caution ceases to have effect.

Personal victims, unless they have expressed a contrary wish, should be informed when a Conditional Caution has been completed or, where it is not completed, about the outcome of subsequent court proceedings.

Recording Conditional Cautions

Pending modifications to the Police National Computer, Conditional Cautions should be recorded in accordance with directions from the Home Secretary.

Appendix 6 Schedule 8 Terrorism Act 2000, selected parts

Para 1 Place of detention

(1) The Secretary of State shall designate places at which persons may be detained under Schedule 7 or section 41.

(2) In this Schedule a reference to a police station includes a reference to any place which the Secretary of State has designated under sub-paragraph (1) as a place where a person may be detained under section 41.

(3) Where a person is detained under Schedule 7, he may be taken in the custody of an examining officer or of a person acting under an examining officer's authority to and from any place where his attendance is required for the purpose of-

(a) his examination under that Schedule,

(b) establishing his nationality or citizenship, or

(c) making arrangements for his admission to a country or territory outside the United Kingdom.

(4) A constable who arrests a person under section 41 shall take him as soon as is reasonably practicable to the police station which the constable considers the most appropriate.

(5) In this paragraph "examining officer" has the meaning given in Schedule 7.

(6) Where a person is arrested in one Part of the United Kingdom and all or part of his detention takes place in another Part, the provisions of this Schedule which apply to detention in a particular Part of the United Kingdom apply in relation to him while he is detained in that Part.

Para 2 Identification

(1) An authorised person may take any steps which are reasonably necessary for-

(a) photographing the detained person,

(b) measuring him, or

(c) identifying him.

(2) In sub-paragraph (1) "authorised person" means any of the following-

(a) a constable,

(b) a prison officer,

(c) a person authorised by the Secretary of State, and

(d) in the case of a person detained under Schedule 7, an examining officer (within the meaning of that Schedule).

(3) This paragraph does not confer the power to take-

(a) fingerprints, non-intimate samples or intimate samples (within the meaning given by paragraph 15 below), or

(b) relevant physical data or samples as mentioned in section 18 of the Criminal Procedure (Scotland) Act 1995 as applied by paragraph 20 below.

Para 5

A detained person shall be deemed to be in legal custody throughout the period of his detention.

Para 6

(1) Subject to paragraph 8, a person detained under Schedule 7 or section 41 at a police station in England, Wales or Northern Ireland shall be entitled, if he so requests, to have one named person informed as soon as is reasonably practicable that he is being detained there.

(2) The person named must be-

(a) a friend of the detained person,

(b) a relative, or

(c) a person who is known to the detained person or who is likely to take an interest in his welfare.

(3) Where a detained person is transferred from one police station to another, he shall be entitled to exercise the right under this paragraph in respect of the police station to which he is transferred.

Para 7

(1) Subject to paragraphs 8 and 9, a person detained under Schedule 7 or section 41 at a police station in England, Wales or Northern Ireland shall be entitled, if he so requests, to consult a solicitor as soon as is reasonably practicable, privately and at any time.

(2) Where a request is made under sub-paragraph (1), the request and the time at which it was made shall be recorded.

Para 8

(1) Subject to sub-paragraph (2), an officer of at least the rank of superintendent may authorise a delay-

(a) in informing the person named by a detained person under paragraph 6;

(b) in permitting a detained person to consult a solicitor under paragraph 7.

(2) But where a person is detained under section 41 he must be permitted to exercise his rights under paragraphs 6 and 7 before the end of the period mentioned in subsection (3) of that section.

(3) Subject to sub-paragraph (5), an officer may give an authorisation under sub-paragraph (1) only if he has reasonable grounds for believing-

(a) in the case of an authorisation under sub-paragraph (1)(a), that informing the named person of the detained person's detention will have any of the consequences specified in sub-paragraph (4), or

(b) in the case of an authorisation under sub-paragraph (1)(b), that the exercise of the right under paragraph 7 at the time when the detained person desires to exercise it will have any of the consequences specified in sub-paragraph (4).

(4) Those consequences are-

(a) interference with or harm to evidence of a serious offence,

(b) interference with or physical injury to any person,

(c) the alerting of persons who are suspected of having committed a serious offence but who have not been arrested for it,

(d) the hindering of the recovery of property obtained as a result of a serious offence or in respect of which a forfeiture order could be made under [section 23 or 23A] ,

(e) interference with the gathering of information about the commission, preparation or instigation of acts of terrorism,

(f) the alerting of a person and thereby making it more difficult to prevent an act of terrorism, and

(g) the alerting of a person and thereby making it more difficult to secure a person's apprehension, prosecution or conviction in connection with the commission, preparation or instigation of an act of terrorism.

(5) An officer may also give an authorisation under sub-paragraph (1) if he has reasonable grounds for believing that--

(a) the detained person has benefited from his criminal conduct, and

(b) the recovery of the value of the property constituting the benefit will be hindered by--

(i) informing the named person of the detained person's detention (in the case of an authorisation under sub-paragraph (1)(a)), or

(ii) the exercise of the right under paragraph 7 (in the case of an authorisation under sub-paragraph (1)(b)).

(5A) For the purposes of sub-paragraph (5) the question whether a person has benefited from his criminal conduct is to be decided in accordance with Part 2 of the Proceeds of Crime Act 2002.

(6) If an authorisation under sub-paragraph (1) is given orally, the person giving it shall confirm it in writing as soon as is reasonably practicable.

(7) Where an authorisation under sub-paragraph (1) is given-

(a) the detained person shall be told the reason for the delay as soon as is reasonably practicable, and

(b) the reason shall be recorded as soon as is reasonably practicable.

(8) Where the reason for authorising delay ceases to subsist there may be no further delay in permitting the exercise of the right in the absence of a further authorisation under sub-paragraph (1).

(9) In this paragraph, references to a "serious offence" are (in relation to England and Wales) to an indictable offence, and (in relation to Northern Ireland) to a serious arrestable offence within the meaning of Article 87 of the Police and Criminal Evidence (Northern Ireland) Order 1989; but also include--

(a) an offence under any of the provisions mentioned in section 40(1)(a) of this Act, and

(b) an attempt or conspiracy to commit an offence under any of the provisions mentioned in section 40(1)(a).

Para 9

(1) A direction under this paragraph may provide that a detained person who wishes to exercise the right under paragraph 7 may consult a solicitor only in the sight and hearing of a qualified officer.

(2) A direction under this paragraph may be given-

(a) where the person is detained at a police station in England or Wales, by an officer of at least the rank of Commander or Assistant Chief Constable, or

(b) where the person is detained at a police station in Northern Ireland, by an officer of at least the rank of Assistant Chief Constable.

(3) A direction under this paragraph may be given only if the officer giving it has reasonable grounds for believing--

(a) that, unless the direction is given, the exercise of the right by the detained person will have any of the consequences specified in paragraph 8(4), or

(b) that the detained person has benefited from his criminal conduct and that, unless the direction is given, the exercise of the right by the detained person will hinder the recovery of the value of the property constituting the benefit.

(4) In this paragraph "a qualified officer" means a police officer who-

(a) is of at least the rank of inspector,

(b) is of the uniformed branch of the force of which the officer giving the direction is a member, and

(c) in the opinion of the officer giving the direction, has no connection with the detained person's case.

(5) A direction under this paragraph shall cease to have effect once the reason for giving it ceases to subsist.

Para 10

(1) This paragraph applies where a person is detained in England, Wales or Northern Ireland under Schedule 7 or section 41.

(2) Fingerprints may be taken from the detained person only if they are taken by a constable-

(a) with the appropriate consent given in writing, or

(b) without that consent under sub-paragraph (4).

(3) A non-intimate sample may be taken from the detained person only if it is taken by a constable-

(a) with the appropriate consent given in writing, or

(b) without that consent under sub-paragraph (4).

(4) Fingerprints or a non-intimate sample may be taken from the detained person without the appropriate consent only if-

(a) he is detained at a police station and a police officer of at least the rank of superintendent authorises the fingerprints or sample to be taken, or

(b) he has been convicted of a recordable offence and, where a non-intimate sample is to be taken, he was convicted of the offence on or after 10th April 1995 (or 29th July 1996 where the non-intimate sample is to be taken in Northern Ireland).

(5) An intimate sample may be taken from the detained person only if-

(a) he is detained at a police station,

(b) the appropriate consent is given in writing,

(c) a police officer of at least the rank of superintendent authorises the sample to be taken, and

(d) subject to paragraph 13(2) and (3), the sample is taken by a constable.

(6) Subject to sub-paragraph (6A) an officer may give an authorisation under sub-paragraph (4)(a) or (5)(c) only if-

(a) in the case of a person detained under section 41, the officer reasonably suspects that the person has been involved in an offence under any of the provisions mentioned in section 40(1)(a), and the officer reasonably believes that the fingerprints or sample will tend to confirm or disprove his involvement, or

(b) in any case, the officer is satisfied that the taking of the fingerprints or sample from the person is necessary in order to assist in determining whether he falls within section 40(1)(b).

(6A) An officer may also give an authorisation under sub-paragraph (4)(a) for the taking of fingerprints if--

(a) he is satisfied that the fingerprints of the detained person will facilitate the ascertainment of that person's identity; and

(b) that person has refused to identify himself or the officer has reasonable grounds for suspecting that that person is not who he claims to be.

Para 11

(1) Before fingerprints or a sample are taken from a person under paragraph 10, he shall be informed-

(a) that the fingerprints or sample may be used for the purposes of paragraph 14(4), section 63A(1) of the Police and Criminal Evidence Act 1984 and Article 63A(1) of the Police and Criminal Evidence (Northern Ireland) Order 1989 (checking of fingerprints and samples), and

(b) where the fingerprints or sample are to be taken under paragraph 10(2)(a), (3)(a) or (4)(b), of the reason for taking the fingerprints or sample.

(2) Before fingerprints or a sample are taken from a person upon an authorisation given under paragraph 10(4)(a) or (5)(c), he shall be informed-

(a) that the authorisation has been given,

(b) of the grounds upon which it has been given, and

(c) where relevant, of the nature of the offence in which it is suspected that he has been involved.

(3) After fingerprints or a sample are taken under paragraph 10, there shall be recorded as soon as is reasonably practicable any of the following which apply-

(a) the fact that the person has been informed in accordance with sub-paragraphs (1) and (2),

(b) the reason referred to in sub-paragraph (1)(b),

(c) the authorisation given under paragraph 10(4)(a) or (5)(c),

(d) the grounds upon which that authorisation has been given, and

(e) the fact that the appropriate consent has been given.

Para 12

(1) This paragraph applies where-

(a) two or more non-intimate samples suitable for the same means of analysis have been taken from a person under paragraph 10,

(b) those samples have proved insufficient, and

(c) the person has been released from detention.

(2) An intimate sample may be taken from the person if-

(a) the appropriate consent is given in writing,

(b) a police officer of at least the rank of superintendent authorises the sample to be taken, and

(c) subject to paragraph 13(2) and (3), the sample is taken by a constable.

(3) Paragraphs 10(6) and (7) and 11 shall apply in relation to the taking of an intimate sample under this para-graph; and a reference to a person detained under section 41 shall be taken as a reference to a person who was detained under section 41 when the non-intimate samples mentioned in sub-paragraph (1)(a) were taken.

Para 13

(1) Where appropriate written consent to the taking of an intimate sample from a person under paragraph 10 or 12 is refused without good cause, in any proceedings against that person for an offence-

(a) the court, in determining whether to commit him for trial or whether there is a case to answer, may draw such inferences from the refusal as appear proper, and

(b) the court or jury, in determining whether that person is guilty of the offence charged, may draw such inferences from the refusal as appear proper.

(2) An intimate sample other than a sample of urine or a dental impression may be taken under paragraph 10 or 12 only by a registered medical practitioner acting on the authority of a constable.

(3) An intimate sample which is a dental impression may be taken under paragraph 10 or 12 only by a registered dentist acting on the authority of a constable.

(4) Where a sample of hair other than pubic hair is to be taken under paragraph 10 the sample may be taken either by cutting hairs or by plucking hairs with their roots so long as no more are plucked than the person taking the sample reasonably considers to be necessary for a sufficient sample.

Para 14

(1) This paragraph applies to-

(a) fingerprints or samples taken under paragraph 10 or 12, and

(b) information derived from those samples.

(2) The fingerprints and samples may be retained but shall not be used by any person except for the purposes of a terrorist investigation or as mentioned in sub-paragraph (2A).

(2A) The fingerprints or samples may be used--

(a) in the interests of national security,

(b) for purposes related to the prevention or detection of crime, the investigation of an offence or the conduct of a prosecution, or

(c) for purposes related to the identification of a deceased person or of the person from whom the material came.

(4) The fingerprints, samples or information may be checked, subject to sub-paragraph (2), against-

(a) other fingerprints or samples taken under paragraph 10 or 12 or information derived from those samples,

(b) relevant physical data or samples taken by virtue of paragraph 20,

(ba) material to which section 18 of the Counter-Terrorism Act 2008 applies,

(c) any of the fingerprints, samples and information mentioned in section 63A(1)(a) and (b) of the Police and Criminal Evidence Act 1984 (checking of fingerprints and samples),

(d) any of the fingerprints, samples and information mentioned in Article 63A(1)(a) and (b) of the Police and Criminal Evidence (Northern Ireland) Order 1989 (checking of fingerprints and samples), and

(e) fingerprints or samples taken under section 15(9) of, or paragraph 7(5) of Schedule 5 to, the Prevention of Terrorism (Temporary Provisions) Act 1989 or information derived from those samples.

(4A) In this paragraph-

(a) a reference to crime includes a reference to any conduct which-

(i) constitutes one or more criminal offences (whether under the law of a part of the United Kingdom or of a country or territory outside the United Kingdom); or

(ii) is, or corresponds to, any conduct which, if it all took place in any one part of the United Kingdom, would constitute one or more criminal offences;

and

(b) the references to an investigation and to a prosecution include references, respectively, to any investigation outside the United Kingdom of any crime or suspected crime and to a prosecution brought in respect of any crime in a country or territory outside the United Kingdom.

(5) This paragraph (other than sub-paragraph (4)) shall apply to fingerprints or samples taken under section 15(9) of, or paragraph 7(5) of Schedule 5 to, the Prevention of Terrorism (Temporary Provisions) Act 1989 and information derived from those samples as it applies to fingerprints or samples taken under paragraph 10 or 12 and the information derived from those samples.

Para 15

(1) In the application of paragraphs 10 to 14 in relation to a person detained in England or Wales the following expressions shall have the meaning given by section 65 of the Police and Criminal Evidence Act 1984 (Part V definitions)-

(a) "appropriate consent",

(b) "fingerprints",

(c) "insufficient",

(d) "intimate sample",

(e) "non-intimate sample",

(f) "registered dentist", and

(g) "sufficient".

(2) In the application of paragraphs 10 to 14 in relation to a person detained in Northern Ireland the expressions listed in sub-paragraph (1) shall have the meaning given by Article 53 of the Police and Criminal Evidence (Northern Ireland) Order 1989 (definitions).

(3) In paragraph 10 "recordable offence" shall have-

(a) in relation to a person detained in England or Wales, the meaning given by section 118(1) of the Police and Criminal Evidence Act 1984 (general interpretation), and

(b) in relation to a person detained in Northern Ireland, the meaning given by Article 2(2) of the Police and Criminal Evidence (Northern Ireland) Order 1989 (definitions).

Para 21 Requirement

(1) A person's detention shall be periodically reviewed by a review officer.

(2) The first review shall be carried out as soon as is reasonably practicable after the time of the person's arrest.

(3) Subsequent reviews shall, subject to paragraph 22, be carried out at intervals of not more than 12 hours.

(4) No review of a person's detention shall be carried out after a warrant extending his detention has been issued under Part III.

Para 22 Postponement

(1) A review may be postponed if at the latest time at which it may be carried out in accordance with paragraph 21-

(a) the detained person is being questioned by a police officer and an officer is satisfied that an interruption of the questioning to carry out the review would prejudice the investigation in connection with which the person is being detained,

(b) no review officer is readily available, or

(c) it is not practicable for any other reason to carry out the review.

(2) Where a review is postponed it shall be carried out as soon as is reasonably practicable.

(3) For the purposes of ascertaining the time within which the next review is to be carried out, a postponed review shall be deemed to have been carried out at the latest time at which it could have been carried out in accordance with paragraph 21.

Para 23 Grounds for continued detention

(1) A review officer may authorise a person's continued detention only if satisfied that it is necessary-

(a) to obtain relevant evidence whether by questioning him or otherwise,

(b) to preserve relevant evidence,

(ba) pending the result of an examination or analysis of any relevant evidence or of anything the examination or analysis of which is to be or is being carried out with a view to obtaining relevant evidence;

(c) pending a decision whether to apply to the Secretary of State for a deportation notice to be served on the detained person,

(d) pending the making of an application to the Secretary of State for a deportation notice to be served on the detained person,

(e) pending consideration by the Secretary of State whether to serve a deportation notice on the detained person, or

(f) pending a decision whether the detained person should be charged with an offence.

(2) The review officer shall not authorise continued detention by virtue of sub-paragraph (1)(a) or (b) unless he is satisfied that the investigation in connection with which the person is detained is being conducted diligently and expeditiously.

(3) The review officer shall not authorise continued detention by virtue of sub-paragraph (1)(c) to (f) unless he is satisfied that the process pending the completion of which detention is necessary is being conducted diligently and expeditiously.

(4) In this paragraph "relevant evidence" means evidence which-

(a) relates to the commission by the detained person of an offence under any of the provisions mentioned in section 40(1)(a), or

(b) indicates that the detained person falls within section 40(1)(b).

(5) In sub-paragraph (1) "deportation notice" means notice of a decision to make a deportation order under the Immigration Act 1971.

Para 24

(1) The review officer shall be an officer who has not been directly involved in the investigation in connection with which the person is detained.

(2) In the case of a review carried out within the period of 24 hours beginning with the time of arrest, the review officer shall be an officer of at least the rank of inspector.

(3) In the case of any other review, the review officer shall be an officer of at least the rank of superintendent.

Para 25

(1) This paragraph applies where-

(a) the review officer is of a rank lower than superintendent,

(b) an officer of higher rank than the review officer gives directions relating to the detained person, and

(c) those directions are at variance with the performance by the review officer of a duty imposed on him under this Schedule.

(2) The review officer shall refer the matter at once to an officer of at least the rank of superintendent.

Para 26

(1) Before determining whether to authorise a person's continued detention, a review officer shall give either of the following persons an opportunity to make representations about the detention-

(a) the detained person, or

(b) a solicitor representing him who is available at the time of the review.

(2) Representations may be oral or written.

(3) A review officer may refuse to hear oral representations from the detained person if he considers that he is unfit to make representations because of his condition or behaviour.

Para 27

(1) Where a review officer authorises continued detention he shall inform the detained person-

(a) of any of his rights under paragraphs 6 and 7 which he has not yet exercised, and

(b) if the exercise of any of his rights under either of those paragraphs is being delayed in accordance with the provisions of paragraph 8, of the fact that it is being so delayed.

(2) Where a review of a person's detention is being carried out at a time when his exercise of a right under either of those paragraphs is being delayed-

(a) the review officer shall consider whether the reason or reasons for which the delay was authorised continue to subsist, and

(b) if in his opinion the reason or reasons have ceased to subsist, he shall inform the officer who authorised the delay of his opinion (unless he was that officer).

(3) In the application of this paragraph to Scotland, for the references to paragraphs 6, 7 and 8 substitute refer-ences to paragraph 16.

(4) The following provisions (requirement to bring an accused person before the court after his arrest) shall not apply to a person detained under section 41-

(a) section 135(3) of the Criminal Procedure (Scotland) Act 1995, and

(b) Article 8(1) of the Criminal Justice (Children) (Northern Ireland) Order 1998.

(5) Section 22(1) of the Criminal Procedure (Scotland) Act 1995 (interim liberation by officer in charge of police station) shall not apply to a person detained under section 41.

Para 28

(1) A review officer carrying out a review shall make a written record of the outcome of the review and of any of the following which apply-

(a) the grounds upon which continued detention is authorised,

(b) the reason for postponement of the review,

(c) the fact that the detained person has been informed as required under paragraph 27(1),

(d) the officer's conclusion on the matter considered under paragraph 27(2)(a),

(e) the fact that he has taken action under paragraph 27(2)(b), and

(f) the fact that the detained person is being detained by virtue of section 41(5) or (6).

(2) The review officer shall-

(a) make the record in the presence of the detained person, and

(b) inform him at that time whether the review officer is authorising continued detention, and if he is, of his grounds.

(3) Sub-paragraph (2) shall not apply where, at the time when the record is made, the detained person is-

(a) incapable of understanding what is said to him,

(b) violent or likely to become violent, or

(c) in urgent need of medical attention.

Para 29 Warrants of further detention

(1) Each of the following-

(a) in England and Wales, a Crown Prosecutor,

(b) in Scotland, the Lord Advocate or a procurator fiscal,

(c) in Northern Ireland, the Director of Public Prosecutions for Northern Ireland,

(d) in any part of the United Kingdom, a police officer of at least the rank of superintendent,

may apply to a judicial authority for the issue of a warrant of further detention under this Part.

(2) A warrant of further detention-

(a) shall authorise the further detention under section 41 of a specified person for a specified period, and

(b) shall state the time at which it is issued.

(3) Subject to sub-paragraph (3A) and paragraph 36, the specified period in relation to a person shall be the period of seven days beginning-

(a) with the time of his arrest under section 41, or

(b) if he was being detained under Schedule 7 when he was arrested under section 41, with the time when his examination under that Schedule began.

(3A) A judicial authority may issue a warrant of further detention in relation to a person which specifies a shorter period as the period for which that person's further detention is authorised if-

(a) the application for the warrant is an application for a warrant specifying a shorter period; or

(b) the judicial authority is satisfied that there are circumstances that would make it inappropriate for the specified period to be as long as the period of seven days mentioned in sub-paragraph (3).

(4) In this Part "judicial authority" means-

(a) in England and Wales, a District Judge (Magistrates' Courts) who is designated for the purpose of this Part by the Lord Chief Justice of England and Wales,

(b) in Scotland, the sheriff, and

(c) in Northern Ireland, a county court judge, or a resident magistrate who is designated for the purpose of this Part by the Lord Chief Justice of Northern Ireland.

(5) The Lord Chief Justice may nominate a judicial office holder (as defined in section 109(4) of the Constitutional Reform Act 2005) to exercise his functions under sub-paragraph (4)(a).

(6) The Lord Chief Justice of Northern Ireland may nominate any of the following to exercise his functions under sub-paragraph (4)(c)-

(a) the holder of one of the offices listed in Schedule 1 to the Justice (Northern Ireland) Act 2002;

(b) a Lord Justice of Appeal (as defined in section 88 of that Act).

Para 30 Time limit

(1) An application for a warrant shall be made-

(a) during the period mentioned in section 41(3), or

(b) within six hours of the end of that period.

(2) The judicial authority hearing an application made by virtue of sub-paragraph (1)(b) shall dismiss the appli-cation if he considers that it would have been reasonably practicable to make it during the period mentioned in section 41(3).

(3) For the purposes of this Schedule, an application for a warrant is made when written or oral notice of an intention to make the application is given to a judicial authority.

Para 31 Notice

An application for a warrant may not be heard unless the person to whom it relates has been given a notice stating-

(a) that the application has been made,

(b) the time at which the application was made,

(c) the time at which it is to be heard, and

(d) the grounds upon which further detention is sought.

Para 32 Grounds for extension

(1) A judicial authority may issue a warrant of further detention only if satisfied that-

(a) there are reasonable grounds for believing that the further detention of the person to whom the application relates is necessary as mentioned in sub-paragraph (1A), and

(b) the investigation in connection with which the person is detained is being conducted diligently and expeditiously.

(1A) The further detention of a person is necessary as mentioned in this sub-paragraph if it is necessary-

(a) to obtain relevant evidence whether by questioning him or otherwise;

(b) to preserve relevant evidence; or

(c) pending the result of an examination or analysis of any relevant evidence or of anything the examination or analysis of which is to be or is being carried out with a view to obtaining relevant evidence.

(2) In this paragraph "relevant evidence" means, in relation to the person to whom the application relates, evidence which-

(a) relates to his commission of an offence under any of the provisions mentioned in section 40(1)(a), or

(b) indicates that he is a person falling within section 40(1)(b).

Para 33 Representation

(1) The person to whom an application relates shall-

(a) be given an opportunity to make oral or written representations to the judicial authority about the application, and

(b) subject to sub-paragraph (3), be entitled to be legally represented at the hearing.

(2) A judicial authority shall adjourn the hearing of an application to enable the person to whom the application relates to obtain legal representation where-

(a) he is not legally represented,

(b) he is entitled to be legally represented, and

(c) he wishes to be so represented.

(3) A judicial authority may exclude any of the following persons from any part of the hearing-

(a) the person to whom the application relates;

(b) anyone representing him.

(4) A judicial authority may, after giving an opportunity for representations to be made by or on behalf of the applicant and the person to whom the application relates, direct-

(a) that the hearing of the application must be conducted, and

(b) that all representations by or on behalf of a person for the purposes of the hearing must be made,

by such means (whether a live television link or other means) falling within sub-paragraph (5) as may be specified in the direction and not in the presence (apart from by those means) of the applicant, of the person to whom the application relates or of any legal representative of that person.

(5) A means of conducting the hearing and of making representations falls within this sub-paragraph if it allows the person to whom the application relates and any legal representative of his (without being present at the hearing and to the extent that they are not excluded from it under sub-paragraph (3))-

(a) to see and hear the judicial authority and the making of representations to it by other persons; and

(b) to be seen and heard by the judicial authority.

(6) If the person to whom the application relates wishes to make representations about whether a direction should be given under sub-paragraph (4), he must do so by using the facilities that will be used if the judicial authority decides to give a direction under that sub-paragraph.

(7) Sub-paragraph (2) applies to the hearing of representations about whether a direction should be given under sub-paragraph (4) in the case of any application as it applies to a hearing of the application.

(8) A judicial authority shall not give a direction under sub-paragraph (4) unless-

(a) it has been notified by the Secretary of State that facilities are available at the place where the person to whom the application relates is held for the judicial authority to conduct a hearing by means falling within sub-paragraph (5); and

(b) that notification has not been withdrawn.

(9) If in a case where it has power to do so a judicial authority decides not to give a direction under sub-paragraph (4), it shall state its reasons for not giving it.

Para 34 Information

(1) The person who has made an application for a warrant may apply to the judicial authority for an order that specified information upon which he intends to rely be withheld from-

(a) the person to whom the application relates, and

(b) anyone representing him.

(2) Subject to sub-paragraph (3), a judicial authority may make an order under sub-paragraph (1) in relation to specified information only if satisfied that there are reasonable grounds for believing that if the information were disclosed-

(a) evidence of an offence under any of the provisions mentioned in section 40(1)(a) would be interfered with or harmed,

(b) the recovery of property obtained as a result of an offence under any of those provisions would be hindered,

(c) the recovery of property in respect of which a forfeiture order could be made under section 23 or 23A would be hindered,

(d) the apprehension, prosecution or conviction of a person who is suspected of falling within section 40(1)(a) or (b) would be made more difficult as a result of his being alerted,

(e) the prevention of an act of terrorism would be made more difficult as a result of a person being alerted,

(f) the gathering of information about the commission, preparation or instigation of an act of terrorism would be interfered with, or

(g) a person would be interfered with or physically injured.

(3) A judicial authority may also make an order under sub-paragraph (1) in relation to specified information if satisfied that there are reasonable grounds for believing that--

(a) the detained person has benefited from his criminal conduct, and

(b) the recovery of the value of the property constituting the benefit would be hindered if the information were disclosed.

(3A) For the purposes of sub-paragraph (3) the question whether a person has benefited from his criminal conduct is to be decided in accordance with Part 2 or 3 of the Proceeds of Crime Act 2002.

(4) The judicial authority shall direct that the following be excluded from the hearing of the application under this paragraph-

(a) the person to whom the application for a warrant relates, and

(b) anyone representing him.

Para 35 Adjournments

(1) A judicial authority may adjourn the hearing of an application for a warrant only if the hearing is adjourned to a date before the expiry of the period mentioned in section 41(3).

(2) This paragraph shall not apply to an adjournment under paragraph 33(2).

Para 36 Extensions of warrants

(1) Each of the following-

(a) in England and Wales, a Crown Prosecutor,

(b) in Scotland, the Lord Advocate or a procurator fiscal,

(c) in Northern Ireland, the Director of Public Prosecutions for Northern Ireland,

(d) in any part of the United Kingdom, a police officer of at least the rank of superintendent,

may apply for the extension or further extension of the period specified in a warrant of further detention.

(1A) The person to whom an application under sub-paragraph (1) may be made is-

(a) in the case of an application falling within sub-paragraph (1B), a judicial authority; and

(b) in any other case, a senior judge.

(1B) An application for the extension or further extension of a period falls within this sub-paragraph if-

(a) the grant of the application otherwise than in accordance with sub-paragraph (3AA)(b) would extend that period to a time that is no more than fourteen days after the relevant time; and

(b) no application has previously been made to a senior judge in respect of that period.

(2) Where the period specified is extended, the warrant shall be endorsed with a note stating the new specified period.

(3) Subject to sub-paragraph (3AA), the period by which the specified period is extended or further extended shall be the period which-

(a) begins with the time specified in sub-paragraph (3A); and

(b) ends with whichever is the earlier of-

(i) the end of the period of seven days beginning with that time; and

(ii) the end of the period of 28 days beginning with the relevant time.

(3A) The time referred to in sub-paragraph (3)(a) is-

(a) in the case of a warrant specifying a period which has not previously been extended under this paragraph, the end of the period specified in the warrant, and

(b) in any other case, the end of the period for which the period specified in the warrant was last extended under this paragraph.

(3AA) A judicial authority or senior judge may extend or further extend the period specified in a warrant by a shorter period than is required by sub-paragraph (3) if-

(a) the application for the extension is an application for an extension by a period that is shorter than is so required; or

(b) the judicial authority or senior judge is satisfied that there are circumstances that would make it in-appropriate for the period of the extension to be as long as the period so required.

(3B) In this paragraph "the relevant time", in relation to a person, means--

(a) the time of his arrest under section 41, or

(b) if he was being detained under Schedule 7 when he was arrested under section 41, the time when his examination under that Schedule began.

(4) Paragraphs 30(3) and 31 to 34 shall apply to an application under this paragraph as they apply to an application for a warrant of further detention but, in relation to an application made by virtue of sub-paragraph (1A)(b) to a senior judge, as if-

(a) references to a judicial authority were references to a senior judge; and

(b) references to the judicial authority in question were references to the senior judge in question.

(5) A judicial authority or senior judge may adjourn the hearing of an application under sub-paragraph (1) only if the hearing is adjourned to a date before the expiry of the period specified in the warrant.

(6) Sub-paragraph (5) shall not apply to an adjournment under paragraph 33(2).

(7) In this paragraph and paragraph 37 'senior judge' means a judge of the High Court or of the High Court of Justiciary.

Para 37

(1) This paragraph applies where-

(a) a person ('the detained person') is detained by virtue of a warrant issued under this Part of this Schedule; and

(b) his detention is not authorised by virtue of section 41(5) or (6) or otherwise apart from the warrant.

(2) If it at any time appears to the police officer or other person in charge of the detained person's case that any of the matters mentioned in paragraph 32(1)(a) and (b) on which the judicial authority or senior judge last authorised his further detention no longer apply, he must-

(a) if he has custody of the detained person, release him immediately; and

(b) if he does not, immediately inform the person who does have custody of the detained person that those matters no longer apply in the detained person's case.

(3) A person with custody of the detained person who is informed in accordance with this paragraph that those matters no longer apply in his case must release that person immediately.